T0244566

Praise for *The Movement*

"A vivid contribution to women's history." —*Kirkus Reviews*

"An indispensable new book that belongs on the shelf of every American woman . . . an absolute page-turning drama."

—Sally Jenkins, *Washington Post* sports columnist and author of *The Right Call* and *The Real All Americans*

"The first truly comprehensive account of the women's movement, underscoring its inextricable links to the civil rights cause and the vital role played by activists of color. [A] spellbinding portrait of a revolutionary time."

—Susan Fales-Hill, executive producer of *And Just Like That* and author of *Always Wear Joy*

"The unvarnished views of how the women's movement got started . . . There is so much insight and explanation here . . . that sheds light on why women today still have a long way to go to achieve real equality."

—Maureen Orth, special correspondent at *Vanity Fair*

"Bingham gives us the gift of private conversations with the extraordinary women who forged our own path to power."

—Katty Kay, *New York Times* bestselling coauthor of *The Confidence Code*

"With her journalist's ear and historian's eye, Bingham has collected the voices of diverse change agents who narrate the story of seismic change in America."

—Elisabeth Griffith, PhD, author of *Formidable* and Substack's "Pink Threads"

"Bingham's sweeping oral history . . . left me with such a powerful mixture of heart-break and renewed resolve. An electrifying blueprint for how determined women can, and do, change the entire world."

—Leslie Bennetts, author of *Last Girl Before Freeway*

"An enlightening record for new generations. And a chilling reminder of rights still under attack today. This is invaluable living history."

—Lynn Sherr, journalist, author, and feminist historian

ALSO BY CLARA BINGHAM

Witness to the Revolution: Radicals, Resisters, Vets, Hippies,
and the Year America Lost Its Mind and Found Its Soul

Class Action: The Story of Lois Jenson and the Landmark Case That
Changed Sexual Harassment Law (with Laura Leedy Gansler)

Women on the Hill: Challenging the Culture of Congress

The Movement

HOW WOMEN'S LIBERATION TRANSFORMED AMERICA, 1963–1973

Clara Bingham

ONE SIGNAL
PUBLISHERS

ATRIA

New York   London   Toronto   Sydney   New Delhi

ONE SIGNAL
PUBLISHERS

ATRIA

An Imprint of Simon & Schuster, LLC
1230 Avenue of the Americas
New York, NY 10020

Copyright © 2024 by Clara Bingham

All rights reserved, including the right to reproduce this book or portions
thereof in any form whatsoever. For information, address Atria Books
Subsidiary Rights Department, 1230 Avenue of the Americas,
New York, NY 10020.

First One Signal Publishers/Atria Books hardcover edition July 2024

ONE SIGNAL PUBLISHERS / ATRIA BOOKS and colophon are
trademarks of Simon & Schuster, LLC

Simon & Schuster: Celebrating 100 Years of Publishing in 2024

For information about special discounts for bulk purchases, please contact
Simon & Schuster Special Sales at 1-866-506-1949 or
business@simonandschuster.com.

The Simon & Schuster Speakers Bureau can bring authors to your
live event. For more information or to book an event, contact the
Simon & Schuster Speakers Bureau at 1-866-248-3049 or visit our website
at www.simonspeakers.com.

Interior design by Joy O'Meara

Manufactured in the United States of America

3   5   7   9   10   8   6   4

Library of Congress Cataloging-in-Publication Data has been applied for.

ISBN 978-1-9821-4421-0
ISBN 978-1-9821-4423-4 (ebook)

Page 559 constitutes a continuation of the copyright page.

For Diana Michaelis
and
In memory of Joan Bingham
(1935–2020)

Contents

Part Two: 1969–1970
{ 1969 }

{ 1970 }

Part Three: 1971–1973
{ 1971 }

{ 1972–1973 }

Introduction

An Opening in History

In 1963, a twenty-year-old American woman could not expect to run a marathon or play varsity sports in college. She could only dream of becoming a doctor, scientist, news reporter, lawyer, labor leader, factory foreman, college professor, or elected official. She couldn't get a prescription for birth control, have a legal abortion, come out as a lesbian, or prosecute her rapist. She almost certainly knew nothing about clitoral orgasm or women's history. She could not get a credit card, let alone a mortgage, without the imprimatur of her husband or father. By 1973, the doors to these options and opportunities had cracked open, and a woman turning twenty in 1973 faced a future of possibilities that no generation before had ever experienced.

"Revolution," "radical change," "tidal wave." How do you describe a period in history when the consciousness of millions of people fundamentally changed? When women for the first time in recorded history found the freedom to be who they needed and wanted to be? This generation of women, as one feminist wrote, found "an opening in history." In a single decade, from 1963 to 1973, thousands of years of human custom and behavior were upended. It was not just political or legal, social or cultural disruption—it was all of that and more. It was a bedroom and a boardroom and an assembly-line revolution—a restructuring of how women and men in America saw each other, a reinvention of roles, and a fundamental identity shift.

This book captures the voices of those who participated in this decade of revolutionary change.

The Movement is a natural sequel to my last book, *Witness to the Revolution: Radicals, Resisters, Vets, Hippies, and the Year America Lost Its Mind and Found Its Soul*, an oral history that contained a single chapter on women's liberation. *Witness* is told primarily from the male point of view, yet it became clear to me as I finished the book that the most profoundly transformative revolution of the late 1960s (the period when *Witness* takes place) was the liberation of half the country's population. I knew then that I needed to return to the well of surviving second-wave feminists (the first wave being the women who fought for suffrage) and rediscover their stories.

Fate took its course in 2017, a year after the publication of *Witness*, when the *New York Times* broke its now-infamous story about Hollywood producer Harvey Weinstein's rampant sexual assaults against dozens of female actors who worked for him. This revelation unleashed a floodgate as thousands of women came forward with their harrowing accounts—long hidden and repressed—of assault and workplace sexual harassment. Started by Tarana Burke eleven years earlier, the #MeToo movement grew exponentially as a new awareness, and intolerance, of sexual violence and gender inequity swept the nation. This was the moment, I thought, for an exploration of the last time American women collectively demanded systemic change.

The Movement is an oral history narrative, which sets it apart from the existing canon of second-wave feminist histories. The women in these pages speak in their own words and tell their own stories.* Some are dead, many are still alive, but they all participated directly in reshaping the role of women in law, politics, racial justice, academia, journalism, healthcare, sexual autonomy, literature, and visual arts. Identifying whom to interview became a multiyear adventure starting in September 2019, when I knocked on the door of eighty-four-year-old Susan Brownmiller's West Village apartment and sat down with one of the great chroniclers of the era. I was all ears. Two and a half years later, I had interviewed more than one hundred women (and some men), whose ages ranged from seventy-five to ninety-seven. Where my interviews didn't suffice, or the subject had died, I searched for their first-person voices in articles, essays, memoirs, archived oral histories,

---

* In order to preserve historic authenticity, some of the language and dialect in this book is outdated and contains slurs that are now considered archaic and offensive.

and speeches. Together, these testimonies deliver the reader directly into the visceral fray of the cacophonous explosion of women's liberation.

For centuries, feminist activists and intellectuals, from Mary Wollstonecraft to Sojourner Truth, John Stuart Mill, and Simone de Beauvoir, tried and failed to beat down the deeply ingrained misogynistic barriers that denied women dignity, independence, and power. But the women in this book differ from their foremothers because they cut their teeth in the civil rights and the Vietnam antiwar movements and applied their sharpened political and organizational skills to spark a new revolution. It began in urban centers and spread across the country with astonishing speed. As Robin Morgan wrote in 1970, "There's something contagious about demanding freedom, especially where women, who comprise the oldest oppressed group on the face of the planet, are concerned."

Fifty years later, second-wave feminism's reputation hasn't aged terribly well. Conventional wisdom boils the movement down to a glamorous Gloria Steinem, a bitchy Betty Friedan, and an amorphous mass of white, middle-class "bra burners." For at least a generation, historians largely ignored the critical role of women of color in the movement and were slow to capture the contributions of lesbian, Native American, Chicana, and Asian feminists—inflicting wounds that have chaffed for decades. Much of feminist literature, as Florynce Kennedy's biographer Sherie Randolph wrote in 2015, "has failed to see Black women as progenitors of contemporary feminism." In an attempt to at least partially correct the record, readers of *The Movement* will hear from Black women leaders Pauli Murray, Shirley Chisholm, Eleanor Holmes Norton, Florynce Kennedy, Aileen Hernandez, and many others who galvanized all women to demand freedom.

The movement was not a monolith. It reflected where women were in the culture at that particular time in history, and in the years that this book takes place the country was at war with itself over racial equality, Vietnam, and the counterculture's youthquake. *The Movement* shows how women from many parts of the political and cultural spectrum adopted the concept of gender equality and made it their own. Socially conservative women who started the National Organization for Women in 1966 differed ideologically from the younger generation of radicals who considered the term "feminist" old-fashioned and called themselves women's liberationists. Many women's groups intersected with and were influenced by Black social justice movements, from the traditional civil rights organizations to the more militant

Black Panthers. Female athletes and artists fought for recognition, creating their own parallel coalitions and actions. Occasionally, these varied and sundry communities found common ground and worked together, but often they did not.

The breadth and complexity of the actors in the women's rights movement and the huge upheaval in the social order they ignited are often belittled and forgotten. There are many explanations for this beleaguered legacy. One is that vicious internal divisions rendered the women's movement vulnerable to attack, and sure enough, in the late 1970s and 1980s, the right wing exploited the beliefs of the radical fringe and demonized all feminists as antifamily. This politically potent backlash successfully chipped away at the movement's hard-fought bipartisan political gains, from universal childcare and the Equal Rights Amendment to reproductive rights.

No single book can possibly convey the whole of this sprawling movement. There were too many feminists, womanists, and varieties of feminisms to attempt a complete approach to collecting voices from every branch and offshoot. Partly because East Coast activists were the influencers with access to media megaphones, there are more of them here than there are Middle American and West Coast voices, and there are more college-educated than working-class women for similar reasons around access to platforms. Visual artists are here, but I could not include pioneering scientists, musicians, or filmmakers, whose stories could easily fill a book of their own. But what *The Movement* does depict is how women started to build a new understanding of the role of women in American society. The book ends in 1973, just as women's liberation began to achieve mainstream political and media attention, and the dizzying and exhilarating changes that occurred in just one decade provided a base from which more diverse—racially and globally—aspects of the movement would expand.

The Movement begins in 1963, several years before "women's liberation" was even a term. Many of its leading actors are now obscure, yet their accounts are electrifying. Readers will hear from the early feminist legal architects: Pauli Murray, Congresswoman Martha Griffiths, Catherine East, and the handful of government insiders who, along with Betty Friedan, catalyzed the creation of the National Organization for Women in 1966. Young radicals spread the word via consciousness-raising groups and take their Yippie guerrilla theater tactics to Atlantic City's Miss America contest in 1968, while athletes Bobbi Gibb and Rosie Casals and artists Faith Ringgold and Judy Chicago break down barriers that kept them from performing fully in the public arena. Shirley Chisholm runs for Congress, Frances Beal writes an influential manifesto explaining the double jeopardy of racism and sexism that Black women endure, and Billie Jean King organizes a group of tennis players to create the first women's pro tour. On the fiftieth anniversary of suffrage, August 26, 1970, many of the groups advocating for different aspects of women's rights converge, and hundreds of thousands of women participate in marches in cities across the country.

Once relegated to church basements and sidewalk picket lines, these new feminists ride a tidal wave that sweeps the nation. Soon after that, Ruth Bader Ginsburg argues her first gender discrimination case before the Supreme Court, Alice Walker and Barbara Smith teach the first college classes in Black women's literature, and *Our Bodies, Ourselves* educates millions of women about previously taboo aspects of their bodies. Women exhibit art in their own galleries and launch *Ms.*, the first mainstream feminist magazine. A University of Maryland graduate student named Bernice Sandler and Oregon congresswoman Edith Green devise Title IX, which opens high schools and universities to women students, faculty, and athletes. That same year, 1972, the Equal Rights Amendment passes the House and Senate with enormous majorities, but its full ratification is eventually halted by a mother of six from Alton, Illinois, named Phyllis Schlafly, who launches her antifeminist campaign. In 1973, the Supreme Court legalizes abortion, and Margaret Sloan and Florynce Kennedy launch the National Black Feminist Organization (NBFO). Finally, in front of a television audience of ninety million in thirty-seven countries, Billie Jean King triumphs over Bobby Riggs in the Battle of the Sexes. King's victory is much more than a tennis match. On that court, the new world order defeats the old.

Ultimately, second-wave feminists were fighting for human rights—and in many cases, their battles were matters of life and death. Tragically, the physical dangers and life-altering burdens women suffered before *Roe v. Wade* can no longer be relegated to history. On June 24, 2022, in *Dobbs v. Jackson Women's Health Organization*, the Supreme Court wiped out forty-nine years of federal protections of abortion rights, and the terrible past roared back into the present, starkly reminding us that misogyny never dies, it just occasionally goes into hiding.

History can inform our future as surely as it chronicles the past. Certainly, when it comes to women's rights there is still so much to achieve. The voices in *The Movement* teach us the colossal debt we owe to these second-wave warriors. It is so easy to take for granted the seismic changes they made, but knowing this history will give us the knowledge we need to continue the struggle for freedom.

NOTE TO READERS

Short biographies of the voices *in The Movement* can be found in the Cast of Characters that begins on page 457.

Part One
{ 1963-1968 }

{ 1963-1966 }

1

Origin Story—*The Feminine Mystique*

Originating from a survey that freelance journalist and suburban mother Betty Friedan sent to her Smith College class of 1942 for their fifteenth reunion, Friedan found that many of her classmates were unhappy housewives experiencing a remarkably similar kind of (often debilitating) depression that she called "the problem that has no name." Friedan's generation (and their mothers) took over men's jobs during World War II, and then in the flush of unprecedented postwar prosperity, they married and migrated en masse to new suburban housing developments, where a new cult of the (white) mother-housewife was aggressively championed by women's magazines and their advertisers. "In the fifteen years after World War II, this mystique of feminine fulfillment became the cherished and self-perpetuating core of contemporary American culture," Friedan wrote. Friedan chronicled the backslide in women's progress that came in the 1950s when the average marriage age for women dropped to twenty, birthrates skyrocketed, and education levels plummeted. By the mid-fifties, 60 percent of women dropped out of college to get married. Friedan's book hit a nerve and sold three million copies in its first three years of publication. Its publication, however, coincided with the civil rights movement in the South, highlighting Friedan's disregard for issues of race and class in her book.

SONIA PRESSMAN FUENTES

I date the beginning of the modern revolution in women's rights—referred to as the second wave of the women's movement—to December 14, 1961. On that date, President Kennedy established the President's Commission on the Status of Women, with Eleanor Roosevelt as chair, to review and make recommendations for improving the status of women.

PAULI MURRAY

And note this: 1963, the President's Commission Report was published.[*] 1963, *The Feminine Mystique* was published.

SONIA PRESSMAN FUENTES

The book was a smash hit. It made one statement: that married women who are living in the suburbs and raising their children and living with their husbands are not happy. That they are not leading fulfilled lives. But it was a powerful statement because nobody went around saying married women with children aren't happy.

TORIE OSBORN

I just remember the buzz. I remember seeing the book when my mother and her two close friends were having tea one afternoon in our house in Haverford, Pennsylvania, and they were just talking and talking. They were college-educated, most of them housewives. I'd never seen my mother so animated in a group of people. The next thing I know, she's writing a column for the *Philadelphia Bulletin*. In '67, she joined the editorial board of the *Bulletin*. That book sparked her career.[†]

FRANCES BEAL

Betty Friedan represented the educated, suburban white woman who was feeling the chains of patriarchy. And to the extent that some of those issues impacted women of color and working-class women, *The Feminine Mystique* was very important. To the extent that it was the push for the

---

[*] The commission, chaired by Eleanor Roosevelt, spelled out the many ways in which women held second-class status in the United States. The eighty-five-page report pressed for reforms in state laws that prevented women from serving on juries or owning businesses and property, and advocated for equal employment opportunities, paid maternity leave, accessible childcare, and higher education and job training.

[†] A graduate of the Smith class of 1948 (six years behind Friedan), Michelle Pynchon Osborn started her twenty-five-year journalism career when she joined the *Philadelphia Bulletin* as a columnist in 1965.

bourgeois women's movement in this country, it had its limitations. I had a much more dismissive attitude toward it when it was first published, because then I was trying to work through both theoretically and politically how you could have a form of oppression that was cross-class. That same oppression impacted wealthy or bourgeois women, middle-class women, and working-class women.

Black women were trying to keep their families together, going out, being domestic workers, and then coming home and trying to feed and clean and do all of that with their own kids. So the double day was very much a reality in the Black community. That was the main difference between whites and Blacks at the time. Black women had the double day and white women didn't.

BOBBI GIBB

When I was growing up . . . I could see how unhappy my mother was because she was a very intelligent woman. She was completely frustrated because she had talents, she had abilities, and she was never allowed to develop them.

She was one of the lucky ones. She went to college. But in those days if you were lucky enough to go to college, you were expected to get engaged your senior year and marry right away because the only way you had of surviving economically was to find a husband, who would then support you and whatever children you had. It was almost like *Pride and Prejudice*. All her women friends would get together and they would drink wine in the afternoon, and they were all on tranquilizers to deal with this sense of, I guess, imprisonment. I read *The Feminine Mystique* and I said, "That's my mother and all her friends. There's no way I can live like this." Remember at that time women had only had the vote for forty years.

KATE MILLETT

I had a master's of arts in English language and literature at Oxford University, and I taught at the University of Waseda in Tokyo, which is a very famous university. But when I got back to America, in the fall of 1963, I not only couldn't teach, I couldn't do anything. I spent six weeks hunting for jobs and was told that if you didn't type, you shouldn't apply. "Don't even come in and fill out the form if you don't type sixty words a minute." Well, I even took that typing test and, struggling heroically, I got twenty-five words a minute and lots of mistakes. After six weeks, the only thing I could pull down was file clerk. Which means you know the alphabet.

I worked for Olsten Temporary and made $1.35 an hour as a file clerk. I was surrounded by young men who you would have snobbishly called "C" students, real mediocre fellows. They were pulling down real salaries and they had offices and desks. So things weren't working out too well for me, and this was one of those moments, when you hear a *click* as feminists say—and everything is clarified.

I had already read Simone de Beauvoir's *The Second Sex** when I was at Oxford, but the book that really turned me on to what was [wrong] with America was Friedan's *The Feminine Mystique*. Having had this terrible experience with employment, I was really angry. De Beauvoir meant an enormous amount to me. But it was theoretical, it was intellectual. Then when I read Friedan's book, I really understood what happened to history, because I had a connection with feminism and the suffragettes through my mother, and through the three-cent stamp of Susan B. Anthony. My mother told us she was the first generation [of women] that voted.

BARBARA SMITH

I could not figure out for the life of me what something called "women's liberation" would be. I could not even wrap my mind around it because, it's like, *white women*? What do white women have to complain about? White women had been the bane of Black women's existence, including the Black women in my family, all of whom had done domestic work, whatever education level they had, and my family was pretty highly educated. Our mother was the only one who went to college, but my aunt was a high school graduate and was the salutatorian of her class in Cleveland, Ohio, in 1932. I mean, these are some really smart people, yet they all did domestic work, and they would tell us the horrors that they had experienced at the hands of white women.

MARGO OKAZAWA-REY

In high school, the mother of my boyfriend and I were very close. Mrs. Wells and I used to watch the daytime soap operas and *The Phil Donahue Show*, which was considered a local program because it started in Dayton, Ohio, where we lived. Betty Friedan was on *Phil Donahue*, talking about her book *The Feminine Mystique* and talking about women's liberation. That

---

*   De Beauvoir, a French existentialist philosopher, published her masterpiece on the long history of female subjugation in France in 1949. It was published in America in 1953.

was the first time I heard about women's liberation. I would love to watch that episode now.

Betty Friedan's work didn't really recognize race and didn't recognize class much, either. I remember Mrs. Wells and I, our eyebrows kind of shot up, and she said, "This woman sounds crazy." And I'm thinking, "Yeah, she sounds crazy." But then I'm thinking, "Hmm . . ."

BYLLYE AVERY

When we as Black women came together, we spoke from our realities and our truths. That white women were kept at home taking care of their children when they wanted to go to work was opposite to Black women, who had been working low-income jobs and they wanted to go home. Well, if the white women were working as maids for Black women, they would have rather stayed home, you see what I'm saying? But I could see some of the threads were the same.

MARGO JEFFERSON

Historically I respected Betty Friedan's contribution. Genuinely. By the time I came to feminism, I was much more interested in the more daring and radical paths. Betty Friedan in that way was very much bound to certain strictures of class, and of race, and of an integrating into the existing power systems. . . . So that's what I thought—it was an historical marker.

2

Civil Rights—Free-dom

Betty Friedan's book was published in a year of great social upheaval. Ever since the Supreme Court's landmark 1954 Brown v. Board of Education decision, heroic efforts by civil rights activists like Rosa Parks; the Little Rock Nine; Greensboro, North Carolina, college students; and Martin Luther King Jr. to challenge the South's Jim Crow segregation laws captured the nation's attention and moral conscience. In August 1963 (three months before President John F. Kennedy's assassination), 200,000 people gathered peacefully in Washington, DC, to pressure the federal government to pass civil rights legislation. The next summer, one thousand students (many from the North) poured into Mississippi to help register Black voters. By the mid-1960s, many women who had worked in the trenches of the civil rights struggle began to see the hypocrisy of a movement that championed male leadership and ignored women's needs for equality. The civil rights movement became a fertile training ground for future feminists.

JO FREEMAN

I didn't actually begin to think about feminism as a social movement until I started reading about the abolitionist movement. I read about how the original woman movement, and you've got to spell this correctly, W-O-M-A-N, that's what it was called pre-suffrage. It came out of the abolitionist movement, and it came because women who tried to be active abolitionists were constantly told to sit upstairs, just watch, don't say anything. It made me wonder, maybe a women's movement will come out of the civil rights movement, the same way that the woman movement came out of the abolitionist movement.

PAULI MURRAY

I was very conscious of the Black brothers and their sexism. In the 1963 March on Washington, no woman had any meaningful leadership role. I don't think any woman was invited to go with the leaders to the White House.

ERICKA HUGGINS

I heard about the March on Washington for Jobs and Freedom. This was 1963, and I was fifteen. I grew up in Washington, DC. So I asked my mother if I could take the bus to get there, and she said, "No, I don't want you to go there." She was afraid. I said, "But Mama, I've got to go." And she knew me well enough to know that if I had decided there was something that I needed to do, I would do it. She was not happy. She didn't look at me or say goodbye when I left.

I stood there and I saw the people who had gathered that day. They were dressed in overalls and getting out of pickup trucks. They would come in church buses with church hats and their finest clothes. They would come in school buses. They came in old, beat-up cars, they came in elegant cars. And some of the people from Maryland and Virginia walked miles to be there.

Then I began to look at the stage, and I recognized that of the speakers who were speaking, none of them were women. In the church my mother went to, I knew that men ran the church, but the women kept it going. The women did all the work. The women made Sunday school happen, the women made the summertime programs happen. The women did it. It was the same in my household. Both my parents worked and they didn't have high-level jobs, but my mother also took care of us three children, and she made life work for us.

Then as soon as I had that thought, looking at the stage and none of the women spoke, Lena Horne moved swiftly to the front of the stage. I describe her as a vocalist, an actress, and an activist. She took the microphone in her hand, and she sang two syllables—*free-dom*—but she sang the first syllable long and the last syllable long, and the syllables just fell like a blanket over all the people. I was watching people raise their heads or lower their heads as if in prayer. *Free-dom.* The words entered my ears and landed in my heart.

And in that moment, I recognized there's something that I need to do, and a vow arose. I will serve people for the rest of my life. It was a spiritual moment for me. I wondered why Rosa Parks didn't speak, why the other women didn't speak. But I knew, even though I didn't have language for it, that there are these hierarchies, and at the top were white men, and women of color were somewhere way low on the ladder.

PAULI MURRAY

A. Philip Randolph, the leader of the march, accepted an invitation to speak before the National Press Club, which at that time excluded all women reporters. They couldn't be members. They couldn't even come downstairs. If they were covering something, they had to do it from the balcony. When these women protested to [civil rights leader] Bayard Rustin about Mr. Randolph's accepting this invitation, he said, "What's wrong with the balcony?" And they said, "What's wrong with the back of the bus?"

ELEANOR HOLMES NORTON

The first feminist that I knew was Pauli Murray. She was a forthright feminist, she'd never married. She had been in the forefront of women's rights for all of her life. And I do believe exposure to Pauli Murray, when we were both studying at Yale Law School, had been important to making me see that the women's movement should be seen in my own judgment as the equivalent of the Black movement for civil rights. I had been focused almost entirely as an African American on civil rights. After all, I'd lived under segregation in Washington, DC. It was pretty hard to be Black in the early sixties and in the fifties and not think of yourself as part of, or needing to be part of, the movement to somehow become equivalent to other people, in this case, white people in their own country. So here came feminists.

PAULI MURRAY

I became aware of sex prejudice in my freshman year at Howard law school in 1941. It came upon me as a terrible shock. I had not grown up in a family where limitations were placed upon women. My whole family tradition had been self-sufficient women. I had never thought of myself in terms of a woman.* I had thought of myself in preparing to be a civil rights lawyer

---

* Murray was active in civil rights as early as 1938, when she protested being denied admission to the University of North Carolina graduate school because of her race. In 1940, she was arrested and imprisoned for refusing to sit at the back of a bus in Virginia. In letters to friends and family and her private journals, Murray (who used the *she/her/hers* pronouns) felt that she was assigned the wrong gender at birth, and

for this cause. I had not been in school, I guess for two or three days, and Professor Robert Ming said, and I can't tell whether he was kidding or being sarcastic, but he said, "We don't know why women come to law school anyway, but since you're here." However you take it, one has to respond, you can't just say that this is really kidding.

Then the second thing was that there was a notice on the bulletin board maybe two or three weeks after school began which said, "All male members of the first-year class are invited to Dean So-and-So's for a smoker." There were only two females in the entire school, one of which was myself. I am so stunned.

So, what I'm really saying is that removing the racial factor, Howard University being a school where the racial factor was not the problem, immediately the sex factor was isolated. So, my whole experience at law school was an experience of learning really for the first time what a crude kind of sexism can be, an unvarnished one. And so, this is the beginning of my conscious feminism, which began at Howard University back in the 1940s.

ELEANOR HOLMES NORTON

There were hardly any Black women or men at Yale Law School, when I entered in 1961. I recognized when I went to Yale that that would be the case. So I was fully prepared. I had applied to Yale because it was the best law school in the country. When I got in, I knew I had to forge ahead, so I did not have any illusions that there would be other Black women or men there. This was, after all, America in the 1960s.

Law schools were virtually an all-male matter. Very much in contrast to today, when about half the law school graduates are women. That speaks to the other professions as well.

PAULI MURRAY

When my PhD classes at Yale Law School began in 1962, I developed all the anxieties of an older woman returning to school and surrounded by bright, mostly male, law students less than half my age. . . . I got to know some of

---

described herself as a "he/she personality." Murray, who suffered from depression, consulted with numerous doctors about receiving hormone treatment and exploratory surgery to see if she had inverted testes, but all her requests were denied. Though she never publicly identified as a lesbian, Murray had a female companion and romantic partner, Irene Barlow, for more than twenty years. Her conviction that she was meant to be a man may explain her heightened sense of injustice when she faced demeaning sex discrimination at places like Howard University Law School.

the younger law students, whose ranks included the new generation of civil rights activists, among them Haywood Burns, Eleanor Holmes [Norton], Inez Smith [Reid], Marian Wright [Edelman], and Clarence Laing. Most of these future leaders were fresh from student sit-in demonstrations and marches against racial segregation in the South, and I was especially glad that my own earlier activism gave me credibility among them and won their respect.

ELEANOR HOLMES NORTON

I went to Mississippi for two summers as a member of the Student Non-violent Coordinating Committee (SNCC).* Many people of my generation dropped out of college to go south because that was the height of the civil rights movement. I was determined to continue my education.

At the same time, I longed to be a part of the civil rights movement. That's when I first met John Lewis. But I didn't want to go to Atlanta where John and others were; that's where SNCC was headquartered. I yearned to go to Mississippi. There I met Fannie Lou Hamer, perhaps the most extraordinary woman I have ever known. She joined SNCC when she was twice our age and became a leader in the Student Nonviolent Coordinating Committee. There weren't many other organizations in Mississippi for her to join, so she joined us. She was one-of-a-kind. She and her husband had been put off a Mississippi plantation where they worked after they had gone to vote. That is what radicalized her.

When I was in Greenwood, Mississippi, the word came that civil rights workers, including Fannie Lou Hamer, had been arrested while insisting on sitting on an interstate bus service, anywhere in the bus they wanted to sit. Lawrence Guyot, who, like me, was a young person in his early twenties, had gone to get Ms. Hamer out of jail, and *he* had been put in jail.†

The first thing I did was to apply my newly acquired legal skills and just ask them as many questions as I could. And I learned that the police chief at Greenwood was a racist to be sure, but that they at least had a relation-

---

* Founded in 1960, the Student Nonviolent Coordinating Committee was a more youthful alternative to Dr. Martin Luther King Jr.'s Southern Christian Leadership Conference (SCLC). One of the largest and more radical civil rights organizations, SNCC conducted freedom rides and voter registration drives all over the South. Mississippi's Lowndes County, home of the largest percentage of Black residents in the state, represented an example of SNCC's challenge: not one Black person had cast a vote there in over sixty years.

† Lawrence Guyot Jr. was an American civil rights activist and the director of the Mississippi Freedom Democratic Party in 1964.

ship with him. And so I called him and I told him, my name was Eleanor Catherine Holmes at the time, I told him about the jailing of Lawrence Guyot and Ms. Hamer, and I told him I was going over to get them out of jail and I asked him to call the police chief at Winona and tell him, "Please don't put this woman in jail too." He apparently did. When I went over, the first thing I did, I saw Ms. Hamer. She had been beaten badly. Lawrence Guyot had been beaten so badly that he had to cover himself when I saw him. I was able to get them both out of jail. That was one of my first experiences in Mississippi.

FANNIE LOU HAMER

After I got beat, I didn't hardly see my family in 'bout a month, 'cause I went on to Atlanta, from Atlanta to Washington, and from Washington to New York, because they didn't want my family to see me in the shape I was in. I had been beat 'til I was real hard, just hard like a piece of wood or somethin'. A person don't know what can happen to they body if they beat with something like I was beat with.

BARBARA SMITH

I was born during Jim Crow, and that was formative to me in relationship to understanding my status and station in the world. Even though I grew up in Cleveland, Ohio, everyone in my family was from the Deep South—a little town called Dublin, Georgia. Because of the great migrations, I had an essentially Southern upbringing in a Northern setting.

I grew up in a racially conscious home, and I got involved in the civil rights struggle as a teenager in Cleveland. In 1964, the civil rights movement in Cleveland was focusing on school desegregation. Amazingly, my sister Beverly and I attended integrated schools.

I met Fannie Lou Hamer in early 1965, because my sister and I decided we wanted to volunteer at CORE, the Congress of Racial Equality. Fannie Lou Hamer came to Cleveland during the early part of that year, and we were invited to come to this party where Fanny Lou Hamer spoke. We got to say a few words to her and it was unforgettable.

SUSAN BROWNMILLER

In 1964, I was enamored of SNCC, we all were. So I volunteered for what is now called "Freedom Summer," but then it was called "Summer Project." Jan Goodman and I both were assigned to Meridian, Mississippi. I came back to New York briefly because it seemed important to vote for Lyndon Baines Johnson, and then I went back to the South and I worked in the Jackson office for the Congress of Federated Organizations (COFO). Everyone felt that the civil rights movement in Mississippi ended after the terrible murders, Goodman, Schwerner, and Chaney [June 1964]. I stayed until 1965.

ROBIN MORGAN

I am one of seven women—three of us white—in the office of CORE* at a joint meeting with SNCC. More than twenty men, Black and white, are present, running the meeting. Three civil rights workers—one Black man and two white men—have disappeared in Mississippi, and the groups have met over this crisis. (The lynched bodies of the three men—James E. Chaney, Andrew Goodman, and Michael Schwerner—are later found, tortured to death.†) Meanwhile, the FBI, local police, and the National Guard have been dredging lakes and rivers in search of the bodies. During the search, the mutilated parts of an estimated seventeen different humans are found. All of us in the New York office are in a state of shock. As word filters in about the difficulty of identifying mutilated bodies long decomposed, we also learn that all but one of the unidentified bodies are female. A male CORE leader mutters, in a state of fury, "There's been a whole goddamned lynching we never even *knew* about. There's been some brother disappeared who never even got *reported*."

My brain goes spinning. Have I heard correctly? Did he mean what I think he meant? . . . Finally, I hazard a tentative question. Why *one* lynching? What about the sixteen unidentified female bodies?

I looked around the room and there were other women, Black and white, Eleanor Holmes Norton was there. And we were all studiously studying the tips of our shoes, and finally I screwed up the courage and I said, "But what about the women?" And all the guys looked at me incredulously as if I had landed from Mars, and said, "Those were probably sex murders, those weren't political." That was the mindset.

---

* Founded in 1942 in Chicago by James Farmer, Pauli Murray, and others, CORE was a civil rights organization that used Gandhian nonviolent civil disobedience tactics to fight racial segregation.

† Three CORE volunteers, Andrew Goodman (age twenty-one) and Michael Shwerner (age twenty-four), both Jewish New Yorkers, and James Chaney (age twenty-one), who was Black and from Meridian, Mississippi, were abducted by the KKK in Philadelphia, Mississippi, on June 21, 1964, tortured, and murdered. After a long search, their bodies were found seven weeks later buried in an earthen dam.

3

Abortion—Secret, Secret, Secret

In 1963, abortion was illegal in every state. Although the birth control pill had come on the market in 1960, birth control was hard to come by. It was illegal in most states for doctors to prescribe it to unmarried women, and even the right for married women to obtain birth control wasn't constitutionally protected in every state until the Supreme Court's 1965 Griswold v. Connecticut *decision. For generations, American women had been managing their unintended pregnancies illegally and putting their lives at risk. As the civil rights movement grew, and* The Feminine Mystique *raised a new awareness of the deficit in women's agency, this disconnect between bodily rights and civil/human rights started to become glaringly obvious.*

SALLY ROESCH WAGNER

I got married in the blue suit that I had bought to go to Mills College. But of course, I couldn't go. I got pregnant right out of high school. This was 1960 in Aberdeen, South Dakota. There was no birth control available. When I went in to get a pregnancy test, my mother asked our family doctor if he would consider giving me an abortion. The doctor was horrified. My mother took a risk asking, and in retrospect I recognized that.

I had to get married, out of town, with a former minister whose wife didn't think there should be any photographs of the wedding because it was a shameful moment. I was a fallen woman. I walked down the aisle and I couldn't stop crying. I just remember walking down, being supported by my father, because I was wearing high heels. I'd never worn them before and I couldn't stand up by myself. I was literally transferred from my father to my husband. It wasn't lost on me that I couldn't stand up by myself. I wept because all my possibilities were gone.

VIVIAN GORNICK

I was growing up among women who were having abortions, and their husbands never knew. Of course, I saw this everywhere in the world that I went as a journalist. Women living these anxiety-ridden secret lives, especially over something like getting pregnant. You got pregnant and you had to get rid of it yourself or you were in the worst despair. Like Tobacco Road, if you were living in a really, really ignorant world, you just had baby after baby after baby. The people I came from were savvy enough so that women had abortions and it was all secret, secret, secret.

When my mother described her own abortions, I never forgot what she told me. She said, "You went downtown to the basement of a nightclub in Greenwich Village, and there, for $10, you had an abortion on a table. And if you were lucky, when you woke up you weren't holding the doctor's penis in your hand."

By that definition, my situation was princely. It was 1963. I was in New York and it was done in an apartment on the Upper West Side by a man who was a medical resident at a hospital in New York. I came to this apartment, and with my legs up against the wall, he scraped me out. He was a dear soul. He was very worried. He wouldn't let me contact him, but he called me every day for a week and gave me antibiotics. It was as good as it could be, but it was illegal and it was frightening.

You just told every woman you knew that you were pregnant and needed an abortion. Like a grapevine. I'd gone back to my own gynecologist, who was an old German-Jewish man on Park Avenue. He fitted me for my first diaphragm, and he remained my doctor for quite a while. When I went back to him and he ascertained that I was pregnant, we both got panicky and he said, "Perhaps you should get married." I said, "No, never. No, no, no, no, that's not a possibility." And he flapped around and he said, "Oh, you young women. You young women, how terrible that you're living like this!" I begged him to help me, and he said, "No." And then he said, "You will find what you need. You all do."

To have an abortion in New York [before 1970] was usually under the conditions that I described. But a lot of women made their way to Puerto Rico or other places in order to have it done in a hospital. There were plenty of places where you could be assured of much safer conditions than what I underwent. But for me, that abortion cost $200 and I had to borrow that from a number of people.

When I think of being forced into living with something on the other side of the law, and there are millions of us who did, the fact of *Roe* being overturned makes you shudder. It really makes you shudder.

ELIZABETH SPAHN

There was a woman who lived in my dorm at Yale, my sophomore year. At one point in the middle of the night, there was banging on our suite door. It was her roommate. She was hysterical, saying, "She's bleeding, she's bleeding! I don't know if we should call the ambulance or not." I went in and the woman was lying on the lower bunk bleeding out. The floor was covered in blood. I said, "We're going to call the ambulance." And her roommate said, "But she just had an abortion. She might get arrested." Abortion was a felony. I said, "Well, she might die." So we called the ambulance and they took her away and she didn't die. She didn't die. But my understanding is she would never be able to have children in the future, which I since learned is a not uncommon side effect of the illegal back-alley abortions. So she'd gotten pregnant and she and her boyfriend had gone to the best that was around, with some back-alley abortion.

FRANCES BEAL

I had my first abortion when I was seventeen. I was still in high school. My boyfriend and later husband, Jimmy, arranged it. It was a backstreet abortion, on the kitchen table. It was horrible because I started bleeding, and I was bleeding, bleeding, bleeding, bleeding, bleeding. And so Jimmy had enough sense to take me to the hospital. We bought a ring and pretended we were married and they wanted to know, "Are you married? You should tell us. Did you do anything? You need to tell us if you did anything. If you did something, we need to know that."

Jimmy had told me, no matter what they say, don't admit that you had an abortion. It was completely illegal. They could put me in jail. I was put in a ward with a lot of other women who had gone through grim botched abortions. Some of them were yelling. I remember a doctor saying to one of the young girls, "Easier going up than coming out, huh?"

4

"Sex" Is Added to the Civil Rights Act

The first legislative victory for women's rights sneaked in through the back door of the Civil Rights Act of 1964, the most sweeping civil rights legislation since Reconstruction. The omnibus bill protected voting rights for Black people and abolished racial segregation in public places like restaurants, hotels, and schools. One section of the bill, Title VII, mandated the end to rampant racial discrimination in employment in the public and private sector. In a last-minute attempt to scuttle the whole bill, a segregationist Democratic congressman from Virginia, Howard Smith, born in 1883, added the word "sex" to Title VII, knowing that it could deter many pro-labor Democrats who wanted to keep outdated protective labor laws for women in place from voting for the bill. Despite Smith's efforts, the legislation passed. The one word that Smith added changed the course of women's history.

MARTHA GRIFFITHS

In 1964, the Judiciary Committee of the House completed their work of many months on the Civil Rights Act. It was a bill designed primarily to give employment rights to blacks,[*] although it did state that employers could not discriminate on the basis of race, creed, or national origin. I was for

---

[*] When using written or published source material like this quote from an article Martha Griffiths wrote, I have kept the original uncapitalized word "black."

the bill. I had known too many qualified black people who had never had a chance to have a decent job simply because they were black.

I intended from the beginning to offer an amendment which would include sex, but I really intended it to apply to the entire Civil Rights Bill. However, on the Sunday before the bill was up, Howard Smith of Virginia, who was the chairman of the Rules Committee, was on *Meet the Press* and May Craig, who was a reporter in favor of the rights of women, asked Smith to offer an amendment which would include sex, and Smith agreed to do so. I was listening to the program, and I realized right then that to have Smith offer it would guarantee that you would get more than a hundred votes, so I decided to let him offer it. What I didn't realize was that Smith would offer it to only one section. Title VII. It was too late to try to amend. I couldn't do both. I couldn't amend, and then get the whole thing passed, so I went with what was there.

PAULI MURRAY

During the closing hours of debate on February 8, 1964, Representative Howard W. Smith, a Virginia Democrat, who chaired the House Rules Committee, introduced an amendment to H.R. 7152 to include the word "sex" as a prohibited ground of discrimination in Title VII, the Equal Employment Opportunities title of the omnibus Civil Rights Bill. Some observers thought Representative Smith's quixotic action was intended as a joke. The amendment had not been considered when Title VII was reviewed in committee and consequently had no legislative history.*

Congressional Record, February 8, 1964, Howard W. Smith

Mr. Chairman, this amendment is offered to the fair employment practices title of this bill to include within our desire to prevent discrimination against another minority group, the women, but a very essential minority group, in the absence of which the majority group would not be here today.

MARTHA GRIFFITHS

During the entire debate there had been little if any laughter. No jokes had been uttered. But when Judge Smith offered the sex amendment and explained it, the House broke into guffaws of laughter.

---

* The legislation contained eleven sections, or "Titles," declaring the end to racial segregation in public accommodations, public facilities, public education, federally funded programs, voter registration, and employment (Title VII), which would become the only title in the bill to include gender as well as race.

SONIA PRESSMAN FUENTES

Well, this was a very interesting development. Smith was a racist who later voted against Title VII and against the whole Civil Rights Act. It's not clear what his motives were. His motives could have been to delay passage of the bill altogether, or to kill it. But he had a good relationship with Alice Paul. Alice Paul, who founded the National Women's Party, was an amazing suffragist feminist, but she was also a racist and she didn't want Blacks getting rights at the expense of women in Title VII. And she was close to Howard Smith. So it's not clear to anybody if Smith was helping out Alice Paul by suggesting that sex be added, or whether he was just trying to scuttle the bill and delay it. But anyway, he made this proposal.

PAULI MURRAY

Smith was called a Southern gentleman. And as I heard it, he said, "I don't know. I just might do that for you ladies." . . . He might in fact have introduced it, kind of half and half, shall I say? But with a kind of chivalry. He had nothing to lose. And he was a sponsor of the Equal Rights Amendment, which is the other thing that I think is interesting about that. If they're going to include some people, why not the women too?

MARTHA GRIFFITHS

Congresswoman Edith Green [D-OR] believed that any amendment would kill the bill. This was the reason given by many who supported the bill and who opposed the amendment, and in most cases, it was probably the real reason. It was also the reason given for more than a hundred years for not applying the Fourteenth and Fifteenth amendments to women.[*]

Congressional Record, February 8, 1964

Mr. [Emmanuel] CELLER [D-NY], chairman of the Judiciary Committee]. Mr. Chairman. I rise in opposition to the amendment.
Mr. SMITH of Virginia. Oh, no.
Mr. CELLER. Mr. Chairman. I heard with a great deal of interest the statement of the gentleman from Virginia that women are in the minority. Not in my house. I can say as a result of 49 years of experience—

---

[*] The three constitutional amendments adopted after the Civil War were the Thirteenth (which abolished slavery), the Fourteenth (which granted US citizenship and the right to "life, liberty, or property" to the formerly enslaved), and the Fifteenth, which granted formerly enslaved men (only) the right to vote. Nowhere in the US Constitution is the word "woman" mentioned.

and I celebrate my 50th wedding anniversary next year—that women indeed, are not in the minority in my house. As a matter of fact, the reason I would suggest that we have been living in such harmony, such delightful accord for almost half a century, is that I usually have the last two words, and those words are, "Yes, dear." Of course, we all remember the famous play by George Bernard Shaw, "Man and Superman"; and man was not the superman, the other sex was.

Celler's opposition to the sex provision was endorsed by the highest-ranking woman in the Johnson administration, Esther Peterson, assistant secretary of labor and head of the Women's Bureau. Ever since the Equal Rights Amendment, which would automatically abolish these protective laws, was first introduced in Congress in 1923, the women's movement was split over this issue.* Republicans who were anti-union and anti–business regulation started an unholy alliance with the pro-ERA feminists in the early years of the ERA. The debate over whether protective labor laws hurt or helped women is one of the main reasons why it took so long for the second wave of feminism to coalesce after suffrage was achieved in 1920. Women were too divided over this issue to find common cause. By 1964, however, that division teetered on its last legs.

MARTHA GRIFFITHS

Various women arose to speak for the amendment, and with each argument advanced, the men in the House laughed harder. When I arose, I began by saying, "I presume that if there had been any necessity to point out that women were a second-class sex, the laughter would have proved it." There was no further laughter. . . .

First, the House voted by a voice vote on the amendment, and then a teller vote was demanded. . . . Judge Smith came to me and said, "Mrs. Griffiths, you should be our counter." So I stood in the middle aisle and counted the "yes" votes. Afterwards, the clerk came to me and gave the scrap of paper on which he had the written record of the chairman. When the vote was announced, it was 168 "ayes" and 133 "nays."

---

* Simply worded, the ERA states that "equality of rights under the law shall not be denied or abridged by the United States or by any State on account of sex." First written by suffragist Alice Paul and introduced in Congress in 1923, and every year since, the bill was opposed by the labor movement and ignored by politicians until Griffiths and other women successfully pushed for a floor vote in 1972.

Obviously, it was too hot to handle for many members, so they absented themselves from the floor.

Up in the gallery a woman's shrill voice cried out, "We made it! We are human!"

PAULI MURRAY

To almost everyone's surprise, the sex provision was adopted by a vote of 168 to 133.[*] Next day the entire civil rights bill was passed and sent to the Senate.

MARTHA GRIFFITHS

When it got over to the Senate, for instance, Bell Telephone came down and lobbied the Senate against it. I had called Liz Carpenter's office[†] in the White House, and I told her that if that amendment came out of the bill, I would mortgage the farm, and I would beat every Democrat who voted against it.

PAULI MURRAY

Senator [Everett] Dirksen, who was the Republican minority leader in the Senate, announced publicly that he would seek a series of amendments to Title VII, one of which was to eliminate the sex provision. This was when our network went into action. Now of that network, I was probably the only person who was free because I didn't work for the government, because you see Mary Eastwood was a government worker, Catherine East was a government worker, Marguerite Rawalt was a government worker.[‡] So I was the guy. Even though I was immersed in my doctoral research at Yale Law School, I put together this memorandum and sent it to Washington. It was a strongly worded document, pointing to the historical interrelatedness of the movements for civil rights and women's rights. . . . It declared: "A strong argument can be made for the proposition that Title VII without the 'sex'

---

[*]   The House passed the Civil Rights Act 290 to 130, and all but one of the congressmen who endorsed the Title VII "sex" amendment (including Representative Smith) voted against the bill.

[†]   Liz Carpenter was Lady Bird Johnson's press secretary.

[‡]   The "underground" triumvirate, Marguerite Rawalt, Mary Eastwood, and Catherine East, were all lifelong civil servants. Rawalt (born in 1895) and Eastwood (born in 1930), both pioneering lawyers, worked for the IRS and the Department of Justice, respectively. Catherine East (born in 1916), was the primary staff member for the Labor Department's Interdepartmental Committee on the Status of Women, where she served as an unofficial information conduit for feminist activists in and out of the federal government. At risk of losing their jobs, Rawalt, Eastwood, and East often conducted their feminist activism outside their workplaces, and often in secret.

amendment would benefit Negro males primarily and thus offer genuine equality of opportunity to only half of the potential Negro work force."

Marguerite and Mary Eastwood worked on trying to get it reproduced and circulated among various people.

JO FREEMAN
Texas Business and Professional Women (BPW) members wrote President Johnson asking his support, Illinois BPW members deluged Senate Minority Leader Everett Dirksen with telegrams, and Murray's memorandum was reproduced and distributed to the President, Vice President, Attorney General and key Senators.

PAULI MURRAY
Marguerite Rawalt knew Lady Bird personally, and we decided there was no point in sending my memo to the president directly because the president would never see it. So I think we had worked out this strategy where Marguerite was going to take it personally and deliver it to Mrs. LBJ. About two weeks later, I got a letter back from Mrs. Johnson's personal secretary, and she said, "I've done some checking around, and I am happy to report that it is the administration's view that the bill should be passed as presently drafted." So this was the tip-off that the administration was at least going to support.

We were jubilant when the historic Civil Rights Act of 1964 became law on July 2, and Title VII contained the "sex" amendment intact.

SONIA PRESSMAN FUENTES
There had been a movement for women's rights started at the Seneca Falls, New York, Convention in 1848, and that really culminated when women got the vote in 1920.

LOUISE "MAMA BEAR" HERNE
I would surmise that the reason why the white women suffragists held their first women's convention in Seneca Falls [in 1848, near the Haudenosaunee Confederacy] is because they were living within a Haudenosaunee world.

My Haudenosaunee foremothers spent thousands of years being part of a democracy, where men rose to leadership through the uterine voice that put them there. The women chose the leaders, and the women told the men what to say, and they also could depose leaders.

Those early suffragists were witnessing something they had never seen before, which was women being revered and women being heard, and women at the forefront of their political spheres. Who would not envy that? And of course, for the early suffragists who were invited to take part in counseling and the political agenda, it probably blew their minds and they said, "We need this for ourselves."

SONIA PRESSMAN FUENTES

After 1920, there were groups of women and organizations who were fighting for women's rights, but they were considered an elite group. It was not a nationwide movement, by any means. So there had been no national movement to eliminate sex discrimination from the workplace or any other place before Title VII was passed. The year before, the Equal Pay Act was passed, which became effective in 1964, and that provided for nondiscrimination in pay based on sex for equal or substantially equal work. Title VII was passed in 1964 and became effective in 1965. But it was a new field for this country.

PAULI MURRAY

Right after Title VII went into effect, and that was in July 1965, I wrote to Marguerite Rawalt and said, "What will it take to get the working women in this country to stand up and fight for their rights? Do you think that the time has come for a national ad hoc committee of women to take the plunge?" So we were already thinking about some sort of national civil rights organization. We had no blueprint for it. . . . But the ground was so thoroughly fertile that when it happened, it just took right off.

5

WRAP—Sex Meets Caste

While feminist lawyers and lawmakers worked to pass legislation in Washington, a new and growing group of younger women—who were more culturally and politically radical—began to wake up to the sex discrimination they were experiencing while participating in the civil rights and antiwar movements.

MARILYN WEBB

I wanted to be a neurosurgeon, but my mother told me that girls couldn't do that. So I majored in psychology at Brandeis, where the whole faculty was pretty much male, except for Eleanor Roosevelt. There were no other women role models. There was no counseling about the future. It was a time when girls had their engagement rings and their silver patterns picked out by the time they graduated. I didn't know what the point was for them to go to college, except to meet husbands. I didn't have that view of myself.

I applied to Harvard and I applied to Chicago—those were the two programs I wanted to go to. Chicago gave me a National Science Foundation stipend. I got a salary plus the scholarship. So, that's why I chose Chicago and entered their PhD program in educational psychology in '64.

I had a professor, Richard Flacks, who taught a class on social movements. The national office of SDS [Students for a Democratic Society]* had moved from New York to Chicago that same year, and Dick Flacks invited a lot of people from the national office to come and speak to our class. So they came to class and talked about Mississippi, and we talked about what we were doing in Woodlawn, and then people ended up marrying each other. Lee Webb, who later became my husband, was the national secretary of SDS at that point.

HEATHER BOOTH

In 1965, my sociology professor at University of Chicago, Dick Flacks, said I might be interested in going to the national SDS meeting, which was being held in Champaign–Urbana, Illinois, because they were going to discuss the so-called "woman question." It was the first national SDS meeting I went to.

LEE WEBB

I had been national secretary of SDS and then had been drafted, but I had received from my draft board in Brookline, Massachusetts, a status as conscientious objector. I was not prepared to fight in Vietnam. I went to Chicago to do my conscientious objector work and help move the SDS national office from New York to Chicago.

I knew Heather Booth well. I introduced her to her husband, Paul Booth. Heather was a student at the University of Chicago. Paul, by that time, was the new national secretary of SDS and he was living in Chicago.

MARILYN WEBB

The National Council meeting was held at the University of Illinois's campus in Champaign–Urbana December 1965. The SDS people were meeting in this big auditorium, and it consisted of mostly guys talking about the draft and the slogan "Women say yes to men who say no." What they were saying is that men who said no to the draft were the ones who got all the girls to fuck them. There were signs made up. It's not that we weren't all against the war, but I thought something was wrong and off in this conversation.

---

* SDS was the largest New Left student organization in the country—founded by Tom Hayden and other activists at the University of Michigan in 1960. Originally an antipoverty organization, SDS soon became an anti–Vietnam War powerhouse, with over 120,000 student members.

HEATHER BOOTH

There were probably a couple hundred people in a large room. At one point, Jimmy Garrett, a Black SNCC staffer I had known in Mississippi, got up and said, "Look, you women aren't going to get it together until you meet on your own." As he left, I thought, "Oh, no. We're Black and white together, we're men and women together, we'll work this out." And after another hour or so, when women would say, "I don't think you listen to me when I speak," the guys would say, "Oh, that's not true," and I realized Jimmy was right.

MARILYN WEBB

Women kept leaving the auditorium and going downstairs to the cafeteria. Somebody said Casey Hayden and Mary King from SNCC had sent us a letter.

HEATHER BOOTH

It was this famous paper that was circulated that November, on the women's position in the movement.

MARILYN WEBB

I was sitting in the cafeteria around several tables and the group kept getting larger and larger. There were about fifty or seventy-five women. The letter from the women in SNCC asked us to consider our own position in SDS as second-class citizens, as they were considering theirs in SNCC, and it talked about the similarities between the social place of women in America and that of African Americans.

> *Sex and Caste: A Kind of Memo from*
> *Casey Hayden and Mary King to a Number of*
> *Other Women in the Peace and Freedom Movements**
> Sex and caste: There seem to be many parallels that can be drawn
> between treatment of Negroes and treatment of women in our society
> as a whole. But in particular, women we've talked to who work in the

---

* Hayden and King were SNCC civil rights activists in the early sixties. A Texan, Casey Hayden (who was married to Tom Hayden from 1961 to 1965) worked closely with SNCC's Ella Baker, and was an organizer for the 1964 Freedom Summer and the Mississippi Freedom Democratic Party. Their memo is considered "the well-spring of the modern women's liberation movement," according to Rosalyn Baxandall and other participants and historians of the movement.

movement seem to be caught up in a common-law caste system that operates, sometimes subtly, forcing them to work around or outside hierarchical structures of power which may exclude them.

MARILYN WEBB

It was a very strong letter laying out a whole ideology about oppression and class structure in terms of society that cut across race lines. What they were saying for the first time that I'd heard it, was that gender cut across those lines too, that gender, like race, made us second-class citizens too.

Sex and Caste: A Kind of Memo

It is a caste system which, at its worst, uses and exploits women. This is complicated by several facts, among them:

1. The caste system is not institutionalized by law (women have the right to vote, to sue for divorce, etc.);
2. Women can't withdraw from the situation (a la nationalism) or overthrow it;
3. There are biological differences. . . . Many people who are very hip to the implications of the racial caste system, even people in the movement, don't seem to be able to see the sexual caste system and if the question is raised, they respond with: "That's the way it's supposed to be. There are biological differences."

MARILYN WEBB

By then, many of us women had grown tired of listening to males grandstand at meetings, of having to do the "shit work" of antiwar and community organizing. We didn't want to be the "women say yes to men who say no." So we started talking about what does this mean for us? It was an aha moment for all of us.*

HEATHER BOOTH

Back on my campus, there was another SDS meeting, and SDS at that point was the largest organization on student rights issues in the country. It was

---

* Women comprised approximately 35 percent of SDS membership, but in 1964, only 6 percent of the Executive Committee were women, and just one of seventeen nationally elected National Council members was a woman. In 1966, no major SDS office was held by a woman.

the leading organization of the New Left. And I was active in it. I was also in student government; I was the head of Friends of SNCC; I headed a tutoring project on campus. So I was speaking at an SDS meeting and one of the male organizers, while I'm talking, said, "Shhh, shut up."

I was so shocked that after I finished speaking, I walked around and tapped each of the women in the group on the shoulder. And I think it was a majority of the group, and I said let's go upstairs. And we left the group and went upstairs and formed WRAP, Women's Radical Action Program.

MARILYN WEBB

We came back to school in January '66, and Heather and I and a couple of other people started a women's group in the South Side. I lived in Hyde Park, and we were meeting in my apartment building. We met for a while and talked with other women besides SDS people, about what it meant to grow up as a female and how our socialization had happened. We didn't really have any language for it. We were just taking off from the conversation at the SDS meeting in that cafeteria, and saying, "Okay, what was it like to be a woman? How were you raised? What were you told by your mother? What were you told by society and the schools you attended?" We were young, well-educated, unmarried, not yet mothers. For me, it was the first time I realized that girls were different.

HEATHER BOOTH

It was kind of electric. Here we were, doing this on our own. We'd have our consciousness-raising discussions, but we would also take on issues on campus. WRAP was the first organization of the new women's movement on a college campus. There were sororities and other things on other campuses, but it was one of the first women's organizations of the emerging women's liberation movement. When we put out our first flier announcing that we were having a meeting, we were flooded. We had more people than could fit into the room. It was a sign.

6

We Just Don't Hire Women— The EEOC's Rocky Start

Opening in 1965, Title VII mandated the Equal Employment Opportunity Commission to eliminate job discrimination. But changing workplace practices for women required disrupting deeply entrenched social norms. Representing both the Democratic and Republican parties, the EEOC's first five commissioners were chairman Franklin Roosevelt Jr., Luther Holcomb, Samuel Jackson, Richard Graham, and Aileen Hernandez, a Black union organizer and member of the California Fair Employment Practices Commission.

AILEEN HERNANDEZ

On the day that we opened our office, July 2, 1965, there were well over two thousand cases that had been delivered to us by the NAACP [National Association for the Advancement of Colored People]. Plus, all the others that were coming from other places, so we were backlogged from the very first day because we had no staff. We had to borrow staff for almost a year.

SONIA PRESSMAN FUENTES

When the Civil Rights Act passed, I had been working for six years at the NLRB, the agency that enforced the National Labor Relations Act. But I felt driven to seek other employment. There was something else I was supposed to do. Ever since I was ten years old, I have thought that my life was saved for a purpose. I was not free to just get married and have a family. I subsequently learned that a lot of Holocaust survivors had that feeling.

So I called my friend's former law school professor, Charlie Duncan, who was the general counsel of a brand-new agency called the Equal Employment Opportunity Commission. We made an appointment. I came into his office and he's sitting behind a desk full of papers. And he says to me, "You see these papers?" I said, "Yes." He says, "Those are all the applications for the one job I have." He says, "I don't know why, but I'm going to hire you." So, that's how I came to the EEOC. And that's when I became conscious of women's rights. I started there on October 4, 1965. I was thirty-six years old. That was the beginning of my life, really.

AILEEN HERNANDEZ

The commission started on a backlog basis. It started with a very iffy leadership; there were people who knew nothing about some of the issues that we were talking about. Certainly nothing about sex discrimination.

Wall Street Journal, June 22, 1965 "Sex & Employment:
New Hiring Law Seen Bringing More Jobs, Benefits for Women"
Picture this—if you can:

A shapeless, knobby-kneed male "bunny" serving drinks to a group of stunned business men in a Playboy Club.

A matronly vice president gleefully participating in an old office sport by chasing a male secretary around a big leather-topped desk.

A black-jacketed truck driver skillfully maneuvering a giant rig into a dime-sized dock space—and then checking her lipstick in the rear-view mirror before hopping out.

Ridiculous? Maybe so. But starting next month female vice presidents and truck drivers as well as male secretaries could well become far more a common sight on the U.S. business scene. . . .

"We're not worried about the racial discrimination ban—what's unnerving us is the section on sex," says a personnel officer at one of the nation's biggest airlines. "What are we going to do now when a gal walks into our office, demands a job as an airline pilot and has the credentials to qualify? Or what will we do when some guy comes in and wants to be a stewardess?"

PAULI MURRAY

In the absence of organized group actions, we had to rely on maximizing our individual efforts. Mary Eastwood and I coauthored a law review article entitled "Jane Crow and the Law: Sex Discrimination and Title VII." . . . We equated the evil of anti-feminism (Jane Crow) with the evil of racism (Jim Crow), and we asserted that "the rights of women and the rights of Negroes are only different phases of the fundamental and indivisible issue of human rights." Our article broke new ground and was widely cited.

MARY EASTWOOD

Ours was the first article that supported interpreting the sex discrimination provision [of Title VII] to give women their rights that they were supposed to have under the law.

PAULI MURRAY

On October 12, 1965, I spoke on Title VII at a conference held by the National Council of Women at the Biltmore Hotel in New York City. I pointed out that the historical significance of the sex provision of Title VII was comparable to that of the Nineteenth Amendment because, if vigorously enforced, it would give women the opportunity of advancing in accordance with their abilities and interests.

BETTY FRIEDAN

I read in the *New York Times* that a woman named Pauli Murray . . . she was Black, and was going to Yale Law School . . . had told an association of women's clubs about this new law which added sex discrimination to race discrimination in employment in Title VII of the Civil Rights Act of 1964. I guess it hadn't even sunk into me that they had added sex discrimination to the law.

But Pauli Murray was giving this speech to this women's club and said, "Unless women march like [Black people did at the March on Washington], we never will have equality." So that struck me as: that's not just talk. There's something there.

I found Pauli Murray at Yale Law School and I went to see her. She told me all about how sex discrimination had gotten in Title VII, and how they were treating it as a joke in Congress. And Martha Griffiths from Michigan had gotten it in. I got in touch with Martha Griffiths, and I started going to Washington and met what I would call an underground of women in government.

MARY EASTWOOD

Betty Friedan was working on a second book. Pauli gave her my name, and Catherine East. So thereafter, Betty made a number of trips to Washington. Catherine and I would have dinner with her almost every time she came. The situation at the EEOC was not good for women because a lot of high-ranking officials were still making fun of the sex provision. They thought it was a fluke, a joke—male Playboy Bunnies, female football tackles, that sort of thing.

They still had "Help Wanted—Men" and "Help Wanted—Women" newspaper advertising. Back in 1965, Catherine and Marguerite Rawalt and I were trying to work on that job advertising issue; we spent our own money publishing a whole lot of fliers for Marguerite to send out to all of her women's club people. We were just trying to get women aroused.

MURIEL FOX

Like every career woman, I had experiences which made me understand all of the discrimination against women. Those of us who wanted good jobs looked under "Help Wanted—Male."

RICHARD GRAHAM

Betty Friedan came by the office, and we talked for a bit. We ran out of time, and I said, "Betty, come home and have supper with us," and she did. I told her about our problems, that we had no constituency on issues of sex discrimination at the EEOC and that this decision on the classified ads was coming up, and the president was very much influenced by groups that had clout and we didn't have any.

There was opposition from President Johnson, because of the newspaper publishers' group. The publishers had a convention down here in Washington. They got to President Johnson. Classified advertising was a very substantial part of a newspaper's revenue, and they didn't want to change the rules.

SONIA PRESSMAN FUENTES

Newspapers liked sex-segregated ads because they got double money, double advertising. So the newspapers fought that one. The EEOC's first holding was ludicrous.

New York Times, September 28, 1965,
"Help Wanted: Picking the Sex for the Job," by John Herbers
WASHINGTON—The Equal Employment Opportunity Commission has ruled that help wanted advertisements published under male and female headings must state that the job is open to either sex—unless the hiring of a man or a woman is "reasonably necessary" to the normal operation of the business. . . .

The regulations said if an ad appearing under the "male" or "female" column did not say the job was open to either sex, "readers may assume that the advertiser prefers applicants of a particular sex, and the commission will regard the advertisement as an expression of preference within the meaning of [the law]."

The commission ruled earlier that it was a violation of the law to advertise for help under "white" or "colored" headings.[*]

BETTY FRIEDAN

Even that first year of Title VII, with very little publicity about the sex discrimination provision except the jokes about it, thousands of complaints were being filed by women in factories and offices. And the field investigators told me it was a cinch investigating those complaints, because the employer didn't even try to deny it, like he did race discrimination. "I wouldn't hire a woman for that job." "We just don't hire women."[†]

SONIA PRESSMAN FUENTES

Shortly after the EEOC opened its doors, stewardesses who had previously filed cases with the New York Commission on Human Rights immediately filed cases under Title VII.

MARY PAT LAFFEY

In 1966, we, the union [Air Line Stewards and Stewardesses Association, or ALSSA], appeared before the Equal Employment Opportunity Com-

---

[*]   The battle over sex-segregated classified ads would drag on for another five years. In 1968, the American Association of Newspaper Publishers (AANP) and the *Washington Star* sued the EEOC, charging that the agency did not have legal authority to change the rules, and in October 1969 NOW filed suit against the *Pittsburgh Press* for refusing to desegregate its ads. That case made it to the Supreme Court in 1973, and in a 5–4 vote, the court ruled that segregating classified job ads by sex discriminated against women.

[†]   By the end of the EEOC's first year, one-third of its complaints were filed by women.

mission, just as it was first appointed. We brought back all the stewardesses who were fired because they were overweight, because they turned thirty-two, or married.

We were the first group of women to appear before the EEOC. They were thinking it's just for Black people. We're saying, "Hey, we want to be married. We want to work after we're thirty-two." We had a gorgeous girl from TWA who testified. She wore this magnificent pink silk outfit that she had made in Rome. She was beauty, not the brains. The real brains at TWA was Maggie McGuire. She's the one who really got them moving.

United Airlines print advertisement

"Old Maid." That's what the other United Airlines stewardesses call her. Because she's been flying for almost three years now. (The average tenure of a United stewardess is only 21 months before she gets married.) But she's not worried. How many girls do you know who can serve cocktails and dinner for 35 without losing their composure? And who smile the whole time like they mean it? (They do.) Not too many, right? That's part of the reason why only one of every 30 girls who apply for stewardess school becomes a United stewardess. But still, since United invented the stewardess back in 1930, we've trained over 15,000 smiling reasons to fly the friendly skies. Maybe that's why more people fly United than any other airline. Everyone gets warmth, friendliness and extra care. And someone may get a wife.

MARY PAT LAFFEY

I grew up in Pittsburgh, Pennsylvania. I am one of five children, Irish Catholic family. I always wanted to travel. That's why I really wanted to become a stewardess, at that time. I thought, "Gee, the world could be my oyster." So Northwest Airlines sent me a ticket to come and be interviewed and I was accepted, and that was it. I was based in Minneapolis. This was in 1958. I was twenty years old.

I showed up for the interview in a gray and white suit, gray and white heels, and a gray and white hat with the veil. White gloves. When I started, we had to wear white gloves with our uniform. We had to wear a girdle, and of course have our nails done and our hair above the collar.

I didn't have a weight problem, but for my colleagues who did have weight problems, it was horrible for them. If they didn't maintain a certain weight, they would be grounded, and if you're grounded, your salary is gone.

There was more money if you flew the international runs. There were girls who were secretly married, and one flight attendant who was on the cusp of being able to hold the international runs turned in the married flight attendants. Of course, we blackballed her for ratting on people.

So that was the awakening of "Good Lord. This is not right. We're working with men who are married and have families. They're our same age, and page fifteen of our contract says that when there is a man on board, he is in charge."

AILEEN HERNANDEZ

We had done preliminary work on one of the cases involving a Northwest Airlines flight attendant who was charging discrimination because she had been fired because she was married. . . . It was one of the first cases we got. . . . Our office made the determination that since they did not fire men for being married, it was clearly discrimination within the meaning of the law.[*]

SONIA PRESSMAN FUENTES

Betty Friedan came to the office, and she happened to come at a time when I was very down about what was going on with regards to women's rights.

My office had four lawyers, the general counsel, Charlie Duncan, the deputy, Dick Berg, who was opposed to women's rights, myself, and a junior attorney called John Dalessio. I read the statute, and the statute said you can't discriminate on the basis of sex. So I thought, naively, that that was part of the statute. Whenever we would discuss something, I would always say, well what about women? What about sex discrimination? So my boss, Charlie Duncan, took to calling me a "sex maniac."

It was heartbreaking because it was like trying to push a big stone up a hill. This was a brand-new concept, that women should be treated equally. This country wasn't geared for that. There were roles for men, and there were roles for women. And there were jobs for men, and there were jobs for

---

[*] In September 1965, the EEOC initially ruled that airlines had the right to fire stewardesses (but not other women who worked for the airline in different jobs) because they considered sex a "bona fide occupational qualification" for stewardesses, and therefore they could be treated differently than male employees. But in 1966, United Airlines fired stewardess Mary Sprogis for getting married. Sprogis filed a complaint that year with the EEOC charging sex discrimination. In August 1968, the commission changed its earlier ruling and found probable cause that United violated the Civil Rights Act of 1964 by discriminating on the basis of sex. Sprogis then filed a federal discrimination suit in November 1968, and in early 1970 a US district court judge ruled that the no-marriage provision was illegal and ordered Sprogis be rehired. The groundbreaking case *Sprogis v. United Airlines* became an important precedent for future sex discrimination cases, and it inspired 475 flight attendants to sue United Airlines in a class action in 1970.

women. Then all of a sudden, this small agency, we had a hundred people at headquarters in the beginning, comes along and we say, "This whole fabric of American life that we have now, we're turning it upside down."

So I took Betty into my office, and with tears going down my face, I told her what was happening. And I said, "What this country needs is an organization to fight for women like the NAACP fights for Blacks."

BETTY FRIEDAN

I remember I went to see Sonia Pressman. She was a counsel of the EEOC, and she shut the door. She said to me with tears in her eyes, "You've got to do something. You're famous now, and people will listen to you. This law could mean everything for women, but it's not being enforced. They're treating it like a joke here. . . . I can't stand the way they joke about women, thinking that they're not going to take us seriously."

I was beginning to see about the discrimination against women in the workplace, and even in the government. And I was beginning to be in touch with the beginning of the feminist underground that was then in Washington who started calling me in the middle of the night, because I was the one that was free.

Pauli Murray would say, "You should start something for women like the civil rights movement. . . ." The others could lose their jobs, but I was free—and also, I could command attention. So I said I didn't see myself starting a women's organization. After all, I didn't even belong to the League of Women Voters, it bored me. I was a writer, a loner. But on the other hand, they were right. Something had to be done.

JO FREEMAN

Everyone gives Betty Friedan credit for starting NOW, and she didn't. These women in the federal government wanted there to be an NAACP for women, but they could not organize it themselves. They thought Betty Friedan could, so they propagandized Betty Friedan about the need for an organization.

BETTY FRIEDAN

I never did write the book, because I started the women's movement instead.

7

We Don't Give Out Birth Control to Unmarried People

They started out as healthcare workers. He sold contraception, and she was a nurse. But what Bill Baird and Faye Wattleton witnessed in the labor and delivery wards of New York City hospitals radicalized them both. They learned firsthand that the scarcity of contraception and safe abortions had created a quiet and growing healthcare crisis for women in America.

BILL BAIRD

I grew up as one of six kids, immigrant parents. Mother from Germany, could hardly speak English, had her first baby at sixteen, and a father from Scotland. They got married as teenagers. It was a marriage from hell, to say the least, because he was an alcoholic. I saw the kind of abuse that my mother went through, and then the death of my sister at twelve because we didn't have money for a physician. It was just so outrageous.

I graduated from Brooklyn College. Then I was hired by a drug company called Sandoz Pharmaceuticals. They're best known for headache drugs, but they're also very well-known for drugs for women after childbirth, like Methergine. It was a drug that will cause the uterus to contract to minimize bleeding.

I found out when I worked for this company—I was Medical Man of the Year for them—that women would say to me, "I will give you my favors, so to speak, if you would let me have some Methergine, because sometimes I'm late with my period." I wouldn't have to be a brain surgeon to realize what they were talking about. They were probably prostitutes, I thought, and they would get pregnant and they needed Methergine to cause them to miscarry.

My oldest brother, Robert, was a pretty well-known physician. He ran the Haven Narcotic Clinic in Harlem on 116th Street, and he let me come in once in a while to listen to the patients. I met a little girl who was only thirteen or fourteen, and she was pregnant and she was a prostitute. I felt so badly for her. At that time, heroin would go through the placental barrier and babies would be born addicted. I thought that was horrendous. Because I always had a belief, since I wasn't wanted and my birth certificate said Baby Baird—I didn't even have a first name—and so that really made me say, "Hey. Every baby should be born loved and wanted."

I got hired by Emko to sell their vaginal contraceptive foam. They said I was a doctor in a lot of newspapers, and they also said I'm a lawyer, and I'm neither. I'm just the most stubborn guy you'll ever meet on the planet earth, but I think that people should stand up for what's right.

FAYE WATTLETON

I wanted to be a nurse. I went to Ohio State at age sixteen and graduated in 1964 with a BS degree in nursing. In 1965, I was at Columbia getting my master's in child and maternal care, and nurse-midwifery. Harlem Hospital was one of three clinical sites. At Harlem Hospital I worked in the prenatal clinics, where women were often coming in quite late in their pregnancy, or on the labor and delivery floor, where I had to deliver at least fifty babies to qualify for my certificate in midwifery. I did my master's on detecting drug use during pregnancy in preparation for caring for fetal drug syndrome babies. My focus was on all of the issues women encounter in low-income communities.

I remember walking into a ward one afternoon while a group of doctors were discussing the prognosis of a pretty teenager. Her condition was terminal, the doctors said. I looked over at her, lying so quiet against the white sheets in a room separated from the large ward of mothers recovering from delivery. It struck me that she was only a few years younger than I. She looked as healthy as any normal teenager, her eyes bright and her skin clear, showing no obvious sign of pain or distress. Though the tubes in her body gave witness to the fact that she was dying, it was hard to believe.

Unable to afford the services of an abortionist, the girl and her mother had concocted a solution of Lysol and bleach and injected it into her uterus. The potent mix of chemicals had been absorbed by her bloodstream, badly damaging her kidneys. Her other vital organs were shutting down and there was nothing that could be done. She was so pretty, so young, and had it not been for one fatal mistake, the world could have been hers.

The year that I was there, approximately 6,500 women entered Harlem Hospital suffering from the complications of incomplete abortion.* One nurse remembered, "There was this one woman . . . she told me she was picked up on a street corner and put in a car blindfolded so she would never know where she had gone. The blindfold stayed on throughout the procedure. Afterwards, she was dropped off, still bleeding, on the same street corner where the whole ordeal had begun. She wound up here with a temperature of a hundred and five degrees, but she made it. We had to call the police, but she wouldn't say anything to them."

BILL BAIRD

The week of President Kennedy's assassination [November 22, 1963], as fate would have it, I was at Harlem Hospital coordinating research about the Emko contraceptive foam. Harlem Hospital was a well-known place for poor people to get abortions. Even though no one would admit it. So while I was there, I heard a woman scream. I ran into the hallway, and I literally saw somebody staggering, covered with blood from the waist down, with an eight-inch piece of coat hanger sticking out of her. I caught her as she slumped to the ground. She said, "My baby. It's my baby." Then all of a sudden, out of nowhere, came some of the orderlies with a gurney, and they just took her right out of my arms and put her onto the gurney. That was the last I saw of her. I found out a little bit later that she had died.

I was incensed when I found out that she was a frequent customer there with abortions because she just didn't know anything about birth control. So I went to Planned Parenthood and said, "Hey, look. I saw a woman die. This is outrageous. You've got lots of money. You organize,

---

* Approximately one million women obtained illegal abortions every year before national legalization in 1973. The number of deaths from complications is a harder number to know, but some experts estimate it to be as high as one thousand a year. We do know that between 1951 and 1962, the number of annual abortion-related deaths in New York City doubled, from twenty-seven to fifty-one, and four times as many women of color died than white women.

you've got power.' I said, 'Would you help me fight this law 1142?"* Their answer to me, shockingly, was, "Oh no, no, no. We don't give out birth control to unmarried people." I said to them, "Why are you doing this only for married people?"

FAYE WATTLETON

The first year out of college I was an instructor in one of the programs in labor and delivery. As hard as it may be to believe, those were the years in which birth control was illegal—before the Supreme Court in *Griswold v. Connecticut*, in 1965, the year after I graduated from college. Mrs. Griswold was the head of Planned Parenthood of Connecticut. The Supreme Court ruled that the Constitution protected married couples to practice birth control.†

I can't say that I was at that point a feminist engaged in the cause, but there was a consciousness about this development—that while it was still not legal for non-married couples to use birth control, now it was okay for the government to stay out of the bedrooms of married couples if they wanted to copulate and use birth control.

Griswold came down while I was teaching labor and delivery nursing. Our encounters with the other side of it in terms of pregnancy termination were when women were miscarrying. There was always the inquiry as to whether it was a natural abortion or whether it was an induced abortion. During those years, there was a consciousness about the rounding up of doctors who were accused of conducting illegal abortions; they were in danger of losing their medical licenses.

Commonly, the illegal abortionist, using a crude instrument or surgical dilator, would open a woman's cervix until contractions and bleeding started, and then send her to the hospital to be "cleaned up."

"We couldn't break the law and risk losing our licenses, so we refused to perform D and Cs [dilation and curettage] unless blood and fetal tissues had already been passed and the suspect 'miscarriage' was already under way when the patient was admitted," one doctor recalled. "This meant that

---

* Section 1142 of the penal code of New York, a holdover from the Victorian-era Comstock laws, criminalized the sale, distribution, or advertising of birth control by nonmedical professionals.

† In some states like Connecticut, puritanical laws from the late nineteenth century were still on the books, rendering all birth control illegal. In 1965, the Supreme Court legalized contraception for married couples in *Griswold v. Connecticut*, yet it remained widely unavailable for unmarried women in many states. The 7–2 decision ruled that the right to marital privacy was protected by the Fourteenth Amendment of the Constitution.

the woman hemorrhaged, and went through a lot of humiliation and pain before she could receive medical treatment, but what could we do?"

In fact, illegality came about because the American Medical Association did not like the competition from nonmedical providers of pregnancy termination. So, they made it illegal to perform pregnancy terminations. That forced anyone who was engaged in inducing pregnancy termination into the underground, whether they were medical doctors or otherwise.[*]

I began to comprehend the sheer force of women's need to end pregnancies they were not prepared to handle, and the tremendous dangers they were willing to face to do so. We were all aware that the dangers fell most heavily on poor women, because women who were well-connected could afford to go to doctors who knew what they were doing. I was also aware that what I heard and saw was only the smallest fraction of the pain that women in Ohio and New York and all over the country were suffering.

HEATHER BOOTH

The person who contacted me was a former boyfriend. He said his sister was pregnant and wanted an abortion, and could I help find a doctor?

I responded, thinking, this is a good deed I can do for a person in need. I got the name of this doctor, Dr. T. R. M. Howard, who had a clinic on Sixty-Third Street. Dr. Howard and I never met, but we talked by phone. On the initial call, all I did was find out, would he do this? What was involved? And I told him the name of the person I was going to give his information to.

Apparently, the abortion was successful. I really didn't think that much more about it. But then someone else must've talked to someone, because I got another call, and then I made that arrangement, and then I got another call. At that point I realized we need to do something about this and I set up a system. My recollection is that this started in 1965.[†]

I was living in a University of Chicago dormitory, but then I moved off campus and built up more of a system, and people would come and

---

[*] When doctors first organized as a group and founded the American Medical Association (AMA) in 1847, the male doctors surveyed the landscape of reproductive care workers and phased out the existing community of female midwives and ob-gyn nurses. Most male doctors at the time did not have much expertise in pregnancy, childbirth, and abortion, which had been left to the female sphere. The AMA then began the process of criminalizing abortion and standardizing medical education, which essentially cut women practitioners out.

[†] Like most urban hospitals, Chicago's Cook County hospital devoted an entire ward to women suffering from medical complications caused by illegal abortions. By the mid-sixties, the hospital treated one hundred women with abortion-related medical emergencies every week.

I would consult with them. Most of it by phone, some of it in person. I found out what was involved in the procedure, what to look out for, and what follow-up to provide the women. I'd talk with Dr. Howard and ask him about how the procedures went, and we would negotiate the price. It was initially five hundred dollars, then I got two for the price of one; we sometimes would get three for the price of one if someone didn't have any money. We developed a trusting relationship over time.

MARGERY TABANKIN

I arrived in Madison, Wisconsin, and had come from this very sort of Stephen Sondheim Jewish family in Newark, New Jersey. All of a sudden, I'm on this huge campus and I'm no longer living at home and being told what to do. I went to work on the student newspaper, and I was experiencing lots of political movements because it was 1965.

It was the spring of '66 when I met this young woman who was pregnant and freaked out. I think she was from Madison, and was a high school student or was just graduating high school. She was a little bit younger than us but not much, and I just didn't know how to help her. I was the kind of person who if you ran into something that you needed to do, you did it, and you tried to figure it out.

So I started asking people on campus, because I knew there were underground abortions being done: "Is there a safe thing you can recommend?" And I can't remember who it was, but it was somebody who was older than me who said yes, I do know, but it's kept under wraps. There's a woman in Chicago named Jane who basically has this very effective underground ability to take care of people and make sure they get safe abortions. So we talked about it. We knew we had to raise some money, and this was really crazy. My college roommate's father made pool cues, so we sold some pool cues to raise money for her.

I'm calling this phone number and this woman answers and I ask for Jane. It turns out, it was Heather Booth. At the time I had no idea who she was. We later ended up becoming incredibly close friends over the years. She asked me a million questions, but she made it happen and it was successful, and the lesson was, the minute you do something like this, somehow you just become the go-to person that people hear about.

I'd say three other people came to me over the few years I was in Madison, and I put them through the Jane network. Having no idea who these people were, except that I trusted them, and they were using very adept health professionals, and I wouldn't worry that she would be on some street corner dying from sepsis.

BILL BAIRD

In 1965, we set up the first birth control group at any college campus in the United States at Hofstra University on Long Island. These college kids would go out with me in the mobile van, which we called the Plan Van, and we would drive into poor areas. They were just great in helping me. They were my strength, because without them there never would have been this movement.

On May 14, I was in Hempstead, Long Island, and I saw these flashing lights. All of a sudden, two police cars. Three police officers including a Sergeant come in and he says, "You're under arrest, Baird." And I said, "On what charges?" "Violation of Law 1142, that you exposed obscene objects, indecent articles." Law 1142 was based on what was called the Anthony Comstock laws that says anyone who prints, publishes, exhibits, or gives any information about birth control or abortion is sentenced to up to one year in jail, and in Massachusetts it was ten years in jail.*

They handcuffed me, jailed me overnight, and that began my fury against these laws that would not only take away my freedom, but the freedom of countless women in New York and later on across the country.†

When my employer, Emko, learned that I would be arrested for teaching birth control to underage kids, Emko told me I would have to stop or I'd be fired. That was a good-paying job. I had four small kids, and I said, "Look. If I want to go bowling at night, that's my business. And if I want to teach birth control with your product, it's my business, not yours." They said, "You're fired." So I said, "Screw you. I'll do what I want to do."

FAYE WATTLETON

Those were also the years in which reproductive rights were emerging because of the technology. For once, oral contraceptives would separate the practice

---

* Anthony Comstock, a puritanical Christian activist, convinced Congress to pass the Comstock Act in 1873, which criminalized mailing obscene literature, contraception, and abortifacients across state lines. The anti-vice crusader enforced the law in his role as special agent for the US Postal Service from 1873 to 1907. Even though a federal court limited the scope of the law when it ruled in 1936 that doctors could mail contraception across state lines, many states had adopted their own versions of the Comstock "chastity laws." To this day, many are still on the books.

† Baird was jailed in New York, New Jersey, and Wisconsin for illegally teaching birth control, but he didn't serve significant time behind bars until he deliberately broke the law in Massachusetts.

of copulation from birth control. You did not have to insert something when you were going to have sex. You could pop a pill.

The oral contraceptive had come forth in the early sixties.* That really did give women a very powerful message to control their reproduction. That has its own history. I only say that one should be a little cautious about ejecting the reproductive rights evolution, which came about in a series of legal proceedings and precedents, from the overall environment of political and social upheaval that was going on on several tracks.

---

* The Food and Drug Administration (FDA) approved the contraceptive pill in 1960, and even though the hormone doses were initially very high, more than six million women were taking the pill by 1965 and celebrating their newfound reproductive freedom. But birth control laws varied state to state, and prescribing birth control to both married and unmarried women was still illegal in many states.

8

There's an Actual Woman Running in the Boston Marathon

Included on the long list of medical, political, and legal limitations on women's lives in the 1960s was athletics. Physical exertion and sweating were considered unladylike, and serious athletic endeavors physically dangerous. Therefore, women were prohibited from participating in most team sports as well as long-distance running.

BOBBI GIBB

The first marathon I ever saw was in 1964. At that time, I had been running with my boyfriend, Will, and the father of one of my high school friends said, "Well, since you like running so much, why don't you go out and watch the marathon?"

"What's that?"

"Twenty-six miles."

"Twenty-six miles? They run twenty-six miles without stopping?" I couldn't believe it. So I went with my dad to Wellesley and we watched the marathon and I just fell in love with it. I wasn't thinking men or women. I was thinking, wow, here are people who feel the same way I do about what it is to be human, the kind of endurance that it takes to run like this.

I was lucky enough to go to college and I loved school. Harvard, Yale, I mean the Ivy League universities were closed to women. Most of the professions were too—you couldn't be a lawyer, you couldn't be a doctor. Later when I tried to apply to medical school, that was in the sixties, they told me I was too pretty. I'd upset the boys in the lab. They had to save the places for men who would actually practice medicine. And obviously I was just going to get married and have kids. I'd graduated from undergrad, I'd taken premed classes, and I got good marks. I mean, there's no reason I couldn't get in. What could you do as a woman? You could be a telephone operator, you could teach school, probably primary school, until you got married, and then you're expected to leave.

I was a woman, therefore I was weak, I was stupid, I was incompetent, I was lesser, I couldn't do anything powerful, like be a doctor. I certainly couldn't run a marathon.

KATHRINE SWITZER

When I was twelve years old [in 1959], I came home one day and said to my dad I was going to be a cheerleader in high school. And he said, you don't want to do that, cheerleaders cheer for other people, you want people to cheer for you. Life is for participating, not spectating. Your school has a field hockey team and you'd be a great field hockey player. I said I can't do that. I've never held a stick in my hand. And he said listen, all you have to do is run a mile a day and you'll be one of the best players. I know you can do it.

He helped measure off a mile in our yard and it was seven laps, and I went out every day in the Washington, DC, hot summer and struggled through the mile. When I tried out for the field hockey team, I was one of the best players because I had conditioning. And I'll tell you, I've been running for fifty-five years and I still think it's magic.

The most amazing thing about that experience was that it wasn't the running, and it wasn't the conditioning, it was the empowerment that it gave me. Every day I ran, I had that sense of victory.

BOBBI GIBB

I just took it for granted that this was a man's sport. At that point, when I started to train, I wasn't thinking, "Oh, I'm going to make a women's statement." I was thinking, I'm following this inner directive that has, for some mysterious reason, told me that I'm going to run the Boston Marathon. I started training the next day.

By then, I had a boyfriend who had a motorcycle. We'd ride out three miles, five miles, whatever, and he'd drop me off and then I would run home. So he helped me measure out the miles, and I would run in the woods with the dogs. I had a geodetic survey map so I could measure how far it was over to the reservoir and back. The idea was to try to run farther and farther every day. I was absolutely committed. I was out there every day, rain, snow, storm, heat.

I was running in nurse shoes. Because of course they didn't have running shoes then, especially for women. It was very hard to get a woman's shoe that wasn't flimsy with a pointed toe and a heel. But nurse shoes were flat. They had broad toes. They were made of leather. They were sturdy. So that was the one shoe I could run in.

The Boston Marathon was the only marathon that I knew of in the country. There were only two or three hundred men from all over the world who came to Boston to run it. There was no New York City Marathon, no Chicago, there were no books on running that I knew of. I didn't know anyone who had run a marathon. There was no running movement. Certainly, for a grown woman to run in public was thought improper. God forbid that she should perspire! And so, I was just going into the unknown, not knowing if my heart would take it, or if I could do it.

KATHRINE SWITZER

There were all these myths that surrounded women who wanted to be athletes—you might get big legs, get hair on your chest, or your uterus would fall out. That was one of the things that set women's running and women's sports back so far, because women themselves were afraid of these myths and were often teased by guys who thought that we were doing something socially objectionable.[*]

BOBBI GIBB

In February 1966, I wrote for my application and I didn't hide my gender or anything. I wrote my married name, and I got a letter back from Will

---

[*] Women runners could run only short distances in the Olympic Games, but in 1960 women were allowed to run the 800-meter race for the first time since 1928, when it was banned because of false health concerns. In the 1960 Rome Summer Olympics, twenty-year-old Wilma Rudolph, a sprinter from the historically Black Tennessee State University's legendary Tigerbelles women's track team, became the first American woman to win three gold medals in one Olympic Games. *Time* magazine declared Rudolph "the fastest woman in the world," and she became an international sensation and role model for future female runners and athletes. The Tigerbelles, including Barbara Jones, Martha Hudson, and Lucinda Williams, won twenty-three Olympic medals and scores of national and international titles. The Olympics didn't allow women to run the marathon until 1984.

Cloney, who was the race director, who said women are not physiologically able to run marathon distances, and furthermore, it's a men's division race. Women are not allowed. There are no marathons for women.

And that's true. There were no marathons for women in those days. I mean, the longest a woman was allowed to run competitively was a mile and a half. At that time I was running forty miles at a stretch, and I get this letter that says women are not physiologically able to run 26.2 miles.

That was the last straw. I was being told, because you belong to a certain class of persons, you're not allowed to be who you are. You're not allowed to do what you love. You're in this box. Here's the box. Here are the bars. I'm sorry, that's as far as you can go. So I knew at that point I was going to make a social statement. I saw that I had a chance to change the way people thought about women. Because if I could run this race that was thought impossible for women to do, it would call into question all the other prejudices and false beliefs that had been used for centuries to keep women subjugated.

So I took a bus back to Boston from California and I arrived the day before the race. I arrived in Boston and my parents actually thought I had lost my grip on reality. I convinced my mother to drive me to the race start, which was an amazing miracle because she had spent her entire adult life trying to get me to conform to the same deadening social norms that made her so miserable. I told her, "Mom, don't you see this is going to help set women free?" Tears came to her eyes. She finally got what I was trying to do and she said, "I'll help you."

I was wearing my good old black tank-top bathing suit with my brother's Bermuda shorts. I didn't want them to know I was a woman right away, so I also wore a blue hooded sweatshirt. I tied my hair back, pulled the hood up over my hair, and I was wearing new boys running shoes, which a friend of mine in San Diego, who was a runner, had suggested. I wish I had worn my nurses shoes because these new boys running shoes gave me horrible blisters. I didn't know you were supposed to break them in. I was thinking to myself, if they see I'm a woman, they're going to arrest me or put me in jail. The most important thing was that I actually demonstrated that a woman can run a marathon, and run it well. I had this huge burden of responsibility sitting on my shoulders. I thought, if I fall down, or if I don't finish, it's going to set women back fifty years.

My mother dropped me off on the outskirts of Hopkinton. The men all started in a pen by the Common. I knew that if I got in the pen, they'd see that I was a woman and pull me out. So I ran around and warmed up behind some buildings for a while, then I found a little clump of bushes as close to the start as I could get.

The starting gun fires and I wait till about half the pack leaves, and I jump into the middle and I start running. Within a few minutes the guys behind me are studying my anatomy from the rear and I can hear them talking, "Is that a girl? Is that a girl?" So I turned around and smiled. I wanted to keep it upbeat and end this stupid war between the sexes and show that we can all do everything together.

So I smiled and turned around and they said, "Oh, it *is* a woman." Then to my great delight, they said, "Oh, I wish my wife, or I wish my girlfriend would run." They were friendly. And then I said, "I'm getting hot. I'd like to take off this sweatshirt, but I'm afraid if they see I'm a woman, they'll throw me out." And they said, "We won't let them throw you out. It's a free road." So they were very protective.

I was probably still somewhere near the border of Hopkinton and Ashland when I threw off my hoodie, never to be seen again. People started to clap and applaud and the women on the sidelines were screaming. One of the reporters saw me running and he phoned ahead. Pretty soon it was being broadcast on one of the local radio stations, and people knew I was coming. They knew there was a woman in the race.

At that point I was running at a sub-three-hour pace but I wasn't pushing myself. I was holding myself back because I didn't know how to run a race. I knew I had to save some energy for the end, so I wasn't pushing at all. I wasn't even out of breath. I was talking with the guys.

Then I get to Wellesley. Well, the women at Wellesley College knew I was coming because it was on the radio, so they were waiting for me. In those days the Wellesley students made a tunnel and two lines of women would line up facing each other and they joined their hands and you had to squinch down and run between the women. They call it the screech tunnel or the tunnel of love.

I could hear these women screaming up ahead of me. When I got closer and they saw there was a woman running, they just went crazy. They were crying and leaping into the air and screaming. And one woman was going, "Ave Maria, Ave Maria." I really felt at that moment that the world would never be the same again. There's an actual woman running the Boston Marathon.

Soon enough, I got these horrible blisters and my pace dropped off because my feet were hurting so bad. I was just tiptoeing along. So the last three miles I felt sort of disappointed because I knew I could have run faster if I had my nurses shoes on.

But anyway, I still did well. I finished in about three hours and twenty-one minutes and forty seconds. I think they figured that was ahead of two-thirds of the pack. So it was a good time. It wasn't as good as I could have run if I hadn't had blisters, but it was still a very good time for that era.

I came down the last stretch and the press was there taking pictures and everybody was screaming and yelling and the governor of Massachusetts, Governor [John] Volpe, shook my hand, and the front-page headlines the next day said "Hub Bride First Gal to Run Marathon." This went out by wire all over the world, and my parents had friends in Malaysia who saw the article.

It was like a pivotal moment where people saw things in a different way. And to me, that is the key thing, and that's what I've been trying to do my whole life, is change people's consciousness. Once the consciousness is changed in one person, then two people, then ten people, then a million people, it becomes a social movement and then you can get the laws changed and then you can get the social system changed and so forth. But it has to start with that change of consciousness.

It wasn't until 1972 that the AAU finally accredited women's marathons and Nina Kuscsik was the first woman to be the official winner of the '72 Boston Women's Marathon. And she was also the woman that brought the petition to the AAU to accredit women's marathons. Now the early runners from '66 to '71 are called the Women's Pioneer Division Marathoners.*

---

* In 1967, Kathrine Switzer became the first woman to be officially timed to run the Boston Marathon. She registered as K.V. Switzer and was given bib number 261, but early in the race, when her gender became apparent, race official Jock Semple tried to pull Switzer off the course. Switzer's boyfriend tackled Semple, freeing Switzer to finish the marathon. She would run thirty-nine more marathons over the next fifty-three years.

9

NOW Rising

Every year since 1963, the Presidential Commission on the Status of Women held a convention in Washington, DC, and women from all over the country came to present reports and speak on panels. Esther Peterson presided over the third annual conference in June 1966. Peterson believed her role was to defend labor laws passed in the early twentieth century that protected women from harsh work hours and conditions. But in many cases these laws had since become legal justifications for blatant sex discrimination in hiring and promotion. Peterson and her union allies fervently opposed the Equal Rights Amendment, and any other changes in their traditional women's agenda, including Title VII. Enter Betty Friedan and Pauli Murray, who had something new in mind.

BETTY FRIEDAN

It was going to be at the Capitol Hilton. I said, "I'll get a press pass to come for that article I'm working on, and we'll all meet and we'll invite to the meeting anyone we see from the different states," because the people that are there are interested in women. . . . How did we know each other? We recognized the honest fire.

MARY EASTWOOD

Prior to the conference, Catherine East and I, at the instigation of Phineas Indritz, drafted a statement for Martha Griffiths to deliver on the House floor attacking the EEOC. Well, not attacking them, but criticizing them for failing to [enforce Title VII for women].

Congressional Record, June 20, 1966

Rep. Martha Griffiths Mr. Speaker,

I am sick of reading the many heartbreaking letters from women trying to earn a living for their families who are denied equal job opportunities because they are women. It is time for the EEOC to wake up to its responsibilities.

Unbelievable as it is, the EEOC interprets the identical words of section 704 (b) of the law as meaning one thing when applied to race or color, but exactly the opposite when applied to sex. . . . It is no different than the regulation issued by the Interstate Commerce Commission permitting railroads to provide separate table service for Negroes in railroad dining cars, which was held invalid by the Supreme Court. . . . The whole attitude of the EEOC toward discrimination based on sex is specious, negative, and arrogant.

PAULI MURRAY

Each conference participant had been furnished with a copy of Congresswoman Martha Griffiths' angry speech. . . . Conference delegates were also angry over the impending expiration of EEOC Commissioner Richard Graham's term on July 1 and the strong rumors that he would not be reappointed. Since he was the one male member of the Commission who had shown sensitivity in dealing with issues of sex bias in employment, Commissioner Graham's imminent departure was seen as calamitous.

By June 29, the second day of the conference, there were enough rumblings of dissatisfaction among activists in attendance to suggest that the time was ripe.

BETTY FRIEDAN

I remember running into Dorothy Haener and Pauli Murray on the escalator the first morning at the Washington Hilton, and agreeing, somewhat less than enthusiastically, that we would invite to my hotel room that night everyone we met who seemed likely to be interested in organizing women for action. I remember inviting Kay Clarenbach. She was the chairman of the Wisconsin Governor's Commission on Women. I invited her to the meeting in my hotel room. I think she brought along Catherine Conroy, who was one of the feminists—we weren't using the word yet—in the Communications Workers. There was Caroline Davis and Dorothy Haener from the United Auto Workers, and the women from Washington—Marguerite Rawalt and the others.

We thought we would figure out a way to pass a resolution at the conference insisting that the president enforce the law on sex discrimination and reappoint Richard Graham, or maybe figure out whether we did need a NAACP for women.

MARY EASTWOOD

There were about fifteen women in the room; some sitting on chairs; some sitting on the floor. I know Pauli would have been smoking.

BETTY FRIEDAN

After Pauli Murray and I explained the whole situation, that maybe we did need a NAACP for women, and a couple of the women said, "Oh no, no, no. We'll [be] having nothing like that!" That sounded too radical. "But we will insist tomorrow at the session that we pass a resolution."

PAULI MURRAY

Tempers flared and we wrangled until after midnight without resolving the basic disagreement. The meeting finally broke up after we agreed—some of us half-heartedly—to Kay's proposal that she draft the resolutions and bring them before the entire conference the following day.

BETTY FRIEDAN

They left in what I felt was sanctimonious disapproval of me for suggesting anything so radical as an independent organization. And Pauli Murray, who'd triggered me first, and my indefatigable friends from the Washington underground and Dorothy Haener from UAW and I just looked at one another and shrugged. *Women*—what can you expect!

PAULI MURRAY

I left Betty Friedan's room that night thoroughly discouraged. . . . I was so depressed that I seriously considered leaving for New York immediately after my panel presentation next morning, without attending the closing luncheon.

But I had not reckoned with the persistent power of an idea whose time had clearly come, and I had not anticipated the radicalization of Kay Clarenbach and Catherine Conroy when their plays for moderate action through existing channels were frustrated.

BETTY FRIEDAN

My phone began ringing at about 4:45 in the morning. First, it was Esther Peterson, who was [assistant] secretary of labor and in charge of the Women's Bureau,[*] saying, "I'm shocked, Betty, what are you doing? Are you trying to destroy our conference? Trying to rouse the women to do unladylike things?"

Then I got a call from one of the women who had been at the meeting. She said, "You were right, and we were wrong. We *do* need to start our own organization for women."

MARY EASTWOOD

Thursday morning, Kay was turned down flat by Esther Peterson, who said, "No resolutions."

BETTY FRIEDAN

Kay Clarenbach, the darling of the Women's Bureau, was absolutely outraged that—with all her politeness, her responsible request, her put-down of my rabble-rousing—she had been told officially that this particular conference of the official status of women commissions of all sovereign states had no power whatsoever to take any action, even pass a resolution, not even on sex discrimination.

PAULI MURRAY

During the luncheon about twenty of us gathered at two tables near the rostrum, carrying on whispered conversations, while just above our heads conference dignitaries were making speeches. . . .

We set in motion a temporary body to be called the National Organization for Women.

---

[*] Founded in 1920 as a division of the Department of Labor, the Women's Bureau monitored working conditions and labor standards for women.

BETTY FRIEDAN

I remember I said National Organization *for* Women because I didn't think it was against men, and I thought men might need to be members. I wanted *now*, because I was sick of all this talk. [We needed] action.

PAULI MURRAY

Betty Friedan hastily scribbled its purpose on a paper napkin: "to take the actions needed to bring women into the mainstream of American society *now* . . . in fully equal partnership with men."

Before the conference ended that afternoon, twenty-eight women had signed up and paid five dollars each for immediate expenses. A telegram bearing the names of the twenty-eight founding members went to the White House, urging the reappointment of Richard Graham . . . and letters were sent to each EEOC commissioner, urging that the discriminatory guideline approving sex-segregated "help wanted" ads be rescinded. Kay Clarenbach was named temporary coordinator of NOW, and along with Caroline Ware, I was elected to a "temporary coordinating committee" of six to assist Kay over the summer in developing the framework for a permanent organization.

BETTY FRIEDAN

We met for an hour before people had to make their planes and agreed we would have a formal organizing conference for NOW in the fall. Kay, who at least had an office and a secretary, would draw up a membership blank, and I would send out invitations to that list I had been compiling. Others would also recruit.

PAULI MURRAY

The birth of NOW had happened so quickly and smoothly that most of the delegates left the conference unaware that a historic development in the women's movement had begun.*

---

* The twenty-eight founders were Ada Allness, Mary Evelyn Benbow, Gene Boyer, Analoyce Clapp, Kathryn Clarenbach, Catherine Conroy, Caroline Davis, Mary Eastwood, Edith Finlayson, Betty Friedan, Dorothy Haener, Anna Roosevelt Halstead, Lorene Harrington, Mary Lou Hill, Esther Johnson, Nancy Knaak, Min Matheson, Helen Moreland, Dr. Pauli Murray (later Rev.), Ruth Murray, Inka O'Hanrahan, Pauline A. Parish, Eve Purvis, Edna Schwartz, Mary-Jane Ryan Snyder, Gretchen Squires, Betty Talkington, and Dr. Caroline Ware.

MURIEL FOX

That summer of 1966, I remember getting this letter. It was a mimeographed, one-paragraph notice, "An Invitation to Join NOW," signed by Betty Friedan and a group of other women and an application blank. This was probably July or something. I sent it back and said, "Of course I'll join," and sent in my five dollars, and said, "Send me two hundred more of these, and I'll be sure to get them out to my business contacts and my friends in American Women in Radio and Television across the country." So NOW sent me two hundred copies, and I guess that's when I came to Betty's attention. Marlene Sanders* told her who I was, because Betty probably didn't remember meeting me. I was the vice president of [the public relations firm] Carl Byoir. So Betty called me in to have a drink at her beautiful apartment in the Dakota [apartment building].

BETTY FRIEDAN

I asked Muriel Fox [who was one of the few women at the top of the public relations profession] and Marlene Sanders and Betty Furness to come to my apartment in New York just before the Washington meeting, and said, "Look, we're going to start a NAACP for women. It's going to be called NOW. It's going to be a women's movement like the civil rights movement."

MURIEL FOX

Betty asked if I would do the publicity and public relations. I said, "Well, I'm awfully busy. I've got two kids, but I'll help." And of course, like everyone that Betty recruited, we ended up working day and night. Thank goodness.

When I came on during that summer, I asked Betty, "Who's going to be the president of the organization?" She said, "Well, of course I am." I was a little surprised, because I thought of Betty as a writer and sort of a firebrand speaker. I didn't think she was quite the image for an organization that was going to try to move the male establishment. I said, "I think Kay Clarenbach would be a better image as the chairman, a professor from the Midwest et cetera." There had also been some talk that maybe Pauli Murray might be the chairman.

---

* Marlene Sanders worked for ABC News and was one of the few female on-air correspondents at the time.

BETTY FRIEDAN

Well, the word was Kay was going to be the president. . . . But Mary East-wood and Catherine East came from Washington to see me in Fire Island to say that they wanted me to be president because I was more radical, and because I was freer.

MARY EASTWOOD

I remember Betty thought it would be better to have it based in either New York or Washington because the press would be—as Betty said—"au courant." So I said, "Why don't you just call Kay Clarenbach up and tell her it's going to be in New York or Washington?" Betty did that. . . . So that's how I got stuck with arranging the organizing conference.

That summer, Pauli and I were in charge of drafting what we called the "constitution," or really the bylaws for NOW.

MURIEL FOX

My husband, Shep, and I drove down to Washington in our car with our two kids. Eric was six and Lisa was four and a half. The night before the conference, a group of us had met in Betty Friedan's hotel room and went over the statement of purpose and made a few little changes. But it was Betty Friedan's document, and we approved the document at our founding conference.

BETTY FRIEDAN

I remember reading the "Statement of Purpose" to the bunch of them the night before, and they made me take out abortion. They said, "It's too soon."

MURIEL FOX

I urge everyone to read that document. It's beautiful and it listed all of the needs of the women's movement. It's still appropriate today, and you can sort of check off what we've accomplished and what we still have to accomplish.

National Organization for Women Statement of Purpose

We, men and women who hereby constitute ourselves as the Na-tional Organization for Women, believe that the time has come for a new movement towards true equality for all women in America, and towards a fully equal partnership of the sexes, as part of the world-wide revolution of human rights now taking place within and beyond our national borders. . . .

We believe the time has come . . . to confront, with concrete action, the conditions that now prevent women from enjoying the equality of opportunity and freedom of choice which is their right, as individual Americans, and as human beings. . . .

MURIEL FOX

That still brings tears to my eyes, it's so beautiful. It was a very important historic moment. For thousands of years, women were second-class citizens and really the property of men. Finally, it was recognized that we should be equals.

MARY EASTWOOD

The *Washington Post* had this community room, called the John Philip Sousa Room. All you had to do was sign up for it if you were a citizen organization of some kind. It was a kind of public service they had. So I thought, because we didn't have to pay anything for the room, having it at the *Washington Post* gave it a little class.

PAULI MURRAY

Thirty-two of us set up the permanent organization of NOW, never dreaming that within less than two decades it would have more than two hundred thousand members and become a potent force in American politics.

MURIEL FOX

We formed task forces on equal employment, legal and political rights, education, poverty, childcare, and religion. Betty recruited the board of directors. Dick Graham became executive vice president. Kay Clarenbach was the chair of the board, and she was a good front person for Betty, who was rather inflammatory and controversial, even then.

Betty asked Aileen Hernandez if she would be executive vice president of NOW. And Aileen agreed she would take the [unpaid] job after her EEOC tenure ended.

BETTY FRIEDAN

We wasted no time on ceremonials or speeches, gave ourselves barely an hour for lunch and dinner. . . . At times we got very tired and impatient, but there was always a sense that what we were deciding was not just for now "but for a century . . ." We shared a moving moment of realization that we had now indeed entered history.

MARY EASTWOOD
We all signed our names on a sheet of yellow paper, and the last name is Aileen Hernandez. Pauli at the time was working as a consultant at the EEOC. She took the paper over to the EEOC and had Aileen sign it. An additional twenty-one women and men signed on as founders at the October 1966 NOW organizing conference in Washington, DC.*

BETTY FRIEDAN
The night after we adopted the Statement of Purpose, Muriel and a half-dozen women economists and lawyers stayed up till five a.m. running off NOW's first press release on Senator Philip Hart's [D-MI] mimeograph machine, and taking them by hand to the newspaper offices.

For Immediate Release
From: NOW
Press Contacts: Muriel Fox, 212-986-6110
Betty Friedan, 212-724-7711
More than 300 men and women have formed a new action organization called National Organization for Women (NOW), to work for "true equality for all women in America" and "a fully equal partnership of the sexes, as part of the world-wide revolution of human rights."

MURIEL FOX
The press release was used on front pages all over the country. Everyone realized this was history except the *New York Times*, who didn't carry the story. So I wrote a letter to Clifton Daniel, who was executive editor of the *Times* at that time. Actually, his wife, Margaret Truman, was a patient of my husband's. I said, "We're not anybody until the *Times* covers us." So, he

---

* Their names were Caruthers Berger, Colleen Boland, Inez Casiano, Carl Degler, Elizabeth Drews, Muriel Fox, Dr. Mary Esther Gaulden (later Jagger), Ruth Gober, Richard Graham, Anna Arnold Hedgeman, Lucille Kapplinger (later Hazell), Bessie Margolin, Marjorie Palmer, Sonia Pressman (later Fuentes), Sister Mary Joel Read, Amy Robinson, Charlotte Roe, Alice Rossi, Claire R. Salmond, Morag Simchak, and Clara Wells.

had one of his top reporters interview Betty Friedan, a wonderful interview, which was published on the women's page right above how to carve your Thanksgiving turkey.

DOLORES ALEXANDER

I was one of three women reporters for *Newsday*, working for the women's pages, and in 1966 I got a press release announcing the beginning of this organization called NOW, and I was very excited about it. The person listed on the press release was Muriel Fox, who was then vice president at Carl Byoir, a very large public relations firm. I called Muriel and she gave me Betty's number and told me to interview her. So that's what I did. I went to interview Friedan, who was living in the Dakota at the time. She was an interesting woman—very haughty, somewhat arrogant, very impatient. I think she felt that I wasn't with an important enough newspaper. But anyway, I went back to the office and wrote a story about it.

After that interview with Betty, she gave me a number of application blanks and I took them back to the office and I signed up every woman that I could find in the newsroom. Now, dues were only five dollars in those days, but if somebody didn't want to join, I said, "Look. I'll pay the dues for you." So, we got a lot of people as members and one woman especially, Ivy Bottini. She was working at *Newsday* as an art director. She joined and she was drawn to it as I was and became also instantly excited and involved and passionate about it.

10

Crimes Against Chastity

Remnants of early colonial-era laws were still on the books in many states in the 1960s. All but ten states, for example, still outlawed "fornication," or sex between two unmarried people, although this was rarely enforced. In Massachusetts, the birthplace of seventeenth-century American Puritanism, a law called "Crimes against Chastity" criminalized unmarried people from receiving information about birth control, even from a doctor. By 1967, the statute was only occasionally enforced, but a group of young radicals enlisted Bill Baird to strike it down.

BILL BAIRD

I got a phone call from Ray Mungo, a brilliant young man. He was the editor of the Boston University student newspaper. "Bill, I read about you in the papers," he said. "We'd love it if you would come here, and challenge our laws." I said, "I can't do it. I've got four little kids. I read the law. It's a ten-year jail sentence—five years for each charge." This was the name of the law: Crimes Against Chastity, Morality, Decency, and Good Order. The law said that if you write an article, or show or display any means of birth control or abortion, or give any information to anyone, it would be a five-year jail term on each charge.

But here's how my thinking went, right or wrong. I said, If I could get heard by the US Supreme Court, here's what I can accomplish: I could knock out the law on birth control, knock out the law on abortion, all based on the same principle of the right of privacy. But I also can maybe knock out the laws on fornication, because if you make birth control legal, you have to fornicate to use it. It said that if you have intercourse, but you're not married, that's illegal. The law clearly said fornication was a one-year jail term in almost all states.

So I thought about it and I said, you know what? I'll come.

So I showed up at Boston University, April 6 at four thirty in the afternoon, and I saw about a dozen police cars. I was active in the peace movement, and I said "Jesus, God, there must be a rally here and the cops are probably making a bunch of arrests." When I went in, I was shocked. There were over two thousand people, the largest audience ever, according to the reporters at Boston University, and there were dozens of police officers there to arrest me. Since I never wrote a speech, I had to think on my feet, "How am I going to handle this?"

One of the things that troubles me to this day, I saw those little faces out there, kids, seventeen, eighteen, twenty, looking like I was somebody who could really help them get their rights. I desperately wanted not to disappoint them. I said to myself now, I better make sure the cops make the arrest under the conditions that I want.

Ironically, on the cover of *Time* magazine on the day of my arrest was a photograph of the birth control pill in a circle, like the woman's symbol of power. So birth control pills were on page one. I picked up that magazine at a newsstand and some instinct just made me pick up St. Joseph's baby aspirin, and I took a St. Joseph's baby aspirin and I glued six tablets onto the bottom of the magazine. On the top, I pasted the real birth control pill. I read the law, "anyone who prints, publishes exhibits, gives any means of information on birth control" would be violating the law, and I wanted to be charged with the easiest thing I thought I could prove would be unconstitutional, which was a violation of free speech.

So when I held it up, the police just frowned at me. No arrest. I said, "All right, you're going to play that game?" I had already held up the diaphragm, the pill, and the IUD and various abortion devices. They made no effort to arrest me. So then I said I had a really small box, and in the box, I had half a dozen or so condoms, which I bought from Zayre's department store. Not a drugstore. It's important that this is in my court record. You can only buy birth control from a drugstore. So I deliberately went to a department store. When I bought the foam I said, "Now, what are they going to do with me? I'm Emko's clinical director, I'm the guy who tells doctors how to use this stuff."

So I said, "Anyone want this?" I had arranged for this nineteen-year-old kid to come up, and she put out her hand and she took the foam and she took the condom.

SUE KATZ

In 1965 I arrived at BU at age seventeen, with a full scholarship. I looked forward to the freedom and independence a big urban university seemed to promise. However, I was in for some unanticipated restrictions. At BU, women were not permitted to wear pants unless a date came to pick us up on his motorcycle and our housemother was around to give dispensation. We had to wear skirts even in the common rooms of the dorm. Our weekday curfew was ten p.m., and on weekends it was midnight. Men had no curfews, of course. Things changed within a year, at least in terms of pants and curfews. I got involved in anti-racism work and the anti–Vietnam War movement. Reproductive rights issues were also in flux.

I was part of the 1967 action at Boston University challenging the law forbidding birth control for single people. By prearrangement a few of us women students took condoms and foam from Bill Baird in a big auditorium full of witnesses in an act of civil disobedience.

BILL BAIRD

The moment I did that, the police came up and had their handcuffs out. I said, "Hold it!" And they said, "What do you mean, hold it?" I said, "I want to show the TV cameras something." And I held up the sales receipt from Zayre's department store and it said, "'Emko foam, $3.09 sales tax.'" This was an illegal sale from a department store. Anyone could buy this, therefore I want to see your attorney general arrested for collecting an illegal tax on an illegal sale."

MYRA MACPHERSON

Of course, the point he was making was that you could buy this anywhere. The illegal part was giving it to an unmarried person.

BILL BAIRD

In my simple head from the slums of Brooklyn I thought, "Look, if I could just get heard, I think I could convince the courts to say that this is a right to privacy issue." I would win without much difficulty, but I had a good chance of risking ten years in jail.

In May of 1969, Baird was convicted of giving birth control aids and advice to unmarried minors and sentenced to three months in jail.

MYRA MACPHERSON

He was then hauled off to one of the worst jails in the country, the Charles Street Jail. When I interviewed Bill for my *Washington Post* story, I tried to ask him about what happened to him in prison, and he clammed up and said, "I was left alone because I was good with my fists."

BILL BAIRD

They gave us a tin cup that we were supposed to bang on the wall to indicate that we were being raped, or sick, or needed help. It was just such an eerie sound to hear everyone banging their tin cups and then being told, "Well, these are the old cells. It's not like the movies where you press a button and the doors slide open." To make a long story short, it was a living hell of a place.

MYRA MACPHERSON

He was in there for thirty-six days, and then he finally got out and he just kept on going.

11

What Was I Wearing?

MARILYN WEBB

I came back to school in January 1967; I had worked the whole vacation on the proposal for my dissertation. I had finished all my graduate coursework and had passed my prelim exams. My PhD dissertation plan was to compare the outcomes of these two preschools I was the director of, the one we had set up, which was run by the mothers, and the one that Saul Alinsky had set up, which was like a traditional preschool. You send your child and we'll teach 'em. Goodbye.

So I went to the person who had been my mentor, Herbert Thelen. He's dead now. He was a big guru in group dynamics, and chairman of the Educational Psychology Department. At the time, he was fifty-four years old. I was twenty-four. He had gotten me this three-year fellowship from the National Science Foundation and had been my mentor in the program.

He said he wanted to come over to my apartment. I said, "Well, okay." So he came over and he said, "I'd like to give you baths." And I said, "I don't think I want to do that. I don't feel very comfortable right now." I basically said, "Could you leave?" I said, "So are you saying you don't want to be on my committee?" And he said, "I want to give you baths." And I said, "Then that's all we have to talk about."

I was devastated, because I really admired him. I needed three people on my dissertation committee, and I went to the next professor I had in mind, who was Larry Kohlberg. His field was the moral development of children. So, I went into Larry Kohlberg's office and as soon as I got there, I gave him my papers and I said, "I really would like you to be on my committee." Then he jumped up, loosened his tie, and ran around the desk. I was terrified. I jumped up, and all my papers fell on the floor. He pinned me to the wall and he started slobbering on my face, and he said to me, "It's quid pro quo."

I don't even remember if I picked up the papers or not. I pushed him away and I ran out the door, and I don't remember anything after that. I thought, this is what it's like being Black. All you can see is a Black person. All he could see was a pretty girl. That's all any of them saw. Pretty girl and then assault. These were professors. I admired them. I had no clue this was the world. It shocked my worldview. All the time I spent trying to be pretty, even though you're trying to be smart and learn and be a professional, it made me feel dirty and like I got the whole thing wrong.

There was a third professor I would have asked, but my classmates said, "There are rumors about him too." I didn't have any options. So I just left. I was humiliated. I was embarrassed for having been a fool, for deluding myself into thinking this was possible.

I thought it was my fault. What was I wearing? Did I look too sexy? What was wrong? And of course that was bullshit. It didn't matter what I was wearing. It was just that's how it was. And who was I to think I could be something different? Maybe if I was Hannah Arendt, who was one of the only women on the university faculty then, but I wasn't. . . . I'm getting upset again.

LEE WEBB

I'd left Chicago and was trying to set up an SDS regional office in Washington at the time. Marilyn and I were sort of an item, and we continued to talk on the phone. Marilyn said she didn't really see a future for her at the University of Chicago and wanted to know whether she could come and live with me in Washington.

MARILYN WEBB

I moved to Washington in the spring of '67. It took about three months until I stopped crying.

LEE WEBB

Getting a PhD was a big deal back then. She left a lot of money on the table.*

MARILYN WEBB

Lee was at the Institute for Policy Studies [IPS], a liberal think tank that had been set up by people who were in the Kennedy administration, and they were very supportive of the New Left, civil rights, and antiwar activists—young people like me. So I started hanging out there.

CHARLOTTE BUNCH

Marilyn Webb was the one who started the first DC consciousness-raising group. She was hanging around IPS too where I was working. She began to talk to me about it, but I wasn't sure yet. I was still partly identifying as one of the guys. I thought it was a compliment when people said to me, "You think like a man, or you're just one of the boys." I was still in the phase where that's what I wanted. I wanted to be accepted.

---

* Encouraged by the #MeToo movement, Marilyn Webb wrote the president of the University of Chicago in 2017, told her story, and asked the university to remedy her past injustice. After rewriting her previously published book to fit a dissertation committee's requirements, Webb was awarded her PhD at age seventy-six and walked in the graduation ceremony with the class of 2019.

12

Black Power—
The Patterns Were Very Similar

The summer of 1967 will be remembered for the violent eruption of race riots and Vietnam War protests. Black Power took over the civil rights movement and rejected its white allies, while New Left organizations like SDS continued to exclude women's rights from their agendas. Looking for recognition and unknowingly working in parallel with the nascent National Organization for Women, these veterans of the civil rights and antiwar movements broke off from their radical male comrades and started their own groups.

FAITH RINGGOLD

The idea was to make a statement in my art about the civil rights movement and what was happening to Black people in America at the time, and to make it superreal. . . . James Baldwin had just published *The Fire Next Time*, Malcom X was talking about "us loving our Black selves," and Martin Luther King Jr. was leading marches and spreading the word. All over this country and the world people were listening to these Black men. I felt called upon to create my own vision of the Black experience we were witnessing. . . . I wanted my paintings to express this moment I knew was history. I wanted to give my woman's point of view to this period.

MICHELE WALLACE

In 1967, Mother wasn't a feminist yet and neither was I. I was fifteen. However, I feel that her work was infused with many of the elements that would later manifest as her feminist consciousness.

FAITH RINGGOLD

My first one-person show at Spectrum was scheduled for December 1967. Since the gallery would be closed during June, July, and August, Robert [Newman] suggested that I use [the space] as my studio. I had sent my daughters to Europe with Mother for the summer. They studied French at the Alliance Française while Mother [a Harlem fashion designer] visited the couturiers in their salons in Paris and Rome. For the first time since the girls were born, I had two months to myself. . . . Every day I painted well into the night in the gallery space. . . . Robert wanted me to depict everything that was happening in America—the cities and the decade's tumultuous thrusts for freedom . . . the climate of America was changing in the summer of '67.* We were moving out of the civil rights period and were at the start of the Black Revolution. In 1966 Adam Clayton Powell Jr. and Stokely Carmichael had sounded the battle cry for Black Power, and by 1967 everyone was taking sides.†

MICHELE WALLACE

My mother taught art to elementary school children at PS 100 in a special program [from 1955 to 1973]. Her students loved her. . . . I was fifteen when she painted *The Flag Is Bleeding, Die,* and *U.S. Postage Stamp Commemorating the Advent of Black Power.* Everybody had to have large paintings then.

FAITH RINGGOLD

The Flag Is Bleeding was eight feet wide and six feet high. By the end of July, I had completed the canvas . . . now I wanted the world to see it. This was actually a very strong image in my mind and the first flag painting in which I showed the complete flag image. The fragile white woman standing in the stripes is the

---

*   In reaction to persistent police brutality and economic inequality, the worst race riots in the nation's history broke out in 158 urban areas across the country. By the end of the "Hot Summer of 1967," the violence claimed eighty-three lives and resulted in seventeen thousand arrests.

†   Published in 1967, *Black Power: The Politics of Liberation in America,* by Kwame Ture (Stokely Carmichael) and Charles V. Hamilton, defined Black Power as a radical way to confront and reform racist society.

peace-maker. The Black man carries a knife, while the white man packs a gun on each hip, ready to draw, Western-style. . . . And why is there no Black woman in this picture? That's because those were the people who were involved in the struggle. The Black woman was left out of it. The white woman was trying to bring the Black and the white man together because she really had no power, and the only way to acquire it was by bringing together the men. There was also a lot of tension and jealousy; the Black man was demonstrating his freedom by being with the white woman, and she was claiming her freedom by being with the Black man. And either way you looked at it, the Black woman was excluded. And there was blood everywhere simply because bad stuff was happening everywhere. Black women were literally out of the picture.

MICHELE WALLACE
The lack of reception for the work by Blacks and by everybody I think had to do with these feminist elements that were there in the work. The thing about it is, that painting is all about gender, race, power, and the Black woman was not in that picture because she didn't have any role in 1967 when Black power exploded. Malcolm X had already been killed. Martin Luther King would be killed in '68. And the Black woman was trying to find herself by attaching herself to these movements, mostly to the Black man.

FAITH RINGGOLD
The opening party was a joy and celebration.

MICHELE WALLACE
Flo Kennedy came.* She was an old family friend. Mom was friends with Flo as well as Flo's two sisters, Fay and Joy. Flo Kennedy did my mother's annulment from my father.

FAITH RINGGOLD
I had called Flo to get some names of people to invite to my exhibition, and she gave me those of Betty Friedan and Ti-Grace Atkinson. . . . Flo

---

* Florynce Rae Kennedy (born 1916) was a radical civil rights activist and lawyer with a knack for organizing colorful political actions. She graduated from Columbia Law School in 1951, and in her private law practice represented the estates of Billie Holiday and Charlie Parker. She used her law degree more politically in the latter half of the sixties, when she represented members of the Black Panthers and pro-choice abortion plaintiffs. An outspoken feminist, Kennedy was a founding member of NOW's New York chapter.

suggested that both could be helpful to me, and further that I should arrange to meet them, join NOW, and get involved in the women's movement. I sent them all invitations to my 1967 show and attempted half-heartedly to reach the two women by phone with no success. Flo came to my opening with some women from NOW. They were all women's liberationists, and I admired them that night for looking the part. They carried with them propaganda about the movement: notices of meetings, plans for feminist actions.

FLORYNCE KENNEDY

I could understand feminism better because of the discrimination against Black people, and the patterns were very similar, almost parallel, so it was easy for me to understand the psychology and the techniques to fight them, you see, because all I had to do is transfer the thinking from the Black community over to the women's community, and you get the same thing: less good jobs and stuck with the kids, and cheaper pay for the same work.

MICHELE WALLACE

Flo was constantly egging my mother on and talking about the women's movement and saying, "Look, you're not going to get anywhere standing behind the men or even working with the men. You're going to have to push your way to the front." But Faith wasn't ready yet.

Black women just really didn't know what to do with themselves, except try to help the men and stand in the back.

The only piece that sold at the American People show was a painting called *The Bridesmaid of Martha's Vineyard*, and it was sold to a guy named James Porter, who was the head of the Art Department at Howard University. He bought it because he was married on Martha's Vineyard, and he asked Faith to change the name from *Bridesmaid of Martha's Vineyard* to *Bride of Martha's Vineyard*, a tribute to his wife.*

---

* It would take fifty years for Ringgold to get the recognition she deserved as an artist. In 2016, the Museum of Modern Art bought her 1967 painting *Die* for its permanent collection, and in 2021 the National Gallery of Art in Washington, DC, purchased *The Flag Is Bleeding*.

HEATHER BOOTH

Stokely Carmichael,* who then became Kwame Ture, mockingly said: "What's women's position in the movement? It's prone." But he wasn't saying that's what it *should* be. Some have misinterpreted that, but what he was saying was that's a stereotype of how many women were treated, and he was exposing it.

> Stokely Carmichael, *New York Times*, April 14, 1996,
> "Formerly Stokely Carmichael and Still Ready for the Revolution,"
> by Karen de Witt
>
> That was a joke. We were on a war front and it was a wartime joke. It had to be a joke because I worked for women like Gloria Richardson of Cambridge, Md., and Ruby Darrow Smith, the executive secretary of SNCC. The general public may not know their names, but these were powerful sisters.
>
> It was the white women in SNCC who spread that because they blamed me for putting whites out of the organization. They ought to thank me. They didn't know they were oppressed until they got pushed out of SNCC and became women's liberationists.

FLORYNCE KENNEDY

I attended all four Black Power Conferences. The first Conference on Black Power was held in Newark in 1967, the second in Philadelphia in 1968, the third in Bermuda in 1969, and the fourth in Atlanta in 1970. There were also Black political caucuses in 1968, and 1972 both in Gary, Indiana, and I didn't miss those either. . . . It's the same gig wherever you are. Whether you're fighting for women's liberation or just Black liberation, you're fighting the same enemies.†

---

* In 1966, Carmichael became SNCC's new leader, coined the phrase "Black Power," and steered the organization away from nonviolent actions and toward a more radical agenda. In July 1967, SNCC asked its white members to leave the organization.

† The last sentence is quoted from *Time*, March 26, 1973. As Kennedy's biographer Sherie M. Randolph writes, "Kennedy's black feminism was shaped by her relationship with the Black Power movement, and she brought the vision of Black Power to the emerging, predominantly white women's movement. As one of the only Black women in NOW, she made Black Power into a pivotal ideological influence on the radical feminist politics that was developing in New York City. She was a bridge builder within these movements, demanding that the women's movement partner squarely with Black Power and continue to participate in anti-war struggles. . . . It never occurred to her that a women's movement would not also fight against racism and imperialism."

FRANCES BEAL

My own view is that SNCC was a part of a generation of activists whose main target was to destroy the formal structure of Jim Crow. And I think what happened is that the level of racism on the part of whites was so strong that many people in SNCC felt that the role of whites at this point was to work in white communities and deal with the racism that existed in white communities, and that that would be the best thing to advance the racial justice movement. White people did have a role, but it wasn't in the Black communities.

I got a job in '67 working for the National Council of Negro Women in New York. They had something called Project Womanpower, and I was initially the secretary of the project. So then they hired a lot of SNCC women because they wanted the activists to carry out this Project Womanpower, which was an attempt to mobilize the potential of Black women around Black women's issues.

MICHELE WALLACE

When Black Power was announced, all the white people were told to go home or go away. And in particular, this was very hurtful and devastating for the white women who had been involved in the civil rights movement.

HEATHER BOOTH

One of the many reasons I moved toward a greater focus on women's issues was partly because the women's movement was emerging, and also, by '66, '67, whites were told it was time we organized in our own communities and Black people needed their own organization. I was a Friends of SNCC student representative (that's what it was called in the North), and I remember the meeting where a number of the very fine Black staff said it was time for Black people to have their own organization, and they wanted the white people out. Initially, I was very taken aback. I felt we had done a great deal for each other, taken many risks for each other, and supported each other. And then I realized that the Black staff who were raising this had sensitivities that I needed to respect.

I still was in a Coordinating Council of Community Organizations, which was the city-wide civil rights group, but my home group, SNCC, wasn't going to be my group anymore. So I went elsewhere. All of that happened at once. But it's not so much like one thing ended and one thing started.

It's like, they all were together, and that's part of why it was a movement. It was a civil rights movement, a women's movement, a Puerto Rican rights movement, an American Indian movement, an antiwar movement, a student movement. And what you felt is that you were part of the *movement*. And I felt it was just a question of what people chose to emphasize, but all of our interests were deeply connected.

JO FREEMAN

By the time I moved to Chicago in '67, I had run into plenty of discrimination. In June or July, someone told me that there was a free school at the University of Chicago, and that two women, Heather Booth and Naomi Weisstein, were teaching a course on women. So I went, and one of the things that they announced was that there was going to be the National Conference for New Politics* in Chicago over Labor Day weekend.

Before going to the conference in August, I went to New York and went around to various antiwar groups, like the Fifth Avenue Peace Parade Committee, for example, and started talking about how we should do something about women. The antiwar women didn't really cotton onto feminism either. They would talk about how men can be drafted and women can't, so we have to worry about the men.†

TI-GRACE ATKINSON

At the New Politics Conference, more than half the people at the convention were women. But the steering committee was all men. Well, I started to get more and more upset. I thought that we should have resolutions on the floor about women, feminist resolutions.

---

* The National Conference for New Politics (NCNP) convention, which took place over Labor Day weekend in 1967, attracted two thousand participants from two hundred liberal and radical civil rights and peace groups who desperately hoped to find a way to unite the fractured movement and promote a unified voice against President Johnson and the escalating Vietnam War. At the peak of its influence, the separatist Black Power movement's agenda dominated the proceedings. White delegates accepted the Black caucus's demand to 51 percent committee representation and convention votes even though they comprised one-sixth of the delegates. H. Rap Brown, SNCC's leader, refused to talk to white delegates.

† By 1967, the Vietnam War had dramatically escalated, and that summer President Johnson announced plans to expand the US troop count to 525,000. By the end of 1967, a total of 19,560 American troops had perished in the war, and opposition to the war began to reach a fever pitch. Martin Luther King Jr. announced his opposition, and former heavyweight boxing champion Muhammad Ali refused the draft and faced jail time. Thousands of young men defied the draft, organized visible, disruptive protests on college campuses and big cities, and stormed the Pentagon.

JO FREEMAN

The people at this conference represented a wide age group. It was full of political activists. I had just turned twenty-three. Shulie [Firestone] was there. She was an art student at the Art Institute of Chicago.

The NCNP hammered out a women's resolution, but Shulie and I went to work on it and we turned it into something more radical than the original resolution.*

TI-GRACE ATKINSON

I went around to get other women. That's where I met Shulie and Jo Freeman for the first time. We all mimeographed their statement, and they were distributing it.

JO FREEMAN

We passed out all these copies of the resolution, and we waited for the women's resolution to be introduced. It was literally at the end of the agenda. They read the original resolution, and we raised our hands expecting to be recognized so we could propose our *substitute* resolution, but the chair didn't recognize us. Instead, he said, "All opposed? All in favor? All opposed? Resolution passed. Next resolution." And then this young man pushed his way in front of me at the microphone. He was instantly recognized, and he said, "Ladies and gentlemen, I want to talk about the forgotten American Indian."

Well, Shulie and I went to the podium, and the person who came down from the podium was the conference executive director William Pepper. I remember this really well. We were protesting the fact that we had not been allowed to promote our substitute motion. Pepper literally patted Shulie on the head and said, "Cool down, little girl. We have more important things to talk about than women's problems."

Needless to say, we were pissed as hell. We had collected the names of the women in the women's caucus, and invited them to a meeting at my apartment on the near-west side of Chicago. So we had this first meeting and we talked about the conference. Some had been there. Some hadn't.

---

* The original women's resolution, drafted by Women Strike for Peace (WSP), blandly recommended that women work toward the peace effort. Freeman and Firestone's resolution demanded that women (because they made up 51 percent of the population) be given 51 percent of votes and committee seats at the convention. They also called for a total "revamping of marriage, divorce, and property laws," and full access to birth control and abortion.

But everyone agreed that the time had come to start doing something more. To stop talking and start acting.

We started meeting at my apartment weekly. It became informally known as the West Side Group.

TI-GRACE ATKINSON
Out of this caucus came women's liberation. Jo Freeman stayed in Chicago and began the first feminist newsletter, *Voice of the Women's Liberation Movement*. Chicago was, for a long time, the heart of women's liberation.*

---

* Atkinson moved to New York and became the first president of the New York chapter of NOW in 1967.

13

Newsweek's Good Girls

As radical women began separating from New Left groups, and NOW started to help blue-collar women and stewardesses challenge workplace sex discrimination, white-collar office "girls" with college educations were experiencing similar barriers to entry and promotion. Even liberal New York publications like Newsweek *were no exception.*

LYNN POVICH

When *Newsweek* started in '33 as the alternative to *Time*, it wanted to be much more politically liberal. Phil Graham, publisher of the *Washington Post*, bought *Newsweek* in '61 and hired Oz Elliott, who came from *Time*, to be the editor in chief. Oz had a group of guys around him who were a lot more open-minded about many things, so that's why *Newsweek* was very much against the war in Vietnam. It was pro–civil rights. We had Black reporters who reported those stories. That's why so many women applied to work there.

NORA EPHRON

I worked on the school newspaper in high school and college, and a week before graduating from Wellesley in 1962 I found a job in New York City. I'd gone to an employment agency on West Forty-Second Street. I told the woman there that I wanted to be a journalist, and she said, "How would you like to work at *Newsweek* magazine?" and I said fine. She picked up the phone, made an appointment for me, and sent me right over to the Newsweek Building, at 444 Madison Avenue.

LYNN POVICH

I graduated from Vassar in 1965, and the job listings were segregated. So it was Help Wanted—Male, Help Wanted—Female. And female jobs were nurse, teacher, secretary, or a training program at Bloomingdale's. Less than 5 percent of women graduates until 1970 went to either medical school or law school, and 3 percent to business school.

We were postwar women raised in that culture of yes, you'll go to college, yes, you'll get married, and yes, you'll raise a family. You may have a job, but not a career. The word "career" was never mentioned. That's what we thought. It wasn't just that the men thought that way, the women thought that way too, with certain exceptions. There were always women who knew that this was unjust and unfair and they were angry about it. But most of us were just happy to have a job at a really great place.

LUCY HOWARD

I graduated from Radcliffe and started looking for a job in New York the summer of '63. I moved in with my friend Sue, who went to Wellesley. She was going to secretarial school. I knew what I didn't want to do, and what I did not want to do was be a secretary. I just didn't want to have to work for somebody like that.

Then I went to an agency and filled out an application, and this nice woman said, "Oh, you went to Harvard. Isn't that interesting?" Because I would put down Harvard because I had a Harvard degree even though we really went to Radcliffe. She said, "I think there may be an opening in the training program at *Newsweek*. Would you be interested?" I thought, "Training program at *Newsweek* magazine, would I be interested? Oh yes, I would." Sounds pretty exciting. I'm going to be trained.

So I put on a nice dress, nice shoes, nice stockings, and had my interview with John McAllister, who was a big, gruff, burly guy who smoked a pipe. He was head of the news desk. He said, "Fine, fine. When do you want to come to work?" Now did I ask anything about what the job would be? No. But this was a job at *Newsweek*.

PETER GOLDMAN

I knew I wanted to be a journalist, so I went to Columbia Journalism School. The other day, I was looking at a class photo from our graduation, and there were more than sixty people in the class, five of whom were women. It was a men's game in those days. When I finished J school I went to work at a newspaper in St. Louis, the *Globe Democrat*, now long defunct. They had precisely two women reporters in a newsroom of probably twenty-five. Then I came to *Newsweek* in 1962. Our top editor, Oz Elliott, had worked at *Time*, and the model was: the writers are men, the researchers and gophers are women.

NORA EPHRON

The man who interviewed me asked why I wanted to work at *Newsweek*. I think I was supposed to say something like, "Because it's such an important magazine," but I had barely read *Newsweek*; in those days, it was a sorry second to *Time*. So I responded by saying that I wanted to work there because I hoped to become a writer. I was quickly assured that women didn't become writers at *Newsweek*. It would never have crossed my mind to object, or to say, "You're going to turn out to be wrong about me." It was a given in those days that if you were a woman and you wanted to do certain things, you were going to have to be the exception to the rule. I was hired as a mail girl, for $55 a week.

There were no mail boys at *Newsweek*, only mail girls. If you were a college graduate (like me) who had worked on your college newspaper (like me) and you were a girl (like me), they hired you as a mail girl. If you were a boy (unlike me) with exactly the same qualifications, they hired you as a reporter and sent you to a bureau somewhere in America. It was unjust but it was 1962, so it was the way things were.

LUCY HOWARD

We'd get these bags of mail and we had a long galley and there were slots for everybody's mail. I did very well. I showed up on time. I could read the letters and I could put the letters in the right box, and that was very important. And the people who were there! Ellen Goodman, Nora Ephron. Everyone who was there was either from a Seven Sisters school or Berkeley.

LYNN POVICH

Newsweek was really fun. The jobs were segregated not only by gender, but by function. The reporters would report and send files to the writers, who would write, and the researchers would fact-check, except researchers could also hand in files if you were in certain departments. Back-of-the-book [culture and business] reporters reported. Very few women got a chance to be promoted to be reporters, even though they were researchers who were reporting.

LUCY HOWARD

Then there was the Elliott girl. The Elliott girl was someone who worked for Oz Elliott. You had to be smart, be pretty, have good legs, know how to make a martini, and not be turned off by any of the jokes that the top editors were telling. They wanted somebody that they found charming and entertaining and decorative.

NORA EPHRON

I was the Elliott girl. This meant that on Friday nights I worked late, delivering copy back and forth from the writers to the editors, until it was very late. We often worked until three in the morning on Friday nights, and then we had to be back at work early Saturday, when the Nation and Foreign departments closed.

LYNN POVICH

So we sort of accepted this. And that was sort of rankling because women were doing more and more reporting and they could show that they could do the job, but somehow they never got raises or promotions.

NORA EPHRON

After a few months, I was promoted to the next stage of girldom at *Newsweek*: I became a clipper. Being a clipper entailed clipping newspapers from around the country. We all sat at something called the Clip Desk, armed with rip sticks and grease pencils, and we ripped up the country's newspapers and routed the clips to the relevant departments. For instance, if someone cured cancer in St. Louis, we sent the clipping to the Medicine section. Being a clipper was a horrible job, and to make matters worse, I was good at it.

Three months later, I was promoted again, this time to the highest rung: I became a researcher. "Researcher" was a fancy word—and not all that fancy at that—for "fact-checker," and that's pretty much what the job consisted of. I worked in the Nation department. I was extremely happy to be there. This was not a bad job six months out of college. . . . There were six writers and six researchers in the department, and we worked from Tuesday to Saturday night, when the magazine closed. For most of the week, none of us did anything. . . . Then, on Friday afternoon, [the writers] all wrote their stories and gave them to the researchers to check. . . . News magazine writers in those days were famous for using the expression "tk," which stood for "to come"; they were always writing sentences like, "There are tk lightbulbs in the chandelier in the chamber of the House of Representatives," and part of your job as a researcher was to find out just how many lightbulbs there were.

SUSAN BROWNMILLER

When I arrived at *Newsweek* in 1963, I was like the first person who didn't have to be a clip girl or a mail girl. They put me right into the Nation department, where I was the fact-checker for Peter Goldman. But he never made any mistakes. I spent two years putting the T in Wyatt T. Walker. He'd write Wyatt Walker and I'd put the T in, Wyatt T. Walker. That's what I did for two years at *Newsweek*.

PETER GOLDMAN

It was the first time in my life, or first time since grade school, when I had actually had female pals. The men in Nation, where I worked, all had cubicles with doors. And the women sat out in what we called the bullpen, just two rows of desks. In the early part of the week there wasn't much to do except send out queries and talk to correspondents. So I spent a lot of time hanging out in the bullpen. I had gone to an all-male college, and mostly male grad school.

I think there was a difference between the back of the book and the front of the book [Nation]. When Nation reporter Tony Fuller moved to the back of the book as a senior editor, he called me one day and said, "Peter, you wouldn't believe this. It's a sexual rodeo up here."

LYNN POVICH

In the mid-'60s when the sexual revolution was in full swing, the magazine was a cauldron of hormonal activity. Women felt as sexually entitled as men, and our short skirts and sometimes braless tops only added to the boil. It was post-pill, and there were a lot of young people. Married or single, it didn't matter.

LUCY HOWARD

Some of the stuff that went on then, you'd be fired for in a split second today. Sometimes people would come up and rub your back, and they would flirt and say they liked your dress, or somebody would call you Dolly. A correspondent from Los Angeles who's movie-star handsome stands right by your desk and says, "I had a great fuck last night. Wanna join me tonight?" That's what it was like.

LYNN POVICH

Many guys looked at us as people they wanted to cheat on their wives with—and many women were happy to accommodate them. The infirmary, two tiny rooms with single beds, was the assignation place of choice. Often a writer would go there to "take a nap" for an hour or two, albeit with a female staffer.

Then Nora left *Newsweek* and went to the *New York Post* because she wanted to be able to write.

14

NOW Swings into Action

By late 1967, just one year after its inception, NOW began to shape its identity and goals, and defending blue-collar women's rights in the workplace—something the EEOC wouldn't do at the time—became its central mission.

MARY JEAN COLLINS

In 1961, I went to Alverno College, a Catholic women's college run by the Sisters of Saint Francis, and there I met two nuns who changed my life completely. I was a history major, and one of my teachers was Sister Joelle Reed, who was one of the founders of NOW. Together, we founded the Milwaukee chapter of NOW in 1967. Sister Joelle Reed was the president and I was the treasurer.

The first NOW event that I went to was the national founding conference in November 1967. Joelle introduced me to Catherine Conroy, who was a leader in the Communications Workers of America union, and another founder of NOW. She said to me, "I want you to go to the NOW conference with me." Off I go with Catherine to Washington, DC. I'll never forget it, because I had never been in a room with women like that; I was just totally blown away. I was probably the youngest person in the room [of 105 people]. I was in my twenties, most of the women in the room were over forty. A lot of the founders of NOW had accomplished as much as any woman could accomplish in the fifties. They were lawyers and PhDs and this and that, but quite a diverse group.

This was NOW's first conference, and what they set out to do was to try to decide what the essence of feminism was, and to define the positions NOW needed to take, and what our strategy would be.

BETTY FRIEDAN
The 1967 NOW convention faced two major crises of decision: the Equal Rights Amendment and abortion.

AILEEN HERNANDEZ
In NOW at that time, we not only had women from a lot of religious groups, we also had an archbishop. A lot of nuns were members of NOW, and they had very strong feelings about what they saw as life.

MARY JEAN COLLINS
Alice Rossi, who was a sociologist from the University of Chicago, gave this incredible paper on abortion and why it was a basic right and had to be a part of our agenda. Here I am this little Catholic kid from Milwaukee. This blew my mind.

Then some people argued that we couldn't come out in support of abortion now because we were too new an organization, and it would get us off the track.

TI-GRACE ATKINSON
The first rift in the movement came over the abortion issue in 1967. The moderates and radicals stuck together, and the right wing of the movement was formed in response to this. NOW lost some of its nuns and Catholic labor union members.

Minutes of 1967 National Conference
of National Organization for Women
Vote on the resolution concerning abortion:
Yes 57
No 14
The resolution was passed.
A motion passed moved by Dr. Alice Rossi that: NOW endorses

the principle that it is a basic right of every woman to control her reproductive life, and therefore, NOW supports the furthering of the sexual revolution of our century by pressing for widespread sex education, provision of birth control information and contraceptives, and urges that all laws penalizing abortion be repealed.

MURIEL FOX

I must say, I thought that it was too early to support abortion rights, and that employment rights were the important issue, and that we would lose the housewives and lose membership. I was wrong. What happened after NOW supported abortion rights was we got tens of thousands of new, younger women, who understood the importance of this issue.

MARY JEAN COLLINS

A bunch of people from Ohio walked out on the abortion issue, including the women who founded WEAL [Women's Equity Action League]. They weren't having that.*

Then the Equal Rights Amendment came up. One of the basic divisions within the feminist movement coming out of suffrage was the question of the Equal Rights Amendment, which the suffrage people wanted, Alice Paul and her group.

MURIEL FOX

Labor union women were among our biggest supporters, and the United Auto Workers did our mailings for us out of Detroit, with Martha Griffiths's approval. The union women said, "Please don't support the ERA."

AILEEN HERNANDEZ

The unions did not want the laws to change. They needed them at the turn of the twentieth century, because women were totally exploited in the job market, didn't get paid, lived under horrible working conditions. So, there was this dilemma: What should we as a movement say about those protective laws? Should we say, "Throw them all out?"

We lost some of our union people for a period of time. But we got a

---

* Founded by Betty Boyer, WEAL became a powerful national organization that focused primarily on employment and educational equity and access. The group often worked in tandem with NOW but avoided taking positions on controversial social issues like abortion.

whole lot of new people coming in, so you got this up-and-down situation while women figured out, How does the movement serve me?

*Out of that conference came Betty Friedan's Bill of Rights for women, including abortion rights, which was considered very radical at the time. It also called for passage of the ERA, enforcement of Title VII, universal childcare, and more.**

MARY JEAN COLLINS

The organization limped out of this convention with a few legs missing, but a clear agenda. What was magnificent about it was they were saying, "We're going to put women first, and see how it falls." These women were kind of middle-age, middle-class women, and yet they were able to take a pretty radical agenda for that time, and put women at the center of things, and try to figure out how to move forward. It was a very courageous meeting.

MURIEL FOX

Two of our most important early lawsuits were aimed at helping blue-collar women working in factories. First was a lawsuit against Colgate-Palmolive aimed to end the practice of separate seniority lists for men and women in factories. And incidentally, we had to fight the labor unions on that issue as fiercely as we fought the corporations.

In November 1965, twenty-eight women, including Thelma Bowe, were laid off despite having more seniority than the men they worked with

---

* Here are some of the other demands in the Bill of Rights for women: "We Demand: III. That women be protected by law to insure their rights to return to their jobs within a reasonable time after childbirth without loss of seniority or other accrued benefits and be paid maternity leave as a form of social security and/or employee benefit. IV. Immediate revision of tax laws to permit the deduction of home and child care expenses for working parents. V. That child care facilities be established by law on the same basis as parks, libraries and public schools adequate to the needs of children, from the pre-school years through adolescence, as a community resource to be used by all citizens from all income levels. VI. That the right of women to be educated to their full potential equally with men be secured by Federal and State legislation, eliminating all discrimination and segregation by sex, written and unwritten, at all levels of education including college, graduate and professional schools, loans and fellowships and Federal and State training programs, such as the job Corps. VII. The right of women in poverty to secure job training, housing and family allowances on equal terms with men, but without prejudice to a parent's right to remain at home to care for his or her children; revision of welfare legislation and poverty programs which deny women dignity, privacy and self-respect. VIII. The right of women to control their own reproductive lives by removing from penal codes the laws limiting access to contraceptive information and devices and laws governing abortion."

at the Jeffersonville, Indiana, Colgate-Palmolive plant. Several women immediately filed complaints with the EEOC, which ultimately was not able to resolve the issue between the company and the women. The EEOC told the women they could sue, which they did on March 30, 1966, filing a class-action lawsuit under Title VII of the Civil Rights Act, arguing that the weight restrictions (women not allowed to lift more than thirty-five pounds) and sex-based layoff policies violated their rights. On June 30, 1967, the US district court judge ruled against the women and in favor of Colgate-Palmolive. One month later NOW filed an appeal.

SONIA PRESSMAN FUENTES

People would file complaints at the EEOC, and they would come across my desk. If I saw a case that looked like it was something, I would call Mary Eastwood, I would call Catherine East. Marguerite Rawalt established a cadre of lawyers who would take these cases on behalf of the women and wouldn't charge money.

MARGUERITE RAWALT

I was chairman of the NOW Legal Committee, and immediately we had to appeal three key cases to the circuit courts of appeals: *Weeks v. Southern Bell, Bowe v. Colgate-Palmolive*, and *Mengelkoch v. State of California* out on the West Coast were all lost under Title VII. They were all union women, and each one of them filed complaints of sex discrimination in different parts of the country and they lost in the district court, in trial court, federal court.

In *Thelma Bowe et al v. Colgate-Palmolive Co.*, the US District Court Southern District Indiana handed down a decision on June 30, 1967, upholding company policy regulations under which women factory workers were confined to lower-paid "finishing" jobs on the grounds that it was proper to "protect" women from jobs requiring the lifting of more than thirty-five pounds. There was no state law involved; the decision was a limitation on the federal statute, Title VII, in its alleged* ban on sex discrimination, which can be broadly expanded to many other restrictions upon women employees.

---

* The EEOC didn't have the ability to legally enforce its sex-discrimination rulings until Congress amended its powers in 1972.

MARY EASTWOOD

There weren't very many women lawyers who knew anything about sex discrimination, or were aware that that was an issue that you should be concerned about. I used to get phone calls from all over the country from women who had been to a lecture of Betty Friedan's, and Betty had given them my phone number. So I would talk to them on the phone and explain that I really couldn't give them legal advice but they could file a complaint with the EEOC.

The first time I met Sue Sellers, Lena Moore, and Anna Casey was shortly after they filed a notice of appeal; they came and stayed at my apartment. Sue Sellers looked like a pleasant grandmother with silver hair. Lena Moore was tall, friendly, and attractive. All these women were in good muscular shape, because they did heavy physical labor at the Colgate plant. We had a meeting with Marguerite Rawalt and Caruthers Berger about how to proceed on their case.

MARGUERITE RAWALT

Sue Sellers was the ringleader. I think she went to the local library to read about this new statute called Title VII of the Civil Rights Act of 1964. She contacted the EEOC and got a complaint form and just went ahead with it. Sue decided, when she filed the complaint, to go ahead and put Thelma Bowe's name on—instead of her own or anybody else's, because as she put it, Thelma was "the oldest girl" in the plant, meaning she had worked for Colgate the longest.

I know that there was a lot of harassment, or at least the women perceived it to be harassment on the part of the men at the Colgate plant. I remember that Sue Sellers was run off the road once, and she thought that it may have been one of her male coworkers. In another instance, one of them fell and got hurt because soap suds were left on the floor for the women to fall on, and they thought that was deliberate on the part of the men. But of course, the men had a lot at stake; they had the best-paying jobs, and the women were trying to get them from them.

Then, one night [in October 1968], three of us were together in an apartment in Washington, DC, when we read about the *Weeks* case* being lost.

---

* Office clerk Lorena Weeks was denied her application for promotion at Southern Bell Telephone in Georgia, because the higher-paying switchman job required lifting more than thirty pounds. State laws prohibiting women from taking jobs that required lifting more than thirty pounds were commonly used as a way to keep women out of higher-paying positions in many blue-collar jobs across the country. Weeks

We called Mrs. Weeks, we didn't know her at all, but we knew that this case couldn't stand. She said she couldn't appeal it because she couldn't afford to hire a lawyer. So we told her that we could do it without any fees, but she would have to agree to stay on the job and we knew it wouldn't be easy, she'd been harassed. She said she would.

Then I called Betty Friedan and I said, look we'll do all this work. We didn't know a thing about this law; it was a new law, it started out in a new field with no precedent. But for heaven's sake somebody ought to pay for the printing of the brief and filing of the appeal, which ran into several hundred dollars, so we explained it to Betty and said, can NOW raise the money? She said, go ahead. I'll get the money some way or another. So we went ahead, and that was two and a half years and every weekend. I don't know how we did anything else.

---

pointed out in her complaint that as a clerk, she had to lift her thirty-four-pound typewriter every day. After several appeals (with help from NOW), Weeks won in 1969 and was granted back pay and the switchman's job.

15

A Program for Radical Women

A suffragist and pacifist, Jeannette Rankin (1880–1973) became the first woman elected to the US Congress in 1916. The first vote Rankin cast, on April 6, 1917, was against the resolution to send American soldiers to Europe to fight in World War I. Rankin's vote against the war cost her her reelection. But she was reelected in 1940, just in time to become the only member of Congress to vote against the declaration of war on Japan after the bombing of Pearl Harbor. Still committed to peace activism at age eighty-seven, Rankin joined her younger compatriots to protest the war in Vietnam one cold day in January 1968.

CHARLOTTE BUNCH

Five thousand women came to Washington, DC, in January 1968 for the Jeannette Rankin Brigade. It was a women's peace event organized by Women Strike for Peace and also Church Women United, who were progressive church women. NOW members were part of the march. I was president of the University Christian Movement at the time, and the church women had negotiated to have one young speaker, so they asked me.

MARILYN WEBB

We knew that this demonstration was going to be moderate, ineffectual, and basically absurd. The brigade organizers had made this deal with Congress that they weren't going to use signs, they weren't going to be creating any ruckus. The way we saw people like Betty Friedan was that they were dealing with the glass ceiling. They wanted to get women to be bankers, lawyers, and doctors. The women in NOW essentially accepted the patriarchy. They were busy meeting with Congress.

CHARLOTTE BUNCH
Most of the women were ten to twenty years older than me.

MARILYN WEBB
We were between the ages of eighteen and twenty-eight, and we had been involved in community organizing, campus organizing, draft-resistance organizing, et cetera. We were talking about a recast of the role of women in society. We wanted to talk about how their roles are defined in marriage, family and social living, how women are treated as a colonized class. We were the generation that did not see the government as our friend and provider. The women who planned the demonstration still had that New Deal faith in their government.

SHULAMITH FIRESTONE
From the beginning we felt that this kind of action, though well-meant, was ultimately futile. It is naïve to believe that women who are not politically seen, heard, or represented in this country could change the course of a war by simply appealing to the better natures of congressmen.

MARILYN WEBB
At our meeting on Sunday night, the day before the brigade, fifty young women from fourteen cities met to discuss their political and personal futures. We had not come to Washington just to participate in a demonstration. We came to see if we could build a movement or a political organization of women capable of developing a program for radical women.

CHARLOTTE BUNCH
I gave a speech on radical young women's views of imperialism at the rally, but while there, I saw a New York group of young radical feminists perform a feminist skit about men and warfare that fascinated me and shocked many. They came through with a coffin. It was a very dramatic interruption and disruption.

SHULAMITH FIRESTONE

We staged an actual funeral procession with a larger-than-life dummy on a transported bier, complete with feminine getup. . . . Hanging from the bier were such disposable items as S&H Green Stamps, curlers, garters, and hairspray. Streamers floated off it and we also carried large banners, such as "DON'T CRY: RESIST!" . . . We had a special drum corps with kazoo and a sheet of clever songs written by Beverly Grant and others. Peggy Dobbins wrote a long funeral dirge lamenting women's traditional role. . . . There were several related pamphlets, including one written by Kathie Amatniek (later Sarachild) which elaborated on the following progression:

> TRADITIONAL WOMANHOOD IS DEAD
>
> TRADITIONAL WOMEN WERE BEAUTIFUL . . . BUT REALLY POWERLESS
>
> "UPPITY" WOMEN WERE EVEN MORE BEAUTIFUL . . . BUT STILL POWERLESS
>
> SISTERHOOD IS POWERFUL[*]
>
> HUMANHOOD THE ULTIMATE!

ROSALYN BAXANDALL

We were the radical-left offshoot saying, "We're not only into telling our men not to fight in the war, we want a movement of ourselves." We were against Women Strike for Peace and their idea of just "Women are peaceful. Women should tell men not to fight in the war." We thought we should have our own movement.

SHULAMITH FIRESTONE

Finally, by way of a black-bordered invitation, we "joyfully" invited many of the five thousand women there to attend a burial that evening at Arlington "by torchlight" of Traditional Womanhood, "who passed with a sigh to her Great Reward this year of the Lord, 1968, after three thousand years of bolstering the egos of Warmakers and aiding the cause of war."

CHARLOTTE BUNCH

The weekend of the Jeannette Rankin Brigade, I went to that meeting Marilyn and Heather Booth arranged, because my college friend Sara Evans and Marilyn were both involved.

The power of listening to the women talking about what they were dis-

---

[*]   This is the first time the slogan "sisterhood is powerful" appeared in feminist literature.

covering resonated with me. I remember them talking about how important those meetings had become for them and how it made them begin to think about women as a constituency.

We spent months convincing ourselves that it was politically okay to meet separately as women and focus on women's concerns. We felt somewhat more secure because we saw a parallel to the arguments of Blacks who had been establishing their right and need to have their own space. Ultimately, the experience was so powerful that it justified itself.

We met every Sunday night for months, and gradually more people would get invited into the group. I remember at one point we decided, "Marilyn, this group is getting too big. We have to start a second group." Then there was a second consciousness-raising group and a third. Marilyn was bringing us a lot of articles and thinking from women in other places around the country.

CATHY WILKERSON

I was a little bit skeptical because I grew up in an all-women's family, with only sisters and my mother, and I already felt very liberated. I was the only woman running a region of SDS, and I was on the national committee of SDS. So I didn't feel that being a woman had held me back.

It became very acrimonious, although it never blew up, because everybody liked each other too much. So everybody argued their positions tremendously defensively because we were all totally defensive about it. My perspective was on a different plane than theirs. I really saw my life as dedicated to activism, to civil rights and antiwar, and all of that stuff. I felt like an outsider.

CHARLOTTE BUNCH

Most of us gradually changed our political work, embraced the term "women's liberation," helped start more consciousness-raising groups, and initiated public action aimed at making people aware of women's oppression.

MARILYN WEBB

We began teaching classes on women's issues to packed sessions at the Institute for Policy Studies, we started a speaker's bureau to go to area churches and college-university campuses, we began an abortion counseling service, started organizing nurses and clerical workers in DC, and began forming seminal thinking for the burgeoning women's movement by writing assorted position papers and articles and getting in touch with other groups—and individuals—around the country that were forming like ours.

ROSALYN BAXANDALL
The New York Radical Feminist meetings were from '68 on. First, we met in my living room at St. Mark's Place. Then the Southern Christian Educational Fund [SCEF] gave us their office at 799 Broadway. Once a week we had a consciousness-raising group there. We learned about consciousness-raising from Kathie Amatniek Sarachild, formerly from SNCC. A lot of women had been very active in the civil rights movement in the South, and they had done a lot of consciousness-raising: going around the room and talking about yourself.

PEGGY DOBBINS
By sharing personal experiences we were discovering that we weren't crazy. We began to evolve a structure in which we went around the room and took turns speaking. Kathie Sarachild introduced a discipline that you weren't supposed to generalize unless you preceded it with a personal experience.

ROBIN MORGAN
We were talking about sex one night. I admitted that on occasion in my marriage I had faked an orgasm. I was convinced that I was the only person in the world sick and perverse enough to have done this. Every woman in the room said, "Oh, you too?"

SUSAN BROWNMILLER
I went to a meeting of New York Radical Women. Kathie Amatniek Sarachild, who was a great believer in consciousness-raising, said, "Let's go around the room, and when you are ready to have a child, do you want a boy or a girl?" And Peggy Dobbin said, "Come on Kathie, you know perfectly well that I had to have the child, and I had to give it away. Because I didn't know how to get an abortion."

And then we went around the room and a lot of people were talking about getting an abortion, and they're all talking about *one* abortion. So I was competitive, right? So I said, "I had three abortions, and the last one was six months ago in Puerto Rico." And I said to my friend Jan Goodman, "I never even told you, did I?" And I hadn't. And then I started to cry. I had never said this out loud before.

ANSELMA DELL'OLIO

NOW was the first group to be founded. We had been reading this stuff written by radical women. We all called them the downtown women. These were the radical feminist groups, they happened out of Chicago—this whole group of women just rose up as one and left that conference and formed a feminist group, and then they came to New York.

Shulie Firestone was one of them, and Anne Koedt. I was viewed with much suspicion by them, because I wore eye makeup and miniskirts, and they all wore jeans and didn't shave under their armpits. I was bourgeois. The only one who walked right up to me at that first meeting and said, "I've heard so many bad things about you, I just knew I had to meet you," was Shulamith Firestone.

If there's one genius that came out of the feminist movement, it was definitely Shulamith Firestone. She was an artist by training, but she was a natural philosopher. She wrote *The Dialectic of Sex* in 1970 and it's still in print, and really is extraordinary for a book written by a twenty-five-year-old art major.

So I made friends downtown and I sat through a few consciousness-raising groups, which I found rather silly. There were like twenty or thirty women in one of those bathroom-in-the-kitchen apartments in the Lower East Side, before the neighborhood became chic. To keep the good talkers from dominating, you got chips. When you used up your chips, you couldn't talk anymore. So we went around and everyone got a chance to speak. It was all very demagogic, because they came out of the extreme Left, they were all Marxists, every one of them.

BARBARA MEHRHOF

Sheila Cronan and I were social workers at the Bureau of Child Welfare on Church Street in Lower Manhattan when we first engaged with feminism. In March, I read the article about the new women's movement in the *New York Times Magazine* with the headline "What Do These Women Want?" It quoted Ti-Grace Atkinson, Betty Friedan, and others.

New York Times, March 10, 1968,
"What Do These Women Want?" by Martha Weinman Lear
Feminism, which one might have supposed as dead as the Polish Question, is again an issue. Proponents call it the Second Feminist Wave, the first having ebbed after the glorious victory of suffrage and disappeared, finally into the great sandbar of Togetherness. . . .

Today NOW has 1,200 members, with a heavy concentration of lawyers, sociologists and educators. . . .

Not all of the new feminist activity is centered within NOW, to its left is a small group called Radical Women—young, bright-eyed, cheerfully militant—which recently splintered off from Students for a Democratic Society . . . the evolutionaries attack concrete issues, tied primarily to employment. They are NOW's pragmaticians, and its overwhelming majority. The militants are its theoreticians . . . they are the movement's intellectual hip, the female version of Black Power. . . .

Their thesis is that true equality for women can come only with profound social revolution. Their haute thinker, and thus the key to their spirit and style, is Ti-Grace Atkinson, president of the New York chapter [of NOW].

MURIEL FOX

That article came at a time when NOW was changing. We were first founded by professional women. These were women and men who had the time, and the status, and the money to travel to board meetings. Later, after the abortion issue was resolved in '67, new people, mostly women, flocked into NOW, and they were much more radical. I remember at the first meeting of the New York chapter of NOW after Martha Lear's article came out, all these women came dressed very strangely. And we looked at each other and said, "Who are these people?" They didn't look like the professional women who founded NOW, there's no question. They looked like a lot of have-nots and radicals. And in some ways that was good for the movement, but it created a lot of friction.

New York Times, March 10, 1968,
"What Do These Women Want?" by Martha Weinman Lear
Miss Atkinson is 29, unmarried, good-looking. She is an analytic philosopher working on her doctorate at Columbia.

"The institution of marriage has the same effect the institution of slavery had. It separates people in the same category, disperses them, keeps them from identifying as a class. . . . To say that a woman is really 'happy' with her home and kids is as irrelevant as saying that the Blacks were happy taking care of Ol' Massa. She is defined by her maintenance role. Her husband is defined by his productive role. We're saying that all human beings should have a productive role in society."

MURIEL FOX

Ti-Grace Atkinson made pronouncements about marriage and children that the other people in New York NOW were horrified by, and they said, "This is terrible public relations." A few months later, we had a big battle.

MARILYN WEBB

By June 1968, our DC Women's Liberation group had decided to plan the first, small national women's liberation meeting in Sandy Spring, Maryland. About twenty attendees included representatives of groups from New York, Boston, Chicago, DC, Gainesville, Baltimore, and others. We began mapping out a cogent feminist theory and decided we needed to have a larger consensus to flesh things out. Then we decided to hold a much larger conference the following November, during Thanksgiving, which ended up being in a YMCA camp in Lake Villa, Illinois.

So we were building up to a national—not really an organization—but at least a cohesive national consciousness. By the time of the conference, position papers were flying all over the country. Women came from New Orleans, Gainesville, Vancouver, Oceanside, New York—there were several New York groups—Chicago, Northside Radical Women's Group, Cleveland, Boston, Durham, North Carolina, Madison, Wisconsin, and Detroit.

JO FREEMAN

They sent notice of the convention less than a month before it was to begin. Nevertheless, over two hundred women attended from twenty states and Canada, most of whom had not previously been involved in women's liberation.

MARILYN WEBB

Kathie Sarachild and Roxanne Dunbar were very vocal about how women are the only constituents they cared about, and they didn't care about the war, they didn't care about civil rights. Women's issues came first.

All of us in Washington Women's Liberation were conscious of the national political issues that were happening around the country. Maybe because of all of the antiwar demonstrations that were happening in Washington. So they considered us sellouts because we were part of the New Left. We considered them completely unrealistic. Like, you can't separate women totally from men, you know? It was a vicious fight.

People like Ros Baxandall and Miriam Hawley were saying that childcare was an important issue and would help us reach larger audiences of women. I asked, are we going to have a mass movement if we tell women that they can't have children? How do you think suburban mothers are going to become part of our movement if we tell them that they've been victimized by their children? They thought I was very counterrevolutionary.

16

Wimbledon—The Men Get All the Money

Tennis originated as an elite club sport, and most players were "amateurs" who were not paid a living wage despite the fact that more and more of them dedicated their lives to the sport. By 1968, a modern age dawned as more players turned "pro" and were compensated according to their talents and audience draw. But "open" tennis also created a new glaring divide between the earnings of men and women players.

ROSIE CASALS

I don't remember when I could not hit the tennis ball; it was the most natural thing that I could ever do. Financially it was always difficult because we had no money. We came from the wrong side of the tracks, none of our kids played tennis, it was a foreign sport. I had a lot of help from a lot of friends from Golden Gate Park. They raised money for me, and I don't think I let them down. The Northern California Tennis Association also helped, but they helped the guys a lot more than they helped the women. So I always needed to raise extra money.

JULIE HELDMAN

I started Stanford in 1962 as a sixteen-year-old who had been competing at tennis since I was eight. I began to win tournaments when I was ten. When I was twelve, I won the Canadian National 18-and-under with buck teeth and a wooden racket. When I was fourteen, I won the US National for 15-and-under. Two years later, I started at Stanford, and I had a goal in mind that I would win the National 18-and-under.

I went to Stanford because I wanted to be in a place where I could play tennis and I could also get an education. But when I got to Stanford, I discovered that the good women tennis players who were going there had already transferred out. There was nobody for me to play with. I don't think there were any women's teams. I was accepted at Stanford as a good athlete, but nobody made a big deal about it. At Stanford, they talked about women getting their Mrs. degree. So, even though Stanford had women and men students since the beginning, women were still the appendage.

What was happening in that era was a young girl's identity depended on how you looked, how you dressed, how you wore your hair, how you wore your makeup. Go back and look at photos of that era. The girls in my classes looked like they were twenty-five years old. By the time I got to be a senior in high school, I too wore my black sweater and my pearls and my puffy hairdo for the class photo. I learned to go to sleep at night with brush rollers in my hair. I gotta tell you how painful that was. I tried to look that way for a while, but it just didn't fit me.

BILLIE JEAN KING

I was one of the lucky ones. My dad knew the coach at Cal State LA, and he said, "If you come to our school, we have Dr. Johnson there. She's the tennis coach and professor as well, and we have a women's team and a men's team that practice together every day from two to five," so I thought that was great. So I went to Cal State LA and got to practice with the men. But down the road, pre–Title IX, someone like Arthur Ashe and Stan Smith who eventually became number one, so did I, had full tennis scholarships. Right there is a huge difference. They're getting their education paid for; we didn't have that privilege.

[In 1967] I was part of [America's] winning Wightman Cup and Federation Cup teams. I also swept the singles, doubles, and mixed-doubles titles at Wimbledon, the pinnacle. My compensation at Wimbledon for all that was a £45 gift voucher. . . . When I came home from my Wimbledon sweep, not a single photographer or reporter was waiting to ask me a thing about it. . . .

I kept pushing for change. I told reporters in the States, "There is no way amateur tennis is going to be available to everyone if only rich kids could play." The USLTA [US Lawn Tennis Association] was content to keep amateur tennis "pure," which to them meant no salaried jobs, no lifeblood endorsement money for players, no reward for playing in tournaments other than the glory of the title and another trophy for the shelf. I could never understand it.

ROSIE CASALS

My first year in '66, I think I made about $3,000 under the table.

BILLIE JEAN KING

I was in Australia in December in 1967 when Wimbledon officials . . . dropped a bombshell: they announced that Wimbledon would be the first major to welcome pros and amateurs, starting in 1968. . . . The All England Club president, Herman David, called amateurism "a living lie."

JULIE HELDMAN

When Wimbledon went pro, that shifted the balance of power, so it eventually all became pro. I didn't take money in tournaments in '68. The organization of everything was so chaotic, and most of the tournaments were still amateur. It turned out to be great for me because I got to play in the Olympics.

A major factor in the beginning of open tennis was that there were several promoters who signed players to contracts where they were given guarantees of how much money they would make.

There was a group called the Handsome Eight, because some of the guys were handsome. And then there was the George MacCall group, which had some of the greatest players of all time, and they also signed women: Billie Jean King, Rosie Casals, Ann Jones, and Françoise "Frankie" Dürr.

BILLIE JEAN KING

I quickly landed my first endorsement, a radio deal with Maxwell House that I wouldn't agree to until I tried their coffee. I was also provided with a Hertz VIP card and my first charge card (AmericanExpress). To me, the cards were a sign of stature. At the time, even working women continued to have trouble getting a credit card or loans unless their husband, father, or employer signed for it.

My two-year contract with George MacCall was $80,000. I was promised more earnings if I surpassed a certain level of prize money at the events we played. George lured Emmo [Roy Emerson] to our group with a guarantee of

$75,000 a year, and I read that Rod Laver had signed up for even more. Was I worth only half of what the top men were paid? You can guess my answer.

ROSIE CASALS
One thing that Billie Jean would always do is go early just before the tournament would start over the weekend, and because she had won Wimbledon before, they would open the gates for her and we would go into the Centre Court. Like a cathedral, it was just beautiful. The seats were empty and she would sit there and reflect and she said, "This is the most beautiful place in the world." I felt that way too.*

In 1968, when Wimbledon finally said we are open, the complexion of the game changed, and we were thrown into a situation where the women and men were once back together again playing tournaments, but what was happening is the men were getting more of the prize money because now there was prize money and commercialism and sponsors. Unfortunately, the women were not really getting anything. All this unrest began to build when the game went open.

BILLIE JEAN KING
When we won Wimbledon, Rod Laver won £2,000, and I won £750. . . . Men ran the tournaments, men made the rules, and they started to get rid of our tournaments. Or if they did have a tournament, the ratio of prize money was around eight-to-twelve-to-one difference. So you could see the writing on the wall that we weren't going to make it the way we wanted to. No chance that we'd be included or treated the same. My former husband, Larry, told me that would happen; he was right about the men. He said, "They'll think it's all theirs. All this money coming into the sport is just theirs."

---

* Rosie Casals was often Billie Jean King's doubles partner from 1966 to 1974, winning many titles with her. They first played Wimbledon in '66, and won in '67, '68, '70, '71, and '73.

17

Colleges Desegregate— I Am Now a Living Relic

Ever since the landmark 1954 Supreme Court decision Brown v. Board of Education, *and later the end of Jim Crow after the Civil Rights Act of 1964, Southern high schools, colleges, and universities were forced to racially integrate, which they did slowly and with much resistance. Meanwhile, a less public form of educational integration was taking place in public and private colleges in the rest of the country where Black students had also been shut out of admissions. By the mid-1960s, the slow process of integrating these institutions' student bodies began, but it was not easy for the first generation of student pioneers.*

BARBARA SMITH

Our guidance counselor thought my twin sister, Beverly, and I should apply to the schools that we were qualified to get into. There was a civil rights movement going on that affected educational institutions, and there were some interventions that happened to coincide with the time we were applying to college that were greatly to our benefit. One of those initiatives was something called the Cooperative Program for Educational Opportunity. Charles E. McCarthy Jr. was the director of the co-op program whose purpose was to get talented, primarily Black students into these elite eastern colleges. He came to our high school, which was one of the best public high schools in the city of Cleveland. I remember meeting him, and he stayed in contact with our guidance counselor. And during that time we were taking PSATs and SATs, and Beverly and I blew the tops off of the tests. When he saw our board scores, Charles E. McCarthy Jr. told our guidance counselor, "Have them apply to every school they want to apply to." So I applied to a lot of the Seven Sister schools.*

The Seven Sister schools would have teas that were organized by the local alumnae chapters. Beverly and I went to a lot of those teas and had a lot of horrible experiences. The teas were in palatial homes because Cleveland had a huge amount of wealth. That was at a time when Black people did not enter front doors. It was made very clear to us that they did not understand why we were there. So here we were, kids in public high school, entering front doors with the notion that we thought we could go to the same colleges as a little white girl who had gone to prep school. Go figure. It was absolutely hellish and heartbreaking.

When I started reading about Mount Holyoke, I was just drawn to it. Mount Holyoke has a different origin story than the other Seven Sisters. It's the oldest of them. And it was started by a visionary individual, Mary Lyon, who drove her horse and buggy around the New England countryside, collecting pennies from farmwives, so that she could start Mount Holyoke. It was originally a seminary.

As far as I'm concerned, I chose the exact right place for me. However, the experience of being there was completely earth-shattering. And that was also true for the tiny handful of Black girls on the campus. There were fewer than thirty of us at Mount Holyoke when I entered in 1965, and there were fourteen or fifteen Black women in my entering class.

The level of work and the volume of work that was expected at Mount Holyoke was staggering. The students who had gone to prep schools were more prepared for the volume—eight hundred pages of reading a week. I mean, just crazy amounts of work. And then there was the fact that I was surrounded by people who were rich. Then there were the racial dynamics. We had some professors who let us know they didn't think we belonged there. But be that as it may, I began to hit my stride. I was a really good student in English, and I took sociology because that was the only place in the curriculum where you could study about Black people, albeit as social problems.

---

* Considered the Ivy League for women, the Seven Sister schools were Barnard, Bryn Mawr, Mount Holyoke, Radcliffe, Smith, Vassar, and Wellesley.

I was a student-activist leader at Mount Holyoke my senior year. There was no Black studies program on any of these campuses at that time. A friend of mine, who became the second Black woman judge in the history of Massachusetts—her name was Marie Therese Oliver—and I decided that we were going to teach a series of seminars on, what at that time we referred to as "Negro" history. So we organized six evening seminars—not for credit. We invited a professor from Smith, who had written one of the definitive works on slavery at the time, Stanley Elkins. We just wrote to him, and he said yes, and he came.

And as I always say, even though I was pretty traumatized, on graduation day in 1969, I thought, "I am now a living relic." I'm a living relic because virtually no Black woman on the face of the globe has ever done what I just did, which is to graduate from Mount Holyoke. I knew that I had rare experiences, and they were painful experiences. But some of them were incredibly positive experiences. It was very mixed.

LINDA BURNHAM

I grew up in a family and community of Black communists in Brooklyn. I graduated from Erasmus High School in 1964. I was sixteen, and I thought I knew everything, but I was really young. But that's not how I saw it at the time. My mom was concerned about where I was going off to college and who was going to be watching over me. At that time, all the young radicals wanted to go to the University of Wisconsin, Madison, which is where I wanted to go. But it was her decision, so I went to Bennett College in North Carolina, an all-girls, historically Black college which was pretty socially conservative. So it was a little bit of a shock actually. I mean, they had us in what was kind of a lockdown, which I guess was the point.

They were trying to churn out ladies who turn into teachers, librarians, or women who could be credible wives for professional Black men. You couldn't wear pants on campus except on Saturday mornings, you had to show up at vespers, you had to put on gloves. They were still working on the values of the fifties. It was kind of fascinating and horrifying. It was not how I operated. So I had to get out of there. I come from a family of strong-willed women, and I'm one of 'em.

My mom had a neighbor who had gone to Reed College, which I of course had never heard of. Somehow, I applied, and they gave me a scholarship. This is when they wanted Black people in college, finally. I think the Ford Foundation was giving scholarships to young Black people to go to colleges. So I ended up at Reed. I didn't even know how to pronounce Oregon.

Reed was quite liberal, and it was almost all white. There were maybe two Black people in the whole school, it was ridiculous, but then again, it was Portland. Reed was white in a way that I didn't know. In my experience of whiteness growing up in New York, you were Jewish, or you were Italian, or you were Irish. Just plain white wasn't in my experience. So it was a kind of a wake-up call about the country.

MARGO OKAZAWA-REY

I was born in 1949 during the US occupation of Japan. My father was an [African American] US military guy, and my mother was a Japanese upper-middle-class woman whose family had already arranged a husband for her. I think it's one of those great love stories where they both made decisions, and part of that decision had to do with wanting me in the world. But they both crossed race, gender, class, nation, all these categories that were not supposed to be crossed, which is really something in that particular moment. I grew up in Japan, and when I was ten years old, my father was transferred to an air force base in Utah.

I really had to think about race in very different ways when we moved to the States. I remember once I ran home to my mom and I said, "The children are teasing me about being Black. And I said, I'm Japanese." And my mom said to me, "Well, you can be Japanese inside, but outside you're Black." She understood the importance of both.

A few years later, we moved to Dayton, Ohio, which was a very segregated city. And because we were Black, we lived in the west side, which is the Black side of town. I went to an all-Black high school. The Blackness I saw there was very complex. That is when I learned what it meant to be African American.

A bunch of these white universities were coming to my all-Black high school to recruit kids to attend. The last college that came to my high school in April of 1968 was Capital University in Columbus, Ohio, a Lutheran college which I guess was trying to do good. They came to my high school and I said, "Can you pay? I don't have money." And they said, "Sure." It was just one of those interventions that completely changed my life trajectory.

I think there must have been five hundred students in the entering class, and ten of us were referred to as "the Black students." White antiwar students and Black students were taking over dorms and administration buildings everywhere. And so, there was this moment when the Black students at my college said we should take over one of the dorms.

At that time, I was confused about my identity, so I just wanted to blend in. I just said, "I'm not going to do that." And I can't remember how I rationalized it, but I remember being against it, not because of the politics, but because I didn't want to stick out any more than I already did. That was the beginning of my identity formation and thinking about what it means to be mixed race because it was the time of Black Power. You were all Black or nothing. I believed that if I said I'm for Black Power, then that means I would have to kill off my mother. And I wasn't going to do that.

BRENDA FEIGEN

I graduated from Vassar in 1966, basically ready to take on the world, and was delighted that I got into Harvard Law School. When I got there, I was thinking, this is great, even though only 6 percent of my class was female: 32 out of 565 students. There were no women allowed in what was called the eating "club," but it was just a restaurant called Lincoln's Inn, where every male student and all of the professors ate. We couldn't get into most of the campus libraries, because at Harvard University they wouldn't let women in.

Then I learned that there was something called "ladies' day," which meant that the professor would only call on women one day of the semester. Ladies' days were really awful. My property law professor, A. James Casner, who the movie *The Paper Chase* was based on, would call on women to answer his question, "Who owns the engagement ring if the engagement is broken off?" In criminal law, they would ask us, how much penetration constitutes rape?

I was getting more and more angry, but still pretty much keeping to myself until one day in constitutional law class, with Paul Freund, who was the most famous constitutional law professor in the country, discussing the 1948 Supreme Court case *Goesaert v. Cleary*, which barred women in the state of Michigan from working as bartenders unless she was the wife or daughter of the male owner of the bar. Professor Freund announced that he agreed with the Supreme Court that this law was totally constitutional, and should just stand on the books.

This was 1968, and I basically stood up and said, "This is outrageous," and I just said what I had to say about it, at which point the professor started to laugh at me, loudly.

Then all the male students were laughing. If there were any women in the class I couldn't see them. I turned around to look at [my boyfriend]

Marc [Fasteau], who was just sitting there. He wasn't laughing or smiling. I ran out of that classroom in tears of rage. That really was the beginning. Even though all kinds of things were happening in the country, for me that was a very personal affront, the fact that Freund was making fun of me. I was furious.

18

Messing with Miss America

ROBIN MORGAN

It was out of that first group, New York Radical Women, that the idea to protest the pageant developed.

CAROL HANISCH

The idea came out of our group method of analyzing women's oppression by recalling our own experiences. We were watching *Schmeerguntz*, a feminist movie, one night at our meeting.* The movie had flashes of the Miss America contest in it. I found myself sitting there remembering how I had felt at home with my family watching the pageant as a child, an adolescent, and a college student. I knew it had evoked powerful feelings.

When I proposed the idea to our group, we decided to go around the room with each woman telling how she felt about the pageant. We discovered that many of us who had always put down the contest still watched it. Others, like myself, had consciously identified with it, and had cried with the winner.

From our communal thinking came the concrete plans for the action. We

---

* The 1965 avant-garde film by two women, Swedish artist Gunvor Nelson and American Dorothy Wiley, is a satiric take on female domestic life. Using film and photo collages, *Schmeerguntz* contrasts images of domestic drudgery with images from women's magazines glorifying the lives of women and housewives.

all agreed that our main point in the demonstration would be that all women were hurt by beauty competition—Miss America as well as ourselves. We opposed the pageant in our own self-interest, e.g., the self-interest of all women.

ROBIN MORGAN

The pageant was chosen as a target for a number of reasons: it is, of course, patently degrading to women (in propagating the Mindless Sex Object Image); it has always been a lily-white, racist contest (there has never been a Black finalist); the winner tours Vietnam, entertaining the troops as a Murder Mascot; the whole gimmick of the million-dollar Pageant Corporation is one commercial shill game to sell the sponsor's products. Where else could one find such a perfect combination of American values—racism, militarism, capitalism—all packaged in one "ideal" symbol, a woman.

SUSAN BROWNMILLER

No one threw herself into it harder than Robin Morgan, who had begun to attend meetings of New York Radical Women. A poet married to a poet, a flamboyant bisexual Kenneth Pitchford, Morgan thrived on the theatrical confrontations pioneered by the Yippies, New Left pranksters led by Abbie Hoffman and Jerry Rubin.* She was a savvy organizer who could fire up the troops, run off the fliers, get the police permits, order the buses, and alert the press. . . . She pulled together the women she was close to, Peggy Dobbins, Judith Duffett, Barbara Kaminsky, Lynn Laredo, Florika Romatien, Naomi Jaffe, Adite Kroll, and went into high gear.†

JUDY GUMBO

I was living with my boyfriend Stew Albert in a cellar apartment on Bleecker Street before going to the Chicago Democratic Convention in '68. In May, Robin Morgan called Nancy Kurshan, Jerry Rubin's girlfriend, and asked if Nancy, Anita Hoffman, and I would come to the Miss America pageant to protest the horrendous way women are objectified as mindless sex ob-

---

* Founded by Abbie Hoffman, Jerry Rubin, and Stew Albert, the Youth International Party, or Yippies, was a media-savvy group that used outrageous theatrical antics like trying to levitate the Pentagon and throwing money from the New York Stock Exchange balcony to get media attention and spread its revolutionary message.

† Morgan's flair for communicating her political views with dramatic humor may have come from her robust career as a child actor. She was best known for playing Dagmar Hansen, starting at the age of eight, in the popular CBS series *Mama*.

jects. I think the two events were a week apart, and doing both at the same time didn't seem possible. Stew would have felt abandoned if I had gone to Atlantic City, so I stood by my man and did not go. Six months later I would've gone in a heartbeat.

ROBIN MORGAN

I can still remember the feverish excitement I felt: dickering with the company that chartered buses, wangling a permit from the mayor of Atlantic City, sleeping about three hours a night for days preceding the demonstration. . . . Each work meeting with the other organizers of the protest was an excitement fix: whether we were lettering posters or writing leaflets or deciding who would deal with which reporter requesting an interview, we were affirming our mutual feelings of outrage, hope, and readiness to conquer the world. We also felt, well, *grown up*; we were doing this one for *ourselves*, not for our men, and we were consequently getting to do those things the men never let us do, like talking to the press or dealing with the mayor's office. We fought a lot and laughed a lot and felt very extremely nervous.

LINDSY VAN GELDER

I'd been on tryout at the *New York Post* a few weeks when this press release from Robin Morgan comes across the city desk saying that they're going to have this demonstration.

I was sent out to meet Robin and the more she talked, the more my mind was going *click, click, click*. At the time, one story getting a lot of respect was guys burning their draft cards. New York Radical Women had planned to have what they called a "Freedom Trash Can" in Atlantic City, where they were going to throw in *Playboy* magazines and girdles and other articles of oppression. I'm a sucker for alliteration, so when I was trying to figure out a way to link this with respectable civil rights protests, I came up with "bra-burning."

New York Post, September 4, 1968,
"Bra Burners Plan Miss America Protest," by Lindsy Van Gelder
Lighting a match to a draft card or a flag has been a standard gambit of protest groups in recent years, but something new is due to go up in flames this Saturday. Would you believe a bra burning?

The scene will be Atlantic City and the annual Miss America Pageant. Stoking the fire are a group of women's liberation demonstrators protesting what they call the "degrading mindless-boob-girlie symbol" of American femininity.

ALIX KATES SHULMAN
We planned the Freedom Trash Can in advance and we brought stuff to throw into it. And then there's the whole question about bra-burning. Initially, we did want to have a bonfire, but when we went to get a fire permit, we were told we couldn't possibly because it was a boardwalk. We could not make the fire *on* the [wooden] boardwalk, we would have done it in the can, but they told us no so we didn't. It's as simple as that. And then Lindsy Van Gelder said that there was going to be bra-burning. I guess she didn't get the word. But the fact is, we did half of a bonfire burning [without the burning] and it was analogous to burning draft cards.

SUSAN BROWNMILLER
The bras were not burned. Lindsy Van Gelder said, "That's going to be my epitaph."

JACQUELINE CEBALLOS
I had my eyes and ears on what was going on with the radical feminists, so I knew that they were going to demonstrate in Atlantic City. NOW was not involved in any of this. They thought the radical feminists were a little nutsy. And to tell you the truth, some of them were.

BETTY FRIEDAN
Because the [radical women] cut their political teeth on the doctrines of class warfare applied to the problems of race, they tried to adapt, too literally, the ideology of class and race warfare to the situation of women. Stokely Carmichael had originated the concept of "Black Power"; separatism, Black nationalism, Black studies programs—all these things could be adapted to women's situations, and that rage, suppressed for so long, could even make them seem plausible.

But there was something about this new, abstract ideology of man hatred, sex warfare, that made me uneasy from the beginning. . . . It seemed, in fact, more sexy than the NOW actions addressed to the concrete social and economic situation of women, but it also seemed to be leading us away from the reality of our movement—and its real possibilities for changing the situation for women.

MARILYN WEBB

We decided, in DC, to plan locally, and then the battles began. People from elsewhere thought they were being manipulated by the people from New York, and people felt they took all the credit for it in New York, when a lot of cities had been involved in the planning.*

CHARLOTTE BUNCH

The New York group was in touch with Marilyn quite a bit, and they invited us to come to Atlantic City. And we thought it was a great idea to demonstrate, because we thought of the Miss America contest as women selling their bodies, and being awarded scholarships based on selling your body. Women shouldn't have to be in a swimsuit contest to get a college scholarship.

ROBIN MORGAN

We assembled in Union Square, where hundreds and hundreds of women suddenly showed up, so we got more buses. That was my first glimpse of *Holy crap! What are we doing here?*

JACQUELINE CEBALLOS

About ten buses lined up in Union Square and they were filled. I sat down next to the wonderful Kathie Sarachild. She changed her name from Kathie Amatniek to her mother's name, Child of Sara. We sang all the way to Atlantic City.

ROBIN MORGAN

Women came from as far away as Canada, Florida, and Michigan, as well as from all over the Eastern Seaboard. . . . About two hundred women descended on this tacky town and staged an all-day demonstration on the boardwalk in front of the Convention Hall [where the pageant was taking place], singing, chanting, and performing guerrilla theater nonstop throughout the day.

JUDY GUMBO

Instead of running a pig for president, which we Yippies did at the '68 Chicago Democratic Convention protest, pageant protesters crowned a live

---

* By September 1968, several early radical women's liberation groups had formed across the country, including Chicago's Women's Liberation Union, Washington, DC's Magic Quilt, New York Radical Women, The Feminists, Cell 16, and Redstockings.

sheep Miss America—a symbol based in the reality that pageant contestants were treated and expected to act like conformist sheep.

New York Times, September 8, 1968, "Miss America Pageant is Picketed by 100 Women," by Charlotte Curtis

Women armed with a giant bathing beauty puppet and a "Freedom trash can" in which they threw girdles, bras, hair curlers, false eyelashes, and anything else that smacked of "enslavement," picketed the Miss America Pageant here today. . . .

The demonstrators, all of whom belonged to what they called the Women's Liberation Movement, were from New York, Washington, New Jersey, and such places as Detroit, Gainesville, Fla, and Bancroft, Iowa. They did their protesting behind police barriers that separated them from 650 generally unsympathetic spectators.

ROBIN MORGAN

There were naysayers on the boardwalk yelling, "You're not pretty enough to get a man!" But then there would be women who would come back and get a leaflet when their boyfriend wasn't looking.

ALIX SHULMAN

I wrote a biography of Emma Goldman, who used to say, "The more opposition I encountered, the more I was in my element." And that's how I felt at the Miss America demonstration. When these guys would yell, "Go back to Russia where you came from," and "You're a bunch of dirty dykes," and "You're so ugly, you're just jealous of Miss America," it just lit me up.

FLORYNCE KENNEDY

I attended the Atlantic City Beauty Contest protest, and was very brazen and very brash and it was the best fun I can imagine anyone wanting to have on any single day of her life.*

---

* Three months earlier in June 1968, Kennedy defended *SCUM Manifesto* author Valerie Solanas in court after she shot and wounded pop artist Andy Warhol. Solanas, who was heralded as a feminist hero by some radical women, served three years in prison and mental hospitals, where she was diagnosed with paranoid schizophrenia.

ALIX KATES SHULMAN

I offered to pay for tickets for protesters to get inside. I had a joint checking account with my husband, and this was the first time I wrote a check without clearing it with him, because he was the breadwinner.

JACQUELINE CEBALLOS

Then when it came time for the beauty pageant, Kathie and a couple of the radical feminists had gotten us in. I went with them.

Television News Anchor *Newsreel* films,
"Up Against the Wall Miss America"

"The new Miss America stands five feet seven inches tall, weighs one hundred and twenty pounds, and measures thirty-six, twenty-four-and-a-half, thirty-six."

ROBIN MORGAN

At night, an "inside squad" of twenty brave sisters disrupted the live telecast of the pageant itself, yodeling the eerie Berber Yell (from *The Battle of Algiers*), shouting "Freedom for Women!" and hanging a huge banner reading WOMEN'S LIBERATION from the balcony rail—all of which stopped the nationwide show cold for ten bloodcurdling seconds.

CAROL HANISCH

I was one of the four women that hung the WOMEN'S LIBERATION banner from the balcony, which was scary but wonderful. I really hated interrupting the outgoing Miss America as she gave her farewell speech. We didn't really mean to be criticizing the individuals—it was the whole idea of beauty pageants that we were criticizing.

ALIX KATES SHULMAN

Although the television cameras did not broadcast it, all the print reporters who covered it did mention it. That was the big accomplishment of that demonstration, to get the words "Women's Liberation" out into the world.

PEGGY DOBBINS

When I was growing up my mother used to hold my head down in the sink and pour on this stinking [Toni home permanent] stuff to make my hair curl. So when we found out that Toni home permanent was the sponsor of the Miss America pageant we decided to sprinkle [permanent solution] along the aisles.

Television News Anchor Newsreel films,
"Up Against the Wall Miss America"

"Shortly before ten Saturday night, police arrested a young woman inside the Atlantic City Convention Hall where the Miss America pageant was being staged. Police say the woman was spraying a foul-smelling vapor about 20 yards from the runway. She was charged as a disorderly person."

PEGGY DOBBINS

I watched the end of the pageant in jail with women who were arrested for prostitution, and I wrote on the wall of my little bunk, "Prostitutes of the world unite, we have nothing to lose but our pimps!" We talked a lot about how being a wife is a form of prostitution.

ROBIN MORGAN

There's an untold story of that protest that I can now tell here. It regards Charlotte Curtis, then editor of *The New York Times* Style Section (for which read: Women's Pages). Curtis was a rarity of that period, a well-known woman journalist. She'd been a foreign correspondent, but that didn't save her from being assigned, on her return, to fashion, flower shows, society. . . .

[After Peggy Dobbins and others were arrested] I stayed on after the buses left, raising bail by phone, and being sent from precinct to precinct in search of where our friends were being held. Finally at three a.m., I learned they'd been released hours earlier, on cash bail put up personally by "some older woman" named Charlotte Curtis.

When I phoned her the next day to thank her, she asked me to keep it quiet, as "these dreary gray guys running the *Times*" would not be amused.

BARBARA MEHRHOF

Everybody knew about NOW, but nobody really knew about women's liberation until the Miss America protest, which I think put us on the map.

MICHELE WALLACE

The radical feminist protest at the Miss America Pageant had gotten a lot of attention in the press in New York. Although the press coverage was designed to turn people off, it did just the opposite for me. I remember that being my initial moment of interest because I had always deeply resented the institution of the Miss America Pageant and had already figured out that life was possible without a bra.

SALLIE BINGHAM*

Bras were big, overbuilt, cotton, cone shaped, heavy, and very hot in the summer. And that was all there was. There wasn't really any choice. If you got some black lace thing, you probably were a whore. When I took off that bra for the first time, I had this physical sense of liberation. That was the beginning of my awakening, that this world—that was insisting that I do and say and wear certain things—was beginning to fall apart.

Albuquerque Tribune, September 12, 1968,
"Burning Brassieres Is Going Too Far,"
by Art Buchwald

The final and most tragic part of the protest took place when several of the women publicly burned their brassieres. . . . Where nature failed, American know-how succeeded and thanks to our scientific ingenuity, it is now impossible for anyone to know where God leaves off and Maidenform takes over.

New York Post, September 9, 1968,
"Female Firebrands," by Harriet Van Horne

These protestants were from the Women's Liberation Front. Their wish, apparently, is to be liberated from their femininity, such as it is. Highlight of their march was a bonfire in a Freedom Trash Can. With screams of delight they consigned to the flames such shackling, demeaning items as girdles, bras, high-heeled slippers, hair curlers and false eyelashes.

FRANCES BEAL

People can laugh about the burning of the bras, which never actually happened, but it symbolized the restricting of women in terms of their dress. I was a person who went to college in the late fifties and early sixties, and was made to suffer through the full girdles, and they were horrible, they

---

* Full disclosure: Sallie Bingham is my aunt—my late father's sister.

would cut into your legs. No jiggle was permitted whatsoever. It was about the liberation of the confining structures of society at large, and girdles in particular. Once I understood that, I never wore a girdle again, and in many ways it was a liberating feeling of no more white gloves on Sunday, no more stockings every day.

ROBIN MORGAN

The pageant has been called the birth of the women's movement, which is (a) totally untrue—NOW was already toiling away—and (b) deeply satisfying.

If it was the birthdate, conception and gestation had been going on for a long time; years of meetings, consciousness raising, thought, and plain old organizing had taken place before any of us set foot on the boardwalk.

But this protest caught the public imagination, and other women learned that we existed. The week before the demonstration there were about thirty women at the New York Radical Women meeting; the week after, there were approximately a hundred and fifty.

My colleagues, my sisters, were not amused. What are we going to do with all of these women? "Well, I don't know," I said. "Let them decide." So we split into groups, and out of that came Redstockings. Then we formed W.I.T.C.H., and there was the October 17 group—that was Ti-Grace Atkinson. There was the group that called themselves The Feminists.* There were humbler groups like the 72nd Street group and the Ninth Street group. All these were Manhattan women. Meanwhile, women were forming lots of groups from other parts of the country. People had come to the demonstration from California and Wisconsin, because we'd done press. They were forming groups all across the country and it was out of hand.

---

* All these groups ascribed to slightly different flavors of radical activism, both in style and ideology. Most remained local, but W.I.T.C.H. (Women's International Terrorists Conspiracy from Hell) "covens" sprang up in Washington, DC, Buffalo, Chicago, and other cities. The Women's International Terrorist Conspiracy from Hell used Yippie-inspired guerrilla street theater to poke fun at and harass their patriarchal adversaries. On Halloween, just a few weeks after the Miss America pageant, W.I.T.C.H. staged its first action. Nancy Kurshan, Robin Morgan, Rosalyn Baxandall, Peggy Dobbins, and others dressed in black witch robes and hats and put a "hex" on the New York Stock Exchange. They oozed Krazy Glue on the locks of the front doors of the exchange at three a.m., and as the morning rush began, the doors wouldn't open and had to be taken off their hinges, causing a delay to the opening bell. Meanwhile, the witches stood outside chanting, "Wall Street, Wall Street, mightiest wall of all street. Trick-or-treat, corporate elite, up against the Wall Street!"

19

The Indomitable Shirley Chisholm

Born in Brooklyn to Barbadian parents in 1924, Shirley Chisholm showed an early interest in political activism when she attended Brooklyn College, graduating in 1946. She earned her master's degree at Columbia Teachers College in 1951 and began her teaching career. But she also got involved in politics by joining the Urban League and the National Association for the Advancement of Colored People (NAACP). In 1964, she would defy hundreds of years of convention and run for the New York State Assembly.

SHIRLEY CHISHOLM

By 1964, there was a vacancy in the State Assembly. I wanted it, and I told the club I felt I deserved it. This was unwelcome news. . . . Some of the men fancied the nomination themselves. . . . By then I had spent about ten years in ward politics and had done everything else but run for office. Starting as a cigar box decorator, I had compiled voter lists, carried petitions, rung doorbells, manned the telephone, stuffed envelopes, and helped voters get to the polls. I had done it all to help other people get elected. The other people who got elected were men, of course, because that was the way it was in politics. This had to change someday, and I was resolved that it was going to start changing right then. I was the best-qualified nominee, and I was not going to be denied because of my sex. . . .

I [was] met with hostility because of my sex from the start of my first campaign. Even some women would greet me, "You ought to be home, not out here." . . . I handled all such hecklers, male and female, the same way. I told them calmly that I had been serving the community for a number of years and now I would appreciate an opportunity to serve it on a higher level, in elected office.

In a three-way contest, Shirley Chisholm won decisively. Women voters turned out in droves for Chisholm, who became the first Black woman elected to public office in Brooklyn. She joined one other Black woman, Bessie Buchanan from Harlem, in Albany where she served in the General Assembly for four years. In 1968, when redistricting created the first majority-Black district in Brooklyn, Chisholm made the bold decision to run for the US Congress, a place where no Black woman had ever served.

SHIRLEY CHISHOLM
Starting in February 1968, I spent ten months doing the only thing I could do: I tramped the streets of Williamsburg, Crown Heights, and Bedford-Stuyvesant, telling my story to the people. I didn't have the money for a conventional congressional campaign; I had to make up for it with hard work. . . . I almost killed myself because I wanted to show the machine that a little Black woman was going to beat it. I wrote a slogan that said it all: "Fighting Shirley Chisholm—Unbought and Unbossed."

CONRAD CHISHOLM
She ran a door-to-door campaign. She got into housing projects. It was one of those campaigns run on a shoestring. Because there were no big donors, nobody wanted her. She's a woman and she's Black? No, no. Big Democratic clubs would give money to the other people.

BARBARA WINSLOW
Her primary opponent, State Senator William C. Thompson, disregarded her so much that he went away on vacation.

SHIRLEY CHISHOLM

When they counted the primary votes, with a very small turn out, I won by about a thousand votes. . . . By this time my Republican opponent was in the field: James Farmer, the former national chairman of CORE, the Congress of Racial Equality. The New York Republicans had seen a golden opportunity in the new Black Brooklyn district, and figured he was just the man to cash in on it for them. Of course, he didn't live in Brooklyn, and never had.

BARBARA WINSLOW

James Farmer was tall and handsome and a great speaker. He also had all the celebrity endorsements—Harry Belafonte, Ossie Davis, Ruby Dee. But Chisholm had the support of the women, and Farmer ran a totally mascu-linist campaign. Remember, it's '68, three years after the Moynihan Report attacks the Black matriarchy, and he played on this.* He said we've got to send a man to Congress. Chisholm went to the women and said you have a chance to do something historic, electing the first Black woman to Congress.

SHIRLEY CHISHOLM

Farmer's campaign was well oiled; it had money dripping all over it. He toured the district with sound trucks manned by young dudes with Afros. Beating tom-toms: the big, Black male image. He drew the television cam-eramen like flies, a big national figure, winding up to become New York City's second Black congressman [after Adam Clayton Powell of Harlem]. His people were flooding the streets. The television stations ignored the

---

* Daniel Patrick Moynihan's 1965 report, *The Negro Family: The Case for National Action*, placed some of the blame for Black economic and social inequality on the strong matriarchal structure found in many Black families. Moynihan, LBJ's assistant secretary of labor (and later a four-term US senator from New York), intended to demonstrate to the president that the landmark civil rights legislation of 1964 and 1965 could not bring true equality to Black Americans unless coupled with economic advancement and opportunity. But Moynihan's many critics accused him of blaming the victim and vilifying Black women for being better educated and employed in higher-level jobs than Black men. Lines like these from the report have gone down in infamy: "In essence, the Negro community has been forced into a matriarchal structure which, because it is so out of line with the rest of the American society, seriously retards the progress of the group as a whole and, imposes a crushing burden on the Negro male and, in consequence, on a great many Negro women as well. . . . Ours is a society which presumes male leadership in private and public affairs. The arrangements of society facilitate such leadership and reward it. A subculture, such as that of the Negro American, in which this is not the pattern, is placed at a distinct disadvantage."

little female who was running against him. One station I called to complain to, came right out and told me, "Who are you?" the man asked. "A little schoolteacher who happened to go to the State Assembly?"

New York Times, April 13, 1969,

"This Is Fighting Shirley Chisholm," by Susan Brownmiller

Bongo drums on the streets—a regular part of Farmer's campaign in Bedford-Stuyvesant—projected an image redolent of Africa and manhood. Farmer's handbills stressed the need for "a man's voice" in Washington. This may have been what the Moynihan Report was talking about, but it didn't sit well with Shirley Chisholm.

The black male mystique stung Shirley Chisholm (she recalls walking into public meetings and being greeted by the catcall, "Here comes the black matriarch!") but the unspoken truth of the Farmer campaign was that Farmer's "black male" image had a double edge. The women of Bedford-Stuyvesant knew without being reminded that James Farmer had a white wife.

BARBARA WINSLOW

Something like 60 to 75 percent of the registered voters in the district were women. Shirley was in every community, religious, school, political immigrant group. She knew she had a fighting chance, because she could mobilize the women.

New York Times, April 13, 1969,

"This Is Fighting Shirley Chisholm," by Susan Brownmiller

Her early heroes were Mary McLeod Bethune, Harriet Tubman, and Susan. B. Anthony. Miss Anthony, the homeliest of the suffragettes, was one of the movement's best speakers. In her Brooklyn campaign, Mrs. Chisholm would reel off a long quotation from Susan B. Anthony when she was bothered by male hecklers on street corners:

"The day will come when man will recognize women as his peer, not only at the fireside but in the councils of the nation. Then, and not until then, will there be the perfect comradeship, the ideal union between the sexes that shall result in the highest development of the race. . . ."

"It always stopped them cold," she reports.

SHIRLEY CHISHOLM

So I went and contacted all the women's organizations that I could get in contact with, white women's organizations, Black women's, Hispanic women's, and I ran on that basis because James Farmer was constantly going against me with this machismo. . . . He said you need someone tough. . . . Shirley Chisholm's smart. She's bright. She's articulate, . . . but she's a frail little woman. . . . That gave me more spunk to show him.

CONRAD CHISHOLM

Another thing that was interesting about her campaign was that 25 percent of her district was Spanish-speaking. She spoke Spanish very well, and the Spanish-speaking people said, you know, Shirley took time out to study our language to represent us. She got all the Spanish votes.

SHIRLEY CHISHOLM

I beat him in the November election 2.5 to 1. . . . I drew 34,885 votes to his 13,777.

Part Two
{ 1969-1970 }

{ 1969 }

1

Take Her Off the Stage and Fuck Her

The 1968 presidential election took place during a bloody and divisive year. In April, Dr. Martin Luther King Jr. was assassinated, followed by Senator Robert F. Kennedy in June. The two shocking tragedies deeply disillusioned King's and Kennedy's millions of admirers and followers. Meanwhile, students across the country, from Berkeley to Madison to New York, expressed their anger over the draft and escalation of the Vietnam War with dozens of bombings and strikes. In April 1968, 720 Columbia University students were brutally beaten and 700 arrested after the weeklong occupation of five campus buildings. The police violence used against the students sparked a nationwide mass student revolt. Then at the August Democratic Convention in Chicago, establishment Democrats nominated Vice President Hubert Humphrey, who was tainted by the Johnson administration's failure to end the war. Outside the convention hall, thousands of young peaceniks protested and were violently beaten by Chicago cops on live television.

By the end of 1968, more than thirty-five thousand American soldiers had perished in Vietnam. Richard M. Nixon, who campaigned on the promise to end the war, narrowly beat Humphrey. On the day of Nixon's inauguration, January 20, 1969, the antiwar movement staged a "counter-inaugural" where a few intrepid feminists dared to state their case.

MARILYN WEBB

When we got to the rally there was a little wooden stage for speakers, which was being guarded by some Mobe [National Mobilization Committee to End the War in Vietnam] members. The stage was cracking and marshals kept trying to keep people off to keep it from collapsing.

ELLEN WILLIS

Dave Dellinger introduces the rally with a stirring denunciation of the war and racism.

"What about women, you schmuck?" I shout.

"And, uh, a special message from women's liberation," he adds.

MARILYN WEBB

It was cold and the tent was a muddy mess. The crowd was young—mostly men—and wanted to get out onto the streets and away from the speeches. Jimmy Johnson of the Fort Hood Three was the third speaker and he was booed down.* We were to follow him. Dave Dellinger was the MC and he announced that women were going to give speeches and that we had asked that the stage be cleared of men. We hadn't, but still, he announced, "All men clear the stage," which included a wounded GI who is in a wheelchair. It would have been nice if he said, "The stage is really rickety so we're trying to get people off the stage so it doesn't fall in." But no, that's not what he said. It was a bad setup. The booing started when they started picking up the guy in the wheelchair.

PAUL LAUTER

What I remember very distinctly was this: Marilyn is a very attractive woman, and for whatever reason, she had decided to wear a short skirt, which showed her off. I was there with my friend Eliza and another friend Alan, who was the peace secretary of the American Friends Service Committee in Baltimore. One of us made some crack about Marilyn's looks and Eliza later said that she really wanted to slap somebody's face but didn't.

---

* In 1966, three army privates, James Johnson, David Samas, and Dennis Mora (one Black, one white, and one Puerto Rican), stationed in Fort Hood, Texas, were the first US soldiers to refuse deployment to Vietnam. The Fort Hood Three became symbols of the growing GI resistance and were celebrated in Pete Seeger's "Ballad of the Fort Hood Three": "Come all you brave Americans and listen unto me / If you can spare five minutes in this twentieth century / I'll sing to you a story true as you will plainly see / It's about three US soldiers they call the Fort Hood Three."

At that point, the feminist movement had made very little penetration into the boys' Left.

DEREK SHEARER

Marilyn spoke kind of haltingly because I think she was nervous. I don't know if she'd spoken in public before, but I also think she sensed that the organizers didn't want her up there.

MARILYN WEBB

I was terrified because I had never given a speech before to a big audience. It was a sea of people. I remember looking at the crowd and thinking, "Oh my God. This is huge." I was a novice. I was a twenty-five-year-old kid.

As soon as I started speaking, the booing started.

"We, as women, have been enslaved by a past that told us that others—the poor, the Blacks—are oppressed. They are," I said. "And we tried to fight everyone's battles. But now we realized that we, too, we as women, are oppressed."

Then the punching began as some men began attacking those booing. The yells and then the slurs grew louder. Sexual slurs. Aggressive attacks that felt scary. It was a mild speech compared with today, but it was likely the first time that feminists described their worldview to a supposedly like-minded crowd. They weren't.

"We are victimized by being cheap labor. We are victimized by being educated to serve others," I said. "We are victimized by having no control over our bodies. We are victimized by having no equality with men. We will take the struggle to our homes, to our jobs, to the streets."

BARBARA MEHRHOF

When Marilyn said something like, "Women will take to the streets," there was pandemonium, because they heard it as a double entendre. Women who walk the street—street walkers. They started cheering, "Take off her clothes. Take her off the stage and fuck her."

ELLEN WILLIS

Her speech is just fairly innocuous radical rhetoric—except that it's a good-looking woman talking about women. The men go crazy. "Take it off!"

PAUL LAUTER

It was very loud. "Take her out back," meaning sexually. "Take her out in back and fuck her."

LEE WEBB

My memory of it is a little different than most people. At some point Marilyn says something like, "We will take to the streets. Women will take to the streets." And there was hooting and hollering amongst the people who were there. I don't know, maybe there were two or three hundred people in the tent. But I remember that when she said those things, there were these two guys standing next to us who were doing a lot of the hooting and hollering. They were white, and they were wearing sports shirts and pants and they had short hair. I always thought that they were undercover cops. When people said that the heckling that greeted Marilyn's speech was an indication of the reactionary character of the antiwar leaders or activists, I always doubted that. The hooting and the hollering wasn't coming from three hundred people. It was coming from probably ten or fifteen people. And I know that at least two of them looked to me like they were undercover agents.

CATHY WILKERSON

Now, I think, obviously, the FBI was involved. It might have been just one FBI agitator and a lot of willing and eager followers, because there were guys in the antiwar movement who were really threatened by women's liberation. At the time, no one knew this kind of manipulation was even a possibility. While the movement leadership—all men—was also upset by the attacks, they didn't join Marilyn on the stage to back her up.

PAUL LAUTER

I think there was a little bit in the way of fisticuffs where people were saying, "Shut up and let her speak," and the other people were saying, "Take her out in back." Yeah, there was some objection. But it was not, I would say, carried out very forcefully.

BARBARA MEHRHOF

These were the people who were going to stop the war and liberate the working class, and this is their attitude toward women. It was just awful. Suddenly these men who were everyone's comrades, especially for the women who had been working in the New Left, suddenly these men were the enemy.

MARILYN WEBB

The guys in the front rows were yelling and then they started hitting each other. I just focused on my speech but the yelling wouldn't stop. They were saying very aggressive rape-oriented things like, "Get her down a dark alley." I started getting scared. I don't remember how far I got through my speech, but at some point Shulie grabbed the microphone and started speaking.

ELLEN WILLIS

When Shulamith Firestone, who is representing the New York group, comes to the mic and announces that women will no longer participate in any so-called revolution that does not include the abolition of male privilege, it sounded like a spontaneous outburst of rage. . . . I was shaking. If radical men can be so easily provoked into acting like rednecks, what can we expect from others? What have we gotten ourselves into?

MARILYN WEBB

Then Dave Dellinger came over and he said, "Get off. Both of you, get off. You're starting a riot. Stop speaking." He grabbed the microphone. It was pandemonium.

PAUL LAUTER

I am not sure that one person started it but it certainly grew. It wouldn't have surprised me if, at least, a few of the guys there were plants, were FBI agents, and saw this as an opportunity to disrupt the whole thing. Which, indeed, it did. It really short-circuited the entire end of the speaking business, nothing was going to happen after that. It was clear that the leaders understood that, which is why people started up Independence Avenue.

Recently, I talked with a draft resister friend who simply attributed the bad behavior to the Left. It took a long time for men on the Left to get it. For me, it was an epiphany and when we finally left the tent, I was delighted to see a couple of women from Bread and Roses* handing out feminism buttons, and happily accepted one and pinned it on my parka for the remainder of the day. It was the first time I self-identified as a feminist.

---

* The Boston-based socialist women's liberation collective Bread and Roses named themselves after the slogan used by women who participated in the 1912 Lawrence, Massachusetts, textile factory strike that demanded better working conditions.

MARILYN WEBB

I was standing there in shock, off to the side of the stage. I had no idea how to process it. I was like, "What just happened?" Lee came over and he said, "I'm so sorry." And he hugged me. And I knew something really bad had happened.

Then I remember him saying, "Let's go back to our apartment." And all these women said, "Can we come too?" They were probably in shock too. We all went back to my apartment. It must've been about forty women.

So we talked about what happened. My mind was in a million pieces. From going to between "I gave an awful speech and I'm a bad speaker" to "How did I get this wrong? I thought that movement men were supportive of us?" And then the phone rang.

To me, there was no doubt. It was Cathy Wilkerson, with her specific cadence of speech. She said, "If you or anyone else ever gives a speech like that, anywhere in the country, ever again, we'll beat the shit out of you."

Cathy and I had once been very close, but she had recently gotten more and more radical and in a few months she would join the SDS offshoot of the Weathermen.* Cathy had been a big figure in our women's group, and then after a time, she wasn't. She was also against my organizing women because she thought it was counterrevolutionary.

On the phone call I thought I heard voices in the background. They had an SDS house around the corner from us, and there were several people who lived there with Cathy. I thought I heard Mike Spiegel and Johnny Lerner in the background, laughing and talking. Then the woman said, "I just want you to keep that in mind." I hung up on her.

JONATHAN LERNER

Marilyn's description of me living in the SDS house with Cathy Wilkerson in DC, participating in the counter-inaugural and witnessing her speech and being extremely obnoxious to her, about which I am deeply chagrined, are accurate. I'd rather not be interviewed about that time, though.

Women's liberation ideas began to be articulated around '67 and '68 within SDS and in the broad Left. It didn't take very long for the women's

---

* Five months later, in June 1969, SDS factionalism between Marxist and Maoist ideologues caused the organization to splinter. When SDS with its 120,000 members imploded, a militant group calling themselves the Weathermen (from a line in Bob Dylan's "Subterranean Homesick Blues": "You don't need a weatherman to know which way the wind blows") took over what was left of SDS. Draft resister and organizer David Harris summed up the movement's transformation: "What had been a movement of nonviolent resistance, civil disobedience, and community organizing freaked out in 1969."

movement to define itself as a distinct thing, but the Left was very recalcitrant about accepting it. It was so new, and in a way disruptive. Sometimes in SDS meetings, there would be fights between men and women. I don't mean physical fights, but women would try to put forth a political platform about women's issues and there were men who would try to argue them down. It was very fraught. It wasn't easy for that first generation of women who were trying to raise feminism within the Left. Women started to flee the Left because they weren't being listened to.

CATHY WILKERSON

I was not at Marilyn's speech and I didn't find out about the phone call until I read about it in Todd Gitlin's book *Days of Rage* in 1987. When I found out about the whole brouhaha with Marilyn years later, it was pretty clear to me that it had all the hallmarks of an FBI operation. They had identified a conflict, and intervened in order to exacerbate that conflict. That's what they did regularly with the Panthers and all kinds of left groups.*

MARILYN WEBB

Years later I was shocked when I happened to run into Cathy and she denied making that call. If it were true that it wasn't Cathy, then whomever was impersonating her did an excellent job of splitting the movement, which was the exact purpose of COINTELPRO. That incident was a perfect example of its intent.

Cathy's and my friendship was over. And everything I thought about the political possibilities of a larger New Left Movement that included both SDS and the women's movement went dead in my brain. It would never happen. I suddenly agreed with Shulie that women needed to organize separately, that we couldn't just be an arm of the larger left. It meant that a separate women's movement was necessary, and that was it. That was the breaking point and that's how I began organizing from then on.

---

* In response to the 1968 student protest at Columbia University, the FBI's secret and illegal program called COINTELPRO (Counterintelligence Program) targeted dozens of New Left groups, including women's liberation. Along with the FBI, the CIA and branches of the armed forces domestic surveillance programs opened files on 23,500 US citizens. The FBI surveilled, infiltrated, and disrupted Black liberation and antiwar groups, as well as veteran, GI, gay, student, environmental, and feminist groups. COINTELPRO targeted food co-ops, health clinics, underground newspapers, communes, bookstores, community centers, and street theaters, using tactics that included spreading divisive disinformation and using infiltrators as provocateurs who encouraged violent, self-destructive behavior. There are voluminous FBI files on almost every women's liberation activist with any public profile, and those files indicate that the FBI hired female infiltrators (all FBI agents were men then) to report on women's liberation activities.

2

Mrs. Chisholm Goes to Washington

Sworn in on January 3, 1969, Shirley Chisholm stepped into the precedent-setting role as the first Black female member of Congress with fierce determination and her signature charm. A national media sensation, Chisholm was inundated with requests for interviews, while many of her white male colleagues treated her like a pariah.

McCall's, August 1970, "A woman who knows all about race prejudice tells why sex prejudice is even more frustrating—and harder to fight," by Shirley Chisholm
Being the first black woman elected to Congress has made me some kind of a phenomenon. There are nine other blacks in Congress; there are ten other women. I was the first to overcome both handicaps at once. Of the two handicaps, being black is much less of a drawback than being female.

BARBARA WINSLOW
She went to Congress. In some ways, for younger people to understand it, it was very much like AOC's [Alexandria Ocasio-Cortez] election. Chisholm was very daring, she was fierce, she was by then a feminist, she was the honorary chair of the National Abortion Rights Action League [NARAL], she introduced the Equal Rights Amendment in Albany and when she got

to Washington. She spoke out against the argument [made by some Black Power activists] that abortion was genocide.

SHIRLEY CHISHOLM

When I got there, I was very, very unhappy. Never before had a Black woman sat in the United States Congress. . . . I felt like I was somebody coming out of the moon. They wouldn't sit with me in the [members-only] restaurant when I would eat . . . you were supposed to go to your delegation's table, but I didn't know where the New York delegation sat. So I sat at an empty table and I ordered my lunch. I was very hungry that day, and the table was crowded with everything that I had to eat. I didn't know it because the tables weren't marked, but I had sat at the Georgian delegation table. The men would come in, and nobody would sit with me. I took out my *New York Times* and read it. They just could not sit at a table, in the House of Representatives, where a Black woman was seated.

SHIRLEY DOWNS

She is just extraordinarily comfortable with a very wide range of people. She exudes this warmth. She always made a point of working with Republicans across the aisle, of working with conservative Democrats. She's a very polite person, and she's very interested in other people's views, even if she doesn't necessarily agree, she will always listen. I think they were surprised because she's so polite.

SHIRLEY CHISHOLM

I had [American] Indians on the staff, I had Blacks on the staff. I had an Italian woman on the staff. I had Puerto Ricans on the staff. I had everything. The real League of Nations staff. And that's what I really wanted so that people can see each other and learn to appreciate each other.

SHIRLEY DOWNS

She's a lady. Mrs. Chisholm is one of these people whose shoes and bags always match, and she's got manners. She would sit in the members lunch room and talk to people and be very forthcoming.

SHIRLEY CHISHOLM

My staff loved the way I dressed. They said, "But Chizzy, you're always so dressed up." I said, "I was raised that way." You see, I tried to bring my life into the clothes so that you could understand me as a person. That was the way that I was reared. My mother, my grandmother always said you must be well attired. You have to have your shoes shined and things like that. But Shirley Downs was the one I had to talk to constantly because she was a product of the sixties. But she was a very smart woman. When we were going places, I had to tell her, "You have to be fashionable today. Two stockings of the same color."

BARBARA WINSLOW

The famous story is that she was put on the agricultural committee and she didn't want to do it.

SHIRLEY CHISHOLM

The first big event in a freshman congressman's career is his assignment to a committee. He is not likely to get the one he wants because length of service, seniority, counts more than anything else. . . . But for the sake of courtesy the leaders of his party ask him which one he prefers. . . . My first choice, naturally, was the Education and Labor Committee. There were some vacancies on the Democratic side, and it would have made sense to take advantage of my twenty years' experience in education by appointing me to one of them. . . . I found out that they had assigned me the Agriculture Committee . . . and my subcommittee assignments were to be rural development and forestry. Forestry!

New York Times, April 13, 1969,
"This Is Fighting Shirley Chisholm," by Susan Brownmiller
Representative Chisholm began her fight to change her assignment from a House Agriculture subcommittee on Forestry and Rural Villages to something more relevant to her Bedford-Stuyvesant community. She approached Speaker John McCormack, who told her, she reports, to accept the assignment and "be a good soldier." She brooded about that for a while, she says, and then decided, "That's why the country is the way it is." Mrs. Chisholm then placed an amendment before the House Democratic caucus to remove her name from the Agriculture Committee, aware that she was taking an unprecedented step—bucking the powerful Wilbur Mills of Arkansas, chairman of the House Ways and Means Committee.

SHIRLEY CHISHOLM

I walked right down on the floor of the House and stood before the members. . . . I realized that I did this without being acknowledged, and I told them that it seems to me that all you know is that no tree grows in Brooklyn. And I don't know one wood from another. I want an assignment that has to do with the people of my district. "You have to take what is given to you." I said no, I'm not going to take it. The next two or three days they gave me Veteran Affairs, and I told them, well that's a smart move. There are far more veterans in the district than trees.

Several of the male members spoke to me afterward in sympathetic terms, as if I had just had a death in the family. "You've committed political suicide," one advised me. That phrase sort of made me feel at home.

It is incomprehensible to me, the fear that can affect men in political offices. It is shocking the way they submit to forces they know are wrong and fail to stand up for what they believe. Can their jobs be so important to them, their prestige, their power, their privileges so important that they will cooperate in the degradation of our society just to hang on to those jobs?

A Congressman from South Carolina . . . used to say to me all the time, "Shirley, you ought to kiss the floor when you come into this Congress. You know why you ought to kiss the floor? Because you getting forty-two-five like me." I said, "What are you saying? You're making forty-two-five like me?" This is all he kept saying, "Forty-two-five."

BARBARA WINSLOW

Members of Congress made $42,500 . . . his point was, how dare you make as much money as me. There was another Southern legislator, who Chisholm's staffer said every time she would stand up to leave a committee meeting, the congressman would clean off her seat.

SHIRLEY CHISHOLM

One day Brock Adams, he was the white congressman from Washington, said, "Every time you come into this chamber, that man from Arkansas starts coughing." So I said maybe he should go to a doctor. Brock Adams said, "He coughs every time you come through [the floor of the House chamber] and then when you get near to him, he puts his handkerchief up and spits in it." I said, "Are you sure?" He said, "We know that."

Brock Adams asked, "When is Shirley Chisholm going to take care of that gentleman?" I had on a beautiful sweater suit, and I went out and purchased a male handkerchief. I put the handkerchief in the pocket of my suit. And sure enough, as I was walking down the aisle, he started coughing, coughing. I had synchronized when to pull out my handkerchief. Just as I got near him, he started coughing and he spat in the handkerchief. I pulled out my handkerchief right there, and spat in the handkerchief in front of his face and said, "Good day." He hasn't done it since.

By the end of March . . . President Nixon announced on the same day that he had decided to build an ABM [antiballistic missile] system, and that the Head Start program in the District of Columbia was to be cut back for lack of money; that was enough for me. I started working on my maiden speech in the House. . . . I had to tell the world that it was wrong to plan to spend billions on an elaborate and unnecessary weapons system when disadvantaged children were getting nothing.

BARBARA WINSLOW

She decided to devote her maiden speech in Congress to explaining why she planned to vote against every defense funding bill until Congress began to vote for programs providing jobs and social welfare. Referring to herself as a teacher and a woman, she said, "As I take this stand today I am joined by every mother, wife, and widow in this land who ever asked herself why the generals can play with billions while families crumble under the weight of hunger, sickness, and unemployment." She concluded, "We must force this administration to rethink its distorted, unreal state of priorities. Our children, our jobless men, our deprived, rejected and starving fellow citizens must come first. For this reason I intend to vote 'no' on every money bill that comes to the floor of this House . . . until our country starts to use its strength, its tremendous resources for people and peace, not for the profits of war."

3

Shattering the Abortion Silence

In the five weeks between Valentine's Day eve and the ides of March in early 1969, three events altered forever the politics of the abortion-rights movement. On February 13, a public meeting of New York's Rockefeller Commission to Review New York State's Abortion Laws was disrupted by radical feminist members of Redstockings who objected to the all-male (and one nun) panel of experts.

The next day, February 14, the brand-new National Association for the Repeal of Abortion Laws (NARAL) held the first-ever abortion-rights conference in Chicago. Amid activists strategizing to repeal state antiabortion laws, Betty Friedan made a passionate proclamation that without reproductive rights women cannot have freedom or equality.

Five weeks later, on March 21, the Redstockings radicals shattered decades of silence when they staged the first abortion speak-out.

BARBARA MEHRHOF

Women's liberation put the whole issue of abortion on the map. The first Redstockings action took place at a hearing about reforming New York State abortion laws. There were fourteen "experts" on the panel and they were all men except for one Catholic nun. They were giving expert testimony to six male members of the New York State legislature about the implications of reforming the abortion law in New York State.

SUSAN BROWNMILLER

On the morning of the February 13 hearing, a dozen infiltrators camouflaged in dresses and stockings entered the hearing room and spaced themselves around the chamber. They called themselves Redstockings.

ELLEN WILLIS

At the hearing, I was nervous. I had deep feminine inhibitions against being nasty and making myself conspicuous. But as the testimony proceeded—a decrepit judge was advocating legal abortion for women who had "done their social duty" by having four children—my adrenaline rose. Then a member of our cadre got up and shouted, "Okay, now let's hear from the *real* experts!" When she finished talking, I started, and I had never felt less inhibited in my life. In another minute, most of the women in the room were angrily demanding to testify. "Won't you act like ladies?" a legislator pleaded, but no one was listening.

SUSAN BROWNMILLER

Joyce Ravitz began to declaim an impassioned oration. Ellen Willis jumped in. More women rose to their feet.

"Men don't get pregnant, men don't bear children. Men just make laws," a demonstrator bellowed.

"Girls, girls, you've made your point. Sit down. I'm on your side," a legislator urged. Raising the temperature a notch higher.

"Don't call us girls," came the unified response. "We are women!"

The hearing dissolved in confusion. When the chairman attempted to reconvene it behind closed doors, the women sat down in the corridor, refusing to budge.

ROSALYN BAXANDALL

They locked us out, and therefore we had our own abortion speak-out at Washington Square church.

BARBARA MEHRHOF

Shulie had just come back from Stockholm, where she had attended the international war crimes tribunal where American veterans testified about war crimes they witnessed in Vietnam. Simone de Beauvoir, Jean-Paul Sartre, and James Baldwin were involved in that too.

So Shulie envisioned something like the Stockholm war trials, but around abortion. The idea was women would go public with what they had not ever talked about in private, their own abortions. Well, that really knocked everybody off their chairs. We agreed that sounded like the right action. But how would we find the women who were willing to testify?

ELLEN WILLIS

We decided to hold our own hearing at which women will testify about their abortions. About a dozen women agreed to speak. Many others refused because they are afraid of static from employers or families.

SUSAN BROWNMILLER

When Redstockings did their first abortion speak-out, Irene Peslikis, who was the main organizer, remembered what I had said at that consciousness-raising meeting and got in touch with me. She said, "Would you come and testify at our abortion speak-out?" I said, "I think I'd make a better contribution by writing about it for the *Village Voice*." And so I did. And the headline was "Everywoman's Abortions: 'The Oppressor Is Man.'" It got on the front page of the *Village Voice*.*

BARBARA MEHRHOF

We all wore dresses. Everyone went back to being a woman, so people had lipstick on. Their hair done. They looked so wonderful. They looked great. They just wanted to look professional for this thing.

ALIX KATES SHULMAN

I was not a testifier but I went to it. It was around the corner from where I lived and I told my husband that I was going to the abortion speak-out and he said that I couldn't speak out because it was *his* abortion too. We had an argument about it. He said, "You can't go, don't go." But I went because by that time, I did whatever I wanted. Then I wrote *The Marriage Agreement*.†

I've had four abortions, and they were never because I didn't use birth

---

* The first alternative weekly newspaper in the country, *The Village Voice* (1955–2018) was based in New York's Greenwich Village and covered arts, culture, and politics with flair, giving its famous, unconventional, and stylish writers free rein to expose, espouse, and muckrake.

† Written in 1969 and first published in the August/September 1970 issue of the underground feminist journal *Up from Under*, Schulman's witty, controversial article proposed that men and women share childcare and housework equally. It was roundly attacked by Norman Mailer, Joan Didion, and Russell Baker, but reprinted in many mainstream magazines like *Life*, *New York*, and *Redbook*.

control. They were all failures of my diaphragm. I went on the pill briefly, but that was when it was in the early days. It was way too much estrogen. My close friend Barbara Seaman, whose work was in the women's health movement, said, "Do not take the pill, you'll get cancer." So I never was on the pill, except for a very short time before I knew her.

So, I always used a diaphragm. But after my fourth abortion, I said to my doctor, "How can I keep getting pregnant when I always use my diaphragm?" He said, "If the man withdraws his penis and then you start again, because your vagina expands during intercourse, the diaphragm can slip out of place. So, if he's going to go in again, you have to reinsert your hand and fix it to make sure the diaphragm is in place." I said, "Why did nobody ever tell me this?" And he said, and I quote, "We can't tell you everything."

GLORIA STEINEM

I went to cover the speak-out as a reporter for *New York* magazine. It was the first time in my life I had ever heard women in public stand up and tell the truth about their lives, parts of their lives that were unacceptable, and just telling the stories, the individual true stories of what it had been like to go out and try to enter a criminal underworld, to endanger yourself, to seek an illegal abortion, all the particular circumstances of each woman.

[I graduated from Smith in 1956], and it was the end of 1956 when I went to London and there—I still didn't have a visa (to travel to India), so I was waiting for a visa, so I was living with a friend and I was working as a waitress in order to survive there. I was such a terrible waitress. . . . And gradually, I realized that I really was indeed pregnant. I kept hoping it would go away. I kept reading books and thinking I could ride horseback or throw myself down a stair, you know, all these kinds of magical thinking, ridiculous notions one has.

I went to a doctor whose name I found just in the phone book in London, who said yes, probably I was pregnant, and gave me pills which would induce a period if I were not pregnant, and of course they didn't. I was at my wits' end. I knew I couldn't tell Blair (my boyfriend), because then this would be a reason, we had to get married. I certainly couldn't tell my family. They couldn't do anything about it anyway. I was quite desperate. I would never, ever, under any circumstances kill myself. But nonetheless, it kind of crossed my mind at that point, because I was so desperate.

Fortunately, just moments before it was too late, I happened to meet an American playwright at some gathering, who was quite an awful man as I remember, and was talking about how he had had to get two of his actresses abortions, because otherwise they couldn't do his production. I said to him, "How did you do that?" He said, "Oh, well, you know, here it's against the law, but if you get two doctors to say that it's against the health or mental health of the woman, you can get permission." So I went back to the first doctor and did not tell him the truth about it. I told him that the man who was the father did not want to marry me—I didn't want to admit that it was my doing—and could he help me? He thought for a long time, and he said all right. He said, "I will do this, but you have to promise me two things. You have to never tell anyone my name, and you have to do what you want to do with your life." I never told anyone, no one—not the woman I was staying with, not anyone—for many, many years, until the women's movement came along and women began to tell the truth about our lives. But I kept it a secret all that time.

> *Village Voice*, March 27, 1969, "Everywoman's Abortions:
> The 'Oppressor Is Man,'" by Susan Brownmiller
> Twelve young women faced an audience of more than 300 men and women last Friday evening and with simplicity and calm and occasional emotion and even humor, told of incidents in their personal lives which they formerly had consigned to the very private. They rapped about their own abortions. . . .
>
> The panelists prepared no speeches for the Friday night open meeting. They set up an unobtrusive tape recorder, kept the lights comfortably dim to encourage conversation, and protected their anonymity by using first names only. The result, which could have been exhibitionistic or melodramatic, was neither—it was an honest rap. And it worked.

ALIX KATES SHULMAN

It was fantastic. It was so moving and so brave of these young women because it was criminal and it broke the taboo. After that it was a national conversation, public conversation on television, wherever. It was a great success in that sense. The church was full, and people from the audience got up and spoke. It was wonderful. Did you know that there's a tape recording of it?

SPEAKER 1

I became pregnant. I slept with a guy during my period and no one ever told me that you could become pregnant when you had your period. The second time (I got pregnant) the guy said, "Well, when I come the second time, the sperms aren't potent at all and you won't become pregnant."

Then the thing about the second abortion that I remember most was this marvelous doctor. I walked in and there was Muzak of Maurice Chevalier going on. He counted the money about five times, looking at it, $700. Then when I got on the table, he said, "You're no nigger. There's no reason to scream." And then he didn't give me any anesthetic and I didn't want to get up from the table. And he said, "Look, I have five patients waiting out there." So I got up from the table and all I felt like doing was being by myself.

So I locked myself in the bathroom there and he sent the nurse in and kept saying, "Look at all these people waiting outside. You must get out of my building." I mean he was just so concerned with all the other women and all the money he had to make. And I was in the bathroom and finally he got the guy who'd gone with me to convince me to come out of the bathroom.

SPEAKER 2

The reason we have the laws that we have now is because men want to make women suffer for their sin. Like a sin to get pregnant and women are forced to carry an unwanted pregnancy. If you do not want the pregnancy, you are faced with a very clear reality and that is that you are sacrificing your life. When you go to a hotel or when you get into a car on Fifty-Fourth Street and Lexington Avenue and you are blindfolded and taken some place, you don't know where, you're not given an anesthetic. The instruments are not even sterilized. You wind up with an infection. You can wind up never being able to have children and this is what women have to go through. This is our debt to society.

And as I said before, we owe society nothing. Society owes us something. And that is to give us the right to decide what we want to do with our own body. The man is the one that screws you and then when you turn to him and say, "Hey, look, sweetheart, I'm pregnant," "How do you know it was me? You never slept with anyone else?"

SPEAKER 4

You are really alone and you are making arrangements with this weird doctor that's not a doctor in New Jersey where you have to not park the car on a certain side of the street and not have regular license plates and you start bargaining about money on the telephone and then you have to sign a statement saying that you are having a polyp removed.

And of course, the typical West New York, New Jersey style, I was told the wrong price and so I had to go back and come back the next day with an extra hundred dollars. He was a very lovely doctor. He had a crucifix in every room and he had a picture of his wife, his family, and all the Italian American societies in West New York, New Jersey, and his wife with a little Madonna around her neck. And they were very sweet. They were very kind. It only cost $900. Of course, I'm still paying off. I went to the bank and I got a vacation loan and I'm still paying that off.

Village Voice, March 27, 1969, "Everywoman's Abortions: The 'Oppressor Is Man,'" by Susan Brownmiller

At one point in the evening, a young man in the audience arose to ask a question: "You keep talking about a woman's right to have a legal abortion," he said. "What about the man's rights, in or out of wedlock? You didn't make yourselves pregnant."

He was told off politely and firmly, "Women have the ultimate control over their own bodies," a Redstocking told him with the patience a weary teacher uses for a dear but exceptionally slow child. Neither he nor any other male in the hall felt like challenging that simple yet not so obvious statement.

GLORIA STEINEM

I was just so transformed by that—that what happened only to women could be taken seriously; that there were other women who were telling the truth about this. I wrote about it without writing about my own experience. But it transformed me, and I began to seek out all the individuals and books and meetings and everything I could find, of what was then the burgeoning women's movement.

SUSAN BROWNMILLER

The Redstockings abortion speak-out was an emblematic event for women's liberation. Speak-outs based on the New York women's model were organized in other cities within the year. The importance of personal testimony in a public setting, which overthrew the received wisdom of "the experts," cannot be overestimated. It was an original technique and a powerful ideological tool, and a political act of courage.

4

Slave of a Slave—Black Women's Liberation

In 1969, women's liberation and abortion rights were often not accepted within the rising Black Power movement, especially among the Black nationalist Nation of Islam. Meanwhile, Black feminists began searching for their place in this new politically charged environment.

FRANCES BEAL

Jim Forman, the former executive secretary of SNCC, came back from the West Coast having met Eldridge Cleaver, and he was just so enthralled with this so-called lumpenproletariat-became-revolutionary. He told us to read Cleaver's new book, it's a great book. So we read the book, right? *Soul on Ice.*[*] And from beginning to end, we were shocked to read about how Cleaver romanticizes raping Black women as practice to get up the nerve to rape white women. That's what we get out of the book. Not about a revolutionary projectory, but something that is demeaning from beginning to end.

---

[*] Published in March 1968, Cleaver's confessional prison memoir described the Black American experience in a new candid, raw voice. *Soul on Ice* delved into the complex, violent history of the sexual dynamic between Black men and white women. The book created a political and literary sensation, and Cleaver became the darling of the Left and spokesman for the Black Panther Party.

Gwen Patton* and I drafted a response to give to Forman. We called it *Soul on Fire*. We tore apart the book. Part of our argument was responding to Forman wanting SNCC to join with the Black Panthers. We were saying, fuck this. We started talking about the women in the South. We had not gone through that in order to now turn around and be put back in this demeaning position by Black men. So the whole question was very clear to us. We were confronted with a lumpen attitude toward women, which we completely rejected and said, this has no place in this revolutionary organization.

BRIAN FLANAGAN

After the student revolt, Eldridge Cleaver gave a speech at Columbia. It was one of his first trips to New York. I remember, because I was with my girlfriend at the time, Sylvia. She was about five years older than me and was a copy editor at McGraw Hill. She had a master's from Columbia and Barnard and was very bright, and my first great love.

Columbia Spectator, "Eldridge Cleaver Derides Election, Candidates 'Pigs,'" October 15, 1968

Two thousand students jammed Wollman and filled adjoining Hewitt Lounge to hear Cleaver's hour long speech. . . .

Cleaver asserted that "the oppressor has no rights that the oppressed are bound to respect" and called for the people "to rise up" and rebel against the present power structure. "We'll burn this motherfuckin' town all the way everywhere if we can't get the programs to re-construct it," he said. "We don't need any more wars on poverty. We need a war on the rich." The crowd in Wollman interrupted Cleaver's speech several times to applaud his comments.

BRIAN FLANAGAN

He was the minister of information of the Black Panther Party. The three main voices in the Panthers were Huey Newton, Bobby Seale, and Eldridge Cleaver. Those were the big three. We were all Panther supporters of course.

---

* Gwen Patton (1943–2017) was a prominent civil rights activist and organizer. As the first female student body president at Tuskegee University, she led students to the Montgomery capitol building to lobby for the passage of the Voting Rights Act. Before college, she worked on voter registration in Montgomery and later became a SCLC and SNCC organizer and a founder and first chair of SNCC's Women's Commission. She also founded the National Association of Black Students and the National Antiwar Antidraft Union.

I can't phrase it exactly, but I remember when he was telling the women in the audience, "Women have a place in this movement; every woman has a position and her position is prone. Don't give it up to the man unless he's a radical." Basically, to withhold sex unless they are really committed to the struggle. I think there were some murmurings from women because it was such an outrageous thing to say. I remember turning to Sylvia and saying as a joke, "Don't worry, I'm real radical."*

ERICKA HUGGINS

Women in the Panthers stood in the same place they stood in society, and women didn't have a lot of power in society. When people ask me about the role of the women in the party, I think they're thinking that it was going to be different because we just showed up one day and joined the Black Panthers. It doesn't work like that. It's systemic. I had been considered a leader in Connecticut and in Los Angeles, but I really wasn't truly understanding what that meant, because it just meant that I took what I was doing seriously.

I would notice there were men who, if I would say, "Can we pick up these chairs and move them over there?" "Nah, I ain't going to do that." And I would have to go get a man to ask the same question. "Yeah. I could help with that." And so I started having conversations with men because I understood how serious the work was that we were doing. I thought to myself before I started the conversations that we're talking about revolution, and do we want to carry this old crap into a new world? I didn't blame men for thinking like that, acting like that, because I know where they got it. Look how society's set up?

I was arrested and I was in prison in New Haven.† But when I came back in 1971, I was working at the Oakland community school, and I was working on the party newspaper with Elaine Brown and Joan Kelley, who were leaders in the party.

---

* True to his word, Flanagan joined the militant Weathermen in 1969.

† After her husband, Black Panther Party leader John Huggins, was murdered in Los Angeles, Ericka Huggins moved to New Haven with their three-month-old daughter, where she founded the New Haven Black Panther Party. She was arrested with six other Panther members in May 1969 and charged with conspiracy to murder another BPP member, Alex Rackley. The conspiracy trial of the New Haven Seven became a focal point for the antiwar, antiracist student movement. Huggins and Bobby Seale were acquitted, but first Huggins served two years in prison.

MICHELE WALLACE

People went crazy when Martin Luther King got killed in 1968 because all of the people who wanted to be militant and violent, they felt as though that was the signal. In other words, if you could kill the prince of peace, obviously, peace was of little use. The Black Panthers said, "Let's get our berets and our guns." There were Panther groups all around. So it was time to have a revolution, as it were. The men were having a revolution that was not going to include us except in a subsidiary, docile, baby-having way.

I lived in Harlem. I began to wear African clothes, long dresses, mainly to prevent men from speaking to me in the streets the way they tended to. There was a lot of sexual harassment everywhere, at school, in the streets, wherever you were. I wanted to be a writer and I wanted to be taken seriously. And I had ideas. Which brought me into conflict with almost every Black man I met.

That's when I became a feminist and my mother became a feminist. The men were so down on the idea of us being in leadership or having an opinion about anything except having babies and walking ten steps behind them barefoot, which was some sort of notion of what it would be like if we were in Africa.

Statement on Birth Control,
Black Women's Liberation Group, Mount Vernon, New York*

September, 11, 1968

Dear Brother:

Poor black sisters decide for themselves whether to have a baby or not to have a baby. If we take the pills or practise [sic] birth control in other ways, it's because of poor black men. . . .

So when whitey put out the pill and poor black sisters spread the word, we saw how simple it was not to be a fool for men any more. . . .

That was the first step in waking up!

---

* Started in 1960, and therefore the earliest second-wave women's liberation group on record, the Mount Vernon/New Rochelle women's group, which also called themselves the Pat Robinson Group and "The Damned," was one of the first to write and publish letters and essays promoting Black feminist theory. Started by leftist psychologist Pat Robinson after her experience volunteering at Planned Parenthood, and attracting Black women domestic workers, welfare recipients, factory workers, teenagers, and grandmothers, the group gave voice to poor Black women with an unapologetic pro-woman, pro-motherhood stance. This letter is a response to the Black Unity Party of Peekskill, New York's statement: "The Brothers are calling on the Sisters not to take the pill. . . . When we produce children, we are aiding the REVOLUTION in the form of NATION BUILDING."

FRANCES BEAL

As women got together and began talking about their role in the society and their role within SNCC, some of us began to see it wasn't an individual problem but a social problem. The other thing that happened at the time, was some of the young men were attracted to the Nation of Islam perspective, and the Congress of African Peoples; LeRoi Jones, who later became Amiri Baraka, talked about how abortion was genocide.* We felt that we needed to take a stand against these guys. First of all, they were never the ones that were already fathers. They didn't have the responsibility of kids. Who was going to take care of this army of babies?

I had gone to high school with a woman named Cordelia. When she was a freshman in college, she went to have an abortion, and she died from the abortion. So here I was, eighteen years old and someone so young as that died because she didn't have access to a doctor. So I did not go along with this thing that abortion should not be a choice that Black women had.

One of the things we had noticed in SNCC too was that in the South there was a sterilization abuse problem amongst Black women, and a number of Black women found that after they had a baby, unbeknownst to themselves, they were sterilized, so they couldn't have more children. So we began to talk about, what right does a woman have to control her own body? I had actually done some research on the various different forms of sterilization abuse that was going on in New York City and the South.

Gwen Patton, May Jackson, Diane Jenkins, and I founded the SNCC Black Women's Liberation Committee. SNCC voted at a meeting in New York in December 1968 to have the SNCC Black Women's Liberation Committee investigate some of the conditions under which Black women function.

We began to have a number of consciousness-raising discussions. We concentrated at first on the abortion question, because there was a lot of activity going on at this period because, in New York in particular, there were enormous meetings and speak-outs where women would get up and talk about their experiences of having an abortion. Some of them were pretty horrible, how they were butchered.

I began to write some short pieces, and to speak in some of the groups

---

* The Nation of Islam opposed abortion and birth control, claiming that it was conceived by white people as part of a plan to reduce the Black population. At the 1967 Black Power Conference in Newark, New Jersey, which was organized by Amiri Baraka (who would father nine children), a resolution passed denouncing the use of birth control by Black women.

around New York City, defending a woman's right to abortion. I did some research and found some pretty horrible statistics about how many Black and Puerto Rican women were actually killed by these illegal abortions.[*]

We also talked about how women on the job were second-class citizens, and were very restricted in the type of jobs that we could have. What I did was to try to pull together a number of those streams. One of my assignments was to look back in history to see what kind of things I could find. Don't forget, there's a plethora of materials now. There was nothing then, nothing.

Earl Conrad's biography of Harriet Tubman [published in 1943] was like a bible to me. Earl Conrad was associated in some way with the Communist Party. He walked around with that book for years and years, going from one publisher to the other, and couldn't get it published. And finally he got it published. To me it's the definitive book on Harriet.

I remember spending time in the Forty-Second Street New York Public Library, and I went to the Tamiment Library at NYU to see what they had there. I just looked everywhere. We didn't have Google at that time, remember, so you had to go to the library, fill out your name, and try to find the books on the subject matter, of which there wasn't very much. I got Earl Conrad's book from a leftist bookstore.

And then I read everything that the CP [Communist Party] wrote about liberation of women, and it was very unsatisfactory. I mean it was satisfactory as far as it called for the equality of women and the liberation of women, but they had this perspective that was throughout the entire socialist world, that the basic thing was the revolution. And then these other "social issues" would come later.

So we decided to publish a pamphlet and called it the *Black Women's Manifesto.* And it had four essays that essentially dealt with Black women's issues. My first draft of *Double Jeopardy* is in there. There is a poem called *For Sadie and Maud,* which was written by Eleanor Holmes Norton. She used to come to a few of our consciousness-raising sessions.

I wrote it, but a lot of the ideas in *Double Jeopardy* came out of the collective process of our consciousness-raising group. I synthesized a lot of it. I had a very strong view on the question of abortion and sterilization abuse. That was my big contribution to the discussion. And the rest of it

---

[*] According to Dorothy Roberts in *Killing the Black Body: Race, Reproduction, and the Meaning of Liberty,* "Half of the maternity-related deaths among Black women in New York City in the 1960s were attributed to illegal abortions."

was a polemic against the polemics that were going on around women at the time. Basically by the nationalists.

Double Jeopardy: To Be Black and Female, by Frances Beal
Unfortunately, there seems to be some confusion in the Movement today as to who has been oppressing whom. Since the advent of Black Power, the black male has exerted a more prominent leadership role in our struggle for justice in this country. He sees the System for what it really is, for the most part, but where he rejects its values and mores on many issues, when it comes to women, he seems to take his guidelines from the pages of the *Ladies Home Journal*. Certain black men are maintaining that they have been castrated by society but that black women somehow escaped the persecution and even contributed to this emasculation.

Let me state here and now that the black woman in America can justly be described as a "slave of a slave." When the black man in America was reduced to such an abject state, the black woman had no protector and was used and is still being used in some cases as the scapegoat for the evils that this horrendous System has perpetrated on black men.

MARGO JEFFERSON

I didn't know anything before I read *Double Jeopardy*. Fran Beal wasn't a name I knew, but that was a knockout. And I felt, all right, all things are possible. There she is, having descended from this visible, but male-dominated and terribly impressive radical, leftist, and Black leftist position and having made her way into feminism with every complexity attached. So that was fascinating. And it was stirring. She was one of those people, Fran Beal, the way she wrote. Again, I would also say Ti-Grace Atkinson and Shulamith Firestone too. They stirred you. They always challenged you. You always felt challenged in that you needed to take hold of yourself, of the world. And just keep questioning and acting. I mean, those are real forms of consciousness-raising, I think.

LINDA BURNHAM

The Black Women's Caucus grew out of dissatisfaction amongst women in SNCC about the role of women in SNCC, and about how women's contributions were viewed, and the whole issue of what women's roles were and should be. Frances Beal was one of the people who played a leading role in forming the Black Women's Caucus, which eventually became the Black Women's Alliance.

FRANCES BEAL

And so the concept that we should have an independent organization that addressed itself explicitly to women's issues emerged in the course of our discussions. That it should be an organization based upon racial identification. And that's where the Black Power aspect came in.

MARGO JEFFERSON

What set us apart from the conflicts that white feminists had was that Black men had also been majorly oppressed. As had Black women, we were in a sense opening up a wedge by saying, "Listen, you've been oppressed, but you have oppressed us too." And that was very hard to say out loud.

There was also a feeling that one way our people protected ourselves from the unjust scrutiny of whites was by not airing our disagreements and differences in public because that would allow white writers, ideologues, politicians to use it in any way they wanted. So all of this was going on and it was difficult. Think of Fran Beal or Flo Kennedy, they were both in their ways working on a new way of looking at the world and analyzing it.

Everything was binary in those days. There wasn't intersectionality. There wasn't the same room to talk about double oppression, triple oppression. We talked it through. I know ways in which being a Black man has been horrible for you, but how did you turn that on women? And how can we make analytic and emotional, and social, and political sense of that? We were just beginning to find those tools.

FRANCES BEAL

And then a number of women come back from their experiences in the Venceremos Brigade in Cuba,* and they were looking for a revolutionary organization, and they had their women's consciousness raised partly by us before they went, and partly by their general sense of being revolutionary women and not being told to sit back and knit booties for their revolutionary babies.

---

* Started in 1969 by SDS, in partnership and solidarity with Castro's revolutionary, anti-imperialist communist regime, the Venceremos (Spanish for "we shall overcome") Brigade sent many young leftist activists to harvest sugarcane in Cuba.

Double Jeopardy: To Be Black and Female, by Frances Beal

. . . perhaps the most outlandish act of oppression in modern times is the current campaign to promote sterilization of non-white women . . . sterilization clinics are cropping up around the country in the black and Puerto Rican communities. . . . The rigid laws concerning abortions in this country are another means of subjugation and, indirectly, of outright murder. . . . Nearly half the childbearing deaths in New York City are attributed to abortion alone and out of these, 79 percent are among non-whites and Puerto Rican women. . . . The lack of availability of safe birth-control methods, and forced sterilization practices, and the inability to obtain legal abortions are all symptoms of a sick society.*

FRANCES BEAL

About six months after forming the committee, we were approached by a number of women who were Puerto Rican who said there was nothing like this in the Puerto Rican community and they said they would like to come into the Black Women's Alliance. So we had a big debate in the organization. And what we were essentially dealing with here was, what were the things that were particularly African American, as opposed to what were the things that were specifically Puerto Rican?

And when we looked at the Puerto Rican sisters, we saw that they were

---

* Involuntary and coerced sterilization of Black, Latina, Native American, and poor women in government-funded hospitals and clinics was prevalent in the first half of the twentieth century (originated by the then-racist population and birth control community) and expanded in the 1960s. Laws allowing involuntary sterilization existed in thirty-one states and were even more draconian in the South. For example, a North Carolina law allowed the state to surgically sterilize welfare recipients, unwed mothers, and women deemed "feeble-minded." Between 1964 and 1966, 64 percent of the women sterilized in North Carolina were African American. In 1961, when Fannie Lou Hamer needed medical attention for a uterine cyst, she was given a hysterectomy at a Mississippi hospital without her consent. Hamer, who (obviously) could never bear children, later testified against Mississippi's sterilization law, calling the procedure a "Mississippi appendectomy." An aggressive program by the federally funded Indian Health Service (IHS) forcibly sterilized up to 25 percent of Native American women, according to one study.

Puerto Rican women suffered the most extreme conditions. By 1965, one study showed that one-third of all Puertorriqueñas between the ages of twenty and forty-nine had been sterilized without their consent. In 1970, Dr. Helen Rodríguez Trías, a Puerto Rican doctor living and practicing in New York City, founded the Committee to End Sterilization Abuse (CESA), which advocated for the repeal of federal sterilization laws. A 1973 lawsuit brought by the Southern Poverty Law Center on behalf of parents of two Black teenagers who were unknowingly sterilized in Alabama exposed that 100,000 to 150,000 poor women were sterilized every year in federally funded programs. The lawsuit, *Relf v. Weinberger*, forced the federal government to reform its regulations, requiring that all women give full consent before being sterilized. But not all hospitals complied, and activists continued to file lawsuits and lobby lawmakers into the late seventies, but often without the support of mostly white pro–reproductive choice organizations.

trying to deal with both their national oppression of living within the United States and a kind of racial and class thing that was separate from just being a part of America as a whole, and then how does your gender fit in when you have this other overriding oppression? And Black women were essentially trying to deal with the same thing: How do you deal with the question of race and class and gender, in terms of what kinds of intersections?

So we finally decided that the two forms of oppression, while not precisely exactly the same—race versus, say, nationality—but the idea of the complexity of women's liberation in that context was fundamentally the same.

I remember it was Keisha Shakur who raised the question, if the organization now was third world, which is the term that we used at that time, then our name should be changed to reflect that. First world being the capitalist world, second world being the socialist world, third world being the anticolonial world. So it went from SNCC to Black Women's Liberation to Black Women's Alliance to Third World Women's Alliance, almost within a year.

LINDA BURNHAM

The Third World Women's Alliance came together as an antisexist, antiracist, anti-imperialist organization. They put out a newspaper called *Triple Jeopardy*, and the intention of that newspaper was to really speak to the ways in which women of color experience the world, and speak to the issues that were not at the time being addressed by the white women's movement, or the mainstream women's movement. And it was the early side of the recognition that women of color faced issues and discrimination and marginalization, not only as women, but also as people of color, as people with a particular class background. Some of this later came to be called intersectionality, which is a very complicated term, but the ideas behind that were formed in these early years, where people were essentially saying, we're whole people, and we can't combat women's issues as though we're unaffected by issues of race. The Third World Women's Alliance was an early articulation of this.

5

Our Bodies, Ourselves

As feminist consciousness emerged and began questioning women's roles in law and the workplace, some women challenged the male medical establishment's dictates about women's health and sexuality. This inquiry got to the core of how women could achieve independence by increasing knowledge about their bodies and reclaiming agency over the childbirth process. A group of feminists in Boston turned their curiosity about women's health, wellness, and reproductive rights into a bestselling book that blew open conventional wisdom and sparked a new, lasting part of the movement.

NANCY MIRIAM HAWLEY
In May of 1969, a number of Boston groups that became Bread and Roses and Female Liberation got together, and I helped organize with folks.

PAULA DORESS-WORTERS
Emmanuel College was run by Catholic nuns. They had a large building and they weren't using it that weekend, so someone asked them if we could. They offered it to us and thought we were just these nice girls. They had no idea.

Flier: Female Liberation Conference, May 9–11,
Emmanuel College, Marion Hall 400 The Fenway
Workshop topics include:

What is Female Liberation?
Women and the Control of Their Bodies
The Family and Children
Professional Women
Capitalism and the Position of the Female
Black Women and the Caste Society
The Role of Psychology in the Oppression of the Female
Liberation of Welfare Mothers
Workshop for High School Girls

Anyone interested can give a workshop. If you would like to meet
with other women to research and discuss these or other topics for
workshops, you should get in touch with us.

NANCY MIRIAM HAWLEY

During the conference, some women from the Women's Health Centers
did self-exams. Well, at that time, women hadn't looked at our genitals. So
with mirrors and plastic speculums we did, with the support of women who
were doing this with other women.

People were doing karate self-defense work. They were from a kind of
intellectual, liberal socialist background, and then some of us were interested
in health issues.

PAULA DORESS-WORTERS

We met in a huge room and I remember Cell 16* women standing up on
windowsills of very tall windows saying, "Down with the nuclear family."
It was very exciting. I took some karate lessons from them.

NANCY MIRIAM HAWLEY

I led a workshop called "Women and the Control of Our Bodies." The
workshop was packed. We talked with one another about the things that
concerned us. Some of us were single, some of us were married, some of

---

* Cell 16 was a Boston-based radical group that started in 1968 and espoused celibacy, separation from
men, and taught self-defense and karate. The group published a journal of early feminist theory called *No
More Fun and Games: A Journal of Female Liberation.*

us had small children. And we were concerned about our health and our family's health. There were no women doctors at that point. Certainly not women ob-gyns.

We talked about wanting to know more about our anatomy, birth control, pregnancy, traumatic deliveries, and terrible postpartum experiences.

PAULA DORESS-WORTERS

There were a lot of talks. I went to one led by Miriam and Nancy Shaw, who was a professor. They were both friends of mine. I wanted to hear what they had to say. They both talked about childbirth, that was a big part of it, but also some people talked about abortion, which was not commonly talked about at that time.

NANCY MIRIAM HAWLEY

After the workshop, some of us who wanted to continue meeting got together and we picked topics that were particularly important to us. We did research. We talked to medical people who were sympathetic. We learned how to use the Countway Library at Harvard Medical School. But the important thing is we continued to meet regularly and talk with one another about our experiences as women. The exploration of evidence-based information of women's experience, and the political analysis, made our work unique.

JANE PINCUS

I had the best doctors in town but I knew nothing about home birth. I knew nothing about midwives, nor did anybody I knew. What I had to guide me was Dr. Lamaze, and a book by Dr. Pierre Vellay called *Childbirth Without Pain*. Two books.

I knew that I wanted to have a natural birth. I took Lamaze classes, which is where I saw a short film showing a baby being born.* I was just amazed by it, but I was ignorant. I went to see my doctor for a regular checkup. He said, "You can have your baby now or wait until you go into labor." I said, "I'll have my baby now." That afternoon I went in and got several doses of

---

* Lamaze is a natural childbirth method developed in the 1950s by French doctor Fernand Lamaze. It was introduced in 1959 to the United States by the book *Thank You, Dr. Lamaze* by Marjorie Karmel. Lamaze childbirth–preparation classes teach a controlled breathing technique that helps women in labor manage their pain without medication.

Pitocin, which caused me to go into labor. This is after you got shaved, had an enema, had my water broken.

I found out a few years later that I had been given too much Pitocin, which gave me what are called tetanic contractions and which were too hard. Then they slowed down the contractions with Demerol. The doctor used forceps to get my daughter Sami out because her heartbeat was going down. I was awake the whole time, but I identified ten unnatural things that happened to me there. Sami couldn't really nurse because she was doped up the first few days.

That was my first birth. Finding out about the dangers of Pitocin fueled my hearty, passionate entry into women's health, because I realized Sami could have died. The Pitocin given to me was too strong, and caused contractions that were slowing my baby's heartbeat. It was stuff that I should never have been given. I should have gone into labor naturally.

NORMA SWENSON

I was pregnant and trying to discuss with my doctor what was going to happen at the delivery, and he said, "We'll give you a little Scopolamine. It's a drug that helps you relax." I wrote it down. I went down the hall and put a nickel in the pay phone, and called the Medical Library. They said, it's a cerebral sedative. It's a hallucinogen. That was the drug of choice for most women in this country for quite a long period of time.

But that was an example of the kind of thing that happened. As soon as the women arrived at the hospital, they were given a tranquilizer of some kind, and then they got sedation. It was considered a great advance when ether was replaced with Scopolamine.

NANCY MIRIAM HAWLEY

When Gina was born, my doctor was running the Cambridge hospital ob-gyn department. I think my husband, Andy, was the first man who was allowed in the delivery room.* He was a doctor that Jane Pincus and Paula Doress-Worters and I all used. He said to one of us, "I want you to know, I stitched you up so tight that your husband is going to have a lot of pleasure." I mean, these are things that were said.

---

* Fathers were customarily not allowed into the labor/delivery room.

LOUISE "MAMA BEAR" HERNE

I was born in a hospital. And at the time that my mother was birthing babies, that was the big transition away from home births into hospitals. But the horror stories that I grew up hearing of women birthing in hospitals and the drugs that they gave women in pregnancy, which also resulted in a few of my cousins being barren and not able to give birth because of the drugs that their mothers took. We also know that there was experimentation going on with our mothers in pregnancy.

BEVERLY KIOHAWITON COOK

Our grandmother was a midwife here on the Akwesasne reservation [in northern New York] and delivered hundreds of babies. They would come to her house, or she would go to their home and stay with them until babies were born and stay with them until the mother was on her feet again. She knew what she was doing. She delivered thirteen of her own children.

JEANNE SHENANDOAH

I grew up here, right where I am now, on Onondaga nation territory, which is in Central New York; it's just minutes south of Cherokee, New York, on an Indian reservation.

My great-grandmother was one of the last midwives in our community. And that last intentional birth, was oh, seventy-some years ago; my great-grandmother attended a birth, and the Onondaga County Health Department from Syracuse, New York, threatened to arrest her. My great-grandmother's name was Adaline Wheelbarrow. She was a well-known midwife in this community, and a basket maker and a farmer. She did not speak a lot of English. The health department intimidated her, and she thought that she would go to jail for doing something that was completely normal. So it shook her up a bit, and there weren't any home births for a number of years here because of that.*

BEVERLY KIOHAWITON COOK

When I was in nursing school, the only births that I had ever seen were women who were being knocked out. They were giving them cocktails of Scopolamine

---

* After the passage of the Sheppard-Towner Act in 1921, the Department of Indian Affairs outlawed home births, and states passed restrictions against home births, taking childbirth out of the hands of midwives and under the responsibility of male doctors in hospitals.

and other drugs that they didn't even know what they were. They didn't even know that they were giving birth at the time. And then once the babies came out of it, they had no memory of their birth. It was barbaric.

I had seen one Lamaze birth, and they cleared out a broom closet for her to deliver in because they didn't have a place to do natural births. It was one of the first ones that they had done, but I got to see what a normal birth looked like. It was natural, whereas the women who were drugged and sedated, they were hooked up to IVs, they didn't know what was happening to them. It was really horrible. That's how women gave birth.

When I finished nursing school in Baltimore I came to meet some people through my cousins who lived in Brooklyn who said, "The Mohawks from Kahnawake are going to take over an abandoned girls camp in the Adirondacks, and they're going to reclaim our land." So, I was like, "I'm in. I'm in."

We were headed up to the Adirondacks, to Caughnawaga, our ancestral territory. It means "people of the flint." Our cause was to reclaim our ancestral lands, and to be sovereign, independent, self-reliant. Go back to the old ways. That was the dream.*

I had graduated nursing school—I hadn't even taken my boards yet—but they said, "We have a doctor in our camp." As it happened, there were a couple pregnant girls in camp. And so they figured that I would deliver the babies. . . . We made friends with these young doctors at a clinic about an hour away. Jeannie Shenandoah was with me at the time. We told these doctors that we were going to be delivering babies, and their eyeballs got really big. And they were like, "Oh, well, this can't be possible. You know, this is very dangerous and anything could happen. Many things could go wrong."

JEANNE SHENANDOAH

We went to different communities and we'd ask, "Anybody want to have their baby at home?"

Our women still held on to the belief of what a holy, sacred time childbirth is—to welcome this new spirit, this new person, onto this earth to live life with us. What a wonderful, beautiful, holy, sacred ceremony that is. I was a midwife for thirty-four years. Home births were all 100 percent illegal in New York State. I could walk down the hallway of our small school in our

---

* The American Indian Movement (AIM) made its most public stand when its members occupied the island of Alcatraz from November 1969 to June 1971. AIM and other Indian freedom groups also marched across the country to Washington, DC, in October 1972 in a protest called the Trail of Broken Treaties.

community, and look right and left and see all these little people that I was so honored to be present to welcome them to life on earth.

Midwifery was coming back into its own again. I worked with women for many years from different communities that were not Native.*

PAULA DORESS-WORTERS

After Hannah was born, I had postpartum depression and it was awful. The doctors didn't say anything that was much more intelligent than what you would read in the women's magazines like *Redbook*. They said, "It's just Baby Blues, you'll get over it." When I wanted to know something, I'd find a book about it. But there were no books that were written for women other than *Baby Blues*. I just felt like it was a black hole and there needed to be more. So I picked my subject.

JANE PINCUS

We wrote up something about each particular reproductive event, and then by word of mouth started to give classes at MIT in January 1970.

NANCY MIRIAM HAWLEY

So in the lounges at MIT—unbeknownst to the administration—we had a very original talk on sexuality where we were talking about masturbation and clitorises for the first time. Things that are not so strange today, but at that point, people weren't talking about masturbation. Women weren't talking about their right to sexual pleasure.

JANE PINCUS

The first class was about sexuality. There were about fifty women there. You could write "masturbation" on the blackboard or "clitoris"— these words were spoken out loud, for some women for the first time.

JOAN DITZION

There was this huge drawing of a vagina with a clitoris and vaginal canals. I'd never seen such a graphic image of women's vaginal anatomy. There

---

* Back-to-the-land hippies who studied and often tried to replicate Native American customs were some of the first non-Native communities to practice natural childbirth. Jeanne Shenandoah became friends with Ina May Gaskin, who had a thriving natural childbirth center on the Farm, a large commune she and her husband, Stephen, founded in 1971 in Tennessee. A midwife for more than thirty years, Gaskin wrote the popular book *Ina May's Guide to Childbirth*.

was this whole discussion about women claiming their own sexuality, knowing about it and understanding the difference between clitoral and vaginal orgasms, which I truly had no real understanding of at that point. It was like, whoa!

The MIT course was transforming.

NANCY MIRIAM HAWLEY

The revolution had been going on, but it didn't hit people in ways in which they could talk about their own experience. So people said, "Can we have copies of the papers you developed for this class?" So we made copies for people. And then people said, "Can we have a book? Can we have them all together?" So we raised $1,500, a lot of money at the time, to get it printed. We went to the New England Free Press, which was a radical place. It was the place for political people to go, and the man who ran the Free Press told us, "We do political things. Women's stuff is not political."

JANE PINCUS

The New England Free Press guys insisted we rewrite whatever we had written, and we wrote a very political last chapter about the capitalist system for the first *Women and Their Bodies*.

JOAN DITZION

It truly was collectively written. We were committed to *we*. Everything was *we*.

NANCY MIRIAM HAWLEY

In December of 1970, the first *Women and Their Bodies* came out.*

Women and Their Bodies:
A Course by Boston Women's Health Collective, 75 cents
Introduction:
One year ago, a group of us who were then in women's liberation (now most of us consider ourselves members of Bread and Roses) got together to work on a laywoman's course on health, women and our bodies. The impetus for this course grew out of a workshop on "women and their bodies" at a women's conference at Emmanuel College in

---

* The 193-page booklet on stapled newsprint titled *Women and Their Bodies* was published by New England Free Press, and the first five thousand copies were distributed by hand at workshops and among friends.

Boston, May 1969. After that, several of us developed a questionnaire about women's feelings about their bodies and their relationship with doctors.* We discovered there were no "good" doctors and we had to learn for ourselves. We talked about our own experiences and we shared our own knowledge. . . . For the first time, we were doing research and writing papers that were about us and for us. We were excited and our excitement was powerful. We wanted to share both the excitement and the material we were learning with our sisters. We saw ourselves differently and our lives began to change. . . .

So after a year and much enthusiasm and hard individual and collective thinking and working, we're publishing these papers. They are not final. They are not static. They are meant to be used by our sisters to increase consciousness about ourselves as women, to build our movement, to begin to struggle collectively for adequate health care, and in many other ways they can be useful to you. . . .

It was exciting to learn new facts about our bodies, but it was even more exciting to talk about how we felt about our bodies, how we felt about ourselves, how we could become more autonomous human beings, how we could act together on our collective knowledge, to change the health care system for women and for all people. We hope this will be true for you, too.

Power to our sisters!!

Nancy Hawley, Wilma Diskin, Jane Pincus, Abby Schwartz, Esther Rome, Betsy Sable, Paula Doress, Jane de Long, Ginger Goldner, Nancy London, Barbara Perkins, Ruth Bell, Wendy Sanford, Pam Berger, Wendy Martz, Lucy Candib, Joan Ditzion, Carol Driscoll, Nancy Mann, and all the other women who took the course and read the papers.

JANE PINCUS

My job was sending out copies of *Women and Their Bodies*. I sent out boxes and boxes to people. That's also part of the magic of it. It was part of women's intense desire to find out about themselves. Miriam always thought we'd sell a million copies, but we had no idea that it was going so far, so fast, and

---

* They asked in-depth questions like: "Think about the time spent with the doctor. Did you like/trust her/him? Did s/he trust you, respect you, listen to you? Did you feel like a participant? Did you feel free to ask questions? If you left with a prescription, did you have a clear idea of the benefits, possible risks, and side effects of the drug? Did you discuss alternatives to that medication? Would you have liked your experience to be different? In what way?"

that it was so incredibly needed and that it would become what it became. I certainly didn't.

BYLLYE AVERY

I was just amazed by *Our Bodies, Ourselves.** I couldn't believe it. Doctors were the gods. You didn't ask any questions. Whatever they told you, you did. Carol Downer went to see her ob-gyn in Los Angeles, she asked him if she could see what he was looking at. He told her that was none of her business. So, when he went out of the room, she stole the speculum and put it in her pocket. She went home and got out a mirror and a flashlight with the speculum, and after that, I always say, the women's health movement was born.†

There was no way for you to get any information because there were no books written for laypeople. There were medical texts that nobody thought about approaching. It was the Boston Women's Health Collective, Carol Downer, and *Off Our Backs*,‡ and all of those other underground women's liberation newspapers that were educating us. They made us aware.

Our Bodies, Ourselves was still a little paperback book that they gave out because I remember they sent us a whole batch of them that we gave out to people at the Gainesville Women's Health Center.

DEMITA FRAZIER

I was noticing the demands for sexuality, through demands for sex on demand, the demand to not pay attention to women's sexual agency, because that's the lie about the so-called sexual revolution. It just meant that we could get fucked without getting pregnant. It didn't mean we were necessarily going to have sexual satisfaction. I had the first edition of *Women and Their Bodies*. It was thirty cents, in 1970. I'll never forget discovering all the things that I discovered.

---

*   The title changed from *Women and Their Bodies* to *Our Bodies, Ourselves* in the second edition.

†   Carol Downer and a group of Los Angeles feminists organized an underground abortion service, similar to Jane in Chicago, called the Los Angeles Women's Abortion Referral Service. At a famous meeting at a feminist bookstore on April 7, 1971, Downer showed the group of two dozen women her cervix. Downer and Lorraine Rothman soon developed a method called the period extractor where menstrual blood could be sucked out of the uterus by a syringe. The technique was also used as a form of self-abortifacient.

‡   Founded by Marilyn Webb and women in DC Women's Liberation, *Off Our Backs* was one of the first (after Berkeley's *It Ain't Me Babe*) monthly feminist newspapers, and the longest lasting. First published on February 27, 1970, *Off Our Backs* had a national circulation and covered women's political and cultural issues for forty years.

Things like how my body was put together, and masturbation. My housemates thought it was hilarious. I'm reading and like, oh, I'll see you all later. Went into my room was like, oh, okay. I couldn't believe it. How come nobody was telling us these things? And then of course you understood why, as you began having sex with men who were only interested in their own pleasure.

TORIE OSBORN

We also read *The Myth of the Vaginal Orgasm* by Anne Koedt.* The whole thing about women's sexuality was so important. It was so radical and it was so new to think about sex separate from intercourse, and not just as a lesbian but just that female sexuality was clitoris-based, not vaginal-based, it was a totally new idea in the early seventies. In *Women and Their Bodies* women were the center. So we learned about all of that, and we learned most particularly about sexuality. We had never been the center of sexuality.

Women and Their Bodies *became a bestseller, with 250,000 copies sold in the first year. The New England Free Press published new editions in 1970 and again in 1971, this time with the new, now-famous title,* Our Bodies, Ourselves.

SALLIE BINGHAM

It was as though we were finally emerging from this murk that we'd all been submerged in. Because the self-hatred that we all were raised with—we were so ashamed of our bodies and had this horrible obsession with weight, which has not left me to this day. This idea that you're always overweight, your rear end is too big, or your breasts are too small. It's just a crippling obsession. And to have this kind of very positive outlook on women's bodies, it just was amazing.

---

* Koedt's essay, first published in *Notes from the Second Year* in 1968, was considered radical for challenging the medical establishment's doctrine that most women achieve orgasm vaginally during intercourse, and if they didn't, they were "frigid." Koedt's exposé explained the then-controversial concept that women are much more likely to achieve orgasm clitorally, thus eliminating the need for the penis in female sexual satisfaction.

BARBARA SMITH

Our Bodies, Ourselves was just so groundbreaking because it was based in valuing women's integrity and a women's right to autonomy. The fact that it was clearheaded and not sensational about sexuality and sex and reproduction, the fact that it took a holistic perspective. *Our Bodies, Ourselves* changed medical practice in the United States. It absolutely changed how people understood what their rights were.

In 1973, Simon & Schuster published the first commercial edition of Our Bodies, Ourselves. *By 1976, 2.5 million copies had been sold and* Our Bodies, Ourselves *appeared on the* New York Times *bestseller list in 1976 and 1977. There have been nine editions since, and the book has been translated into thirty-one languages.*

———————

6

NOW Lesbians Come Out

The day of the Stonewall Inn riot, June 28, 1969, is widely understood as the start of the gay rights movement. Before the movement, intrepid out lesbians and gay men might join the Daughters of Bilitis or the Mattachine Society, but these organizations functioned more as support than political-action groups. In 1969, sodomy (oral and anal sex) between consenting adults was illegal in forty-nine states, and gay people faced employment discrimination and open social rejection from the mainstream. Lesbian mothers frequently lost custody of their children in divorce cases. Even in progressive social justice organizations like SDS, NOW, and the Black Panthers, homophobia was rampant. But by 1969, the hypocrisy of NOW demanding women's rights while ignoring gay women's rights began to pull the organization apart.

JACQUELINE CEBALLOS
We kind of knew that some of the women in NOW were lesbians, but none of us ever discussed our sexual preferences. Then a young woman came to town by the name of Rita Mae Brown.

DOLORES ALEXANDER
I went to a meeting in Sheridan Square—the apartment of Helen Leeds, who was a lawyer and member of NOW. There's this young woman sitting

cross-legged over by the windows who didn't say anything during the meeting, but at the end, announces, "Well, as your vocal neighborhood lesbian . . ." I'm like, "Oh shit, there goes the Long Island chapter"—because I had invited two women from Long Island to come in to see what we were about.

RITA MAE BROWN
I got a scholarship at NYU and double-majored in English and Classics, which is how I wound up in New York, from Florida. I heard about NOW and was interested, and thought, "Well, I'll go to a meeting and listen." Of course, everybody there was in their thirties or forties, and I was about nineteen. But I listened and I thought, you know, there's something to this. I'm not a housewife. I'm not angry. I didn't surrender my life to have a husband and children, and I don't think women all surrender their lives, but those women in the room certainly felt they had.

So I started going to NOW meetings and soaked it up, and realized Betty Friedan is a bully—brilliant, but a bully who had to be the center of attention.

DOLORES ALEXANDER
Rita Mae never stopped saying the word "lesbian" and never stopped outraging everyone. Rita also loved to tell you how poor she was and that she slept in a car and she was a student at NYU, and that she was a writer and a poet. Very self-assured, cocky little person, and very likable and funny. She was the only one who said the word "lesbian."

BARBARA LOVE
I thought, Wow, wow, wow, wow! And she was wearing some see-through blouse and a Phi Beta Kappa key. And I said, "I want to talk to you about this. Can we get together after the meeting?"

JACQUELINE CEBALLOS
She was this beautiful young girl, dressed in a very, very delicate feminine little blouse. She looked so sweet and lovely, like she just came out of college. After I finished talking, she said to me, "There are a lot of lesbians in NOW, and you don't acknowledge them, and you all don't know."

IVY BOTTINI
The problem was that Betty Friedan, still the most influential feminist leader in the country, had made it clear that she didn't want lesbianism associated

with feminism. I don't know that she had a problem with individual lesbians themselves. It was just that she and many other feminist leaders were convinced that anything involving "those deviant lesbians" could easily be scorned and dismissed by mainstream society. The lesbian-baiting accusations that all women's libbers were lesbians had been enough to frighten some women, even straight women, away. Real, live, out lesbians in the movement, Friedan and other leaders were convinced, would kill the cause. Friedan was a little crazy on this topic.

MURIEL FOX

It was a question, should NOW get involved in this issue or will it distract from our main issue of sex discrimination of women? I felt that way. I'm not sure I was right. We all certainly believed that there should be no discrimination on the basis of sexual orientation, but we felt it was a separate issue. But the lesbians wanted to make it a major feminist issue with NOW. We had a couple of years of heated arguments, and then they won.

RITA MAE BROWN

I figured, why don't you shock them? Why don't you rattle their chain a little bit? Because here they are talking about women's liberation and then they're turning around and oppressing other women, whether they were women from Spanish-speaking cultures or Black women or women from the lower classes. I mean, there was no recognition whatsoever that not everyone came from a nice white middle-class home.

ANSELMA DELL'OLIO

Rita Mae had worked for me on the Feminist Theater.* She had been my assistant. She was what the Italians call a *peperino*, a real peppery live wire. She lived out of her car for a while. She had no money. She was real hardscrabble, ambitious and fun, and very militant in her lesbianism.

RITA MAE BROWN

Betty called me a redneck. And I replied, "Well, this redneck reads Latin and Greek. What about you?" Shut her up for a couple of minutes. But at any rate, she was awful to anyone that didn't bow down to her. She scared

---

* Anselma Dell'Olio founded the New Feminist Repertory Theater in 1969, which staged a series of pop-up feminist plays and musicals.

the lesbians in NOW, and there were quite a few. But they didn't want to upset her.

ROSALYN BAXANDALL

From the beginning, the press was calling us gay. And a lot of women in the movement *were* gay. They had more time to spend, as men and children didn't drain their energies. So, the movement began being known as gay. And splits started happening—horrible splits.

JACQUELINE CEBALLOS

What can I say? She was a seducer and a charmer, and she told—not only me—she told Ti-Grace and several others that she was going to turn on every officer in NOW. She apparently had some success. A lot of the women were beginning to experiment. It was the age of sexual freedom.

I brought her into the movement and then she started trying to make it a lesbian movement. I said, "It won't be a movement if you make it a lesbian movement, Rita Mae, it just won't be." She didn't understand that. This was a women's movement. It wasn't a gay movement.

DOLORES ALEXANDER

Betty was awful about it. In June of '69, I remember we went to California to a NOW board meeting.* When we were in San Francisco, she walks into this meeting and she nearly has a fit because who does she see there but Del Martin and Phyllis Lyon,† and they looked gay to her and so she said to me, "Get rid of them. Don't let the press see them. Put them in the back." Difficult to do, you know.

But it was true. The press was using that word to bait us. And everyone who was opposed to us was using that word to bait us. And women were afraid of it. Who wanted to be called a lesbian?

BETTY FRIEDAN

I was considered square, uptight, old-fashioned, conservative, etc., about lesbianism; and considering my Middle American background, maybe I was.

---

* At the time, Dolores Alexander was a closeted lesbian and the executive director of NOW.

† Del Martin and Phyllis Lyon started the first lesbian organization in the country, the Daughters of Bilitis (DOB), in the fifties, and edited the DOB's publication the *Ladder*. They were the first openly lesbian couple to join NOW and were legally married in San Francisco in 2008.

I think everyone has a right to sexual privacy—and to each her/his own (as long as it doesn't hurt or exploit anyone else). But it was both hurting and exploiting the women's movement to try to use it to proselytize for lesbianism because of the sexual preferences of a few. This could only subordinate the great issue of equality for women, the opportunity and institutional changes that all women so desperately need. As president of NOW, I never knew, or wanted to know, any woman's sexual preferences.*

DOLORES ALEXANDER

Over the months and then the next couple of years, it became apparent to me that yes, the movement was loaded with lesbians and they were the most competent, the hardest workers of all.

Ivy Bottini and I were driving to Washington, DC, to a NOW meeting and Ivy confessed to me that she was a lesbian, and that she had started a relationship with a woman and she would eventually leave her husband and her two daughters. My attitude was, Okay Ivy, I still love you, I won't tell anybody else because you're going to get yourself into so much trouble, it's not going to be worth it.

IVY BOTTINI

I decided it was time that NOW as an organization confronted its own homophobia and acknowledged and addressed lesbian concerns. I knew as the president of NYC NOW, I had a position I could act from.

RITA MAE BROWN

Ivy Bottini, a mother from Malvern, Long Island, and Dolores Alexander represented a far less rigid type of feminism. Up until then, the show had been a three-way game of kickball between Betty, Ti-Grace [Atkinson], and Flo [Kennedy].

IVY BOTTINI

In the summer of 1969, I suggested to the steering committee we sponsor a lesbian program. At first they were shocked. NOW had never used the

---

* At the First Congress to Unite Women in November 1969, Friedan called lesbians in NOW the "lavender menace," which was a play on the McCarthy anti-communist slur "Red Menace." Not only did Friedan think identifying NOW with lesbians would hurt the movement's ability to expand by attracting mainstream American housewives, she also suspected that lesbians were CIA plants and part of a plot to destroy the women's movement.

word "lesbian" in any of its activities, pronouncements, or publications. But I convinced them that it was important. With their backing, I began to organize a panel on lesbians in defiance of Friedan's wishes.

With this attention to lesbians, I was on to something that was in the air, but I hadn't realized it. The riots at the Stonewall Inn in Greenwich Village had taken place at the end of June that year, but, at the time, I, and many others, didn't take a lot of notice of them.*

In 1969, I wasn't totally out. I was out within the lesbian community but not to the world. Not to the movement. This was not unusual. . . . If I had a fling with another NOW activist, we kept it quiet. NOW was definitely not welcoming such affairs, and I was devoted to NOW. I didn't want to lose my place in it.

BARBARA LOVE

Ivy was kind of matronly looking, she had two children, she was married, and she lived in the suburbs—she was perfect. Well, she was a lesbian and they didn't know it. You know, we were still sick in the eyes of the American Psychiatric Association.† NOW was no different from the whole of society then.

IVY BOTTINI

When I opened the NOW public forum entitled "Is Lesbianism a Feminist Issue?" in September of 1969, I knew we would hit a nerve. The basement room of the church on West Eighty-Third street . . . was packed with two hundred and fifty to three hundred women instead of the fifty or so who usually attended our programs. . . . Lesbianism in the women's movement was clearly an issue whose time had come. The excitement, the sense of being at a transgressive, transformative event, was palpable.

Fourteen women were on the panel, all active feminists, plus me as the

---

* On June 28, 1969, police made what was a routine vice raid at the Greenwich Village Stonewall Inn, a well-known gay bar. This time the customers fought back, sparking a riot that continued for several days and marking the birth of the gay rights movement. Just by chance, Rita Mae Brown and Martha Shelley were walking in Greenwich Village that night and witnessed the beginning of the Stonewall riot. Shelley, a member of Daughters of Bilitis, helped organize a series of follow-up protests as part of a new mix-gendered umbrella organization called the Gay Liberation Front.

† When the American Psychiatric Association published its first *Diagnostic and Statistical Manual of Mental Disorders* (DSM) in 1952, homosexuality was classified as a mental disorder, a form of "sexual deviation." After lobbying from the newly organized gay rights community (including Barbara Love, who had a master's degree in psychology and was actively involved in challenging the APA), the APA dropped the classification in 1973.

moderator. . . . Only two of the women on the panel were out lesbians, Barbara Love and Sidney Abbott, who in 1971 published *Sappho Was a Right-On Woman*. I didn't introduce myself as a lesbian. I had the courage to host the forum at that point but not to go public myself. . . .

All agreed that yes, lesbianism was a feminist issue and homophobia was wrong. . . . One panelist would tell of a lesbian who lost her kids in a custody dispute. Others would then chime in, "Yes, I heard it happens all the time." Other panelists would add, "I know somebody who got fired." "Gatherings could be raided by police, in bars, or at private parties. . . ." "She couldn't even visit her partner in the hospital." "She had a nervous breakdown." The list went on and on. It was as though each statement was a great discovery. And for many women it was . . . Somehow talking about it at all in such a public forum, even with all the traumas of lesbian lives, was electrifying.

From that forum on, Betty Friedan disliked me for publicly associating NOW and the women's movement with lesbianism.

7

Code-Name Jane

While debates raged within NOW over whether the organization should take on the cause of lesbian rights, a group of feminists in Chicago were quietly practicing what they preached when it came to reproductive rights.

HEATHER BOOTH

By 1968, there were too many calls coming through for Jane and I couldn't respond to the demand. I was trying to get a graduate degree, I was married and expecting my first child, I was teaching full-time, I was doing other movement work, and I needed more people to take this on. So, at the end of every political meeting I attended, I announced, "If you want to work on abortion, come see me." When I had about fifteen women who said they were interested, we convened a meeting. I explained how I did the counseling, and what I had learned from the doctor. I passed on all that information to these women who were in the planning group, and then I left.

LAURA KAPLAN

I had a friend in college at the University of Chicago who got pregnant at the very beginning of a relationship. She saw an ad someplace for Jane and called, and went and got an abortion. Afterwards, she came to my apartment, and she was so excited by this experience that she was almost bouncing off the walls. She was blown away. So, she took me to meet her counselor who said the group was starting a new counselor-training session, and I joined as a counselor. I thought, "Well, here's a way into the women's movement."

MARTHA SCOTT

I was a mom with four children and I was not particularly interested in the women's movement until my friend took me to a Jane meeting and I said, well, that is something I would like to get involved in. It appealed to me a lot more than the other political activity that was going on.

LAURA KAPLAN

First, we had counselor-training sessions in which you learned a little bit about the group, but not too much. You only knew what you needed to know. As you were brought more into the inner circle, you learned more and more until you knew everything.

We never called anybody patients because that's a medical term. We were creating a much more equalizing experience. So, we called people counselees. We described what an abortion was, what it felt like, who would be there. We knew that people were terrified by the unknown, and so we wanted to make it as transparent as we could.

MARTHA SCOTT

The way it worked is you would go to a meeting and people who had contacted the Abortion Counseling Service's names were written out on cards. You chose a card and you called that person up. You said, "Hi, I'm from Jane. Do you think you'd want to get together?" Then I would invite that person to my home and we would have a counseling session. I would say, "You are scheduled for such and such a time." Then we would spend maybe an hour talking about what she wanted to do and what it was going to be like and how she got herself in this situation. Then we gave out a fair amount of literature talking about abortion rights.

LAURA KAPLAN

We had "the front" and then we had "the place." At the front, they could bring anybody they wanted with them. People brought their kids, their husbands, their mothers, friends, whoever they wanted for support. It was in one of our apartments. There was a big table full of food and usually there would be about five people there at a time. Then just the women who needed abortions were driven to what we called the place, which was usually another apartment that belonged to one of us, or one of our friends. Occasionally, we rented apartments. The abortions took place there, in bedrooms on regular beds, and then afterwards the women were driven back to the front where they reunited with whomever they brought for support. Then the post-abortions meds were given to them with instructions and afterwards, their counselor followed up with them for the next two weeks to make sure they were okay.

MARTHA SCOTT

I lived in a big house in Hyde Park, which was often used as the front. My kids were young at this point, but my husband, who was a night worker, was around during the day and picked up a lot of the slack for me with the kids. He did an awful lot.

The women who did the administrative job of organizing the information were called Big Jane. The people who answered the phone were Little Jane. First, we used an answering service and then we used a tape-recorded answering machine, which cost a whole lot of money and somebody helped us buy it.

ALICE FOX

I had gone to the University of Chicago and I was living on the north side of Chicago with a new boyfriend, who ultimately became my husband, and whom I now have two children with. But at that point, it was a new relationship and I wasn't about to have a baby with him.

I saw an advertisement in one of the women's liberation newspapers that said, "Pregnant? Call Jane." So, I called, honestly, not knowing anything except I knew I had to take care of it. A very nice woman called me back and I gave her the information, my last period, et cetera. Then someone else counseled me about what would happen all along the way. I just remember following one step after the other. The interview was so respectful and informative. I felt totally comfortable and safe. It had the most un-illegal feel to it of anything. It wasn't shady. For the abortion itself, I was told exactly what would happen. I didn't find it unbearably painful or anything like that.

My memory was that I was wearing a blindfold because the doctor, or the man, didn't want to be identified. I was in an apartment on a bed with a plastic sheet, so that the sheets didn't get bloody. The woman who I already had been speaking with was sitting next to me holding my hand, telling me exactly what was going to happen. At that time, I think we were told he was a doctor. He certainly wasn't identified by name. He was nice enough and he was telling me what he was doing. Everything was told in this very calm, patient way, and it didn't take very long. Then it was over, and I was fine.

I was kind of elated by this whole thing. It was remarkable. I had a medical issue that I took care of by myself for the first time in my life, and I was fine. And these people were amazing. Let me tell you, they changed my life. I became a medical professional because of them. I got involved with the group as a counselor. I wanted to learn the skills so that I could help other people.

MARTHA SCOTT

After I had joined the service, I got pregnant. I already had four children and one of them was severely disabled. I thought, I really can't have any more. My gynecologist said, "Well, I can't help you, but I'll give you a number." He told me to call Jane. I did not say, "Oh, I know all about them." I said, "Thank you very much."

I had an abortion by this person who said he was a doctor, but who we later learned wasn't a doctor.

JUDITH ARCANA

As the service evolved, some of us, me included, began to do more than referrals and counseling. By the end of '70, beginning of '71, we had an excellent relationship with a particular abortionist we called "Mike," whom I liked very much. The two main Janes, Jody Parsons and Ruth Surgal, had been the initial contact for this guy who turned out to be easily the best abortionist we had ever worked with. The deal we cut with Mike was, "You come down in your price and let us in so that we learn more about how to do the procedure."

The first thing that I did was observe. Then I sat by the side of the bed and held the woman's hand and kibitzed with him and her during the abortion itself. I did that a couple times. Then I learned how to give shots. Of course, I already knew how to put in a speculum. I remember very clearly when Mike taught me how to dilate a cervix. He was a good teacher. The more we learned, the more we wanted to learn. Soon, several of us had enough experience assisting him that we started doing it ourselves.

MARTHA SCOTT

It was an apprenticeship. You watch for a long time and then little by little you do it, and then you're doing it. Within about a year and a half, a lot of abortions were being done by people in the Abortion Counseling Service and I was one of the people who got trained to do that.

I don't know how else to put this, but since I had learned in a situation where I felt comfortable, and I had the experience of things working well, I thought, I can do this. I believe an abortion is a very easy thing to do, and I believe it is possible to do it safely.

JUDITH ARCANA

Then in 1971, he disappeared. He went away probably for lots of reasons. One of the reasons was that the mob was leaning on him and he refused to give them a cut.

LAURA KAPLAN

Once he was gone, we dropped the price to $100 or what you could afford, and that ended up being an average of $40 or $50 an abortion.

MARTHA SCOTT

When it was just the group of us working, we would do between seventy-five and a hundred a week. We worked three or four days a week and would do maybe twenty or twenty-five abortions a day. Our volume increased because our prices went down.

JUDITH ARCANA

We had these people's lives in our hands literally. The responsibility was enormous. We had to be *really* good all the time. If we hurt someone we would be turned into back-alley butchers in the newspaper.

LAURA KAPLAN

There was a real sense that we were empowering ourselves to do something out of the box, and we were creating the circumstances where the women who came to us could empower themselves by making decisions about what kind of life they wanted to lead, and they could take action to make that happen.

8

The Next Great Moment in History Is Theirs

VIVIAN GORNICK
I got a job at the *Village Voice* and the very first piece that I ever wrote was "Women's Liberation: The Next Great Moment in History Is Theirs." The editors sent me out to investigate, as they said, these women's libbers, these "chicks." They actually said chicks in those days. Their intention was that I would come back with a tongue-in-cheek, ironic account of these new political crazies in the Village. It was November 1969.

So I went out and within a week, I met many women who ultimately became quite famous: Susan Brownmiller, Kate Millett, Ti-Grace Atkinson, Shulamith Firestone, Alix Shulman, Phyllis Chesler. Everybody was just milling around in New York and talking a mile a minute. I interviewed them and in two seconds I got converted.

I was then in my early thirties and I was feeling incredibly aimless, not knowing what on earth to do with myself. I wanted to write, but I didn't have either the mental or emotional energy to just do it. I was married at the time, but I didn't take my marriage seriously, but I didn't know that I wasn't taking it seriously. Other people seemed to find an identity, no sooner were they married, but that never happened to me. I just felt like I was floating adrift in the world. After interviewing all these fantastic women, I immediately saw myself as a woman in history. It's like a light went on in my head and I saw what everyone else was seeing: that we were born and raised to become mothers and wives and not very much else.

Village Voice, November 27, 1969, "Women's Liberation: The Next Great Moment in History Is Theirs," by Vivian Gornick
. . . to have instilled in women the belief that their child-bearing and housewifely obligations supersede all other needs . . . is to have accomplished an act of trickery, an act which has deprived women of the proper forms of expression necessary to that force of energy alive in every talking creature, an act which has indeed mutilated their natural selves and deprived them of their womanhood, whatever that may be, deprived them of the right to say "I" and have it mean something. This understanding, grasped whole, is what underlies the current wave of feminism. It is felt by thousands of women today, it will be felt by millions tomorrow. You have only to examine briefly a fraction of the women's rights organizations already in existence to realize instantly that they form the nucleus of a genuine movement complete with theoreticians, tacticians, agitators, manifestos, journals, and thesis papers, running the entire political spectrum from conservative reform to visionary radicalism, and powered by an emotional conviction rooted in undeniable experience, and fed by a determination that is irreversible.

VIVIAN GORNICK

It was like a moment of conversion and I never looked back. And what you discovered, of course, was that the women who became really serious feminists suddenly were burning over. It wasn't like we discovered what we were discovering in a laissez-faire way. It felt like life and death.

I never became an activist like many others. I didn't join New York Radical Women. I didn't join anything actually. All I did was write. But I had the *Village Voice*. I had a platform. And so, from that moment on, every single thing I wrote was written from the point of view of a woman who suddenly saw the world in terms of sexism.

I was constantly in touch with feminists through general meetings, through parties, through dinners, through endless conversation about it all. We were all involved with it morning, noon, and night. It was overwhelming. And it was like that for a good many years.

Village Voice, November 27, 1969, "Women's Liberation:
The Next Great Moment in History Is Theirs," by Vivian Gornick

From NOW we move, at a shocking rate of speed, to the left. . . . For instance, there is WITCH (Women's International Terrorist Conspiracy From Hell), an offshoot of SDS. . . . There is Cell 55. God knows what they do. There are the Redstockings, an interesting group that seems to have evolved from direct action into what they call "consciousness-raising."

And finally, there are the Feminists, without a doubt the most fiercely radical and intellectually impressive of all the groups. This organization was begun a year ago by a group of defectors from NOW and various other feminist groups, in rebellion against the repetition of the hierarchical structure of power in these other groups. . . .

But there's one great thing about these chicks: if five feminists fall out with six groups, within half an hour they'll all find each other (probably somewhere on Bleecker Street), within 48 hours a new splinter faction will have announced its existence, and within two weeks the manifesto is being mailed out. It's the mark of a true movement.

VIVIAN GORNICK

After the article was published, I got mail from all over the country and from every class of people. I got fan mail on these key-punch tickets from women who were working as clerks. And I also got mail on embossed stationery from women in the fanciest suburbs of American life. A woman from the Midwest, whom I could picture wearing white gloves and a navy-blue blazer, with a 1950s bouffant hairdo, wrote me, "Oh my dear, if I'd only had you to talk to twenty years ago." It was really thrilling. It was shocking. Everyone at the *Voice* was taken by surprise by the amount of response to that piece. And for a long time, that piece was iconic.

Certainly, it changed my life. It gave me my work. It became a ballast of thought and feeling, and it gave me purpose. It gave me a way to see the world that became all useful. I'd say we burned with it and that felt often like its own form of oppression. You felt that pressing on you. It was very alive.

9

The Boston Tea Party of Women's Health

BARBARA SEAMAN

I first learned about the dangers of estrogen when my aunt Sally died of uterine cancer at the age of forty-nine. As we stood by her hospital bed, her cancer doctors warned us, her sisters and her nieces, to "never take Premarin" because we might have the same "susceptibilities." They told us it had been known from the 1930s that estrogens frequently bring on cancer in the endometrium of menopausal women. Sally did have a tough menopause, but I was horrified that her gynecologist failed to inform her of this risk so she could decide for herself if it was worth it.

That is how I became obsessed with informed consent. I wrote about health and medicine from the point of view of patients, not just the doctors and the pharmaceutical industry. My first articles were on breastfeeding and natural childbirth.

For example, when my son was born, I told my obstetrician that I planned to breastfeed. But he said I didn't have the right personality, too educated. The infant formula companies, after all, had persuaded doctors in the 1950s that their product was "nutritionally superior" to mother's milk.

Then I discovered that many women were getting sick on the birth control pill, and their doctors pooh-poohed it as "all in their mind" and probably due to a fear of sexual liberation. In 1969, I published my first book, *The Doctor's Case Against the Pill*. Publication was delayed by several drug companies that tried to get an injunction against it. The judge at last denied the injunction, and some of my fellow science writers told the story of the campaign against me. It caught the interest of Senator Gaylord Nelson [Democrat from Wisconsin], who asked me to send him a letter on why he should hold hearings in the Senate on the dangers of the pill.

MARILYN WEBB

When I was in Chicago, I was taking the pill and then I gained a lot of weight. So I stopped, and then I started asking myself questions about the pill, like what was it doing to your body, your metabolism? Then, in 1969, Barbara Seaman wrote this book *The Doctor's Case Against the Pill*, which was about how potentially dangerous the pill was.

BARBARA SEAMAN

In about 1950, when she was about eighty-eight, Margaret Sanger, the founder of Planned Parenthood, was introduced to Gregory Pincus [a reproductive scientist from Massachusetts]. She raised approximately $150,000 . . . to get Pincus started on research toward a universal contraceptive. He conducted his historic 1956 Puerto Rican clinical trials, in which hundreds of mostly impoverished Puerto Rican women were given the newly developed pill experimentally. . . .

When the Pincus pill was introduced under the brand name Enovid, women embraced it as a marvel, for after the word "no" it was the most effective and convenient reversible contraceptive ever devised. It also held alluring health benefits, particularly the relief of painful menstruation.

Beneath the surface, however, Enovid was a chemical swamp, for, amid sworn assurances of safety, it began its commercial life as a massive overdose. Only after millions of women had taken Enovid—and thousands had died or had been disabled by blood clots—was it discovered that the amount of hormones in the pill was ten times what is needed for contraception.

ALICE WOLFSON

One of the early demonstrations I recall organizing was a picket line outside of DC General Hospital, the only publicly funded hospital in Washington, DC. We were protesting the disproportionate numbers of Black women who were being maimed and were dying from botched abortions.

It was in the context of these citywide health actions that I first heard about the Nelson pill hearings.

All of us had taken the pill, and this was obviously before any longitudinal studies. Aside from weight gain, which everybody had, my hair started to fall out. I went to a dermatologist and I said, "What's happening?" He said, "I have no idea." I went to several doctors and none of them related the hair loss to the pill until I made the connection. The other women in the group had experienced similar problems. We were curious. We went to the Hill to get information. We left having started a social movement.

MARILYN WEBB

I was pretty much the de facto leader of DC Women's Liberation at that point, but other people were leading other groups under the umbrella organization that we called Magic Quilt. Judy Spellman and Alice Wolfson wanted to do health. They announced that they wanted to go to the pill hearings and did I want to go too? I said, "Yeah, I'd like to find out more information." And at the time I was seven months pregnant, and I was worried about what the pill might have done to my child.

ALICE WOLFSON

In those days, you could just walk into Senate hearings. We just walked in and we were seated. There were about fifteen of us in the whole group to start with.

MARILYN WEBB

We sat there for a bunch of hours, and it was one man after the next, talking about their studies.

UPI, January 15, 1970, "Doctor Warns Congress on Dangers of 'Pill,'" by William B. Mead

WASHINGTON—A gynecologist told Congress today widespread use of birth control pills "has given rise to health hazards on a scale previously unknown to medicine."

"Nine million American women are consuming these compounds almost as automatically as chickens eating corn," unaware the pills may cause cancer, blood clots, diabetes, or arteriosclerosis, said Dr. Hugh J. Davis.

ALICE WOLFSON

As the testimony unfolded, we were appalled. Not a single woman was testifying, not a single pill user, not a single female researcher. All of the information that was coming out was frightening. "Estrogen is to cancer what fertilizer is to wheat," said one scientist.

ANNE FENTY

JAN FENTY

One by one, different women in our group started saying, "Why are there no women on the panel?" "Why are you using women as guinea pigs?" It was spontaneous, because we were just so angry.

> *Wisconsin State Journal*, January 24, 1970,
> "Pill Hearings Disrupted by Women Protesters"
> WASHINGTON (UPI)—A group of lank-haired, mini-skirted young women broke up a Senate hearing Friday on the safety and effectiveness of birth control pills.
> The protesters, members of Washington Women's Liberation, shouted questions and demanded the right to testify until Sen. Gaylord Nelson was forced to recess the hearing and clear the room.

ALICE WOLFSON

The cameras turned to us, and away from the senators. They wouldn't let us go on. They stopped the meeting.

MARILYN WEBB

They ushered us out, and the press followed us out and interviewed us. It was a big deal, but the ultimate result was even bigger.

JAN FENTY

I remember meeting the next day with Senator Gaylord Nelson in his office and he was very respectful and listened to what we had to say.

BARBARA SEAMAN

Of all the witnesses whose Senate testimony was interrupted by the protests, only one, Dr. Philip Corfman of the National Institutes of Health, paused to confirm the legitimacy of the shouted questions. And it was Dr. Corfman who, in the late 1980s, finally prevailed on manufacturers to withdraw all brands of oral contraceptive containing more than fifty micrograms of estrogen.

ALICE WOLFSON

The demonstrations, with national and international attention, had succeeded. For the first time in pharmacological history, patients were given the right to know of the potential health-threatening side effects of a prescription drug.

BARBARA SEAMAN

Alice Wolfson and her colleagues had trained in the civil rights, student, and antiwar movements. Their Senate action became the Boston Tea Party of women's health. In 1975, the National Women's Health Network was officially cofounded by Ms. Wolfson, Belita Cowan, Dr. Mary Howell, Dr. Phyllis Chesler, and me. It became the central switchboard for the hundreds—and then thousands—of activist and self-help groups then dealing with women's health rights and body issues.

10

Goodbye to All That

ROBIN MORGAN

So there I was one day in January 1970, a young mother, in my office at Grove Press, where I was an editor. Jane Alpert called me and said, "We've all been complaining about *Rat*,* and I think we're going to seize it. Will you come with us and give it legitimacy?" I was slightly older by two or three years than most of the women I hung with. I was never in SDS. I was in MDS, which was Movement for a Democratic Society, which was the old people who were not campus-based. I was quite delighted, because I'd had many run-ins with Jeff Shero, who was the editor of *Rat Subterranean News*. They had become this porn-infested boy thing, a lot of rock and roll, a lot of R. Crumb, less politics, and profoundly sexist.

So we took it over. We marched in and we said, "Out, get out." We threw them out, and they thought it was amusing. They didn't understand they weren't coming back. We changed the locks, we seized the bank account—I mean we were radicals. We knew how to do this kind of thing. Then we did the women's issue, which became quite famous.

I wanted the Left to be pure and to be feminist and to be good for

---

* *Rat Subterranean News* was one of New York's most popular underground newspapers in 1970, along with the *East Village Other* and *The Rag.*

women. I felt women were the real Left and I felt that if we could transform the consciousness of the Left we could change this country. "Goodbye to All That," came out very fast, in one whole night. I cried while writing it. I mean I just sobbed.

"Goodbye to All That" was crossing a bridge and burning it behind me. I thought none of these people will speak to me again and I don't care.

"Goodbye to All That," by Robin Morgan

So, *Rat* has been liberated, for this week, at least. . . . I wanted to write about—the friends, brothers, lovers in the counterfeit male-dominated Left. The good guys who think they know what Women's Lib, as they so chummily call it, is all about—who then proceed to degrade and destroy women by almost everything they say and do: The cover on the last issue of Rat (front and back). The token "pussy power" or "clit militancy" articles. The snide descriptions of women staffers on the masthead. The little jokes, the personal ads, the smile, the snarl. No more, brothers. No more well-meaning ignorance, no more cooptation, no more assuming that this thing we're all fighting for is the same; one revolution under man, with liberty and justice for all. No more.

ROBIN MORGAN

This literally nauseated me to write, and my palms would sweat with fear and trembling and I'd go and throw up, and then go back to the typewriter and get it down. I would lie to myself and say, "You don't have to publish it, just get it down." Then once it was down, I knew I had tricked myself.

"Goodbye to All That," by Robin Morgan

Goodbye to the illusion of strength when you run hand in hand with your oppressors; goodbye to the dream that being in the leadership collective will get you anything but gonorrhea. . . . Goodbye to Hip culture and the so-called Sexual Revolution, goodbye forever to the notion that a man is my brother who, like Paul [Krassner],* buys a prostitute for the night as a birthday gift for a male friend, or who,

---

* One of the founders of the Yippies, Paul Krassner was a charismatic member of the counterculture and a member of Ken Kesey's psychedelic Merry Pranksters. A writer and a satirist, Krassner founded and edited the irreverent alternative magazine *The Realist*.

like Paul, reels off the names in alphabetical order of people in the women's movement he has fucked, reels off names in the best locker-room tradition—as proof that *he's no sexist oppressor.*

Let it seem bitchy, catty, dykey, Solanasesque, frustrated, crazy, nutty, frigid, ridiculous, bitter, embarrassing, man-hating, libelous, pure, unfair, envious, intuitive, low-down, stupid, petty, liberating. We are the women that men have warned us about.

ROBIN MORGAN

You have to remember the comments coming out of the male Left at this point—and I refer to it as the male Left even though we were in it as women. Everywhere you looked there were guys saying obnoxious things. Either just ignoring women things, just the generic male pronoun, or the assumption that the draft—which I might add affected only men—was a universal issue, but childcare, which ought to affect everyone because it's the next generation, was a fringe issue. To talk about rape was to be a frigid hysteric. The homophobia was enormous. To raise the issue of a leftist guy hassling a woman, sexually harassing a woman, raping a woman was to invite censure on the woman.

"Goodbye to All That," by Robin Morgan

Goodbye, goodbye forever, counterfeit Left, counterleft, male-dominated cracked-glass mirror reflection of the Amerikan Night-mare. Women are the real Left. We are rising, powerful in our unclean bodies; bright glowing mad in our inferior brains; wild hair flying, wild eyes staring, wild voices keening; undaunted by blood we who hemorrhage every twenty-eight days; laughing at our own beauty we who have lost our sense of humor; mourning for all each precious one of us might have been in this one living time-place had she not been born a woman. . . .

We are rising with a fury older and potentially greater than any force in history, and this time we will be free or no one will survive. Power to all the people or to none. All the way down, this time.

Free Kathleen Cleaver! Free Kim Agnew!
Free Anita Hoffman! Free Holly Krassner!
Free Bernardine Dohrn! Free Lois Hart!

Free Donna Malone! Free Alice Embree!
Free Ruth Ann Miller! Free Nancy Kurshan!
Free Leni Sinclar! Free Dinky Forman!
Free Jane Alpert! Free Dinky Forman!
Free Gumbo! Free Sharon Krebs!
Free Bonnie Cohen! Free Iris Luciano!
Free Judy Lampe! Free Robin Morgan!
Free Valorie Solanas!*
Free our sisters! Free ourselves!

ROBIN MORGAN

So we published it, and within a day the shit hit the fan.[†] I mean the phone began ringing off the hook. I received anonymous death threats from quite a few revolutionary brothers. Some of them are still alive and around and should be ashamed. But they would call and say, "You're a fucking cunt, you're going to be dead, and if the cops don't get you, we will."

People came by and informed me that they were reprinting it in the *Berkeley Barb* and lots of other publications. It became this odd badge of honor among male Left newspapers, "We can print this, we can handle self-criticism."

JUDY GUMBO

I recall Stew [Albert] storming into our bedroom. . . . In one hand, he waved a crinkled copy of a late January issue of the *Rat*. He yelled, "Look where your punk-ass women's liberation shit has got us now!" . . . Robin Morgan had published a rant. In it, she denounced the conspiracy defendants[‡] the

---

*   All of these women were associated in some way—either as girlfriends, wives, and/or participants—with the male-dominated Left (except for Kim Agnew, who was the vice president's rebellious daughter).

†   "Goodbye to All That" was first published in the February 6–23, 1970, issue of *Rat Subterranean News*, which featured a cover story of an interview with Afeni Shakur, one of the two women indicted in the Panther 21 trial, which started in New York on February 2, 1970.

‡   The Chicago Eight (later Seven) conspiracy trial *United States v. Dellinger et al.* opened on September 28, 1969, and lasted five months. It was called "the political trial of the century." The defendants, Bobby Seale (who was bound and gagged in the courtroom and then dropped from the case), Abbie Hoffman, Jerry Rubin, Dave Dellinger, Tom Hayden, Rennie Davis, and their lawyer William Kunstler put the Vietnam War on trial and turned the courtroom into a stage for counterculture comedy performances, which became a daily national television sensation. Stew Albert, Judy Gumbo's boyfriend, was an unindicted co-conspirator in the trial. Gumbo (born Judy Clavir, and given her nickname by Black Panther leader Eldridge Cleaver, who originally called her "Mrs. Stew") worked for the defendants in their trial office, answering phones and sending the daily trial transcripts to the press. Hoffman, Rubin, Dellinger,

male counterculture, environmentalists, and ultimately every man on the planet for their patriarchal domination of women. Robin blamed Abbie for ditching his wife Shirley like any philandering movie star. She castigated Jerry for cashing in on media celebrityhood while Nancy remained unknown. She condemned Paul Krassner for joking about an instant pussy aerosol can and reeled off names of movement women Paul had slept with. . . .

Then I saw it: "Free Gumbo!" I confess—I felt relieved. Had I not made Robin's A-list of women who needed to free ourselves, I would have wallowed in that same distress about being second tier that I'd suffered during the Conspiracy Trial. . . . Stew's "women's liberation shit" remark was for me an amulet moment. I stood up on my mattress to give myself height equal to Stew's and, quoting Robin as my authority on all things misogynist, screamed at him.

"You see my name there? You know what that means? You're an asshole sexist pig and I need to free myself. So there!"*

MICHAEL KAZIN

I remember I was living in this apartment with all women in Cambridge, Massachusetts, when "Goodbye to All That" came out. It was painful, because they were saying, "Michael, you know, I think she's talking about you."

Later, I wrote in my book *American Dreamers* that "Goodbye to All That" became as widely known as any document by a woman radical since the 1848 declaration at Seneca Falls.

ROBIN MORGAN

I could never have imagined that "Goodbye to All That" would have released such rage of leftist women that had been boiling all this time. I had not assumed that women would step forward and it would be like, "I am Spartacus!" That was an amazing thing.

Hayden, and Davis were convicted on February 18, 1970, of intent to riot at the 1968 Chicago Democratic convention. They appealed, and their convictions were overturned in 1972.

* Judy Gumbo broke up with Stew Albert a few months after the publication of "Goodbye to All That." She moved to Boston and joined the women's liberation movement. Gumbo and Albert married seven years later.

11

Newsweek Girls Revolt

LYNN POVICH

We did it in the ladies' room. We did it in our apartments. We closed the door in somebody's office who was staying late and we would say something like, "We noticed that your file was totally used in the story but you were never credited." If they responded, then we'd say, "Well, we're thinking about doing something about this and organizing."

So all of the first women we talked to agreed, and we were about fifteen when we decided, "We need a lawyer. We need somebody to tell us what our options are." There was no employment law at that time. First, we went to Harriet Pilpel, who was a famous lawyer and a senior partner at the firm Greenbaum, Wolff & Ernst, which specialized in First Amendment issues, but she said that she didn't know anything about employment law.

We then approached Florynce Kennedy, the flamboyant civil rights lawyer and fiery feminist who had defended Valerie Solanas. Greeting us in her apartment in the East Forties wearing her signature cowboy hat, Flo had lots of ideas of what we could do, including sit-ins and guerrilla theater, but most of them were too outrageous for us. She also discussed how much money we would need, which made us realize we should think about a pro bono lawyer.

So then we thought, "Well, I guess it's like a civil rights case so we should go to the ACLU." And that's when we found Eleanor Holmes Norton, who was the assistant legal director for the ACLU based in New York. We called her up and four of us went down there and that's when she opened the magazine to the masthead. She looked at it—then looked at us—and said, "The fact that there are all men from the top category to the second from the bottom and virtually all women in the last category proves prima facie that there's a pattern of discrimination at *Newsweek*. I'll take your case."

ELEANOR HOLMES NORTON

I was assistant legal director at the American Civil Liberties Union in New York. *Newsweek*, at the time, was hiring the best of the best women and employing them as researchers. They were hiring the men as reporters and writers. It was one of those extraordinary cases a civil rights lawyer yearns for. It was a two-track system: one for women and one for men. But saying that is one thing when there had not been many lawsuits of the kind brought, in fact I don't know of any at that time, certainly not involving an entire group of women at a great corporation.

This was a very important case because it was as blatant as cases where Blacks experienced differential treatment from whites. So I met with the women, and though they tended to understand that there was discrimination going on—why else would they have come to the ACLU?—they were very hesitant about moving forward. They feared retribution. So the first thing I had to do was to involve them not only in the legal matter, but in raising their consciousness as women. This was a pathbreaking case and they could not be punished because the statute had an element against retaliation.

LYNN POVICH

Eleanor was perfect for us. She was a veteran civil rights lawyer and a self-avowed feminist, she was smart, shrewd, and sharp-tongued. She had this Afro that was out to here and she was five months pregnant with her first child. She was only thirty-two years old but she was already an extraordinarily accomplished lawyer. After clerking for Judge A. Leon Higgenbotham Jr., the first Black judge on the US District Court, she joined the ACLU in 1965 where she wrote amicus briefs for Julian Bond, Muhammad Ali, and Adam Clayton Powell. She was tough and very sharp. What interested Eleanor in our case was that she had been defending a lot of union cases in the South, but she had never taken on, as she told us, a class action in a profession where the judgments are subjective. So I can write a story and my editor can not like it. And I don't know whether it's because it's not good or because there's something else operating here. She told us, "I'll take your case, but you've got to get organized. It can't just be your small group."

Another reason Eleanor took our case was that we were the first women in the media to sue and, it turned out, the first female sex discrimination class-action suit.

ELEANOR HOLMES NORTON

I must say it took some meetings and consciousness-raising first. These women had a lot to lose. Perhaps if they stayed, they could rise in the ranks. *Newsweek* was the crème de la crème, they were sitting at the best news magazine in the country. They wanted to remain there and yet they wanted to get beyond the discrimination that was there. So it was important to foster the notion of solidarity, that no single woman should ever have to do this, but if all of us do it then we have something real here. I wanted them to sign on as a class or else I couldn't move forward.

LYNN POVICH

Then we opened it up to more women because we felt it was very important that we all decide together. Remember, this was the women's movement where everybody had to have an opinion and it all had to be collial and cooperative. We met in people's apartments and Eleanor came and said, "Here are your options. You should file this class-action suit as a class because you all are all the same. You're doing the same jobs. You more or less come in with the same credentials as the people who are above you."

In fact, Pat Lynden was one of our best cases. She went to Columbia Journalism School with Paul Zimmerman. They both graduated the same year and he got hired as a writer and she got hired as a researcher. I mean, it was so blatant. It was just sort of amazing.

First, Eleanor said, "We're going to have to toughen you girls up. You are very privileged people and you are very homogeneous. You're all white, you're all educated. You don't even know what's going to happen to you. You better be prepared. Who knows? You could be punished. It's not going to be easy. Daddy's not going to save you. You've got to take off your white gloves."

ELEANOR HOLMES NORTON

These women understood intellectually that they held the winning hand, but psychologically they certainly did not. So my participation in this case was as much about consciousness-raising as it was about legal advice to these women. They recognized one thing, that there had never been a case like this. It's amazing that this statute, Title VII, had the word "sex," as well as the word "race," and yet women almost never sued under the Civil Rights Act. So the way to understand these women is to understand the pioneering role they were playing.

LYNN POVICH

There were five or six Black women researchers at the time. We went to them as we were opening up to recruit more people.

DIANE CAMPER

There was a feeling that there had been all these conversations going on among the white women about agitating for more women to be reporters and we [Black women] were an afterthought. At the time, there was more identity with race than gender. People just didn't see the strategic advantage of joining in.

LYNN POVICH

There were two Black women who worked in the letters department who signed. But for some reason, I don't know why, we didn't tell Eleanor that the Black women researchers had decided not to join, because had she known, she would've gone to them and gotten them to join our action. Because Eleanor believed very strongly that Black women should be part of the women's movement, and she would've convinced them to do it.

There was a lot of discussion. I remember Fay Willey said, "Why don't we just go and talk to Kay Graham?* She's a woman, she'll understand this."

We thought, "Look at the circumstances of her life. She took over her family business and she was always unsure in those early years." I mean, this was 1970. She'd only been running the company for six or seven years, and she always deferred to the men. So, we thought, "No, I don't think so."

OSBORN ELLIOTT

In March 1970, *Newsweek* ran its first cover story on women's lib—and even at that late date we found it necessary to explain to our readers what it was all about, and who the feminists were. . . . Planning the story, we

---

* Katharine Graham was the owner of the *Washington Post* and *Newsweek*.

realized that it should be written by a woman—but as we looked around the New York staff, we concluded (correctly) that we had no woman then qualified to do the job. And so, for the first time in *Newsweek*'s history, we commissioned an outsider to write the cover story—reporter Helen Dudar of the *New York Post*, who happened to be married to our own star writer, Peter Goldman.

LYNN POVICH

I was the only woman writer and I was a junior writer. I'd never written a cover story so I wasn't going to be the one. So they hired Helen Dudar, who was a really fabulous writer at the *New York Post*. And Helen had never covered this topic, but she could do anything. She could do the reporting and she could also write quickly.

And who did they assign to be her research assistant? Judy Gingold. Judy is in this odd position of being really the leader of the class action. She started the whole thing.

PETER GOLDMAN

Helen had come up in an era when women were not welcome in most newsrooms, but she started at *Newsday* on Long Island, and then moved to the *Post*. I think she was one of the great journalists of her day. But because she had made her own way, and in hard times, she thought, at first, that the young feminists needed to get over it and make their own way. She read Betty Friedan, and the literature generally had some impact on her, but the cover she wrote was a life-changing experience for her. It was a journey of self-discovery.

LYNN POVICH

The moment that *Newsweek* said, "We're going to hire Helen. We're doing the cover story on the women's movement." We thought, "Aha!" Being good journalists, we knew the publicity would get them, more than anything else.

Six weeks later we had this Sunday-night meeting before *Newsweek* came out on Monday morning to sign the complaint, and to write the press releases before our press conference at nine a.m. at the ACLU offices. The "Women in Revolt" cover story came out on Monday, March 16.

Eleanor wanted three researchers to answer questions. Somebody said, "Well, you should speak." I said, "No, I'm the only one who's gotten through. I should not speak."

We decided it would be Lucy Howard, Pat Lynden, and Mary Willis. They went off to decide what they were going to say, and what they were going to wear. That was the most important thing.

LUCY HOWARD

We wanted it to be a surprise. It's always better to catch people off guard, so they're not prepared. We didn't want them to know because they could have stopped it. And they were totally off guard. I mean they knew something was coming, but they thought maybe we were going to stage a protest and dance on their desks or something. But they soon learned that we were serious. We had a good lawyer. This is a serious action. And they were shocked, shocked, shocked.

I remember Sunday night very well—I was sitting in my bathtub crying, because I thought, "Oh dear God, I can't do this. What am I doing?" That morning, as I was getting dressed and getting my hair done, I was thinking, "You've just got to stop crying," because my eyes were going to be all red and that would look terrible.

OSBORN ELLIOTT

The women sent their letter to Kay Graham, and filed their complaint, and held their press conference, and made headlines around the world. *Newsweek* had the distinction of being the first media organization to be so confronted by the women's movement.

New York *Daily News*, March 17, 1970,
"Newshens Sue *Newsweek* for 'Equal Rights'"

Forty-six women on the staff of *Newsweek* magazine, most of them young and most of them pretty, announced yesterday that they were suing the magazine, charging it discriminates against them because of their sex.

Most of the 46, in minis, midis, maxis and pants, gathered at the American Civil Liberties Union offices here to explain that they were "systematically discriminated against in both hiring and promotion and are forced to assume a subsidiary role simply because they are women."

The girls also asked Mrs. Katharine Graham, president of the Washington Post Co., parent corporation of *Newsweek*, to negotiate the dispute. . . .

Later, editor in chief Osborn Elliott denied the women's charges and said the whole thing was a matter of tradition. He said the magazine was thinking of changing the tradition.

New York Times, March 17, 1970, "As *Newsweek* Says, Women are in Revolt, Even on *Newsweek*," by Henry Raymont
"Women in Revolt," reads the caption of *Newsweek*'s current cover story, and so they are—right in the magazine's own offices. . . .

A slim, miniskirted reporter wearing a field jacket repeatedly shouted "Right on! Right on!" as Eleanor Holmes Norton, assistant legal director of the A.C.L.U. and lawyer for the employees, read the complaint.

By contrast, some 30 young women of the *Newsweek* staff who were present at the news conference were neatly and almost conservatively dressed. More were college graduates in their mid-20s.

KATHARINE GRAHAM
I was away at the time [on vacation in the Bahamas] and got a phone call from Fritz Beebe [chairman of the board] and Oz Elliott together, telling me about the complaint. "Which side am I supposed to be on?" I asked—to which Fritz quickly responded, "This is serious. It isn't a joke."

LUCY HOWARD
When we went into the office after the press conference, we were met with total silence until we encountered Oz, who invited Pat and me, "Come to my lair, my dears," and questioned us about, "How could you do this to me? Why did you do this? Oh, this is terrible." After that, everyone just kind of avoided us, until a cable came in from the San Francisco bureau.

LYNN POVICH
Some of the correspondents in the field sent congratulatory cables. "The all-male San Francisco bureau (and chief stringer Karen McDonald) say right on, sisters," read a telex.

PETER GOLDMAN
My attitude was, go for it. We were in a "movement" frame of mind and as soon as the women lit the match, it was obvious. The top editors, who we

called the Wallendas,* regarded it as a management problem, and they were quite angry about the revolt. But the men I knew sympathized, which were mostly the guys on the eleventh floor, Nation section. I think we were all wearing blinders up to that moment, and the women forced us to take the blinders off. It became clear, thanks to the women's revolt, that what we had been living in was a caste system, and that it was wrong.

ELEANOR HOLMES NORTON

When I went in to meet with *Newsweek* executives, I insisted that Kay Graham be among them, and that the women be with me. That's how I opened negotiations. By the way, Kay Graham later became a good friend of mine.

OSBORN ELLIOTT

A couple of days after their press conference, I met with all forty-six of the angry women in *Newsweek*'s reception area Top of the Week, a large room on the fortieth floor of the building . . . finally in came the women's lawyer—highly articulate, tough, militant, black—and pregnant. It was Eleanor Holmes Norton, who since then has become a top government official in equal opportunity areas.

"Delighted you could join us, Mrs. Norton," I said, looking up at her in the front row. "First, I'd like to say a few words to the women of *Newsweek*."

"I'm sorry, Mr. Elliott," replied Mrs. Norton, "but this is *our* meeting, and on this occasion, we must insist on the women's prerogative. *We* will do the talking." . . .

Our negotiations—interrupted by sudden, dramatic, and quite effective outbursts of anger from the skillful Mrs. Norton—dragged on for months.

ELEANOR HOLMES NORTON

Newsweek eventually reached out for a settlement. The rest is the history of the integration of women into the high sectors of America's signature publications.

---

* Nicknamed after circus stunt performers the Flying Wallendas, who walked on high wires without a net, *Newsweek*'s top editors were considered by their underlings to be at the height of their power, but if they slipped, they had a long way to fall.

LYNN POVICH

Two months after we filed our complaint, ninety-six women at Time Inc. would file a sex discrimination complaint against *Time, Life, Fortune,* and *Sports Illustrated.* In the next few years, women sued their employers at the *Reader's Digest, Newsday,* the *Washington Post,* the *Detroit News,* the *Baltimore Sun,* the *New Haven Register,* and the Associated Press. In 1974, six women at the *New York Times* filed sex discrimination charges on behalf of 550 women and in 1975, sixteen women at NBC initiated a class action lawsuit covering 2,600 present and past employees.*

---

* One week after the *Newsweek* announcement, on March 18, 1970, one hundred women (many of them members of New York Radical Feminists) staged a dramatic eleven-hour-long sit-in at the office of the editor in chief of *Ladies' Home Journal.* They presented John Mack Carter with a long list of demands, which included filling its glossy pages with issues that mattered to modern women beyond the usual "children, church, and kitchen" topics.

12

Betty's Last Stand

The indefatigable and impossible Betty Friedan presided over NOW for four years. She traveled across the country from Kansas to Maine, Texas to Alabama, spreading the gospel of women's equality. But inside NOW, she made more enemies than friends. By 1970, it was time for a change, but before Betty stepped down, she came up with an inspired idea for how to make the National Organization for Women a household name.

BETTY FRIEDAN

I was going to step down as president of NOW. I'd been spending virtually full time as an activist for nearly four years . . . and Aileen Hernandez wanted to run for president. A Black woman—and a good administrator—could be right for NOW at this time. . . . In 1970, there were about three thousand members of NOW in thirty cities.

AILEEN HERNANDEZ

I got asked by members of NOW in early 1970 if I would run for the presidency. Betty had been president from 1966 until 1970 and there were some people who were very upset with her personality, and they didn't want the presidency of NOW to become a permanent position. So, they asked if I would run and I said yes, I would, and I got elected. That was in March of 1970, in Chicago.

MURIEL FOX

It was a legitimate change of office. It wasn't a battle. Her term of office ended. She probably missed all the publicity, but she got a lot of publicity anyway because she was Betty Friedan. She was a very difficult person. She was hostile, she was neurotic, and very hard to get along with. She made a lot of people miserable. She hung up on them or shouted at them. They quit, or they complained. I think sometimes maybe angry people make revolution, and Betty Friedan made our revolution and deserves the credit.

AILEEN HERNANDEZ

One of my goals was to make sure that the movement for women's rights would include all women. I felt that there needed to be a whole lot more work done with women of color and poor women. This is where I had spent most of my life working, and so I thought it was important to do that. I stayed as president until 1971, which is about all the time I could give if I was also going to earn any money, and went back and did my business after that.

BRENDA FEIGEN

I joined NOW after I went to the First Congress to Unite Women. I had just passed the Massachusetts bar exam, and not long after that I received a phone call from Lucy Komisar, NOW's national vice president for public-ity: Would I please consider running for national legislative vice president? They needed a lawyer to fill the position. Shortly after that call, I was on a plane to Des Plaines, Illinois, headed to NOW's 1970 annual convention, where I was handily elected to the legislative position. . . .

As national vice president of legislation for NOW, my responsibility was to ensure that the Equal Rights Amendment would be passed by Congress and sent to the states for ratification that year. It had been introduced every year since 1923 but had never made it out of Congress. And its wording had remained the same: *Equality of rights under the law shall not be denied or abridged by the United States or any state on account of sex.* . . .

The newly elected president, Aileen Hernandez, a former commissioner of the EEOC, was Black, so I hoped that lesbians would be welcomed and more women of color would join NOW. NOW's focus would continue to be mostly on working women's issues, such as twenty-four-hour childcare and equal pay for equal work, as well as the ERA and abortion rights.

BETTY FRIEDAN

The media was still treating the women's movement as a joke. And fear of ridicule still kept a lot of women from identifying themselves as feminist, from identifying with the women's movement. . . .We needed an action to show them—and ourselves—how powerful we were. . . . We needed an action women could take in their own communities without much central organization. A woman from Florida, Betty Armistead, had written me . . . reminding me that the fiftieth anniversary of the vote was August 26, 1970.

MURIEL FOX

At the end of our conference, Betty Friedan said, "We're going to have a march on August twenty-sixth, the anniversary of women's suffrage, and we're going to march all over the country." Aileen Hernandez, who I was standing next to, said, "Oh my God, we're going to have to do all that work." She hadn't consulted with anybody, Betty just said it, and the media picked it up.

Betty Friedan speech, "Call to Women's Strike for Equity," March 31, 1970

Our Movement toward true equality for all women in America in fully equal partnership with men has reached a point of critical mass. All of us this past year have learned in our gut that sisterhood is powerful. The awesome power of women united is visible now and is being taken seriously, as all of us who define ourselves as people now take action in every city and state, and together make our voices heard. . . .

I therefore propose that we accept the responsibility of mobilizing the chain reaction we have helped release for instant revolution against sexual oppression this year, 1970. I propose that on Wednesday, August 26, we call a twenty-four-hour general strike, a resistance both passive and active, of all women in America against the concrete conditions of their oppression. On that day, fifty years after the amendment that gave women the vote became a part of the Constitution,* I propose we use our power to declare an ultimatum on all who would keep us from using our rights as Americans. I propose that the women who are doing menial chores in the offices cover their typewriters and close

---

* The Nineteenth Amendment may have granted all women the vote in 1920, but most women of color were not permitted to vote because of racist, restrictive voting laws in Southern states. It was not until the 1965 Voting Rights Act became law that women (and men) of color could fully participate in the American electoral system.

their notebooks, the telephone operators unplug their switchboards, the waitresses stop waiting, cleaning women stop cleaning, and everyone who is doing a job for which a man would be paid more—stop—every woman pegged forever as assistant, doing jobs for which men get the credit—stop.

MARY JEAN COLLINS

This was March 31. So, I was like, "Oh my God. This is only five months away, right? We're supposed to do this massive thing in only five months?" I was elected NOW's Midwest regional director organizing in thirteen states.

People were grumpy, but nobody said, "We can't do this. Why didn't you talk to somebody ahead of time?" But it was the best idea ever in the history of the world, because it doubled the size of the women's movement. It launched the women's movement because people just did it. We didn't even know what we were doing, but we knew we wanted to do it. So, what we did was we went to all the other women's liberation groups and we organized people to be part of it.

BETTY FRIEDAN

I was told that I spoke for nearly two hours. . . . It was late in the afternoon, and intense. I was so tired when I finished that I held on to the lectern. I ended, knowing it was so—"I have led you into history. I leave you now—to make new history." They gave me a standing ovation.

13

Shut Out of Academia

While almost every white-collar professional job sector severely limited female participation, academia was one of the most egregious of all. But in 1970, an unknown graduate student at the University of Maryland started turning the entrenched male-dominated system on its head.

BERNICE SANDLER

I had always wanted to be a professor. I was in the department of counseling and personnel services, and taught some courses while I got my doctoral degree. The year I got my doctoral degree, 1969, at the University of Maryland, there was a huge expansion in the department—seven openings, and they didn't even consider me. Meanwhile, six or seven men got their doctorates at the same time as me, and all of them got job offers. I couldn't understand this. I went to one of the guys on the faculty whom I knew fairly well, and I said, "Hey, how come they didn't even think of me?" and he was very frank, he said, "Well, let's face it, Bunny, you come on too strong for a woman."

I went home and I wept and said, "Oh my God, I never should have spoken out at meetings." I just blamed myself. My then husband was very good; he named what had happened. He said, "It's not you, it's them, it's sex discrimination." I thought I'd never been discriminated against and that this would certainly not happen to me. Particularly because I was so smart. I mean, I laugh at that now.

So, I started reading and, because there wasn't anything about women, I started reading up on what the Blacks had done in terms of civil rights and I quickly learned that sex discrimination was not illegal. I read a booklet from the Commission on Civil Rights, which was evaluating civil rights enforcement of various laws. Then I found a footnote about an executive order that the president initiated and it said something like: this order covers contractors, people with contracts with the government, and it prohibits discrimination on the basis of race, color, religion, and national origin. And then there was a footnote, and being an academic, I always read footnotes. I read the footnote at the back of the book, and it said, "This executive order was amended" to add "sex" effective on such and such a day.* I literally screamed aloud in the house.

EDITH GREEN

One of the first times that I realized that a change had to be made, we had a panel of state school superintendents testifying before the [education] committee and one of the superintendents started telling us about special programs for disadvantaged boys and what a great success it had been and then two other superintendents joined in. They had this similar program. You take turns on the committee questioning. When it was my turn I said to them, "Do you mean that you had classes only for disadvantaged boys?" "Yes." "Well, was there not a need to have classes for disadvantaged girls?" This probably was in the late sixties. The answer, "The boys are going to have to be the breadwinners." But there were no classes for disadvantaged girls. The highest rate of unemployment was among Black girls between sixteen and twenty-one. It is certainly established that there were lots and lots of girls who were selling their bodies in order to buy the bread and butter they needed. I remember saying: "Couldn't you have classes and include both boys and girls?" "Well, it's better to have it this way."

Later, I raised the question on violation of the law, under the Civil Rights Act, that there is to be no discrimination on the basis of sex and here you are spending federal funds on boys and not on girls. I had to reread the Civil Rights Act. All education programs were excluded, so it was perfectly legal to discriminate in any education program against girls or women. That was the first thing that made me determined that I was going to change the law so that they could no longer discriminate.

---

* Executive Order 11246, which prohibited race discrimination in the federal government and by federal contractors, was amended in 1968 to include sex discrimination too. The executive order was signed by President Johnson, after lobbying from Esther Peterson, Betty Friedan, and Muriel Fox of NOW, but it was never enforced.

BERNICE SANDLER

I called the Office of Federal Contract Compliance at the US Department of Labor and I said, "I want to find out if this executive order covers colleges that have federal contracts." The woman who answered the phone said, "Let me put you through to the director, Vincent Macaluso." He said, "Why don't you come in and we'll talk about it." I was thinking to myself, I was really worried, "Is this guy coming on to me, or does he really want to talk about it?" because nobody had ever shown that kind of interest in my thoughts. I came in and saw him; he was delighted to see me. He said, "This is what you need to do. You need to gather all of the information that's out there." I said, "There isn't much information out there." He said, "It doesn't matter, you need to have a whole pack of stuff, because no one's going to read it anyway." He said, "If it's thick, people will believe that there's a problem." That was brilliant but it was absolutely true. Together we planned the first complaint against universities and colleges, and the strategies to bring about enforcement of the executive order.

At the end of the meeting he said, "You have to meet Catherine East. She's housed in the Women's Bureau. She's also working on women's issues, and you'll really like her." Catherine was the hub. She put me in touch with other women in academe. Think of the time when there were no women's newsletters at all. There were none. There were no women's caucuses in any of the disciplines. Women's studies was . . . maybe Sheila Tobias was teaching a course and maybe Florence Howe was teaching a course. But there was no women's studies network. So how were we going to get in touch? Through Catherine. She knew the laws, and she taught me a lot in the beginning because what did I know? Nothing!

I did a quick survey at the University of Maryland, pretending I was doing research. I went around to a bunch of departments and said I need a list of the faculty and I need to know which ones were men and women, and they gave it to me. I was afraid to say I was making a complaint. So I had that study, and there had been one done at Columbia and the University of Chicago.*

There was a group called the Women's Equity Action League, WEAL, which was developed by a woman named Betty Boyer, an attorney, who had been involved in the early setup of NOW. . . . But she quickly realized that the abortion issue and the demonstration issue might keep some women

---

* The University of Chicago had granted only four women tenure in the sociology department in the history of the school. In 1969, women members of the American Sociological Association reported that out of the 188 graduate schools across the country, women earned 30 percent of the PhDs but were only 4 percent of the full professors.

out of the women's movement. I think she was absolutely brilliant in that estimate, because I would not have joined NOW at that point. They did look radical to me. So Boyer provided a very good service for letting us get our feet wet in the women's movement in a very "safe" environment.

WEAL was there for me, they made me their chair of the Action Committee on Federal Contract Compliance. I was the entire committee. In any event, I get all of this material and, this is 1969; there is no Kinko's. I'm not affiliated with the university anymore, where there were just a few Xerox machines, and what am I gonna do? So my husband was being funded by the Ford Foundation and a woman he knew there agreed to take all the materials and surreptitiously have them copied by the Ford Foundation. And we ended up with two hundred copies of a stack of papers that was probably about eighty pages long.

This included the study I had done, just showing patterns of discrimination—the higher the rank, the fewer the women; the more prestigious the department, the fewer the women.

EDITH GREEN

I was also keenly aware of the difference in salaries that were paid to women professors in colleges and universities. This was impressed on my mind more, during these years, by women who came to me. The old-boy syndrome, which I am sure you have heard of. When there is a vacancy in a department or if there is to be a promotion, it was not advertised and the word was passed by mouth, and there were more male mouths around, and therefore women who might have received the promotion never heard about it.

BERNICE SANDLER

I started in '69 and I filed my first complaint in January 1970. I put out a press release and it was picked up by the *Saturday Review of Literature*. A lot of academics read it: there was no *Chronicle of Higher Education* at the time. We got maybe two or three sentences and it had my name in it—for further information, contact—and I started getting letters from people. I made the decision that I'm never going to be hired in academia, so I might as well file these charges because they were not going to hire me anyway. So, I had that kind of freedom, and through the executive order, I could sign the complaint and never mention who sent me the information.

What I would tell them is, "Okay, check the percentage of men and women at each rank in your department and a few departments like music, psychology, English; because that's where many women got their degrees."

And I said, "Get this data and I'll send in the complaint." A copy of every complaint I sent to the Labor and Health, Education and Welfare Departments went to Representative Edith Green, Representative Martha Griffiths from Michigan, and Representative Shirley Chisholm.

Martha Griffiths gave the first speech on the floor of the Congress concerning discrimination against women in education.

Representative Martha Griffiths, Congressional Record, March 9, 1970

Mr. Speaker, it is a national calamity that agencies of the Federal Government are violating our national policy as well as the President's executive orders, by providing billions of dollars of Federal contracts to universities and colleges which discriminate against women both as teachers and as students. . . .

Half of our brightest people, the people with talent and capacity for the highest intellectual and fruitful endeavors, are women. They encounter pervasive discrimination when they try to enter college—when they apply for graduate and advanced training—when they attempt to join the faculties of our most esteemed universities and colleges—and if they finally succeed in becoming teachers, they get less pay and fewer promotions than their male colleagues.

The University of Pennsylvania, for example, has only four departments with more than two women, and twenty-six departments with no women at all. Similar incredible examples exist in many universities and departments in practically all areas of higher education.

BERNICE SANDLER

So, I'm filing complaints like mad and Congresswoman Edith Green gets interested. Then Edith Green decides she'll introduce a bill and I get called in by her staff member. I mean, it was so heady, because here I am a little Jewish girl from Flatbush. So, I worked with Green's chief of staff Harry Hogan on the hearings in terms of who to invite, because I knew all the people. I also testified at the hearings.

EDITH GREEN

We started a series of hearings on June 17, 1970. There had never been any hearings in the House of Representatives before on discrimination on the basis of sex.

BERNICE SANDLER

When Edith Green held seven days of hearings, very few [male] members came to those hearings. One or two showed up as a courtesy, but they didn't stay.

> **Representative Edith Green, House of Representatives,**
> **Special Subcommittee on Education, Wednesday, June 17, 1970**
> The subcommittee will come to order for the further consideration of legislation that is under the jurisdiction of this subcommittee. . . . Section 805 would amend the Civil Rights Act to prohibit discrimination on the basis of sex in federally financed programs and would remove the exemption presently existing in Title VII of the Civil Rights Act with respect to those in education. . . .
>
> It is to be hoped that the enactment of the provisions would be of some help in eliminating the discrimination against women which still permeates our society. . . . It seems ironic that in a period when we are more concerned with civil rights and liberties than ever before in our history— that discrimination against a very important majority—women—has been given little attention . . . despite the growth in the number of women working today, the proportion of women in the professions is lower in this country than in most other countries throughout the world. While the United States prides itself in being a leader of nations, it has been backward in its treatment of its working women.
>
> Professionally, women in the United States constitute only 9 percent of all full professors, 8 percent of all scientists, 6.7 percent of all physicians, 3.5 percent of all lawyers, and 1 percent of all engineers. . . .
>
> We have been concerned, and rightly so, about discrimination against the Negro in our society—about the Negro man who averages $5,603— only 69.9 percent of the average [annual] earnings for a white man.
>
> But I hear little concern expressed for women who average only 58 percent in comparison. The average wage in the United States is: Negro women, $3,677; white women, $4,700; Negro men, $5,603; white men $8,014. . . .

DR. HARRIS

I am Ann Sutherland Harris, assistant professor of art history in the Graduate Facilities of Columbia University in the City of New York. . . . Much of my evidence concerning discriminatory practices against women in higher education is drawn from my knowledge of the situation at Columbia University. My research merely confirms my long held suspicion, however, that the situation at Columbia is merely typical of comparable high-endowment, high-prestige universities in the United States. . . . I have been astonished—and disheartened—to discover how uniform the pattern of discrimination is. In whatever proportion the women are to be found, the women are always at the bottom. . . .

I would like to try and convey to the committee by means of some quotations made by academic men about academic women the sexually negative atmosphere in which women live and work as students, staff, and faculty. . . .

When President Nathan Pusey of Harvard realized that the draft was going to reduce the number of men applying to Harvard's graduate program, he exclaimed: "We shall be left with the blind, the lame, and the women."

DR. MURRAY

Madam Chairman and Mr. Hathaway, I am Pauli Murray, a professor of American studies at Brandeis University. I must say to the Committee that I put my credentials in my prepared statement* partly out of pressure from my colleagues and partly because I hoped they would make the male members of the subcommittee take me seriously. . . .

The emergent revitalized women's rights/women's liberation movement is no historical accident. It was born of the involvement of women in the civil rights movement of the 1940s, 1950s, and 1960s. Because it affects a literal majority of the population, it has a revolutionary potential even greater than the black revolt. It has the compelling force of an idea whose time has come, and neither ridicule nor verbal castigation can delay it. At present it has a controlled fury and a passion which is at times frightening when one realizes the depth of frustration from which it comes. . . . Women are appealing, demanding, organizing

---

* This is the impressive biographical data that Pauli Murray submitted to the committee: A.B., Hunter College; L.L.B., Howard University; L.L.M., University of California; J.S.D., Yale University. Former deputy, Office of Attorney General, Department of Justice, State of California; former associate, Paul, Weiss [Goldberg], Rifkind, Wharton & Garrison; member of Political and Civil Rights Committee of President's Commission on Status of Women (1962–63); former consultant, Equal Employment Opportunity Commission. Founder and member, National Organization for Women (NOW); member, Women's Equity Action League (WEAL); member, subcommittee on Women's Rights, American Bar Association; member, Commission on Women in Today's World, Church Women United; life member, National Council of Negro Women; life member, National Association for the Advancement of Colored People (NAACP). . . .

for, and determined to achieve acceptance as persons, as full and equal partners with men in every phase of our national life.

. . . Just as blacks have found it necessary to opt for self-definition, women are seeking their own image of themselves nurtured from within rather than imposed from without. I am led to the hypothesis that we will be unable to eradicate racism in the United States unless and until we simultaneously remove all sex barriers which inhibit the development of individual talents. . . . It demands that we women . . . keep before us the goal of liberating our own humanity and that of our male counterparts. It demands from those who hold formal power—predominantly white males—something closely akin to conversion, the imagination, and vision to realize that an androgynous society is vastly superior to a patriarchal society—which we now are—and that the liberation of women through legislation, through a restructuring of our political and social institutions, and through a change in our cultural conditioning may well hold the key to many of the complex social issues for which we do not now have answers. . . .

It is my special responsibility, however, to speak on behalf of Negro women who constitute about 93 percent of all nonwhite women, and I wish to call to your attention an article which appeared in the March 1970 Crisis published by NAACP, "Job Discrimination and the Black Women," by Miss Sonia Pressman, senior attorney in the Office of General Counsel of the Equal Employment Opportunity Commission and an expert in the law of race and sex discrimination.

This document presents the special problems of Negro/black women because of their dual victimization by race and sex-based discrimination coupled with the disproportionate responsibilities they carry for the economic and social welfare of their families compared with their white counterparts. . . . The Negro woman has a higher rate of unemployment, a higher incidence of poverty, a greater proportionately economic responsibility and less overall opportunity than white women or black or white men. . . .

The organization for action against discrimination, is taking place particularly among the professional and academic women and women in the higher industrial occupations climbing the ladder to the higher paying jobs.

The lower economically paid women, I don't think, are as well organized. They are not often in trade unions. When they are black women, very often they are organized in the welfare rights organizations to some extent, but the tragedy of black women today is that they are brainwashed by the notion that priority must be given to the assertion of black male manhood and that they must now stand back and push their men forward.

What this means, in essence, is that while the militant rhetoric is that we are rejecting the values of white society; on the other hand, we are holding on very definitely to the patriarchal aspect of white America, and I think it is tragic and I stand against it. . . .

My own struggle for higher education through college and law school apart from scholarships for tuition was financed by working as a waitress, dishwasher, elevator operator, night switchboard clerk, and bus girl in a large hotel in Washington during World War II. In the last job the waiters whom we bus girls served were all Negro males, but they tipped us only 25 cents per night.

Our salary of $1.50 per night plus a second-class meal supplemented by what we could steal from the kitchen constituted our weekly wage. If anyone should ask a Negro woman what is her greatest achievement, her honest answer would be, "I survived."

SUSAN RENNIE

In 1970, when Congress begins hearings and they're starting to go after universities for discriminating against women, Columbia was their test case. And by golly, there weren't many women in their faculty.

One of my professors in the political science department was appointed the executive vice president, and he came to me and said, "How would you like it if we brought you into the administration? You're smart. Everybody knows that you are very strong on women's issues." And he said, "We could make you assistant vice president for academic affairs." I thought, well, here we go. Here's an adventure. Why not? My salary would triple. So I became the assistant vice president for academic affairs at Columbia.

They wanted to say to the federal government, "Look, we're changing, and we have brought a woman into a high administrative position, two down from the president." At meetings, I remember they couldn't decide whether or not I was a secretary.

14

Congress Hears the ERA

One month before Representative Edith Green's hearings on sex discrimination in education, Senator Birch Bayh held three days of hearings on the ERA. Starting on May 5, 1970,* a cavalcade of representatives from all walks of the women's liberation movement testified in favor of the constitutional amendment that had first been introduced in Congress in 1923, yet had never before been the subject of a congressional hearing.

BRENDA FEIGEN

Shortly after I assumed the position of national vice president of NOW, I received a call from Senator Birch Bayh, the Democratic Senator from Indiana. I had interned for him in 1965 between my junior and senior years at Vassar. That was really a wonderful experience where I got to spend the summer in Washington and got to know him. He was working on the amendment that gave people the vote at age eighteen (from twenty-one). Suddenly the phone rang, it was early 1970, and it was Birch Bayh telling me that he was the chair of the Senate Subcommittee

---

* The first day of the ERA hearings occurred the day after thirteen unarmed students were shot and four killed by the Ohio National Guard at Kent State University in Ohio. The students were protesting President Nixon's announcement of the American invasion of Cambodia. In response to the student massacre, seven hundred campuses across the country were shut down by 2.5 million outraged, striking students.

on Constitutional Amendments, and would I like to organize the "pro testimony" for his hearing on the Equal Rights Amendment in May. I said sure, and that was the beginning of my more organized focus on the Equal Rights Amendment.

After a party in New York at my brother Richard's place, where I met Gloria Steinem, and I had seen her do a really good job defending feminism on the *David Susskind Show*, I decided to call her and find out if she would like to testify because Bayh wanted some well-known people. She was well-known as an intelligent journalist with good political connections. I got her number from my brother and called her, and she said, "Okay, if you'll write my testimony." I happily agreed.

Birch Bayh, Subcommittee on Constitutional Amendments of the Committee on the Judiciary, United States Senate on S.J. Res. 61, May 5, 1970

I think it is fair to say that today begins an all-out effort to secure a long overdue objective—equal rights under the law for men and women.

The amendment we are considering provides that "Equality of rights under the law shall not be denied or abridged by the United States or by any State on the account of sex." The amendment would outlaw discrimination on account of sex in the same manner and to the same extent that we prohibited discrimination on account of race, religion or national origin in the 14th amendment 100 years ago. This amendment would be a sorely needed step in striking down laws still on the books that deny more than half our population the right to first-class citizenship. . . .

The range of discrimination against women is not limited to areas of pay and employment. State laws in Illinois and seven other States provide that women attain the age of majority at 21, while men attain majority at 18. . . . Many States impose limitations on jury service. State property laws are a jumble of restrictions, many dating to the 12th century, wholly out of tune with the role of women in modern American society. For example, California and Nevada require married women to follow a formal procedure of obtaining court approval before they may engage in independent businesses.

BRENDA FEIGEN

I reviewed the transcripts from past years' ERA floor debate.* I studied legal writings on the ERA, concluding that it would, in fact, go further than the Fourteenth Amendment's Equal Protection Clause. Three officers of NOW were scheduled to testify during that first day of hearings, and I was one.

Aileen Hernandez, Senate ERA hearing, May 5, 1970

My name is Aileen Hernandez, and I am the national president of the National Organization for Women. I and my sisters in this new feminist organization appear before you today with decidedly mixed emotions. We are infuriated by the cavalier manner in which the gentlemen of the Congress have treated the question of equality for women for 47 years since the Equal Rights Amendment to our Constitution was first introduced. We are saddened by the fact that an amendment is needed, because our male founders and male-dominated courts refuse to accept women as people in setting forth and interpreting the guarantees of freedom in the Bill of Rights. Gentlemen, we are enraged. We are dedicated and we mean to become first-class citizens in this society.

BRENDA FEIGEN

I was young, just twenty-six, and I remember speaking on behalf of all women demanding equal protection by the Constitution, just as men were. The Supreme Court, in various sex discrimination cases that had come before it, starting with Myra Bradwell's suit (in 1873) against the state of Illinois, which wouldn't let women become lawyers, had failed us miserably, never deeming such discrimination a violation of the Equal Protection Clause of the Fourteenth Amendment.

Brenda Feigen, Senate ERA hearing, May 5, 1970

My name is Brenda Feigen Fasteau. I am legislative vice president of the National Organization for Women. I am also a lawyer and a

---

* Although the ERA had been introduced in every Congress since 1923, it made no legislative traction until this hearing in 1970.

recent graduate of Harvard Law School. . . . I will tell you a little about my own experience, much of which might never have happened if Congress had acted on this amendment earlier. Being a woman at a professional school was an infuriating experience throughout which I was treated like an unwelcome phenomenon. Job interviews conducted through the [Harvard] law school placement office make every other insult mild in comparison. Of the law firms which I interviewed for jobs, four told me that they simply would not hire a woman. Several firms stated that women were hired to do only probate, trust, and estate work, the traditional domain of "lady lawyers." I am angry at these men, and I am not the only one. Across the country millions of women and self-confident men are joining together to fight the insidious oppression which has held women back for thousands of years, oppression which results from discrimination disguised as chivalry and protection.

Shirley Chisholm, Senate ERA hearing, May 5, 1970

Mr. Chairman, colored minority group Americans are not the only second-class citizens in this country. More than half of the population of the United States is female, but women occupy only two percent of the managerial positions. They have not even reached the level of tokenism yet. No women sit on the AFL-CIO Council or the Supreme Court. In Congress we are down to one Senator and 10 Representatives.

People have often asked me why I feel that American Blacks and American women have received such treatment. I believe it is because American institutions were created by white males and that the freedom, equality, and justice that they mentioned and fought for was intended, albeit consciously, for them and them alone.

This is the reason that I believe that an amendment such as the one presently under consideration has not been passed by the male-dominated Congress in the past. . . . May I remind you, gentlemen, you are the power, and as such you are then the focal point of the struggle. It is not the intention of American women to become a nation of Amazons. We will no longer, however, be denied our rights as human beings equal in all respects to males.

Birch Bayh, Senate ERA hearing, May 5, 1970

I agree with everything you said Mrs. Chisholm. . . . I might have one reservation with your remarks, which is that although I really cannot blame you for feeling frustrated relative to the task before us, I hope it will not be a futile effort.[*]

---

[*]   Forty-three witnesses testified at Bayh's three-day-long hearing.

15

New York Legalizes Abortion

In early 1970, a group of five feminist lawyers challenged the constitu-tionality of New York's antiabortion statutes in a first-ever class-action lawsuit. More than three hundred plaintiffs claimed that a law banning women's right to abortion violated their constitutional rights as citizens. A year earlier, New York's branch of NOW drafted legislation to repeal New York State's 1828 abortion ban that was introduced in the State Assembly. The bill and the lawsuit—one that hoped to repeal state law, the other ambitiously challenging the US Constitution—moved forward on parallel tracks. Meanwhile, by chance of timing and luck, two young lawyers in Texas became the first to bring an abortion-rights case to the Supreme Court.

NANCY STEARNS

I graduated from UC Berkeley in '61, and I got my master's in '63, and then I went to the South for a year. I was an office worker in the Atlanta headquarters of SNCC. I left at the end of the Mississippi Summer Project, the summer of '64.

Over the period of time I was there, I came to the conclusion that if I really wanted to be useful, I needed a skill, and I concluded that the most sensible degree to get was a law degree. So I went to NYU Law School in 1964, and I graduated in '67. I had guys in the class saying things to me like, "Why are you here? Why are you taking up a seat that a man could have? You're only here to marry a lawyer," all the same bullshit that women had to deal with in those days in professions.

When I was in law school, I read a law review article by an incredible woman lawyer named Harriet Pilpel,* who did legal work for Planned Parenthood, about how restrictions on abortion were unconstitutional, and it just made a great deal of sense to me.

I was just one of many who saw it as totally fundamental to a woman being able to truly be free and truly participate in society. New York's law (enacted in 1828) only allowed for abortion if it was "necessary to preserve the life" of the woman. It was one of the stricter ones. If you had enough money, you could get a psychiatrist or two, however many the hospital required, to write a letter and say you were going to kill yourself if you were forced to bring your fetus to term.

SUSAN BROWNMILLER

Nancy Stearns was "ready for women's stuff" in the summer of 1969. . . . Her activism made her a natural for the newly formed Center for Constitutional Rights, where Arthur Kinoy became her mentor. Most civil rights attorneys specialized in defense cases, but Kinoy went on the offensive by initiating federal lawsuits with massive numbers of plaintiffs.

NANCY STEARNS

The summer of '69, I went to a meeting of a group of women in New York called the Women's Health Collective. They were talking about a variety of issues, and one of the issues was abortion. I raised the question of starting a lawsuit to challenge New York's law. At that point, I don't know that any of us thought that we'd win it, but we saw it as an organizing tool.

SUSAN BROWNMILLER

Stearns proposed that they organize in a new way around abortion. Instead of waiting for rulings in *Belous*† and *Vuitch*,‡ they could go on the offensive

---

* Born in 1911, Harriet Pilpel graduated second in her class at Columbia Law school in 1936 and served as general counsel for the ACLU and Planned Parenthood. She was involved in twenty-seven US Supreme Court cases, including the 1965 case that legalized birth control for married couples, *Griswold v. Connecticut*, for which she wrote the Planned Parenthood amicus brief.

† Nine doctors in California were convicted in 1968 for referring their patients to an abortion clinic, and in *People v. Belous* (September 1969) the California Supreme Court ruled that the state's one-hundred-year-old abortion law was unconstitutional.

‡ In 1969, Washington, DC, doctor Milan Vuitch, who had previously been arrested sixteen times on abortion charges, was convicted of providing an abortion to a woman whose life was *not* endangered.

in federal court. "Let's bring an affirmative case in New York on behalf of the people who are really harmed," she urged. "Not the doctors, the women." She laid out her plan.

NANCY STEARNS

At that point there had been some challenges to abortion laws in other states [like *Belous* and *Vuitch*], primarily emerging from criminal prosecutions of either doctors or abortion counselors. Women were never in court themselves. It was as if we were irrelevant. The relevant people were the doctors, who were men, and the abortion counselors, who were primarily men.

I felt like the crucial people who should be challenging it were missing. And that was why I wanted to bring a lawsuit where it wouldn't be people defending themselves against prosecution. It would be people going to court and saying, my rights are violated.

Legislatures were virtually all male. Courts were virtually all male. So a woman could not be part of the government mechanisms that ultimately made the decisions that controlled her life. That means you are not an equal member of society. We were saying that not only was her right to liberty being violated, her right to the equal protection of the laws was being violated.

We spent the summer going around to the different boroughs in New York. I was the lawyer. We had a doctor, June Finer, and a health organizer, Rachel Fruchter. We would talk to small groups of about ten to fifteen women at a time. I would talk about the legal implications of abortion, June would talk about medical, and Rachel would talk about abortion and women's healthcare as a political issue. Then we would ask people if they wanted to talk about their experiences in the healthcare system in general, and the way they were treated by doctors, many of whom were sexist, and if anybody wanted to talk about abortion, they could. Then after that, we would tell them that we were planning on doing this lawsuit, and did they want to sign up as plaintiffs? We got 350 people.

He argued that the DC law was unconstitutionally vague, and in 1971, the US Supreme Court in *US v. Vuitch* ruled in his favor and overturned his conviction.

SUSAN BROWNMILLER

Stearns enlisted four more women attorneys, including Diane Schulder, an early member of New York Radical Women, and Flo Kennedy, always on hand to "kick ass" (as she would like to say) and carry the banner for women of color. [Carol Lefcourt, Ann Garfinkle, and Emily Goodman also joined the legal team.]

DIANE SCHULDER AND FLORYNCE KENNEDY

The *Abramowicz* case (referred to this way because the first plaintiff, in alphabetical order, was Dr. Helen Abramowicz) was argued before [federal] Judge Edward Weinfeld on October 28, 1969, by Nancy Stearns. On that day, the courtroom was filled with plaintiffs and other sympathetic women. Most of them were young, white, college-educated women, some of whom brought their children. Many of whom carried coat hangers.[*]

NANCY STEARNS

We packed the Southern District courtroom with women. I was arguing for our case, and our legal team was all women. All the other people who spoke were men in dark suits. You rarely had a courtroom full of women in the federal court, and you rarely had a courtroom where there were a group of women lawyers.

> United States District Court
> For the Southern District of New York
> HELEN ABRAMOWICZ M.D., *et al.*, on their behalf and on behalf
> of all others similarly situated, Plaintiffs
> v.
> LOUIS J. LEFKOWITZ, *et al.*, Defendants
> Plaintiffs Brief
> *1. The New York Abortion Laws Violate*

---

[*] The plaintiffs were mostly ordinary "female citizens" who sought abortions, but some were also doctors (like the lead plaintiff, Dr. Helen Abramowicz), lawyers, psychologists, social workers, husbands, and ministers. The case was precedent-setting because it was the first lawsuit filed on behalf of victims of the state's abortion ban, and the first to make the argument to male judges, who had virtually no personal understanding of what it was like to experience an unwanted pregnancy, that the law violated their constitutional rights. The large class of 350 (mostly) women presented their case about how the New York abortion ban law was discriminatory. The decision would have an impact beyond New York State borders because *Abramowicz v. Lefkowitz* was filed in federal court, and the plaintiffs asserted that the New York law violated rights guaranteed by the US Constitution, and as a result the case could make its way on appeal to the Supreme Court.

Plaintiff Women's Rights to Life,
Liberty, and Property Guaranteed by
the Fourteenth Amendment to the
Constitution

Under the Fourteenth Amendment to the Constitution,* no State may . . . "deprive any person of life, liberty, or property, without due process of law." The Courts have not yet, however, begun to come to grips with the fact that approximately half of our citizenry is systematically being denied these guarantees of the Fourteenth Amendment. However, that is exactly the effect of the New York abortion laws. The Federal Courts must not shrink from redressing the constitutional wrongs perpetrated on women.

For the first time, the Federal Courts have the opportunity to give serious and full consideration to the degree to which laws such as those challenged herein, which deny a woman the control of her reproductive life, violate her most basic constitutional rights. . . .

EMILY GOODMAN

I joined the legal team of women working with Nancy Stearns. The federal judge said there could be hearings, but not all in the courthouse, because these hearings would involve maybe hundreds of women. These would be women who either had abortions, illegal abortions in different parts of the country, or left the country, or couldn't get abortions, and tried self-abortion with various consequences, women who had babies that they really didn't want, women who had babies and placed them for adoption. So, we covered every possible contact that women had with abortion, and everyone was invited to a speak-out, which was part of the case.

SUSAN BROWNMILLER

The lawyers for the women's suit challenging the New York abortion law won a huge concession in January 1970 when they got the green light to take personal testimony at the federal courthouse.

Diane Schulder, who had heard me blurt out my story at New York

---

* Adopted in 1868, after the Civil War, the Fourteenth Amendment to the Constitution granted former male slaves the rights that accompany US citizenship—including voting rights. However, the full range of citizenship rights was not granted to women—of any race—and women would not gain the right to vote, for example, until 1920.

Radical Women, asked me to come down and be deposed. Flo Kennedy conducted the questioning. She neglected to tell me that a reporter for the *Times* was present in the hearing room; it was an odd sensation to read about my abortions in the next day's paper.

New York Times, January 27, 1970, "Women Testify in Abortion Law Test"

A 34-year-old writer told a Federal court hearing yesterday that she had three abortions between 1960 and 1967 because having an illegitimate child "would have been the end of my life."

The plaintiff's lawyers represented a class-action suit brought by more than 100 people, mostly women, who have had some experience, either professional or personal, with abortions.

The suit argues that the abortion law deprives women of their fundamental right to private decisions and violates freedom of speech and freedom from religious coercion.

FLORYNCE KENNEDY

The all-woman lawyer team worked with a minimum of friction. Nancy Stearns drew the papers and wrote the major part, if not all of the briefs, except that Emily Jane Goodman wrote an amicus curiae brief. Diane Schulder did yeoman service on the depositions.

DIANE SCHULDER AND FLORYNCE KENNEDY

The following testimony is from the official transcripts of depositions taken on January 14, 15, and 23, 1970, in the case of *Abramowicz v. Lefkowitz*. . . .

Examination by Nancy Stearns

Q: Would you indicate your age, what your circumstances were? Was this before or after you had finished school?

A: I was out of college. . . . I went to Wellesley, and I had been abroad for a year. I got pregnant and came back and was going to get married, but really didn't want to get married. I didn't know how to go about getting an abortion. . . . One psychiatrist in Birmingham counseled me to go to a home for unwed mothers and have the baby. . . . You had to pay $80 a week. It was on the Upper East Side. It was a fairly comfortable place.

Q: How many women were there?

A: About sixteen . . .

I gave the baby up, which is what everybody in the home did. . . . I prepared to think of myself as a breeder. I was just breeding babies for someone else to take rather than think of myself as a mother who abandoned her baby. But the guilt . . . for months after I left the home, I'd wake up in the night crying and sort of rocking my pillow.

Q: Was it obvious to you that some of the women needed psychiatric assistance?

A: Yes, there was one woman who was about thirty-five, who was a lawyer. She was a Vassar graduate, a lawyer who had been working as a legal secretary and who was in a catatonic state the whole time she was in the home. She was totally withdrawn and frightened. There was another woman, also about thirty-five, who was pregnant with a child of her boss who had tried to get an abortion. Most of the women in the home, except those who were Catholic, had tried to get an abortion.*

NANCY STEARNS

A successful court case is stories. Part of trying to build a case that says why all of these laws violate the Constitution and violate women's rights is to talk about the details of the impact they had on women and then try to tie that to something the Constitution says. That's the guts of it. It's people's lives.

DIANE SCHULDER AND FLORYNCE KENNEDY

It was not until New York women took the affirmative action in the courts and on the streets that the New York Legislature acted. . . . An important concomitant to the court case had been the organizing of new women's liberation groups and actions. It became obvious that the abortion issue was

---

*   Dozens of women recited their traumatizing and humiliating stories like this one while being constantly objected to as "irrelevant" by opposing counsel. Women recounted being blindfolded and butchered in Washington, DC, some were raped by their abortionists, those who could afford to flew to Puerto Rico, Japan, and London for abortions. Some were kicked out of college because they were pregnant, and others lost their jobs and were forced onto welfare. Florynce Kennedy and Diane Schulder published many of these graphic depositions in their 1971 book *Abortion Rap*.

one that could mobilize large numbers of women across the country. . . .
A group of women called People Against Abortion Laws planned a mass
demo of women to be held on March 28.

This was the first time in many decades that New York had seen masses
of women in the streets on women's issues.

SUSAN BROWNMILLER
A week before the Cook bill was brought to the floor in Albany . . . two
thousand New Yorkers streamed to Union Square. . . . The air was thick with
FREE ABORTION ON DEMAND/NO FORCED STERILIZATION
posters. . . . All eyes were on Albany the following week.

*By April 1970, the political pressure had reached a fever pitch. While the
legal challenges made their way through the courts, New York lawmakers had
tried and failed since 1968 to pass abortion reform legislation. But things
changed when the New York branch of NOW drafted a bolder bill repealing
the abortion ban law (before twenty-four weeks). That bill was introduced
in the state assembly by Republican Constance Cook and Democrat Franz
Leichter, and it was accompanied by lobbying by a wide coalition of more
than fifty organizations, from NOW, NARAL, and PAL (People to Abolish
Abortion Laws) to religious groups like the New York Council of Churches
and the American Jewish Congress. The strength in numbers began to move
the political dial. Large street protests in Albany and Manhattan, combined
with grassroots campaigns targeting legislators with calls and letters from
constituents, signaled to anyone paying attention that a critical mass of
righteous women were no longer going to take no for an answer.*

Newsday, April 11, 1970, "Abortion Reform
Is Here: What Happened?," by Jon Margolis
At the end of the roll call, the off-again, on-again bill seemed to have
failed in the Assembly by one vote. But as Speaker Perry Duryea, Jr
(R-Montauk) told the clerk to announce the results, Assemblyman
George Michaels rose in his place, and said to someone who told him
to keep still. "I must speak."

George Michaels is not one of the well-known legislators. He is
a Jewish Democrat from Auburn, a city which is about 70 percent

Catholic, overwhelmingly Republican. . . . But he had another constituency. During an earlier abortion debate he had revealed that his daughter-in-law, a former social worker, had not spoken to him for a month after he voted against reform last year. Now he revealed that one of his three sons had called him a "whore," [and] that another had pleaded with him not to let his vote kill the bill.

In the final moments of the roll call, Michaels had quickly considered that facing his constituents in November with a yes vote was a lesser risk than facing his family on Passover a week from Monday with a no vote. His glasses off, his hands rubbing his wet eyes, his emotions overpowering him Michaels said: "I must have peace in my family."

UPI, April 11, 1970, "Abortion Reform Bill Approved by Assembly," by Clay F. Richards

"I fully appreciate that this may terminate my political career, but I cannot in good conscience stand here and thwart the obvious majority of this house," Michaels said. "What's the use of getting elected or re-elected if you don't stand up for something?" . . . As he changed his vote from negative to affirmative a shout went up in the packed chamber. Then Duryea cast the deciding 76th vote as promised beforehand and announced, "The bill is passed."

Secretaries and other young women standing in the back of the chamber let out shrieks and cheers.*

EMILY GOODMAN

The new law mooted out our whole case. So, it was good news and bad news. My strongest recollection is that we were furious that no credit was given to the organizing that made this possible. It was as if no women were involved—that it didn't take blood, sweat, and tears.

When New York liberalized its state abortion law, and the lawsuit was dropped, Stearns's case lost its chance to make its way to the Supreme Court and set a national constitutional precedent. But New York became the first state in the nation to decriminalize abortion, and women from all over the country who could afford to travel flocked to the state for

---

* As he predicted, Michaels lost his reelection bid because of his abortion vote. Hawaii, New York, Alaska, and Washington would be the only states to legalize abortion before *Roe v. Wade* in 1973.

safe abortions.* Hawaii and Washington State also legalized abortion in 1970, but only for state residents, and Alaska followed in 1971. Knowing that she had pioneered a powerful legal strategy, Stearns took her class-action formula to other states.

NANCY STEARNS

I started working closely with people in New Jersey, Connecticut, Rhode Island, and a little bit in Massachusetts, and I gave my papers to people in Pennsylvania, and Georgia, and Texas.

When it was time to turn to Connecticut, I called Catie Roraback because who would know more, and who would understand using a lawsuit as an organizing tool better than Catie?

Catie Roraback was one of the lawyers on *Griswold v. Connecticut*, which was the case that struck down the ban on birth control, a very, very crucial case. I got to know Catie because I met her when I was working for SNCC in the South and we got to be good friends.[†]

Catie was the one who said, "Look, these men," because the judges were all men, "they don't understand. They don't get what abortion is. They don't get what the problems are, and we have to educate them." She was determined to have them hear witnesses. She said, "Look, unless their wives or their daughters told them, the judges don't understand what it means to be afraid of being pregnant and having your whole life change." I mean, it's why you need women judges. It's why you need Black judges. It's why you need Asian American judges. It's why you need a diverse judiciary, because if it's all upper-middle-class white men, their view of the society is that of upper-middle-class white men, and that's what it was in those days.[‡]

---

*   After the new law went into effect July 1, 1970, New York became a destination for women from all over the country to receive legal, safe abortions. In the first twelve months, 139,042 abortions were performed in New York State, 50,919 were for residents and 88,123 were for nonresidents. Of the non-residents traveling to New York for abortions, 79,309 were white women and 8,352 were non-white. The demand for legal, safe abortions became obvious by the end of 1972, when nearly 350,000 women traveled to New York for abortions.

†   A shrewd litigator, legendary civil rights lawyer, and political activist, Catherine Roraback (born in 1920) had successfully represented Ericka Huggins, who was acquitted in the New Haven, Connecticut, Black Panther trial.

‡   In 1970, only 4 percent of lawyers and 1 percent of judges in the United States were women, and non-white judges were just as scarce. Constance Baker Motley (1921–2005) was the first Black woman to serve as a federal judge. She was appointed by President Johnson in 1966 to New York's Southern District, and her confirmation was held up for seven months by Mississippi's pro-segregationist senator

In Connecticut, we put witnesses on the stand. We had to educate the judges, and we did, and it worked.*

ELIZABETH SPAHN

I may have been one of the zillions of plaintiffs in *Abele v. Markle*, I don't know. The way I remember being involved is they wanted people to do radio call-in shows, interviews with newspapers and television, and having one of the Yale superwomen would be good PR.† And so somebody asked me if I would do it, and I said, "Sure." I didn't want to be a star, but when it's something like abortion, I'll be the first Marine on the beach, and I'll let them shoot at me for a while. And then pretty soon, the sisterhood shows up and then there are lots and lots of, lots of us on the beach.

NANCY STEARNS

I heard about the case *Roe v. Wade* before it was filed because I received a call from a lawyer in Texas, Sarah Weddington. My recollection is she told me about her client and that she was going to be going into court and asked me if I would send her my papers that outlined the legal theories we were using. Weddington's case was different from ours because her plaintiff was

---

James Eastland because of Motley's work on desegregation cases like *Brown v. Board of Education*. In 1962, Motley became the first Black woman lawyer to argue before the Supreme Court, in *Meredith v. Fair*.

*   The lawsuit argued that the Connecticut abortion ban unconstitutionally discriminated against women because it "classifies . . . women not as full and equal citizens but as limited and inferior persons—persons denied the right to choose a lifestyle or an occupation other than one consistent with bearing all the children they conceive." On April 18, 1972, the US District Court ruled (2–1) in favor of the plaintiffs (whose numbers had risen to two thousand). The decision is worth quoting here because of its acknowledgment of the newly changed status of women, which informed and influenced the Supreme Court's January 1973 *Roe v. Wade* decision. It is also a telling and sharp contrast to the June 24, 2022 (almost exactly fifty years later), Supreme Court ruling that reversed *Roe v. Wade*. The *Abele v. Markle* decision stated: "In Connecticut, statutes prohibit all abortions . . . unless necessary to preserve the life of the mother or the fetus. . . . We think that by these statutes Connecticut trespasses unjustifiably on the personal privacy and liberty of its female citizenry. Accordingly, we hold the statutes unconstitutional in violation of the Ninth Amendment and the Due Process Clause of the Fourteenth Amendment.

"The decision to carry and bear a child has extraordinary ramifications for a woman. Pregnancy entails profound physical changes. Childbirth presents some danger to life and health. Bearing and raising a child demands difficult psychological and social adjustments. The working or student mother frequently must curtail or end her employment or educational opportunities. The mother with an unwanted child may find that it overtaxes her and her family's financial or emotional resources. The unmarried mother will suffer the stigma of having an illegitimate child. Thus, determining whether or not to bear a child is of fundamental importance to a woman."

†   Spahn was in the first class of women to enter the all-male Ivy League bastion of higher learning in New Haven, Connecticut. Out of 4,586 undergraduates, Yale enrolled 575 female students in September 1969.

an individual pregnant woman who was looking to get an abortion and needed to go into court to obtain a temporary restraining order, which is not an easy thing to do, to block the law from being enforced against her. There were kernels of what we were arguing in New York, but it landed more on rights like privacy than liberty.

Privacy is a very passive right. You're just saying, I need this realm around me that's private that the government can't get involved in. Liberty is saying, I have a life. I have to be able to live my life to the fullest. And unless you get off my body, I will not be able to live that active life.

SARAH WEDDINGTON

I took comfort in the knowledge that many other people around the country were as frustrated with the law as we were, and I began to see our efforts in Texas as one piece of a national patchwork. . . . Around the nation, the big advances seemed to be coming from courtrooms, not legislative halls. Shouldn't we be following the example of those who were winning, and file a court challenge? A lawsuit was an obvious route . . . but my total legal experience consisted of a few uncontested divorces for friends, ten or twelve uncomplicated wills for people with little property, one adoption for relatives, and a few miscellaneous matters. I had never been involved in a contested case. The idea of challenging the Texas abortion law in federal court was overwhelming.

SUSAN BROWNMILLER

In January 1970, a friend of [lawyer Linda] Coffee's who handled adoptions steered the clientless litigants to Norma McCorvey, a hard-luck itinerant bartender in Dallas who lacked the resources to cope with her third pregnancy in six years. McCorvey's first child lived with her parents; the second had been given up for adoption at birth. . . . The twenty-two-year-old was already too late for a routine termination. Over four months pregnant and showing when she met the two lawyers at a Dallas pizza parlor.

SARAH WEDDINGTON

She had never finished the tenth grade, was working as a waitress, and knew she would lose her job if her pregnancy continued. She could barely support herself, much less a child. I sympathized with her plight, and we agreed that it was unfair that many women—teachers, stewardesses, and others—lost their jobs if they became pregnant. That was something else we wanted to change.

Linda and I explained the Texas antiabortion law and told her why we felt it was wrong. She had found an illegal place in Dallas, she admitted, but she didn't like the looks of it. She had no money to travel to another state. As the conversation continued, Jane Roe [Norma McCorvey's new pseudonym] asked if it would help if she had been raped. We said no; the Texas law had no exception for rape. . . .

Jane Roe asked what being a plaintiff would involve. First, we told her, a minimal amount of time. In fact, she signed a one-page affidavit stating her situation. She never had to answer written or oral questions from the opposing lawyers. She did not attend any of the court hearings. . . . Linda and I were donating our time, and we were covering the expenses.

LINDA COFFEE

The main argument was that such a broad prohibition of abortions is an unreasonable infringement on the woman's personal right to decide whether or not to bear children. And that the state could not show that it had any legitimate interest in making such a broad proscription of abortions. . . . The constitutional authority for this so-called broad right of privacy, which has always been considered to be, since the case of *Griswold v. Connecticut* [in] 1965, the contraceptive case, has been considered to be the Ninth Amendment.

SARAH WEDDINGTON

On March 2, 1970, Linda and I spent the evening working on last-minute details and changes. When we finished, our first case was captioned: "In the United States District Court for the Northern District of Texas, Dallas Division—Jane Roe, Plaintiff, v. Henry Wade, District Attorney of Dallas County, Defendant." The next day it was docketed as case number 3-3690-B. It became known as *Roe v. Wade*.

On May 22, 1970, Weddington and Coffee argued their case in front of a three-judge panel, which included one female judge whom Coffee had clerked for, Sarah T. Hughes. By June 17, the US district court ruled that the Texas abortion law was unconstitutional because it deprived women of their Ninth Amendment right to privacy to choose whether to have children. But the court would not grant an injunction prohibiting the district attorney from prosecuting doctors who performed abortions. Weddington and Coffee appealed the case to the US Supreme Court.

16

We Are Your Worst Nightmare, Your Best Fantasy

NOW convened the first Congress to Unite Women in November 1969 with the hope to find common ground between the increasingly divided moderate and radical wings of the movement. At the second congress, just six months later, the smoldering adversity ignited when lesbians demanded acceptance and recognition.

KARLA JAY

The Second Congress to Unite Women got underway on May 1, 1970, at 7 p.m. at Intermediate School 70 on West Seventeenth Street in Manhattan. About three hundred women filed into the school auditorium.

RITA MAE BROWN

The organizers of the second congress, who chose not to invite lesbians (unless they were in the closet), were dumb enough to invite the media.

So we dyed T-shirts lavender and printed *Lavender Menace* on them. Once all the girls got seated, we cut the lights. Well, that scared the shit out of them.

MARTHA SHELLEY

What happened was we had our Lavender Menace T-shirts under our other clothes, and at a certain signal—I don't know who gave the signal, Donna

Gottschalk flipped the light switch and threw the whole auditorium into darkness. And when she flipped the lights on again, people had posted these posters that said, "Take a Lesbian to Lunch," "Superdyke Loves You," "We Are Your Worst Nightmare, Your Best Fantasy" around the room and we had taken off our other clothes and we were wearing our Lavender Menace T-shirts.

KARLA JAY

I was planted in the middle of the audience, and I could hear my coconspirators running down both aisles. Some were laughing, while others were emitting rebel yells. When the lights flipped back on, both aisles were lined with seventeen lesbians wearing their Lavender Menace T-shirts. There were hoots of laughter and I joined the others in the aisles. Then Rita yelled to members of the audience, "Who wants to join us?"

"I do; I do," several replied.

Then Rita also pulled off her Lavender Menace T-shirt. Again, there were gasps, but underneath she had on another one. More laughter. The audience was on our side.

MARTHA SHELLEY

We ran up and grabbed the microphone and said, "We want our issue addressed." The woman who was in charge of the microphone up there said, "Well, what does everybody else think? Do we want to continue with the speakers that we have invited? Do we want to open up this issue?" And everybody wanted to open up the issue. So we made speeches. I was one of them. I still have a picture of myself standing there holding a microphone and shooting off my mouth.

RITA MAE BROWN

I said, "There wasn't much light in this room, but there was heat." And that's how I started. I just said, this is not the way to do this. We need to find common cause. I couldn't tell you word for word what I said. And I said, you're doing to us what men do to you. That got through.

And then other people spoke, and some of the women in the audience really began to listen. They really began to get it, partly because the people who spoke were respectful. Nobody was screaming and hollering and talking about how terribly abused they were. That gets you nothing. And I think we made a real difference. I'm proud of that moment. I actually am.

PHYLLIS CHESLER

They then led a speak-out on lesbianism—the oppression of women who were lesbians, the hard work that they did in the movement, and being forced to hide in the movement was not acceptable. They talked about needing a home in the movement.

ANSELMA DELL'OLIO

When they rushed the stage and were all in their Lavender Menace T-shirts, I thought it was kind of fun, but I felt bad for Betty because she kind of got a raw deal. You know? It was an unfortunate thing to say but I understood exactly where she was coming from. She didn't want the movement to be taken over by the lesbians. She thought that was a mistake. It was going to turn off the 90 percent of the country that isn't. You know?

She was worried about a movement that was promoting lesbianism as the only way to be a true feminist. We got a lot of that in the movement at that point, by the way. There was a lot of pressure to sleep with women. Like you're not a real feminist if you don't, and you're hung up. I allowed myself to be raked in a couple of times and then said, "Sorry. Not my cup of tea."

RITA MAE BROWN

Our position paper, "The Woman-Identified Woman," hit this congress like a bombshell. Seven of us worked on it.

> "The Woman-Identified Woman," by Radicalesbians[*]
> By virtue of being brought up in a male society, we have internalized the male culture's definition of ourselves. That definition consigns us to sexual and family functions, and excludes us from defining and shaping the terms of our lives. . . . We are authentic, legitimate, real to the extent that we are the property of some man whose name we bear. To be a woman who belongs to no man is to be invisible, pathetic, inauthentic, unreal. He confirms his image of us—of what we have to be in order to be acceptable by him—but not our real selves.

---

[*] The authors of this manifesto were Rita Mae Brown, Cynthia Funk, Lois Hart, Karla Jay, Artemis March, Ellen Shumsky, and Barbara XX.

KARLA JAY

"Woman-Identified Woman" became an oft-reprinted classic because it summed up so much of what we as radical lesbians thought about ourselves. It started by defining a lesbian as "the rage of all women condensed to the point of explosion." The true lesbian, we wrote, acted "in accordance with her inner compulsion to be a more complete and freer human being."

"The Woman-Identified Woman," by Radicalesbians

Only women can give to each other a new sense of self. That identity we have to develop with reference to ourselves, and not in relation to men. This consciousness is the revolutionary force from which all else will flow, for ours is an organic revolution. . . . It is the primacy of women relating to women, of women creating a new consciousness of and with each other, which is at the heart of women's liberation, and the basis for the cultural revolution. Together we must find, reinforce, and validate our authentic selves.

KARLA JAY

Though the manifesto was in some ways a daring and radical assertion of lesbian pride, in other ways it was cautious and conservative. Nowhere does the document discuss lesbianism in terms of sexual behavior. We chose to downplay our sexuality because our primary goal was to make a political point, and back then the vision of a lesbian in bed conjured up an image of perversion, not radicalism.

MURIEL FOX

Many people said, "We must say that lesbianism is a feminist issue." And some of us, including me, thought it was too early for that; we would turn off the housewives. And within two years the people who said lesbianism was a feminist issue won. At the NOW national conference in 1974 when I was elected chair of the board, NOW voted that lesbianism was a feminist issue.

RITA MAE BROWN

The congress shot me up and out as though from a cannon. Women knew who I was. My deeds flashed across the country to other women. Whether they scorned or admired me, people began to realize I had a few things to offer.

SUSAN BROWNMILLER

I call it the Congress to Divide Women. I didn't get to the congress until Sunday because I was working. When I walked in, looking for a warm bath of sisterhood, Susan Frankel, from my consciousness-raising group West Village-One, greeted me with a nervous warning, "They're organizing a petition against you." At a class workshop, they decided to have a petition against me for seeking to rise to fame on the back of the women's movement.[*]

PHYLLIS CHESLER

The Chinese Cultural Revolution in Feminist America is what I called it.

SUSAN BROWNMILLER

My accusers, some of whom I recognized, were trembling as they read their resolution aloud. When they got to the part about me, I leaped up and bellowed, "That's *my* name you're using, *sisterrrs!*" Necks craned. The class-workshop women looked away and continued reading, arm in arm.

After they finished, discussion on the resolution was brief. Rita Mae Brown spoke for it. Eyes flashing, she skipped down the aisle, rapping about growing up in the South as poor white trash. For her finale, she sassed, "We don't need spokespeople and we don't need leaders. All women can speak, and all women can write." Her rhetoric brought down the house. Rita Mae, at twenty-five, was not yet a published author.[†]

When the applause for Rita Mae died down, the NOW women rose in my defense. The resolution was defeated by a comfortable margin. I was to watch the radical women's movement turn on its own people many times during the next decade. Eventually I grew fairly philosophical about it. A certain amount of cannibalizing seems to go with the territory whenever activists gather to promote social change.

---

[*] At the same conference, Anselma Dell'Olio announced she would be leaving the women's movement. She presented her paper, "Divisiveness and Self-Destruction in the Women's Movement," in which she described the vicious attacks she suffered from her radical fellow feminists for giving speeches and appearing on television.

[†] Rita Mae Brown's first book, the bestselling lesbian coming-of-age novel *Rubyfruit Jungle*, was published in 1973 and would become a classic in its genre. She went on to have a prolific writing career. Among several books and screenplays, Brown has also written fifty-six mysteries, many of them featuring cats.

17

The Whitney Isn't With-It

FAITH RINGGOLD

It was not until 1970 that I got involved in the women's movement. In this year I became a feminist because I wanted to help my daughters, other women, and myself aspire to something more than a place behind a good man. The "Liberated" Biennale, the Whitney demonstrations, and the Flag Show* were my first out-from-behind-the-men actions. In the 1960s I had rationalized that we were all fighting for the same issues and why shouldn't the men be in charge?

The first demonstration at a museum by a group of Black artists was in 1968 in front of the Whitney Museum—the people at the Whitney asked that question: "Oh, how many Black artists are there?" And the Black artist was constantly in the position of trying to number and say how many we are. Well, what happened is that when the opportunities increased for the Black artist, I thought I was included in that. But I found out later that they really meant men.

---

* Faith Ringgold, one of the organizers of the "People's Flag Show," an art exhibition that protested the war in Vietnam at the Judson Memorial Church in New York in November 1970, was arrested with white male artists Jon Hendricks and Jean Toche and charged with desecration of the flag. They became known as the "Judson Three," and members of the Left rallied to their defense. They were convicted, but the ruling was eventually overturned.

MICHELE WALLACE

In the fall of 1969, I went off to Howard University, a place designed to acquaint you with the shortcomings of Black female status if ever there was one. Between the fraternities and the Black Power antics, misogyny ran amok on a daily basis down there.

In the spring of 1970, I transferred to City College of New York. In my absence, New York had become a seething hotbed of all kinds of feminist activity. Faith and I were very shortly radicalized within the frenetic and inclusive goings-on of the downtown art scene. . . .

In every conversation with every man I met, they wanted to explain to me, "Sister"—everything was "Sister"—"Sister, your mind is messed up. These white women have gotten to you." And there was no concept that there could possibly be feminism that wasn't white.

I wanted to be a writer and I wanted to be taken seriously. And I had ideas. And so that brought me into conflict with almost every Black man I met.

I founded WSABAL in 1970 when I was eighteen years old. It stands for Women Students and Artists for Black Art Liberation and it developed under my mother's direction and prompting and support. My idea was to found a Black feminist art organization, but I knew there weren't that many Black women who were interested in feminism. Trying to get them together on anything was like trying to herd cats. So I named it WSABAL because it meant that you didn't have to be Black; you didn't have to be a woman; and you could be a student. I mean it was simply for Black art liberation. So that was me and my mother and whomever else we could round up at the time—a daring bank of people.

LUCY LIPPARD

I first met Faith Ringgold in 1968 when she was already a force to be reckoned with, having made civil rights paintings and good trouble for several years. She was smart, unafraid, and glamorous in her African garb, becoming a visible figure in the early feminist protests of New York's art institutions and joining Black colleagues in demanding that MoMA open a Martin Luther King Jr. Wing. In 1970, she was a cofounder of the Ad Hoc Women's Artists' Committee with Brenda Miller, Poppy Johnson, and, finally, me.

MICHELE WALLACE

So the Ad Hoc committee protested at the Whitney. They had an annual every year, every other year it was sculpture or it was painting. That year was sculpture.

LUCY LIPPARD

The percentage of women artists in the Whitney Annual was pathetic. We wrote them and we said come visit women's studios and you can find more good art. And then they did go to more women's studios and so there were really quite a few more women in that Annual.* We sent out a press release before the Whitney Annual that said the Whitney was founded by a woman and the head of the board of trustees was a woman and the Whitney was going to have 50 percent women in all their exhibitions, and 50 percent non-white, which is not a term I would use anymore.

MICHELE WALLACE

I wrote from WSABAL to the Whitney with the names, phone numbers, and addresses of five or six Black women artists that I would recommend that they include in their sculpture biennial.

FAITH RINGGOLD

[Betye] Saar and [Barbara] Chase-Riboud became the first Black women to be in the Whitney Annual; more to the point, they were the first Black women ever to be exhibited at the Whitney Museum of American Art.†

We decided to demonstrate during the opening to make our point. We had to get our demonstrators inside, since the opening was by invitation only, so we printed fake tickets and distributed them outside the museum on the night of the opening to anyone who wanted to demonstrate. A guard with an ultraviolet detector confiscated over a hundred forged tickets; nevertheless, we got in a lot of people. Once inside, we mingled with the crowd. Museum officials knew something was afoot as rumors began to spread that there was to be a demonstration that night.

At a predetermined time, Lucy Lippard and I began to blow our whistles.

MICHELE WALLACE

There were whistles and there were eggs. Women had raw eggs and they

---

* In 1969, only 8 of the 143 artists exhibited in the Whitney Annual were women. After protests from the women's art groups, the 1970 Annual numbers improved, with 21 women artists out of 103 exhibitors. Between 1965 and 1970, the Museum of Modern Art exhibited seventy-one one-man shows, and *one* one-woman show; none was by Black artists. On the West Coast, the statistics were no better. In 1971, only 1 percent of work shown at the LA County Museum of Art was by women artists.

† In 1972, the Washington, DC–based abstract painter Alma Thomas (born 1891) would become the first Black woman artist to have a solo show at the Whitney.

would put them in different places. So, if you touch them, of course you get egg yolk all over. Our eggs were black. My mother boiled our eggs and painted them black, and in red 50 PERCENT was painted on the egg.

FAITH RINGGOLD

The women came toward the center of the main gallery on the second floor. We continued to blow. The people gathered around us and we formed a big circle sitting on the floor. Then we got up and walked around chanting "Fifty percent women, fifty percent women."

Throughout the show we demonstrated every weekend, blowing police whistles and singing off-key.

LUCY LIPPARD

We picketed every Saturday for four weeks. We projected women's slides on the façade of the Whitney. We put unused Tampaxes in the bathroom, marked 50% WOMEN. We painted 50% WOMEN on the mirrors in the ladies room with lipstick. We did fake docent tours. We found out if you just dressed decently, which most of us didn't usually, and stood in a corner with three or four people around you, and started talking about the art, that people would gather thinking you were the docent. And then we could give them all our propaganda.

Flier:

TO THE VIEWING PUBLIC FOR THE 1970 WHITNEY AN-
NUAL EXHIBITION:

Don't Despair!

If this exhibition leaves you cold, if you find that it doesn't have much life, or meaning, or excitement for you, don't jump to the conclusion that you're "just not with it"! There's another possibility: THE WHIT-
NEY ISN'T WITH IT!!!! . . .

WE'RE NOT SATISFIED! WE WANT MORE! WE HAVE BEEN DEMANDING FIFTY PER CENT, AND WE'RE GOING TO KEEP RIGHT ON UNTIL WE GET IT.

Even we don't know the potential of women artists in this country, because we've never had a chance to find out. ON TO FIFTY PER CENT!!!

MICHELE WALLACE

We would go into the museums and just disturb the peace. That was the idea. We did it at the Guggenheim and at the Museum of Modern Art.

LUCY LIPPARD

We really went at MoMA: we wanted a women's wing, we wanted a people-of-color wing, and the MoMA sort of had talks with us.

LYNN HERSHMAN LEESON

We had nothing to lose because they wouldn't even look at the work, much less show it, much less buy it, much less write about it. You had to do outrageous things like that. You had to really throw yourself into the culture and not look back.

MICHELE WALLACE

The women's art movement was by itself. What I would call the mainstream of the progressive feminist movement had very little interest in art. I mean, there was one person, Pat Mainardi, who was a painter. She was in Redstockings. Pat Mainardi was very important to my mother.

Everybody came to our house to meet Mom. But for the most part, there wasn't a lot of overlap between visual art and these other forms of progressive politics in the women's movement.

HARMONY HAMMOND

One of the things that grew out of those actions was something called the Women's Art Registry. When we would try to hold a museum or a gallery accountable and ask, "Why aren't there more women in the show?" They'd say, "Well, we didn't discriminate. There would be more women if we only knew who they were." Once we had the registry, we'd say, "Here's six hundred for starters. Sit here and look at these." It was that aggressive in the beginning. I mean it was there for anyone to use and it was used by a lot of people. Because instead of going around to studios, you could go through all these slides and reduce it down to a number of artists that perhaps you were interested in for an article or a show.

LUCY LIPPARD

A Women's Art Registry made it clear that a large number of female artists were working on a par with men.

18

An Idea Whose Time Has Come

By sheer coincidence, three distinct feminist victories fought by different activists in different cities collided on one day—August 10, 1970. The Equal Rights Amendment passed with wide margins in the US House of Representatives, feminists occupied the Statue of Liberty, and New York mayor John Lindsay signed a law banning the city's "Men's Only" bars and restaurants.

IVY BOTTINI

The ERA simply stated, "Men and women shall have equal rights throughout the United States and every place subject to its jurisdiction. Congress shall have power to enforce this article by appropriate legislation." Doesn't sound all that radical, right? Yet, until 1970, the ERA had been stuck for twenty-five years in a congressional committee controlled by Emmanuel Celler, the Democratic congressman from Brooklyn. Twenty-five years!

To get the ERA going, my chapter of NOW organized a picket line at Celler's home [in Brooklyn]. After a week of demonstrators in front of his house from early morning well into the evening, Celler finally invited another NOW member and me in to negotiate with him. I guess he saw the angry women and the handwriting on the wall.*

---

* The chairman of the House Judiciary Committee, Brooklyn Democrat Emmanuel Celler (age eighty-

MARTHA GRIFFITHS

When I went to Hale Boggs, who was then the majority leader, and he was from Louisiana, to ask him to sign the ERA discharge petition he said to me, "Now, Martha, when you get to number two hundred, I'm going to sign it. I want to be number two hundred." Well, every day I went in and the first thing I did was look at the discharge petition and see who had signed it.

We had a tremendous lobbying effort. The National Business and Professional Women, the largest group of organized women in America in any club, were having a convention in Hawaii. When I began to get the discharge signatures, I would call them every night and tell them who had not signed, and the next morning they would have a breakfast meeting, and they would tell the entire convention. Virginia Allan and Marguerite Rawalt did this. They would tell them that I had called, that these people hadn't signed, and they should send telegrams immediately, and they did. It was an absolutely incredible performance because those women lived all over the country. There were clubs in every congressional district.

Every congressman was getting a message to sign the discharge petition. When I had gotten to about 150, I had gone to Jerry Ford, who was then the minority leader, and told him, "Jerry, the Republican Party endorsed the Equal Rights Amendment first, not the Democratic Party, and you have very few signers on this discharge petition, so you're really going to look very bad. Please get some signers." Well, he didn't do anything until I got two hundred, and when I got two hundred and I had gotten Hale Boggs to sign it, I was called off the floor . . . and when I came back in, I could hardly get in the door. There was a line of people in front of the Speaker's desk, and I asked someone what it was, and they said, "This is the group that's signing the discharge petition on equal rights." . . . Jerry had gotten seventeen signers for me, and at that moment, that amendment was on the floor. We only had an hour's debate, which worked out to the very best, because all who wanted to speak wanted to laugh at it, and I could not have stood two hours of laughter.

---

two), was Representative Martha Griffith's nemesis, whom she had butted heads with over the sex provision in Title VII in 1964. Celler was a civil rights supporter, but a dyed-in-the-wool sexist. During his twenty-two-year reign as chairman, Celler refused to hold hearings on the Equal Rights Amendment, or to allow the bill to reach the House floor for a vote. A discharge petition required signatures of more than half of the members of the House, which meant a minimum of 218. With its success, the bill could be released from the committee's jurisdiction and sent to the floor for a vote.

Congressional Record, August 10, 1970

Mrs. GRIFFITHS

Mr. Speaker, for 47 consecutive years this amendment has been introduced into the Congress of the United States. For 26 years both parties in their political conventions have endorsed it; the Republican Party has endorsed it for 30 years. Yet it has been 22 years since the Judiciary Committee of the House has even held a hearing on it. On the eve of the 50th birthday of women suffrage, it appears reasonable to me that the proponents of this legislation, who are more than a majority of this House, have a right to have this legislation discussed. . . .

The Supreme Court . . . has on not one single occasion granted to women the basic protection of the 5th or the 14th amendment. The only right guaranteed to women today by the Constitution of the United States is the right to vote and to hold public office. . . . I ask you, Mr. Speaker, to support the discharge motion; to vote for the motion for immediate consideration. . . . Let me paraphrase the greatest suffragette of them all—Sojourner Truth, "Ain't I a woman?"

Mr. CELLER

Mr. Speaker, I rise in opposition to the discharge petition. . . . What we are being asked to do is to vote on a constitutional amendment, the consequences of which are unexamined, its meaning non-defined, and its risks uncalculated. . . . According to Prof. Paul Freund of the Harvard Law School . . . every provision of law concerning women would raise a constitutional issue which would have to be resolved in the courts. . . . Can we afford to grope in the dark without any concrete evidence? . . .

Feminists clamor for equal rights. Nobody can deny that women should have equality under the law. But ever since Adam gave up his rib to make a woman throughout the ages, we have learned that physical, emotional, psychological and social differences exist and dare not be disregarded.

Neither the National Women's Party nor the delightful, delectable and dedicated gentlelady from Michigan [Mrs. Griffiths] can change nature.

Let me say there is as much difference between a male and a female as between a horse chestnut and a chestnut horse—and as the French say, "Vive le difference." Any attempt to pass an amendment that promises to wipe out the effects of these differences is about as abortive as trying to fish in a desert—and you cannot do that.

There is no really genuine equality, and I defy anyone to tell me what "equality" in this amendment means. Even your five fingers—one is not equal to the other—they are different.

Mr. GERALD R. FORD

Mr. Speaker, this amendment should really be unnecessary. But it clearly is mandatory because women today do not have equal rights. This amendment will give them those most valued rights—the rights to a job, to a promotion, to a pension, to equal social security benefits. . . . There is no denying that these rights are different for women than for men.

The great French writer Victor Hugo said: "Greater than the tread of mighty armies is an idea whose time has come." There is no question that the Women's Equal Rights Amendment is just such an idea. Its time has come just as surely as did the 19th Amendment to the Constitution 50 years ago, giving women the right to vote.

New York Times, August 11, 1970, "Equal Rights Plan for
Women Voted by House 350-15," by Eileen Shanahan
WASHINGTON, Aug. 10—The House of Representatives, by the overwhelming vote of 350 to 15, passed today a constitutional amendment prohibiting discrimination on the basis of sex. It was the first time that the House had ever voted on the amendment, which has been introduced every year since 1923. The one-sidedness of the vote surprised supporters of the amendment. Even though a two-thirds majority is required for approval of a constitutional amendment, there were more than 100 votes to spare.

MARTHA GRIFFITHS

I felt that I was going to win. I can count as easily as anybody, and I had the votes counted. . . . I never thought of it particularly as a vast historic moment which it really was. I never thought of it in terms of, this is really the wave of tomorrow. I never considered that part. All I knew was that I had a job to do, and I had done it.*

---

* The Senate then passed an amended bill that exempted women from the military draft—the most controversial issue raised by the ERA. This amended ERA didn't fly with Representative Martha Griffiths and her coalition, so the bill didn't advance. She would work to bring it up for another vote the following year.

IVY BOTTINI

Another one of our significant actions took place in early August of 1970 at the Statue of Liberty. On August 10, 1970, one hundred or so women gathered at the lower Manhattan pier to take the tourist boat to the Statue of Liberty, splitting up into two boats to be less conspicuous. When both boats arrived on Liberty Island, I took my larger group up the hill from the boat ramp to the grassy area at the foot of the statue.

JACQUELINE CEBALLOS

We didn't have any trouble running upstairs. We had strong women like Rita Mae Brown. When we got to the top of the stairs we couldn't get into the balcony. The guards stopped us. Mayor Lindsay called and he said, "Let the women do what they want to do." So, give Mayor Lindsay the credit. So, then we got onto the balcony.

IVY BOTTINI

As I looked up from the ground, I saw the fifteen or so women gather on the pedestal. I could see a lot of bustling movement as they removed their bulges, which were actually sections of an oil cloth banner that they had wrapped around their bodies in pieces. They then attached the segments and stretched them out along the top of the pedestal. Within minutes they had dropped and hooked to the railing a forty-foot-long, four-foot-high banner.

> New York *Daily News*, August 11, 1970,
> "Miss Liberty Ours, Say Gals," by Anthony Burton
>
> The Statue of Liberty was drafted into the women's liberation move-ment yesterday. . . . The involuntary induction at her home on Liberty Island in the Upper Bay began at 10:40 a.m., when a banner saying, "Women of the World Unite!" was unfurled immediately, below Miss Liberty's feet by a group of women's rights activists. Alongside, other banners fluttered down, reminding viewers that the women's lib groups are planning a national strike on Wednesday, August 26.

IVY BOTTINI

Then they raised their fists. It was spectacular. That was until I saw three police boats and two fire boats coming toward us. For the first time, it oc-curred to me that we were on federal land and could go to federal prison. . . .

From the deck of one of the boats, one police officer yelled up at us through a megaphone, "What are you doing up there?"

I shouted back, "We're walking and we're singing."

His reply, "How long do you think you will be?" . . . A few minutes after this conversation, the fire boats began to shoot streams of water out into the air just as they did at times of civil celebrations, and then those boats and the police boats started their sirens. They were joining in our demonstration!

JACQUELINE CEBALLOS

Bella Abzug was running for Congress. Everybody knew Bella and loved her, and she came and visited the island because she realized it was important for her to be there and of course she would get a lot of press.*

SHERRYE HENRY

When I moved to New York from Memphis in 1968 and then divorced in 1970, I cared about women's issues, but it never occurred to me to call myself a feminist. That was too far out for me, until I got divorced. And then suddenly a number of things happened. I bought a little apartment across the street from where we had lived at 6 West Seventy-Seventh but I couldn't get a mortgage, because women weren't allowed to get a mortgage unless they had a man to sign for them, which was a real problem for me. And then when I went to get a credit card, I couldn't get a credit card, because you couldn't get an AmericanExpress card without a man signing for you. So, it just seemed like every place I turned, I was hamstrung, because I was just a woman.†

Then, at the same time, I found out that women were discouraged from serving on juries in New York because they were considered too emotionally disturbed during their menstrual cycles, and couldn't be counted on to give

---

*   This was not the first time that feminists protested at the Statue of Liberty. At the October 28, 1886, unveiling ceremony, a flotilla of ships crowded in the waters by Liberty Island underneath the 305-foot-tall copper statue of the Roman goddess Libertas, a symbol of freedom and democracy. A boat carrying two hundred suffragists, wishing to highlight the hypocrisy of the celebration in a nation where women did not have the right to vote, flew the suffrage flag on the bow and unfurled a large white banner emblazoned with the words "New York State Woman Suffrage Association."

†   Before the passage of the Equal Credit Opportunity Act in 1974, banks and credit card companies routinely denied women access to credit unless a father or a husband cosigned for them. This practice often placed women, regardless of their salary or education level, at the mercy of their fathers and/or husbands in order to conduct most business dealings.

a good verdict.* I also found out at exactly the same time that if a woman was raped, she couldn't bring charges against the guy unless she had a witness who had seen the rape.†

MURIEL FOX

One of our big issues was Title II on public accommodations, which said you cannot discriminate in public accommodations on the basis of race, but not sex.‡ McSorley's was a bar in New York that didn't let women in, so we picketed that along with the Oak Room restaurant at the Plaza Hotel.§

SHERRYE HENRY

One evening, soon after I moved to New York, my friend Barbara Howar and I were walking down Fifty-Seventh Street on our way to dinner. We were a little early, so we decided to have a drink first at the Russian Tea Room, which was a favorite of mine. I loved the Tea Room. The place was empty, so we shuffled up onto bar stools and ordered our drinks. But the bartender said, "No, no, no. I can't serve you. We don't allow unaccompanied women at our bar." I said, "Well, wait a minute. There's a homeless man in the gutter outside. If we invited him to join us for a drink would you serve us then?" We didn't wait for an answer. We just walked out of there. We were both so pissed. It turned out that just at that time, I had taken a new job at Channel 13. I was on air twice a week and one of the first subjects that I produced for myself was the problem of certain restaurants and bars in New York City that wouldn't allow women to come in unaccompanied. So,

---

* Jury service in New York was voluntary for women but mandatory for men. Many states prohibited or discouraged women from serving on juries until the Supreme Court ruled in 1975 in *Taylor v. Louisiana* that it was unconstitutional to exclude women from jury duty.

† Up until 1974, New York's rape laws were some of the most draconian in the country, and rape victims were required to show "corroborating evidence"—either physical evidence or a witness.

‡ Title II of the 1964 Civil Rights Act prohibits discrimination in public accommodations on the basis of race, color, religion, and national origin, but it does *not* mention sex. States slowly reversed their bans on sex discrimination in public places, which New York did in August 1970.

§ A sample of the many restaurants and bars across the country that restricted or prohibited women in 1969 include Stouffer's in Pittsburgh; Schroder's Cafe in San Francisco; Whyte's, Sardi's, and P.J. Clarke's in New York; the London Chop House in Detroit; The Retreat in Washington, DC; Wales Coffee Shop and the Bull and Bear in Chicago; the Clam Broth House in Hoboken; the Biltmore Hotel bar in New York; the Continental Plaza bar in Chicago; the William Penn bar in Pittsburgh; the Monteleone bar in New Orleans; the Men's Grill in Oakland's Leamington Hotel; and the Viking Room of Minneapolis's Radisson Hotel. During "Public Accommodations Week," between February 9 and 15, 1969, NOW staged "eat-ins" and "drink-ins" in cities all over the country to expose the "men's only" gender discrimination in public places where men were conducting business.

I asked the owner of the Russian Tea Room to come, a woman by the name of Faith Stewart-Gordon. I had the son of the owner of McSorley's Old Ale House, and I had the maître d' of the men's bar at the Hilton Hotel—all these places that wouldn't allow women to come in unaccompanied.

So, I ended up, at ten o'clock at night, on a live show with these two guys and Faith Stewart-Gordon in front of me. And I asked each one of them why they wouldn't let women come in. And when I got to Faith she said, "Well, my husband owned the restaurant. I've only gotten this in his estate, but he never wanted women at the bar because he thought it would lower the decorum of the bar." And I said, "Well, Faith, let me tell you *my* story." So I told her my story of being turned away from the Russian Tea Room bar, and I said, "Faith, would I have lowered the decorum of your bar?" And the truth is that she didn't like the situation, and she banged on her chair. And she said, "Damn it, women can come into my bar from now on."

New York *Daily News*, August 11, 1970,
"14 High Heels Stir Sawdust at McSorley's," by John Toscano

Behind the bar in McSorley's Old Ale House is an ancient ledger whose crackled, yellow pages record the tavern's history since it opened on Feb. 17, 1854.

Danny O'Connell Kirwan, whose mother owns the bar but has never set foot inside, opened the musty ledger at 3PM yesterday and wrote: "God bless us all on this occasion."

The occasion was a new city law barring sex discrimination in public places. And when Mayor Lindsay signed it yesterday afternoon, McSorley's threw in the bar towel and admitted female drinkers for the first time in 116 years. . . .

"We've been waiting for this for years," said long-haired Amanda Biddle who stood patiently outside the ale house at 15 East Seventh Street for two hours before the bill was signed into law.

The male customers greeted the invasion glumly, but refrained from carrying out earlier threats to douse the new patrons with ale. "We have to act like gentlemen at the wake," a red-bearded drinker said.

MURIEL FOX

Another cause we adopted around this time was the airlines. United Airlines had what they called an "executive flight" between New York and Chicago— one flight in the morning and one flight in the evening—and women were not allowed on that executive flight. A mailroom boy could get on it, but not a woman executive. And they'd have the stewardesses lighting cigars for the men—imagine the situation.

United Airlines advertisement

Relax after a busy day on this special DC-6 Mainliner flight. You'll enjoy the informal, club-like atmosphere. Smoke your pipe or cigar, if you wish, and make yourself comfortable by using the pair of slippers provided. A full-course steak dinner is table-served by the two stewardesses aboard. It's a delicious meal, prepared by experienced Continental chefs.

MURIEL FOX

NOW fought this. We filed legal complaints and did press releases. I wrote a letter to the CEO of United Airlines on my Carl Byoir vice president letterhead to show that I was somebody substantial attacking these executive flights. And when the CEO of United Airlines got it, he called the CEO of my agency over the weekend and complained. Monday morning the Carl Byoir CEO took me into his office and chewed me out. He was right, I should not have used the company letterhead.[*]

The first day that the Oak Room opened its doors to women, I had lunch there with my brother and it was no big deal. The world didn't end. This happened so many times. We would open things up and it worked out fine.

---

[*]   NOW filed complaints with the Civil Aeronautics Board and picketed the Chicago headquarters of United Airlines in 1969, with signs like "Go Fly Yourself." United ended the men-only flight, which they had operated since 1953, in 1970.

19

Don't Iron While the Strike Is Hot— Women's Strike for Equality

IVY BOTTINI

The August 26 Women's Strike for Equality which Betty announced in March was the project that kept me busy during the planning of the Statue of Liberty caper. The idea was to have women all over the country go "on strike" from their regular activities for the day and rally and march against women's inequality instead.

Another group that unexpectedly took an interest in the march was the FBI. They tried to recruit Jill Ward, one of the women training to be a march marshal, to be an informant. Their method was not very subtle. During the training period for the marshals, Jill lost her wallet. She was greatly relieved when she got a call from a guy who said he had found it. He suggested they meet at a local café where he would return it to her. She went. The man did indeed have her wallet, but he also had an agenda. It seems he had somehow stolen the wallet in order to get to talk to her. He informed her that he was FBI and offered her $750 a month, a lot of money in those days, to spy on NYC NOW. National NOW was kind of the public relations wing of the movement, but my chapter, NYC NOW, was the center of many of the large, organized actions. We had no idea why the FBI chose her. Maybe the FBI knew she had little money and thought she could be tempted. They were wrong. Jill refused the offer and came back and reported it to the chapter. Such attempts at infiltration were scary and disturbing, but at least they meant we were making some of the people who had power in the country pretty uncomfortable.

As president of NYC NOW, I was one of the major coordinators for the New York City march, expected to be the biggest in the country. It was quite a job. It took months of preparation to coordinate with the city and all the different women's organizations that wanted to take part. Yes, all these disparate feminist factions were fully united about something. Even Black women's organizations that had seen NOW and the women's movement in general as pretty much exclusively concerned with the issues of white middle-class women became part of the march.

ALIX KATES SHULMAN

We didn't know whether we'd be the same old handful multiplied by ten or a hundred or a thousand. We knew there were more groups than we could count. We knew that our supporters were everywhere by that time, because everywhere we took our message, we were treated like heroes almost as often as we were shouted down as devils. But we didn't know who was actually willing to take a stand, who would be willing to get out there and show their face. We knew what the police thought. They had refused the parade committee a permit to occupy more than one lane of Fifth Avenue.

MARY JEAN COLLINS

We didn't even know what we were doing, but we went to all the other groups in Chicago and we organized people to be part of it. We got the civic center, it's now the Daley Center, got the sound system, got this, got that, started organizing the leaflets, putting stuff up on the street everywhere.

Ann Scott was the NOW legislative vice president. She came up with that saying, "Don't Iron While the Strike Is Hot." Then Mary Ann Lupa made the poster with the iron. We put those up. We called it skulking in the middle of the night. We'd plaster the poster and leaflets up on telephone poles all over the city in the middle of the night, avoiding the police.

The press really helped. There was an article on the front page of the *Sun Times* the morning of the march. There was huge press a couple of days ahead of time. So, that was part of it.

Time, August 31, 1970, cover story

THESE are the times that try men's souls, and they are likely to get much worse before they get better. It was not so long ago that the battle of the sexes was fought in gentle, rolling Thurber country. Now the din is in earnest, echoing from the streets where pickets gather, the bars where women once were barred, and even connubial beds, where ideology can intrude at the unconscious drop of a male chauvinist epithet. This week, marking the 50th anniversary of the proclamation of the 19th Amendment granting women the vote, the diffuse, divided, but grimly determined Women's Liberation movement plans a nationwide protest day against the second sex's once and present oppression.

ALIX KATES SHULMAN

It started at Columbus Circle and then we marched down Fifth Avenue. I had my kids with me in the stroller. All these early feminist groups were there who had split off from each other in successive epiphanies, and the new ones I'd never heard of, grouped together for the first time. NOW, who'd organized the march, and Betty Friedan, who'd called for the strike, led off with a group of aged veterans suffragists, heroes from the first wave of feminism. Now we're in our eighties like those aged suffragists whom I so appreciated when they led off the strike.

They gave us a permit for one lane, but after we assembled, it was clear that we were going to take up the entire Fifth Avenue. At first, they tried to stop us, but they didn't have a chance, and we started marching all the way across Fifth Avenue. People were hanging out of windows in the buildings above. They were waving flags for us. There were some hecklers, but mostly it was only people who supported us.

JACQUELINE CEBALLOS

We demonstrated all morning, all over town and we told everybody to meet at four o'clock to start the march at Columbus Circle and then march down Fifth Avenue. I'll never forget. I had been on the Upper West Side, and when I turned the corner onto Fifth Avenue you couldn't see the end of the line. It was packed. We had been given a little route on one side of the street. We weren't supposed to go onto the street.

CAROLE DE SARAM

I joined Pat Lawrence and Marion Gannet, who lived in Queens near my home, and met them on the morning of August 26. They had with them the now famous "Women of the World Unite" banner they hung off the Statue of Liberty on August 10. As we gathered on one side of Fifth Avenue and Fifty-Ninth Street, thousands of women were appearing from all over. I still get chills remembering it. There was a bus of nurses from Connecticut wearing their nursing caps, women with baby carriages, all ages and types of women converging on Fifth Avenue, and entering into the park. We lined up behind the Socialist Workers Party women who had helped plan the march and had experience with anti–Vietnam War marches.

Traffic on Fifth Avenue was chaotic, with cars honking horns and unable to move. The Socialist Workers Party women shouted "Start marching and don't stop!" Surging forward behind them, we marched with the banner onto Fifth Avenue with Jacqui Ceballos marching in front of the banner, hollering at us "Move to the left and right with the banner!" and "Don't stop!"

JACQUELINE CEBALLOS

Carole De Saram, who was up in the front—blond, lovely, beautiful—had said, "When the whistle blows, let's take over the whole street." When the whistle blew, we just moved through. It was unbelievable.

CAROLE DE SARAM

The police tried to stop us, but we shouted and chanted, "Move on over or we'll move on over you!" until we took over Fifth Avenue with the banner. The crowds cheered and we marched on. It was exhilarating to see the thousands of people on the avenue.

BETTY FRIEDAN

Mayor Lindsay wouldn't close Fifth Avenue for our march, and I remember starting that march with the hoofs of policemen's horses trying to keep us confined to the sidewalk. I remember looking back, jumping up to see over marchers' heads. I never saw so many women; they stretched back for so many blocks you couldn't see the end. I locked one arm with my beloved Judge Dorothy Kenyon (who, at eighty-two, insisted on walking with me instead of riding in the car we had provided for her), and the other arm with a young woman on the other side. I said to the others in the front ranks, "Lock arms, sidewalk to sidewalk!" We overflowed till we filled the whole of Fifth Avenue. There were so many of us they couldn't stop us; they didn't even try.

JACQUELINE CEBALLOS
There were women like Dale Williams, who's no longer here. She had a big job in a Fifth Avenue building and she heard the women marching, "I'm coming down!" Many of them joined us. We'd say, "Join us, join us!" The line was absolutely fantastic. We took over the whole avenue.

ALIX KATES SHULMAN
Redstockings and the feminists and New York Radical Feminists, all pioneers then, Big Sisters and Black Women's Liberation and the National Coalition of American Nuns, and RAT, Radical Lesbians and Gay Activist Alliance and New Yorkers for Abortion Law Repeal, and Women In Childcare and Newsreel Women's Caucus and Media Women and Women Artists in Revolution.

And the Third World Women's Alliance and Spanish American Feminists and Women's Strike for Peace and Jeannette Rankin Rank and File and the YWCA and the Emma Goldman Brigade and the Alice Crimmins Brigade and the Stanton-Anthony Brigade and the League of Women Voters and High School Women's Coalition and the Lesbian Food Conspiracy and Betsy Ross Junior High Women's Liberation and Women in Publishing and Scuff Women and CORE Women and SNCC Women and SWP Women and the Young Socialist Alliance and International Socialist Women and Daughters of Bilitis, and half of Brooklyn, and It's All Right to Be a Woman theater and *Off Our Backs* and *Up From Under*, and *It Ain't Me Babe* and Afra and Lilith and the Group and Multitudes to Obliterate Misogyny. That's MOM.

And Columbia Barnard Women's Liberation and Queens College Women's Liberation and Brooklyn Women's Liberation and Westside Women's United and Westchester Women's Liberation and Bronx Feminists and Revolutionary Childcare Collective and Youth Against War and Fascism, YAWF, and Women of the Venceremos Brigade, who did harvesting of sugarcane in Cuba, and Spartacist Women and Maoist Women and National Welfare Rights Organization and Women Versus Connecticut and Professional Women's Caucus and Women for Bella Abzug and Women's International League for Peace and Freedom and the Joan Byrd Bail Fund and Independent Radical Women's Caucus, and hundreds of unidentified women wearing buttons of their own design, and hundreds of unaffiliated women carrying signs and women without labels and Men for Women's Rights, and a few independent men too.

BRENDA FEIGEN

It was amazing when I watched the crowds of women taking over all of Fifth Avenue, we just said, "we" being the collective multitudes, "Screw it," and we went through the entire avenue.

HOWARDENA PINDELL

I mean it was wall to wall. I remember just walking next to a white woman. And she was friendly. I don't remember seeing many Black women. But I remember it was really packed.

VIVIAN GORNICK

I was there and it was thrilling.

BRENDA FEIGEN

Gloria and I decided that we wanted to go to the march and have antiwar signs because we were very much opposed to the war, and Betty Friedan was running around saying neither the war nor lesbianism were feminist issues. That was Betty's big contribution to this whole huge mess. We were basically backlashing against it with these My Lai massacre signs.

New Yorker, September 5, 1970, "Liberation"

The harshest and grimmest sign was carried by Gloria Steinem, the beautiful feminist and writer for *New York* magazine. It showed a picture of victims of the My Lai massacre,* with the caption "The Masculine Mystique."

ALIX KATES SHULMAN

On the sidewalks and from windows of buildings along the route, people held up signs, unfurled banners and cheered, "Don't cook dinner tonight,

---

* Gruesome photographs taken by US Army photographer Ronald Haeberle of the bodies of several hundred Vietnamese civilians (mostly women and children) from the village of My Lai slaughtered by American infantrymen in 1968 became powerful images that exposed the savage immorality of the war.

starve a rat today. Clean the streets of rapists and sex murderers. Liberté, égalité, sororité. Don't iron while the strike is hot. Uppity women unite. Free our sisters, free ourselves." A few heckled and jeered and a few others giggled and many just stood and watched, but mostly the people along the streets chanted and cheered men and women alike, held up the clenched fist of solidarity or just grinned happy supportive grins.

FRANCES BEAL

We, the Third World Women's Alliance, were involved in that march down Fifth Avenue on August twenty-sixth of 1970. And there were fifty thousand women, and we carried a sign that said, "Hands off Angela Davis," because at that time, she was underground and the FBI was looking for her.* And we were approached by some people from NOW who said, "Take down that sign, because Angela Davis has nothing to do with women's liberation." So, we essentially responded, "She has *everything* to do with the kind of liberation we're talking about," in terms of being a political activist fighting oppression. So, you can see that there were some differences of opinion about that.

But on certain issues, we saw we could unite with people. The right to abortion, for example, was one of those things. There were certain things that spread across the classes that made up the different women that were for women's liberation, or feminists, if you wish. But they did not have to challenge the class structures that existed in society, and we felt that we had to do those things. So, it's not uncommon for us to see most of the women's movement made up of women of sort of middle-class or up backgrounds, whereas the working-class women, white and Black alike, but poor white women in particular, have very much been ignored by the women's movement, in the sense that it's a class of women that they have not put their money behind.

ELEANOR HOLMES NORTON

I marched down Fifth Avenue. As I recall it, I think I wore some kind of turban to send a message to Black women that we should be as much in-

---

* On August 9, 1970, Black communist intellectual Angela Davis, who was accused of providing the gun that her friend Jonathan Jackson used in an attempted jailbreak and murder of a judge at a Marin County courtroom, went underground. She was placed on the FBI's Ten Most Wanted List, and a nationwide manhunt ensued. Davis was captured two months later, on October 13. But in those few weeks, she became a cause célèbre and a powerful symbol of Black revolutionary resistance. While in prison in 1971, *The Black Scholar* published Davis's groundbreaking essay "Reflections on the Black Woman's Role in the Community of Slaves." "Free Angela Davis," became a rallying cry in left-leaning circles during her imprisonment and celebrated trial. Davis was acquitted on June 4, 1972, of all charges.

volved with women's rights as we should be with our rights as Black women, because Black women had not been fully enlisted in the women's rights movement at the time.

LYNN POVICH

Eleanor became the city Human Rights Commissioner in April 1970, she couldn't be our lawyer anymore, so Mel Wulf, who was the head of the ACLU, became our lawyer until we signed the agreement with *Newsweek* the morning of August 26, 1970, which was the day of the Women's Strike for Equality.*

Our office was on Fiftieth and Madison. So we joined the march. I don't remember if we had signs. Most people came out of their offices. The offices were just empty in Midtown. . . . There were women streaming out of buildings and onto the street and we took over the whole of Fifth Avenue.†

IVY BOTTINI

I was exultant and deeply moved, especially when I stepped off the street and stood up on tiptoes on the sidewalks as the march turned a corner to head for the rallying point. Stretched in front of me and behind me, filling the streets in all directions from sidewalk to sidewalk, were marchers who had joined in our cause. We had indeed created a serious and joyous—at least that day—movement and I had been a part of it. I was almost brought to tears. The anti–Vietnam war and civil rights movements were important, but this, I thought to myself, was the real revolution. We were changing people's lives. Everyone's.

HEATHER BOOTH

The march in Chicago was enormous. It was in a large square in front of the Civic Center building. It was the largest one-place demonstra-

---

* The agreement, which Eleanor Holmes Norton negotiated, was a memorandum of understanding in which *Newsweek* promised that it would make "substantial rather than token changes" to promote women as reporters, writers, and editors, but the agreement did not include specific goals or timetables. In 1972, after very little progress, fifty-one women filed a second discrimination complaint against *Newsweek* with the EEOC and the New York State Division of Human Rights. By June 1973, management agreed that one-third of the magazine's writers and domestic reporters would be female by December 1974, and the process of truly integrating women into the more senior levels of the editorial department began.

† Full disclosure: I worked as a reporter in *Newsweek*'s Washington bureau from 1989 to 1993, and filed stories regularly to Lucy Howard, who was a senior editor. I also knew Lynn Povich, who was also a senior editor and the first woman senior editor in the magazine's history. At the time, I knew nothing about their class-action lawsuit that benefited the next generation of women journalists, like me.

tion that I had seen to that point; and it was clear that this really was a movement.

MARY JEAN COLLINS

I was the master of ceremonies, or mistress of ceremonies, so I said whatever I said, and then I introduced each of the speakers. I walked up the stairs to the stage, and then to the podium, and I looked out at the crowd and it filled the entire plaza and the streets. Everything was filled. I was totally blown away. I couldn't believe it. I just couldn't believe what I saw. I would have been happy probably, with five thousand people, but it was huge. It was just an incredible experience. So, we did our speeches. Heather spoke on childcare, somebody else spoke on abortion. We had ten or eleven, twelve speakers, and all of the groups who turned people out, they were given an opportunity to speak.

HEATHER BOOTH

Our group had one speaker. One of the projects the Women's Liberation Union worked on was a group called Women Employed, which was about improving women's conditions in the workplace. And one of the targets for that was Kraft Foods, which wouldn't let women be in management positions because to be a manager you had to drive one of the little yellow trucks, and only men were allowed to drive the trucks. Women's hands, they said, were so much more suited to be secretaries because they had little fingers for the keys for the typewriters. So there was a whole suit against Kraft. One of the women—I think from Swift, a packing plant, another food corporation—brought her child to work, and was fired. She told the demonstration, and a group of the people from the demonstration went back with her to protest at Swift and she got her job back. So again, it was this message that if you organize, you can win.

MARY JEAN COLLINS

We had Black speakers. There was Clara Day, who was an international rep for the Teamsters Union. She was a very strong feminist and active member of NOW. Addie Wyatt was from the Amalgamated Meat Cutters Union. She was active in NOW, and in PUSH*—she was our connection

---

* The Chicago-based People United to Save Humanity advocated for Black self-help, social justice, and

to Reverend Jesse Jackson. She was very helpful with the Black community. I mean, people have the wrong idea that this was only a white movement. At least in Chicago, we had a lot of Black participation from the union women primarily. We didn't only speak for the women who were trying to get management jobs, we tried to make things better for the women who were doing clerical and factory jobs.

UNITED STATES DEPARTMENT OF JUSTICE
FEDERAL BUREAU OF INVESTIGATION
Office: Washington, D.C.
Title: Women's liberation movement
Information concerning—Miscellaneous, Period of Activity May 1–October 30, 1970
On August 26, 1970, Special Agents of the FBI observed the following in connection with the above-described scheduled activity for the day: . . . At 11:20 a.m. WILMA SCOTT HEDIE, Chairman and National Board Member of NOW, made several announcements regarding the day's activity . . . the demonstrators which swelled in numbers en route to about 900 marched to Farragut Square via Connecticut Avenue, N.W. The participants carried placards inscribed as follows: "Women Strike for Free Abortion on Demand; Twenty-Four Hour Child Care Centers; Women Unite for the Right to Control Our Own Bodies; Women are People Too; Men to be Sure of Your Masculinity Use Masculine Hygiene Deodorant; Liberated Mommies Make for Healthy Kids; Our Founding Fathers Were Male Chauvinists." . . .

The program at Farragut Square commenced at approximately 11:40 a.m. with musical and singing entertainment. Speeches then followed which dealt with equal rights for women. A petition was circulated for signatures which would be presented to Senator MIKE MANSFIELD at 3 p.m. today by the group, demanding equal rights for women inasmuch as an equal rights amendment was then under consideration by Congress. . . . Before the demonstration terminated

---

civil rights. In 1971, Jesse Jackson renamed the organization Operation PUSH, and it eventually merged with the National Rainbow Coalition. Dr. T. R. M. Howard, who assisted Heather Booth and the Jane underground abortion organization, served on the board of directors.

an announcement was made that ETTA HORN of the NWRO [National Welfare Rights Organization] would lead a group to the D.C. Women's Detention Center. . . . The group marched up and down in front of the center chanting "Freedom," "Free Our Sisters." . . . No arrests were made.

GINNY BERSON

I went to the rally on Farragut Square and I heard this woman speak, her name was Joan Carmody. She was on the stage, and she came out as a lesbian. This was thrilling to me. People knew her. She was part of the lesbian community, and I didn't even know there was a lesbian community. I got her phone number and I called her up and I said, "I can't tell you who I am, but I want to tell you how important it was to me to hear you say that you were a lesbian from the stage and thank you for doing that." I remember that made a big impression on me.

LYNN POVICH

We went down to Bryant Park on Forty-Second Street behind the New York Public Library, where Eleanor [Holmes Norton] was one of the speakers. I don't remember what she said. I don't think she talked about the *Newsweek* case. But what we all realized was that it wasn't just us. It was like all these women were facing the same thing, and that gave us steam and confidence and support to feel like we had done the right thing.

New Yorker, September 5, 1970, "Liberation"

When a representative of the Third World Women's Alliance attacked the strike's sponsors as "reformist" and went on to say, "The only answer is revolution—to smash the capitalist monster through armed struggle," the crowd listened politely, but when Eleanor Holmes Norton stood up, she was more enthusiastically received. "I wear the dress of my African forebears not to be senselessly symbolic but to emphasize that black women have a stake in equality for all women," she said. "Sex, like color, is a meaningless criterion and an oppressive criterion when it is made a condition for a job. Women, like me, want to work for reasons of self-fulfillment, but like men, most men, women work because they have no choice. The average working woman is thirty-nine years old and lives with a husband who needs her salary to supplement his income. Do these sound like women with time on their hands?"

JACQUELINE CEBALLOS

When we got to the New York Public Library and had a stage, that's when Betty Friedan talked.

Betty Friedan speech

After tonight, the politics of this nation will never be the same. By our numbers here tonight, by women who marched curb-to-curb down Fifth Avenue—women who had never marched before in their own cause with veterans of the first battle for the vote with young high school students, Black women with white women, housewives with women who work in factories and offices . . . we learned. We learned the power of our solidarity, the power of our sisterhood. . . . We learned that we have the power to restructure the social institutions that today are so completely man's world. . . . We faced the enemy and the enemy was us, was our own lack of self-confidence, was woman's self-denigration. . . .

The meaning of the strike is that we have no more time to waste in navel-gazing rap sessions, we have no more time to waste in sterile dead ends of man hatred. . . . This is not a bedroom war. This is a political movement and it will change the politics. . . . We serve notice, in our strike here tonight, that any senator who dares to trifle in any way with the Equal Rights Amendment trifles with his political future, for women will not forgive and will not forget. . . .

In the joy on every woman's face here tonight, in the sense that all of us have that we are sisters, that all women are beautiful, in our ability to transcend the lines of nation, class, man-made politics and race that divide us, in our affirmation of ourselves as women, we have felt a transcendent joy tonight. . . .

In the religion of my ancestors, there was a prayer that Jewish men said every morning. They prayed, "Thank thee Lord, that I was not born a woman." Today I feel for the first time, absolutely sure that all women are going to be able to say, as I say tonight: "Thank thee, Lord, that I was born a woman."

MURIEL FOX

It was in all the papers and all the nightly news shows. I mean, it was a huge event. The anchor for ABC News said after the story about the march, "Now we'll go on to less trivial events." But the world understood this was a major revolution. . . . And of course, that march really was a turning point. Millions of women had their consciousness raised by that march, and they participated in marches all over the country. And that was really the moment when we became part of the mainstream American existence.

MARY JEAN COLLINS

It transformed the women's movement. We doubled our membership that day, period. I mean, it made it mainstream in a different way. It brought in just a huge number of people who became involved. It was amazing. So, Betty's idea was brilliant.*

BETTY FRIEDAN

On August 26, it suddenly became both political and glamorous to be a feminist.

---

* NOW's membership grew exponentially for the next few years. In 1972, just four years after its inception, NOW reached eighteen thousand members and then more than doubled to forty thousand by 1974. Just one year later, in 1975, the organization's ranks reached sixty thousand.

20

Women's Lob—The Tennis Boycott

ROSIE CASALS

Well, I did not participate in the women's march in New York City—I was playing in the US Open in Forest Hills. Billie Jean and I were a little bit at odds as to whether we really wanted to go that route. I said, "Look, we should be a part of all this that's happening with women." Even though they're not talking about sports, they're talking about other things, pay equity in the workforce and schools. I always felt that we were part of it. We were just the sporting part of it and we had a platform, which was the US Open, where things were changing and women were fighting and we had been getting a lot of press for what we were wanting to do.

BILLIE JEAN KING

Rosie was ready to have women's tennis hop on the bandwagon. I thought we had to be more strategic. I wanted to speak out in a way that was strong, but I also wanted people to listen, not tune us out. . . . While I strongly supported the women's movement, it was not in a wholesale way early on. Parts of the early feminist movement felt too extremist or elitist to me, too devoid of women of color.

ROSIE CASALS

After tennis became open, the complexion of the game changed and we were thrown into a situation where the women and men were back together again playing tournaments, but what was happening is the men were getting more of the prize money because now there was prize money and commercialism and sponsors. Unfortunately, the women were not getting their share of the money and recognition. That's when all of the unrest began.

JULIE HELDMAN

Everybody knew the name Jack Kramer. He signed a great deal with Wilson Racquet Company and his was the most popular racquet in the United States. He also did some broadcasting and he was really good at it. He was young, he was handsome. He was a good broadcaster and he had this famous racquet. So, he became a man who had power and he built on his power.

When tennis became open, Jack became an early advocate for the men to have their own tennis association, which became the ATP [Association of Tennis Professionals], and he had his own tennis tournament in Southern California called the Pacific Southwest.

ROSIE CASALS

Throughout that whole summer of 1970, the women were very unhappy, and we were meeting, talking, trying to find the right way to move forward and communicate to the right people that we were not happy. It all came to a head at the US Open in 1970 there at Forest Hills.

BILLIE JEAN KING

We learned that the men's US Open winner would get $20,000, compared to just $7,500 for the women's champ, which mirrored what the other Grand Slams were offering. Our concerns spiked again when Jack Kramer, never one to conceal his contempt for female players, convinced the ILTF [International Lawn Tennis Federation] to set up a $1 million International Grand Prix tennis circuit for 1971 with Pepsi as a sponsor. Only a handful of the twenty-five new Grand Prix events would be open to women. . . .

Worse, when I asked USLTA [United States Ladies Tennis Association] officials how their 1971 schedule for us was shaping up, they told me there were only two tournaments scheduled for women between October 1970 and March 1971. That was a deeply troubling moment. The livelihoods of women players everywhere were at stake.

JULIE HELDMAN

Because there were so few tournaments for women, these empty weeks were just terrible. Soon it went all the way through the ranks of women players that there was beginning to be nowhere to go and no money to be made. Then, in August 1970, Jack Kramer announced that the prize money for the Pacific Southwest tournament two weeks after the US Open would be eight-to-one in favor of the men.

BILLIE JEAN KING

He planned to offer a $65,000 purse to the men versus $7,500 for the entire women's field.

JULIE HELDMAN

The men's winner will make $12,500 and the women's winner will make only $1,500.

In fact, in some of the rounds, it was twelve-to-one, and there was no money for the women unless they got to the quarterfinals. So, if you were a regular tour player, there was very little chance that you'd get anything at all. No other tournament gave the women such a raw deal.

Kramer announced that the reason he didn't want to have much prize money for the women was because women didn't sell tickets.

JUDY DALTON

So, we decided that we would put together a questionnaire. We asked everybody who came through the gates of the Forest Hills Club if they would fill in the questionnaire.

The most important thing we asked, from my point of view, was "Would men come to women's-only tournaments?" And 49 percent of the men said yes, they would.

BILLIE JEAN KING

Of the 278 people who returned the questionnaires—94 women and 184 men—about half said women's tennis was just as interesting as men's. Eighty-two percent of men preferred seeing men and women play in the same tournament. One-third of the men and half the women thought the prize money distribution should be equal. This was something we could build on. This was data, not hearsay. . . .

I wasn't playing at the 1970 US Open because I was recovering from my second knee surgery. . . . I was still on crutches by the US Open, so I agreed to work the tournament as a television commentator for CBS. Sports broadcasting was just opening up to a few women. Maureen Connolly had announced some Wimbledon matches on BBC broadcasts, and the Olympic swimmer Donna de Varona retired from competition at the age of seventeen and in 1964 became the first female sports broadcaster on an American network when she joined ABC's *Wide World of Sports.*

ROSIE CASALS

Billie Jean would come to the locker room and spend time there. We got to the point where we said, "Okay, what are we going to do about the Pacific Southwest? Are we going to boycott? Are we going to find another tournament?"

BILLIE JEAN KING

Rosie and I started polling the women players to see if we could agree to protest Kramer's prize money decision. I called [my husband] Larry for advice, and he suggested we talk again to Gladys Heldman. Rosie, Nancy Richey, and I had lunch with Gladys on the West Side Tennis Club terrace during the US Open and asked her for help.

JULIE HELDMAN

My mother, Gladys Heldman, started *World Tennis Magazine* in 1953 as a thirty-one-year-old married woman with two children. She liked to say that other women would come up to her and say, "Isn't it nice your husband lets you work?" But my mother was a force of nature. It was never what my father would let her do, it was where her energy was pushing her.

She started playing tennis when I was three months old and became good enough to be the Texas state champion. Then she got into tennis journalism completely on her own, started the magazine, and became a major promoter of the sport. Tennis was a minor sport then. There was baseball, football, basketball, and then there was nothing. Soccer wasn't anything in the States. Golf was an elite sport, played at clubs, and tennis was an elite sport too.

ROSIE CASALS

We told Gladys Heldman, "Look, we want to make a statement and we will boycott the Pacific Southwest and Jack Kramer."

BILLIE JEAN KING

Gladys was a brilliant, self-made, well-connected power broker in a male-dominated world who founded her magazine at the age of thirty-one and turned it into the bible of our sport. She was tireless, generous, glamorous, eccentric, narcissistic, creative, and just plain wonderful. . . .

It was decided that Gladys would try to persuade Kramer to increase the women's purse. She spoke to him twice. The first time, he refused to talk to her about it. The second time he told her, "Fine, if the women players don't like it, I won't give them *any* prize money." Gladys's report back to us was "Kramer's an ass." . . .

On September 6, Rosie and I led a locker room meeting to discuss whether to boycott Kramer's event. Everyone hated the prize money disparity, but once again a lot of women were afraid. What if we upset our national associations? What if we were banned from Wimbledon or the other majors? We were pretty hotly divided, and I was getting pretty exasperated, when Gladys burst through the door with a big smile on her face and almost sang, "Ladies! I've got news!"

JULIE HELDMAN

Within days, my mother had organized a tournament in Houston, Texas, where my parents were about to move. It would be at this new club, the Houston Racquet Club. They were a gung-ho club that was just getting going and they wanted to have tournaments in order to attract crowds.

My mother went to Jack Kramer at the US Open and said, "Do you have a problem if women have a tournament during the Pacific Southwest? It'll be solely women and you said you didn't care about women." Answer: "No," he said, "I'm not that kind of guy."

ROSIE CASALS

Fortunately, Gladys's friend was the CEO of Philip Morris, Joseph Cullman III. She went to him and said, "Will Philip Morris support our tournament if we have a tournament in Houston at the same time as the Pacific Southwest?" He said, "Yes, I will. We have a new cigarette coming out, Virginia Slims, and we'll do it under that brand." Of course, *now* everybody would balk at the fact that a cigarette company would sponsor a women's event or any sporting event, but I'll tell you what, if it wasn't for them, women's tennis would not be where it is today.

JULIE HELDMAN

My mother said, "I have a sponsor." And at this meeting she said Virginia Slims—which was a women's cigarette brand owned by Philip Morris—offered to put in several thousand dollars, and that was all, into this very first tournament, but would also provide incredible marketing. They would send down their very best people to support the tournament in terms of publicity. The club agreed that the tournament would be called the Virginia Slims Open.

BILLIE JEAN KING

The next day, Rosie, Ceci [Martinez], and eight other players announced our intentions to reporters from around the world at the annual Lawn Tennis Writers Association luncheon. They distributed a three-point manifesto in which we said we were seeking "prize money commensurate with that of men, equal exposure in center court matches, and better treatment by the news media, which subordinates women's tennis to the men's game." We weren't even arguing for equal pay at that point. . . .

The news of our revolt made headlines around the world, including the front page of the *New York Times*. Numerous other outlets printed the results of our survey. It was the first time a large segment of the general public had an insight into how unfairly the women players were being treated.

Washington Post, September 8, 1970,
"Tennis Girls Plan Boycott," by Mark Asher

Women's Lib reached tennis today. Some of the top women players announced they will boycott, or girlcott if you please, the Pacific Southwest championship at Los Angeles starting Sept 19. . . .

In a random survey of 2 percent of Sunday's [US Open] crowd of 13,116, the public overwhelmingly disapproved. Only 13 percent of the men and 6 percent of the women polled favored separate tournaments.

BILLIE JEAN KING

Once again, most of the top male players abandoned us.

New York Times, September 8, 1970,
"Women Tennis Stars Threaten Boycott Over Unequal Purses"
John Newcombe of Australia, who headed the now defunct International Tennis Players Association, thinks women players have little cause for argument in regard to their demands for more prize money.

Arthur Ashe was even more adamant on the subject. "Men are doing this for a living now. They have families, and they don't want to give up money just for girls to play. Only three or four women draw fans to a tourney, anyhow, so why do we have to split our money with them?"

BILLIE JEAN KING

I wasn't about to remain quiet. When Bud Collins reached me, I fired back in the *Boston Globe*, "I sell more tickets than Stan Smith. I think I'm a more exciting player and more people want to see me play."

The players who agreed to compete in Houston that week were Rosie Casals, Nancy Richey, Kerry Melville, Judy Dalton, Val Ziegenfuss, Peaches Bartkowicz, Kristy Pigeon, Patti Hogan, and me.

JULIE HELDMAN

I was not planning to play the tournament. I had ripped apart my elbow and I couldn't play, but I was planning to cover the tournament as a journalist for the *Houston Chronicle* because, certainly, nobody could have known the tennis world better than I did.

So, it all seemed fine and the night before the tournament, before the eight women competitors were going to get on airplanes and fly to Houston, Stan Malless, that disgusting guy from the USLTA Sanction Committee, called every woman and said if you get on the plane and go play in Houston, you will be suspended so that you won't be allowed to play in other USLTA-sanctioned events like Wimbledon and the US Open.

ROSIE CASALS

The Houston Racquet Club, which was very strongly supported by the USLTA, was threatened and they said, "If you host the women and the Virginia Slims, we will take away your sanctions."

JULIE HELDMAN

Then Stan Malless said, "If the women want to play the tournament, you can play an amateur tournament and have it not be a pro tournament. You can take money under the table, as much as they'll pay you, but you can't be a pro tournament." There was no rule about that. It was a rule they made up for women, for us. They thought that we would back down, and not one of us backed down.

BILLIE JEAN KING
Every five seconds, something was changing. We're going to get suspended, we're not going to get suspended. The club's going to get a sanction, the club's not going to get a sanction. There was all this turmoil, it was very tumultuous. So the players there were talking a lot about what could we do.

JULIE HELDMAN
The meeting went on for a really long time, including several hiatuses where Billie Jean and Nancy both phoned Alastair Martin, who was the president of the USLTA and said, "Are you really going to suspend us?" He said, "Yes, we will." So they were trying to see every different possibility. Did we really have to do this?

BILLIE JEAN KING
I talked to Gladys, and I said, "Why don't you just sign us?" And she said, "I can't afford you." I said, "Well, can you afford a dollar?" I said, "Because it's just as binding as a trillion." She said, "You'd do that?" And I said, "Yeah, we'd do that. Are you kidding? We've got nothing to lose, let's go. We had no other choice. We were going to be out. So nine of us signed that $1 contract.*

JULIE HELDMAN
The day that all hell broke loose, I decided in the early afternoon that I'd go over and see how the tournament was going. I arrived there and found out that women's tennis had been turned upside down and that everybody had signed to be contract pros with my mother. . . . I knew that there was no choice but to stand up for all the women together, so I immediately decided that I would join them.

---

* Without a contract, the women would have had to revert back from being professional players who could accept prize money to amateurs.

BILLIE JEAN KING

We lined up and the *Houston Post*'s Bela Urgin snapped a photo that became iconic: It shows Gladys holding up our contracts and eight of us players holding up our $1 bills and smiling. We became known as the Original Nine.

JULIE HELDMAN

I've always regretted that I wasn't in the iconic 1970 photo of the Houston players who rebelled against the men who ran the USTA.

ROSIE CASALS

That's how the Original Nine became the Original Nine, because there were nine very strong individual women who decided that for a change, they would be together on this. We all felt the same, we all were willing to sacrifice whatever it was that we had, because we felt we had a lot to gain.

JULIE HELDMAN

The only way to really join them was to play the tournament. But I couldn't play the tournament because I was injured. So, I came up with the idea that I would play one point, lose the point, shake hands, and Billie Jean offered that I could play the point against her. So, Billie Jean and I went on a side court. She served softly. I hit back softly. We both pitty-patted back and forth. She said something like, "Isn't that enough?"

So, I hit the ball in the net, which was absolutely against every instinct that I had. I went up to the net, we shook hands, and I was eligible to be suspended because I became part of the group that was a contract pro. I stood up for something I believed in that was incredibly important, and for the future of women's tennis. We didn't know it was going to become as big as it became, but it was something we stood up for and we believed in.

ROSIE CASALS

I'm happy to say that I won, and I made $300 more in prize money than Stan Smith won at the Pacific Southwest winning the men's singles. We were able to make that statement. I think that cemented the fact that we made the right decision, because from that, of course, we were suspended. That meant you could not play Wimbledon, you could not play any of the Grand

Slams, and that was giving up a lot. These were the tournaments that held the most money, they held the most prestige that really shaped your career.

JULIE HELDMAN

During the tournament, Mom contacted tournament promoters around the world, scoping out their interest in running women's pro tournaments. . . . On September 26, 1970, finals day at the Virginia Slims of Houston, the 1971 women's schedule was a blank slate. One month later, Mom sends all the Houston players a letter. In such a short time, she's gained firm commitments for seven new tournaments and a few more maybes, starting in January 1971. This is beyond extraordinary.

There was the absolute convergence of luck and destiny and determination because, on January 2, 1971, cigarette advertising on TV and radio was outlawed. All of a sudden, cigarette advertising money needed to find a place to go. It was a perfect combination for a women's tennis tournament and a women's cigarette. It was perfect for them. For us, everybody had to, at some level, say, "I'm not going to smoke. I'm never going to smoke. This is nuts." We went to bed with the devil, and the devil saved us.

BILLIE JEAN KING

Two weeks after [the Houston tournament], four of us held a press conference at the Philip Morris headquarters in New York to announce the Virginia Slims/World Tennis professional women's circuit for 1971, and Gladys uttered a memorable line to the assembled press. "You've heard of Women's Lib? This is Women's Lob."

Making Cunt Art

In a California state college, a woman who had just renamed herself Judy Chicago explored a new form of artistic expression and started the first-ever feminist art class.

**Poster for Judy Chicago's one-woman show
at Cal State Fullerton, October 23–November 25, 1969**
Judy Gerowitz hereby divests herself of all names imposed upon her through male social dominance and freely chooses her own name: Judy Chicago

JUDY CHICAGO
Back in the end of the sixties, there were almost no women artists who were visible at all. At the same time, by the end of my first decade of professional practice, I was just completely fed up. I was fed up with being told I couldn't be a woman and artist too. I was fed up with the idea that no matter what I did, I couldn't get anywhere. I couldn't get any institutional support. And then the women's movement started and I saw that it meant that I could be myself, but I didn't know how, because I'd so disconnected my impulses from myself in order to be taken seriously. So I had to figure out how to reconnect without sacrificing the formal control I had developed in the first ten years of my career.

I was in the throes of my early research on women's history and discovering that there was this whole history that I knew nothing about, and I wanted the time to look at it. I read through women's novels, systematically looked for women's art, read women's biographies. I thought, if I teach young women and I help them make art without having to do what I did, maybe I can figure out how to reconnect myself. But that took a couple of years.

I knew when I went to California State University at Fresno and proposed this women's class, I knew what I was really wanting to do, but I didn't say that to the head of the art department. I just said, I've gone through ten years of professional practice. I went to school with all these women, none of them made it into professional practice. I'd like to try and help young women traverse this course from school to professional practice and be able to succeed. Well, that sounded good and pretty benign. I didn't say I want to create an alternative art making.

SUZANNE LACY

I ended up at Fresno State because I had a boyfriend going there. Fresno had a fairly decent grad program in psychology, and I got right in. At that point feminist organizing was beginning in psychology. I went to the founding meeting of the Women's Psychology Associates at an American Psychological Association annual conference in Washington, DC. I met a lot of women psychologists who were just starting to ask questions of Freud's attitudes toward women. In graduate school, I taught a course in feminist psychology, which was very new then, for my graduate peers, and rabble-roused as much as I could every time Freud came up in a class, and I was known as "that angry woman."[*]

At Fresno, I ran into Faith Wilding, who was there as a graduate student in English literature. Her husband was a teacher. She was probably the only other person at Fresno that knew anything about feminism. We proceeded one day to stick up signs all over campus saying, "Feminist meeting tonight." There must have been thirty or forty women who showed up. Faith and I sat there dumbfounded and looked at each other and said, "What do we do now?"

---

[*]   Many feminist psychologists accused the influential founder of psychoanalysis of misogyny, as evident in Sigmund Freud's (1856–1939) theory that women suffered from "penis envy," were passive, dependent, and morally inferior to men.

FAITH WILDING

And then Judy Chicago came to Cal State Fresno. I had no idea who she was. . . . Somebody told Judy she had to meet me, so she came storming into my house in Fresno. I was doing crafts. I was doing a lot of pottery. I was doing weaving—traditional female things. She walked into my living room and there was this huge loom, and I was sitting at it. She was spouting all of these ideas at me for things we should do. And I said something fearful—"No we can't do this," which at that time was a stance of mine—and she started screaming at me, "You want to sit on that weaving bench forever and be a faculty wife? Forget about it!" and she stomped out of my house.

But we managed to get together and she told me about her idea of starting a feminist art program so somehow it ended up that she was the teacher and I was her assistant.

SUZANNE LACY

I applied that spring of 1970, after a year of graduate school. Judy brought about fifteen students together. The first thing she did was ask us to buy work boots. Then she taught us how to deal with Realtors, as we canvassed Fresno to look for an abandoned space to make into our studio. We found this huge old theater outside of town and, with our work boots, began to transform it. Judy taught us carpentry. I was certainly familiar with tools and stuff, but I'd never learned how to sheetrock. We built ourselves an art studio.

FAITH WILDING

It was like a little experimental think tank. We were sort of stumbling into this whole field, or whatever you would call it, of the idea of feminist art.

SUZANNE LACY

Judy would give us assignments having to do with topics, for example, like rage. Like, "How do you feel when you're walking down the street with men leering at you?" We made art of our experience.

FAITH WILDING

We would meet every week and we would choose a subject, and we tried to make art out of it after. We talked about our fathers or sex or money or rape or whatever the subject was, Judy would give us the assignment, "Go home and make art out of it." It was all very experimental and unorthodox. Now it seems like nothing, but then it was very radical. And

performance and happenings of course started in the sixties, but it still
was not a discipline. So, we started doing performances, very direct, often
crude performances.

JUDY CHICAGO

When people put people down by calling them cunts, it means that cunt is
an image of contempt. That is what a cunt is. Well, we have to get hold of
our own image, take it over. That's why I changed my name, because I took
hold of my own identity and I said, "Henceforth, I shall determine who I
am. I *reject* the definition society has given me, because the definitions society
has given me are nonoperable. They are incorrect, they are crippling, they
are dehumanizing. So, I take hold of my identity, I take hold of my cunt,
henceforth I shall say what cunt is. I shall build cunt myself."

FAITH WILDING

In her efforts to explore female sexual imagery Chicago was now working
with us in the studio making a cut paper "cunt alphabet." . . . We vied with
each other to come up with images of female sexual organs by making
paintings, drawings, and constructions of bleeding slits, holes, and gashes,
boxes, caves, or exquisite vulval jewel pillows. Making "cunt art" was exciting, subversive, and fun, because "cunt" signified to us an awakened consciousness about our bodies and our sexual selves. Often raw, crude, and
obvious, the cunt images were *new*: they became ubiquitous in women's
art in the seventies, and they served as precursors for a new vocabulary for
representing female sexuality and the body in art.

SUZANNE LACY

Ti-Grace Atkinson came to Fresno and we prepared a cheerleading reception
for her. We went down to the Fresno airport prepared to do our "C-U-N-T"
cheers—with the pink cheerleaders—and off the plane came forty or so
Shriners as we were screaming, "Give us a *C*, give us a *U*." Right behind
them came this giant leggy woman wearing sunglasses at six o'clock at night
and carrying a cigarette holder. She had buckskin pants and a giant fur coat.
That was Ti-Grace Atkinson, who sat there sort of bemused while we were
performing madly for her. It was quite an evening. Judy and she had a real
run-in. The gist of it was Ti-Grace felt that everybody, male or female, who
had anything to do with patriarchy was completely screwed. Judy's position
was to work with the men in your life.

JUDY CHICAGO

I felt that it was important for the women to learn about the work of women of the past, identify with their lives, and use their achievements to extend their own. I personally wanted to see the work and examine it for clues that could help me in my own art. We organized a research seminar, and the women began to go to local libraries, and then to libraries in Los Angeles, where they went through books, making lists of all the names of the women artists that they found. We quickly discovered that there was an enormous amount of information about women artists that had never been collated—so much, in fact, that I cried because I felt deprived of my rightful heritage.

SUZANNE LACY

We had a series of courses. We had reading studies, feminist art history and studio art. That's when we first started discovering people like Frida Kahlo, Mary Cassatt, and other women artists, who were uncovered subsequently or simultaneously—I'm not sure which—by art historians. Several women we discovered by rooting through used bookstores. I remember when Nancy Youdelman came to class one time with the book of the 1893 Chicago World's Fair and the first Women's Building. This was revolutionary to us. We pored over this and other books and found photographs in esoteric places.

JUDY CHICAGO

So here I am in Fresno with the Feminist Art Program. We have our own studio. And I'm thirty years old. And some of my students like Suzanne Lacy and Faith Wilding, they're only five years younger than me. So, there's not that big age gap, but I'm the teacher and they're the students, and they're dependent on me for support. And all of this energy is coming out, this bottled-up subject matter energy. It's kind of terrifying.

And at the same time, I didn't want to at all impede it. So, I really needed some help and some support myself. And I didn't really know who I could turn to. I had met Miriam Schapiro in San Diego at a party. And out of the blue, I just called her up and I told her that I was working with these young women, I was trying to help them be artists, which was true. And she got interested. I arranged for her to give a lecture in Fresno. And she came up, and she came to the studio. Mimi always had a real gift in terms of critique. I have a gift in terms of helping people find their voice in their content. But Mimi was always better than I was once that happened.

MIRIAM SCHAPIRO

Well, in the interim between my staying the extra year teaching art at UCSD [University of California at San Diego] and then leaving and going to CalArts, I met Judy Chicago. The difference between the atmosphere that I was living in and the atmosphere that she had created was astonishing to me. I felt she was involved in an appropriate historical change. And I think that what I reacted to was really part of what was necessary for the future.

JUDY CHICAGO

Mimi and [her husband] Paul [Brach, the dean of visual arts] proposed that I bring my program to CalArts. And they offered to let some of the girls, the students, come to CalArts. And Mimi helped them prepare their portfolios. By that time, I was ready to start the next phase of my imagery, which was *Red Flag, Through the Flower*, paintings, and then the *Great Ladies* series, where I was trying to figure out how to use my form language to express women's history.

FAITH WILDING

I remember driving through the streets of Fresno with Judy, and she would say, "God, can you imagine? This might be a course that could be taught in all schools!" . . . or "Can you imagine if women would start becoming artists on the same level as men?" She'd spin off these fantasies and I'd sit there thinking, this is not going to happen.

JUDY CHICAGO

At CalArts we were to have studio space, private quarters, tools, equipment, course support money for projects and materials, an art historian, and a budget to continue our work in assembling female art history archives. This was to be the first time that a school of art was addressing itself specifically to the needs of its female students by incorporating an educational program designed and run by women.

Mimi and I were interested in the possibility of starting with a large-scale art project. . . . Our art historian [Paula Harper] had suggested a project that we were quite enthused about, the designing of a house. Women had been embedded in houses for centuries and had quilted, sewed, baked, cooked, decorated, and nested their creative energies away. . . . Could the same activities women had used in life be transformed into the means of making art?

We broke up into teams and scoured the city for appropriate spaces. Three of the women spotted an old, run-down mansion near downtown Los Angeles. . . . On a bright November morning, twenty-three of us arrived at Mariposa Street armed with brooms, saws, ladders, hammers, and nails. "Womanhouse" had begun.

CHRISTINA SCHLESINGER

Womanhouse was spectacular. They took over an abandoned house in downtown LA and they gave rooms to all the students to make art in. Every room had been transformed into some statement about being a woman. I remember going to that opening and how it was so exciting and there were long lines of women waiting to get into it.

FAITH WILDING

Womanhouse with its sickly pink kitchen, its woman trapped in the sheet closet, its bride crashing into the wall, and its endless homage to costume, makeup, and domesticity could also be understood as a sharp critique of the confinement of female creativity to a limited sphere. Womanhouse was a new kind of art making which took private and collective female experience as its subject matter. . . . It was in fact the first public exhibition of "feminist art."

CHRISTINA SCHLESINGER

The kitchen that had eggs on the walls that looked like breasts, and Faith Wilding was doing the ironing.

LINDA NOCHLIN

There was Judy Chicago's unforgettable *Menstruation Bathroom* with its wall-to-wall Kotex and vivid red-and-white décor.

JUDY CHICAGO

We resolved to put together the bits and pieces that we found and to make an archive at CalArts. Mimi used to have her assistant check out the books that the women had found in the library, take them to CalArts, make slides from them, then return them. Out of her pocket and mine and with the work of young students, we put together the first West Coast file on women artists' work.

Throughout the fall of 1971 we met frequently. One weekend, we had a marathon, and all showed each other our work.

CHRISTINA SCHLESINGER

CalArts had a weekend when they invited women artists from all over California to come and show slides. There must have been at least a hundred women there. The room was full. I mean, that seems like nothing, but it was huge. I remember everybody's sitting there and everybody's showing their slides. It was mind-blowing for us. Anybody who was there remembers it because it was the first time. And it was really exciting. It was really run by Arlene Raven—she was beautiful and a lesbian.

That weekend burned in our memories. Just walking into that room, and the energy, and never being in a room full of women before. I felt isolated both as a lesbian and as an artist on the East coast, but when I got to California, suddenly there was a community there. Suddenly I wasn't alone. It's ordinary now, but once upon a time, it was revolutionary.

JUDY BACA

I went to Arlene Raven's slideshow, which was a moment of transformation for me. I remember it being over a hundred women, and sitting on the floor with Christina [Schlesinger]. I remember Arlene starting to show these slides. I'd been through many art history classes and I had a master's in art, but I had never seen any of these pieces.

People like Romaine Brooks, Elizabeth Catlett, and Emily Carr. One right after the other of women's art. And I remember just kind of being wowed by these women's work, and the number of them. And how they had remained invisible.

I was like, how could there be so many accomplished women that I never saw? I don't remember if she had Frida in that group. But at the same time, maybe a little later, Chicanos were starting to resurrect Frida Kahlo and put her in altars, and beginning to say, look, there are women who were amazing artists that were never respected or acknowledged.

22

Sexual Politics Lights a Fuse

By 1970, the mainstream media—from newspapers and magazines to book publishers—began to see that the women's rights movement had captured enough of the zeitgeist that its leaders and its messaging were in demand. That year alone, a tidal wave of books written by Black and white women, most of them now classics, entered popular culture and changed popular culture—along with the millions of minds reading these books—forever.

ROBIN MORGAN

The year 1970 hit like a meteor. I was working as an editor at Grove Press, and writing. My book of poems was coming out. I had already begun assembling *Sisterhood Is Powerful,* which I'd started because starting back in '67 and '68 our various CR groups would take trips to campuses, and hand out these mimeographed papers that people were writing, some of the classics like "The Politics of Housework" by Pat Mainardi and "Resistances to Consciousness" by Irene Peslikis and those early papers. And we were getting bursitis from lugging around these goddamn shopping bags. So I thought we need a cheap, available book that anybody can pick up that can be in airports, and even newsstands as well as bookstores, so that we don't have to lug these mimeographed papers around. Also, books go where you can't follow.

So, I tromped into my little CR group and I said, "I think we need a book, and I can assemble a book, and I want *your* piece in it and *your* piece in it and *your* piece." And while people were enchanted at the idea of having their pieces in it, they didn't want me to do a book. Because here we encounter for the first time the downwardly mobile anti-intellectualism of that period, where the only use for a typewriter, one was told, was to drop it out a window on the head of a cop. Get rid of all your books, they're bourgeois. This is the beginning of the rise of Weatherthink.* . . . Keep in mind that I was going ahead and doing the book even though my own women's group said I shouldn't. Years later they said, "Well, how good that you didn't listen to us." But at the time, it hurt.

FRANCES BEAL

I was called by Robin Morgan, who said that she was doing *Sisterhood Is Powerful* and she wanted an essay on Black women. And I said I would take a few of the things I had already started and pull together an overview, and that's how *Double Jeopardy* was born. An earlier version was in our *Black Women's Manifesto*, which was a thick pamphlet that we mimeographed and we sold in some bookstores and passed out at meetings.

ROBIN MORGAN

My old friend from SNCC days, Eleanor Holmes Norton, agrees to write one of a number of essays I plan to include on Black women. Another pal from the civil rights days, Elizabeth Sutherland Martinez, is happy to organize a section on Latinas.

I watch a woman being interviewed on William F. Buckley's TV show. She's presented as a feminist Roman Catholic theologian by Buckley, himself an archconservative Catholic. . . . She mops the floor with him, wrings him out, and proceeds to dust up the Vatican. I must have *her* in this anthology. I track her down. Her name is Mary Daly.

I hear about a woman who's a sculptor and also an academic; she's writ-

---

* "Weatherthink" refers to an antiauthoritarian, militant style of discourse used by members of the Weathermen organization and others Leftists. On March 6, 1970, three members of the Weathermen died when an explosive they were building accidentally detonated and blew up a town house, which belonged to Cathy Wilkerson's father in Greenwich Village. After the catastrophic event, the group's leaders were wanted by the FBI, and they all went underground, becoming famous outlaws. They scattered all over the country, living in secret collectives and using fake identification, and continued their bombing campaign of targeting government facilities and banks (but not people). Wilkerson manage to escape the blast and lived as a fugitive for the next ten years.

ing her dissertation on what she calls "sexual politics" in literature. I get in touch with her, read a draft, ask if she'd be willing to have an excerpt of it appear in a women's anthology. She thinks that's a great idea, confessing she yearns to publish the dissertation as a book, "even if nobody wants to read an academic thesis." I say she should try, and maybe the excerpt will help her land a book contract. Her name is Kate Millett.

KATE MILLETT

I called up Betty Prashker [an editor] at Doubleday, who had politely refused to publish the little pamphlet I wrote with the education committee of NOW but had offered to read whatever I wrote next. She did. She liked the first chapter and offered me an advance of four thousand dollars.

> ### *New York Times*, March 8, 1970, "Books to Liberate Women," by Marylin Bender
>
> Isn't it ironic that the book publishing industry which has always underpaid, underrated and underemployed the second sex, should now be gallantly courting the women's liberation movement?
>
> Almost every major publisher either has a feminist under contract or wishes he did. . . . The first of the new wave of feminist books is Kate Millett's "Sexual Politics," which Doubleday will publish in July.
>
> The single biggest category of women's liberation books is the anthology. Basic Books has Vivian Gornick, a staff writer for *The Village Voice*, and Barbara K. Moran, a writer-editor, soliciting contributions for "Fifty-One Percent: The Case for Women's Liberation." Like Robin Morgan's book for Random House [*Sisterhood Is Powerful*], it will probe every aspect of sexual discrimination from economic to psychological, and will include a critique of Sigmund Freud, one of women's liberation's arch villains. . . .
>
> Other scheduled anthologies are New American Library's . . . "Anthology on Black Women," by Toni Cade (for August, 1970), which will cover the distinctive strain of black women's liberation.

LETTY COTTIN POGREBIN

I was about to publish my first book, *How to Make It in a Man's World: A Survival Manual for the Girl Who Wants It All.* At that time, I had a queen-bee approach to pretty much everything. I saw the world through my own very nearsighted glasses. I didn't understand class and gender. My editor,

Betty Prashker, took me out to dinner and warned me that I was going to get attacked, and she tried to explain women's liberation to me. Then she gave me a briefcase packed with papers and pamphlets including the manuscript for a book called *Sexual Politics*, which she was publishing six months ahead of my book. She said, "Read this. You're an English American lit major. Kate Millett looks at 'women's lib' through the prism of literature, so you'll get this. Even if you don't get Anne Koedt's *The Myth of the Vaginal Orgasm*," which by the way I certainly did get, "and you don't understand sisterhood, start with Kate Millett and then read all these other radical position papers by all these radical women's groups all over the country who are springing up and are yelling back at people like you who are complicit. You are collaborators in the patriarchy."

These were the women who radicalized me. I learned from them. I used part of their thinking to formulate my own.

New York Times, August 17, 1970,
"Women's Lib Wooed by Publishers," by Grace Lichtenstein

Less than a month after publication, "Sexual Politics" by Kate Millett, a manifesto of the new feminism, has sold upward of 15,000 copies and is in its fourth printing. The paperback rights have been sold for $75,000. It is also a Book-of-the-Month Club alternate selection for November.

Meanwhile, other women's liberation activists have found themselves besieged with contract offers from book publishers. . . . In addition to the Millett book, more than a dozen titles dealing with the subject are scheduled for publication this fall and winter. . . .

JO FREEMAN

Her face was on the cover of *Time* magazine. That was the kiss of death.*

Time, August 31, 1970

Until this year, with the publication of a remarkable book called *Sexual Politics*, the movement had no coherent theory to buttress its intuitive passions, no ideologue to provide chapter and verse for its assault on patriarchy. Kate Millett, 35, a sometime sculptor and longtime bril-

---

* *Time*'s cover image of Kate Millett, painted by the New York feminist portrait artist Alice Neel, was the first time that a feminist had been put on the cover of a major national news magazine.

liant misfit in a man's world, has filled the role through *Sexual Politics*. "Reading the book is like sitting with your testicles in a nutcracker," says George Stade, assistant professor of English at Columbia University. He should know; the book was Kate's Ph.D. thesis, and he was one of her advisers. . . . In a way, the book has made Millett the Mao Tse-tung of Women's Liberation.

ALIX KATES SHULMAN

Kate Millett's pivotal book just lit a fuse that exploded in controversy all across the country. As one of the strongest, and certainly the best publicized of the movement books—more than Shulamith Firestone's *Dialectic of Sex** or the collection of movement papers, Robin Morgan's *Sisterhood Is Powerful*, or Vivian Gornick's and Barbara K. Moran's *Woman in Sexist Society*—*Sexual Politics*, and Kate with it, were both celebrated and vilified. When Kate's picture appeared (against her explicit wishes) on the cover of *Time* magazine, despite a lot of backbiting and envy inside the movement . . . we all knew what a remarkable victory Kate's book had achieved for our side—especially when it was attacked by Irving Howe in a long, mocking essay in *Harper's* magazine. The degree to which *Sexual Politics* shook up the opposition (and gratified us) can be guessed by Howe's writing that "there are times when one feels the book was written by a female impersonator," or, again, that Millett writes like "a little girl who knows nothing about life."

Time, December 14, 1970,
"Behavior: Women's Lib: A Second Look"

To Critic Irving Howe, the book is "a farrago of blunders, distortions, vulgarities and plain nonsense," and its author is guilty of "historical reductionism," "crude simplification," "middle class parochialism," "sexual monism," "methodological sloppiness," "arrogant ultimatism" and "comic ignorance." Howe's attack seemed certain to stir up an unholy war between the sexes. For it was directed against both the bible and the high priestess of the Women's Liberation movement: *Sexual Politics* and its author, Kate Millett . . .

---

* Firestone, who was twenty-five years old when she wrote *The Dialectic of Sex*, attributes the root of female oppression to the nuclear family, childbirth, and childrearing, and she posits that women will be free of oppression only when children can be reproduced outside the womb. Unsurprisingly, her radical views received mixed reviews in the mainstream press.

MARGO JEFFERSON

I ordered the hardback, which as a young person one didn't buy a lot of hardbacks, and read it voraciously. First of all, she was taking on the canon. It was D. H. Lawrence, Henry Miller, Norman Mailer, taking on the presumptions that vast, far-reaching, and often vicious misogyny presented mythologically, presented sexually, presented in some very compelling language, but it was puerile and cruel. She was taking on the whole myth of what is required in terms of gender and sexuality to be a real artist, which of course also meant a real male.

BARBARA SMITH

That particular Christmas of 1970, I was in graduate school, and one of my dear aunts who knew how much my sister and I loved to read gave me a gift certificate to a wonderful local bookstore. And what did I buy with that gift certificate? *Sexual Politics.* Even though I was not involved in the women's movement, I read *Sexual Politics* by Kate Millett, and I was amazed by it. . . . I was stumbling over myself with excitement because I was in graduate school in English, I was familiar with many of the authors she was writing about. Her perspective on their work was completely out of the box.

PHYLLIS CHESLER

I stood up in the Sheridan Square Bookstore and I couldn't stop reading *Sexual Politics* and *The Dialectic of Sex* and Germaine Greer's book *The Female Eunuch*, which also came out in 1970. That book doesn't really stand the test of time. Shulie['s] and Kate's books do. It was extraordinary. It was like suddenly all the pieces clicked into place and it all made sense.

HONOR MOORE

Reading *Sexual Politics* was like having your head blown off, oh my God. I had been someone who read all of Norman Mailer and I was like, "How could I have read that stuff?" She was calling out the sexism of how the women were treated in all those works of fiction that were the canon. And by extension the position of women in the culture around us. It was a huge click moment. Suddenly someone was articulating, in hundreds of pages, what we had articulated in groups and in short pieces and in radical newspapers.

ALIX KATES SHULMAN

Reading *Sexual Politics*, you get a strong sense of us versus them. The book was a thrown gauntlet, then a weapon in a battle, and we fired it off as often as we could. The book is written *from* us *to* them rather than to us.

LEE WEBB

Marilyn and I were recruited to move to Goddard College in Vermont, where Marilyn set up a women's program and I set up a radical studies program. By this time, Marilyn and I were beginning to separate. I became active in a male consciousness-raising group, where we read Kate Millett's *Sexual Politics* and studied it. I thought it was one of the most impressive books I had ever read. I think the aha moment for me was realizing the degree to which men's minds and psychologies were distorted in a way that was bad for them, by sexism and the sexual division of labor, the sexual constructs of personality and behavior and roles and responsibilities.*

In 1970, feminist books like The Female Eunuch, Sexual Politics, The Dialectic of Sex, *and* Sisterhood Is Powerful, *written by white women, sold commercially and were widely reviewed and debated. But that same year, an even more impressive crop of books, written by Black women, many soon to become paragons of literature, like Toni Morrison, Alice Walker, Audre Lorde, and Toni Cade Bambara, were published quietly. But in time, their audiences and influence on politics, culture, and literature would balloon in size.*

MICHELE WALLACE

It was in 1970 that Black feminism really began to emerge as an autonomous discourse with the publication of the anthology *The Black Woman*, edited by noted Black feminist author Toni Cade Bambara, and the organization of such groups as Third World Women's Alliance, led by Frances Beal. In 1971, *The Black Scholar* published an article called "Reflections on the Black Woman's Role in the Community of Slaves," which was written by Angela Davis in her prison cell, kicking off the Black feminist critique in the social sciences.

---

* *Sexual Politics* remained on the bestseller list for more than three months, and was reissued in 1990, 2000, and 2016. It has been called "the bible of women's liberation."

MARGO JEFFERSON

That was a lot to take in. I was reading women writers from everywhere obsessively and almost exclusively. It was like the great inform-yourself-educate-yourself project, which was exciting.

FRANCES BEAL

Toni Cade had seen the *Black Women's Manifesto* and wanted it for her anthology *The Black Woman*. And so that's how it got published there. Since then, it has been published again and again, and it's used over and over in Black women's studies courses.[*]

> **Toni Cade Bambara, preface to *The Black Woman: An Anthology***
> This . . . is a beginning—a collection of poems, stories, essays, formal, informal, reminiscent, that seem best to reflect the preoccupations of the contemporary Black woman in this country. . . .
>
> For the most part, the work grew out of impatience: an impatience with the all too few and too soon defunct Afro-American women's magazines that were rarely seen outside of the immediate circle of the staff's and contributors' friends. It grew out of an impatience with the half-hearted go-along attempts of Black women caught up in the white women's liberation groups around the country. . . . And out of an impatience with the fact that in the whole bibliography of feminist literature, literature immediately and directly relevant to us, wouldn't fill a page. . . .
>
> The question for us arises: how relevant are the truths, the experiences, the findings of white women to Black women? Are women after all simply women? I don't know that our priorities are the same, that our concerns and methods are the same, or even similar enough so that we can afford to depend on this new field of experts (white, female).

MARGO OKAZAWA-REY

For a long time, I was just trying to just fit in, date guys, not make waves. When I came out, I remember saying to myself, "There's no place where

---

[*]   Toni Cade was a Black feminist writer, activist, and intellectual (1939–1995) who in 1970 added the West African name Bambara when she found it written on a notebook that belonged to her great-grandmother. Another important title written by a Black feminist author and published in 1970 was Celestine Ware's *Woman Power: The Movement for Women's Liberation*.

you're going to fit in because you've just defied all the categories." And so I said to myself "I want to be part of helping create spaces for people like me." And that's how I got engaged in activism. The women's movement enabled me to do that in different ways, to think and act completely outside the box.

I was living in collectives in Boston, getting involved in work with battered women. There were all these opportunities for us to engage in political work. There was a holding environment for all of us to just do an experiment and learn and create things that hadn't existed before. And at the time our textbooks were the writings of Toni Morrison and Toni Cade Bambara, because we were also really very much moving toward Black feminism because the white women's movement didn't do a good job of dealing with race, right? And we all also wanted to just have our own space.

Los Angeles Sentinel, December 17, 1970,
"New Books: Powerful Novel on Black American Womanhood"
"The Bluest Eye," by Toni Morrison, Holt, Rinehart & Winston, $5.95
Toni Morrison has written an exceptionally fine novel, an extraordinarily fine first novel. It is a more vivid and skillfully handled treatment of black American womanhood than Maya Angelou's "I Know Why the Caged Bird Sings."

New York Times, November 13, 1970,
"Three First Novels on Race," by John Leonard
Miss Morrison exposes the negative of the Dick-and-Jane-and-Mother-and-Father-and-Dog-and-Cat photograph that appears in our reading primers, and she does it with a prose so precise, so faithful to speech and so charged with pain and wonder that the novel becomes poetry. . . . I have said "poetry." But "The Bluest Eye" is also history, sociology, folklore, nightmare, and music.

MARGO JEFFERSON
In fiction at that time [1970], Alice Walker and Toni Morrison were publishing *The Bluest Eye* and *The Third Life of Grange Copeland*, I'm talking about pre-*the* books they were best known for. These were the breakthrough books.

MARGO OKAZAWA-REY

Toni Morrison was one of our guiding lights. I remember when her first book, *The Bluest Eye*, came out. We saw our families in the characters. For example, my grandmother and some of other people's mothers and aunts had been domestics. So we could relate to working for white people and wanting to have blue eyes, internalizing wanting to be white. None of us had done that, but we could recognize the push to be that, and to be straight. Audre Lorde, of course, was an important guiding light for us as well.

MICHELE WALLACE

The steady flow of novels and poetry by Black female authors—Maya Angelou's *I Know Why the Caged Bird Sings*; Toni Morrison's *The Bluest Eye* and *Sula*; Alice Walker's *The Third Life of Grange Copeland, In Love and Trouble, Once*, and *The Color Purple;* Toni Cade Bambara's *Gorilla, My Love* and *The Salt Eaters*; as well as the poetry of Nikki Giovanni, Audre Lorde, Sonia Sanchez, June Jordan, Lucille Clifton, Sherley Anne Williams, and others too numerous to name—represented a momentous paradigm shift not only in Black feminism but in the women's movement overall.

23

We Are One

Fame was a double-edged sword for members of the women's liberation movement. Writing with a byline, appearing on television, having a distinctive public voice conflicted with the movement's antihierarchical, communal ethos. Becoming a star invited the jealousy and judgment of your peers and the king-making media. But when Kate Millett admitted that she was bisexual, her fall from grace was more like a crash.

KARLA JAY

When the forthcoming publication of Kate Millett's *Sexual Politics* was announced in the *New York Times* July 20, 1970, many activists hailed it as the first mainstream feminist analysis of literature, and Kate was anointed by the media as a new light. But to a few Radicalesbians, publishing in mainstream venues was collaborating with the enemy. When Kate appeared at one of the Radicalesbians meetings that fall, she was greeted by an unsigned leaflet [everyone I interviewed believed Rita Mae Brown to be its author] that had been planted on all the chairs before the start of the meeting. The leaflet accused Kate of several "crimes." First, the book was too expensive. . . . Second, Kate had "described herself as trying to be a bridge between Women's Liberation, N.O.W., and our group." The mimeo pointed out that since many members of Radicalesbians were also members of feminist groups, we didn't need her as a "bridge."*

ANSELMA DELL'OLIO

Kate had a consciousness-raising group that she worked with and debated ideas with, which then went into the book. That group tried to force her not to sign her book because signing a book was being a capitalist pig basically. In other words, you were hogging all the limelight for yourself. She was a literature professor who had never published anything, and she said that it was her thesis. How could she not sign it? Well, I of course totally supported her. I said that's nuts, sign that book and don't even listen to them, that's just stupid and jealous.

KARLA JAY

Radicalesbians determined not to let her become a media celebrity. That December Kate was "outed" (that word did not exist until the late 1980s) as a bisexual by Ann Sanches of Radicalesbians during a talk Kate gave at Columbia University. During the question-and-answer period, Ann stood up in the audience and asked Kate more than once whether she was a lesbian; Kate finally, but reluctantly admitted she was bisexual.

MARGO JEFFERSON

First, she said, "Actually, I'm bisexual." And this young woman pressed her. I've seen confrontations and even denunciations at political meetings, but this was maybe the first of its kind that I'd seen. Basically, the young woman was saying, "It matters that you take this stand. Are you willing to say even if you are bisexual? Yes, I am a lesbian?" And Kate said, "Yes, okay." And that basically was her outing, so to speak.

KARLA JAY

Suddenly Kate was no longer the darling of the media.

---

*   In her memoir *In Our Time*, Susan Brownmiller writes that Radicalesbians member Martha Shelley told her that Rita Mae Brown wrote the anonymous letter attacking Millett. "I was there early, setting up the room, when Rita Mae put the unsigned paper on people's chairs. To my everlasting shame, I didn't stop her," Brownmiller wrote, "The statement attacked Kate for being a star and selling out to the male press, which of course as soon as Rita Mae could possibly do [sell out], she did." Rita Mae Brown denied the charge.

Time, December 14, 1970,
"Behavior: Women's Lib: A Second Look"

Ironically, Kate Millett herself contributed to the growing skepticism about the movement by acknowledging at a recent meeting that she is bisexual. The disclosure is bound to discredit her as a spokeswoman for her cause, cast further doubt on her theories, and reinforce the views of those skeptics who routinely dismiss all liberationists as lesbians.

KATE MILLETT

Time magazine first put me on the cover in August, and then in December, they said, "She has admitted, confessed to being a bisexual." It was a way to burst the bubble. It was a way to manipulate the movement, by manipulating me. So, they more or less said in December that my book now didn't make any more sense. Two months before, they said that it was so smart and terrific. It was now dishonored and invalid, why? Because I was a bisexual—admitted and confessed.

IVY BOTTINI

Many feminists, including me, were furious at the [*Time*] attack with its fake high morality, homophobia, and racism.

So as the president of NYC NOW, I decided to hold a ("Kate Is Great") news conference and invited the movement's movers and shakers to condemn the media's efforts to dismiss Millett and the book. This was the first time the leaders of the women's movement addressed the topics of bisexuality and lesbianism in a mainstream, public forum.

FLORYNCE KENNEDY

First thing I know, somebody was inviting lots of women in the movement to a press conference and, except for a few movement rabbits, just about everybody was there.

Women were three or four rows deep. Crowded round Kate. Every area was represented. Ti-Grace Atkinson, feminist philosopher and lecturer, Gloria Steinem, editor and lecturer, Barbara Love, editor of *Foremost Women in Communications*, later author of *Sappho was a Right-On Woman* (with coauthor Sidney Abbott), Ruth Simpson of DOB (Daughters of Bilitis), Sally Kempton, writer, and, of course, innumerable organized and individual lesbian women and other feminists.

KATE MILLETT

Finally, we said, "We are one, and shoulder to shoulder, and brother and sister with gay liberation. We agree to the same analysis of society that they do."

New York Times, December 18, 1970,
"The Lesbian Issue and Women's Lib," by Judy Klemesrud

The Lesbian issue, which has been hidden away like a demented child ever since the women's liberation movement came into being in 1966, was brought out of the closet yesterday.

Nine leaders of the movement held a press conference at the Washington Square Methodist Church to express their "solidarity with the struggle of homosexuals to attain their liberation in a sexist society." ...

The 36-year-old Miss Millett ... read a statement that she said had been prepared last Monday night at a meeting of about 30 women representing such groups as the National Organization for Women (NOW), Radical Lesbians, Columbia Women's Liberation and Daughters of Bilitis.

The statement said, in part:

"Women's liberation and homosexual liberation are both struggling toward a common goal: A society free from defining and categorizing people by virtue of gender and/or sexual preference. 'Lesbian' is a label used as a psychic weapon to keep women locked into their male-defined 'feminine role.' The essence of that role is that a woman is defined in terms of her relationship to men. A woman is called a Lesbian when she functions autonomously. Women's autonomy is what women's liberation is all about."

KATE MILLETT

We made a very fine, reasoned, principled, argued response. However, personally, everybody went nuts. My mother in Minnesota was like, "What will the neighbors say?" At Bryn Mawr, nobody came to my classes anymore when I was teaching there. I became notorious overnight, and we stopped selling the book real fast.

But we had made the united political front. We had theoretically and politically done the right thing. Then everybody went home and had a nervous breakdown, because who didn't feel unambivalent about this? Many of these women were lesbians. They were throwing themselves out of the closet with this statement.

IVY BOTTINI

I was there. It was guilt by association. I considered that press conference my public coming-out.

KATE MILLETT

Even if the statement was theoretical, and impersonal, and abstract, it still brought up mountains of confusion in those who were gay. But in those who were straight, the same thing, because women were crossing the line between gay and straight like jaywalking in those years. I mean there was an enormous surge of sexual energy within the women's movement. We were falling in love with each other. Why not? We loved each other. I mean, we had to explore all these possibilities.

IVY BOTTINI

That afternoon, after the news conference, I went to work at *Newsday*, as usual. Once I got there, it came to me that since our panel had gotten a lot of coverage, all my coworkers would know about me by now. They had to have seen the news. . . . I took a deep breath and went straight to my desk. Nobody said anything. I got to work.

Later that day, as usual, I went to check the mockup of the pages that I had designed before they were actually printed. This involved walking through two heavy, leather doors into a large room filled with the din of linotype machines. Generally, when I came into the room, the machines would be making a racket. . . . This day, as soon as I opened the doors and walked in, the machines went quiet. . . . As I plodded down the long corridor, I thought to myself, "Oh no, they're going to kill me for being gay." I finally got to Joe, who was in his usual blue shirt with, as usual, a cigar in his mouth. . . .

He looked at me, leaned back in his chair, took the cigar out of his mouth, and said, "Hell of a press conference, Bottini." He brought his chair back down and showed me the pages printed from the chase for me to check. The machines went back on. I breathed a sigh of relief.*

JO FREEMAN

Kate used her royalties from her *Sexual Politics* to buy a Christmas tree farm near Poughkeepsie, and she ran a writer's camp there and she raised and sold

---

* In an anti-lesbian coup orchestrated by Betty Friedan, Ivy Bottini was voted out of her position as president of New York NOW in April 1971 and replaced by Jacqueline Ceballos.

Christmas trees. So, in December instead of grading term papers, she was on the streets of Manhattan selling Christmas trees. That's what happened. She was an early prominent feminist. At a time when the academic world didn't want to have anything to do with feminists.

ANSELMA DELL'OLIO

I stayed friends with Kate as I did with Shulie Firestone and I saw what happened to both of them. They both lost their minds. At least Kate got hers back, Shulie never did. Shulie ended up in and out of Bellevue. It just pushed them over the edge, it was just too much. They couldn't keep it together—it just blew their minds apart.

24

The Military Is Only for Men

When a young Air Force physical therapist stationed in Alabama asked for equal housing dispensation, she walked into a wall of barriers she never knew existed, and eventually started a tidal wave of legal change.

SHARRON FRONTIERO-COHEN

I was born in 1947 and grew up in Massachusetts in a Catholic, blue-collar family. I went to UMass for the first two years and then I transferred to University of Connecticut for their physical therapy program. My senior year of college, I needed money, so I applied for the Air Force Institute of Technology scholarship, which basically paid me a salary to just be on tap for the next three years. I graduated in '69 and went to basic training in Texas. Then I reported for active duty at Maxwell Air Force Base in Montgomery, Alabama.

Maxwell was a big retirement base. It was also the university of the Air Force. It really was a lovely place to be stationed because it had a lot of high-ranking officers. I had a hometown boyfriend, whom I probably should not have married looking back at all the things you do when you're very young. I was twenty-two. I loved him. We were both very young. So, I went home on leave and got married. When we came back to Montgomery together, I applied for a housing allowance because I knew everybody working in my physical therapy clinic who was married got a housing allowance.

I was being paid about $500 a month and the housing allowance would've been about $120 a month. My husband was on the GI Bill—he was a student at Huntington College in Montgomery, and he had a part-time job as a night watchman in a vinegar factory.

There was no married housing on base, so we had to live off base. Everybody else who was married also lived off base, and the men got a housing allowance. So, I expected it and went looking for it, and was told no. I was a good little girl, I was doing things the right way. There weren't that many women in the service; there weren't that many married women.

I went to four or five of the personnel people, the money people, and worked my way up to the commander of the hospital and the base commander. By then I pretty well knew that it was going to be no. They would tell me, "I'm sorry, we can't do this. You're a woman." I mean, they were telling it to me straight to my face. And it was just going over my head because I thought, this just can't be right. You must be mistaken. I was hearing, "You don't belong here at all, the military is for men, you're lucky we let you come here at all." And I just thought that was ignorance.

It was actually my husband who said, "Enough is enough." He was quicker to be fed up than I was and said, "Let's just get a lawyer and see what we can do." At that point, I had no intention of suing. There was a law firm in town that did civil rights work that was called Levin and Dees. Eventually they would rename themselves the Southern Poverty Law Center. Everybody knew about them. We called up and made an appointment and went in and Morris Dees was off somewhere, but Joe Levin was there.

JOE LEVIN

I have a pretty clear recollection of Sharon coming into our office at the Southern Poverty Law Center in November 1970. She gave us the straightforward story about how she and her husband were denied the housing allowance that all the married men got. At that point, the firm had dealt only with race-discrimination cases.

SHARRON FRONTIERO-COHEN

I was still insistent that this was just some kind of glitch, and if Joe Levin would find the right statute and write the right letter, this would all be cleared up. But he said, "No, it won't. What you've bumped into is a federal statute.* There's nothing you can do except file a lawsuit."

---

* The statute on the books spelled out a clear double standard. All wives of servicemen were deemed

JOE LEVIN

She had tried all of the procedures that were made available to her within the Air Force. None of them had worked. She was just dead determined to get this resolved. She was not going to leave it alone. We filed the suit in a three-judge court pretty quickly on December 23, 1970.

SHARRON FRONTIERO-COHEN

I didn't do it because I was a rebel. I was not carrying a feminist banner up a barricade. But when Joe said, "There is nothing to do except change the law," it was the first time that I totally understood that this was not individual. It was part of the structure.

Then I started to notice the brouhaha about women's rights that was going on around me. Later, I would join a consciousness-raising group. But I never was much of a joiner. I never was a person who was going to be a street-active feminist.

For me, it was a lot like going to the optometrist. When they put the lens in front of your eye and you say, "This is clearer now!" There's that moment when suddenly it comes into focus. Everything you've already known, everything that's been around you, but you haven't been paying attention to, suddenly comes into focus.

JOE LEVIN

We filed it in the district court, where we argued that the due process clause of the Fifth Amendment did not permit discrimination on the basis of sex by the government, by the military. There'd been no case that would support that up until that point.*

Joe Levin would soon find himself collaborating with a feminist legal scholar named Ruth Bader Ginsburg.

"dependents" and therefore eligible for medical and housing benefits, regardless of their income. But husbands of servicewomen had to prove that their wife earned more than half the couple's combined income in order to be eligible for the same benefits.

* The due process clause of the Fifth Amendment, protecting people from being deprived of "life, liberty, and property without due process of law," applies to actions of the *federal* government and is analogous to the due process clause of the Fourteenth Amendment, which applies to actions of *state* governments.

RUTH BADER GINSBURG

In 1970, students at Rutgers, where I was teaching mainly civil procedure, asked for a seminar on women and the law.* So I undertook to read anything one could find on the subject in case reports and legal texts. That proved not to be a burdensome venture. So little had been written, one could manage it all in a matter of weeks. . . .

At the end of 1970, less than ten law schools offered electives in this field. Students in many law schools were clamoring for a course on women and the law. I had put together a set of materials for my students at Rutgers. The Supreme Court had never seen a gender classification it didn't like or at least that it didn't think was constitutional. It was an amazing time to be alive and a lawyer.

---

*   Ginsburg entered Harvard Law in 1956 as one of nine women out of five hundred students. Unable to get a job at a law firm or a clerkship because she was a woman, she started teaching at Rutgers Law School in 1963, where she was one of only two full-time female faculty members. In 1971, she helped one hundred female employees file a class-action pay discrimination suit against the university, which they won. Ginsburg moved to a tenured position at Columbia Law School in 1972.

Pauli Murray, key legal architect of the civil rights and women's movement and cofounder of the National Organization for Women. Photographed in 1970 when she was a professor at Brandeis University. (AP)

Left to right: Rep. Martha Griffiths (D-MI), Maine newspaper reporter May Craig, Rep. Howard Smith (D-VA), and Rep. Katharine St. George (R-NY) celebrate after the House voted 168 to 133 to include "sex" along with race in Title VII of the 1964 Civil Rights Act, prohibiting employment discrimination. (Bettmann Archive/Getty Images)

Mississippi Freedom Democratic Party delegates singing at a rally on the boardwalk outside of the Democratic National Convention, Atlantic City, NJ, August 10, 1964. Women, left to right: Fannie Lou Hamer, Eleanor Holmes Norton, and Ella Baker.

(©1976 George Ballis /Take Stock/TopFoto)

Bobbi Gibb nears the finish line on Boylston Street and becomes the first woman to run and complete the Boston Marathon, April 19, 1966.

(Fred Kaplan/*Sports Illustrated* via Getty Images)

Group portrait of NOW founders at its organizing conference in Washington, DC, October 30, 1966. Betty Friedan is far-right, front row. (Vince Graaf/ Schlesinger Library, Harvard Radcliffe Institute)

The American Peopl Series # 18 : The Flag is Bleeding, 1967
© Faith Ringgold 1967
72 x 96 inches
oil on canvas
Artist's Collection

Faith Ringgold's 1967 painting *The Flag Is Bleeding*. (© 2024 Faith Ringgold/Artists Rights Society [ARS], New York. Photo courtesy of Faith Ringgold/Art Resource, NY)

Feminists protest outside the 1968 Miss America beauty pageant, Atlantic City, NJ. They threw items symbolizing female oppression, like uncomfortable girdles and bras, in the Freedom Trash Can, but because they could not obtain a fire permit, no bras were burned.

(Alix Kates Shulman Papers, David M. Rubenstein Rare Book & Manuscript Library, Duke University. Photograph copyright Alix Kates Shulman; used with permission)

Feminist protesters holding signs illustrating how the Miss America pageant degrades women by objectifying them as pieces of meat, Atlantic City, NJ, on September 7, 1968. (AP)

Marilyn Webb with Susanne Orrin Jackson (holding baby) stand backstage before Webb's speech at the counterinaugural demonstration (January 1969), where she was booed off the stage. (Courtesy of Marilyn Webb)

Rep. Shirley Chisholm (D-NY), the first Black woman elected to the US Congress, and her all-female staff on Capitol Hill, whom she fondly called "The Chisettes," 1969. From left to right: Alice Panneli, Karen McRory, Travis Cain, Shirley Chisholm, Shirley Downs, Cathryn Jones (Smith), and Pauline Baker. (Courtesy of the Shirley Chisholm Estate)

Francis Beal, cofounder of the SNCC Black Women's Liberation Committee and the Third World Women's Alliance and author of *Double Jeopardy: To Be Black and Female*, speaking at the Militant Labor Forum in New York City, July 17, 1970.

(Howard Petrick)

Four members of the all-female litigation team that took the first class-action abortion rights case, *Abramowicz v. Lefkowitz*, to federal court in New York in 1970. From left to right: Carol Lefcourt, Diane Schulder (Abrams), Florynce Kennedy, and Emily Jane Goodman. (Edith Gould)

Rita Mae Brown (far right)
participating in the Lavender
Menace action, which challenged
NOW to accept lesbians at the
Second Congress to Unite Women,
New York, 1970.

(Photo by Diana Jo Davies, Manuscripts and
Archives Division, The New York Public Library)

Faith Ringgold (right) and her
daughter Michele Wallace (middle)
at the Art Workers Coalition
Protest, Whitney Museum, 1971.

(Jan Van Raay)

The original founders of the Boston Women's Health Book Collective, who started teaching a class on women's bodies that eventually turned into the iconic women's health manual *Our Bodies, Ourselves.* (Courtesy of Our Bodies, Ourselves)

One hundred feminist activists occupy the Statue of Liberty and unfurl a huge "Women in the World Unite!" banner at the base of the statue, August 10, 1970. (Bettmann/Getty Images)

In the largest protest in women's history, feminists march in New York City on August 26, 1970, on the fiftieth anniversary of the passing of the Nineteenth Amendment, which granted American women suffrage. NOW called on women nationwide to "strike for equality," and hundreds of thousands of women took the day off work and marched in cities all over the country. (Jean Pierre Laffont)

Tens of thousands of women from diverse parts of the women's liberation movement block traffic and march down Fifth Avenue on August 26, 1970. (John Olson/ The LIFE Picture Collection/Shutterstock)

A member of the Third World Women's Alliance stands holding a sign at the Women's Strike for Equality in New York, 1970.

(Keystone/Getty Images)

Forty-six women employees of *Newsweek* hold a press conference on March 16, 1970, to announce they are suing the magazine under the 1964 Civil Rights Act. Charging discrimination in jobs and hiring, they said they were "forced to assume a subsidiary role simply because of their sex." Seated left to right: employees Patricia Lynden and Mary Pleshette; their lawyer, ACLU legal director Eleanor Holmes Norton; and employee Lucy Howard. (Bettmann/Getty Images)

Billie Jean King (left) and Rosie Casals display their doubles trophy after beating France's Francoise Dürr and Great Britain's Virginia Wade, 6–2, 6–3, at the Wimbledon ladies' doubles final, July 4, 1970. (Popperfoto via Getty Images)

On September 23, 1970, tennis players hold up one-dollar bills after signing a contract with *World Tennis* magazine publisher Gladys Heldman to turn pro and start the Virginia Slims tennis circuit. From left, standing: Valerie Ziegenfuss, Billie Jean King, Nancy Richey, and Peaches Bartkowicz. From left, seated: Judy Tegart Dalton, Kerry Melville Reid, Rosie Casals, Gladys Heldman, and Kristy Pigeon. Gladys Heldman replaced her daughter, Julie Heldman, who was injured and unable to pose for the 1970 photo. (Bela Urgin/Houston Post Collection/Houston Metropolitan Research Center/Houston Public Library)

August 4, 1971

Kate Millett (author of *Sexual Politics*) and Gloria Steinem (cofounder of *Ms.* magazine) taking a lunch break on the sidewalk near the entrance to the New School in downtown Manhattan, a frequent meeting place for feminist panels, August 4, 1971.
(Jill Krementz)

Pulitzer Prize–winning author, poet, and activist Alice Walker photographed in Central Park on August 12, 1970, the same year her first novel, *The Third Life of Grange Copeland*, was published. (Bettmann/Getty Images)

Ruth Bader Ginsburg, the first female full professor at Columbia Law School, photographed in class on January 18, 1972. As cofounder, with Brenda Feigen, of the ACLU Women's Project, Ginsburg litigated more than two dozen Supreme Court cases challenging sex discrimination laws. She became the second woman to serve on the Supreme Court (1993–2020). (Courtesy of Columbia Law School)

Gloria Steinem, Rep. Shirley Chisholm, Betty Friedan, and Rep. Bella Abzug (standing) at a press conference on July 12, 1971, announcing the formation of the National Women's Political Caucus. One of their goals was to have women compose half of the delegates to the 1972 presidential conventions. (Charles Gorry/AP)

Ms. magazine staff meeting, June 1972. From left to right: Letty Cottin Pogrebin, Gloria Steinem, Margaret Sloan-Hunter, Suzanne Levine, Mary Thom, Harriet Lyons, Patricia Carbine, and Ruth Sullivan. (Nancy Crampton)

Shirley Chisholm campaigning for president in downtown Miami as she joined sugarcane workers picketing the Talisman Sugar Corporation offices on February 24, 1972. (Jim Kerlin/AP)

Gloria Steinem (center) and Bella Abzug (right) applaud Senator George McGovern after he addressed the feminist caucus at the Democratic National Convention on July 10, 1972. McGovern betrayed his feminist supporters and refused to endorse abortion rights. (Bettmann/Getty Images)

Mug shots of four out of the seven members of the Chicago underground abortion network, code-name Jane, who were arrested on May 4, 1972. From left to right: Sheila Smith, Martha Scott, Diane Stevens, and Judith Arcana. Called the "Abortion Seven," they faced more than ten years in jail for providing illegal abortions. Their case was dismissed after the Supreme Court legalized abortion nationally in January 1973. (Chicago Police Department)

**6-4, 6-3, 6-3,
And No Love
For Bobby . . .**

Daily News front page, September 21, 1973, announcing twenty-nine-year-old Billie Jean King's straight three-set victory over fifty-five-year-old Bobby Riggs in the "Battle of the Sexes" at the Houston Astrodome, in front of thirty thousand spectators and ninety million worldwide television viewers.

(*New York Daily News* via Getty Images)

Margaret Sloan, cofounder of the NBFO, speaking in New York on August 25, 1973.

(Bettye Lane/Schlesinger Library, Harvard Radcliffe Institute)

The Combahee River Collective, a more radical offshoot of the NBFO, started in Boston in 1974. Left to right, bottom: Demita Frazier and Helen Stewart. Left to right, top: Margo Okazawa-Rey, Barbara Smith, Beverly Smith, Chirlane McCray, and Mercedes Tompkins. (Courtesy of Margo Okazawa-Rey)

Part Three
{ 1971-1973 }

1

You've Come a Long Way, Baby

BILLIE JEAN KING

We knew this would be one of our dreams come true if we could make this happen.

JULIE HELDMAN

What happened was the marketing and the advertising people at Virginia Slims came up with unbelievable things. They had a drawing of a woman with short hair in a short skirt, flapper kind of outfit. In one hand was a cigarette in a cigarette holder, and in the other hand was a tennis racket. At the end, they came up with the slogan, "You've come a long way, baby." Nobody in the tennis world seemed to take into account that the word "baby" was demeaning. They called the girl "the Ginny."

BILLIE JEAN KING

The first tournament was in San Francisco and the second one was in Long Beach, and then we moved around in Southern California. We sold out.

Philip Morris made the difference. They had the money, the marketing expertise. Joe Cullman, the CEO of Philip Morris, believed in women, believed in us and our future. So, we were really lucky to have these people in our lives who actually cared. It wasn't just sponsorship, it was a real partnership.

JULIE HELDMAN

My mom was like the Wizard of Oz, sitting at home in her giant round bed, running the magazine and running the women's pro tour. Those were two more-than-full-time jobs that she took on. She was the publisher of her *World Tennis Magazine*, but she was always looking for new tournaments, always looking for new sponsors. And when the tours started in '71, there were like eight tournaments. And then she got a ninth one, which was to be played at Caesars Palace, the biggest tournament ever, with $40,000 in prize money. Then there was another one after that in San Diego and then we all went off to play in Europe, and she even got a tournament in Venice.

BILLIE JEAN KING

We racked up fourteen tournaments in the first three and a half months of 1971 alone, almost one a week. I won the first five, beating Rosie each time in the final. The pace was grueling. . . . Our Slims events were played everywhere from college gyms and rec centers to Caesars Palace in Las Vegas, which felt like the big time even though sand came blowing off the desert onto our outdoor court.

JUDY DALTON

The tournaments were tough. If you lost, you went to the next tournament location and you did all the publicity, you went to the radio stations.

BILLIE JEAN KING

The players were willing to do anything. We were willing to do interviews for magazines, TV, and radio. We got no sleep. We signed every autograph before we left the court every night. We did whatever it took.

We would take a car to a local newspaper to try to get some coverage, and they usually said no. It was usually a white guy with a cigar. . . . I mean, it was hysterical. I used to sit there and try not to laugh, and I'd say, "Would you have someone cover our tournament?" And he'd say no.

So I started thinking about it and asked, "Well, do you have a stringer or an intern?" And they'd say, "Oh yeah, we've got them." And I said, "Well, could you send one of them every night? It'd be great if it was the same person so they'd get to know the people running the tournament as well as get to know us." And they said yes. And I said, "Well, if they write a good article or whatever, would you give them a byline? These kids, it would mean a lot to them." They said, "If it's good, we will." And that's another way we built relationships, because those little guys in the beginning became the big guys later. So you never know.

ROSIE CASALS

It was definitely an uphill battle. If any of the sports reporters had to write about tennis, they thought that was a punishment. They knew baseball, basketball, all of that, they knew nothing about tennis. We had to educate them. We had to tell them who we were, what we were doing, 15-40, deuce, what the hell is that? There was hardly ever a woman reporting on women's tennis.

JULIE HELDMAN

Six months into the tour, my mother hired a tennis dress designer. He was this absolute character, a six-foot-six, very thin, very gay designer who lived in London. His name was Ted Tinling. The original deal was that the dresses would have the Ginny on them so that, basically, they would be advertising both the tour and the cigarettes. The dresses were fabulous. Each one was different. Ted was famous for that. They would be very fitted, and very feminine—they were outrageously adorable. He had this class that everybody loved, so they made him the person who announced the players as they walked onto the court. He became this very special, extra marketing tool. He was also brilliant, funny, and filled with stories—very few of which were true.

ROSIE CASALS

All of it was packaging. Selling a product, selling our tennis, selling our feminism, selling the entertainment part of it, because that's what we were. Entertainers. We played in all these wonderful arenas that everybody said, "Well, did you fill them?" We filled the Forum, we filled Madison Square Garden, we filled all these arenas in the seventies. We would have spotlight, introductions, with music, the whole thing. Then, of course, Ted Tinling would say, "I'm going to make you a dress that is going to bring out your personality." I was flashy, so my dress had lamé and velvet and sequins. We had all of these wonderful things that would shine and sparkle in the spotlight and everybody had their own style that reflected their personalities. It was all geared toward entertainment, and that's what we felt we were selling. We were selling women who were successful, who were attractive, who performed at the highest level, and we did a good job of it.

BILLIE JEAN KING

In December of 1970, I told Larry, "I'm going to try to make $100,000 because if I can make a lot of money, people will notice the tour. They will notice that women are good players, who are powerful." Money talks. Everyone understands money, whether you're a teacher, a factory worker, or the president of a corporation. So, it was really important for me to break the $100,000 mark. I knew it would take most of the year, I'd have to get really lucky with some of the wins, but I crossed over a hundred thousand in the last tournament of the year, and made $117,000. For the first time, a lot of women players were making real money, and we were determined to keep it going. . . . Practically overnight, we were trying to change a tennis structure that had existed for a hundred years and buck chauvinism at the same time.

ROSIE CASALS

Behind the scenes, we were such a close family.

BILLIE JEAN KING

We protected each other whether we were gay, straight, the biggest star, or the lowest qualifier. We were like a traveling family, complete with all over-lapping storylines, dramas, loves and neuroses, and we kept things in-house.

ROSIE CASALS

Every one of the players knew that I was gay, and that Billie Jean was gay. Everybody knew that. But it was not for any conversation outside the locker room. We were all friends. Chris Evert comes in, she's sixteen, or seventeen—young. She understands, no problem. But it wasn't something you could talk about, especially when you're trying to launch the Virginia Slims tour. The sponsors would want you to be a certain way and saying that you were gay was not acceptable.

JULIE HELDMAN

It was not only not okay to be gay, it wasn't okay to look gay.

It was okay to look like this pretty young girl who would shake her booty, but if you admitted to being gay in the 1960s and 1970s, you would be ostracized. Billie Jean King has said frequently that she struggled with being gay and not being able to talk about it.

BILLIE JEAN KING

It's hard to convey how oppressive it was. Hardly anyone in public life was out then, that I can remember, except a handful of authors and activists such as James Baldwin, Audre Lorde, Gore Vidal, Rita Mae Brown, Larry Kramer, and later, Harvey Milk, the first openly gay elected official in California. . . .

I was in a delicate position because I was our fledgling tour's leading player and spokesperson, a woman known for calling out hypocrisy. . . . My reputation was built on being a truth-teller and pioneer. Now I was living a lie and hating myself for it. The fact that I was lying out of necessity didn't lessen my shame or dissonance about it. I didn't even feel that I could go to therapy to sort it out. The psychiatry manuals still said gays were "deviants." . . .

My parents were homophobic. My religious upbringing told me that homosexuality was wrong. And yet, if I was being honest, I didn't feel like a sinner. So what *did* that make me? All I knew was that I was still married to a man but in a relationship with a woman and if it was revealed, it would be a catastrophe.

I had made $117,000, which was huge. The president called me, congratulated me. Nixon's from California and I'm from California, so he was proud as punch that it was me. We got the sponsor, which made all the difference. You had nine of us who were fantastic people, all different. Everyone's very smart, and we were willing to give up our careers for the future generations.

The three things we said were number one, any girl born in this world, if she's good enough, would have a place to compete. Number two, that we wanted to be appreciated for our accomplishments, not only our looks. And number three, we wanted to be able to make a living playing tennis.

The players today have no clue. I mean, it's so different now. It's so great now. Oh my God, they're making a living, they're living our dream, and they're making big bucks, really big. And women usually get the same amount as men.

2

In the Room Where It Happened

*Almost no women held elected office in America. In 1971, just 4.7 percent of all state legislators were women, and only seven out of the country's thirty thousand mayors were women. In the US Congress, only 15 of the 535 members of Congress were women. When a brassy New York lawyer named Bella Abzug was elected to Congress in 1970, she and her supporters launched the first real effort to deliver political power to women by running women for office.**

ESTHER NEWBERG

I had been running political operations for Arthur Goldberg for Governor in the 1970 campaign against Nelson Rockefeller. My friend Ronnie Eldridge called me up and said, "Okay. Arthur Goldberg lost, and Bella Abzug's looking for an AA [administrative assistant]. Do you want to go back to Washington?" I said, "I would go back to Washington. I think it might be fun." She says, "I've arranged for you to have an interview on Bank Street," where Bella's town house was. I get to Bank Street, I walk in, and someone tells me to go into the bedroom, where Bella was literally pulling on a girdle.

She was talking a mile a minute, and we started to talk. "I want some-

---

* For comparison, in 2024, there were 417 female mayors (in cities with populations over 30,000), twelve governors, and 151 members of the Congress (25 in the Senate and 126 in the House).

one who's worked in Washington and Ronnie speaks highly of you. I need you to go to Washington before I get there and hire legislative assistants who can figure out how to add my agenda to other bills. There's got to be a way. Those Southerners can do it, and I want to know how to do it too." So smart. So, I did. I went to Washington, and I hired the staff. We were all women.

She was sworn in by Shirley Chisholm with five hundred women in attendance all over the steps of the Capitol, just to make a point. She represented the most left-wing district in the history of the Congress, Manhattan's Upper West Side, so she was good to go.

The very first bill that she ever introduced was a bill to withdraw the troops from Vietnam. That was her most important issue—getting out of the war. Way more than feminist issues, at the beginning. It's not that she came late to feminism, but she had been a founder of Women Strike for Peace. When I worked for Robert Kennedy in '66, '67, and '68, she came to our offices with the head of Women Strike for Peace.

She never tried to wear her hat onto the floor of the House. That was such a myth. But every single newspaper ran stories, "Bella Tries to Wear Her Hat." No, she didn't. She wore it to the floor and then she took it off. They just tortured her in little ways like that.

She was always putting in votes to end the war, and they mostly didn't pass because Nixon had the Republicans. After one of those votes, we were coming back from the House floor, and we were coming up the escalator, and going down on the other side were Hale Boggs and [Speaker of the House] Carl Albert. Carl Albert was my height, which, by the way, is not very tall. As he passed, he said to Bella, "Better luck next time, Bella." And she looked at him and said, "Fuck you."

I said, "Well, there goes my inside parking pass, Bella. You can't say that to the Speaker." I loved her even though she made me insane. I can tell you exactly the number of years, weeks, and days that I worked for her.

BELLA ABZUG

My slogan for my first campaign was "This Woman's Place is in the House." I wanted to make clear to the public, when I was running, that there was something wrong with just having eleven women out of 435 in the House of Representatives. And I was willing to strike at what was a myth as to where a woman's place was. Even to raise it very sharply. Now, other women had run for Congress before me, but they were not, as I was, the product of a time where there was a women's movement. And so, I had that responsibility, and I was willing to risk it.

When I got there, there were a lot of misconceptions about what I was. I mean, some people thought I was somebody that walked out of my kitchen into the Congress. I was an activist in the peace movement, and I brought that opposition into the House very strongly. And they kept saying, why do you keep raising it? I said, because we can't go on this way. And they understood after a while. They knew that I was skillful, and my training as a lawyer and an activist was very helpful. I learned the rules fast.

GLORIA STEINEM

The National Women's Political Caucus was begun by Congresswomen Bella Abzug, Shirley Chisholm, and Patsy Mink.* They were clear from the beginning that the caucus was to be a representative coalition of adult American women, and it was representative by state, race, and ethnicity, including African and Asian Americans as well as American Indians. This was the first such representative national gathering, and it has yet to be replicated. Perhaps even more remarkable, it was subsidized by funds voted upon by the US Congress.

JILL RUCKELSHAUS

We needed to be in the room where it happened. That's what the caucus was all about.

Women were really good at organizing, and getting lists, and making strategy, and putting on events, and seeing things through, and handing in budgets. We knew how to do all of that. But there wasn't anywhere to go with it. You weren't going to run for office.

When the women's movement decided to focus on politics, and getting more delegates to the national conventions, and trying to get language into the platforms, the Women's Political Caucus was formed to get more women elected to office.

LETTY COTTIN POGREBIN

When my book *How to Make It in a Man's World* was published, the editor of *Ladies' Home Journal* called me up the day after I got a rave review

---

* Elected from Hawaii in 1959, Democrat Patsy Mink was the first woman of color, and first Asian American woman, to serve in the US House of Representatives.

in the *New York Times*. This was April 10, 1970, and Lenore Hershey, the editor who worked under the editor in chief John Mack Carter, said, "I'd like you to write a column for us called 'The Working Woman.' We want everything you wrote about in your book, but make sure that it's useful. Make it utilitarian." I said, "Could I write about how to ask for a raise?" "Yes." "When to quit?" "Yes." "What's it like to work with other women? What if you have a male chauvinist boss?" "Yes. Anything you want." So, I said yes.

I had the column for ten years, and it pioneered all the issues that we at *Ms.* eventually covered in depth. The column appeared and in late spring of 1971 I got a call from Betty Friedan, who at that moment was *the* American feminist, period. She said, "This is Betty Friedan. I was just at the hairdresser. I read your column. On July 10, a group of us are going to Washington, DC, and we're going to start something called the National Women's Political Caucus. And I'd like you to come and be my writer."

I was already covering everything of interest to working women, so naturally I should also be up to speed on legislation, politics, and litigation and who was doing what on behalf of women. So, I jumped at it.

LIZ CARPENTER

A phone call from Shana Alexander [editor of *McCall's*] alerted me: "Betty Friedan thinks the feminist movement has gone as far as it can go until it gets some political clout behind it. You know more about politics than anyone I know. Will you talk to her if she calls?"

It was the spring of 1971. I had been out on the road selling my book *Ruffles and Flourishes: The Warm and Tender Story of a Simple Girl Who Found Adventure in the White House.* "Sure, I'll talk to her." She did, and about ten minutes later, spouting forth in the rapid staccato . . . the need to elect more women, the need to pass legislation that would help women work, the desperate need to make Congress aware of all the inequities the working woman faces. I was impressed with Betty's sharp mind and intense focus on the problem. "There's going to be a meeting next weekend with a core group on the Hill. All the women's organizations will be represented there. Three congresswomen, Bella Abzug, Shirley Chisholm, and Patsy Mink, and of course, Gloria Steinem. I hope you'll be there too."

So I went. Bella opened the meeting by asking everyone to stand up and say why they were there. Of course, all eyes were on Gloria in blue aviator glasses and miniskirt, dramatic and cool with her soft voice and waist-long blond hair. These trademarks were already making news in *W* and other New York literary media. Betty Friedan, a very different type, sporting a frowsy blouse, long skirt, and an "earth mother" look. . . . When Gloria spoke, everyone was quiet. "Looking around this room, I see there is at least one thing we all have in common—a vagina." I jumped about two feet. I had never heard that word except in my gynecologist's office. . . . When it came to my turn, I introduced myself as having covered the Hill for sixteen years and worked in the White House for Lyndon and Lady Bird Johnson for the past five. . . .

Over the next few weeks, a small group of us kept meeting for long hours in grimy offices . . . there was growing tension between Betty on one side, and Bella and Gloria on the other . . . their strong and clashing personalities and enthusiasms burst out like gunfire in our long, tedious nightly meetings. Betty, having energized the women's movement with her book, was understandably possessive. Bella, whose clout as congresswoman from New York gave us all greater entrée and a podium, was unyielding in her own strong beliefs. Gloria, softer-spoken and conscious of her large following among young women throughout the country (Gloria lookalikes were everywhere, wearing aviator glasses, long hair, ribbed turtlenecks), was equally unrelenting in her position that the women's movement had to embrace every female issue.

BELLA ABZUG

Gloria Steinem, Shirley Chisholm, and I have this major difference of opinion with Betty as to what the nature of a women's political movement should be. She seems to think we should support women for political office no matter what their views, and we don't. I feel our obligation is to build a real political movement of *women for social change*. I don't think we're at the level where we have to fight to get just *any* woman elected. . . . But because she tends to regard herself as "the" leader of the women's movement, Betty is impossible sometimes.

ESTHER NEWBERG

I think Bella liked Gloria better than Betty because she was pretty, and she was feminine, and she was very strong on all the issues that Bella cared about. Betty was just a bully. Literally.

It was horrible. She was competitive. Betty took credit for the whole women's movement, and Bella was important too and she also wanted credit.*

LIZ CARPENTER

Betty felt that Bella and Gloria were "separatists" and "anti-men," narrowing the movement with radical chic cliches of the time. She saw the movement more as part of the general drive for equality and civil rights. . . . I had never been around so many strong women shouting at each other, but I had never been around a revolution before.

BELLA ABZUG

On July 10, 1971, when our founding conference of the National Women's Political Caucus (NWPC) opened at the Washington Hilton, some three hundred women from all over the country—a mix of elected officials, community activists, feminists, Democrats, Republicans, radicals, union women, homemakers, students, Blacks, Hispanics, and lesbians—were on hand.

LETTY COTTIN POGREBIN

Bella turns up at the Hilton. I knew her because I had knocked on doors and passed out pamphlets for her campaign. I loved her. She was a wild woman. She was a powder keg. She was totally sui generis.

BELLA ABZUG

After an early appointment at the House Beauty Shop, I arrived at the conference at about ten o'clock. This was the plenary session. It was very impressive—there were women from all over the country—California, Texas, Alabama, Kentucky, Michigan, not just New York.

I said it in my speech, and I'll say it again here, this was truly a historical meeting—easily as significant as the first little convention for suffrage in Seneca Falls more than a hundred years ago. The presence here in Washington of three hundred women from twenty-six states serves notice to everyone that women will no longer accept second or last place—politically, socially, economically, or humanly. And though we may, as a unit, have some trouble working out our organizational and tactical problems, there is one thing that we're all in perfect agreement on: women should

---

*   Friedan and Steinem graduated from Smith College fourteen years apart—Friedan in 1942, Steinem in 1956.

be fully represented in the political power structure as both a matter of right and a matter of justice. . . .

One of the put-downs that has continually plagued the women's movement is the charge that it speaks only for white middle-class women. To the contrary, there has always been an acute sensitivity to the need for representing the interests of all women. As one of the keynote speakers at the first NWPC meeting, I said the hope of building an effective women's political movement lay in "reaching out to include those who have been doubly and triply disenfranchised—reaching out to working women, to young women, to Black women, to women on welfare—and joining their strength with that of millions of other American women who are on the move all over this country, demanding an end to discrimination and fighting for their rights as full and equal citizens."

Fannie Lou Hamer, a Black woman who had been involved in the struggle to get Mississippi's Freedom Delegation of Blacks officially seated at the 1964 Democratic convention, was pointed in her remarks to us: "America is sick," she said. "Something has got to change in this country."

Fannie Lou Hamer speech

Now, something has got to break in this country. We have got to have some changes and we can't keep standing around waiting for the white male . . . not only changes for the Black man, and not only changes for the Black woman, but the changes we have to have in this country are going to be for liberation of all people—because nobody's free until everybody's free. . . .

If you think about hooking up with all these women of all different colors . . . with the majority of women of voting strength in this country, we would become one hell of a majority. And this is something that should have been done for a long time because a white mother is no different from a Black mother. The only thing is they haven't had as many problems. But we cry the same tears and under the skin it's the same kind of red blood.

Shirley Chisholm speech

No one gives away political power. It must be taken, and we will take it. If women and minorities ever got together on issues and on their own tragic underrepresentation in the places of power, then this country would never be the same. I believe we have taken a step in that direction.

Gloria Steinem speech

This is no simple reform. It really is a revolution. Sex and race, because they are easy, visible differences, have been the primary ways of organizing human beings into superior and inferior groups, and into the cheap labor on which this system still depends. We are talking about a society in which there will be no roles other than those chosen, or those earned. We are really talking about humanism.

Betty Friedan speech

Women who have done the political housework in both parties, who have been ignored by the very men they have elected, know what we in the women's movement have learned when we've tried to get priority or money appropriated or even legislation enforced on issues like childcare, abortion, or sex discrimination: What we need is political power ourselves. With men composing 98 or 99 percent of the House, Senate, the State Assemblies, and City Halls, women are *outside* the body politic. . . .

The women's liberation movement has crested now. If it doesn't become political, it will peter out, turn against itself and become nothing. . . . It is time to move up from the menial housework of home, office, school, factory and political party. It is time to have a voice in human destiny, to find and use our fullest human power.

LETTY COTTIN POGREBIN

At the end of the day on Saturday, Betty sent me off to write a position statement. She said, "We're going to need a mission statement summarizing everything that you've heard. Just do a draft." So, I went looking for an empty room to work in, and I opened the door and sitting by herself at a table was Gloria Steinem. Now I knew Gloria because I read her voraciously. I read her in *New York* magazine, I read her in *Show* magazine; I mean, she was my idea of fabulous. So, I was backing out of the room in my humble way. And she said, "Come in. I'm Gloria."

I said, "I'm Letty, and Betty Friedan asked me to write up a statement of purpose." She said, "Come sit here. I'm writing up a statement of purpose too." And this is so typically Gloria, she said, "We'll work on it together." And my brain was saying, "Are you fucking kidding me? I'm supposed to sit here and work with you? I've got to leave." She went, "No, no, no. It'll be fun."

We worked together until about three o'clock in the morning. In the middle of the night, it was so freezing cold from the overly air-conditioned rooms that they do in hotels that we wrapped ourselves in the felt tablecloths that were on the tables. As you might imagine, at the end of the night we were friends. And then she said, "I'm working with a group of women and we're going to start a magazine, and we don't really know if it's going to be a newsletter or a magazine, but we're just starting to talk and we're having a meeting on Monday in Tudor City." It was at Brenda [Feigen] Fasteau's apartment. That was fifty years ago.*

LIZ CARPENTER

I had been "drafted" by Shana and Betty to be the contact person with the press. Monday morning, the story of our meeting and the five-column picture of the speakers ran on page one of the *Times*, the *Star*, and the *Post*. What a picture! Betty Friedan, jubilant that the feminist movement was going to get some political clout and attention. Bella Abzug in hat, looking determined and purposeful. Shirley Chisholm, mellow and wise. Gloria Steinem, looking younger and more serene than any of us.

New York Times, July 12, 1971,
"Goals Set by Women's Political Caucus," by Eileen Shanahan

The Women's National Political Caucus, a new organization dedicated to increasing the political power of women, announced today the guidelines it will use in deciding what candidates it will support for public office.

The guidelines emphasize "the elimination of sexism, racism, violence and poverty." They also call for an immediate withdrawal from Vietnam. . . .

Of the 21-member council, seven members are black and one is Indian. Eleven are Democrats, two are Republican and the rest have no political affiliation or do not state it.

Mrs. Abzug declared at a news conference that "a new political force was born."

---

* One month after the NWPC conference, *Newsweek* anointed Steinem the women's liberation movement's new leader and spokeswoman and put her on its August 1971 cover. Just one year after the *Newsweek* women filed their discrimination lawsuit, the magazine still didn't have a woman staff writer to pen the Steinem cover story, which disappointingly focused more on her beauty and glamorous boyfriends than her feminist activism. A reluctant star, Steinem refused to sit for a cover photo.

LIZ CARPENTER

Meanwhile, in San Clemente, President Nixon met with his cabinet and found that Secretary of State Bill Rogers had arrived that morning from Washington with the eastern newspapers. Rogers threw the papers on the table for all to see. "It looks like vaudeville," someone said. "Who is Gloria Steinem?" asked President Nixon. Secretary Rogers replied jovially, "Oh, she's one of Henry Kissinger's girlfriends."

Helen Thomas from UPI, who was within hearing distance, pounced on those words and the wire stories began.

BELLA ABZUG

"Obviously," I commented at the time, "the president and his advisors are accustomed to viewing women only in terms of flesh shows." Gloria issued a statement saying she was not then and had never been a girlfriend of Kissinger, nor, in fact, was she a woman friend.

A few months earlier, Vice President Spiro Agnew, speaking at a fund-raiser in Maryland, had delivered what he thought was a crowd-pleaser by exhorting Republicans "to keep Bella Abzug from showing up in Congress in hot pants." My response, which proved to be accurate on both counts, was that "hot pants will disappear from the national scene, along with Mr. Agnew and Mr. Nixon."

In 1971, when the NWPC was just getting started, we had no paid staff and no money—just enthusiastic volunteers and a vision of what had to be done. Most of the women who attended the conference went home and began to organize state and local caucuses. . . . In a speech to the National Press Club a week later, I was able to report that caucuses were being formed in fifteen states. . . . In the next twelve years, the caucus grew to a membership of more than seventy thousand women, with a professional staff headquartered in Washington.

New York Times Magazine, August 22, 1971, "What the Black Woman Thinks About Women's Lib," by Toni Morrison

What do black women feel about Women's Lib? Distrust. It is white, therefore suspect. In spite of the fact that liberating movements in the black world have been catalysts for white feminism, too many movements and organizations have made deliberate overtures to enroll blacks and have ended up by rolling them. They don't want to be used again to help somebody gain power that is carefully kept out of their hands. They look at white women and see them as the enemy—for they know that racism is not confined to white men. . . .

The winds are changing, and when they blow, new things move. The liberation movement has moved from shrieks to shape. It is focusing itself, becoming a hard-headed power base, as the National Women's Political Caucus in Washington attested last month. Representative Shirley Chisholm was radiant: "Collectively we've come together, not as a Women's Lib group, but as a women's political movement." Fannie Lou Hamer, the Mississippi civil-rights leader, was there. Beulah Sanders, chairman of New York City-wide Coordinating Committee of Welfare Groups, was there. They see, perhaps, something real: women talking about human rights rather than sexual rights—something other than a family quarrel, and the air is shivery with possibilities.

3

The Past Is Studded with Sisters

As the great awakening unfolded for women in politics, law, health, sexuality, art, and sports, women scholars began to uncover a wealth of history and literature that had been dismissed by the male academy and collecting dust in attics and libraries for decades. The discovery of the hidden history of women political activists, writers, artists, and intellectuals would eventually evolve into an entirely new field of study and, more important, a revelation of self-discovery.

SALLY ROESCH WAGNER

I was getting my master's in psychology at California State University, Sacramento, when we opened up the campus during the Cambodia–Kent State Strike City in May 1970, and held alternative classes. Women's studies grew out of that. We created an alternative education because we were so excluded from the curriculum. The first women's studies class that I cotaught with Jeanne Knofel, as part of the Experimental College, was Women in Psychology. This year will be the fifty-first year that I've been teaching this class.

When Jeanne and I proposed the class to the psych department, they rejected it after the Freudian on the faculty had a hissy fit. But John Doolittle, a tenured professor, thought it sounded like a good offering, so he put it in the schedule under his name. He came to the first class, then turned it over to us and we taught it. I remember the students were hungry for the information and the chance to have a women-taught class from a feminist perspective. There was only one woman faculty member in the psych department then, and she taught like the boys.

I was in psychology, and at one point I had an equal number of English credits and psych credits. Who did I read in English? I read dead white men. Who was I studying in psychology? Dead white men, and a few living. So, I wondered, did women really *not* do anything? Or was that just what we were taught? We women graduate students would compare our academic areas, and ask each other, "Are you studying any women?" And all of a sudden the invisible became visible, that absence which we hadn't even recognized as an absence because it was so universal, became apparent. And then it was, "Okay, what *have* women done?" And then we started finding the women.

The program that I helped found at California State University, Sacramento, was, as far as we were able to tell, the third women's studies program in the country and the first in the country to offer a minor in women's studies.*

LINDA NOCHLIN

Shortly after my return from a year in Italy with my husband and baby to my familiar job in the Vassar art history department, a friend showed up in my apartment with a briefcase full of polemical literature. "Have you heard about women's liberation?" she asked me. I admitted that I hadn't . . . but that in my case it was unnecessary. I already was, I said, a liberated woman and I knew enough about feminism—suffragettes and such—to realize that we, in 1969, were beyond such things. "Read these," she said brusquely, "and you'll change your mind." That night, reading until two a.m., making discovery after discovery . . . my consciousness was indeed raised, as it was to be over and over again within the course of the next year or so. . . . It was rather like the conversion of Paul on the road to Damascus: a conviction that before I had been blind; now I had seen the light.

BRENDA FEIGEN

Back in 1970, I'm at Vassar with Gloria, who has just given the commencement address, and I saw my old friend Linda Nochlin, whom I'm very fond of. I had taken her art history course 101 at Vassar in the early sixties. I

---

* The first two women's studies programs were founded at San Diego State College (now called San Diego State University) and Cornell in 1970.

ended up going up to Linda and saying, "Linda, my brother Richard [who was an art dealer] doesn't think there are any great women artists. Why are there no great women artists?" She said, "Let me think about that."

LINDA NOCHLIN

A few months later . . . I posted the following notice on the bulletin board in the art history office at Vassar: "I am changing the subject of the Art 364b seminar to: The Image of Women in the 19th and 20th Centuries. I have become more and more involved in the problem of the position of women during the course of this year and think it would make a most interesting and innovative seminar topic. . . . This would be a pioneering study in an untouched field."

BRENDA FEIGEN

January of '71 I was walking by a newsstand and I notice the *ARTnews* cover story with the headline: "Why Have There Been No Great Women Artists?" written by Linda Nochlin. Linda really was a pioneer in describing why women weren't great women artists, because they weren't exposed or they couldn't paint nudes, they couldn't be anywhere.[*]

ELIZABETH SPAHN

Women's history didn't exist. I mean it existed, but it had been suppressed. It had been lost, hidden. We didn't know it.

Elga Wasserman's[†] office had given a grant to the Sisterhood Yale Women's Center to make some proposals for the curriculum. We were doing research on the history part of it because the argument was, there isn't any women's history. I think the chair of the History Department at Yale said, "You might as well have the history of dogs," or maybe it was children. I can't remember. But his point was, there's nothing to teach. So, we were researching and gathering materials to show that there was in fact *some* history, that there were *some* things to read and events and topics to explore.

I went to the *W* section of the card catalog at Sterling Library. Do you remember what a card catalog is? I spent a lot of time in the *W*'s. And when

---

[*]   Nochlin's 1971 article helped launch the new field of women's art history, and in 1976 she and fellow academic Linda Sutherland curated a first-of-its-kind exhibit at the LA County Museum of Art: *Women Artists: 1550 to 1950*.

[†]   Elga Wasserman served as special assistant to the president of Yale for the education of women from 1968 to 1972.

I found call numbers, I'd go up in the stacks and I'd wander around. Oh my God, I was so happy, playing in the books. Here's a book about Emmeline Pankhurst—I wonder who she is? Literally, I had no clue and apparently the chair of the History Department didn't either.[*]

We started looking into doing research on women's suffrage—both the British and American movements. I literally remember sitting in Sterling Library and I had found a book about the American women's suffrage movement written by this person Elizabeth Cady Stanton, whom I'd never heard of, but my name is Elizabeth K. Spahn, so there's sort of a vibey resonance there. And I started reading the book; it was called *The Woman's Bible*.

The Women's Bible, by Elizabeth Cady Stanton and the Revising Committee, Introduction, 1898

From the inauguration of the movement for women's emancipation the Bible has been used to hold her in the "divinely ordained sphere," prescribed in the Old and New Testaments. . . .

The Bible teaches that woman brought sin and death into the world, that she precipitated the fall of the race, that she was arraigned before the judgment seat of Heaven, tried, condemned, and sentenced. Marriage for her was to be a condition of bondage, maternity a period of suffering and anguish, and in silence and subjection, she was to play the role of a dependent on man's bounty for all her maternal wants, and for all the information she might desire on the vital questions of the hour, she was commanded to ask her husband at home. Here is the Bible position of woman briefly summed up.

ELIZABETH SPAHN

Holy moly. Talk about an epiphany. There she was talking to me a hundred years later. She's speaking to me and she's saying, "Listen, this patriarchal religion stuff, let me tell you about the Bible." And she's so radical. And she's so clear and she writes beautifully and with such passion. Then I started studying Stanton and Anthony. And then of course I discovered

---

[*] Emmeline Pankhurst (1858–1928) was a militant British suffragist who founded the Women's Social and Political Union in 1903. The group's members, which included Pankhurst's daughter Christabel, staged hunger strikes and conducted bombing and arson campaigns. Pankhurst was arrested and jailed many times. In 1918, women over the age of thirty gained the right to vote in Britain, two years before the United States. But it would take until 1928, the year of Pankhurst's death, that women over the age of twenty-one could vote.

their racism, which did not make me happy. Unearthing your own history is always fraught with peril.* But they also could literally talk to you across the centuries. I was really happy to discover that we were not alone.

SALLY ROESCH WAGNER

One part of my course that I hated teaching was history, so I would bring in somebody who would lecture on the suffrage movement. A friend of mine was writing a paper on the woman's suffrage campaign in South Dakota in 1890, and she said, "There's a woman who was doing stuff in Aberdeen," South Dakota, where I grew up. "Did you ever hear of a woman named Matilda Joslyn Gage?" I said, "Well, my mom has a friend named Matilda Gage." I called up my mom and said, "Is your friend Matilda old enough to be a suffragist?" It didn't seem feasible. She said, "No, but her grandmother was an important suffragist."

I said, well, "I wonder if Matilda has any stories about her grandma? Would you set up a meeting for me with her when I come back home this summer?" I almost didn't go. It was a hot day and I didn't have air conditioning in my VW van. I didn't want to go into town. But I thought, well, I'll go in for an hour, get a story that I can share with my friend, and then I'll come back. I walked into her front parlor and she's showing me her grandma's furniture and her picture, and I'm rolling my eyes. Then she takes me into the dining room, where she's brought out all of her grandmother's papers and letters. She was the namesake and the only living grandchild of Matilda Joslyn Gage, and she had her father's correspondence, her aunt's correspondence to their mother, and Matilda's writing to her children. She had family photo albums, published and unpublished manuscripts by Gage, and bound volumes of her writings.

I was like, "Wow, this is cool." So, I started digging in. Matilda's handwriting is not easy, but I was able to read it, and one of the first letters was about how Mrs. Stanton is the Benedict Arnold of the movement. At that moment I was hooked. Susan B. Anthony and Elizabeth Cady Stanton were the leaders of the suffrage movement, and they were the only ones we knew about at the time.

---

* Susan B. Anthony (1820–1906) and Elizabeth Cady Stanton (1815–1902), two of the most prominent early suffragists, worked closely with abolitionists to end slavery, but when the Fifteenth Amendment granted Black men but not women the vote, Stanton and Anthony unleashed a torrent of racist statements and allied themselves with Southerners. Their racism created a split in the suffrage movement and alienated their Black abolitionist allies like Frederick Douglass and Mary Church Terrell.

I stayed there all day long trying to discover if Gage was important. I'm finding all these letters that have the officers of the National Women's Suffrage Association listed on the letterhead, and Gage's name is on every single one, along with Stanton and Anthony. As I read more and more of the correspondence, it became clear that she was a major figure.

And it dawned on me that it's craziness that the rest of the world is telling you one thing, but here's this evidence—take the evidence and work with it.

We had just gone through a really painful split in the women's studies program in Sacramento, and here was Gage talking smack about Anthony and Stanton.

And then I find newspaper articles where Gage is being interviewed about what's going on within the movement. "You girls are fighting, huh?" the reporter asks. And she tells the reporter, "We just have a difference of opinion about how to approach women's rights. Both sides are for women's rights, we're just working for it in different ways." And it was like, bingo, there's our answer. We publicly show a united front but deal with our conflict privately.

Here is a feminist foremother reaching across the ages and telling me what we should be doing. And it was like, boom. I'm ready. This woman who hated history became a born-again historian. My love affair with Matilda directed the whole rest of my life.*

MICHELE WALLACE
When I was a kid, the only Black feminist I knew was Sojourner Truth, and I didn't know much about her. Those of us who first became Black feminists in the early seventies knew so little about the Black women—the artists, intellectuals, and feminist activists—who had come before us. It took a long time to find the record they had left.

BARBARA SMITH
African American literature was not taught at historically white colleges and universities anywhere during that period. Black literature was taught at historically Black colleges and universities, but not even necessarily in the

---

* In 1978, Wagner earned one of the first PhDs in the country for work in women's studies, from the University of California, Santa Cruz. The title of her dissertation: "That Word Is Liberty: A Biography of Matilda Joslyn Gage."

context of Black studies. It might've been taught in the context of an American literature course. In other words, these fields had not yet been defined.

We were demanding Black studies at Mount Holyoke. One of the articles that I wrote for the school newspaper was about why we need Black studies. This was a dream that all students of my generation had, and that we were advocating for, because it didn't exist where we were getting our higher education. I didn't miss anything. I didn't skip classes or not read the catalog carefully. There was nothing. I wanted to study Black literature and I found the most wonderful professor. He's in that group of my three favorite professors of all time. My English advisor at Mount Holyoke. He shaped my career and was wonderful. A young white man named Richard Johnson. Sadly, deceased.

I ended up doing an independent study with him about four Black writers who were considered to be among the most significant Black writers at the time. It was Ralph Ellison, James Baldwin, Richard Wright, and Leroy Jones. Jones had not changed his name to Amiri Baraka at that point.

I went to grad school knowing that I wanted to teach African American literature. I was not in grad school to teach the Europeans. I went to grad school to teach *my* literature.

My first semester at the University of Connecticut, they offered a seminar in women's literature. This is 1971. It was one of the first courses offered in women's literature in a graduate program in the country. I don't remember any Black students at the University of Connecticut in my grad program. I asked my seminar professor if she had any suggestions for Black women writers who I might do my final paper on. She had no suggestions at all. Think about it. Even though it may seem appalling and of course I was upset because I'm on a mission, and I'm taking a women's literature seminar and my interest is African American literature and my professor can't help me.

Anyway, she did give me Gerda Lerner's *Black Women in White America: A Documentary History*, which is a transformative book. That was one of the books that built the field of women's studies, particularly women's history. And of course, I was fascinated by the book and read it deeply, and I'm thinking, "This is an incredible book. What can I do with this? I need to come up with a seminar topic."

ALICE WALKER

When I started teaching my course in black women writers at Wellesley (the first one, I think, ever), I was worried that Zora Neale Hurston's use of Black English of the [nineteen] twenties would throw some of the students off.

It didn't. They loved it. They said it was like reading Thomas Hardy, only better. In that same course I taught Nella Larsen, Frances Watkins Harper (poetry and novel), Dorothy West, Ann Petry, Paule Marshall, among others. Also, Kate Chopin and Virginia Woolf . . . because they were women and wrote, as the Black women did, on the condition of humankind from the perspective of women.

BARBARA SMITH

Fast-forwarding to summer of 1972, *Ms.* magazine started publishing in '72 and I was a charter subscriber. I wasn't in the movement, but I was doing the reading, and Alice Walker was affiliated with *Ms.* magazine early on. I knew who Alice Walker was because I had read her poetry in *Harper's Magazine.* When I saw she was teaching a course in Black women writers at Wellesley, I wrote to her and I asked if I could audit her class. By the time she taught it again in the fall of '72, she was teaching at UMass Boston. I audited her class. That's when I got bit by the bug.

> Alice Walker, Sarah Lawrence commencement speech, 1972
>
> I found that the majority of Black women who tried to express themselves by writing and who tried to make a living doing so, died in obscurity and poverty, usually before their time. . . . Zora Neale Hurston, who wrote what is perhaps the most authentic and moving Black love story ever published, died in poverty in the swamps of Florida, where she was again working as a housemaid. She had written six books and was a noted folklorist and anthropologist, having worked while a student at Barnard with Franz Boas.[*]
>
> The young person leaving college today, especially if she is a woman, must consider the possibility that her best offerings will be considered a nuisance to the men who also occupy her field. . . . If she is Black and coming out into the world, she must be doubly armed, doubly prepared. Because for her there is not simply a new world to be gained, there is an old world that must be reclaimed. There are countless

---

[*]   Walker reintroduced Zora Neale Hurston and her forgotten 1937 novel, *Their Eyes Were Watching God,* to the American literary world in the 1970s and is largely responsible for the recognition of Hurston as one of the most heralded Black women writers of the twentieth century. Walker found Hurston's unmarked grave in 1973 in Fort Pierce, Florida, and installed a gravestone on which she had inscribed, "Zora Neale Hurston / "A Genius of the South / 1901– – –1960 / Novelist, Folklorist Anthropologist." Walker's essay describing her quest to discover Hurston's life history and grave site, "In Search of Zora Neale Hurston," was published in *Ms.* in March 1975.

vanished and forgotten women who are nonetheless eager to speak to her—from Frances Harper and Anne Spencer to Dorothy West—but she must work to find them, to free them from their neglect and the oppression of silence forced upon them because they were Black and they were women. . . .

Historians are generally enemies of women, certainly of Blacks, and so are, all too often, the very people we must sit under in order to learn. Ignorance, arrogance, and racism have bloomed as Superior Knowledge in all too many universities. . . .

But it is a great time to be a woman. A wonderful time to be a Black woman, for the world, I have found . . . because the past is studded with sisters who, in their time, shone like gold. They give us hope, they have proved the splendor of our past, which should free us to lay just claim to the fullness of the future.

BARBARA SMITH

That fall of '72 is when I first found out about Zora Neale Hurston, Ann Petry [who wrote *The Street*], and the novel *Jubilee* [by Margaret Walker] for the first time. I did my seminar paper for that course at the University of Connecticut on Ann Petry, who is just one of my favorite writers of all time. I said to myself, "The next time I teach," because I'd already had teaching experience as a teaching assistant, "I'm going to teach a course in Black women writers."

The next year, I got hired at Emerson College to teach composition, but the wonderful woman who was head of the English Department said, "And what else would you like to teach?" I said, "I want to teach African American literature." She said, "Fine." I had promised myself that someday, I would teach a course in Black women's literature, and one year later, that's exactly what I was doing.[*]

FLORENCE HOWE

When I began at Goucher College in Baltimore in 1960, I taught what I had been taught: the male-centered curriculum, male writers, male perspectives, about mainly male worlds.

Then in 1969, when the women's movement hit US campuses, students

---

[*]   Barbara Smith became an influential Black women's literature scholar and public intellectual, and published the first article about Black feminist literary criticism in 1977, "Toward a Black Feminist Criticism."

asked why there were no women writers in the eighteenth-century course I taught. I had to admit that I knew of none, that I had studied only men. That's when I knew something was wrong.

Early in 1970, three university presses asked me to write a biography of Doris Lessing. I told them I wanted to begin another project: a series of one hundred short biographies about dead women, to be written by living ones, including Doris Lessing. They all turned me down, saying, "There's no money in it."

Then my husband, Paul Lauter, who was teaching at the University of Maryland at the time, said, "Why not do it ourselves?" He thought of the name, the Feminist Press—and it sounded magical.

Without telling me, Baltimore Women's Liberation announced the Feminist Press's existence in its newsletter. When I returned from a month at Cape Cod, I found more than a hundred letters, some with checks and cash, in my street mailbox, addressed to the Feminist Press. The letters indicated that Baltimore Women's Liberation had also announced that the Feminist Press would publish children's books as well as the biographies I had suggested. Fifty people attended the first meeting of the Feminist Press in my living room on November 17, 1970.

PAUL LAUTER

And then slightly later, but not much, we began to publish work by women writers who had been lost and basically forgotten. Like Rebecca Harding Davis's *Life in the Iron Mills* and Charlotte Perkins Gilman's *The Yellow Wallpaper*. Those became very significant and not only in the Feminist Press, but in the women's movement.

FLORENCE HOWE

By 1973, I was hunting for the rights to Zora Neale Hurston's work. I had been going to secondhand bookstores and buying up all the copies I could find of *Their Eyes Were Watching God* and lending them to my students, since the book was out of print. When I couldn't find anyone who knew who controlled Hurston's rights, I asked Tillie Olsen if she could reach Alice Walker, who had written an essay for *Ms.* about Hurston's unmarked grave in Florida. Tillie called Alice and she made a lunch date, and I discovered that she, too, was looking for Hurston's heirs, since she had finished collecting material for an anthology.

Alice offered the Feminist Press the anthology she called *I Love Myself*

When I Am Laughing and Then Again When I Am Looking Mean and Impressive: A Zora Neale Hurston Reader, even though we were paying no advances at all. I remember the meeting with Alice and her agent, Wendy Weil, who could not believe Alice wanted to sign our contract.

RUTH ROSEN

As part of my five-year fellowship at Berkeley, I was to be a teaching assistant, and in the second or third year, you could teach small seminars, and I taught the first women's history course at Berkeley, it was probably 1970.

We were changing the way history was written, and we were changing what history was. My colleagues in my graduate student class were starting labor history, they were starting Black history, they were starting urban history, and I was starting women's history. Our whole generation was creating new fields of history.

It was like a whole group of women who had gone to college suddenly discovered women's history at the same time, yet there was very little women's history to teach. I made my class into a research seminar so that the students could do research on subjects and read one another's work and tell one another what they found.[*]

HONOR MOORE

When I came to New York, I started to scrawl poems. Then I started writing them. I got inspired by Sonia Sanchez[†] and Adrienne Rich. Sonia, for her direct address in her first collection called *Homecoming* (1969), which I found in the *Rat* office when it was taken over by women's liberation. It was a yellow and black pamphlet with very radical, direct-address poems that inspired me. I didn't know much about literary poetry. I knew a little about the New York School poets. You just can't imagine how hard it was to get a hold of a woman writer to read. Really, all we had was Sylvia Plath, so all we wrote were suicidal poems, even if we weren't suicidal. But we sort of were, because we didn't have a life.

I wrote without the company of other women poets until December 11, 1971, when some women got in touch with me, and said, "We're doing a

---

[*]   Ruth Rosen's first book of feminist history, *The Maimie Papers*, about a nineteenth-century prostitute, was published by the Feminist Press in 1978.

[†]   Civil rights activist and poet Sonia Sanchez also taught one of the first courses on African American literature at San Francisco State University in 1966.

women's liberation poetry anthology." So together we organized these massive women's poetry readings in a big room at the now-razed Loeb Student Center at NYU, because someone was a graduate student at NYU.

In those days, the poetry reading came from the Beat movement, through the Black Arts movement, into the women's liberation movement. So, it was a thing for a political movement to have poetry as part of it, and as it happened, we had some great poets among us.

The first reading was packed, with many of us sitting on the floor. Twenty-one women read—most of us had not published books and some, like me, had not published at all; others had appeared in *Rat*, *Moving Out*, and other women's liberation papers and journals. The ecstatic, celebratory night ended only when the building closed. Six more group readings followed the next winter. And first it would just be the gang of us, but then we'd have Carolyn Kizer and June Jordan and Sonia Sanchez, whose books had been published by trade publishers.

Robin Morgan would read a poem and everybody would stand up and scream and shout and carry on. My friend Mary Silverman said, "For me, the women's movement was poetry." It was so exciting. Those years gave me my belief in myself as a writer because it was quite extraordinary to really connect with your readers and have them come right back at you immediately to respond to a poem.

I would say this went on for about four years. There were also all of these anthologies coming out, like Florence Howe's *No More Masks*, which was more literary, and *We Become New*, which was more political. *Amazon Poetry* came out later, which was radical lesbian.

By the later seventies, Audre Lorde and Adrienne Rich were bringing thousands of people to a reading or a speech.

MICHELE WALLACE

At various events around town, I met Audre Lorde, Toni Morrison, Alice Walker, June Jordan, Nikki Giovanni, and Sonia Sanchez, who all seemed to me stunningly attractive, articulate, and bigger than life. I encountered Walker, who seemed shy and retiring, at meetings of Black feminists. Even then, to fledgling Black women writers, Morrison was a queen.[*]

---

[*] Toni Morrison, an editor at Random House from 1967 to 1983, published her first novel, *The Bluest Eye*, in 1970. She would go on to write ten more novels and many other books. Morrison won the Pulitzer Prize for her 1987 novel, *Beloved*, the Nobel Prize for Literature in 1993, and the Presidential Medal of Freedom in 2012.

I was traveling around with my mother to conferences. You know, I'm a poet. I was writing poetry and at all the readings that I went to, there were two Black women, me, and Audre Lorde. She was very grand, very regal.*

ROBIN MORGAN

What is happening here is not only a feminist renaissance, but because of that feminist renaissance, a renaissance of art. Art has the possibility of becoming alive again, relevant to real people's real needs, to suffering, to human emotion and possibility; of becoming something accessible, something you live with. In terms specifically of language, words are being used today that simply weren't possible before—umbilical cord, vagina, tampon, diaper, kitchen sink—a whole new treasure chest of words and the images attendant on them that are now possible in a poem.

KIRSTEN GRIMSTAD

I was teaching German to male undergraduates at Columbia and completing my doctoral exams and after the doctoral exams were over, Patsy Geisler, who oversaw all the teaching assistants, crossed paths with Catharine Stimpson, the founding director of the Barnard Women's Center, who asked her if she could recommend someone to become the editor of this new bibliography of women's studies. I was a Barnard graduate, so Patsy mentioned me.

The whole field of women's studies was just getting started, but the burgeoning scholars of women's studies were very busy, because all of history, all of literature, all of art had to be looked at now through the feminist lens. So there was a lot of work to be done, and it was just pouring out.

So an annual bibliography of women's studies would keep track of it all. This bibliography was not going to just have scholarship, it was going to have women's activist projects too, because we have to put scholarship and activism together.

So I made a questionnaire and sent it out to women's organizations all over the country. I wanted to know what activism they were engaged in. I got

---

* In 1977, Alice Walker and June Jordan started a Black feminist literary collective called The Sisterhood. Margo Jefferson and Michele Wallace were among the thirty members who met once a month for two years. Wallace, who worked at *Newsweek* with Margo Jefferson, was one of the youngest members of the group. In 1978, at age twenty-seven, Wallace published her explosively controversial first book, *Black Macho and the Myth of the Superwoman.*

back all sorts of exciting information. Every city had a feminist newspaper, there were women's centers everywhere, women's bookstores popping up everywhere. There were anti-rape groups, and publishing companies—the Feminist Press, but also KNOW Inc.[*] My real epiphany was discovering all of this.

And if you put it all together: the scholarship, the conceptual reorganization of our understanding of ourselves and our world, plus the diverse ways in which women were taking their lives and their future into their own hands, what we saw was a whole alternative culture. There was the dominant culture where men had privilege and power, and then there was this alternative culture, women's culture, where women were not answering to men anymore. It was like saying, "Oh the heck with you, we're going to just do it ourselves."

Among the people who were on the board of the new Barnard College Women's Center was Susan Rennie. She was the assistant vice president for academic affairs at Columbia. She was their token woman. She had completed her doctorate in the political science department. She's originally from South Africa.

SUSAN RENNIE

I was at the Barnard Women's Center for a meeting, and in the door walks this young woman and she's got a motorcycle helmet under her arm and long flaming-red hair. I said, "Whoa, who is this?"

Kirsten said, "I have this questionnaire that I sent out a few months ago. There's a lot going on in women's studies, but the thing that is so interesting," she said, "I had one box in the questionnaire asking if there are other women's activities on your campus," and she was getting back answers saying they weren't just on campus, but also in town.

I mean, in places like Eugene, Oregon; Iowa City; Oakland, California; and Los Angeles: all of these things were happening. It still gives me goose bumps to think about this. It was all activism and self-help.

These are women saying, we want to be able to change our married names, so we're going to start a group to fight for this, because we can't do it legally, or going to teach women to use speculums to look at their own insides. Or in North Carolina, we are starting a collective to write

---

[*] Founded in 1969 by members of the Pittsburgh chapter of NOW, KNOW Inc. was a publishing collective that issued a newsletter and published women's studies books.

and publish children's short stories because we don't like what our female children are reading.

I said, this is absolutely incredible. Everybody in New York thinks that what is important in the world is happening in New York, but nobody hears about the scale of what was touching so many different aspects of women's lives.*

---

*   Grimstad left her husband, and she and Rennie became lovers, quit their jobs, and spent the summer of 1973 driving twelve thousand miles to dozens of towns and cities across the country. They documented the blooming new feminist ecosystem of bookstores and newspapers, farm communes, mechanic shops, poster collectives, and art galleries. *The New Woman's Survival Catalog: A Woman-Made Book* was published in late 1973 and became a bestseller. Grimstad and Rennie then moved to Los Angeles and started the monthly feminist publication *Chrysalis*, which published out of the Women's Building from 1977 to 1980.

4

Reed v. Reed and the Birth of Feminist Jurisprudence

By late 1971, Brenda Feigen, Gloria Steinem, and Ruth Bader Ginsburg's worlds collided. While Feigen and Steinem cooked up the idea for Ms., Ginsburg, a professor at Rutgers Law School, began to launch a systematic and strategic attack on the large body of laws that treated men and women differently. Feigen would soon join Ginsburg on her journey to reset the legal landscape.

RUTH BADER GINSBURG

At the same time [that I was teaching the course "Sex Discrimination and the Law"], the New Jersey affiliate of the American Civil Liberties Union began to refer to me complaints of a kind the affiliate had not seen before: teachers forced out of the classroom when their pregnancy began to show, women whose employers provided health insurance with family coverage only for male employees, and parents whose school-age daughters were excluded from publicly funded educational programs open only to boys. I was lucky to be in the right place, at the right time.

The cases we picked were carefully selected. The first one was *Reed v. Reed*.

Sally Reed was a divorced woman with a teenage son. When her child was young—the legal expression of tender years—she had custody. When the boy reached his teens, his father said now it's time for him to be prepared for a man's world. Sally Reed fought giving custody to the father but lost. As it turned out, sadly, she was right, the boy became severely depressed in his father's custody. One day he took out one of his father's many guns and committed suicide. Sally wanted to be appointed administrator of his estate.

They were from Boise, Idaho, and the law read: "As between persons equally entitled to administer a decedent's estate, males must be preferred to females." So, we had the ideal law to challenge—the ideal real-life situation. All of the 1970s gender discrimination cases in which I was involved had that kind of plaintiff.

Sally Reed took her case through three levels of the Idaho courts on her own dime. The ACLU didn't get into the act until the Supreme Court. . . . I called Mel Wulf, who I knew from summer camp days. He was then the legal director of the ACLU. I told Mel, I would like to write the brief in Reed. He replied, "Ruth, we will write the brief." "We" meaning Mel and me. And so we did, with the aid of students from Yale Law School, Columbia Law School, Rutgers Law School, and NYU.

In preparing Sally Reed's appeal to the Supreme Court, I placed on the brief the names of two women. One was Dorothy Kenyon, who had represented Gwendolyn Hoyt,* the other was Pauli Murray,† the lawyer, poet, novelist, and later minister who had long fought for racial and gender justice. Both were then too old to be part of the fray, but people of my generation owed them a great debt, for they bravely pressed arguments for equal justice in days when few would give ear to what they were saying.

The Supreme Court unanimously declared Idaho's male preference statute unconstitutional. *Reed v. Reed* was the turning point case. Decided in November 1971, Sally Reed's case invalidated an Idaho statute that afforded men (in this particular case, Sally's estranged husband Cecil) an automatic preference over women for estate administration purposes.

---

* Convicted by an all-male jury of second-degree murder for killing her abusive husband in Florida, Gwendolyn Hoyt believed that if women served on juries she would have received a more lenient sentence from her peers. In *Hoyt v. Florida* in 1961, the Supreme Court rejected Hoyt's claim, ruling that it was constitutional for a state not to require women to serve on juries because of their role in "the center of home and family life." ACLU lawyer Dorothy Kenyon wrote the brief on behalf of *Hoyt*. In 1975, the court overturned the 1961 decision. In *Hoyt v. Louisiana,* the court ruled that excluding women from jury service is unconstitutional.

† Pauli Murray and Mary Eastwood's 1965 "Jane Crow and the Law," which explained the historical and legal parallels between racism and sexism, and Murray's ACLU brief for the Alabama jury race and sex discrimination case *White v. Crook* in 1966 provided the legal foundation on which Ginsburg built many of her gender discrimination cases.

BRENDA FEIGEN

I was a vice president of NOW. It was 1970. I got a job in New York in the litigation department at a big corporate law firm, Rosenman, Colin, Kaye, Petschek, Freund and Emil. But I couldn't just sail through my life as a corporate lawyer. That's what drove me in that moment to run to Gloria's apartment and say, "Listen, we have to do something. I have an idea."

The idea was something I got from Dick Goodwin, who told me about Bobby Kennedy and organizing people on a local level to fight for certain issues. I felt that NOW was addressing the Equal Rights Amendment and abortion rights from the top down, but I thought there needed to be a group that would encourage women to confront sexist issues in their own communities. I went up to Gloria's apartment and we decided that we were going to start something that would address the local issues that women had, like childcare, and stereotyping in textbooks, and whatever else women felt they needed to fight sexism in their own personal worlds. We could help them mobilize around those kinds of issues. We could connect groups in different parts of the country that were struggling with the same problem.

We worked out what to call it. Gloria wanted the word "sisters" in it. So we called it Sisters: The Women's Action Alliance.

GLORIA STEINEM

It became more and more clear to me that I couldn't really publish what I wanted to publish in the magazines that were existing. I don't think that I would have quite had the nerve to think about starting another magazine if it hadn't been for two things. One was that we started to go around to speak. The whole idea that there was only interest in the women's movement among a few crazy people in New York and California turned out to be quite the opposite. There was a great hunger and interest everywhere we went. I was afraid to speak in public so I asked a friend who was not afraid to do much of anything by herself, Dorothy Pitman Hughes, an African American woman who had started what may have been the first multiracial, nonsexist childcare center. I had written about her for *New York* magazine, and then we became friends.

I asked her if she wanted to come with me, because I was thinking, okay, I don't have any children, and perhaps women will find my life experience too distant, and this is her specialty. I'm sure I was thinking about the fact that we were a white woman and a Black woman together, but I didn't fully understand how important that was to audiences. It was so clear, the moment we started, that we both got audiences together that neither one of us would have got separately; that it became even more of an advantage than either one of us had thought about. We had a lecture agency who would book us and I could see that there was this enormous interest in places like Wichita, Kansas, which stands out in my mind because there were, like, five thousand people there.

I hate to generalize this much, but in the eyes of the media, I think the women's movement was viewed as white females, the civil rights movement was viewed as Black males, and Black females got left out of both, when in fact, obviously they were essential in both. And so we became committed to speaking in pairs. "Feminists come in pairs like nuns," we used to say.

By speaking together at hundreds of public meetings, we hoped to widen the public image of the women's movement created largely by its first home-grown media event, *The Feminine Mystique*. Despite the many early reformist virtues of *The Feminine Mystique*, it had managed to appear at the height of the civil rights movement with almost no reference to Black women or other women of color. As a result, "white middle-class-movement" had become the catchphrase of journalists describing feminism in the United States. And ignoring the fact that Pauli Murray had the idea for the National Organization for Women as "an NAACP for women," and that Aileen Hernandez had followed Betty Friedan as its president. Both were Black feminists.[*]

And then we started the Women's Action Alliance, which was an effort to answer questions that came—like how to start a childcare center—from women who didn't have the time or the ability or the desire, perhaps, to join an organization like NOW. They just wanted a question answered. So, the Women's Action Alliance started as a kind of information source.

BRENDA FEIGEN

The Action Alliance was going on for a while before Gloria said, "I should just do a newsletter for this." By this time, Gloria had become quite well known and I thought that we should capitalize on that and spread the word much more than a little newsprint publication would be able to do. I said, "We don't need that, it should be a slick magazine." She said, "We will never get advertising." I said, "Yes, you will."

---

[*] After Dorothy Pitman Hughes had a child and could no longer travel constantly, Black civil rights and feminist advocates Margaret Sloan and Flo Kennedy became regular speaking companions of Steinem, who from the beginning of her involvement in the women's movement was always particularly conscious of the issues of race and poverty and how they intersected with feminism.

Gloria decided she'd have a meeting in her apartment, which was a floor of a brownstone on East Seventy-Third Street. We announced it, and the place was jammed with women.

GLORIA STEINEM

All of us who were writing for *New York* or other magazines began to meet and to try to invite other women editors and lots of people, to see if people wanted another place to publish. And overwhelmingly they did.

BRENDA FEIGEN

Every woman you'd ever seen a byline of, like Susan Brownmiller, Adrienne Rich, Robin Morgan, Jill Johnston, Jane O'Reilly, all came. The next meeting was in my apartment, which was this great place in Tudor City that looked out over the East River. It was completely jammed with women journalists, writers, wannabe writers. After each woman spoke about what she wanted to write but hadn't been able to get approved by male editors and publishers, I thought we had enough proof. That sealed the deal; we decided to start the magazine.*

VIVIAN GORNICK

Radical feminists like me, Ellen Willis, and Jill Johnston had a different kind of magazine in mind. We came out against marriage and motherhood. Gloria was uptown; we were downtown. She hung out with establishment figures; we had only ourselves. It very quickly became obvious at that first meeting that they wanted a glossy that would appeal to the women who read the *Ladies' Home Journal.* We didn't want that, so they walked away with the idea.

GLORIA STEINEM

In trying to think of a title for the magazine, *Sojourner* was one, after Sojourner Truth, but we discovered people thought it was a travel magazine. *Sisters* was another, but then they thought it was Catholic. A virtue of *Ms.* was that it was short, so it left more room for cover lines. At the time, I had only ever seen "Ms." in secretarial handbooks from the 1950s, where

---

* In the five years between 1968 and 1973, according to Anne Mather's "A History of Feminist Periodicals," 560 feminist publications had sprouted up across the country, but none had significant national newsstand distribution.

it was recommended as a way of dealing with the unfortunate situation in which you didn't know the marital status of the person you were writing to.

So that was really the start of *Ms.* magazine. We did a mock-up of it, and we went around trying to raise money, which was impossible. The idea of a feminist magazine seemed crazy to people, but especially one that was controlled by its staff.

BRENDA FEIGEN

Then I got a call from Mel Wulf, the legal director of the ACLU national office, who said, "We're starting a Women's Rights Project with Professor Ruth Bader Ginsburg, would you be willing to consider coming in as director with her?" I said, "Oh my God, I've just announced the formation of *Ms.* magazine. You're going to have to let me think about this," which I did for about three weeks. I was flattered, because I had practiced law for only about six months before I left to start the Alliance. I talked to Gloria about it. She had no doubts. Lots of women were qualified to run the Alliance but few, if any, feminist lawyers were around to do the job at the ACLU. I took the job.

I knew that Ruth had gone to Harvard Law School ten years before me. She was in the class of '59 and her class was only 3 percent women. I knew it was horrible for women then; it was barely any better by my year.

I made a point of reading the Supreme Court's opinion in *Reed v. Reed*. It was a unanimous decision for Sally Reed, and Ruth had written the brilliant brief for *Reed*, the brief that was the beginning of what I call feminist jurisprudence. She was laser-focused on getting sex to be treated the way race was treated, with the strictest standard of review. The justices agreed that women were a "protected" class, deserving recognition under the Equal Protection Clause of the Fourteenth Amendment.

Because of *Reed*, a new age was dawning for women, and I was excited by the thought that I might be able to help in that revolutionary struggle.

5

Ms. and the Cultural Click

KATHARINE GRAHAM

My friendship with Gloria Steinem was an important influence. . . . Being younger, she had been shaped by the 1950s, a very different time from my own frame of reference. I had watched the burgeoning women's movement, of which she was a distinguished leader, from afar at first and was put off by the pioneering feminists who necessarily, I now suspect, took extreme positions to make their crucial point about the essential equality of women.

I couldn't understand militancy and disliked the kind of bra-burning symbolism. . . . Gloria kept telling me that if I came to understand what the women's movement was all about, it would make my life much better. In time it inevitably dawned on me, and how right she was! Later, when Gloria came to me for funds to start up *Ms.* magazine, I put up $20,000 for seed money to help her get going.

GLORIA STEINEM

Clay Felker at *New York* magazine,* who always did a big double issue at the end of the year, recognized that the women's movement was news. So he said that if we—this hearty little band of people—did an issue of this

---

* Felker, a legendary magazine editor and publisher, cofounded the weekly magazine *New York* in 1968 and was one of the few editors in New York at the time who took women writers and editors seriously.

new magazine and gave him thirty pages of it as a sample to bind into his year-end issue, he would pay for the production of the other hundred pages, and we would have a sample issue. And that's really how it happened. So there was one preview issue of *Ms.* in late December 1971.

JANE O'REILLY

To give Clay credit, he would encourage women, including me, to write anything. He did, and that was true across the board.

NANCY NEWHOUSE

I remember Clay saying he was going to put *Ms.* magazine inside *New York* magazine, and everybody on the *New York* staff was like, what's he talking about? Everybody was just stupefied. Gloria had tried to get funding to start the magazine, and she got nowhere. That's where Clay's intuition came in. A) he admired Gloria, but b) it was something he wanted to do because he had started *his* magazine, and she wanted to start *her* magazine. He had totally positive feelings about Gloria and what she was trying to do.

Clay assigned Rochelle Udell and me to work on the *Ms.* insert. I didn't even know Rochelle because she was in the art department, but she was bright and nice. We were delighted to be put on this big project. We were in charge of the editorial and design production, and we worked hard to meet the deadline. Gloria would come in and see that Rochelle and I were still at the office at ten o'clock at night, and knowing how hard we were working, she gave us both a silver ring with the female symbol on it. I wish I could find it.

JANE O'REILLY

I remember sitting in Gloria's living room, and there were lots of people there discussing all the different important areas that would be covered, and what stories we should write for the preview issue. Of course, we thought we'd never get a second edition, so we had to put everything in.

So I'm sitting there thinking, "Oh, I never thought about that," and "Oh, do I have to think about being a lesbian?" And someone said, "I guess we should have an article about housework." And everybody went, "Ugh." And I said, "I'll do it." I knew I could write about housework, and at least I could be funny. So, that's how "The Housewife's Moment of Truth" got started.

It had been a busy summer, so I was in effect skimming the froth off my summer. For example, the woman on the boat to Fire Island who said, "Isn't he wonderful? He took out the garbage." All of the anecdotes in the story had happened in the previous few months. So I was just picking up what I'd seen. I just sat down and I started typing, and then I thought, "Click." And there's my contribution to the English language.

Ms., Spring 1972, "The Housewife's Moment of Truth," by Jane O'Reilly

On Fire Island my weekend hostess and I had just finished cooking breakfast, lunch, and washing dishes for both. A male guest came wandering into the kitchen just as the last dish was being put away and said, "How about something to eat?" He sat down, expectantly, and started to read the paper. Click! . . .

In New York last fall, my neighbors—named Jones—had a couple named Smith over for dinner. Mr. Smith kept telling his wife to get up and help Mrs. Jones. Click! Click! Two women radicalized at once! . . .

Last summer I got a letter, from a man who wrote: "I do not agree with your last article, and I am canceling my wife's subscription." The next day I got a letter from his wife saying, "I am not canceling my subscription." Click! . . . In the end, we are all housewives, the natural people to turn to when there is something unpleasant, inconvenient or inconclusive to be done.

GLORIA STEINEM

Jane described a moment when a woman who's been piling up things on the stairs to take to the second floor watches her husband walk around them as he climbs the stairs, and she thinks, *He has two hands!* It was a prototypal "click" of realizing unfairness.

JANE O'REILLY

The "click" idea just came to me. I didn't know it would be the best idea I'd ever had.

BILLIE JEAN KING

Sometime in late 1971, Larry and I had a lunch conversation with the editors of a new magazine called *Ms.*, which was set to launch in early 1972. . . . Sometime after our first get-together, an envelope from the magazine arrived at the apartment that Larry and I had in California. It was in a stack of mail that Larry handed to me after I got home, and he told me I would probably want to support the petition inside the envelope because, he said, "It will help legalize abortion." The Supreme Court's *Roe v. Wade* ruling was almost two years off.

I got pregnant in early 1971 six weeks into the Virginia Slims tour. . . . I played two more tournaments and nearly threw up on the court at the second one in New York City. That's when I called Larry and flew back to California to take a pregnancy test. It came back positive. *Oh dear God,* I thought. *Now what do I do?* . . . I'd always wanted to have children and still did—but not then. Our marriage was too shaky, and our lives were so complicated and unpredictable. Also, I now realized my attraction to women wasn't going away.

California was one of a handful of states that had legalized abortion before *Roe v. Wade*, as long as it was a "therapeutic" abortion performed by a doctor in a hospital. But any woman who wanted an abortion had to go before a medical committee first and explain why she believed that her pregnancy would "gravely impair" her "physical or mental health."

Arguing to a dozen or so people I had never met why I qualified for an abortion remains one of the most degrading experiences of my life. But there was still another indignity: the law required that my husband sign a consent form.

BARBARALEE DIAMONSTEIN-SPIELVOGEL

The abortion petition was Gloria's idea. She asked me to do it because she thought that people would trust me. At the time, I was the first director of cultural affairs for New York in Mayor John Lindsay's administration. I remember having several meetings in my apartment with about four or five people figuring out what we should do. I made lists of prominent women. I sent them letters. They didn't answer. I called them up. I knew a lot of them, otherwise, I'm not sure what we would've done. In my letter, I deliberately did not ask if they had abortions, because this was not meant as a test of anything except solidarity for the concept. It wasn't meant as a confessional and should not be interpreted that way.

NORA EPHRON

I remember that Gloria called me and said they were doing a statement that was inspired by what the Danes had supposedly done during World War II, wearing Jewish stars, daring the Nazis to arrest them all.

LETTY COTTIN POGREBIN

I thought it was especially important because as a wife and mother of three, I could not easily be accused of being a "baby killer." Almost all my friends had had abortions. I wanted everyone to admit it.

BARBARALEE DIAMONSTEIN-SPIELVOGEL

Several people, as you would imagine, did not want to be identified with such controversy. It wasn't like a signing on because you were the smartest girl in the class. There was nothing honorific about it. It took courage.

BILLIE JEAN KING

I said okay, that I would take a look. But it was Larry who actually signed my name on the petition and sent it back without telling me he had done so—or me knowing that the petition allowed *Ms.* to publish my name along with a list of other prominent women signees under the headline "We Have Had Abortions." The fifty-three others included Steinem, the playwright Lillian Hellman, the historian Barbara Tuchman, the singer Judy Collins, and the writers Anaïs Nin, Susan Sontag, and Grace Paley.

Ms., Spring 1972, "We Have Had Abortions:
These 53 American Women Invite You to Join Them in a Campaign for Honesty and Freedom," by Barbaralee D. Diamonstein
Last year, 343 prominent and respected Frenchwomen were willing to sign a public manifesto declaring that they had undergone abortions. This act *del revolte* dramatized their individual determination to take their lives and liberation into their own hands. It also showed their willingness to stand with and to speak for their less well-known sisters who were forced to suffer unwanted pregnancies or illegal abortions in silence. . . .*

In fact, at least one of every four women in the United States has had an abortion. Until the recent legal reforms in two states (New York and Hawaii), all of those had to be either therapeutic or illegal. . . . There has been untold suffering, especially on the part of poor women who

---

*   In the French "Manifesto of the 343," 343 French women, including actress Catherine Deneuve and writers Simone de Beauvoir and Marguerite Duras, declared that they had had illegal abortions. Written by de Beauvoir, the manifesto was inspired by the 1960 "Manifesto of the 121" calling for Algerian independence from colonial France. It proclaimed: "One million women in France have abortions every year. Condemned to secrecy, they do so in dangerous conditions. . . . Society is silencing these millions of women. I declare that I am one of them. I declare that I have had an abortion."

must resort to self-induced or butchered abortions. . . . During the first nine months of the new legal abortion program in New York, "deaths from childbirth" dropped by at least 60 per cent.

To save lives and spare other women the pain of socially-imposed guilt, 53 respected women residents in the United States have volunteered to begin the American Women's Petition by signing the statement below. . . . Because of the social stigma still wrongly attached to abortion, many women in public life, or with husbands in public life, have felt unable to join us. . . . But we invite all women, from every walk of life, to help eliminate this sigma by joining us in this petition, and signing the statement below. The complete list will be sent to the White House, to every State Legislature, and to our sisters in other countries who are signing similar petitions for their lawmakers.*

SUZANNE LEVINE

Letty was a friend of mine, and they were looking for somebody who could put out the magazine, and at the time, I was the managing editor of a magazine in Seattle called *Sexual Behavior*. I read the preview issue of the magazine, which included among such classics as "Click! The Housewife's Moment of Truth" by Jane O'Reilly and "I Want a Wife" by Judy Syfers, but I fixated on a list of celebrity names under the headline "We Have Had Abortions." It took a lot of courage back then to admit to what was a crime. In the corner was a coupon which readers could fill out to add their name to the list. I filled it out with pride and relief that I wasn't alone (I hadn't admitted to my crime before). And the loveliest thing is that by the time we were opening those envelopes, I was managing editor at *Ms.* and I got to see my envelope opened.†

---

* On a personal note, I first read all fifty-three names of the petition while writing this chapter in February 2023, and was astounded to see my mother's name, Joan Bingham, on the list. In 1971, my mother lived in New York working as a freelance photographer. She was not famous, but she happened to be friends with Barbaralee Diamonstein. I knew that my mother, who was widowed with two children at age thirty-one in 1966, had traveled to London for an abortion, but she never told me that she lent her name to this historic *Ms.* petition. Maybe so many decades later she had forgotten, and unfortunately, I will never know how she felt at the time that the first issue of *Ms.* hit the newsstands. She died in October 2020, at age eighty-five, before I had the chance to ask her.

† The September '72 issue of *Ms.* ran a new petition with 1,425 signatures. Levine remained managing editor of *Ms.* until 1988, when the magazine, which still exists, became a nonprofit.

BILLIE JEAN KING

I was blindsided when the list was printed.

In late February 1972, Mark Asher, a sports reporter for the *Washington Post*, asked me about [the abortion] while I was promoting a tournament in Maryland. I told him how I truthfully felt: "If every woman who had an abortion would come out and say so, then it wouldn't be such a social stigma." I also asked him not to make a story out of my procedure. He did. The article was picked up all over the country, including the *Los Angeles Times*, the newspaper that slapped down on my parents' doorstep every day. The headline was "Billie Jean King Defends Her Abortion—and Women's Rights."

I got tons of hate mail. But the worst part was that I still hadn't told my parents about my abortion. My brother Randy told me only recently that angry people sent letters to him at Candlestick Park, where he pitched for the San Francisco Giants, calling me a "baby killer," a "murderer," and more. One package that arrived was filled with plastic fetuses.

JULIE HELDMAN

I remember that story very well, because I beat Billie Jean in a tournament the next week in Washington, DC. People were all over her. There was a guy at the *Washington Post*, Mark Asher, who read *Ms.* magazine and accused her of being a money-grubber. It was vile. So she was giving a press conference in advance of the Washington, DC, tournament, and Asher shows up. And Billie Jean sees him, knows who he is and says, "I won't continue with this press conference, unless he leaves." And he wouldn't leave. So she walked out.

But the more extraordinary thing that happened is I ended up playing Billie Jean in the second round of that tournament, and she had been doing something that pissed me off to no end, which was she would hit a serve or hit a ball and then go *thump, thump, thump* with her feet, as if she were going to go to the net. And she was a great net rusher, but she wouldn't go to the net. She was just making this disturbing sound. It was against the rules, and nobody was calling her on it because she was the great Billie Jean. So Vincent, my boyfriend at the time, who was a lawyer, looked up the rules and he found "Rule 15B." He got me completely prepped. So I'm playing Billie Jean in the second round. She hits the serve, *thump thump thump*, the serve bounces in the service box. I catch it, turn to the umpire, and I say, "I claim rule 15B, that was an interference with play."

The umpire's looking like, what the hell is 15B? I say, "You have a choice. If you think she meant it, the interference, you can give the point to me, or you can play it over again." "We will play it over again." So from that moment on, I got her rattled. Nobody made a legal stance in the middle of a point. And I beat her. And I'm sure part of the reason she got rattled was all that was going on about women's lib and *Ms.* magazine and her abortion and her sexual identity. She gave a press conference and said she had an infected toe and that was why she lost. But the reality was far more complicated.

BARBARALEE DIAMONSTEIN-SPIELVOGEL
I had no idea that Billie didn't know that her name was on the list . . . that's horrible.

JULIE HELDMAN
When the first edition of *Ms.* magazine came out in January of '72, Billie Jean was in effect outed for having had an abortion.

BARBARALEE DIAMONSTEIN-SPIELVOGEL
For the first six days after publication starting at six a.m., my phone rang off the hook with sportswriters from all over the world asking about Billie Jean King. They wanted to know, was it really true? Well, needless to say, I wasn't saying anything about anything.

So much attention was paid in such an outsized way to Billie Jean King that it overshadowed everything else. I had no idea it would create that response. She was really the star of center court and quite a remarkable woman, more than just an athlete. She knew if she said something it might be repeated and have value to a wider world. The press reaction revealed that Americans love sports more than anything else.

GLORIA STEINEM
It was chaotic and scary because we were afraid that we would not succeed and we would disgrace the movement. Or that we couldn't properly represent the movement because we were the only national feminist publication at the time, so we were a forum, and it wasn't as if everybody in the same issue felt the same way. They didn't.

The preview issue of *Ms.* came out at the very end of '71 [on December 20]. We cover-dated it Spring 1972 because we were afraid it was just not going to sell and [it would] be an embarrassment to the movement. So, we didn't even call it January, we called it Spring, in the tried-and-true news-stand method of dating everything forward.

LETTY COTTIN POGREBIN

We were quivering in our shoes, thinking, "Oh my God. It'll be sitting there for months and months, and nobody will buy it."

GLORIA STEINEM

But it sold out. It was supposed to be on the newsstands for three months, and [its three hundred thousand copies] sold out in a week.

LETTY COTTIN POGREBIN

We had a deal with the newsstand owner's association that *Ms.* would be displayed for eight weeks, and it sold out everywhere in eight days. Not just in New York and Chicago and San Francisco and Miami, but everywhere; in Lawrence, Kansas, in Baton Rouge. It was incredible.

JANE O'REILLY

My story was on the cover with my name in big letters and they sent me off on a publicity tour.*

GLORIA STEINEM

We had no money to advertise the preview issue, so we all went out on the hustings to talk about the magazine to the media.

DEMITA FRAZIER

When the first issue of *Ms.* came out, Gloria came to Chicago because she and Margaret Sloan† were doing some kind of gig, and we had a party at our house to celebrate the magazine. We all got the very first copy of *Ms.* when it was still part of *New York* magazine. I lived in Margaret's big, beautiful house in Chicago with a bunch of lesbian feminists. Because Chicago

---

*   The cover image, which Steinem fought for over Felker's objections, was an illustration of the Indian goddess Shiva as a tearful, pregnant woman with eight arms holding a phone, frying pan, duster, iron, steering wheel, mirror, typewriter, and clock, with the cover line "Jane O'Reilly on the Housewife's Moment of Truth." Most of the early flood of letters to the editor were in reaction to and in solidarity with O'Reilly's article. The term she invented, "Click," was quickly adopted as a popular feminist term.

†   Margaret Sloan, who traveled the country giving talks about the intersection between feminism and race with Gloria Steinem, moved from Chicago to New York and become a founding editor at *Ms.* Barbara Smith's sister Beverly also worked briefly on the magazine staff.

Lesbian Liberation was white and Black women together, one of the great things about Margaret's house was that it drew all the Black lesbians from Chicago Lesbian Liberation for parties, for talking discussions, cultural sharing. It was wonderful.

So at the party, we're all sitting around drinking and other things, and hanging out. Gloria is on the floor next to me, she's twenty years older than me. I will never not be loyal to that memory, because she always made a point of making sure that there were women of color at the table. I can't say that for everybody who was involved, because I did get to meet a lot of people. But there were always Black women's voices included in *Ms.* from the beginning.

LETTY COTTIN POGREBIN

We got these reports back that were just stunning about how it was being discussed on local news. I went to Boston for five days of interviews to promote the magazine when it first came out, and everyone else hit the road too. Sonya Hamlin had this big television show in Boston* and she programmed five days just on *Ms.* Several of us traipsed up to Boston, and then we went all over the country. Well, the women everywhere were just grateful beyond belief. They were fawning all over us. I mean, "How great, how wonderful, my mother, my daughter, my aunt, everybody loves this. We've started a consciousness-raising group." Women just opened up to us, but a lot of the men were still smarmy, and they couldn't help ridiculing us.

Harry Reasoner [the ABC evening news anchor] said we would never last. "I'll give it six months, before they run out of things to say." He then apologized five years later when we were still around.

Boston Globe, December 22, 1971, "The First Issue of Ms . . .
a Pity!," by James J. Kilpatrick (syndicated column)
This first issue of *Ms.* breathes of a selfishness that beggars description. It is like looking at the slides of carcinoma in a cancer magazine. . . . A single tone vibrates through the whole of this first edition. It is C-sharp on an untuned piano. This is the note of petulance, of bitchiness, of nervous fingernails screeching across a blackboard. The feminists of

---

* *The Sonya Hamlin Show*, launched in 1970 on Boston's WBZ-TV, was the first television show to focus entirely on women's changing roles.

this enterprise . . . do not cry; they merely mewl. They whine. They carp. They exude a flatulent self-pity. . . .

It seems beyond their comprehension that a woman could preserve her integrity as a woman and still enjoy the role of wife, mother, and homemaker. What this sad magazine requires, at the outset, is a more descriptive name, closer to the nature of the movement it serves. Call it, perhaps . . . Barren.

LETTY COTTIN POGREBIN

I think that *Ms.* was seen as mainstream by radical feminists and seen as radical by most other people. *Ms.* had a foot in both worlds.

VIVIAN GORNICK

People in Redstockings started calling Gloria and *Ms.* enemies of the movement because the "message," from the radicals' point of view (and here I include myself), was too watered down. But I hated the Steinem-bashing. I wrote a piece to say, "If you don't like *Ms.*, start a magazine of your own."

MARGO JEFFERSON

Vivian Gornick speaks intelligently about *Ms.* and it sums up how I felt. It was an accomplishment in terms of the mainstream world of journalism, and the mainstream world of feminism as a political movement. I think that that serves a real purpose, but it has its real limits in terms of daring.

CHARLOTTE BUNCH

Ms. came along as the super-mainstream project. At first, we were pissed off, we felt like we've been doing this work for years with publications like *Off Our Backs* and the *Furies,** and now here's this magazine with all this money and the New York publishing world. But very quickly, I began to see, "Well, here's a place that can give us access to a much wider audience in America."†

---

*   In 1971, Charlotte Bunch and Rita Mae Brown (who were lovers) started a militant lesbian separatist collective in Washington, DC, called the Furies, named after the goddesses of vengeance. About two dozen women lived together in a commune on Capitol Hill, renounced men and male children, and began to develop a theory of lesbian feminism. The collective dissolved by the end of 1972, but in January of that year it published the first edition of their influential newsletter, *The Furies*, which lasted for two years.

†   In 1974, Bunch would help found and edit *Quest: A Feminist Quarterly*.

SUZANNE LEVINE

The hardest consideration was this was a movement for all kinds of women at all stages of their lives, and all stages of consciousness. I felt my mission was to cover all the territory, and to break new ground.

JANE O'REILLY

Literally thousands of letters were delivered to the office every day. Everybody would have a huge pile of letters next to their desk. It seemed every single woman in America who ever saw an issue or heard of one wrote a long letter.

SUZANNE LEVINE

The letters came in big mail bags. Margaret Sloan was there at the very beginning, and she worked on the letters. She would open them all and pull out the ones she thought more people should read and pull out the ones that needed answers.

GLORIA STEINEM

We were getting much more mail than, say, *McCall's* or some much bigger magazine. We were always hooked on the letters. You couldn't stop reading them. We printed as many as we could.*

RUTH ROSEN

Ms. acted like a bulletin board, and it got a lot of women to know about these issues that they would never have known about, because they were not in consciousness-raising groups, they were not in cities, they had never been part of the New Left, but they learned about these things through *Ms.*

---

* Twenty thousand letters streamed into the *Ms.* office in response to the preview issue, along with twenty-six thousand subscription requests. Ultimately, Steinem found enough financial backing and advertising to launch the monthly magazine with three hundred thousand subscribers and four million readers.

6

National Childcare—Nixon Says No

On Capitol Hill, Congresswomen Bella Abzug and Shirley Chisholm and members of the Women's Political Caucus pushed their colleagues to pass legislation for women. But when it came to universal childcare, they ran into a road block from the White House.

BELLA ABZUG

I held a special hearing on childcare centers in the auditorium of the Veterans Administration building, where my New York office is located. For hours . . . Shirley Chisholm and I listened to the testimony of women hospital workers, elevator operators, telephone workers, post office employees, and others. They desperately told us that they can't work and take care of their kids at the same time. In effect, they said that either we get them childcare centers or they're going to be forced to go on welfare. One woman who works at night in the post office was so frustrated that she begged us to do something already and stop talking. "Please don't study us anymore," she said. "We have been studied to death."

Ten billion is a trifling amount when you consider that since the Second World War this country has spent more than one trillion dollars for military purposes alone. . . . We could have a universal childcare program in this country for what it costs to maintain the military for a month and a half.

When it comes to childcare, the United States is at a primitive stage compared to countries like Israel, Denmark, Sweden, and Russia. We have more than four million working women with children of preschool age. We have countless other women with young children who are on welfare because they have no other choice.

Chisholm and I introduced a model comprehensive childcare act and succeeded in getting key sections attached to a bill sponsored by Senator Walter Mondale, the Minnesota Democrat.

AILEEN HERNANDEZ

One of the things that we're very concerned about that relates to Black women is the question of childcare. One way of keeping women out of the job market is to not provide childcare facilities. Most women do very strongly feel their protective role as mothers. They're not about to go into jobs unless they have some reasonable assurance their children will be taken care of while they're gone. Now, Black women have been making do without organized childcare for a long time because they've had to work. They've had no choice. There were whole generations of latchkey kids, trained to wear the key around their necks and go home from school and stay there.

We don't provide childcare services in the United States. We are incredibly backward in this area.

PATSY MINK

The Republicans worked with us constantly on the development of the bill. The administration came in with all sorts of revisions, and we would revise it; they'd come in with another set, and we would be angry, but we would revise it. I mean, this went on for almost a year.*

I was aware of enormous amounts of mail being generated in the last three months of our deliberations, by right-wing groups and right-wing newsletters where people would clip out a section from these newsletters, i.e., the Liberty Lobby and groups like that. And so we did get a huge amount of mail saying that we were stealing mothers from their children

---

* Representative Patsy Mink (D-HI), who as a young practicing lawyer struggled to find childcare for her daughter in Honolulu, first introduced a national childcare bill in 1967. Her efforts picked up steam in 1971 when she partnered with Senator Walter Mondale (D-MN) and Representative John Brademas (R-IN), who cosponsored the $2 billion Comprehensive Child Development Act of 1971 (CDA) that called for building a nationally funded network of childcare centers. The bill would have been the largest, most important piece of social legislation since Social Security.

and turning childcare centers into communes; vicious scare tactics. So, it was an organized thing. It just didn't happen by itself.

BELLA ABZUG
Well, we did it. The House and Senate have both finally passed a childcare law as part of an overall antipoverty bill. The vote was 210–186 [and then 63–17 in the Senate]. The next step is the White House. Since it's the single most important piece of social legislation to come out of this Congress, Nixon has already made it clear that he's not happy with it, and that he's considering a veto. It would be a perfect opportunity for him, after all, to express his disdain for women, minorities and youth—all of whom are benefited by this bill—in one swoop. This time our people-be-damned president is even toying with some new victims: children.

New York Times, December 10, 1971, "President Vetoes
Child Care Plan as Irresponsible," by Jack Rosenthal
WASHINGTON, Dec. 9—In a stinging message, President Nixon vetoed today a Congressionally initiated bill to establish a national system of comprehensive child development and day care.

The proposal, he said, was characterized by "fiscal irresponsibility, administrative unworkability and family-weakening implications."

The President said that he objected to committing, without wide national debate, "the vast moral authority of the national Government to the side of communal approaches to childrearing over against the family centered approach." . . .

"Good public policy requires that we enhance rather than diminish both parental authority and parental involvement with children."

PATSY MINK
The most conservative member on our committee had agreed to the bill and had recommended that the president sign it. I doubt these individuals would double-talk. The Office of Child Development endorsed the final product. And I believe the reason the head of OCD quit shortly after the veto was because he was thoroughly humiliated.

WALTER MONDALE
Worse than the veto was the harsh language Nixon used in the veto message. He accused us of "Sovietizing" American youth. He said our bill would take

the responsibility of child-rearing away from parents. It was plainly designed to scare people, poison the conversation about helping families, and dip into the nation's stew of cultural resentments. Even for Nixon, it was surprising.

In time we learned the full story behind Nixon's veto. Pat Buchanan, then Nixon's chief speechwriter and a shrewd guy, latched on to the issue. He advised Nixon that if he was going to oppose the legislation, he might as well use the issue to rally cultural conservatives. The other piece of the puzzle was that Nixon had announced his groundbreaking trip to China, which was not popular with his conservative base. I always thought that vetoing our bill, and casting himself as the defender of traditional American values, was his way of mollifying the conservatives and creating a little maneuvering room to make the China trip.

Whether Nixon and Buchanan knew it or not, they had tapped into deep currents in American society. Families were changing, as was the role of women in the economy, the resentment was stirring against the liberal establishment that seemed to threaten traditional values. The abortion rights and antiwar movements had already prompted a backlash among conservative Americans, who saw in them contempt for their values and the nation's institutions. . . . I believe that episode helped launch the religious right as a political movement and Nixon's veto was one of the triggering events for the culture wars that would consume American politics for the next three decades.*

---

* Mondale tried again in 1973 and then 1975 to pass a federally funded childcare bill, but by then the issue had become a lightning rod for social conservatives, who waged successful disinformation campaigns against the bill that passed in the Senate but could never pass in the House. The conservative backlash against the women's movement, which would come into full bloom in opposition to the ERA, got its start with the childcare bill in 1971. To this day, America still has no federally funded childcare system, which Senator Mitch McConnell (R-KY) called "toddler takeover" in December 2021, when a similar bill failed yet again to pass in the Congress.

7

Shirley Chisholm Runs for President

The primary campaign to nominate the Democratic Party's presidential candidate in 1972 was the most "democratic" in the party's history. Traditionally, primaries were not much more than a showcase for candidates, while the real decision making took place behind closed doors by the party's white, male, mostly Southern power elite. That's what happened in 1968 when LBJ's vice president, Hubert Humphrey, who did not run in the primaries, was given the nomination by an archaic party apparatus that was woefully out of touch with the insurgent antiwar and Black freedom movements. After the bloody scene enacted on live television of Chicago's Mayor Daly's police brutally beating demonstrators in Lincoln Park, many demoralized Democrats sat out the election and Republican Richard Nixon won.

A major overhaul of the system followed, which opened up the delegate-selection process to women and minorities and empowered voters in primary states to choose their own candidates. The time was ripe for politicians of all stripes to consider a presidential run in this fertile new ground.

SHIRLEY CHISHOLM

Running for president was not my idea originally. It was a number of college students who started me thinking seriously about it, against what I first thought was my better judgment. It began as far back as 1969, my first year in Washington. Before the end of my second term in the House, I had spoken on well over one hundred campuses in forty-two states, and on most of them someone had asked me, "Why don't *you* run for president in '72?"

SHIRLEY DOWNS

Shirley Chisholm basically makes up her mind herself. She doesn't go running around consulting with people. She is the most inner-directed person I know. She just consults herself and then tells you.

ROBERT GOTTLIEB

You have to remember, back in 1971, we were in the throes of the revolution in this country. Richard Nixon reflected the very worst in American politics, Vietnam was still going on and thousands and thousands of people my age were dying because white politicians were sending them off to war. Heroes of mine, Martin Luther King, Bobby Kennedy—they were dead. It was a violent time.

And here's this Black woman taking on the establishment in Washington on the Vietnam War, on Head Start, she was out there fighting on every single issue that I cared about. I thought, "Now there's somebody whom I could really admire."

SHIRLEY CHISHOLM

Young radicals failed to capture the Democratic Party in 1968; the party's traditional liberals put up Hubert H. Humphrey, who put his arm around Chicago mayor Richard Daly, the author of the police riot during the 1968 convention, confirming the kids' belief that conventional politics is an absurdity. After 1968, some young people turned off politics. They waited for 1972 to see if next time would be different. As 1972 came closer, they began to suspect strongly that it was not going to be. The same old faces came forward with the same old song and dance.

CAROLYN SMITH

She said, "I think I'm going to do something no one's going to believe." I said, "What is that?" "I'm going to run for president." So I said, "President of what?" She said, "For your understanding Mrs. Smith, I'm going to run for president of the United States." I said, "Are you kidding?" She said, "Call in the staff. I have an announcement to make."*

---

* The only women to run for president before Chisholm were suffragist Victoria Woodhull in 1872

ROBERT GOTTLIEB

I interned for Chisholm the summer of '71, and I went to DC during Christmas break to say hello to the staff, and the congresswoman asked me to come into her office and she said she's going to run for president in 1972. Well, first of all I couldn't believe it. Then she said that she would like me to join the campaign as National Youth Coordinator. I immediately said, "Of course I'm going to join you." But I had one problem. I was in the middle of my senior year at Cornell. But how could I not join the crusade to shake up this country?

CAROLYN SMITH

I thought she was out of her ever-loving mind. I was not the only one. Shirley Downs thought she had lost it too.

SHIRLEY CHISHOLM

I realized at the moment I made the decision that all hell was going to break loose. The Black politicians were going to say that's a woman, and we don't want her because she is getting out there ahead of us. The white politicians were going to say, who does she think she is? She doesn't have the backing of business, and she doesn't have the backing of unions. The only thing that I was doing was responding to hundreds of frustrated, disillusioned citizens in this country who are both Black and white. So one of the reasons why I made the decision was because people were saying we want you. . . .

The ratification of the Twenty-Sixth Amendment giving eighteen-year-olds the vote in 1971 had a tremendous effect on my candidacy because I had many, many college people, college seniors and juniors and sophomores, pushing me.

ROBERT GOTTLIEB

The voting age had just changed from age twenty-one to eighteen in July 1971, and we were given a week off at Cornell to go back to our local communities to register people to vote.

---

and then Margaret Chase Smith, Republican senator from Maine, in 1964. The only Black person to run for president before Chisholm was abolitionist Frederick Douglass, who spoke at the 1888 Republican convention and received one roll call vote.

BELLA ABZUG

While the Women's Caucus was not ready yet to support any particular candidate, Shirley—and we had a lot of discussions about this—felt that as an individual she should undertake a symbolic campaign to show that a woman should be considered for president. She told me that if she could raise the money, she would run in certain primaries, notably Wisconsin.

CONRAD CHISHOLM

Shirley Chisholm knew that she could not become the President of the United States, but she wanted to prove a point. She wanted to show them.

New York Times, January 26, 1972,
"New Hat in Ring: Mrs. Chisholm's," by Frank Lynn

Representative Shirley Chisholm announced her candidacy yesterday for the Democratic Presidential nomination—the first black woman to seek a major-party Presidential nomination.

The Brooklyn Democrat picked an unusual setting to announce her candidacy —Bedford-Stuyvesant parochial school auditorium.

Shirley Chisholm announcement speech, January 25, 1972

I am not the candidate of Black America although I am Black and proud. I am not the candidate of the women's movement of this country, although I am a woman, and I am equally proud of that. I am not the candidate of any political bosses or fat cats or special interests. I stand here now without endorsements from many big-name politicians or celebrities or any other kind of prop. I do not intend to offer you the tired and glib clichés that for too long have been an accepted part of our political life. I am the candidate of the people of America. . . .

Those of you who were locked outside of the convention hall in 1968, those of you who can now vote for the first time, those of you who agree with me that the institutions of this country belong to all of the people who inhabit it. Those of you who have been neglected, left out, ignored, forgotten or shunted aside for whatever reason, give me your help at this hour. Join me in an effort to reshape our society and regain control of our destiny as we go down the Chisholm Trail of 1972.

New York Times, January 26, 1972,
"New Hat in Ring: Mrs. Chisholm's," by Frank Lynn

On the stage with her were a score of black community leaders and Mr. [Percy] Sutton, City Councilman William Thompson; Representative Ronald V. Dellums, Democrat of California; Betty Friedan, the women's liberation leader, and Howard J. Samuels, chairman of the city's Offtrack Betting Corporation, who said he was merely "paying his respects to a courageous woman," not endorsing Mrs. Chisholm.

Later, at a Washington repeat of the announcement ceremony, Representatives Charles Rangel of Harlem and Bella Abzug, a women's liberation leader, took similar stances. They told reporters that they were encouraging Mrs. Chisholm but not endorsing her.*

SHIRLEY CHISHOLM

One surprise came from my sister congresswoman from New York, Bella Abzug. . . . [At my Washington announcement] after my statement, [Congressmen] Parren Mitchell and Ron Dellums spoke; they gave me strong and moving endorsements. Then Bella made a strange statement, largely about movements and the underprivileged in politics. She said little about my candidacy, except that it was "an idea whose time has come," if I remember correctly.

Later a reporter asked her whether she had endorsed me or not. Bella hedged. She said she supported "the idea" of my candidacy and would support me in those states where I was running (at the time she appeared to think I was going into only three or four primaries). Bella never offered to campaign for me in Florida, North Carolina, or even New York, for that matter. It was a letdown, and also bewildering if she intended to sit on the fence, why did she ask to appear with me when I made my announcement for the presidency?

ESTHER NEWBERG

Bella wasn't really an ally person. That's why she didn't support Shirley Chisholm for president in 1972. She liked playing with the people that

---

* Chisholm entered a crowded primary field of establishment white male candidates that included South Dakota senator George McGovern, former vice president Hubert Humphrey, Maine senator Edmund Muskie, Washington senator Henry M. "Scoop" Jackson, Alabama governor George Wallace, and New York mayor John Lindsay. Representative Patsy Mink from Hawaii also entered the race, but only for a few months.

were actually going to get it done. She wasn't going to endorse Shirley because she wasn't going to win.

JILL RUCKELSHAUS

Shirley announced her run for president, and the National Women's Political Caucus couldn't support her. Bella talked to me for a long time about why we couldn't endorse Shirley. It was important that Shirley ran, but she wasn't going to be nominated. Bella was really the one who helped us all understand that if we wanted to use our political leverage for the issues we cared about, we needed to be in the game and that meant supporting the party nominee. It turned out to be McGovern. I don't think Shirley could accept that. That was a betrayal. We could've endorsed her. We should've.

BETTY FRIEDAN

Shirley Chisholm won the nation's respect for her campaign for the presidency. I made a quixotic fool of myself, maybe, going into subways at seven a.m. to run as a delegate for Shirley Chisholm in my own district.* . . . I fought bitterly and expressed disgust out loud when the National Women's Political Caucus refused to endorse Shirley Chisholm's candidacy. Shirley Chisholm didn't say anything; she just resigned.

GLORIA STEINEM

Florynce Kennedy and I supported Shirley Chisholm's candidacy wherever her name was on the ballot, and only supported McGovern where it was impossible to vote for Chisholm. For instance, Flo, I, and others ran in New York as delegates pledged to Shirley Chisholm, even though this angered the McGovern campaign (which I worked for in 1968),† which had to spend money publishing the fact that we were pledged to Chisholm, not

---

* Friedan actively campaigned as a Chisholm delegate, but her efforts were seen as self-serving and racially tone-deaf. Her speeches turned off Black voters, and she upset Chisholm's staff by raising money for her own delegate campaign needs but not sharing with the cash-strapped national campaign. Friedan's worst faux pas came when she planned to bring a flatbed truck to Harlem and host a "Traveling Watermelon Fest." Flo Kennedy, who detested Friedan, sarcastically suggested that she serve "fried chicken and watermelon," but Friedan purportedly did not get the joke. Chisholm's campaign canceled the event, but only after Friedan had already issued a press release. Friedan's racial ignorance and insensitivity only exacerbated mistrust between Black and white feminists on the Chisholm trail.

† Steinem wrote speeches and fundraised for McGovern's 1968 presidential campaign, but she never thought that McGovern took her, or women's issues, seriously.

McGovern. Of course, our Chisholm slate lost, as we knew it would, but it was worth every bit of effort to every one of us on it.

FLORYNCE KENNEDY

Shirley Chisholm is fabulous. When I thought there could be a Feminist Party supporting Shirley Chisholm, I set it up on November 3, 1971, at Queens College. We went to Florida in connection with her campaign. I don't care whether we lose or win. The struggle is what's important. I never think that people are ridiculous when they are serious, and if they're trying to make a gain in the same area that I'm in.

> *Atlantic Sun*, Florida Atlantic University, January 18, 1972
>
> This year Florida is going to be the place where the action is, so "go baby!" was the main thrust of Florynce Kennedy's speech at the University Theater. The outspoken black radical feminist attorney urged everyone to start working in anti-establishment politics, and stop perpetrating the "horizontal hostility" that splits minority groups. . . . Flo Kennedy strongly endorsed Shirley Chisholm's candidacy for President. . . . She thinks it would be good for people interested in gay, women's and black liberation, other oppressed minorities, ecology groups, and antiwar people to all get together and combine efforts.

MICHELE WALLACE

We were absolutely and completely for her. Mother did a series of paintings called *Political Landscapes*, supporting Shirley Chisholm.

FAITH RINGGOLD

In the spring of 1972, I had been invited to a benefit [at Flo Kennedy's house] to raise money for Chisholm's presidential candidacy. For this event I made the first *Political Landscape* paintings on which I inscribed a supporting message for Chisholm. . . . She told an audience in a speech in 1970 in Washington, DC: "I don't want you to go home and talk about integrated schools, churches, or marriages if the kind of integration you're talking about is Black and white. I want you to go home and work to fight for the integration of male and female, human and human." . . . I sold them, and contributed the money to her campaign fund.

MICHELE WALLACE

We wore Shirley Chisholm buttons. Men would say, "Got to have a brother first. You need a brother."

SHIRLEY CHISHOLM

Two of the most prominent members of the women's movement and the NWPC, Betty Friedan and Gloria Steinem, wound up supporting me and running (unsuccessfully) as Chisholm delegates in Manhattan. . . . The charming, dynamic editor of *Ms.* magazine is often on television talk shows as a spokeswoman for the women's movement, and naturally she began to be asked whom she supported for president. She would say, "I'm for Shirley Chisholm—but I think that George McGovern is the best of the *male* candidates." This hybrid endorsement began to exasperate me, and finally, after she had done it again on a television program in Chicago, on which we both appeared, I told her, "Gloria, you're supporting either George McGovern or Shirley Chisholm, I don't mind if you are supporting George. If he is your candidate, so be it, but don't do me any favors by giving me this semi-endorsement. I don't need that kind of help."

GLORIA STEINEM

I never understood how Shirley expected me to support her in states where she wasn't running. So, what I was doing was supporting her in the states where she was a candidate, and supporting McGovern in the states where she wasn't a candidate. Even then, I would always say he was the best white male candidate. I wrote a major position speech for her which she liked and used without changing a word. I raised money for her campaign. We often worked together.

BARBARA WINSLOW

There was not a single member in the Congressional Black Caucus, except Ron Dellums, who supported her. The Black men didn't support her, except Al Sharpton, who did. Rosa Parks supported her candidacy and raised money for her.

The irony is the Congressional Black Caucus men said, because Chisholm was a feminist, she wasn't really Black. And yet she had the support of the Black Panthers, and in '72, you couldn't find a more machismo Black organization, and she was the only person in the Black Congressional Caucus who stood up for the two Black women radicals Angela Davis and Joan Bird.

WILSON RILES

At the National Black Political Convention in Gary, Indiana (in March 1972), Blacks were seriously considering whether or not to have a Black presidential candidate to galvanize support for all of those delegates across the country, but they weren't able to settle on anyone. So, it was very difficult because Shirley was seen as a divisive person within that group because she did also bring a lot of women support and some Hispanic support too, so they couldn't tie her up. They couldn't control what she would be about. Unbought and unbossed, like she said.*

SHIRLEY CHISHOLM

I didn't attend that meeting in Gary because I knew that it was going to be a real confrontation. I had already started to run, and I knew that they didn't want me to run because I was a woman. No woman had a right to run for president before a Black man. So I sent my campaign staffer Thaddeus Garrett to be my representative.

BARBARA WINSLOW

A young man at the Gary conference who worked for her was wearing a Chisholm button, and got denounced for supporting Chisholm. Everybody, including people whom we viewed with great love, like Julian Bond, just said, someday we would like a Black woman, but not that one.

SHIRLEY CHISHOLM

I didn't pay them any mind and that angered them. They gave out to newspaper editors and reporters the story that she was stubborn, that she's just going on an ego trip. I remember one Black politician said to me, "You

---

* The National Black Political Convention brought ten thousand participants on March 10–12, 1972, to Gary, Indiana, for an historic political reckoning. Every important Black leader, from Jesse Jackson, Amiri Baraka, Bobby Seale, Coretta Scott King, Julian Bond, and Louis Farrakhan to Muhammad Ali and Harry Belafonte, attended. The conference produced the Gary Declaration, which ends with a call to action: "We begin here and now in Gary. We begin with an independent Black political movement, an independent Black Political Agenda, and independent Black spirit. Nothing less will do. We must build for our people. We must build for our world. We stand on the edge of history." Chisholm would later be accused, by Jesse Jackson and others, of sabotaging the Black leadership's efforts to put a strong (male) presidential candidate forward by unilaterally declaring her candidacy without asking for their approval.

foolish woman, you can't win." I said, "Foolish or not, I am still going to run for the presidency of the United States." And that got him. I don't know what it was in me, but I felt that I had been called upon by women, by many Black people, by students to make this run. And I had to do it.

New York Amsterdam News, March 11, 1972, "The Amsterdam Interviews the Candidates: Candidate Shirley Chisholm"

Q: Black leaders have complained you're fouling up the strategy by waging a hopeless campaign for convention delegates that in some states could frustrate black delegates who want to put pressure on the major white candidates, such as Edmund Muskie, Humphrey, McGovern, etc. What is your comment on that particular statement?

A: My candidacy was initiated over 6 months ago by several women's groups, student groups and black masses and Puerto Rican masses—not the black or white political bosses. . . . I am not disrupting any black movement . . . of course, I have been a scapegoat politically for many different forces for the past 20 years. This is nothing new to me. . . . All I know is that it's very difficult for some people to realize that, although I'm black and although I'm a woman, I do have a following in this country who are faithful to me and it's up to me to decide whether or not I want to take advantage of this opportunity, and that's how the candidacy emerged.*

ROBERT GOTTLIEB

So, I'm twenty-one years old. I'm a senior in college. I'm raring to go and my first trip was to North Carolina to go to some colleges to try to organize students. I had to wait until we received the boxes of bumper stickers and brochures from the printer that we could hand out. On the outside of the box there was a "Chisholm for President" bumper sticker. I took a plane to Raleigh, North Carolina, and I went to pick up my bags and the box of brochures and bumper stickers from the luggage carousel. Scrawled all over the box was "Nigger go home."

I suddenly realized that this is serious stuff and people hate Shirley Chis-

---

* The editorial board of the *New York Amsterdam News,* one of the most prominent Black newspapers in the country, endorsed Chisholm's candidacy in the March 11, 1972, issue.

holm for who she is, having nothing to do with her stance on Vietnam, or women's rights, or what was happening to minorities in this country. That isn't why people wanted to send her home or kill her. It was because she was a Black woman, and how dare she run for president. . . . Back then we were feeling the hatred, the division, the animosity, the fear, every day.

VICTOR ROBLES

I served her as a staff person for ten years, and when she ran for president, I was the one person who traveled almost twenty-five states in the union with her before the attempted assassination of George Wallace.*

George Wallace was extremely shocked and surprised that she actually went to his bedside. I mean, can you imagine a Black woman going to see George Wallace? But that's Shirley Chisholm. I remember when George Wallace said to her with his Southern drawl, he kept saying, "But Mrs. Chisholm, you came to visit me." And her answer was simple, "George, you're a brother, aren't ya?"

No other Black leader went to visit George Wallace, but she did. But knowing her, she went to visit not George Wallace the racist—she went to visit George Wallace because he was a presidential candidate like she was. I mean all of the other presidential candidates, who were white, visited him, regardless of how liberal they were. One, he was a colleague, and she was a Christian woman, and that was a Christian thing to do. Our culture teaches us that your enemy is still your brother. Shirley Chisholm was living out her Christian faith. After that, they became friends.†

SHIRLEY CHISHOLM

I must have gone to about seventy-five college campuses during the course of my campaign. I just went from campus to campus. And at practically every college I went to, the auditoriums were filled and students were packed on the outside looking through the windows, it was fantastic.

---

* George Wallace, the racist, segregationist governor of Alabama and Democratic presidential candidate, was shot on May 15, 1972, at a campaign event at a mall in Wheaton, Maryland, by a white man named Arthur Bremer. Wallace was paralyzed from the waist down for the rest of his life. He dropped out of the campaign (after winning with 42 percent of the vote in the Florida primary) and gave a speech at the Democratic convention in Miami from a wheelchair. Nixon assigned the Secret Service to protect all the other primary candidates after the assassination attempt.

† Wallace and Chisholm were such political polar opposites that her fifteen-minute bedside visit spurred rumors, which she would deny for years, that she and Wallace had colluded in a secret delegate deal.

ROBERT GOTTLIEB

She had a speech impediment that was very pronounced, but what always amazed me is that you can be in front of an audience and you know that's what they're thinking when she first comes onstage. By the time she finished talking, they loved her. Her physical appearance or her speech impediment disappeared from their minds because her message and the way she delivered it was so powerful. And it doesn't matter what time of night it was, how many times she had given the same speech, it didn't matter how tired she was, once she got herself wound up and became the preacher, it would sound fresh every single time because she really believed it.*

SHIRLEY DOWNS

In her campaign, there were Blacks, Hispanics, women, gays, and Chisholm would have to go out on the campaign trail and negotiate between people who had come together for her campaign because they were novices and hadn't been involved in politics. This was a maiden voyage for everybody.

SHIRLEY CHISHOLM

I had a Washington office. And I had little satellites in about sixteen or seventeen states. And heavens, they fought. They fought like cats and dogs. Because I ran into opposition and furor to the Black people and the white women. The white women would say, we're putting her up for president, we're raising most of the money, and we should have a say in the campaign. And the Black people would say, she's one of us. She's our sister.

---

* Chisholm could draw big crowds at her campaign events, mostly of Black and white students, hippies, and women. At a rally in Los Angeles, 1,750 attended, and 300 were turned away because of space restrictions.

8

The ERA Passes with Flying Colors

What started out as a pipe dream in 1923 became a runaway victory by 1972, when the House and Senate passed the Equal Rights Amendment with overwhelming majorities. Title VII and court rulings against workplace discrimination marked the beginning of the end of discriminatory "protective" labor laws for women, which had split the women's movement for decades. By 1972, the concept of treating women equally under the law was no longer the reliable laugh line it had been for the male legal and political establishment.

In just a few years, the women's movement had grown powerful in size, stature, and political influence, and the ERA became a popular bipartisan bill, with only a handful of elderly, conservative white male legislators standing in its way. In the House, the ERA's mightiest foe, New York Democrat and Judiciary Committee chairman Emmanuel Celler, would lose his seat in a primary challenge to Elizabeth Holtzman in June 1972, partly because of his staunch opposition to women's rights. This left North Carolina Democratic senator Sam Ervin (born 1896), who was on the brink of fame for his role as chairman of the Senate Watergate investigation. A former segregationist and unreconstructed male chauvinist, Ervin had managed to block passage of the ERA in the Senate for two years, until he could no longer withstand the political wave that swept the Senate on March 22, 1972.

MARTHA GRIFFITHS

When we got the ERA into the Senate the first year and it didn't pass, and then we got it back there the second year,* we knew that a tremendous effort had to be made. . . . Gladys O'Donnell [president of the National Federation of Republican Women] and myself met regularly. The Business and Professional Women worked very hard. Then we had this little Carol Burris who went to every one of those Senate offices every morning. She knew exactly what was happening, exactly what kind of mail was coming in. She knew who was opposing it and who wasn't, so that we had an absolutely fantastic information service. If the Senate had ever realized what we knew about what was going on in those offices, I swear that they would have fired every employee, because we knew everything that was happening to them, and we knew exactly where to apply the pressure. We knew exactly which states to call up, whom to organize, and so forth, but you see, we never had that when we hit the state legislatures.

JO FREEMAN

The Equal Rights Amendment brought them [women] out in droves . . . more than fifty national organizations supported it, and the Ad Hoc Committee alone sent out over forty thousand letters to presidents of varying organizations asking them to write their congressmen and publish items on the ERA campaign in their newsletters. All of Common Cause's 215,000 members received a letter to do the same, and a battery of volunteers made over fifty-one thousand phone calls on Common Cause's WATS [Wide Area Telephone Service] lines. The Business and Professional Women's Clubs sent at least one hundred thousand letters to state officers and local club presidents, and served as the spearhead of the pass-ERA drive in many locales where feminist organizations were anathema.

The result was that some congresspeople received as many as fifteen hundred letters a month, and Congressperson Tip O'Neill of Massachusetts was quoted as saying that the ERA had generated more mail than the Vietnam War. The coordinated effort worked so well that, according to one key member of the Ad Hoc Committee, "Toward the end, it got so you could make twelve phone calls and get five to ten thousand letters." The lobbying

---

* After the ERA failed to leave the House in 1970, Griffiths restarted the process, and the clean ERA (with no exceptions) passed the House again, on October 12, 1971, by a vote of 354–24 and was immediately sent to the Senate.

effort was similarly intense, with twenty to thirty-five full- and part-time volunteers literally living in the halls of Congress. A couple of women devoted a full two years of their lives to the ERA campaign.*

MARTHA GRIFFITHS

Then I went to see senator after senator after senator. I went to see [John] McClellan of Arkansas and [James] Eastland of Mississippi. I saw all the Southern senators and begged them to vote for it. We had other people who were pressing them to support the Equal Rights Amendment, as well as the mail they were getting. In the end, I think they would have passed it if for no other reason than to get rid of that terrible pressure, because they were getting tired of it.

Of all the senators, Sam Ervin was the least chivalrous, and he was the most determined against it; and of course, it was part and parcel of Ervin really. He wouldn't meet with me.

On February 19, a month before the Senate vote, Phyllis Schlafly, a conservative Republican activist, sent Senator Ervin a letter wishing him success defeating the amendment. She also included a copy of her conservative monthly newsletter, in which she addressed the ERA for the first time.

Phyllis Schlafly Report, February 1972, "What's Wrong with 'Equal Rights' for Women?"

Women's lib is a total assault on the role of the American woman as wife and mother and on the family as the basic unit of society. Women's libbers are trying to make wives and mothers unhappy with their career, make them feel that they are "second-class citizens" and "abject slaves." . . . They are promoting abortions instead of families.

Why should we trade in our special privileges and honored status for the alleged advantage of working in an office or assembly line? Most women would rather cuddle a baby than a typewriter or factory machine. . . .

---

* Dubbed "Crater's Raiders," a group of more than twenty women organized by Virginia NOW member and veteran political activist Flora Crater coordinated closely with Representative Martha Griffiths and an underground network of congressional secretaries and staffers to lobby members of Congress on a regular basis. Also, the mail campaign of Marguerite Rawalt's Women United group coordinated with ninety-two pro-ERA organizations, which mailed over five million letters to congressional offices.

Women's libbers do *not* speak for the majority of American women. American women do *not* want to be liberated from husbands and children. We do *not* want to trade our birthright of the special privileges of American women—for the mess of pottage called the Equal Rights Amendment. . . .

And why should the men acquiesce in a system which gives preferential rights and lighter duties to women? In return, the men get the pearl of great price: a happy home, a faithful wife, and children they adore. . . . Let's not let these women's libbers deprive wives and mothers of the rights we now possess.

Tell your Senators NOW that you want them to vote NO on the Equal Rights Amendment. Tell your television and radio stations that you want equal time to present the case FOR marriage and motherhood.*

Congressional Record, Senate, March 22, 1972

Mr. Ervin, Mr. President, the pending amendment reads as follows:

At the end of section 1 add the following sentence: "This article shall not impair the validity, however, of any laws of the United States or any State which extended protections or exemptions to women."†

I am constrained to offer this amendment because I remember how faithfully my own mother performed the obligations devolving upon her as a wife and mother. I am also constrained to offer this amendment because of my realization that my life has been made happy by a wife who has stood beside me for many years and has faithfully performed all of the obligations devolving upon her as a wife and mother.

My own mother and my own wife have given me the capacity to comprehend what Rudyard Kipling said in his poem entitled "Mother o' Mine" from "The Light That Failed."

---

* By September 1972, Schlafly had a mission and an organization called STOP (Stop Taking Our Privileges) ERA, and she organized one hundred women from across the country to come to St. Louis to plot their strategy to kill the amendment. By early 1973, STOP ERA groups (made up of Christian, socially conservative women) were in twenty-six states, and Senator Sam Ervin's Senate office became its communications hub.

† In the days leading up to the final vote on March 22, Ervin introduced nine amendments that would have weakened the ERA. They included: exempt women from the military draft; exempt women from military combat units; exempt protective legislation; exempt wives, mothers, widows; exempt laws that don't require men to pay for their children; exempt privacy; and exempt sexual offenses. All nine amendments were defeated, but they would soon provide the blueprint for Schlafly's successful countermovement.

If I could, I would compel every Member of the Senate to read the poem before he votes on this amendment.* If every Member of the Senate would read it before he casts his vote, I am confident that he would have great difficulty in voting to rob wives and mothers and widows of the protections which commonsense and reality and the experience of the human race have placed around them, to enable them to perform their roles as wives and mothers, to give necessary nurture and training to their children. . . .

Mr. President, in appraising the objectives of the militants, we are confronted by the question whether there is any rational basis for reasonable distinctions between men and women in any of the relationships of undertakings of life.

We find in chapter 1, verse 27, of the Book of Genesis this statement which all of us know to be true:

God created man in His own image. In the image of God, created He him. Male and female, created He them.

Congressional Record, Senate, March 22, 1972

Resolved by the Senate and House of Representatives of the United States of America in Congress assembled (two-thirds of each House concurring therein), that the following article is proposed as an amendment to the Constitution of the United States, which shall be valid to all intents and purposes as part of the Constitution when ratified by the legislatures of three-fourths of the several States within seven years from the date of its submission by the Congress:

ARTICLE —

Section 1. Equality of rights under the law shall not be denied or abridged by the United States or by any State on account of sex.

Section 2. The Congress shall have the power to enforce, by appropriate legislation, the provisions of this article.

Section 3. This amendment shall take effect two years after the date of ratification.

---

* At the time, there was only one female senator, Maine Republican Margaret Chase Smith, who encouraged her colleagues to vote for passage of the ERA.

Charlotte Observer, March 23, 1972,
"Women Triumph as Senate Passes Rights Amendment:
Sam Ervin Implores Forgiveness," Associated Press

WASHINGTON—The Senate Wednesday completed congressional approval of a constitutional amendment giving women equal rights—including the right to be drafted into the military forces if Congress wishes.

The lopsided 84-8 vote was greeted by a high-pitched war whoop or two from women in the gallery hailing a triumph at the end of four decades of effort. . . . The states have seven years in which to act. . . .

"The significance of women as a new and powerful political force is demonstrated by the overwhelming margin of passage of the amendment," said Rep. Bella Abzug D-NY, chairwoman of the caucus. . . .

"Forgive them, Father, they know not what they do," said Sen. Sam Ervin, D-NC, in concluding his unsuccessful fight for a host of amendments. This brought a hiss from around the gallery which was dominated by women three to one.

JILL RUCKELSHAUS

I remember being in Anne Armstrong's office at the Republican National Committee, she was the cochair, and everyone in that office cheered for the ERA going to the states. I'll never forget it. When our little office started the cheering, all the secretaries who were smart, terrific women said, "What's that?" And we told them and they said, "Great." So, women knew. Women were watching.*

New York Times, March 23, 1972, "Equal Rights Amendment
Is Approved by Congress," by Eileen Shanahan

Hawaii became the first state to ratify the amendment when the state Senate and House of Representatives registered its approval at 12:10 P.M. Hawaiian standard time. . . . Confidence that ratification would be achieved swiftly was expressed by a number of supporters of the amendment. Senator Birch Bayh, Democrat of Indiana, who

---

* President Nixon quietly endorsed the ERA when he sent a letter to Senator Hugh Scott (R-PA), encouraging him to vote for the amendment on March 18, 1972.

led the Senate fight for the amendment, said he thought it would be ratified "with dispatch."

Present on the Senate floor when the amendment passed was Representative Martha W. Griffiths, Democrat of Michigan, who is generally given the largest single share of credit for enacting the amendment. . . . Mrs. Griffiths sat at the back-row desk usually occupied by Senator Edmund S. Muskie, Democrat of Maine, keeping her personal count of the roll call.

MARTHA GRIFFITHS

The next day I was sent a lei of orchids, and I wore them over to the House floor and made a speech saying Hawaii had ratified. . . . Then I went to state after state urging people in state legislatures to ratify.*

JO FREEMAN

There was no organized opposition [to the ERA] except for labor, and that was breaking up [the AFL-CIO endorsed the ERA in 1975]. Although the ERA had been around for years, the fact that it had only recently become "public" meant that it had not acquired any politics. With few exceptions, people could not determine their attitude toward the ERA by virtue of who else was for or against it.

JILL RUCKELSHAUS

Phyllis Schlafly was a defense person. She had studied nuclear weapons, she knew about all the treaties and the defense budget. And then she stumbled across the women's issue that the people in her hometown Alton, Illinois, were getting excited about. She wanted to be elected, but she lost a couple of runs at the House in '52 and '60.

So, she built this great STOP ERA movement and was wonderful at it, really, really good at it. I can't give Phyllis enough credit, she was really clever. They had committees, they knew how to organize, they had phone trees, and that was STOP ERA. They tapped into the religious right, and abortion would soon become a very big thing.†

---

*   By April 1973, thirty states had ratified the ERA. The process slowed down in 1974, with only three more, and then two more by 1977, for a total of thirty-five—leaving just three more states needed to ratify the constitutional amendment by the seven-year deadline, 1979, which was then extended to 1982.

†   Married to a lawyer, mother of six children, and author of several books on national defense, Schlafly was a politically ambitious two-time congressional candidate and perennial Republican convention

MURIEL FOX

The ERA was not considered that revolutionary. Richard Nixon supported it, and it was in the Republican platform right up to Ronald Reagan in 1980. Then the counterrevolution, led by Phyllis Schlafly, very successfully defeated the ERA. We did not see it coming.

JILL RUCKELSHAUS

It was not controversial at all. It raced through legislatures without much fuss, until these rumblings came out of Illinois: STOP ERA!

We ERA people were very complacent. We were so sure that we had history and this huge vote in the House and Senate on our side, and this early ratification in thirty states. And we couldn't believe this buffeting we were getting. Phyllis made something enormous out of practically nothing. It could've just been women wringing their hands in Alton after church, but she turned it into something.

BIRCH BAYH

Phyllis Schlafly, she is one woman I really despise. She is the personification of evil in my mind because she was responsible for killing the ERA by going into state legislatures with housewives who'd bring baskets of just-baked bread onto the floor—I remember the Illinois legislature—and say, "Senators, Senators, don't make me have to go to work; I want to stay home with my children." We came up three votes short because of her.[*]

---

delegate. Her 1964 self-published book, *A Choice Not an Echo*, lauding conservative Arizona senator Barry Goldwater and trashing elite Rockefeller Republicans, sold three million copies. But when Goldwater lost in the Republican primaries that year, Schlafly's political star faded with his. She had not yet engaged in feminist issues and didn't know about the ERA until she was asked to participate in a debate about the amendment in Connecticut in December 1971. Schlafly soon discovered that opposing the ERA had political legs, and she embraced her new antifeminism crusade.

* Bayh is referring to the last three states needed to ratify the ERA, one of which hinged on passage in the Illinois state legislature, which required a three-fifths majority in order to pass constitutional amendments. The state legislature voted many times to pass the ERA between 1972 and 1982 but never managed to reach the required three-fifths majority. In a final dramatic vote, ERA supporters staged a thirty-seven-day hunger strike, but five days before the July 30, 1982, deadline the legislature's vote failed to pass the three-fifths-majority hurdle, and Schlafly's well-organized forces defeated the amendment once and, very possibly, for all.

9

Bill Baird's Supreme Court Victory

By late 1971, Bill Baird, who had endured thirty-six days in Boston's grim Charles Street Jail for handing contraceptive foam to a Boston University student in 1967, found himself in the chambers of the US Supreme Court listening to his attorney, Joseph Tydings, argue Eisenstadt v. Baird. *The November 17, 1971, oral argument took place just one month before twenty-seven-year-old Texas lawyer Sarah Weddington argued her case before the Supreme Court, asserting that Texas law violated her pregnant client Jane Roe's constitutional right to have an abortion. These two seminal cases would soon liberate the reproductive lives of millions of American women for decades to come.*

Baird's case would also play a role in Roe v. Wade. *Justice William Brennan circulated his pro-Baird draft opinion to his colleagues the morning of Weddington's first oral argument. In it, Brennan explained that women in Massachusetts had a right to privacy, just as married couples did, to use birth control. Brennan would be joined by all but one justice in his resounding final opinion that once and for all legalized the use of contraceptives for single women.*

EISENSTADT, SHERIFF v. BAIRD
Argued November 17–18, 1971—Decided March 22, 1972
MR. JUSTICE BRENNAN delivered the opinion of the Court.

Appellee William Baird was convicted at a bench trial in the Massachusetts Superior court under Massachusetts General Laws . . . first, for exhibiting contraceptive articles in the course of delivering a lecture on contraception to a group of students at Boston University and, second, for giving a young woman a package of Emko vagina foam at the close of his address. . . .

If under *Griswold* the distribution of contraceptives to married persons cannot be prohibited, a ban on distribution to unmarried persons would be equally impermissible. . . . If the right of privacy means anything, it is the right of the *individual*, married or single, to be free from unwarranted governmental intrusion into matters so fundamentally affecting a person as the decision whether to bear or beget a child.

BILL BAIRD

I was in the courtroom for the oral argument, and then on March 22, when the decision came down, reporters called me from all over the place. "If the right of privacy means anything, it is the right of an individual to be free to decide whether to *bear or beget a child*." Those were the powerful lines that went down in history and were used over and over in hundreds of other cases.

MYRA MACPHERSON

It took from the beginning in 1967, when Bill Baird gave her the contraceptive, until 1972 to get *Eisenstadt v. Baird*. It legalized contraception for unmarried people. As amazing as it seems, it took that long for that. It established a right to privacy that had not been established before.

Brennan's iconic phrase—*to bear or beget*—led directly to *Roe* ten months later. And that opened the floodgates. It was mentioned five times in the *Roe v. Wade* majority opinion and has been cited in over fifty-two other Supreme Court cases between 1972 and 2002. It was even sighted in the ruling that legalized same-sex marriage in 2015, *Obergefell v. Hodges*.

BILL BAIRD

My case affected millions of women, millions. But not a single movement fighter on a national level said, "Bill Baird, thank you for fighting for our rights."*

MYRA MACPHERSON

One would think that this Supreme Court decision would have made him extraordinarily famous. But I think he was considered too bizarre, too extreme. He would do things like turn up at anti-choice rallies with his eight-foot cross. I could never understand why Betty Friedan so despised him. After *Roe v. Wade*, he had three abortion clinics on Long Island, and they were firebombed.

---

* Despite his significant contribution to women's reproductive rights, Baird was kept at arm's length by the women's movement, whose leaders were suspicious of his self-aggrandizing zealotry. Baird operated as a one-man crusader and didn't tend to coordinate or strategize with women's groups, but he took umbrage when he wasn't thanked for his efforts on the behalf of women. Betty Friedan loathed him and accused him of being a CIA plant, and Robin Morgan called him a "male-supremacist." Vilified by the Catholic Church and the antiabortion movement, Baird also didn't get the love he felt he deserved from his ideological allies. The fact that he was a man didn't help. In March 1973, he picketed outside NOW's New York headquarters, denouncing its members for "blatant sexual chauvinism."

10

Ginsburg Stuns the Supreme Court

The political and legal battle to attack the constitutionality of laws that prohibited women from equal treatment took place simultaneously. While the ratification of the ERA would ultimately stall after the spring of 1972, Ruth Bader Ginsburg would succeed in systematically dismantling statutes that treated women differently from men, and vice versa. After the 1971 victory in Reed v. Reed, *Ginsburg, with Brenda Feigen, her co-director of the ACLU Women's Rights Project, took* Frontiero v. Richardson *as a "friend of the court" and many other landmark gender discrimination cases to the Supreme Court as direct counsel.*

JOE LEVIN

We lost the *Frontiero* case in the three-judge court by a two-to-one vote on April 5, 1972. But Judge Frank Johnson wrote a beautiful dissent; he supported our position all the way. The majority argument basically was that the due process clause did not apply to the federal government or to the military. We decided to appeal it to the Supreme Court. To tell you the truth, I didn't think there was any way in hell that the Supreme Court would take the case.

SHARRON FRONTIERO-COHEN

Joe took the case and ran with it and I didn't hear too much more about it until we lost and then he said, "Well, the next step is the Supreme Court." I said, "Fine."

BRENDA FEIGEN

Ruth and I continued to put our emphasis on winning equal rights for women in the many cases that were coming to us. Even though the principal work of the ACLU was litigation, lobbying for the ERA remained a priority. Sex discrimination litigation would be forever changed once the amendment was ratified. To Ruth, in those days too: "The ERA is the bedrock issue. . . . Without it the Supreme Court has no gun at its head." One day, while the ERA was still in the ratification process, Ruth told me about a sex discrimination case that the Supreme Court had just agreed to review. The case was *Frontiero v. Richardson*.

JOE LEVIN

At that time, we at the Southern Poverty Law Center had lots of litigation going on. I was basically running the place because my partner Morris Dees had gotten engaged in the George McGovern presidential campaign, so he was going to be of no assistance. I got a call from Brenda Feigen, who was with the ACLU Women's Rights Project in New York, who said they wanted to get involved. Long story short, after some conversations with a guy named Mel Wulf, who was the legal director of the ACLU at the time, and with Brenda, I agreed to let them do it. Mel told me then that the head of the women's rights group, Ruth Ginsburg, would be the one handling it.

What happened was we had a fundamental disagreement over how to argue the case. We thought that the court could find for us on the basis of a *rational basis test*, which is a much less strict basis than the one that Ruth wanted to do. She wanted to argue what they call *strict scrutiny*. Well, strict scrutiny is a tougher argument to make. If it's rational basis, you have to prove less in order to be successful in arguing that the due process clause protects women's rights in the military. This case was going to decide things in a large way across the board, because it was the first federal case that was attacking the federal government. The one in Idaho, *Reed v. Reed*, was a state case.

BRENDA FEIGEN

We wanted the Court to apply the highest level of scrutiny to sex discrimination cases. That meant that in order for a distinction based on gender to be upheld, a court would have to rule that there was a "compelling state interest" in keeping that distinction on the books. Every race discrimination case in recent years had been examined under the strict-scrutiny standard to see if there was a "compelling state interest" in maintaining whatever the particular racial classification was.

But all that Ruth had been able to secure in *Reed* was that there had to be a "rational state interest" in maintaining a sex-based classification. That meant that the lowest standard of review could be applied, and that if there were any logical reason (it certainly didn't need to be compelling) for maintaining the distinction on the basis of gender, a court could uphold the provision containing that distinction.

In *Frontiero*, however, it certainly would cost the government money to add benefits for husbands like those so far provided only to wives. We worried that the Court might deem avoiding a higher cost to the government for paying for a husband's housing not just administratively convenient but also a *rational* state interest. Therefore, we wanted the Court to apply the highest level of scrutiny because this was our chance to ensure that sex discrimination would become just as reprehensible as race discrimination. Afterall, the Equal Rights Amendment hadn't yet been ratified.

The brief was just monumentally important. We had a couple of months. I remember [my husband] Marc [Fasteau] and I would draft a section and Ruth would edit it and revise it. This brief was brilliant, and the most mind-boggling part of it was when she uses these sexist expressions of all of these hugely important men of history, from Thomas Jefferson,* Alexis de Tocqueville, William Blackstone,† Alfred Lord Tennyson, to Grover Cleveland. It just was very cool to be able to quote what all these very famous men had to say about the inferior place of women in society.

And then to move through that to Elizabeth Cady Stanton and her Declaration of Sentiments‡ and the Grimké sisters.§ I mean, it was just bril-

---

* Thomas Jefferson: "Were our state a pure democracy there would still be excluded from our deliberations women, who, to prevent deprivation of morals and ambiguity of issues, should not mix promiscuously in gatherings of men."

† William Blackstone, 1768: "By marriage, the husband and wife are one person in law: this is, the very being or legal existence of the woman is suspended during the marriage, or at least is incorporated and consolidated into that of the husband; under whose wing, protection, and *cover*, she performs everything; and is therefore called in our law a *femme-covert.*"

‡ Declaration of Sentiments, 1848: "The history of mankind is a history of repeated injuries and usurpations on the part of man toward woman, having in direct object the establishment of an absolute tyranny over her. . . . He has compelled her to submit to laws, in the formation of which she had no voice."

§ Sarah and Angelina Grimké, daughters of a wealthy South Carolina plantation owner, rejected their slave-holding family, moved to Philadelphia, and spent the rest of their lives eloquently writing and speaking out for abolition and women's rights.

liant and it wasn't just about finding cases, it was about her vision, which was how you persuade these nine old men justices that something has to be changed. You don't just talk about case law because we don't have case law on our side. What we had was the human condition and the way women were treated in society.

JOE LEVIN

I got a subsequent call from Mel Wulf saying, "Would you be willing to let Ruth Ginsburg argue part of the case as an amicus?" And I said, "Let me think about that one." You got a total of thirty minutes of argument before the Court, and they wanted ten minutes of argument. I wanted to be civil about this, so I told them, "Yes, you can have ten minutes of oral argument. I'll open the argument with maybe fifteen minutes of opening argument and I'll do ten minutes or so of rebuttal." They agreed to that.

BRENDA FEIGEN

For the upcoming argument, I was tasked with bringing all the case books to Court on the shuttle so the cases she was citing would be accessible. We got to Washington and walked up the steps of the Supreme Court. You entered through these marble columns and walked down a hall lined with marble statues of old white men. We were led to the council table and I was sitting to her left and I put all the casebooks down on the table in front of me. Pretty soon we heard the "Oyez! Oyez! Oyez!" and in filed the justices in order of seniority, and they took their seats. Of course, Thurgood Marshall was the only person of color.

Joe Levin went first. There was just nothing inspiring about him whatsoever.

JOE LEVIN

There was a lot of tension and I was certainly nervous, but I'll tell you the truth, when I got up to make the argument, I felt pretty comfortable, and I felt comfortable during the rebuttal. I thought the questions that they asked were good questions. I listened to that recording once. I felt like I did an okay job, especially for somebody who'd never done it before, and who was only twenty-nine years old.

RUTH BADER GINSBURG

The first case I argued at the Supreme Court was *Frontiero v. Richardson*. It was a divided argument.* I was so nervous. In those days the Court sat in the afternoon and the morning and *Frontiero* was an afternoon argument. I didn't dare eat lunch. I had a very well worked-out opening sentence. And then I looked up at the bench and realized I had a captive audience. They had no place to go. They had to listen to me and I knew a lot more about this than they did.

BRENDA FEIGEN

Then Ruth was asked to step up and speak. In this extremely articulate, slow, modulated voice, she delivered the brilliant oral argument with not a pause for my cases, my citations, my anything.

Ruth Bader Ginsburg, Supreme Court oral argument, January 19, 1973

Mr. Chief Justice and may it please the Court.

Amicus views this case as kin to *Reed v. Reed* 404 U.S. The legislative judgment in both derives from the same stereotype.

The man is or should be the independent partner in a marital unit.

The woman with an occasional exception is dependent, sheltered from bread winning experience. . . .

To provide the guidance so badly needed and because recognition is long overdue, amicus urges the Court to declare sex a suspect criterion.

Appellees concede that the principle ingredient involving strict scrutiny is present in the sex criterion.

Sex like race is a visible, immutable characteristic bearing no necessary relationship to ability.

Sex like race has been made the basis for unjustified or at least unproved assumptions, concerning an individual's potential to perform or to contribute to society. . . .

Women today face discrimination in employment as pervasive and more subtle than discrimination encountered by minority groups. In vocational and higher education, women continue to face restrictive quotas no longer operative with respect to other population groups.

---

* A divided argument means that different lawyers for the same party present different parts of the oral argument.

Their absence is conspicuous in Federal and State Legislative, Executive, and Judicial Chambers in higher civil service positions and in appointed posts in federal, state, and local government. . . .

Sex classifications do stigmatize when as in Goesaert against Cleary 235 U.S.,* they exclude women from an occupation thought more appropriate to men. The sex criterion stigmatizes when it is used to limit hours of work for women only. . . .

These distinctions have a common effect. They help keep woman in her place, a place inferior to that occupied by men in our society. . . .

In asking the Court to declare sex a suspect criterion, amicus urges a position forcibly stated in 1837 by Sarah Grimke, noted abolitionist and advocate of equal rights for men and women. She spoke not elegantly, but with unmistakable clarity. She said, "I ask no favor for my sex. All I ask of our brethren is that they take their feet off our necks."

BRENDA FEIGEN

There was not a single question. Nothing. Their faces were just deadpan, there was not a single reaction among any of them. I am thinking "Oh my God," but I looked at them and I thought, "You know what? These guys are blown away by this. They have never seen a performance like this before."

RUTH BADER GINSBURG

As it turned out at that first argument, not a single question was asked. Amazing for the Court. And I wondered, I still wonder, why. Were they indulging me? Or was I really opening their eyes? The problem we had was that judges who in those days were overwhelmingly men, they considered themselves good fathers, no doubt they were, good husbands, so what is this sex discrimination about? I mean they knew about race discrimination. That was bad. My mission was to open their eyes to the reality. As Justice Brennan put it so well, too often the pedestal on which women were thought to stand turned out to be a cage.† Getting them to understand that was a challenge. It was also exhilarating. The other arguments I had prompted a series of questions. But that first one . . . I felt like a teacher lecturing. The

---

*   In *Goesaert v. Cleary* (1948), the Supreme Court upheld a Michigan law that prohibited women from working as bartenders unless they were the wife or daughter of the establishment's owner.

†   Brennan's exact words in the decision were: "There can be no doubt that our Nation has had a long and unfortunate history of sex discrimination. Traditionally, such discrimination was rationalized by an attitude of 'romantic paternalism,' which, in practical effect, put women not on a pedestal, but in a cage."

effort was to show the arbitrariness of gender-based classifications. And that men as well as women could be the target.

BRENDA FEIGEN

I've subsequently seen oral arguments in the Court and nothing has come close to this delivery. I mean, there've been good arguments, but this was just fantastic. After she finished, I leaned over and said to her, "You're going to be the next Democratic appointee to this court." I just knew it. And there we were in 1973. Exactly twenty years later, I would be right. Her husband, Marty, came over to her and gave her a big kiss and was grinning.

11

Who Are These Girls?

On December 13, 1971, two female lawyers with pregnant clients in Texas and Georgia brought their cases to the US Supreme Court. Sarah Weddington argued Roe v. Wade, *and Margie Pitts Hames argued* Doe v. Bolton.* *Meanwhile, scores of abortion rights cases were making progress in state courts, and the country was seething with change and tilting toward freedom. But none of this was apparent to the women in the Chicago Abortion Counseling Service (code-name Jane), who were busier than ever helping desperate women terminate their unwanted pregnancies.*

JUDITH ARCANA

It was May 3, 1972. I was driving somebody else's car and going back and forth between the front and the place. That was in the period when we actually rented an apartment to be the place, because for a long time we just borrowed two apartments every day that we worked. We were hitting up all of our friends.

I was a nursing mother. My son was six months old, and he was with

---

* Ten months later, on October 11, 1972, Hames and Weddington made their oral arguments a second time to the court because two new justices, Lewis Powell and William Rehnquist, had not yet been seated for their first arguments.

Eileen [another Jane], who was doing my babysitting with the bottles of breast milk that were in the fridge.

MARTHA SCOTT
We were at this apartment that we had rented in South Shore, which is south of Hyde Park. There were a bunch of us working. I don't believe I was doing an abortion. I was getting somebody ready.

JUDITH ARCANA
That day, there was one Jane working the front, and there were five Janes at the place either doing D&Cs or inducing miscarriages. There would be five or six women at the place at any given time who were undergoing medical procedures, and lots of people at the front.

I was taking this woman who had just had an abortion back to the front. We said goodbye and walked out of the apartment. We took the elevator down eleven flights and when the elevator doors opened, there were two big white guys wearing trench coats and shiny black shoes standing in the lobby. They looked like they were sent from central casting to play homicide detectives.

They flashed their badges and asked the woman I was with, "Did you just have an abortion?" and she burst into tears. I said to her, "Don't worry. You don't have to talk to them if you don't want to." Right away they knew that I was the criminal, and she was the victim. Then she led the cops to the apartment upstairs.

They said something like, "We're going to detain you," and one of them took me out to the paddy wagon in the parking lot and put handcuffs on me and hooked the handcuff onto some device on the wall.

The first thing I thought was, "They're going to take my child away from me. They're going to say I'm an unfit mother because I'm a criminal and because I was doing abortions, and that's against mothers." Because that's the way those people think. Then I worried about what was happening upstairs in the apartment.

MARTHA SCOTT
There was a loud knock on the door. It was really a heavy knock and it was exactly what you expect to happen with the police. When someone opened the door, she shouted, "It's the cops! It's the cops!" People started throwing the [medical] instruments out the window. Somebody else started tearing up the cards with the women's names and information.

A bunch of big guys came in, looked around, and kept on saying, "Where is he? Where's the doctor?" We were just a bunch of girls. The feeling was, "Who are these girls?" Then we were all carted down to the police station.

JUDITH ARCANA

I don't know how long I was in the police van until, all of a sudden, all of the Janes from the place got in the van with me. Another group of cops had gone to the front. Once they had rounded up everybody at both locations, they had about forty-two people including small children. That was a scene. Oh my God.

We all wound up in the Cottage Grove police station. The Janes were all cuffed and kept separately from each other for a while. I got hooked onto another anchor on the wall like a medieval prisoner. It was really creepy. Plus, my breasts were filled with milk.

The bust was at about three p.m. We were in the police station for a long time, but by midnight, we were taken downtown to the women's lockup. This was when it was at 1121 South State Street. It was the famous women's lockup. We got fingerprinted, we got our mug shots taken.

MARTHA SCOTT

We were put in a holding cell with a whole bunch of women who were, by and large, prostitutes. That was an education in itself. One of the ladies said, "What are all you white ladies doing in here?"

JUDITH ARCANA

They said to us, "What are you in for?" and we said, "Abortion." And they said, "Ooh." And then we said, "What are you in for?" And they said, "We didn't do anything." And we said, "Well, we didn't do anything either."

Our cell had a tiny, tiny sink, like a doll's sink, almost, and a toilet. Everything was filthy. I milked my breasts into the sink, that's why I have this vision of it so clear in my head.

My husband's law partners helped us all get released the next day. Mind you, we were all white. That's an important point. If we had been Black, we'd still be there.

Chicago Daily News, May 4, 1972, "Nab 7 in Abortion Raid:
Women Seized in Cut-Rate Clinic"
Seven Chicago women were arrested Wednesday on charges of operating
an illegal low-cost abortion clinic out of two Southside apartments.

Chicago police learned of the clinic from a woman whose sister reportedly was scheduled to have an abortion there Wednesday and did not want her to undergo the operation.

Homicide investigators said the clinic only charged about $100 for the operation and handled as many as 15 patients per day. None of the women who performed the operations was a licensed physician, police said.

JUDITH ARCANA

The other women in the Service mobilized immediately: they got bail money ($2,500 for each of us), and they got the abortions done for the women who were scheduled that day.

The seven women—Susan Gallatzer, twenty-one; Abby Gollon, twenty-seven; Judith (Arcana) Pildes, twenty-nine; Madeline Schwenk, thirty; Martha Scott, thirty; Sheila Smith, twenty-two; and Diane Stevens, twenty-three—were each charged with three counts of performing abortions and three counts of conspiracy to perform abortions. Each violation carried the potential of ten years' jail time. Joining other movement outlaw groups like the Chicago Seven and the Panther 21, the women were called the Abortion Seven.

JUDITH ARCANA

During the time between the bust and the grand jury, we were interviewing lawyers. All but one were men, of course. The men were, in different ways and with different tones, so condescending that it was impossible. How could we possibly hire these guys to represent us when they couldn't even see us?

LAURA KAPLAN

Then the seven interviewed [Jo-Anne Wolfson]. She was one of the top criminal lawyers in Chicago. She had defended other radicals [like the Black Panthers] and her position was clear: "There's no reason for any of you to go to jail. My job is to keep you out of jail, not to fight the issue of abortion."

Until Jo-Anne told them about it, they were not aware of the Supreme Court's pending decision in *Roe v. Wade.* . . . Since the oral arguments in December 1971, the Supreme Court had been deliberating.

JUDITH ARCANA

This is what Jo-Anne looked like the day she came to court for us. She was wearing canary-yellow pants, a canary-yellow sleeveless sweater, she was carrying a canary-yellow patent leather briefcase, I don't remember her shoes unfortunately, and she was wearing silver bangles. This is a white woman with a deep tan—silver bangles on her arms and from her ears and she talked like God. She was so smart and so sharp and she looked like that. It was fabulous.

LAURA KAPLAN

By the time we got busted, we were getting almost three hundred calls a week, so we had people waiting for weeks for their abortion, and they kept on calling after news of the bust. So we went back to our normal way of operating. It was incredibly intense. Eventually, a number of the seven women who were busted came back to work while the case was in progress.

JUDITH ARCANA

Because *Roe v. Wade* was being considered by the Supreme Court, Jo-Anne did whatever she could to stall the case.

12

On the Chisholm Trail

Strapped for cash, Shirley Chisholm relied on an army of rainbow coalition volunteers to secure her name on the ballot in eight states, set up events, and help her spread her utopian message of peace and freedom. But what she couldn't prepare for was being a target of President Nixon's corrupt "dirty tricks" campaign.

BARBARA LEE

I was an activist. I was a revolutionary. I was a progressive Black woman, Black Student Union president at Mills College, and community worker with the Black Panther Party. I helped serve kids' breakfast; I'd bag groceries; I dragged my two little kids to survival rallies. We did everything in terms of community service.

So, I was not going to register to vote; there was no way I was going to get involved in politics. I didn't think the two-party system was working; it wasn't working for me. I mean, I was on welfare, trying to get through school. My kids went to class with me. I didn't have money for childcare, so I had to drag them to class.

I had a class in government with Professor Dr. Frances Mullins, "Candidates, Campaigns and Constituents," and part of the course requirement was to work in a presidential primary campaign. Then it was McGovern, Muskie, Humphrey, and whomever else. I said, "Flunk me, I'm not working on any of these guys' campaigns." I never flunked a class in my life, but I was willing to flunk this government class. So, at the same time as this class that I'm flunking, as the BSU president, I invite Congresswoman Shirley Chisholm, the first African American woman elected to Congress, to speak to the student body and to the Black Student Union.

SANDRA GAINES

In '72, I was a junior transfer at Mills College from a community college. I had a Ford Foundation fellowship as a single parent, raising three sons, and I was on welfare. Not quite the image of Mills. Barbara Lee was also a student. We were called "resumers." . . . Prior to the event when Shirley came to speak, I didn't know who she was. I don't even know how Barbara knew about her to be quite honest.

BARBARA LEE

Shirley came out and she spoke. First of all, she spoke fluent Spanish; a lot of people don't know that. She talked about immigrant rights. She talked about education because she was an educator. She was against the Vietnam War. She was an unbelievable candidate. She talked about coalition-building. And she was one of the first board members of NARAL; she was pro-choice all the way. I mean, Shirley Chisholm was a phenomenal lady. She was speaking, and I'm saying I've never heard a member of Congress speak like this. Then she said she was running for president. It was like, really? Because of course, the news just didn't cover her.

So, I went up to her later and said, "I didn't know you were running for president. I have this class in government. I'm trying to pass it." I said, "You sound like a candidate I could work for and try to pass this class." She looked at me and said, "Wait a minute." I had a big Afro, jeans, power to the people. She said, "What are you talking about? You've got to get involved in politics because if you're not on the inside trying to make changes, you're going to just continue to raise Cain. And change comes from the pressure." But, she said, "You're smart enough to be in there helping us change the system. You need to register to vote."

I said, "Not me. That's bourgeoisie. I'm a revolutionary, so I'm not going to register to vote. Do I have to do that to work in your campaign? I'm just trying to pass this class." She said, "Yes, you do."

She took me to task. I said, okay, took a deep breath. And she really mentored me. And that encounter with her at the student union ballroom that night where she spoke, really changed the trajectory of my life because I told her, "Okay, who do I call? What do I do? Where's your campaign housed?" She said, "I don't know. I'm leaving it up to my local supporters. I don't have a lot of national money. This is a grassroots campaign."

SANDRA GAINES

What she was saying in her message was, become involved and make a difference. So I looked around and I ran for student body president and Barbara Lee ran for the head of the BSU. I think we called it the Black Feminist Alliance.

BARBARA LEE

I went back and I talked to my professor and said, "Okay, I found a candidate. I'll try to pass this class. What do I do?" She said, "That's up to you. That's the point of the class, figure it out." So, I figured it out. I organized the Northern California Shirley Chisholm presidential primary campaign from my class at Mills College in Oakland, along with other students there. I got an A in the class.

WILSON RILES

I had come home from the Peace Corps in Senegal and began work for a political campaign management firm, and basically resigned from my job and went to work for Shirley as the Northern California coordinator. I saw her campaign as important symbolism that needed to be pushed and moved forward. But then meeting her in the flesh and hearing what she had to say, her commitment and depth of knowledge about what was happening in the Black community, with poor people in this country, then that symbolism turned into visceral reality that was very powerful and important.

SANDRA GAINES

What attracted me to Shirley was she was just so audacious about what was right. I never had any illusions that she was going to win and become president. And I'm sure she didn't either. But I certainly believe that this was a time and a place and that our country needed these issues to be heard, and they needed to try to form some sort of coalition to get more than token attention from the politicians, and to try to change the Democratic Party platform.

No other politician has had that kind of effect on me personally. Not even Martin Luther King, to be honest, as Shirley had on me as a person. I went into education. I'm still a teacher.

BARBARA LEE

I went on to the Democratic convention in Miami as a Shirley Chisholm delegate. And the rest is history. That's how I got involved in politics and haven't turned back since.*

WILSON RILES

I was told that I would have to do a lot of fundraising, because there wasn't going to be any money coming out of the national campaign. I ended up getting one check after one month's work and then nothing after that.

SANDRA GAINES

Our campaign office was a little ragged dump, but it was great for us. . . . I'm sure there were some undercurrents going on with so many different factions trying to come together and make this coalition basically of the have-nots. We were trying to increase the vote in Alameda County. We had the feminists and the Black Panthers supporting us.

WILSON RILES

The Black Panther Party was doing a lot of the voter registration, a lot of the street work, getting the literature out, going door-to-door. There was a strong group of students from Mills College that were the core campaign.

Around the beginning of the campaign effort, it was very clear that there was this schism taking place between the leadership among the Black community and the women's movement, in terms of who Shirley was and what Shirley was about. . . . She wanted support from the Black man but she wasn't going to kiss their ring so to speak, so they didn't appreciate that about her. But the women continued to support her.

SHIRLEY CHISHOLM

The rivalry between Black men and white women campaign workers, which was troublesome in Florida, North Carolina, and other states, became bitter

---

* Barbara Lee worked as a staff member for Congressman Ron Dellums before she was elected to Congress in his Berkeley/Oakland district in 1998. In 2023, she announced her candidacy for Dianne Feinstein's former California Senate seat, but lost to Rep. Adam Schiff in the primary.

hostility [in California]. . . . The same kind of disagreements plagued the Los Angeles area, where my Southern California campaign coordinator, Arlie Scott, a University of Southern California history professor, did a vigorous and capable organizing job, only to provoke a barrage of criticism from Blacks who said she and the other white women were dominating the whole scene. Some, I am told, were even threatened physically. . . .

One militant Black group, however, endorsed me strongly—the Black Panthers. National chairman Bobby Seale said I was "the best social critic of America's injustices to run for president from whatever party," and promised that the Panthers' full membership would work for me.

New York Times, April 28, 1972, "Huey Newton Backs Race by Mrs. Chisholm"

Huey P. Newton, leader of the Black Panther party, today called for "every black, poor, and progressive human being" to support the candidacy of Representative Shirley Chisholm. . . . "The social trend of power by the people for more control of the economic, political, and social institutions within this society is the basic goal." . . . Mr. Newton . . . said the party is "putting down the gun" to work within the system for the good of the black community. During a three-day campaign last month, the Panthers registered 11,000 new voters.

ARLIE SCOTT

The Black Panthers were evolving as an organization by 1972, and they were getting into electoral politics. Huey Newton wanted to throw a fundraiser for Shirley Chisholm in his Oakland penthouse apartment, but he wasn't that thrilled about the Secret Service being there. And vice versa. But we worked something out and they both gave a little.

It was in the beautiful penthouse overlooking the whole city, there were a lot of people there and the Secret Service was discreetly in the back. It was very exciting.

WILSON RILES

I don't think a lot of people recognized that the Black Panthers used the Chisholm campaign to test their political machinery. So, in 1973, they ran Bobby Seale for mayor [and Elaine Brown for City Council] and they had learned a lot about the mechanics of how to do that by working in the Shirley Chisholm campaign. And Bobby's race in Oakland changed the face of Oakland. Bobby didn't win, but in 1977 we ended up with our first Black mayor, Lionel Wilson.

ARLIE SCOTT

She came to California the very day that George Wallace was shot in Maryland. And before that, we had gotten hate mail, vicious mail, from people in Orange County and other conservative areas. They were threatening violence.

And we had just gotten other mail—one on Humphrey's letterhead sent to Chisholm delegates, saying the Chisholm campaign wants to stop McGovern, so instead of voting for Chisholm, you ought to vote for Humphrey.

You can't imagine the impact one letter like that, going out to all the delegates had. It made the white women, Black women, Black men who were in the leadership distrust us, and there were rumors that Shirley was only a stalking horse, she's not serious.

And there was another letter that was written on Shirley Chisholm stationery that was supposedly signed by me and one that was signed by the office manager telling people that they ought to vote for McGovern. All we could do was get on the phone right away and try to tell people that we didn't know where the letters were coming from. The McGovern and Humphrey campaigns were saying, "We didn't do it." But our group was furious with Humphrey, furious with McGovern, and had no idea at the time that it was coming from the outside. Well, we found out later, after the campaign.

CAROLYN SMITH

Then there was the biggest lie that she had been in an insane asylum. I don't know where they got that from, because she's never had a nervous breakdown, to my knowledge, and to hers either. Oh, the lies just popped up!

ARLIE SCOTT

Later, I found out that it was part of the whole Watergate thing.*

---

* G. Gordon Liddy, the Committee to Re-elect the President's dirty-tricks mastermind, initially suggested a wide range of covert operations aimed at "ratfucking" Nixon's political opponents. Among his many sabotage schemes was Operation COAL, which aimed to *help* Chisholm's campaign, the idea being that she didn't have a chance of winning the primary but maybe she could hurt McGovern. In the end, Liddy and Donald Segretti must have chosen to do the opposite and attack Chisholm directly.

To Sac Los Angeles July 26, 1973
Urgent From Director FBI

UNSUB: SPURIOUS NEWS RELEASE CONCERNING REPRESEN-TATIVE SHIRLEY CHISHOLM, CALIFORNIA PRESIDENTIAL PRIMARY 1972 ELECTION LAWS.

The office of special prosecutor Archibald Cox, U.S. Department of Justice, has requested an investigation be conducted into the allegation that news releases made in Los Angeles during the past presidential primary campaign indicated that Representative Shirley Chisholm (D-NY), a presidential contender, had been in and out of mental institutions. . . . Consultation with Mr. Cox's staff revealed the only information available to their knowledge is a UPI news release dateline 5/31/73 at Los Angeles which reads as follows: "Press release stationary was stolen from the office of Senator Hubert Humphrey's campaign office shortly before the June 6, 1972 presidential primary and circulated with false statements, it was disclosed today. <u>BLANK</u> Humphrey's California campaign said a closet was broken into on June 4 and about 1,000 blank copies of the form used for press releases were removed. The next day the news media received what appeared to be news releases from Humphrey's headquarters.

ARLIE SCOTT

I had a visit from a couple of FBI agents who were investigating Nixon's dirty tricks and Don Segretti. . . . They took all this stuff because they had reason to believe that it had just been part of the Watergate thing. I never heard back from them.*

BARBARA WINSLOW

No other candidate had such smears, so to speak, against them. Nothing that repulsive. And she never spoke of it, never. I can only assume that it hurt her deeply and she didn't want it known.

---

* Donald Segretti was Liddy's lead operative behind an elaborate political sabotage campaign designed to disrupt and turn the Democratic candidates against each other during the primaries. The burglary and break-in at the Democratic National Committee's headquarters in the Watergate building on June 17, 1972, turned out to be just the tip of the iceberg. The Nixon's Committee to Re-elect the President (CREEP)'s illegal "dirty tricks" effort started as early as the New Hampshire primary in February, and forged campaign stationery was frequently used to cause confusion and hostility between the candidates. On October 1, 1973, Segretti pled guilty to three counts of conspiracy and distributing campaign literature without identifying the source. He served four months in prison. Liddy was convicted of conspiracy, burglary, and illegal wiretapping and sentenced to six to twenty years of prison (he only served four and a half).

CAROLYN SMITH

She had never been audited by the IRS until after she ran for president, and then, until she retired in 1983, they audited her every single year.

WILSON RILES

We did surprisingly well in California. I think we had about twelve delegates, about half from Southern California, and half from Northern California. Most of them from the Dellums district in Northern California. And neither the McGovern or Humphrey folks had a majority of the delegates. . . . We were essentially the balancing number of delegates as the whole California delegation was carved up, so we felt that we were in a critical position as far as the whole convention was concerned.

> *Chisholm's name was on the primary ballot in eight states, and she received votes in a total of fourteen states (because of write-ins). Even though the campaign had raised only $300,000, she stayed on the campaign trail long after other losing candidates dropped out. Chisholm won 2.7 percent of the popular vote and only twenty-eight delegates.*

13

The Education Act's Surprise—Title IX

EDITH GREEN

The 1972 Education Act amended various education acts in several ways. Title IX was the part of the bill which probably has caused the greatest amount of trouble for colleges and universities of any section of the '72 act. It prohibits discrimination on the basis of sex in any educational program. We had Patsy Mink and Shirley Chisholm on the full committee. I remember the room was packed in the full committee and Al Quie (R-MN) opposed it. He said, "If this passes you are going to have male stewards on airplanes." I can still remember the laughter.

PATSY MINK

We tried to get a civil rights bill [amendment], but the Justice Department intervened and said, no, we cannot support an amendment of the Civil Rights Act; why do you not put this measure in the education bill? And really that is the genesis of Title IX. It was not a surrender, but it was a concession to the Department of Justice.

BIRCH BAYH

The main reason I got involved in Title IX is when you looked at all the discriminations in the Equal Rights Amendment discussion, the one that leaped out at me was education. I had inherited the mantle—rightly or wrongly—as the number one defender of women's rights. I was proud to have it.

BERNICE SANDLER

So, what happened is as the bill proceeded through the Congress, a group of us had a meeting with Mrs. Green, and we asked, "We're here, Representative Green, you tell us what you want us to do for lobbying and we'll do it." And she said, "Don't. This bill is going to pass, and if you start lobbying for it, people are going to ask questions and realize what Title IX will do. Trust me." And she was absolutely right.*

Congressional Record, February 28, 1972

Mr. Bayh, Mr. President . . . The amendment is as follows:

Sec. 1001. (a) No person in the United States shall, on the basis of sex, be excluded from the participation in, be denied the benefits of, or be subjected to discrimination under any education program or activity receiving Federal financial assistance.†

BERNICE SANDLER

When Title IX passed in both the House and Senate by June '72, maybe ten of us, and I'm not exaggerating, knew that it was going to cover athletics. But again, no one had done the study of how bad athletic discrimination was at either college or K–12, and so we really didn't know that much about it. My understanding of Title IX's impact on sports was something like this: "Isn't this nice! Because of Title IX, at the annual Field Day Events in schools, there will be more activities for girls." Part of the reason was that our definition of discrimination was very narrow, focusing primarily on admissions and employment. The NCAA [National College Athletics Association] wasn't involved; this was an education bill, who was looking?

And remember, this is before computers, you can't get information out that quickly unless you send it or call everybody. So, most of the education

---

*   By the time the amendment became law, Sandler had filed sex discrimination cases against more than 350 colleges.

†   After two years of legislative sausage-making, the final draft of Title IX of the Education Amendments Act of 1972 covered all educational programs that receive federal funding, from pre-K to graduate schools, with exemptions in admissions for single-sex, religious, and military schools and universities and private undergraduate colleges.

world and the athletics folks didn't know and it got through. After Title IX passed, they were very surprised when they found out what it would really do.

BILLIE JEAN KING

Without the word "activity" in those thirty-seven words of Title IX, we wouldn't have women's sports. Senator Birch Bayh told me that they debated whether to leave it in or take it out, and they went back and forth on it. And I remember him telling me, "I'm so happy we left it in because we had no understanding of what this was going to do for women." He said, "I really didn't know it was going to do this great job."

DONNA DE VARONA

The athletic groups didn't want it. I mean, you look at UCLA, they had to put a women's locker room in Pauley Pavilion. There were a lot of structural changes, cultural changes that had to happen. You had to build the pipeline. Girls had to realize their potential. You have to get competitive, you have to field teams, you have to invest, you have to change a culture.

Before Title IX, one in twenty-seven girls played sports. Now, one in almost three do. That's the difference. But that's why the guidelines of Title IX were important, but everybody games the system because you can't have equality overnight. That's where the male leadership was right. You can't just open the door and pour money in, if you don't have the feeder system, but you have to create it and you have to open the door to do it.[*]

> The bill took a decade to implement, but ultimately it opened up college and graduate school student admissions and faculty jobs to women. Its most visible and unintended consequence was to create a new world of athletics for girls and young women. Representative Edith Green retired from Congress in 1974, leaving the job of protecting Title IX from a constant barrage of legislative attacks to Senator Birch Bayh and Representative Patsy Mink.

---

[*] In 1974, Billie Jean King started the Women's Sports Foundation, whose original mission was to promote and protect women's athletics under Title IX. Olympic gold medal swimmer Donna de Varona became the foundation's first president.

BERNICE SANDLER

In '72 they didn't know that athletics was going to be covered by Title IX. But once they found out—athletics is very important, it's big money, okay. It's power, I mean a lot of football coaches make more money than the president. And it's emotional; I mean, this is macho stuff and "these women are going to take it away from us" kind of thing. So, that's very visible as the regulation gets developed because people are aware of that. The change in admissions came without the same kinds of opposition.

Pauli Murray letter to Bernice Sandler

Dear Bunny!* When you're written up in the history of this era, they should refer to you as the little woman who started the Academic Sex Revolution. . . . Cheers, and in Sisterhood—Pauli.

By 2016, women became a majority of law students; by 2017, they were a majority of new medical students and 57 percent of all college and university students. By 2018, women filled almost half of all full-time faculty jobs. Twenty-five years after the passage of Title IX, women's athletic scholarships grew from less than $100,000 to $200 million. The number of girls participating in high school athletics grew from three hundred thousand in the school year 1971–1972 to three million in 2021–2022.

---

* Bunny was Bernice Sandler's nickname.

14

Woman Power 1972 at the Democratic Convention

History was made at the 1972 Democratic and Republican national conventions—which both convened in Miami in July and August. They were the first US national party conventions in the history of the American Republic in which women held positions of power. Just a few months after the passage of the Equal Rights Amendment and Title IX, the National Women's Political Caucus (NWPC) rode a wave of popular support, and Shirley Chisholm made history as the first woman presidential candidate to run a full primary campaign. At the Democratic convention in July, a full 40 percent of the delegates (1,212) were women, and 15 percent were Black—three times more than in 1968. Yvonne Brathwaite Burke, a Black California congressional candidate, was named Democratic National Committee vice chair, and the NWPC successfully lobbied the party to adopt a fifteen-point Rights of Women plank in the party platform. George McGovern's staff nicknamed the women "The Nylon Revolution," and they would soon battle over abortion rights on the convention floor.[*]

---

[*] This was the first time that a women's rights agenda had ever been adopted by a national party platform. The fifteen-point-plan included ratification of the ERA, the eradication of job discrimination on the basis of sex, increasing educational opportunities for women and minorities, job training, amending Social Security, childcare, and eliminating barriers for women to credit, mortgages, and property ownership.

BRENDA FEIGEN

Gloria, Marc, my brother Richard, and I had all run as Chisholm delegates on the Upper East Side, but we lost and therefore were not delegates at the convention. Gloria and I flew to Miami and checked into this really dumpy hotel, the Betsy Ross. We shared a room. There was no shower curtain, the paint was peeling, the lightbulbs had no shades. . . . Gloria mused that we wouldn't be in the room very much.

Theodore H. White, *The Making of the President 1972*

The National Women's Political Caucus had taken over as headquarters the third floor of the derelict, sea-sprayed Betsy Ross Hotel. . . . The Betsy Ross was the power center. Mimeograph and Xerox machines spewed out leaflets in thousands; the switchboard at the Betsy Ross Hotel jammed; fuses blew; and each night, after dark, couriers boarded the busses to travel north on Collins Avenue and persuade night clerks of the forty or more major hotels to stuff mailboxes or let them slip leaflets under delegates' doors. 'WOMAN POWER 1972' . . . When the convention broke up, woman power 1972 was real.

BETTY FRIEDAN

I went to both conventions as a reporter: a maneuver by Bella had replaced the caucus steering committee by special convention "spokeswomen"—Gloria Steinem at the Democratic, Jill Ruckelshaus at the Republican.

BRENDA FEIGEN

The Policy Council of the NWPC chose Gloria to be its spokesperson at the Democratic convention. Neither Gloria nor I had been present during the vote, and Gloria expressed no pleasure at having been awarded the honor.

Esquire, November 1972, "Woman," by Nora Ephron

Two weeks before the convention, the NWPC council met to elect a spokesperson in Miami and chose Gloria Steinem over Friedan. The election was yet another chapter in Friedan's ongoing feud with Steinem. . . . Just how well the caucus will do in its first national election remains to be seen. . . . There were battles still to be fought at the convention—the South Carolina challenge* and the abortion

---

* The thirty-two-member South Carolina delegation had only seven female members, and the NWPC,

plank—but the first was small potatoes (or so it seemed beforehand) and the second was a guaranteed loser.

Harper's Magazine, October 1972,
"McGovern the Big Tease," by Germaine Greer[*]

When I got to the National Women's Political Caucus meeting in the Napoleon Room at the Deauville Hotel on Sunday morning, Gloria Steinem was speaking, and the controlled jubilance of her tone pushed my tormenting hopes up to a fever pitch. She spoke of councilmen being ousted by housewives, of women forming 46 percent of the attendance at precinct meetings in one state. "The political process has been changed," she sang, "and it will never be the same again." . . . Bella Abzug took over, vowing staunchly . . . that women would not be McGovern's sacrificial lamb. . . . Bella brought up the question of the minority report on control of one's reproductive destiny. To bring abortion into the Democratic party platform might be unwise, she argued, but the issue concerned a fundamental human right that could not be denied by those who chose to live by a different code. . . . There was a brief debate on the subject; some delegates argued that it was a state matter, and inappropriate therefore in the party platform . . . Bella's . . . windup left us in even more doubt about how the women were to proceed: it was our overriding priority to dump Nixon, she said, even if we had to waive the immediacy of certain demands. "Womanpower is a growing thing that must live."

Boston Globe, July 11, 1972, "Women Delegates Caucus, Hopefuls Woo Their Votes," by Ellen Goodman

The women's caucus held a meeting yesterday and the candidates came. They came not for chivalry but for votes.

---

led by floor leader Bella Abzug, insisted on a vote to force the state to include more women in its delegation. This vote would be a public show of the newfound political power of the women's caucus, and McGovern promised he would help deliver the votes. But for arcane reasons having to do with their fear of losing the "California Challenge," where McGovern needed the crucial 271 delegates in the winner-take-all state, the women were blindsided by McGovern's strategists, who worked secretly to defeat the South Carolina measure.

[*] Greer's and Ephron's coverage of the convention for *Esquire* and *Harper's* represented a new style of magazine writing called New Journalism, which included first-person, experiential, and therefore much more engaging and entertaining writing. Hunter S. Thompson's drug-fueled, colorful coverage of the 1972 election for *Rolling Stone*, which was almost entirely white male–focused, represented the New Journalism of the seventies on steroids.

And that's a measure of political power.

A full third of the women delegates filled the Carillon Hotel ballroom as the candidates came to woo them: first Terry Sanford, then Hubert Humphrey, Shirley Chisholm and George McGovern. George Wallace sent a friend of his wife. Only Edmund Muskie didn't show.

ARLIE SCOTT

The Women's Caucus at the Democratic convention met in a huge room with a podium where the candidates would talk about women's issues. The big issue was not only proportional representation, but also support for a pro-choice plank in the platform. That was very, very important to everybody.

Esquire, November 1972, "Woman," by Nora Ephron

Betty has publicly announced her drive to run Chisholm for Vice President. The ballroom of the Carillon Hotel, packed full of boisterous, exuberant delegates, activists and press, gives her suggestion a standing ovation; minutes later, it is hissing Chisholm with equal gusto for waffling on the California challenge.*

Boston Globe, July 11, 1972, "Women Delegates Caucus, Hopefuls Woo Their Votes," by Ellen Goodman

The women stood on chairs applauding and shouting for the only female candidate, their McGovern and Humphrey buttons shaking.

"This shows where you stand in our hearts," said Liz Carpenter, herself a Humphrey supporter.

Off Our Backs, September 1972, by Vivien Leone

WE WANT SHIRLEY! Up went the beautiful soprano chant. It was tears-in-the-throat-making. Up rose the steering committee from their proscenium seats and they all-in-a-row kissed her. Magic!

---

*   In an attempt to keep her hard-earned California delegates and defeat McGovern's winner-take-all California challenge, Chisholm joined forces with the ABM (Anyone But McGovern) coalition, which put her in an unholy alliance with conservatives Humbert Humphrey and George Wallace. This infuriated members of the liberal Black caucus and the women's caucus, both of whom had already endorsed McGovern.

Boston Globe, July 11, 1972, "Women Delegates Caucus, Hopefuls
Woo Their Votes," by Ellen Goodman

Mrs. Chisholm tried to convince the women to put their votes where
their "hearts" were.

"You know deep in your hearts, you put me beside any candidate
and I have a deeper commitment to those issues that are important to
us than any of them. You have to make the decision whether your commitment to women is going to go down the line for a woman candidate
or whether women go for the male candidate like they always do."

Fewer than two dozen female delegates are voting for Mrs. Chisholm,
but more than 400 applauded.

"That's why I'm clapping so hard," said one Michigan feminist
delegate. "I'm clapping out the guilt. But this is politics and she's not
going to win."

Off Our Backs, September 1972, by Vivien Leone

Into the meeting strode the bloodless figure of George McG, and the
crowd screamed . . . even though a year ago most of the screamers had
hardly heard of South Dakota . . . and this figure with all the fervor
of a Madame Tussaud's Wax Museum, is Against The War (Rah!), and
Is A Man, and consequently is A Serious Candidate. The alternative
adjective is "realistic."

Esquire, November 1972, "Woman," by Nora Ephron

Beaming, while he is graciously introduced by Liz Carpenter, "We
know we wouldn't have been here if it hadn't been for you," she says.
"George McGovern didn't talk about reform—he did something about
it."* The audience is McGovern's. "I'm grateful for the introduction
that all of you are here because of me," says the candidate rumored to
be most in touch with women's issues. "But I really think the credit
for that has to go to Adam instead . . ." He pauses for the laugh and
looks genuinely astonished when what he gets instead is a resounding
hiss. "Can I recover if I say Adam and Eve?" he asks.

---

*   In reaction to the 1968 Democratic convention, which, engineered by party bosses behind closed
doors, nominated Vice President Hubert Humphrey, who had not run in the primaries, instead of Senator Eugene McCarthy, who had, McGovern and Representative Donald Fraser spearheaded a set of party
reforms. The McGovern-Fraser Commission would change the nominating rules in 1972 to make them
more democratic and representational, including increasing the number of women and Black delegates.

Harper's Magazine, October 1972,
"McGovern the Big Tease," by Germaine Greer

There were a few cries of "Shame!" and "Pig!" but you would have thought they were more endearments. He swung into an explanation of the California delegate dispute and into his stock speech on Vietnam. Suddenly there was an interruption. Jacqui Ceballos, deadly pale, was on her feet just below the stage.

"What about the right to control our own bodies?" she cried. "We'll never be free until we have that!"

I could hear her from where I was standing, halfway down the hall, but Bella and Gloria (who were sitting next to him on the stage) stared glassily out into the room, as if they were deaf or entranced. Without a microphone, Jacqui could not hope to compete with McGovern's hugely amplified voice.

ARLIE SCOTT

We started shouting "What about abortion? What about abortion, Senator?" Of course, that's the Chisholm people.

Harper's Magazine, October 1972,
"McGovern the Big Tease," by Germaine Greer

He faltered, and in the brief silence Jacqui's voice wailed, "We must control our bodies, otherwise we'll never be free." McGovern resumed, sailing crescendo into the familiar finale: "I want us to resolve that once that tragedy is put behind us, never again will we send the precious young blood of this country to die trying to bail out a corrupt dictatorship."

ARLIE SCOTT

He closed his book, ended his speech, and stood up. And two women, two big leaders in the women's movement [Gloria and Bella] were sitting right next to him and he never mentioned abortion and they stood up with him and started applauding. And everyone stood up and started applauding and we were still shouting. It wasn't just Chisholm people. How can you even go to the women's caucus and not even mention it?

Harper's Magazine, October 1972,
"McGovern the Big Tease," by Germaine Greer

Why had Bella and Gloria not helped Jacqui to nail him on abortion? What reticence, what loserism had afflicted them? I wondered if they had already made some sort of a deal. They may have thought they had . . . but what on earth would they get in exchange. . . . [What] could be worth it?

ARLIE SCOTT

Afterwards, you could hear shouts of Shirley MacLaine [who worked for McGovern] and Bella arguing. So, the women didn't get what they wanted.

BRENDA FEIGEN

We still had to convince George McGovern to get behind the minority plank for abortion rights. As Gloria stayed up that first night drafting the statements of the three women who would introduce the plank [one of whom was Eleanor Holmes Norton], she made sure that the focus was on reproductive rights in general, including decrying involuntary sterilization for poor women and ensuring access to birth control by everyone. We, of course, ignored Shirley MacLaine, who was claiming that our insistence about abortion, however it was phrased, would cost McGovern the nomination.

Harper's Magazine, October 1972,
"McGovern the Big Tease," by Germaine Greer

For me, the clearest case of funk was the railroading of the abortion issue. . . . The delegates who were for McGovern first and the interests of the group they represented second argued that abortion was a state matter and had no place on a federal platform, which was irrelevant.

Tuesday night, the fight over the abortion plank—which was referred to as the human-reproduction plank because it never once mentioned the word abortion—produced the most emotional floor fight of the convention.

BRENDA FEIGEN

We were on the floor of the convention and Gloria decided she needed to talk to Gary Hart because he was the only way she was going to get through to McGovern. She went up to him and he started screaming at her. I was right there. He was screaming about how abortion is going to destroy McGovern's whole candidacy. And she started to cry.

Then Nora Ephron descended on us, and I said, "We've got to get out of here," and then the press started to come up with all the cameras. So, I got her out of there and we left.

Esquire, November 1972, "Woman," by Nora Ephron
At four in the morning, Bella Abzug was screaming at Shirley MacLaine, and Steinem, in tears, was confronting McGovern campaign manager Gary Hart: "You promised us you would not take the low road, you bastards."

MYRA MACPHERSON
I was on the floor constantly reporting for the *Washington Post*, and I got Gloria Steinem screaming at Gary Hart saying, "You bastard, you've taken the low road."

Washington Post, July 12, 1972, "Sisters vs. Sisters:
Abortion Battle Turns Bitter," by Myra MacPherson
Sen. George McGovern, a man under the gun, chose not to risk defeat in November on a controversial issue. . . . McGovern strategists—Gary Hart, Frank Mankiewicz, Gordon Weil, Matty Troy—told their delegates that there was a Humphrey-Wallace coalition voting yes to saddle McGovern with an embarrassing and possibly defeating plank, and the votes began dropping sharply. . . .

As the yes votes increased, some states switched several times. Abzug shook her fist at the New York delegation and threatened them if they changed any more. "I ask you, don't distort the vote and sabotage our law in New York and other places" . . . In the end, many of the pro-abortion delegates did cave in. [Sissy] Farenthold [of Texas] said, "My delegation started out split, and in the end, it was 33-to-1. That one was me."

Esquire, November 1972, "Woman," by Nora Ephron
The roll call on the plank was held largely at Betty Friedan's insistence. . . .
The plank went down to a thoroughly respectable defeat, 1572.80 against 1101.37 for.

Washington Post, July 12, 1972, "Sisters vs. Sisters: Abortion Battle Turns Bitter," by Myra MacPherson

The battle began after 2 a.m., and wound up around 4:30 a.m. It left some of the purists in McGovern's camp disillusioned. "McGovern's double-crossed everybody," said one female delegate. Mankiewicz could not suppress his smile at their victory. . . . "We have good bench strength," he joked, knowing full well that no matter how mad the women were with the tactics, they had no other place to go. Even as her voice broke in disappointment, Mrs. Abzug said, "Of course I'll support McGovern to defeat Nixon."

After their loss last night, one NWPC member said, "We got everything we asked for except abortion, so I suppose people will say, 'see, those women just aren't effective: they lost on abortion.'" . . .

Former White House aide Liz Carpenter said, "We are being heard more and more. This convention is a victory for us. We don't have to have every single woman delegate with us to be effective. And we don't have to agree and get along. Heck, if the American Revolution waited for *everyone* to like each other, we'd still be at Bunker Hill."

MYRA MACPHERSON

That was a page one story. I finished it at like seven in the morning. We had those little tents, where everybody was working. Everybody was handing in their copy, and to [editor Richard] Harwood's credit, he rang the bell and he said, "Best story of the day is Myra's."[*]

SHIRLEY CHISHOLM

At first the McGovern strategists said they would keep hands off the issue and let it be "a vote of conscience" for each delegate. But this was not to be . . . the [abortion] plank, which probably would have been defeated even if McGovern had honored his promise to keep aloof, was heavily defeated. Abzug, Steinem, and others were furious. They had considered McGovern wishy-washy on abortion, but now they felt betrayed. Like the Blacks, the women had failed to get it together at Miami; too many had made com-

---

[*] The *Washington Post* and *Boston Globe* (but not the *New York Times*) ran the abortion story on their front pages, written by female reporters assigned to cover the women's caucus. But generally, women reporters were underrepresented and not taken seriously by the macho "boys on the bus" political press corps. Of the 7,500 press passes issued at the convention, 1,000 were for women, and most of those were secretaries and "go-girls" for the television networks.

mitments to a candidate ahead of time, and their adherence to him made it impossible for them to work effectively for their cause.

Harper's Magazine, October 1972, "McGovern the Big Tease," by Germaine Greer

As Flo [Kennedy] said bitterly, "Honey, if you'll fuck for a dime, you can't complain because somebody else is getting a fur coat." Womanlike, they did not want to get tough with their man, and so, womanlike, they got screwed.*

GLORIA STEINEM

Then came the question of whether or not Shirley Chisholm wanted to have her name put in nomination at the convention for the vice presidency. Because we—"we" means the National Women's Political Caucus, the poor people's caucus, the Black caucus, and the Hispanic caucus, all of which met in coalition—all wanted to have a coalition candidate for the vice presidency on the floor of the convention, as a show of strength and also because there was some little hope that we might actually have a vice presidential candidate. We certainly had much more support than [Thomas] Eagleton, who finally ended up being the candidate.†

I was hoping that Shirley Chisholm would agree to have her name put in vice presidential nomination. We waited and waited until the very last minute, until she made her decision. When she said, "No," then Sissy Farenthold became the candidate. I was supposed to give her nominating speech. Of course, this took place in the middle of the night. I arranged to split my time with a representative from each of the other caucuses, so that Fannie Lou Hamer gave part of the nominating speech, and a Chicano man, who had served with Sissy in the state legislature of Texas, gave another part. Among the three of us, we represented the major caucuses of

---

* Abortion, which would not become legal until January 1973, was a hot-button political issue in 1972, which the Nixon campaign eagerly exploited. In an effort to win the blue-collar Catholic vote, which traditionally leaned Democratic, Nixon's team, following White House speechwriter Patrick Buchanan's "Assault Book" pointers, labeled McGovern soft on amnesty (for Vietnam War draft resisters) and pro abortion and drug legalization. The plan was to link McGovern to the radical, antiwar, feminist counterculture disdained by many Middle Americans. During the primaries and general election, McGovern was frequently smeared with the triple-A label: "Acid Amnesty Appeasement."

† Missouri senator Thomas Eagleton, who supported Muskie in the primary and was antiabortion, dropped off as McGovern's vice president eighteen days after admitting he had been treated with electric shock therapy. Sargent Shriver replaced Eagleton on the ticket, but the Eagleton bungle irreparably damaged the McGovern campaign.

underrepresented groups. It was a great moment, actually, because it was very clear that this was an important coalition.

SHIRLEY CHISHOLM
Through all of this, I was not on the floor; I spent most of the time seeing people in my hotel rooms.

BARBARA WINSLOW
Chisholm ended up with 152 delegate votes and she became the first woman in the Democratic Party to have her name placed in nomination.[*]

SHIRLEY CHISHOLM
When I got to the convention hall, it was lit up by noise. That was a wonderful moment for me, to see the way all of the delegates received me at the convention. . . . Because I had felt that someday, a Black person or a female person should run for the presidency of the United States, and now I was a catalyst of change.

---

[*]   On the first-ballot roll call vote, delegates handed McGovern the nomination with 1,729; Jackson, 525; Wallace, 382; and Chisholm, 152 (others 224). Chisholm's extra delegate votes came from people who had voted for other candidates in the primary but switched to Chisholm at the convention.

15

Exhibiting Art by and for Themselves

By 1972, feminist artists evolved from protesting institutions like the Whitney and LA MOCA to creating their own galleries, conferences, and databases. The West Coast and East Coast feminist art worlds began to cross-pollinate, and together they created a vibrant, new, revolutionary art form.

FAITH RINGGOLD

Shirley Chisholm had really been the woman who first inspired the Political Landscape Series. . . .

In the fall of 1972, I painted my first cloth-framed paintings. . . . I named them The Feminist Series and they were also my first acrylic paintings. On these painted landscapes, I printed in gold paint statements made by black women, dating from slavery times until the present. I found these statements in Gerda Lerner's *Black Women in White America*, a book published in 1972. Lerner's book came at a time in my life when I really needed to know about the past feminist history of black women. I felt renewed when I discovered that, along with Harriet Tubman and Sojourner Truth, there were many other black women who were in the vanguard of the feminist movement.

. . . Back in the early seventies black women were in denial of their oppression in order to be in support of their men. This made it very important for me to put the works of these valiant black feminists in my art so that people could read them and be as inspired as I had been. . . .

In 1971, realizing how difficult it was to achieve anything alone, I decided to create a black women's art group. Kay Brown and I founded Where We At, which turned out to be a non-activist although socially conscious women's exhibition group.*

HARMONY HAMMOND

Women artists were just not represented by galleries, and the gallery system at that time was where new emerging art and artists were shown. So, effectively, we were locked out. And that gave a message that women's art wasn't as good as men's.

So two artists who were frustrated because they couldn't get galleries to respond to their work, Susan Williams and Barbara Zucker, decided that they would start a co-op. There was a core group then of maybe six women initially, and then with Lucy Lippard's help, they made fifty-five studio visits and invited artists to become members of the gallery that was just forming. I was one of those artists.

HOWARDENA PINDELL

The art world was almost solidly white and male. The white women who were shown were usually the child of, or wife of, or girlfriend of a white male artist.

Lucy Lippard asked to visit my studio and she said, "Oh my God, you're really good." And then she invited me to do things. One of the things being the women's exhibition at the Aldrich Museum that Adrian Piper and I were in.†

HARMONY HAMMOND

We rented a space in SoHo, and we renovated it ourselves. We had no funding.

---

* In the summer of 1971, Kay Brown, Jerrolyn Crooks, Pat Davis, Mai Mai Leabua, Dindga McCannon, and Faith Ringgold planed the first Black women's art exhibition at the Acts of Art Gallery in Greenwich Village. Ringgold left the group after one year, but the cooperative grew to thirty artists who stayed together for eleven years.

† In April 1971, Lucy Lippard curated the first all-woman museum show, featuring twenty-six artists at the Aldrich Museum in Connecticut. The show was not reviewed by the mainstream art press.

HOWARDENA PINDELL

A.I.R. was a ground-floor space at 97 Wooster Street. We all chipped in. I was one of the initial twenty members of A.I.R., and I named the gallery. First, I came up with EYRE gallery named after Jane Eyre, and then it turned to A.I.R. [Artists In Residence].

HARMONY HAMMOND

The gallery began to form its structure as a feminist collective, everybody helped, we had to agree on everything, the endless circle. We all had to contribute financially a certain amount to get into the gallery, and then a monthly payment. For me as a single mom, trying to make a living and paying my $21 a month was very different from another artist in the gallery whose husband earned a good living.

And there was a lot of discussion about how political the gallery should be. Everybody didn't agree. Some were strident and very political and militant, and others said, "No, no, no, we have to tone that down." Feminism meant many different things to these women, and their reasons for being in the gallery were different. Some saw it as a totally separatist, all-women's space. Some saw it as a stepping-stone to a commercial gallery. All of this had to get navigated and negotiated, feminist-style.

Initially, we were almost all entirely white, and nearly all middle-class women. There was one African American woman in the gallery.*

HOWARDENA PINDELL

The feminist movement was where my work was first shown. The Black community at the time generally rejected abstract art. It is different now, as the Black community embraces diversity of artistic expression.

My first show was with Harmony Hammond. I had the back of the gallery, and she had the front. I exhibited my large spray paintings. Several of them were exhibited the summer of 2019 at Victoria Miro Gallery in London and were finally sold after all these years.

HARMONY HAMMOND

A bunch of us traversed the United States and began to form feminist art

---

* Founding artists were Rachel bas-Cohain, Judith Bernstein, Blythe Bohnen, Agnes Denes, Daria Dorosh, Loretta Dunkelman, Harmony Hammond, Anne Healy, Laurace James, Nancy Kitchell, Louise Kramer, Rosemary Mayer, Patsy Norvell, and Howardena Pindell.

networks, all over. A.I.R. was a model for other feminist art galleries, and women's co-ops opening in other cities. I went to Chicago, I talked to artists there, and I said, "Look, we did it. You can do it." Then two women's galleries opened in Chicago. There was WARM in Minneapolis, Muse in Philadelphia. They were all over the place. Two more opened in New York too.

JUDY CHICAGO

On November 28, 1973, we opened the Women's Building, named after the first Women's Building at the 1893 World's Columbian Exposition at Chicago.

SUZANNE LACY

The Women's Building was a grand experiment. It was located in the old Chouinard Art Institute, which we took over. The Feminist Studio Workshop* was the heart of the place, and it had thirty or forty students a year. There were also various galleries. We had, for a while, a printing press and sisterhood bookstore. Once again, we did a whole lot of carpentry, renovating the place.

LUCY LIPPARD

I came out to the Women's Building [from New York]. They painted all their tools pink while they were building it. As I recall, there was sort of a bookstore and a café and lots of studios and groups and all hell was breaking loose. It was wonderful.

JUDY CHICAGO

When the building opened, my exhibition the *Great Ladies* also opened.[†] For the first time, my work was in a context that could really illuminate it. . . . For a solid month before the opening, I suffered from depression, anxiety attacks, even rashes. I felt that the opening of the building and the exhibition of my new work truly revealed my commitment, my ideas, and my values, and I was afraid they would be rejected. Five thousand people attended the opening. I could hardly believe the crowds when I arrived. . . .

---

* Judy Chicago resigned from her faculty job at CalArts and teamed up with art historian Arlene Raven and graphic designer Sheila de Bretteville. In 1973, they opened the Feminist Studio Workshop, an independent feminist art school.

† Chicago's *Great Ladies* series were large canvases with sprayed acrylic, each dedicated to a different woman in history like Queen Victoria and Christine of Sweden.

People embraced me and cried and told me how moved they were by what I'd done. I couldn't believe it. I was being myself—really myself—and not only was nothing terrible happening, but I was receiving the acknowledgment I had been deprived of for so long.[*]

JUDY BACA

I became friends with Judy Chicago and Suzanne Lacy. Judy Chicago was doing the Feminist Studio Workshop, I was directing the first citywide mural project. This was the middle of the Che Guevara moratorium, and the beginning of Brown people starting to speak out. But the Chicano movement had no consciousness about women, and to claim yourself a feminist was really not a good thing. I mean, almost none of the Chicano women would say they were feminists. It meant that you were basically allied with white women and that you were not working for the economic issues that were facing our community.

White feminists would be interested in abortion rights. Well, you would not see a self-respecting Chicana saying that. You're not going to be advocating for abortion. Babies were one of the best things that happened to us, right? Children were the prizes and precious commodities of our families. So it took a long time before women felt they had the right over their own bodies, and I don't know that they do yet. They're still Catholic. They're still religious.

So I began straddling these two movements—the feminist movement and the Chicano movement. And in a sense, I was not accepted by either, because I didn't conform in either case. . . . Feminist writing and the feminist thought really informed my thinking and my capacity to expand beyond what was a very nationalist, limited vision in the early Chicano movement. I call the men "Chicanosauruses."

So Suzanne and Judy asked me to do a show, and I organized the first Chicano show at the Women's Building. I brought in five women who I was already working with producing murals, and we put up this exhibition that was called *Las Venas de la Mujer*.

---

[*] Throughout the seventies, the Women's Building remained a hub of feminist artistic expression, hosting musicians, poets, writers, as well as performance and studio artists, including movement luminaries such as Kate Millett, Alice Walker, Audre Lorde, Rita Mae Brown, Meg Christian, Holly Near, Margi Adam, and Cris Williamson. Meanwhile, Judy Chicago enlisted four hundred women artists and artisans (1974–1979) to help her create a monumental installation, featuring thirty-nine lost women in history, called *The Dinner Party*, which now resides permanently at the Brooklyn Museum.

That's when I made the *Tres Marías* piece, which the Smithsonian owns now. And it's traveling everywhere. That piece has had this resurgence—forty years later, it's come of age. So I produced that piece for the show, and that solidified my relationships with the Women's Building.

I was fortunate enough to have key people in my life that opened windows for me so that I began to see, wow, it's possible to be different. It's about really trying to figure out, what is freedom? What does it mean to be free, to be who you are? Isn't it?

16

The Supreme Court Legalizes Abortion

Victorious after his forty-nine-state reelection landslide, but just eigh-teen months away from resigning over the Watergate scandal, President Nixon celebrated his inauguration on January 20, 1973. Two days later, former president Lyndon Baines Johnson, age sixty-four, died in Texas of heart failure. Johnson's death upstaged the other big news of January 22: the Supreme Court's 7–2 ruling to legalize abortion. The Roe v. Wade *decision vindicated years of legal and political struggle by women's rights activists and would become one of the high-water marks for the women's movement.*

SARAH WEDDINGTON
Monday, January 22 . . . at ten a.m. Eastern Standard Time, the Supreme Court had announced that by a vote of seven to two the Texas antiabortion statutes had been ruled unconstitutional as violating the constitutional right of privacy. The plaintiffs in *Doe v. Bolton* had also won most of their points, but the importance of that opinion was overshadowed by the breadth of the *Roe* decision. Supreme Court decisions set the supreme law of the land; the decisions in *Roe* and *Doe* affected the laws of every state that had provisions similar to those of Texas and Georgia. Abortion was no longer illegal.

Pandemonium broke out. The phones erupted with press calls, congratulatory calls, calls requesting information about the decision. . . . Linda [Coffee] got the news on the radio while driving to work.

CBS Evening News, January 22, 1973

Walter Cronkite: "In a landmark ruling, the Supreme Court today legalized abortions. The majority, in cases from Texas and Georgia, said that the decision to end the pregnancy during the first three months belongs to the woman and her doctor, not the government."

"Thus, the anti-abortion laws of 46 states were rendered unconstitutional."

SARAH WEDDINGTON

There were spontaneous celebrations for the Court's decision around the country. Reactions from many recognized women leaders flashed across newswires. People often tell me that they remember vividly where they were when they heard about two events: the death of President John F. Kennedy and the decision in *Roe v. Wade*. That decision represented a change of immense proportions in the lives and futures of American women.

SUSAN BROWNMILLER

The downtown feminist restaurant Mother Courage erupted in a spontaneous party on the night in January when the *Roe v. Wade* decision came down. . . . *Roe* fostered the euphoric delusion that the women's revolution was an unstoppable success. A new day had dawned; anything was possible.

SARAH WEDDINGTON

The copy of the *Roe* opinion sent by the Court arrived a few days after the decision. It was a thrill to hold the document [Harry] Blackmun wrote for the Court. I skimmed the main points. . . . The opinion got even better from my perspective when Blackmun began to write about privacy:

> The right of privacy, whether it be founded in the Fourteenth Amendment's concept of personal liberty and restrictions upon state action, as we feel it is, or, as the District Court determined, in the Ninth Amendment's reservation of rights to the people, is broad enough to

encompass a woman's decision whether or not to terminate her pregnancy. The detriment that the State would impose upon the pregnant woman by denying this choice is altogether apparent.

I wanted to stand and cheer!

I checked off the significant points: There is a constitutional right of privacy: pregnancy is fundamental; the State had no compelling reason to prohibit abortion to the extent the antiabortion laws had provided. The Texas laws were unconstitutional.

The Court could have stopped there, but it added what is called dictum. . . . In the dictum the Court revealed what it considered appropriate state regulations of abortion. . . . The Court went on to outline a scheme for state regulation and procedures a state might implement if it chose to act. These suggestions were based on a trimester approach to pregnancy.

LINDA COFFEE

If the Court hadn't used the trimester approach, there would have been litigation for years and years. During this time, women would have continued not to be able to have abortions, there would have been untold suffering. And just from a practical viewpoint, I'm really glad they did it. I really think it was justified under the circumstances, although I admit it's unusual, and I'm sure it comes close to being legislation by the Supreme Court.

NANCY STEARNS

It was fabulous. I mean fabulous. We saw the shortcomings, but it was very exciting. I was excited that we now had a constitutional right to abortion. But I was disappointed that we had to search for the right to liberty in it, that it wasn't front and center. And I also realized that what's called the "trimester trilogy" was complicated and was going to present problems down the road.

BRENDA FEIGEN

Roe was a very, very mixed bag. We were delighted that women had the right to get abortions, but constitutionally, I thought it was worrisome.

We were sort of surprised because it came up really fast and nobody asked Ruth. Nobody asked her for her input.

RUTH BADER GINSBURG

At the time of *Roe v. Wade*, this issue was all over the state legislatures. Sometimes, the choice people won, sometimes they lost, but they were out there organizing and getting political experience. I think it would have been healthier for that [political] change to have gone on. . . . Texas had the most extreme law in the nation; the Court could have decided the case before it, which is how the Court usually operates. It should have said that the Texas law is unconstitutional. There was no need to declare every law in the country addressing abortion, even the most liberal, unconstitutional. That's not the way the Court usually operates. It doesn't take giant steps. . . . I know there was a very strong Right to Life movement long before *Roe* came down; it continued after. But now there is a target that was not there before *Roe v. Wade.*

17

Ginsburg (Nearly) Wins *Frontiero* Big

While reproductive rights made their legal leapfrog, Ruth Bader Ginsburg continued to plug away at what would be a decade-long unraveling of dozens of federal sex-based statutes. From 1972 until 1980, from her post at the ACLU's Women's Rights Project, Ginsburg dismantled gender-based classifications, many of which "protected" women by assuming men to be the breadwinners, and wives and widows their dependents. She worked on briefs in twenty-four Supreme Court cases and personally argued six before the Court. Reed v. Reed *in 1971 became the first of many victories. Next would be* Frontiero v. Richardson *(1973) and then* Weinberger v. Wiesenfeld *(1975).* "The objective," she explained, "was to show the Court that women were not favorites of the law, that they were hemmed in by the law's restrictions."*

---

*   Stephen Wiesenfeld's wife, Paula, a public school teacher in New Jersey, died giving birth to their son in June 1972. When Wiesenfeld filed for Social Security benefits, he discovered that only widows could receive what was called the "mother's insurance benefit" while caring for a young child, but widowers (regardless of how much their wives had paid into Social Security) could not. Ruth Ginsburg met Wiesenfeld in late 1972 and took his gender discrimination case against the Social Security Administration all the way to the Supreme Court, which unanimously decided for Wiesenfeld in 1975. As a result of their work together on the case, Ginsburg and Wiesenfeld developed a lifelong friendship.

RUTH BADER GINSBURG

On May 14, 1973, in *Frontiero v. Richardson*, the Court moved forward more swiftly than many had anticipated; in effect, it served notice that sex discrimination by law would no longer escape rigorous constitutional review.

New York Times, May 15, 1973,
"Air Force Woman Wins Benefit Suit," by Warren Weaver Jr.

WASHINGTON, May 14 —The Supreme Court ruled today that female members of the armed services were entitled to the same dependency benefits for their husbands as servicemen have always received for their wives. The vote was 8 to 1.

The decision fell just short of a major triumph for the women's rights movement because the Court divided, 4 to 4, on the critical issue of whether discrimination based on sex is as constitutionally offensive as that based on race or national origin.

RUTH BADER GINSBURG

In *Frontiero*, in which Rehnquist was the only dissenter, Brennan had pushed to have sex declared a suspect classification.* Four signed onto that. Four isn't five. The executive director of the ACLU, Aryeh Neier, came to tell me, "You won *Frontiero* big. Four signed onto sex as a suspect classification." I said, "Oh, that's it? We're not going to get a fifth?" . . . The remaining justices, although they came out the right way, wouldn't go that far.†

---

* Designating sex as a "suspect classification," as race is, would mean that laws imposing sex-based distinctions would be permissible only if the government could provide a "compelling interest" in treating those groups differently.

† The split ruling in *Frontiero* meant that a majority agreed that the Air Force's policy favoring servicemen over servicewomen violated the Constitution, but they disagreed about the level of scrutiny to apply to sex discrimination cases going forward. Four members—a "plurality"—wanted to adopt Ginsburg's proposed strict scrutiny, but the other four members wanted to retain the "rational basis" standard adopted in *Reed v. Reed*, which was more deferential to the government's decision to favor certain groups.

The split ruling resulted in the Court's applying a new, "intermediate" scrutiny that treated sex-based distinctions by the government more skeptically than under "rational basis" review, but more permissively than "strict scrutiny." Under that standard, the government would be permitted to treat men and women differently only if it could show that such differential treatment bore a "substantial relationship" to a statute's goals.

BRENDA FEIGEN

We won on the merits. Women Air Force officers were going to get the benefits for their husbands. But we did not win the standard review that Ruth was so keen on. It was a victory, but not for what we were doing in the Women's Rights Project.

The justices were on our side. Everybody—except Rehnquist—was for throwing the statute out. But it was the way in which they did it. How much scrutiny are they going to give to that statute? We wanted the strictest scrutiny, they wanted the lowest level of scrutiny.

Justice Brennan wrote for the plurality saying that sex *should* be a suspect classification and therefore there should have to be a compelling state interest in order to keep this distinction. . . . That encouraged my conviction that we needed the Equal Rights Amendment.

JOE LEVIN

This is before cable news and social media. I heard about the decision from a reporter who called and asked me some questions about it. It was an eight-to-one decision that the regulation supporting this treatment of women officers differently than men officers was unconstitutional and violated the due process clause. Ginsburg and Feigen didn't win the strict scrutiny argument. . . . I just recall a real sense of satisfaction. I don't think I fully appreciated the extent to which the case would have that level of importance down the road.

New York Times, May 22, 1973,
"A 'Flaming Feminist' Lauds Court"

GLOUCESTER, Mass.—When Mrs. Sharron Frontiero, who describes herself as "a flaming feminist," heard about the recent Supreme Court judgment that female military personnel were entitled to the same dependency benefits for their husbands as servicemen for their wives, she burst out with a joyous, "Hot damn!"

The High Court's judgment came as somewhat of a surprise to the 26-year-old physical therapist, who was a first lieutenant at Maxwell Air Force Base, Ala., when she filed the class action suit in December, 1970. . . .

In a moment of reflection, Mr. Frontiero added that while it took time and money, "the one real good thing about it was that it gave a real lift to the feminist movement. We like to think we've helped do something concrete rather than just talk."

BRENDA FEIGEN

Ruth was still determined, but she thought the best way to do this whole thing was the double-edged-sword approach. If men are discriminated against and women are discriminated against, these guys in the Court are going to get it, and we're going to get the standard, eventually, that we wanted in *Frontiero**.... That wouldn't happen until the VMI case in 1996, three years after she got on the Court. She wrote the decision.†

---

* After *Frontiero*, Ginsburg applied an incremental approach of filing case after case to challenge government laws and policies that favored one sex over another. Part of her strategy was to bring claims on behalf of men to challenge sex-based laws, in hopes to show that stereotypes about men's and women's societal roles harm everyone. In several cases, she represented widowers who were denied government benefits because of rules that presumed only women need financial support when a spouse dies—*Weinberger v. Wiesenthal* (challenging a rule granting Social Security survivor benefits for childcare to mothers but not fathers), *Kahn v. Shevin* (challenging a state property tax assessment benefiting widows but not widowers), and *Califano v. Goldberg* (challenging a Social Security rule that gave survivor benefits to widows but not widowers)—as well as a case brought on behalf of a male criminal defendant who alleged he was denied a fair trial because state law excluded women from serving on juries (*Duren v. Missouri*).

† Ginsburg became a Supreme Court justice in 1993 and wrote her first opinion in the 1996 *U.S. v. Virginia Military Institute* case. VMI, a federally funded military school, did not accept women cadets. In a 7–1 decision, the Court ruled against VMI. The Court did not explicitly adopt the "strict scrutiny" standard for gender cases that Ginsburg and Feigen had sought with *Frontiero*, but it did so implicitly, demanding that the government show an "exceedingly persuasive justification" for sex-based rules going forward. VMI, the Court ruled, could not meet that standard; its exclusion of all women from the citizen-soldier ranks based on a stereotype that women were, as a group, ill-suited to its "adversarial method" of training.

18

FBI Closes Its WLM Files

After years of hiring informants and conducting illegal undercover sur-
veillance, J. Edgar Hoover's FBI agents failed to gather the evidence they
needed to prove that women's liberation posed a threat to national security.
By the end of 1972, the FBI began shutting down their "revolutionary
activities" offices across the country.

United States Department of Justice
Federal Bureau of Investigation
12/20/72   **Office: New York, New York**

Character: INTERNAL SECURITY—REVOLUTIONARY
ACTIVITIES
Synopsis: The New York Women's Liberation Center (NYWLC),
currently located at 243 W. 20th Street, NYC, is allegedly staffed by
homosexual women working to improve the rights of women homosexuals, and have not attempted to significantly influence the WLM.
Current investigation reflects no evidence to indicate the WLM is
dominated or influenced by any revolutionary group. . . .

[BLANK] advised on [BLANK] that the more radically motivated
women in the NYC area are no longer organizing around women's

rights issues because these women realize that many of the concepts and demands of the WLM are being listened to and acted upon at city, state, and federal levels. Many feel that the women's movement has passed from a highly emotional street display of outrage, to a stage where numerous women in society generally accept most of the WLM concepts. . . .

United States Government   1/24/73
Memorandum
To: Acting Director, FBI
From: SAC, Boston
Subject: Women's Liberation Movement
The following informants, who are familiar with certain phases of revolutionary activity in the Cambridge-Boston, Massachusetts, area have advised that they have no current information concerning the Women's Liberation Movement. . . . In view of the fact that no pertinent information has been developed in recent months concerning the WLM, further inquiry appears unwarranted at this time and the file at Boston is being closed based on this communication.

United States Department of Justice Bureau of Investigation

January 31, 197   Office: Baltimore
Title: Women's Liberation Movement

Character: Internal Security–Revolutionary Activities
Details:
1. Activities
On [BLANK] advised that the Women's Liberation Movement (WLM) in the Baltimore area has become a social club for about [BLANK] members. [BLANK] advised the group meets at 3028 Greenmount Avenue once a month and holds "women's dances." [BLANK] stated the group does not have officers or any radical aims. [BLANK] advised that the only purpose of the WLM is a place where the group can meet and "have fun."

[BLANK] advised that there is no current political or revolutionary activity on the part of the WLM in Baltimore

Los Angeles Times, February 6, 1977, "FBI Investigation of Women's Lib Groups Disclosed," by Norman Kempster

WASHINGTON: Using female informers to provide details its male agents could not obtain, the FBI investigated women's liberation groups for at least four years—learning among other things that a New York group used actor Paul Newman's telephone credit card.

The investigation, which apparently ended in the spring of 1973, never resulted in any criminal charges. But it provided a catalog of information about the political beliefs and sexual preferences of activist women throughout the nation.

In response to a Freedom of Information Act request, the FBI made public 1,377 pages from its file on the women's liberation movement, or WLM as it was known to the FBI. . . . The file showed that the investigation was conducted by FBI offices in Los Angeles, San Francisco, Washington, Baltimore, Boston, Cincinnati, Seattle, Philadelphia, Chicago, Newark, St. Petersburg, Fla, and other cities.

Ms. Magazine, June 1977, "The FBI Was Watching You," by Letty Cottin Pogrebin

Are you now or have you ever been a member of the Women's Movement?

If so, you may find yourself in the 1,377 pages of memos, reports, teletypes, tape transcripts . . . gathered between 1969 and 1973, in the files of the Federal Bureau of Investigation under the subject heading: Women's Liberation Movement (WLM). . . . Within its pages you may find your name (misspelled perhaps), your address, and in a few instances, a physical description of yourself, your clothing, and behavior. . . . This particular "FBI Story" is a paranoid's fantasy come true. "They" kept tabs on "us" with the aid of special agents, informers, observers, infiltrators . . . *

---

* The FBI WLM files were discovered in 1977 after the *LA Times* and *Ms.* magazine filed a Freedom of Information Act request, following the shocking revelations of the 1975 Church Committee hearings, which exposed the FBI's illegal COINTELPRO operation that ultimately resulted in the indictment of forty-six agents and high-ranking bureau officials.

19

The Battle of the Sexes

JULIE HELDMAN

Bobby Riggs tapped into antifeminist sentiment in America. He said, "I'm a fifty-five-year-old guy. I can beat any woman tennis player in the world."

BILLIE JEAN KING

Bobby Riggs was one of my heroes because he won the Wimbledon triple crown in '39. He was mixed-doubles partner with Alice Marble, who helped me and coached me, so I had that connection. . . . I understood his need for attention. He didn't get the proper attention when he was number one in the world, which was during World War II when they didn't have Wimbledon for five years. He saw us women tennis players getting all this attention and he wanted it, and rightly so. . . .

He followed me around for two years. I said, "No, I don't want to play you." First of all, to beat a guy that old is not an athletic feat at all, okay?

New Castle News, February 23, 1973,
"Women Challenged," by Milton Richman, UPI

Bobby Riggs says, "No woman ever lived who could compete with a man on an equal basis—even a 55-year-old man. There's lots of talk about Women's Lib. They feel they're worth as much as the guys, but they can't play a lick if they can't beat a 55-year-old guy."

ROSIE CASALS

Bobby Riggs went after Billie Jean, and she said, "No, no." and then he went after Chris [Evert] and Chris said, "No, no." Margaret Court, because she liked money, said, "Yes, yes."

BILLIE JEAN KING

I said to Larry, "I know Margaret will win easily. But if she doesn't, then I will have to play him."

JULIE HELDMAN

At that stage, Billie Jean and Margaret Court were the top two players in the world. Billie Jean symbolized women's liberation in sport. Margaret Court was a really interesting other figure. She was muscular, strong. She was a fabulous tennis player.

She had two children. She took off for a year, had babies, came back and played. Nobody did that. And yet at the same time, she spouted outrageous nonsense, like: "Women shouldn't get as much money as men. Men are superior." Meanwhile, she's traveling around the world with her husband and she's the only one working.

ROSIE CASALS

Margaret was not a feminist. She did not believe in the things that we believed, and the fight that we fought. But she definitely got the benefit of it.

JULIE HELDMAN

Margaret had no idea what she got into. She didn't realize that Bobby Riggs was the ultimate hustler.

ROSIE CASALS

She really did not prepare. I think she didn't realize what it entailed and what repercussions there were. She's just thinking of the money and winning. She's number one. She was playing her best tennis, but when I saw how she played, she was so nervous. Why? Because she hadn't prepared.

Riggs and Court played on Mother's Day, May 13, 1973, at a tennis club near San Diego. CBS aired the match live. Before taking on the fifty-five-year-old Riggs, the thirty-year-old Australian had won eighty-nine

*out of her last ninety-two matches. Several days of media hype preceded
the game, and several celebrities attended, including Barbra Streisand,
who christened the match by singing Helen Reddy's 1971 feminist pop
hit "I Am Woman."*

JUDY DALTON

As soon as Margaret got on the court, Bobby Riggs came out with a bunch
of flowers and she curtsied to him. I said to my husband, "That's it. She's
gone." She had no idea how clever he was. She thought he couldn't play.

JULIE HELDMAN

He threw her junk, and she was off to start with, and she never came back.

ROSIE CASALS

Billie Jean and myself had been playing in Japan, and on the way back,
we stopped in Hawaii. They used to have these little TVs in a chair in the
airport where you put in a quarter and then the TV would kick on. I remember turning it on and catching the end of the match and seeing that
Margaret had lost.

*It was called the "Mother's Day Massacre." Bobby Riggs beat Margaret
Court 6–2, 6–1 in only fifty-seven minutes and landed on the cover of*
Sports Illustrated *the next week with the headline "Never Bet Against
This Man."*

JULIE HELDMAN

He beats her badly, and it starts ricocheting around the tennis world because
Bobby Riggs goes to the press and says, "I'm fifty-five. I beat the number
one in the world. I can beat Billie Jean."

BILLIE JEAN KING

So Margaret loses, and I tell Larry, "Okay, go make a deal. But can we
wait until after Wimbledon?" Wimbledon was just coming up, and we
had just formed the WTA [Women's Tennis Association] four days before
Wimbledon.

JULIE HELDMAN

First of all, it was so horrifyingly frightening that Margaret would lose so badly to him. She was known to get nervous in the crunch, but it was really hard to get her nervous, because she was so good. But still, there was the worry; maybe Billie will lose to him too, and then we will lose everything.

BILLIE JEAN KING

I won the triple crown at Wimbledon that year, which is very unusual; that's singles, doubles, and mixed doubles. I think the only reason was, I was so excited that we had our WTA. We were finally all together, we had one voice, and now we could negotiate. I also had great doubles partners—Rosie and Owen Davidson.

After Wimbledon, we made the announcement. I knew the country would go nuts. I knew it'd be crazy and I knew it'd be about social change. But I also knew I had a unique opportunity. This would be the most people that I would ever play in front of, and I had a chance to spread the word. And I knew it was so important that I win. I had to win.

ROSIE CASALS

Billie Jean took it in and said, "I'm going to be fit," which she was, "I'm going to play a certain weight," which she did. She concentrated; everything from that point on was dedicated to her playing Bobby on that center stage.

BILLIE JEAN KING

All these things were happening in '73, it was an unbelievable year. It was a year after Title IX passed, so I knew deep down this match would help keep Title IX strong for us. I knew I had to win because they already had lawsuits; John Tower, the senator in Texas, wanted revenue-producing sports not to be a part of Title IX. I'm like, "I have to win this match for Title IX, for tennis, for women, for men too really, for everyone to start the discussion that you always want to be inclusive." Plus we're only in our third year of professional tennis, and for two years before '73, we only had two women's tours, and I knew we could not have that happen again.[*]

---

[*] In 1973, approximately fifty thousand male college students had sports scholarships compared to only fifty women, and in a 1973 *Sports Illustrated* survey, most girls could not name even a handful of women athletes.

JULIE HELDMAN

We had to give way to Billie Jean's fame. She walked around and she was just covered with reporters, it was like ants on a candy bar. And she had to be protected back then. I mean, she had to have somebody walk her from here to there.

Then two weeks before she played Bobby Riggs, I beat her [at the US Open in Forest Hills]. And I was over-the-top thrilled, but horrified by the way the reporters were just jumping all over me. "If she loses to you, is she going to lose to Bobby Riggs? What did you do to harm her that made her lose?" It was a slap in the face.

ROSIE CASALS

At that time, of course, enters Jack Kramer. ABC, who's going to televise it, wants me and Kramer as the commentators, so we could have some friction on and off the court.

Billie Jean said, "Look, if you have Jack Kramer there, I will not play. He cannot have a platform in which he's going to bash women's tennis and me." That part went all the way up until the last moment. The night before the match, ABC said, "Okay, you win," and they brought in Gene Scott, who was not a Jack Kramer.

Boston Globe, September 20, 1973, "Lady v. Wrinkled Tiger in Tennis Tussle Tonight"

Never have so many people witnessed in person a game of tennis, if that's what it is.

"It's more, much more—the battle of the sexes," trumpeted Bobby Riggs for the 2,081,917th time yesterday, "Man against woman; sex against sex; an old one-foot-in-the-grave champion against the current Wimbledon champion. People can identify. Husbands argue with wives, bosses with secretaries. Everybody wants to bet." (The odds are 2½–1 Riggs, according to Jimmy-the-Greek Snyder who arrived from Las Vegas.) . . . The winner will take at least $200,000, the loser half that amount.

"Are you sure you can win, Dad?" asked his [Riggs's] 16-year-old son, Billy.

"Son, no broad is gonna best me . . . I'll tell you why I'll win," says Riggs. "She's a woman, and they just don't have the emotional stability. She'll choke just like Margaret Court did."

JULIE HELDMAN

It was men versus women—the battle was going on everywhere. Literally, mothers and daughters were fighting against husbands and sons. The husbands were saying, "Oh, you women are no good," and the women were saying, "I'm for Billie Jean."

ROSIE CASALS

Before the match I talked to her: I said, "You're going to win. Aren't you?" She said, "Yes, I'm going to win." She looked at me with those baby blues. I knew because I'd seen it before. We've been down by five–love, forty–love, triple match point, and she said, "We're going to win this," and I believed her, and we won.

So, I knew that she was going to win, and I predicted it would be in three sets.

Tucson Daily Citizen, September 21, 1973, "Now Billie Jean's 'King' of Hustlers," Associated Press

King made her entrance on a carriage, bourne by four muscular [shirtless] males like a reigning Egyptian queen.

Riggs then entered riding in a rickshaw, pulled by several pretty "Bobby Boosters" with "Sugar Daddy" on the backs of their blouses. Riggs presented Mrs. King with a giant candy sucker with "Sugar Daddy" written on the side.

Riggs got a brown baby pig from Mrs. King.

JULIE HELDMAN

I think there were thirty-seven thousand people at the Astrodome, the most ever to watch a tennis match and people with signs, cheering. They say ninety million people watched it on television in thirty-seven countries.

ROSIE CASALS

Bobby was exhausted by the time he got to the match, because he'd been partying and socializing and not really practicing and getting in shape. At least his coach, Lornie Kuhle, said that, and I think that was the case.

JULIE HELDMAN

When she saw that he looked a little bit unfit she decided to run him and run him and run him. And by the end, he was exhausted and she was a better player than he was.

ROSIE CASALS

I was up in the ABC booth with the god of television sports, Howard Cosell. Mind you, he knew nothing about tennis. Of course, I was me and I would say what I wanted to say. I said that Bobby was a male chauvinist pig and he didn't deserve to be there, and that he was probably just enjoying getting all this publicity on the women's coattails, and the only reason that he's doing this is because he wants to make money.

But to think that somebody at his age of fifty-five, running around with women and being an idiot and saying the same stupid things like, "Women belong in the kitchen," and "Women belong in the bedroom," and all these stupid things that he said, of course, I'm going to say something about it and I did. I got so much hate mail for months after that. Stacks of them, "Rosie, you were so cruel. You were so obnoxious. You were so, whatever."*

> **New York _Daily News_, September 21, 1973, "Billie Jean King Outlibs the Lip: Wallops Riggs in Straight Sets 6-4, 6-3, 6-3 and No Love for Bobby . . ."**
> In their "Battle of the Sexes" at the Houston Astrodome, last night, Billie, 29, took mere two hours and five minutes to destroy 55-year-old hustler's myth of masculine superiority before an exuberant crowd of 30,000 fans.

> **_Boston Globe_, September 21, 1973, "Love at Last Sight . . . ," by Bud Collins**
> HOUSTON—Susan B. Anthony, Elizabeth Cady Stanton, Joan of Arc, Amelia Bloomer, Emmaline Pankhurst, Carrie Nation, Molly Pitcher and a lot of other bygone heroines must have been rocking on that great court in the sky last night when their spiritual descendant, Billie Jean King, landed on Bobby Riggs like a ton of mascara.

> **_Tucson Daily Citizen_, September 21, 1973, "Now Billie Jean's 'King' of Hustlers," Associated Press**
> Screaming, delirious women's-libbers lit up more brightly than the rocket shooting Astrodome scoreboard last night when Mrs. King showed the devastating swiftness that won her five Wimbledon titles

---

* Because of Casals's combative commentary, the Boston ABC affiliate received 133 complaints and the _Boston Globe_ fielded forty calls complaining about Casals. One of her best insults: "Anyone built like a duck can't be an athlete."

in defeating self-proclaimed male chauvinist Riggs, 6-4, 6-3, 6-3 in the internationally televised battle of the sexes tennis extravaganza.

BILLIE JEAN KING

Every single day since that day, the Bobby Riggs match comes up. Women tell me that it gave them self-confidence, and for the first time in their lives they started to dream about what they wanted to do with their lives. They said that they felt powerful for the very first time and went and asked for raises that they never had the courage to ask for before.

The men were reflective. Sometimes they had tears at least in their eyes, and they said, "You know, you really made me think differently. I have a daughter and I want her to have the same as my son."

When I met President Obama, he said he was twelve years old, and how the match affected him in bringing up his two girls. So, I know that for both genders at that time, now all genders, that it made a difference. It made people ask hard questions. "How do you want this world to look? Do you really want half the population not to have the same opportunities?" And the answer: it's pretty hard to say no.

20

A Model for Political Action

While clearly a momentous victory, the Roe v. Wade *decision had a nuanced impact on the Janes—the underground abortion providers in Chicago—and unintended consequences for all women.*

JUDITH ARCANA
The state of Illinois dropped our case a few months after the *Roe* decision, and our lawyer got our records expunged.

LAURA KAPLAN
The state didn't need to drop the case. They could've tried them for practicing medicine without a license, but none of the women who were getting abortions the day of the bust would testify.

MARTHA SCOTT
It was an enormous relief. Enormous relief. We seven Janes still could have been prosecuted, but we knew that once *Roe v. Wade* happened, we would be okay.

LAURA KAPLAN
After New York legalized, our demographics changed quickly. Some women could afford to get on a plane at O'Hare Airport and fly to New York and

flying back. But that wasn't the case for young women, poor women, and women who couldn't even get away for a day because of whatever their circumstances. So, we kept operating until the first legal clinics opened in Chicago.

We felt bad about it because we knew people were going to get the same, shitty medical care they'd always gotten in clinics, and they would be treated like patients. We framed what we were doing in the context of women taking control over their lives, and their destiny, and that was not going to happen at a clinic.

HEATHER BOOTH

Between 1965, when I first started, and when *Roe* became the law of the land, the women in Jane performed eleven thousand abortions.

LAURA KAPLAN

After we folded, we all went back to our own lives. The housewives, the mothers, went back to being housewives and mothers, and we all went in different directions. I have to say, some of my strongest friendships—women I would trust with my life—are from those days.

I was living in an apartment with a fireplace, and Eileen Smith came over. We had both done Big Jane for a long time, and we built a fire in the fireplace. We had hundreds of three-by-five cards with women's names and phone numbers and addresses, their last monthly period, all that information.

We put on a Bob Dylan record and read the names to each other, and then tossed the cards into the fire. Because we thought, "This is none of anybody's business."

ALICE FOX

If you think about a model of political action that is based in human experience and personal need, Jane was it. Right now, people are feeling the need to respond to repressive, hostile, and misogynistic policies. What happens if things turn and we're no longer given the freedom to make those choices that seemed a short time ago, to be taken for granted?

NANCY STEARNS

The problem was, after the *Roe* decision our side went home. We did not realize the intense organizing power of the Catholic Church, because it was Catholic money and doctrine that was behind the opposition at that point. Now it's more complex, because it's evangelicals too. We did not see how they were going to chip away, chip away, chip away, and of course that's exactly what happened.

21

We Were Beautiful Black Women

By 1973, as a critical mass of Black women began to adopt the principles of women's rights, a group of New Yorkers, spearheaded by Margaret Sloan and Flo Kennedy, began to organize and discuss how to define feminism for themselves.

MARGO JEFFERSON

By 1973, I had not yet found a group of Black women whom I knew well enough to form a consciousness-raising group with. And I had decided I didn't want to be the only Black woman in a consciousness-raising group. So, I started talking to friends, but not formally. I have no recollection of how NBFO [National Black Feminist Organization] first started. I really don't. Margaret Sloan was there. Flo Kennedy was there. And groups of us coalesced from all over: artists, lawyers, political people. Someone would tell someone, who would tell you there was a meeting going on. So you'd go.

Ms., May 1974,
"Black Feminism, a New Mandate," by Margaret Sloan
The moment was on a Sunday in May. About 30 of us sat in closeness because the room was not big enough. We had known about this day

for a long time and had made plans, well in advance, to be there. It was the day that would change our lives . . . and we knew it.

We were married. We were on welfare. We were lesbians. We were students. We were hungry. We were well fed. We were single. We were old. We were young. Most of us were feminist. We were beautiful Black women.

MARGO JEFFERSON

Flo Kennedy was this extraordinary, maybe the first really visible Black woman who had been on the forefront of civil rights, Black power, and the women's movement. Both its white and Black branches. Born the same year as my mother, 1916, Flo Kennedy was everywhere. And she was dazzling. I'll never forget the day she said to an NBFO meeting, it may have been at our organizing weekend. She said something like, "When Black women tell me feminism is a white woman's thing, I tell them; you've spent all these years, all these centuries, imitating every bad idea white women came up with—about their hair, their makeup, their clothes, their duties to their men. And now, they finally come up with one good idea—feminism—and you decide you don't want anything to do with it!" It was so brilliant.

Ms., May 1974,
"Black Feminism, a New Mandate," by Margaret Sloan

It was a busy three hours. We all had so much to say. Our relationship with the feminist movement, our participation in the Black Movement. We listened. We laughed. We interrupted each other, not out of disrespect, but out of that immediate identification with those words and feelings that we had each said and felt . . . many times alone. We had all felt crazy and guilty about our beliefs. And yet, all the things that have divided Black women from each other in the past, kept us from getting to that room sooner, seemed not to be important. . . . We knew that we were creating our own "herstory," and we had never been in a situation where there were so many Black women who understood feminism.

MARGO JEFFERSON

We broke down into smaller groups, and I would meet regularly with about four or five other women. And we would go from political discussions to a consciousness-raising meeting. The kinds of discussions that would later take a wonderful, poetic form in Ntozake's *For Colored Girls.** But we would also have serious organizational meetings because we were all trying to start this organization. So, it was whatever we needed to do.

I don't want to speak for the women in NBFO, but what we wanted to do was find, declare, make viable for ourselves, and for the world, and very specifically a Black feminism that took up issues, contradictions, conflicts, questions that with very few exceptions white feminists were not taking up.

MARGARET SLOAN

Ironically, I don't really think most of us thought of founding an organization; we just decided that we had such an experience spending the day talking with each other we'd like to hold a conference to bring as many women from the East Coast as possible—Black women—to talk about feminism.

DEMITA FRAZIER

Margaret Sloan left Chicago to move to New York after she and Sharon Ritchie broke up in the winter of '71. About a year later, Margaret and some women in New York began talking about forming the National Black Feminist Organization, and Margaret sent me a set of guidelines that they were using for Black feminist consciousness-raising groups. So, Sharon, myself, and a couple of other women in Chicago began having these Black feminist consciousness-raising groups, which were awesome.

MARGARET SLOAN

One of the biggest changes that's happened has been the change in the minds and hearts of women and that's a kind of organic change that's necessary to get about a feminist revolution. Anyone who wants to form a chapter of the NBFO has to first be in a consciousness-raising group. We just think that that's paramount and you can't organize if you believe your lips are too big, if you believe your hair is nappy and your face is ugly. You can't organize. You don't even go out there and demand your rights if you

---

* Written by twenty-eight-year-old Barnard graduate Ntozake Shange, *For Colored Girls Who Have Considered Suicide/When the Rainbow Is Enuf* is a play based on a series of poems set to music and dance that premiered off-Broadway in 1976 and then moved to Broadway. It was a critically acclaimed sensation. Margo Jefferson remembers going to see the play at least four times.

believe that. So we believe consciousness raising is essential to any woman. White women have had the time—during the six or seven years that we've been organizing in terms of feminism. There isn't a white woman I've met that hasn't been in some kind of CR group—and most Black women I meet have not been in them. It's important for Black women to create that space once a week, that they sit down with other Black women and say: "Hey, this is what I'm feeling."

DEMITA FRAZIER

We loved that we got to pick what we talked about, and it was amazing because one of the things that we talked about was colorism. We also talked about the importance of looking at domestic violence as a way of empowering women survivors. Because it turned out three of us came from alcoholic backgrounds and another two of us had had domestic violence be part of our lives. It was a small group, about eight of us altogether, I shouldn't use the word "seminal," I always hate that word. But it was the beginning of a very important process that then got carried over, and we used some of the same guidelines in Combahee [River Collective].*

MARGARET SLOAN

That summer, the media did another job on Black women. There were a lot of articles depicting the relationship of Black women to white women, none of which were written by Black women, by the way. A famous news magazine had a terrible article misquoting Black feminists. There was a Black magazine that had an article saying women's lib has no soul. It was written by a white male psychiatrist. And these kinds of things really messed us up. There was also a civil rights leader who was going around the country saying that the recent Supreme Court decision on abortion *Roe v. Wade* meant genocide for Black women. We were furious. Everybody was talking for Black women but us.

So we said we're going to call a press conference. We're going to tell them we have this organization, it's a national organization. I love the arrogance of Black women because we just kind of did it. Everybody came.

---

* The more politically left group was named by Barbara Smith after Harriet Tubman's Civil War military campaign in South Carolina that freed more than 750 slaves, which was (and may still be) the only military campaign in US history planned by a woman. Barbara and Beverly Smith, Demita Frazier, and others wrote the Combahee River Collective Statement, which explained that race, gender, class, and sexuality were "interlocking" problems.

All the press came because they were hungry like piranhas. They just knew we were going to cut up everybody: trash white women, trash Black men, trash everybody. So everybody came, even the German press, I mean the room was more press there than we were. It was only fifteen of us. They said to us, "Miss Sloan, how many women do you have as members?" And we said: "Potentially millions, next question?"

Chicago Tribune, August 25, 1973, "Blacks Refocus," by Yla Eason
"We refuse to let the women's movement be given to white women," said Margaret Sloan, a former Chicagoan when announcing the formation of the National Black Feminist Organization, a group formed recently in New York to challenge the "white middle class" image of the Women's Liberation Movement.

"It's too bad that our blackness will have to give credibility to the liberation struggle, but I think it will," she continued. An editor for *Ms.* magazine, Sloan said about 30 women had been meeting since March discussing the "enormous amount of pressure and guilt" placed on the black women not to join the movement.

New York Amsterdam News, August 25, 1973,
"Women Launch New Group"
"This organization could not have been formed when the women's liberation movement started five or six years ago because Black women had to deal with the pressures of the civil rights movement then," [New York Human Rights] Commissioner [Eleanor] Norton said. "It took time to clear up the confusion between the differences and similarities between the civil rights movement and the women's movement," she added.

Miss Sloane read the organization's statement of purpose: "The movement has been characterized as the exclusive property of so-called white middle class women. And any Black woman seen involved in this movement has been seen as selling out and dividing the race.

"Black feminists resent these charges and are therefore establishing The National Black Feminist Organization. Black women have suffered cruelly in this society from living the phenomenon of being Black and female in a country that is both racist and sexist."

Mrs. Norton announced that NBFO would conduct consciousness-raising sessions among black women to help them get rid of negative images of themselves. The organization founders said that already chapters have been formed in San Francisco, Cleveland and Chicago.

MARGARET SLOAN

We never expected to get the response that we did. The next day we received over two hundred calls from Black women around the country saying, "Where have you been?" "I feel so alone, there's no group I can identify with, is there a chapter in my city?" And then the next day, we got another two hundred calls.

BEVERLY SMITH

I was living in New York and worked briefly for *Ms.* magazine, where I met Margaret Sloan. She was instrumental in founding the National Black Feminist Organization and she told me about the conference they were having in November. I immediately told my sister about it. She was very enthused.

BARBARA SMITH

Beverly told me that we had to attend this conference, and of course I was in. I was teaching Black women's literature, so I was interested. I wasn't involved in the women's movement. My sister Beverly actually went to NOW meetings in New York City. I never did that. I had been so burned by white women, and I just felt like the white women's movement was not a place for me. I couldn't see myself in it, even though I understood the issues and was reading about it.

BEVERLY SMITH

It was wonderful, I would say there were maybe about three hundred women there. To finally be with so many Black women who were interested in feminism was a phenomenon.

BARBARA SMITH

It was amazing. It was held at Riverside Church. And many people who are luminaries of the Black feminist movement and of Black feminism, were there. Alice Walker was there, June Jordan was there. Shirley Chisholm and Eleanor Holmes Norton were there. Faith Ringgold was there with her daughter Michele Wallace. Those are the people I remember.

BEVERLY SMITH

It just felt like this is a place I can do political work, work for the things I'm concerned about and interested in, and feel comfortable. We can talk about sexism and stuff that happened through the lens of Black women and not feel like we are the odd people out.

BARBARA SMITH

Because my sister and I, and this is true, I'm sure, for virtually everybody who was there, had never been around so many Black women who wanted to talk about gender and race simultaneously, who were politically motivated around our actual lived experiences.

And we felt like we had found a home. There was exhilaration, excitement. It was just an overwhelmingly transformative experience and a beautiful experience.

My sister and I were so excited about it. And we felt like we had found a place where we could be our authentic selves and be concerned about and work on the issues that we actually knew were important and not take a second seat to anyone. Even though it was called the First Eastern Regional Conference, it was a national conference. People came from as far away as California.

ALICE WALKER

I realized at the National Black Feminist Organization conference that it had been much too long since I sat in a room full of Black women and, unafraid of being made to feel peculiar, spoke about things that matter to me. We sat together and talked and knew no one would think, or say, "Your thoughts are dangerous to Black unity and a threat to Black men." Instead, all the women understood that we gathered together to assure understanding among Black women, and that understanding among women is not a threat to anyone who intends to treat women fairly. So the air was clear and rang with earnest voices freed at last to speak to ears that would not automatically begin to close.

New York Times, December 2, 1973,
"Black Feminists Hold Parley Here," by Barbara Campbell

Black women from across the country—professionals, blue collar workers, mothers, housewives and students—attended the first black women's liberation conference here yesterday.

"Five years ago," said Mrs. Eleanor Holmes Norton, the city's Commissioner of Human Rights, "you couldn't have gotten five women to come here. They would have been too embarrassed."

But now, Mrs. Norton said, many women have overcome their fear of appearing divisive, by isolating their own needs and goals from the black-liberation movement and have "stopped being closet feminists."

MICHELE WALLACE

At the conference at Riverside Church, Faith and Alice Walker led a workshop on the arts. We were just learning about who Alice Walker was. I always considered her famous really from the first moment I met her and read her work.

BARBARA SMITH

The central core of the conference's activities were the Saturday morning and afternoon workshops. The subjects were varied, but were consistently crucial to Black women's experiences. They included "Black Women and Welfare," "The Image of Black Women in the Media," "The Black Woman Addict," "Abortion and Sterilization," "The Triple Oppression of the Black Lesbian," "Black Woman and the Cultural Arts," and a day long consciousness-raising session called "Stepping Out to Sisterhood."

ALICE WALKER

I thought about friends of mine whose views do not differ very much from mine, but who decided not to come to the conference because of fear. Fear of criticism from other Black people (who, I assume, consider silence a sign of solidarity), and fear of the presence of lesbians. The criticism will no doubt be forthcoming, but what can one do about that? Nothing, but continue to work. As for the lesbians—a Black lesbian would undoubtedly be a Black woman. That seems simple enough. In any case, I only met other Black women, my sisters, and valuable beyond measuring, every one of them.

BARBARA SMITH

This was prior to coming out. I was nervous being around people who said that they were lesbians. I don't think I was particularly homophobic, but I certainly knew that I could never be a lesbian because I knew that that would mean I was throwing away my entire life, everything I had worked for, everything that my family had worked for, all of their expectations. I would lose my connection to the Black community. I would be a persona non grata. I would be akin to a criminal. I would be a lowlife. And that was exactly what I thought. I've written about that.

Meeting other Black lesbians helped me to realize that "Oh, so you can be a wonderful person and be a Black lesbian. You can be racially conscious and racially identified and be a Black lesbian." So, it was really through the women's movement, and through being involved in Black feminism, that I got the support to finally grapple with this terrible secret and to come out.

Off Our Backs, December–January 1974, "Black Feminists Up Front," by Fran Pollner

Men were excluded. White female press were excluded from the workshops and plenary sessions, and black female press were told not to report on them. . . . Objections centered mainly around two issues: the racism of white women and angry reluctance to be affiliated with the women's movement, and the absence of any emphasis on aligning with black men to fight the general oppression of black people. . . .

Doris Wright and Laurie Sharp, both members of NOW, described their experiences with that group—which included constantly being mistaken for one another.

Doris Wright: "White women are well-intentioned in trying to reach black women, but they weren't coming from the same direction. There was no real understanding, no cultural communication. I can't be concerned with making it on Wall Street—not that NOW doesn't try to do something about child care and welfare, but it's only attracted white middle class women."

During an unscheduled question-and-answer session after [Flo] Kennedy's speech, hostility toward white women was sharply expressed by several women.

One said that white feminists approach black women for the sole purpose of getting into their homes and into bed with their husbands. Kennedy replied that, "Our rejection of white feminists shouldn't be based on that.

We can make coalitions with white women, deal with their racism, and stick our toes in the asses of the individual women who go after our men."

BARBARA SMITH

So the people who were there from Boston, none of whom I knew, we met, as I remember, in the stairwell at the church. And we made a plan to start meeting in early 1974. The conference was in late November of 1973. We did have a meeting in January of 1974, and that's how the Boston chapter of the NBFO started.[*]

Off Our Backs, December–January 1974,
"The Morning After," by Anne Williams

Calling her, "The woman who picked up the rock thrown by Tubman and Truth, and brought black women into the 20th century as women," Eleanor Holmes Norton introduced speaker Shirley Chisholm to the Saturday open session of the NBO conference.

ALICE WALKER

And then to hear Shirley Chisholm speak: to feel all of the history compressed into a few minutes and to sing "We love Shirley!" a rousing indication of our caring that we could not give to Sojourner Truth or Harriet Tubman or Mary McLeod Bethune. To see her so small, so impeccable in dress, in speech, and in logic, and so very black, and to think of her running for president of this country, which has, in every single age, tried to destroy her. It was as if, truly, the faces of those other women were just beneath the skin of Shirley Chisholm's face.

Bay State Banner, December 20, 1973, "Chisholm Advises
Feminists at New York Conference," by Shirley Simpson

In an atmosphere permeated with enthusiasm and excitement, the Honorable Shirley Chisholm rose to the podium to a rousing standing ovation that grew into a rhythmic chant. "We love Shirley!" and lasted a full three minutes.

"We are not here to speak about any division between black men and black women. The realization is indeed that we are going to eventually

---

[*]   In 1975, the Boston NBFO chapter broke off from the national organization over the issue of socialism and lesbianism to become the Combahee River Collective.

become an incomparable people and we need the sisters and brothers holding each other up and marching on to victory. . . . Goals like the nationalization of day care centers in this country and minimum wage legislation are such that we can unite with other groups, such as the women's liberation movement. Why are we in favor of these goals? Because they are part of survival. Black women have been unable to accept many of the focuses of the white women's movement because they are not geared to survival. That is the reason for the National Black Feminist Organization coming together."

Ms. Chisholm closed with a challenge exhorting black women across the nation to participate in all kinds of social, economic, and political movements: "Dare as you have always dared—but dare in numbers sufficient to have an effect on yourselves and others in this society."

ALICE WALKER

And we talked and we discussed and we sang for Shirley Chisholm and clapped for Eleanor Holmes Norton and tried to follow Margaret Sloan's lyrics and cheered Flo Kennedy's anecdotes. And we laughed a lot and argued some. *And had a very good time.**

---

* The NBFO expanded so quickly that within a year it had more than three thousand members and ten chapters across the country, but it lacked the funding and infrastructure needed to support the influx of members. Structural and organizational problems, combined with internal ideological disagreements, led to its dissolution in 1976, but not before spawning strong local Black feminist organizations in cities including Chicago, San Francisco, and Boston.

Cast of Characters

Bella Abzug (1920–1998), labor and civil rights lawyer, women's rights leader; graduate of Columbia University Law School (1944); founder and national legislative coordinator of Women Strike for Peace (1961–70); Democratic congresswoman from New York (1971–77); cofounder and cochair of the National Women's Political Caucus (NWPC) (1971).

Dolores Alexander (1931–2008), journalist, lesbian, feminist activist; served as the executive director for NOW but resigned in 1970 due to the homophobic beliefs of the organization in its early days; co-owner with Jill Ward of Mother Courage, a popular feminist restaurant in New York City (1972–1975).

Judith Arcana (1943–), author, reproductive rights activist, teacher of women's health and sexuality, member of the Chicago underground abortion service, code-name Jane, one of the seven women arrested for performing illegal abortions on May 3, 1972.

Ti-Grace Atkinson (1938–), radical feminist activist and writer; second president of the New York chapter of NOW (1967–1968); founder with Florynce Kennedy of The Feminists; author of *Amazon Odyssey* (1974).

Byllye Avery (1937–), women's healthcare activist; cofounder of Gainesville Women's Health Center and Birthplace; founder of the National Black Women's Health Project (1983); 1989 recipient of the MacArthur Foundation's Fellowship for Social Contribution.

Judy Baca (1946–), feminist visual artist, community activist, and professor; cofounder in 1976 and artistic director for the Social and Public Art Resource Center (SPARC) in Venice, California, known for creating the monumental *Great Wall of Los Angeles* public mural in Los Angeles (1975). After receiving little recognition from the art world for decades, Baca's work has been purchased by the Smithsonian and exhibited at the J. Paul Getty Museum in Los Angeles in 2022.

Bill Baird (1932–), early reproductive rights pioneer and agitator who fought to legalize birth control, culminating in the Supreme Court case *Eisenstadt v. Baird*, 1972, and to empower minors to obtain abortions without parental consent in *Baird v. Bellotti I and II*, 1976–1979.

Toni Cade Bambara (1939–1995), African American novelist, poet, social activist, screenwriter, and editor of the landmark book *The Black Woman: An Anthology* (1970); professor at Rutgers University and Spelman College.

Rosalyn Baxandall (1939–2015), feminist activist; founding member of New York Radical Women (NYRW); member of Redstockings, Women's International Terrorist Conspiracy from Hell (W.I.T.C.H.), and Coalition for Abortion Rights and Against Sterilization Abuse (CARASA); author and American and women's studies professor.

Birch Bayh (1928–2019), progressive Democratic senator from Indiana (1963–81) who championed women's rights and sponsored the ERA and Title IX; the only senator to author two constitutional amendments (the Twenty-Fifth and Twenty-Sixth).

Frances Beal (1940–), feminist pioneer; member of Student Nonviolent Coordinating Committee (SNCC), where she founded the Black Women's Liberation Committee in New York in 1968; leader of the Third World Women's Alliance (1970); author of the landmark 1969 Black women's manifesto *Double Jeopardy: To Be Black and Female*.

Ginny Berson (1946–), radical lesbian feminist activist, member of lesbian separatist Washington, DC, collective The Furies (1971–1973), and cofounder of feminist music company Olivia Records.

Sallie Bingham (1937–), author (of novels, plays, essays, biographies), feminist activist, and philanthropist who founded the Kentucky Foundation for Women and the Sallie Bingham Center for Women's History and Culture at the Duke University library.

Heather Booth (1945–), early civil rights, antiwar, and feminist activist; member of SNCC; cofounder of Chicago Women's Liberation Union (CWLU) (1969); founder of Chicago underground abortion service, code-name Jane (1969–1973); lifelong progressive political organizer.

Ivy Bottini (1926–2021), feminist lesbian activist; New York NOW president (1968–1970); worked in the design department of *Newsday* for sixteen years and designed NOW's logo, which is still used today.

Rita Mae Brown (1944–), lesbian feminist activist and author; member of Redstockings and NOW; founding member of lesbian separatist Washington, DC, collective The Furies (1971–1973); author of bestselling lesbian coming-of-age novel *Rubyfruit Jungle* (1973); author of many novels, screenplays, and fifty-six mysteries, many featuring cat protagonist Sneaky Pie Brown.

Susan Brownmiller (1935–), civil rights and radical feminist activist; early chronicler of the women's liberation movement in the *Village Voice* and the *New York Times*; author (among others) of the landmark work on rape *Against Our Will* (1975) and her memoir of the movement, *In Our Time* (1999).

Charlotte Bunch (1944–), feminist lesbian activist, author, and academic; cofounder with Marilyn Webb of Washington, DC, Women's Liberation Movement (DCWLM) (1968); founding member of lesbian separatist Washington, DC, collective The Furies (1971–1973); founder and first editor in chief of *Quest: A Feminist Quarterly*; professor of women's studies and founder of the Center for Women's Global Leadership at Rutgers University.

Linda Burnham (1948–), writer and political activist; member of the Angela Davis Defense Committee and the Third World Women's Alliance; cofounder and director of the Women of Color Resource Center (1990); director of National Research for the National Domestic Workers Alliance.

Diane Camper (1948–), lawyer, journalist, civil rights and urban affairs specialist; Washington correspondent for *Newsweek* covering the Supreme Court and the federal judiciary; member of the *New York Times* editorial board (1983).

Liz Carpenter (1920–2010), journalist, feminist political activist, Democratic party operative, and first woman executive assistant to Vice President Lyndon B. Johnson; Lady Bird Johnson's press secretary; cofounder of the National Women's Political Caucus (NWPC) (1971); and cochair of ERAmerica.

Rosie Casals (1948–), professional tennis player; one of the Virginia Slims Original Nine; doubles partners with Billie Jean King, winning US hardcourt and indoor tournaments, and reaching the semifinals in the Grand Slam Singles at Wimbledon ('67, '69, '70, '72) and the US Open (1970–1971); winner of 112 professional doubles tournaments (the most in history after Martina Navratilova).

Jaqueline Ceballos (1925–), feminist activist, board member of NOW (1967–1973), and president of the New York chapter of NOW (1971); NOW's delegate to the United Nations Conference on Women in Mexico (1975); cofounder and president of the Veteran Feminists of America (1992).

Phyllis Chesler (1940–), feminist activist, psychologist, academic, and author; cofounder of the Association for Women in Psychology (1969); author of the landmark bestselling book *Women and Madness* (1972); cofounder of the National Women's Health Network (1975); professor of psychology and women's studies.

Judy Chicago (1939–) (born Judith Cohen), pioneering feminist artist and educator; founder of the first Feminist Art Program (FAP) at Fresno State College (1970); cocreator with Miriam Schapiro of Womanhouse (1972) and the Los Angeles Woman's Building (1973); creator of the iconic feminist art installation *The Dinner Party* (1974–1979); prolific artist whose work was not fully valued by collectors and the art establishment until she was in her eighties.

Conrad Chisholm (1916–2009), husband of Representative Shirley Chisholm (1949–1977); private investigator specializing in negligence-based lawsuits.

Shirley Chisholm (1924–2005), teacher, politician, feminist, and civil rights leader; member of the New York State Assembly (1965–1968); the first Black woman elected to the US Congress (1969–1983); cofounder of the National Women's Political Caucus (NWPC) (1971); first African American to run for president (1972); cofounder of the National Black Women's Political Caucus (1983).

Linda Coffee (1942–), lawyer; argued, with Sarah Weddington, the precedent-setting US Supreme Court case *Roe v. Wade*; member of the Women's Equity Action League (WEAL).

Mary Jean Collins (1939–), feminist activist; president of Chicago NOW; Midwest regional director for the NOW-sponsored Women's Strike for Equality (August 26, 1970); deputy director for Catholics for Free Choice (1985–1993).

Beverly Kiohawiton "Kasti" Cook (1953–), Saint Regis Mohawk Tribal Council elected Chief, Upstate New York; midwife and nurse practitioner (1984–2013); nationally and internationally known leader in the environmental and reproductive justice movements.

Judy Dalton (1937–), Australian professional tennis player; winner of nine major doubles titles; runner-up in ten major doubles tournaments; Wimbledon singles semifinalist (1968); one of the Virginia Slims Original Nine.

Donna de Varona (1947–), two-time Olympian (1960, 1964), two-time gold medal winner for swimming (1964); holder of eighteen world records; the youngest sportscaster and one of the first female sportscasters for a national network (ABC) (1964); first president of the Women's Sports Foundation (1974).

Anselma Dell'Olio (1941–), feminist activist, author, theater and film director, and critic; early New York NOW member (1966); founder and director of the New Feminist Repertory Theater (1970).

Carole De Saram (1939–), feminist activist; longtime member of the NOW leadership, including president of New York NOW (1974); active in helping single women gain credit from banks, led successful boycott against Citibank, and participated in the 1971 Wall Street "zap" action; banker who helped form the Women's Credit Union.

Barbaralee Diamonstein-Spielvogel (1932–), historian, author, television producer, preservationist; White House assistant (1963–1966); New York City's first director of cultural affairs (1966–1972); the longest-serving New York City Landmarks Preservation commissioner (1987–1995); progressive philanthropist.

Joan Ditzion (1943–), feminist health activist, cofounder of Our Bodies, Ourselves collective (1970); Ditzion wrote the first-edition chapter, "Our Changing Sense of Self," in the book *Our Bodies, Ourselves*, and has had a hand in writing and editing all nine editions; geriatric social worker.

Peggy Dobbins (1938–), feminist activist, artist, sociologist, and author; cofounder of New York Radical Women (1967) and Women's International Terrorist Conspiracy from Hell (W.I.T.C.H.) (1968); assistant professor of sociology at the University of Alabama, Tuscaloosa.

Paula Doress-Worters (1938–), feminist health activist; member of Bread and Roses; cofounder of Our Bodies, Ourselves collective (1970); contributor to all editions of the book *Our Bodies, Ourselves*; resident scholar in women's studies at Brandeis University.

Shirley Downs (1942–), legislative aide for Shirley Chisholm; worked with staffers for Congresswomen Patsy Mink and Bella Abzug to advance women's equity policies.

Mary Eastwood (1930–2015), pioneering women's rights lawyer and Justice Department attorney (1960–1979); worked on the President's Commission on the Status of Women (1962–1963); coauthored the influential article "Jane Crow and the Law: Sex Discrimination and Title VII," with Pauli Murray (1965); one of the twenty-eight original founders of NOW (1966); worked behind the scenes on some of the most important early gender discrimination cases.

Osborn Elliott (1924–2008), editor in chief of *Newsweek* (1961–1976).

Nora Ephron (1941–2012), celebrated essayist, humorist, author, screenwriter of fourteen popular films (many of which she produced and directed), including *When Harry Met Sally*, *Sleepless in Seattle*, and *Julia and Julia*; got her start at *Newsweek*, the *New York Post*, and *Esquire*.

Brenda Feigen (1944–), feminist activist lawyer; vice president of NOW (1970); founding member of the National Women's Political Caucus (NWPC) (1971); cofounder of the Women's Action Alliance (1971); codirector with Ruth Bader Ginsburg of the ACLU's Women's Rights Project (1972).

Jan Fenty (1935–), feminist activist; member of the Magic Quilt, and the Washington, DC, collective that published *Off Our Backs*, one of the first and longest-lasting women's liberation newspapers (February 1970–2008); her son Adrian Fenty was mayor of the District of Columbia (2007–2011).

Shulamith Firestone (1945–2012), radical feminist activist and writer; cofounder with Jo Freeman of the West Side Group in Chicago (1967); cofounder with Ellen Willis of Redstockings; cofounder with Anne Koedt of New York Radical Feminists in 1969 after leaving Redstockings; author of *The Dialectic of Sex* (1970).

Brian Flanagan (1946–), radical left political activist; member of SDS, the Weathermen organization, and the Prairie Fire Organizing Committee; pool shark; former bar owner; *Jeopardy!* champion; wine consultant.

Alice Fox (1948–), women's health activist; trained as a physician's assistant in women's health; member of the Chicago underground abortion service, code-name Jane.

Muriel Fox (1928–), public relations executive at Carl Byoir & Associates; co-founder of NOW (1966); cofounder of the National Women's Political Caucus (NWPC) (1971); board chair of Veteran Feminists of America.

Demita Frazier (1952–), radical antiwar, Black power, and feminist activist and organizer in Chicago and Boston; active in the Black Panther Party Breakfast Program and the Illinois Women's Abortion Action Coalition; cofounder of the Combahee River Collective (1974); coauthor of the Black feminist manifesto the Combahee River Collective Statement (1977); and lifelong social justice activist.

Jo Freeman (1945–), civil rights activist, member of the Southern Christian Leadership Conference (SCLC); cofounder with Shulamith Firestone of the West Side Group in Chicago (1967); founder of the first women's liberation newsletters: *Voice of the Women's Liberation Movement* (early 1968); author (among others) of *The Politics of Women's Liberation* (1975) and editor of *Women: A Feminist Perspective* (1975–1995), a leading text in women's studies courses.

Betty Friedan (1921–2006), journalist, author, often called the "mother" of the modern women's movement, Friedan wrote the landmark bestselling book *The*

Feminine Mystique (1963), which helped launch second-wave feminism; cofounder and first president of NOW (1966); cofounder of the National Women's Political Caucus (1971).

Sharon Frontiero-Cohen (1950–), Air Force lieutenant and physical therapist who sued the US secretary of defense in 1970 for gender discrimination. She won her case *Frontiero v. Richardson*, argued in the Supreme Court by Ruth Bader Ginsburg (1973).

Sonia Pressman Fuentes (1928–), first woman lawyer in the Office of General Counsel at the Equal Employment Opportunity Commission (EEOC) (1965); influential in convincing Betty Friedan to start NOW; cofounder of WEAL (1968).

Sandra Gaines, campaign staffer for Shirley Chisholm's 1972 presidential campaign in Northern California; former welfare mother of three; educator.

Bobbi Gibb (1942–), lawyer, artist, runner, and the first woman to run the Boston Marathon, illegally, in 1966.

Ruth Bader Ginsburg (1933–2020), pioneering feminist lawyer, law school professor at Rutgers University (1963–1972) and Columbia University (1972–1980); cofounder of the ACLU's Women's Rights Project with Brenda Feigen (1971); served on the bench of the US Court of Appeals for the District of Columbia (1980–1993); Supreme Court justice (1993–2020).

Peter Goldman (1933–), writer and contributing editor for *Newsweek* for forty-five years; author of several *Newsweek* presidential campaign books, novels, and a biography of Malcolm X.

Emily Goodman (1941–), feminist activist lawyer, specializing in representing women in divorce cases; New York State Supreme Court judge, both criminal and civil divisions (1988–2012).

Vivian Gornick (1935–), radical feminist journalist who chronicled the women's liberation movement in the *Village Voice*; coeditor with Barbara Moran of the anthology *Women and Sexist Society: Studies in Power and Powerlessness* (1971) and author of (among many others) *Fierce Attachments: A Memoir* (1987).

Robert Gottlieb (1950–), Cornell student who worked for Shirley Chisholm's campaign as national youth coordinator and field director (1972); attorney.

Katharine Graham (1917–2001), owner and publisher of the *Washington Post* (1963–1991) and *Newsweek*; the first woman publisher of a major American newspaper in the twentieth century; the first female Fortune 500 CEO (1972); her autobiography, *Personal History*, won the Pulitzer Prize in 1998.

Richard Graham (1920–2007), equal-rights activist; deputy director of the Peace Corps (1963–1965); one of the first five commissioners of the Equal Employment Opportunity Commission (1965–1967); cofounder of NOW (1966) and its first vice president; president of Goddard College (1975–1976).

Edith Green (1910–1987), ten-term Democratic member of Congress serving from Oregon (1955–1974); sponsor/author of 1963 Equal Pay Act; instrumental behind passage of Title IX, the 1972 Equal Opportunity in Education Act.

Germaine Greer (1939–), British radical feminist writer and public intellectual; famous for her bestselling book *The Female Eunuch* (1970).

Martha Griffiths (1912–2003), lawyer, judge; the first Democratic woman elected to Congress from Michigan (1954–1974); "Mother of the ERA" who fought for women's rights in Congress.

Kirsten Grimstad (1944–), professor, college administrator, German scholar, editor of Barnard Women's Center's *Women's Work and Women's Studies* (1971); coauthor with Susan Rennie of *The New Woman's Survival Catalog* (1973) and *The New Woman's Survival Sourcebook* (1975); cofounder with Susan Rennie, editor, and publisher of *Chrysalis: A Magazine of Women's Culture*, which published out of the Women's Building in Los Angeles (1977–1981).

Judy Gumbo (1943–), radical political activist and member of the counterculture antiwar group the Yippies (Youth International Party) (1968); girlfriend of Yippie Stew Albert; started one of the first women's liberation groups in Berkeley, California.

Fannie Lou Hamer (1917–1977), nationally recognized civil rights leader; women's rights and community organizer; granddaughter of slaves and one of twenty children of sharecroppers from Mississippi; arrested and beaten for registering Black residents to vote; cofounder of the Mississippi Freedom Democratic Party (MFDP) (1964); cofounder of the National Women's Political Caucus (NWPC) (1971).

Harmony Hammond (1944–), feminist artist, activist, author, curator, professor; founding member of A.I.R. Gallery, New York City's first women's cooperative art gallery (1972); coeditor of *Heresies: A Feminist Publication on Art and Politics* (1977); author (among others) of *Lesbian Art in America: A Contemporary History* (2000).

Carol Hanisch (1942–), radical feminist activist and writer; founding member of New York Radical Women (1967); helped organize Gainesville Women's Liberation in Florida (1969–1973); managing editor of *Feminist Revolution*, the Redstockings book (1975).

Nancy Miriam Hawley (1942–), feminist health activist; leader of the first workshop on women and their bodies (1969); founding member of Our Bodies, Ourselves collective (1970); wrote the chapter on sexuality and contributed to the birth control chapter in the first edition of the book *Our Bodies, Ourselves*; psychotherapist and life coach (since 1976).

Julie Heldman (1945–), professional tennis player; one of the Virginia Slims Original Nine; winner of twenty-two singles titles and three medals (gold, silver, and bronze) at the 1968 Mexico City Olympics.

Sherrye Henry (1935–), television and radio broadcaster; the first woman in America to broadcast television editorials; the host of "Woman!" for New York's WCBS-TV (1971–1973); host of WOR *The Sherrye Henry Show* (1973–1998); author of *The Deep Divide: Why American Women Resist Equality* (1994).

Aileen Hernandez (1926–2017), union organizer; civil and women's rights activist; one of the first five commissioners of the Equal Employment Opportunity Commission (EEOC) (1965–1967); cofounder and second national president of NOW (1970–1971).

Louise "Mama Bear" Herne (1961–), condoled Mohawk Bear Clan Mother; member of the Mohawk Nation Council, Haudenosaunee Territory in central New York and southern Canada; spiritual leader, school teacher, practitioner of alternative medicine.

Lucy Howard (1940–), started working at *Newsweek* in 1963 as a mail girl, clipper, and researcher; after taking part in the 1970 class-action lawsuit against *Newsweek*, Howard remained at *Newsweek* until 2002, where she rose to senior editor of the National and International sections.

Florence Howe (1929–2020), author, publisher, professor; "Mother of Women's Studies," Howe taught one of the first women's studies courses at Goucher College; cofounder and president of the Feminist Press (1970–2000); Howe wrote many essays and twelve books, mostly regarding women's studies and literature.

Ericka Huggins (1948–), social justice activist, educator, writer; member of the Black Panther Party and founder of its New Haven chapter; director of the Panthers' Oakland Community School (1973–1981); first woman and African American to serve on the Alameda County board of education; professor of sociology, women's studies, and African American studies in the Peralta Community College District (2008–2015).

Karla Jay (1947–), lesbian and gay studies pioneer; member of Redstockings (1969); member of the Gay Liberation Front (GLF); participant in the Lavender Menace action; editor and contributor to several anthologies regarding lesbianism and feminism; English professor and director of the women's and gender studies program at Pace University (1974–2009).

Margo Jefferson (1947–), Black feminist writer, academic, and literary critic; cofounder of the National Black Feminist Organization (NBFO) (1973); theater and book critic for *Newsweek* (1973–1978) and the *New York Times* (1993–2006); winner of the Pulitzer Prize for Criticism (1995); author of (among others) *Negroland: A Memoir* (2015).

Laura Kaplan (1947–), women's health activist and community organizer; member of the Chicago underground abortion service, code-name Jane; author of *The Story of Jane: The Legendary Underground Feminist Abortion Service* (1997); founding member of the Emma Goldman Women's Health Center; board member of the National Women's Health Network.

Sue Katz (1947–), writer, women's rights and lesbian activist, and martial arts master; in 1967 she participated in an action at Boston University with birth control activist Bill Baird.

Michael Kazin (1948–), SDS leader at Harvard and Weather Underground member; professor of history at Georgetown University; coeditor of *Dissent*; author of seven books on American political history, including *What It Took to Win: A History of the Democratic Party* (2022).

Florynce "Flo" Kennedy (1916–2000), Black radical civil rights and feminist activist and organizer, lawyer who represented civil rights leader H. Rap Brown (1961) and Valerie Solanas (1968); challenged with a group of feminist lawyers the constitutionality of abortion law in New York (1969); member of NOW, founder of the Feminist Party (1971); founding member of the National Women's Political Caucus (NWPC) (1971); founder of the Coalition Against Racism and Sexism; cofounder of the National Black Feminist Organization (NBFO) (1973).

Billie Jean King (1943–), professional tennis player, feminist activist, and author; ranked number one tennis player in the world five times and winner of seventy-one singles championships and thirty-nine major titles: one of the Virginia Slims Original Nine; winner against Bobby Riggs in the "Battle of the Sexes" (1973); founder of the Women's Sports Foundation (1974); author of six books.

Suzanne Lacy (1945–), feminist multimedia artist, writer, educator; performance faculty member at the Feminist Studio Workshop at the Los Angeles Woman's Building.

Mary Pat Laffey (1938–), flight attendant for forty-two years; union representative and plaintiff in discrimination lawsuit against Northwest Airlines.

Paul Lauter (1932–), civil rights activist, writer; professor, cofounder with his wife, Florence Howe, of Feminist Press (1970).

Barbara Lee (1946–), attended Mills College as a single mother of two; Shirley Chisholm campaign staffer in Northern California, and delegate to the 1972 Democratic convention; legislative staff member for US Congressman Ron Dellums (1975–1986); first Black woman to represent Northern California in the State Assembly (1990–1996); member of the US House of Representatives (1998–2025).

Lynn Hershman Leeson (1941–), award-winning (including the Guggenheim Fellowship) multimedia and performance artist, known for her early performance piece *Roberta Breitmore* (1973–1978); creator of six films including *!Women Art Revolution* (2010).

Jonathan Lerner (1948–), activist, journalist, novelist; member of SDS and founding member of the militant Weathermen organization.

Joe Levin (1943–), military intelligence officer, lawyer, and cofounder of the Southern Poverty Law Center (1971); argued the *Frontiero v. Richardson* case before the Supreme Court on Sharron Frontiero-Cohen's behalf (1973).

Suzanne Braun Levine (1941–), feminist journalist and editor; founding editor of *Ms.* (1972–1988); editor of the *Columbia Journalism Review* (1989–1996); and author of *Inventing the Rest of Our Lives: Women in Second Adulthood* (2005), among other books.

Lucy Lippard (1937–), writer, art critic, feminist activist; curator of more than fifty exhibitions; author of twenty-three books on art, feminism, politics, and place; cofounder of the feminist art movement in New York; cofounder of the Heresies Collective and its journal, *Heresies*, and Printed Matter, Inc.

Barbara Love (1937–2022), feminist lesbian writer, editor, and activist; early member of NOW; coauthor with Sidney Abbott of *Sappho Was a Right-on Woman: A Liberated View of Lesbianism* (1972); writer and editor of *Feminists Who Changed America, 1963–1975*, an encyclopedic book with biographies of 2,200 second-wave feminists.

Myra MacPherson (1934–), journalist who wrote for the Style section in the *Washington Post*, often covering the women's movement (1968–1991); author of, among others, *Long Time Passing: Vietnam and the Haunted Generation* (1984).

Barbara Mehrhof (1942–), feminist activist, social worker, writer, educator; member of New York Radical Feminists, Redstockings, and The Feminists; contributor to *Notes from the Second Year* and *Notes from the Third Year*; cocoordinator of Women Against Pornography (late 1970s).

Kate Millett (1934–2017), author, academic, feminist activist, artist; early member of New York NOW and chair of the education committee (1966–1970); founder of Columbia University Women's Liberation; early member of Downtown Radical

Women; author of (among many others) *Sexual Politics* (1970), a bestseller and key text of the second-wave feminist movement that catapulted Millett to notoriety.

Patsy Mink (1927–2002), lawyer, legislator, women's rights activist; the first Asian American to practice law in Hawaii; first woman of Asian descent to be elected to the US House of Representatives (1965–1977 and 1990–2002); worked on childcare, education, and women's rights; cofounder of the National Women's Political Caucus (NWPC) (1971); played a key role in protecting and enforcing Title IX.

Walter Mondale (1928–2021), lawyer and Democratic party politician; US senator from Minnesota (1964–1976); forty-second vice president of the United States under President Jimmy Carter (1977–1981).

Honor Moore (1945–), poet, playwright, memoirist, professor, editor of poetry, plays, and manifestos of the women's movement. Author of, among other works, *The Bishop's Daughter* (2009), *Our Revolution* (2019), and several poetry collections; editor with Alix Kates Shulman of *Women's Liberation! Feminist Writings That Inspired a Revolution & Still Can* (2021).

Robin Morgan (1941–), poet, author, feminist activist, and former child actor; cofounder of New York Radical Women (1967–1969) and cofounder of W.I.T.C.H. (1968); editor in chief of *Ms.* (1989–1994); author of more than twenty books, including the acclaimed anthology that she edited, *Sisterhood Is Powerful* (1970); cofounder (with Gloria Steinem and Jane Fonda) of the Women's Media Center (2005).

Pauli Murray (1910–1985), celebrated Black legal scholar and strategist; civil rights and feminist activist; poet, writer, and professor; founding member of Congress of Racial Equality (CORE) (1942); one of two women and first in her class at Howard University Law School (1944); denied admission to University of North Carolina because she was Black and to Harvard Law School because she was a woman; served on the civil rights committee of the Presidential Commission on the Status of Women (1961–1963); the first woman and African American to receive a doctorate from Yale Law School (1965); cofounder of NOW (1966); ordained the first Black woman Episcopal priest (1977).

Esther Newberg (1941–), Democratic political operative for, among others, Senator Robert F. Kennedy (1966–1968) and Congresswoman Bella Abzug (1971–1973); veteran literary agent at ICM/CAA.

Nancy Newhouse (1936–), editor at *Home and Garden* and *New York*; at the *New York Times*, editor of Living/Style department (1978–1989), the Travel section (1989–2004), and the "Hers" column (1977–2004).

Linda Nochlin (1931–2017), pioneering feminist art historian and Vassar College professor, where she taught one of the first courses in women's art history; known for her 1971 *ARTnews* piece, "Why Have There Been No Great Women Artists?" and *Women Artists: The Linda Nochlin Reader* (2015).

Eleanor Holmes Norton (1937–), civil rights and feminist lawyer and activist; attorney with the American Civil Liberties Union (1965–1970); first woman to chair the New York City Commission on Human Rights (1970–1977); first woman to head the EEOC (1977–1983); delegate to the US House of Representatives, representing the District of Columbia (since 1991).

Margo Okazawa-Rey (1949–), feminist activist, author, and educator; member of the Daughters of Bilitis (1973) and founding member of Combahee River Collective (1975).

Jane O'Reilly (1936–), journalist, newspaper columnist, author; cofounder of *Ms.*, for which she wrote the first cover story, "The Housewife's Moment of Truth," and coined the term "Click!"

Torie Osborn (1950–), lesbian feminist activist, community organizer, author, and music producer; member of the Chicago Women's Liberation Union (CWLU); cofounder (with Robin Tyler) of the West Coast Women's Music and Cultural Festival (1980); first female executive director of the Los Angeles Gay and Lesbian Center (1987–1992).

Jane Pincus (1937–), artist, author, and cofounder of the Our Bodies, Ourselves collective (1970); she edited almost every edition of the book *Our Bodies, Ourselves* and wrote about pregnancy and birth.

Howardena Pindell (1943–), visual artist, feminist, curator, and educator; curator in the Department of Prints and Illustrated Books at the Museum of Modern Art (1967–1979); founding member of A.I.R. Gallery, the first New York women's cooperative art gallery (1972); professor at the State University of New York, Stony Brook (1979–2020).

Letty Cottin Pogrebin (1939–), feminist activist, cofounder, contributor, and editor of *Ms.* (1971–1989); author of twelve books; editorial consultant for *Free to Be . . . You and Me*, with Marlo Thomas (1972).

Lynn Povich (1943–), journalist; one of sixty women to file the landmark sex discrimination case against *Newsweek* (1970), which she chronicled in *The Good Girl's Revolt* (2012); first woman senior editor at *Newsweek*; editor in chief of *Working Woman*; producer at MSNBC.

Marguerite Rawalt (1895–1989), early feminist lawyer (class of 1933, George Washington Law School); staff lawyer for the IRS (1935–1965); first woman president of the Federal Bar Association (1941); appointed to the President's Commission on the Status of Women (1961); cofounder of NOW (1966) and of NOW Legal Defense and Education Fund; charter member of WEAL (1968); president of WEAL Educational and Legal Defense Fund (1972).

Susan Rennie (1939–), visual artist, professor, coauthor with Kirsten Grimstad of *The New Woman's Survival Catalog* (1973) and *The New Woman's Survival Sourcebook* (1975); cofounder with Kirsten Grimstad of *Chrysalis: A Magazine of Women's Culture*, which published out of the Women's Building in Los Angeles (1977–1981).

Wilson Riles Jr. (1946–), politician and community activist; Northern California coordinator for Shirley Chisholm's 1972 presidential campaign; member of the Oakland City Council (1979–1992).

Faith Ringgold (1930–2024), feminist visual artist, activist, and author; member of Women Artists in Revolution (WAR) (1969); cofounder (with daughter Michele Wallace) of Women Students and Artists for Black Art Liberation (WSABAL) (1970); cofounder of Ad Hoc Committee of Women Artists (1970) and the National Black Feminist Organization (NBFO) (1973); cofounder of the Black women artists group Where We At (1971); writer and illustrator of seventeen children's books; recipient of twenty-three honorary doctorates and more than eighty awards.

Victor L. Robles (1945–), staff member for Congresswoman Shirley Chisholm; ran Chisholm's Brooklyn district office (1970s); member of the New York State

Assembly (1979–1984); member of the New York City Council (1985–2001); city clerk of New York (2001–2007).

Ruth Rosen (1945–), journalist, author, professor, and historian of gender and society; member of Berkeley Women's Liberation (1968–1972); taught the first seminar in women's history at the University of California, Berkeley (1971); author of (among others) *The World Split Open: How the Women's Movement Changed America* (2000).

Jill Ruckelshaus (1937–), Republican feminist activist; founding member of the National Women's Political Caucus (NWPC) (1971); head of the White House Office of Women's Programs (1972); commissioner for the US Commission on Civil Rights (1980). Married to Illinois Republican congressman and two-time EPA director William Ruckelshaus.

Bernice Sandler (1928–2019), women's rights activist; member of WEAL (1969–1971); considered the "Godmother of Title IX," she was instrumental in the creation of Title IX (along with Senator Birch Bayh and Representatives Edith Green and Patsy Mink).

Miriam Schapiro (1923–2015), painter, sculptor, printmaker, and feminist art pioneer; cofounder with Judy Chicago of the Feminist Art Program (1970); cocreator with Judy Chicago of Womanhouse (1972); leader of the Pattern and Decoration art movement.

Christina Schlesinger (1946–), painter and muralist, feminist art activist; cofounder of the Social and Public Art Resource Center (SPARC) in Venice, California (1976); part of the Guerrilla Girls (early 1990s).

Diane Schulder (Abrams) (1937–), New York feminist activist and lawyer specializing in women's matrimonial law; taught the first "Women and the Law" course (1969) at the University of Pennsylvania; author, with Florynce Kennedy, of *Abortion Rap* (1971).

Arlie Scott (1937–), feminist political activist; California coordinator for the Shirley Chisholm presidential campaign (1972); active in NOW leadership as member of its national board of directors (1973–1979); Democratic convention coordinator (1976); and organizer of first ERA march in Washington, DC (1977).

Martha Scott (1942–), mother of four, member of the Chicago underground abortion service, code-name Jane, and one of the seven women known as the Chicago Seven, arrested May 3, 1972.

Barbara Seaman (1935–2008), journalist, author, and founder of the National Women's Health Network (1975); author of *The Doctor's Case Against the Pill* (1969) and *Free and Female: The Sex Life of the Contemporary Woman* (1972).

Derek Shearer (1946–), activist, professor, US ambassador to Finland; freelance journalist and columnist for *Ramparts*; director of the McKinnon Center for Global Affairs at Occidental College.

Jeanne Shenandoah (1945–), citizen of the central New York's Onondaga Nation; midwife, herbalist; active in natural childbirth and homebirth movement; member of Hodenosaunee environmental task force; vice president of the Matilda Joslyn Gage Foundation.

Martha Shelley (1943–), lesbian feminist activist, poet, author; member and later president of the Daughters of Bilitis (DOB) (1967); early member of the Gay Liberation Front (1969); key organizer of the Lavender Menace zap at the Second Congress to Unite Women (1970); produced *Lesbian Nation*, a New York radio show (1972–1974).

Alix Kates Shulman (1932–), radical feminist activist, novelist and essayist; member of New York Radical Women (1967), Redstockings (1968), and W.I.T.C.H. (1968); author of (among others) *Memoirs of an Ex-Prom Queen* (1972).

Margaret Sloan-Hunter (1947–2004), lesbian feminist and civil rights activist; early editor at *Ms.*; joined the Congress of Racial Equality (CORE) at age fourteen; cofounder of National Black Feminist Organization (NBFO) (1973).

Barbara Smith (1946–), lesbian feminist activist, author, scholar, and pioneer of Black women's studies; coeditor of *All the Women Are White, All the Blacks Are Men, But Some of Us Are Brave* (1982); editor of *Home Girls: A Black Feminist Anthology* (1983); member of National Black Feminist Organization (NBFO) (1973);

cofounder of the Combahee River Collective (1974); cofounder of Kitchen Table: Women of Color Press, the nation's first publisher for women of color (1980).

Beverly Smith (1946–), Black feminist activist and health advocate, writer, academic, and theorist; member of (CORE); member of (NBFO) (1973) and cofounder of the Combahee River Collective (1974) with her twin sister, Barbara Smith; instructor of women's health at the University of Massachusetts, Boston.

Carolyn Smith (1939–), close aide and administrative assistant for US congresswoman Shirley Chisholm (1969–1983); accountant who served as chief audit executive for the Columbus, Ohio, City School's Office of Internal Audit, and on the Board of Trustees of the Financial Accounting Foundation.

Elizabeth Spahn (1949–), lawyer, feminist activist; one of the first women to attend Yale University (1969); law professor at New England Law Boston (1978–2014); a legal expert in international bribery and corruption and international women's issues.

Nancy Stearns (1939–), lawyer, abortion rights, and civil rights activist; NYU Law School graduate (1967); staff attorney at the Center for Constitutional Rights; professor at Rutgers University (teaching Ruth Bader Ginsburg's Women in the Law course) (1972–1981); assistant attorney general in the Environmental Protection Bureau of New York (1981–1995); since 1996, principal attorney in the Law Department of the New York State Supreme Court; cabaret singer.

Gloria Steinem (1934–), journalist, feminist activist, and organizer; celebrated public speaker, cofounder, and editor for fifteen years of *Ms.* (1971); cofounder of the National Women's Political Caucus (NWPC) (1971), the Women's Action Alliance (1971), the Ms. Foundation for Women (1972), and Voters for Choice (1979); author of (among others) *Outrageous Acts and Everyday Rebellions* (1983).

Norma Swenson (1932–), natural childbirth activist and lecturer; president of the International Childbirth Education Association (1966); coauthor of the childbirth chapter for many editions of *Our Bodies, Ourselves* starting in 1971; first director of the Boston Women's Health Collective's international programs, and consultant to the World Health Organization on women's health.

Kathrine Switzer (1947–), champion marathon runner, women's sports activist, and television sports commentator; first registered woman to run the Boston Marathon, even though it was illegal (1967); ran the Boston Marathon nine times, including in 1972, when it was first legal for women; won the New York Marathon in 1974; has run forty-one marathons.

Margery Tabankin (1948–), political, peace, and justice activist; first woman president of the National Student Association (1971–1972); Director of VISTA (Volunteers in Service) (1977–1981); executive director of the Hollywood Women's Political Committee (1988–1994) and the Barbra Streisand Foundation (1987–2014).

Lindsy Van Gelder (1944–), feminist journalist; reporter for the *New York Post* and early chronicler of the women's liberation movement; founded Media Women with other feminist reporters (late 1960s); contributing editor *Ms.*

Sally Roesch Wagner (1942–), feminist organizer, activist, author, and scholar; cofounded one of the first college women's studies programs at California State University, Sacramento (1969); one of the first students to earn a PhD in women's studies (1978, University of California, Santa Cruz); author of *Sisters in Spirit: Haudenosaunee (Iroquois) Influence on Early American Feminists* (2001) and editor of the anthology *The Women's Suffrage Movement* (2019); founder and director of the Matilda Joslyn Gage Foundation (2000).

Alice Walker (1944–), internationally celebrated author, poet, and activist; first African American woman to win the Pulitzer Prize for Fiction (1983); winner of the National Book Award (1983) for her 1982 bestselling novel, *The Color Purple*; author of seven novels, four collections of short stories, and several volumes of essays and poetry; coined the term "womanist" in 1979: she describes women of color as "womanists" rather than feminists.

Michele Wallace (1952–), feminist writer, cultural critic, activist, and professor; cofounder (with her mother, artist Faith Ringgold) of Women Students and Artists for Black Art Liberation (WSABAL) (1970) and National Black Feminist Organization (NBFO) (1973); author of (among others) *Black Macho and the Myth of the Superwoman* (1978); president of the Faith Ringgold Society.

Faye Wattleton (1943–), reproductive rights activist and nurse-midwife; the first African American and youngest president of Planned Parenthood Federation of America (1978–1992); has received fifteen honorary doctoral degrees.

Lee Webb (1941–), civil rights and political activist, journalist; national secretary of SDS (1963); founder of the Center for Policy Alternatives (1976); vice president of the New School University (1998).

Marilyn Salzman Webb (1942–), feminist activist, organizer, professor, author, and journalist; cofounder of the first women's consciousness-raising group in Chicago (1966); founding member of Washington, DC, Women's Liberation Movement (DCWLM) (1968); cofounder, writer, and editor of early feminist and longest-running newspaper *Off Our Backs* (1970); cofounder and executive director of one of the first women's studies programs at Goddard College (1970); cofounder of Sagaris Institute (1975); editor-in-chief of *Psychology Today*.

Sarah Weddington (1945–2021), attorney, law professor; women's rights and reproductive health activist; member of the Texas House of Representatives (1973–1977); represented "Jane Roe" in the landmark *Roe v. Wade* case before the US Supreme Court that legalized abortion in 1973.

Faith Wilding (1943–), Paraguayan American multidisciplinary artist and professor; teaching assistant in Judy Chicago's Feminist Art Program (FAP) at California State University, Fresno (1970); participated in Womanhouse (1972).

Cathy Wilkerson (1945–), antiwar and civil rights activist; SDS organizer and officer, member of the militant Weathermen organization; lived underground to escape capture from the FBI from 1970 to 1980; served eleven months in Bedford Hills Correctional Center; high school math teacher for twenty years in Brooklyn, New York.

Ellen Willis (1941–2006), journalist, feminist, author, and political activist; the first rock music critic for the *New Yorker* (late 1960s–1970s); member of New York Radical Women (1968); cofounder (with Shulamith Firestone) of Redstockings (1969); founding member of Coalition for Abortion Rights and Against Sterilization Abuse (CARASA) (1977); editor of *Ms.* (1972–1975) and the *Village*

Voice (1984–1990); contributor to numerous publications and author of several books of collected essays.

Barbara Winslow (1945–), feminist activist, professor; founding member of the Reproductive Rights National Network (1978–1984); cofounder of the women's studies programs at the University of Washington and Seattle Community College; biographer of Shirley Chisholm and founder and former director of the Shirley Chisholm Project at Brooklyn College.

Alice Wolfson (1941–), women's health and abortion rights activist; attorney; founding member of Washington, DC, Women's Liberation Movement (DCWLM) (1968–1977); participated in the disruption of the US Senate birth control pill hearings (1970); cofounder of the National Women's Health Network (1975).

Acknowledgments

I was born the year this book begins, in 1963, and joined that first generation of women to benefit from the monumental changes it records. As a child in New York City, I grew up inhaling the fumes of the women's movement and idolizing Shirley Chisholm and Bella Abzug—my city's noble and boisterous congressional representatives. Without much thought or gratitude, I walked down the red carpet that this generation before me paid so dearly to roll out. It didn't take long into research for *The Movement* for me to be struck by reminders of how many more life options I had than women in the generation before me.

Case in point: one of my first jobs after graduating from college in 1985 was as a reporter in the Washington, DC, bureau of *Newsweek*, where I covered the White House. During my years at the magazine, I knew nothing about the sex discrimination class action that forty-six women employees had filed against the magazine in 1970. Flash forward to 2022, when I interviewed Lucy Howard and Lynn Povich, both respected senior editors at the magazine when I was there. Little did I know when I was filing stories to them that they were plaintiffs in the lawsuit—the first of its kind—that forced the magazine to hire or promote qualified women as reporters, writers, and editors. Understanding the scope of the debt my generation—and all who come after—owe to the brave, brilliant, and sometimes whacky outcasts who made up the second wave feminists fueled my five-year-long adventure to meet their leaders and participants.

Many people helped me with this book, but I owe everything to the more than one hundred women (and some men) who trusted me enough to plumb the depths of their memories and share their personal stories. Their names are listed chronologically, beginning on page 519, and that list serves as a blueprint of my journey reporting this book, as one conversation led to the next in a zig-zag patchwork across the country. My lengthy, in-person interviews ended abruptly in March 2020. I remember driving to Jo Freeman's apartment in Brooklyn on March 11, where we talked and leafed through her boxes of saved papers from the 1960s and '70s. Little did we know that four days later, the pandemic shutdown would bring our worlds to a crashing halt. For the next year and a half, my interviews were relegated to Zoom. But each discussion delivered new revelations and uncounted moments of outrage and excitement. I already miss those magical encounters—whether on Zoom with Barbara Smith and Charlotte Bunch, or in Frances Beal's Oakland nursing home, or Lucy Lippard's living room in Galisteo, New Mexico.

Still, many of the voices in *The Movement* belong to women who are no longer alive, or with whom I could not manage to meet, and several crucial archives harbored many of their vivid, first-person histories. The Harvard-Radcliffe Institute Schlesinger Library's Tully-Crenshaw Feminist Oral History Project and Smith College's Voices of Feminism Oral History Project were essential resources that helped fill many gaps, and I am grateful to those libraries for committing the considerable resources to capture these historic stories. I also relied on the archives and oral histories found at the Library of Congress, the National Archives, Veteran Feminists of America, Duke University's Sallie Bingham Center for Women's History & Culture, and several other universities. I extend my appreciation to the many librarians and archivists at those institutions who helped me pry these stories out of dusty files.

Over the five years it took to research and write this book, I relied on the able help of dedicated researchers, starting with Eloise Lynton and followed by Sasha Zients, Jess Schwalbe, Charley Burlock, Kendrick Pratt, Rachel Garbus, and Ceceile Kay Richter. For more than two years, Fernanda Amis provided invaluable research, insights, and creativity to this project. Lisa Chase helped me shape early drafts, Tim Rockwood copyedited them, Jack Bales meticulously assisted with endnotes and bibliography, Crary Pullen sleuthed for photographs, and Emily Feder and Suzanne Williams played a hand in presenting *The Movement* to the world.

Esther Newberg, my indomitable agent since 1995, is not only a character in the book who recounts her experience as Congresswoman Bella Abzug's first chief of staff, but she is also *The Movement*'s godmother and advocate. One Signal Publisher's founder, Julia Cheiffetz, believed in the early concept of the book and shepherded my research and writing process. Abby Mohr expertly edited multiple drafts, and the exceptionally talented Jenny Xu helped pull the book over the finish line. I am grateful to be in the hands of the skillful and professional team at Simon & Schuster's Atria Press, including Libby McGuire, Falon Kirby, Maudee Genao, Aleaha Reneé, Kathleen Rizzo, Danielle Mazzella di Bosco, Joy O'Meara, and Elisa Rivlin.

I will be forever in debt to my friends who reached into their rolodexes (as if such a thing still exists) to help me connect with people I needed to interview. They include Joe Conason, Charles Kaiser, Nancy Steiner, Charlotte Sheedy, Esther Newberg, Leslie Bennetts, Holly Peterson, Joe Armstrong, Cecile Richards, Julia Pershan, Lisa Beattie Frelinghuysen, Tim Rockwood, Jane Kramer, Steve Wasserman, Sherrye Henry, Honor Moore, Betsy West, Geralyn Dreyfous, Elizabeth Sackler, Sallie Bingham, Gillian Thomas, Peggy Siegal, and Rachel Garbus. The story Sandy Gotham Meehan told me about graduating from Stanford but not being able to get a credit card inspired the second working title of the book, *Lit by Hellfire*, and Vicki Gordon, always full of ideas, miraculously came up with *The Movement*'s final title.

While I found the process of reporting *The Movement* an exciting adventure, the solitude of writing proved a lonely endeavor. Alleviating this burden were a handful of dear friends who took time out of their busy lives to read drafts of the manuscript and provide critical insights and corrections. In the summer of 2022, my beloved aunt Eleanor Bingham Miller and Tom Weinberg carefully critiqued the first raft of pages, while my daughter, Diana Michaelis, patiently listened to me read early chapters. Later in the process, I relied on the skilled advice of my dear friends David Michaelis, Emily Bingham, John Burnham Schwartz, Aleksandra Crapanzano, Susan Sommer, and Gillian Thomas. My sister-cousin Emily Bingham talked me off several ledges and, with firm patience and considerable talent, pushed me to make the book better. Jennifer Maguire tirelessly read every single draft while prodding and coaching me on each twist and turn of the book's development during our daily phone calls. Her attentive, generous friendship sustained me.

A posse of fast friends provided much-needed emotional and moral support, and I am so fortunate to have them in my life. They include: Natalie Williams, Stephanie Cabot, Cary Netchvolodoff, Carolyn Strauss, Mary Zients, Claudia Silver, Courtenay Valenti, Katherine Goguen, Jacqueline Kinghan, Virginia Moseley, Mary Beth and Chris Harvey, Ariadne Calvo-Platero, Perry Peltz , Liz Massie, Sarah Lyall, Stephen Reily, Nancy Steiner,

Mary Zipser, Vicki Gordon, Leslie Bennetts, Laura and Bob Peabody, Billy O'Farrell, Michael Kafka, Laura Yorke, Electra Toub, Holly Peterson, Chris Isham, Charles Kaiser, Jon Meacham, Jimmy Hunt, Marcus Lovell Smith, Karin Day, Todd Klein, Matt Arnold, Katty Kay, Jane Mayer, Tom Carver, Morgan Entrekin, Elisabeth Schmitz, Alexandra Styron, Patricia Allen, Mahnaz Ispahani Bartos, Sherrye Henry, Annie Stackhouse, Eva Timmerman, Pamela Bell, Mary Berner, Sally Whaling, Deb Futter, Bill Cohan, Martha Sherrill, Sally Hall, Sally Horchow, Peter Soros, Drew and Jessica Guff, Sarah Slusser, George and Leslie Biddle, Michele Bernhardt, Amanda Penarrieta, Nan Huson, Kris Monroe, and Veronique Ory.

Many life-altering events took place during the making of this book: the COVID pandemic, my mother's death at age eighty-five, and moving in with my husband, Joe Finnerty. Through all these changes and transformations, I relied on my extended family for love, support, and entertainment. After ten years of marriage, I have happily adopted Joe's large, loving tribe of five siblings, their spouses, and children as my own. Their matriarch, Alice Ann Finnerty, is a model of leadership and warmth. I am grateful to be in the business of coparenting with the wise and empathetic David Michaelis and Nancy Steiner, Amy Finnerty and Tunku Varadarajan, and I count myself lucky to be part of the fabric of the lives of my remarkable stepchildren, Katherine, Alice, and Sam Finnerty.

My three children, Jamie, Henry, and Diana, bring deep joy, purpose, and boundless love to my life. Jamie (twenty-eight) and Henry (twenty-six) fill my heart with pride and gratitude for the thoughtful, sensitive, self-aware men they have become. I singled out their bold, adventurous sister, Diana (twenty-three), for the book's dedication because I hope her future will be informed and shaped by the history this book brings forth. Diana stands on the shoulders of her grandmothers, Joan Bingham and Diana Tead Michaelis, and great-grandmothers, Mary Bingham, Helen Stevens, Clara Tead, and Martha Michaelis, who managed to carve out their own versions of freedom and independence despite the social forces in play at the time of their coming of age.

From start to finish, Joe Finnerty lived every day of this book with me. His steadfast love gave me the confidence and courage to persevere. I relied constantly on his good judgment and superior editing skills, as well as his lively humor and broad intelligence. I cherish every moment of walking through life with Joe with every inch of my heart.

—Brooklyn, May 2024

Notes

1. Origin Story—*The Feminine Mystique*

4 *I date the beginning*: Sonia Pressman Fuentes, *Eat First—You Don't Know What They'll Give You: The Adventures of an Immigrant Family and Their Feminist Daughter* (Indiana: Xlibris, 1999), 124.

4 *And note this*: Pauli Murray, interview in the Pauli Murray Oral History, June 16, 1983, part 2, transcript, 5, Southern Oral History Program, Wilson Library, University of North Carolina, Chapel Hill, NC; Pauli Murray, *Song in a Weary Throat: Memoir of an American Pilgrimage* (1987; repr., New York: Liveright, 2018), 452.

4 *The book was a smash hit*: Author's interview with Sonia Pressman Fuentes, May 15, 2020.

4 *I just remember the buzz*: Author's interview with Torie Osborn, February 24, 2021.

4 *Betty Friedan represented*: Author's interview with Frances Beal, May 21, 2021.

5 *When I was growing up*: Author's interview with Bobbi Gibb, October 31, 2019.

5 *I had a master's of arts*: Kate Millett, interview by Jacqueline Ceballos, January 7, 1991, transcript, 3–4, Tully-Crenshaw Feminist Oral History Project, Schlesinger Library, Radcliffe Institute for Advanced Study, Cambridge, MA.

6 *I could not figure out*: Author's interview with Barbara Smith, June 14, 2021.

6 *In high school*: Author's interview with Margo Okazawa-Rey, June 7, 2021.

7 *When we as Black women*: Author's interview with Byllye Avery, September 22, 2021.

7 *Historically I respected*: Author's interview with Margo Jefferson, June 9, 2021.

2. Civil Rights—Free-dom

8 *I didn't actually begin*: Author's interview with Jo Freeman, March 11, 2020.

9 *I was very conscious*: Pauli Murray, interview in the Pauli Murray Oral History, June 16, 1983, part 1, transcript, 4, Southern Oral History Program, Wilson Library, University of North Carolina, Chapel Hill, NC.

9 *I heard about the March*: Author's interview with Ericka Huggins, July 26, 2021.

10 *A. Philip Randolph, the leader*: Pauli Murray, interview, Southern Oral History Program, June 16, 1983, part 1, 4.

10 *The first feminist that I knew*: Author's interview with Eleanor Holmes Norton, January 25, 2022.

10 *I became aware*: Pauli Murray, interview by Genna Rae McNeil, February 13, 1976, interview G-0044, transcript, 65–66, Southern Oral History Program (#4007), Wilson Library, University of North Carolina, Chapel Hill, NC.

10n *Murray was active*: Rosalind Rosenberg, *Jane Crow: The Life of Pauli Murray* (New York: Oxford University Press, 2017), 119–21; Pauli Murray Center for History and Social Justice, https://www.paulimurraycenter.com/pronouns-pauli-murray.

11 *There were hardly any*: Author's interview with Eleanor Holmes Norton.

11 *When my PhD classes*: Murray, *Song in a Weary Throat*, 449.

12 *I went to Mississippi*: Author's interview with Eleanor Holmes Norton.

12n *Founded in 1960*: Mark Whitaker, *Saying It Loud: 1966—The Year Black Power Challenged the Civil Rights Movement* (New York: Simon & Schuster, 2023), 2.

13 *After I got beat*: Howell Raines, *My Soul Is Rested: Movement Days in the Deep South Remembered* (1977; repr., New York: Penguin Books, 1983), 254.

13 *I was born during Jim Crow*: Author's interview with Barbara Smith.

13 *In 1964, I was enamored*: Author's interview with Susan Brownmiller, September 24, 2019.

14 *I am one of seven women*: Robin Morgan, *Demon Lover: The Roots of Terrorism* (New York: Washington Square Press, 1988), 223–24; author's interview with Robin Morgan, March 5, 2014.

3. Abortion—Secret, Secret, Secret

15 *I got married*: Author's interview with Sally Roesch Wagner, May 26, 2021.

16 *I was growing up*: Author's interview with Vivian Gornick, February 10, 2022.

17 *There was a woman*: Author's interview with Elizabeth Spahn, July 27, 2022.

17 *I had my first abortion*: Author's interview with Frances Beal, May 21, 2021.

4. "Sex" Is Added to the Civil Rights Act

19 *In 1964, the Judiciary Committee*: Martha W. Griffiths, "Appendix I," 1, a typed copy of an undated, unpublished article on sex in the Civil Rights Act, included with transcripts of oral history interviews with her, 1977–1979, in Griffiths, Martha W., folder 2, box I:5, Transcripts, Former Members of Congress, Inc., Oral History Interviews, Manuscript Division, Library of Congress, Washington, DC.

20 *During the closing hours*: Murray, *Song in a Weary Throat*, 462.

20 *During the entire debate*: Griffiths, "Appendix I," 6.

21 *Well, this was a very*: Author's interview with Sonia Pressman Fuentes.

21 *Smith was called*: Pauli Murray, interview, Southern Oral History Program, June 16, 1983, part 2, 2.

21 *Congresswoman Edith Green [D-OR] believed*: Griffiths, "Appendix I," 10.

22 *Various women arose*: Griffiths, "Appendix I," 6, 10.

23 *To almost everyone's surprise*: Murray, *Song in a Weary Throat*, 463–64.

23 *When it got over*: Martha W. Griffiths, interview by Fern S. Ingersoll, October 29, 1979, 79, in Griffiths, Martha W., folder 1, box I:5, Transcripts, Former Members of Congress, Inc., Oral History Interviews.

23 *Senator [Everett] Dirksen, who was*: Pauli Murray, interview, Southern Oral History Program, June 16, 1983, part 1, 7; Murray, *Song in a Weary Throat*, 646.

24 *Texas Business and Professional Women*: Jo Freeman, *The Politics of Women's Liberation: A Case Study of an Emerging Social Movement and Its Relation to the Policy Process* (Indiana, iUniverse, 1975), 179.

24 *Marguerite Rawalt knew Lady Bird*: Pauli Murray, interview, June 16, 1983, part 1, 7.

24 *There had been a movement*: Sonia Pressman Fuentes, interview by Liz Alpert, December 19, 2013, transcript, 3. *Oral History of Sonia Pressman Fuentes*. Oral history interviews of Sonia Pressman Fuentes conducted by Liz Alpert for the American Bar Association's Women Trailblazers in the Law Project. Chicago: American Bar Association, 2013–2014.

24 *I would surmise that the*: Author's interview with Louise "Mama Bear" Herne, September 13, 2021.

25 *After 1920, there were*: Sonia Pressman Fuentes interview by Liz Alpert, December 19, 2013, transcript, 3.

25 *Right after Title VII*: Pauli Murray, interview, June 16, 1983, part 1, 2.

5. WRAP—Sex Meets Caste

26 *I wanted to be a neurosurgeon*: Author's interview with Marilyn Webb, February 3, 2020.

27 *In 1965, my sociology*: Author's interview with Heather Booth, October 15, 2019.

27 *I had been national secretary*: Author's interview with Lee Webb, January 31, 2020.

27 *The National Council meeting*: Author's interview with Marilyn Webb, January 22, 2020.

28 *There were probably*: Author's interview with Heather Booth, October 26, 2018.

28 *Women kept leaving*: Author's interview with Marilyn Webb, January 22, 2020.

28 *It was this famous paper*: Author's interview with Heather Booth, January 8, 2013.

28 *I was sitting in the*: Author's interview with Marilyn Webb, January 22, 2020.

28 *Sex and caste: There seem to be*: Casey Hayden and Mary King, "Sex and Caste: A Kind of Memo," History Is a Weapon, https://www.historyisaweapon.com/defcon1/sexcaste .html.

29 *It was a very strong*: Author's interview with Marilyn Webb, January 22, 2020.

29 *It is a caste system*: Hayden and King, "Sex and Caste."

29 *By then, many of us*: Author's interview with Marilyn Webb, January 22, 2020.

29n *Women comprised approximately*: Sara Evans, *Personal Politics: The Roots of Women's Liberation in the Civil Rights Movement and the New Left* (1979; repr., New York: Vintage Books, 1980), 112.

29 *Back on my campus*: Author's interview with Heather Booth, October 26, 2018.

30 *We came back to school*: Author's interview with Marilyn Webb, January 22, 2020.

30 *It was kind of electric*: Author's interview with Heather Booth, January 8, 2013.

6. We Just Don't Hire Women—The EEOC's Rocky Start

31 *On the day that we opened*: Aileen Clarke Hernandez, interviewed by Larry Crowe, April 12, 2007. The HistoryMakers Digital Archive, session 1, tape 5, story 2, https:// www.thehistorymakers.org/sites/default/files/A2007_134_EAD.pdf.

31 *When the Civil Rights Act*: Author's interview with Sonia Pressman Fuentes; Sonia Pressman Fuentes, interview by Liz Alpert.

32 *The commission started*: Aileen Clarke Hernandez, interviewed by Larry Crowe, session 1, tape 5, story 2.

33 *In the absence of organized*: Murray, *Song in a Weary Throat*, 472.

33 *Ours was the first article*: Mary Eastwood, interview by Muriel Fox, March 7, 1992, transcript, Tully-Crenshaw Feminist Oral History Project, Schlesinger Library, Radcliffe Institute for Advanced Study, Cambridge, MA.

33 *On October 12, 1965*: Murray, *Song in a Weary Throat*, 476.

33 *I read in the* New York Times: Betty Friedan, interview by Sue Horton, April 26, 1992, transcript, 85, Tully-Crenshaw Feminist Oral History Project, Schlesinger Library, Radcliffe Institute for Advanced Study, Cambridge, MA.

34 *Betty Friedan was working*: Mary Eastwood, interview by Muriel Fox, 4.

34 *Like every career woman*: Muriel Fox, interview by Jacqueline Ceballos, January 1991, transcript, 18, Tully-Crenshaw Feminist Oral History Project, Schlesinger Library, Radcliffe Institute for Advanced Study, Cambridge, MA; Muriel Fox, interview by Wenxian Zhang, Alia Alli, Jennifer Ritter, and Maureen Maensivu, November 25, 2010, transcript, Rollins College Archives, Winter Park, Florida.

34 *Betty Friedan came by*: Richard Graham, interview by Sylvia Danovitch, July 8, 1992, oral history project of the Equal Employment Opportunity Commission, transcript, 22, Library of Congress, Washington, DC.

34 *Newspapers liked sex-segregated*: Author's interview with Sonia Pressman Fuentes.

35 *Even that first year*: Betty Friedan, *It Changed My Life: Writings on the Women's Movement* (1976; repr., Cambridge, MA: Harvard University Press, 1998), 99.

35 *Shortly after the EEOC*: Author's interview with Sonia Pressman Fuentes.

35 *In 1966, we, the union*: Author's interview with Mary Pat Laffey, June 1, 2020.

36 *"Old Maid." That's what*: Nell McShane Wulfhart, *The Great Stewardess Rebellion: How Women Launched a Workplace Rebellion at 30,000 Feet* (New York: Doubleday, 2022), 59.

36 *I grew up in Pittsburgh*: Author's interview with Mary Pat Laffey.

37 *We had done preliminary work*: Aileen Hernandez, interview by Sylvia Danovitch, 39.

37n *In September 1965*: Wulfhart, *The Great Stewardess Rebellion*, 56, 96.

37 *Betty Friedan came to the office*: Author's interview with Sonia Pressman Fuentes; Sonia Pressman Fuentes, interview by Liz Alpert.

38 *I remember I went*: Betty Friedan, interview by Sue Horton, 85. Friedan, *It Changed My Life*, 77.

38 *Everyone gives Betty Friedan*: Author's interview with Jo Freeman.

38 *I never did write*: Betty Friedan, interview by Sue Horton, 87.

7. We Don't Give Out Birth Control to Unmarried People

39 *I grew up as one*: Author's interview with Bill Baird, April 15, 2020.

40 *I wanted to be a nurse*: Author's interview with Faye Wattleton, November 18, 2020; Faye Wattleton, *Life on the Line* (New York: Ballantine Books, 1996), 93.

41n *Approximately one million women*: Leslie J. Reagan, *When Abortion Was a Crime: Women, Medicine, and Law in the United States, 1867–1973* (Berkeley: University of California Press, 1997), 214; Linda Greenhouse and Reva B. Siegel, eds., *Before Roe v. Wade: Voices That Shaped the Abortion Debate Before the Supreme Court's Ruling* (New York: Kaplan Publishing, 2010), 3; Glenn Kessler, "Planned Parenthood's False

Stat: 'Thousands' of Women Died Every Year Before Roe," *Washington Post*, May 29, 2019.

41 *The week of President Kennedy's*: Author's interview with Bill Baird.

42 *The first year out of college*: Author's interview with Faye Wattleton.

43 *The person who contacted me*: Author's interview with Heather Booth, October 26, 2018.

43n *Like most urban hospitals*: Reagan, *When Abortion Was a Crime*, 210.

44 *I arrived in Madison, Wisconsin*: Author's interview with Margery Tabankin, November 1, 2018.

45 *In 1965, we set up the first*: Author's interview with Bill Baird.

45 *Those were also the years*: Author's interview with Faye Wattleton.

46n *The Food and Drug Administration approved*: Andrea Tone, *Devices and Desires: A History of Contraceptives in America* (New York: Hill and Wang, 2002), 233.

8. There's an Actual Woman Running in the Boston Marathon

47 *The first marathon*: Author's interview with Bobbi Gibb.

48 *When I was twelve years old*: Kathrine Switzer's narration in *Boston*, a documentary produced and directed by Jon Dunham (LA Roma Films, 2017).

48 *I just took it for granted*: Author's interview with Bobbi Gibb.

49 *There were all these myths*: Kathrine Switzer's narration in *Boston*.

49n *Women runners could run only:* Margo Jefferson, *Constructing a Nervous System: A Memoir* (New York: Pantheon Books, 2022), 92–96.

49 *In February 1966*: Author's interview with Bobbi Gibb.

9. NOW Rising

53 *It was going to be*: Betty Friedan, interview by Sue Horton, 88; Friedan, *It Changed My Life*, 101.

54 *Prior to the conference*: Mary Eastwood, interview by Muriel Fox, 31.

54 *Each conference participant*: Murray, *Song in a Weary Throat*, 478.

54 *I remember running*: Betty Friedan, interview by Sue Horton, 89.

55 *There were about fifteen*: Mary Eastwood, interview by Muriel Fox, 10.

55 *After Pauli Murray and I*: Betty Friedan, interview by Sue Horton, 89; Friedan, *It Changed My Life*, 102.

55 *Tempers flared and we wrangled*: Murray, *Song in a Weary Throat*, 479.

55 *They left in what I felt*: Friedan, *It Changed My Life*, 103.

55 *I left Betty Friedan's room*: Murray, *Song in a Weary Throat*, 479.

56 *My phone began ringing*: Betty Friedan, interview by Sue Horton, 89.

56 *Thursday morning, Kay*: Mary Eastwood, interview by Muriel Fox.

56 *Kay Clarenbach, the darling*: Friedan, *It Changed My Life*, 103.

56 *During the luncheon*: Murray, *Song in a Weary Throat*, 480.

57 *I remember I said*: Betty Friedan, interview by Sue Horton, 90.

57 *Betty Friedan hastily scribbled*: Murray, *Song in a Weary Throat*, 480.

57 *We met for an hour*: Friedan, *It Changed My Life*, 104.

57 *The birth of NOW had*: Murray, *Song in a Weary Throat*, 480.

58 *That summer of 1966*: Muriel Fox, interview by Jacqueline Ceballos, 21.

58 *I asked Muriel Fox*: Betty Friedan, interview by Sue Horton, 91.

58 *Betty asked if I would*: Author's interview with Muriel Fox, April 28, 2020.

59 *Well, the word was Kay*: Betty Friedan, interview by Sue Horton.

59 *I remember Betty thought*: Mary Eastwood, interview by Muriel Fox, 19.

59 *My husband, Shep*: Author's interview with Muriel Fox.

59 *I remember reading*: Friedan, interview by Sue Horton, 91.

59 *I urge everyone to read*: Author's interview with Muriel Fox.

59 *National Organization for Women*: "Statement of Purpose," National Organization for Women, https://now.org/about/history/statement-of-purpose/.

60 *That still brings tears*: Author's interview with Muriel Fox.

60 *The* Washington Post *had this*: Mary Eastwood, interview by Muriel Fox, 28.

60 *Thirty-two of us set up*: Murray, *Song in a Weary Throat*, 480.

60 *We formed task forces*: Author's interview with Muriel Fox.

60 *We wasted no time*: "Founding of Now," National Organization for Women, https:/350fem.blogs.brynmawr.edu/about/history/founding-of-now/.

61 *We all signed our names*: Mary Eastwood, interview by Muriel Fox, 35.

61 *The night after we adopted*: Friedan, interview by Sue Horton, 91; Friedan, *It Changed My Life*, 105.

61 *The press release was used*: Author's interview with Muriel Fox.

62 *I was one of three*: Dolores Alexander, interview by Kelly Anderson, March 20, 2004, transcript, 14, Voices of Feminism Oral History Project, Sophia Smith Collection, Smith College, Northampton, MA.

10. Crimes Against Chastity

63 *I got a phone call*: Author's interview with Bill Baird.

65 *In 1965 I arrived at BU*: Sue Katz speech at Boston University conference on Women's Liberation, March 27–29, 2014.

65 *The moment I did that*: Author's interview with Bill Baird.

65 *Of course, the point he*: Author's interview with Myra MacPherson, February 11, 2020.

65 *In my simple head*: Author's interview with Bill Baird.

66 *He was then hauled off*: Author's interview with Myra MacPherson.

66 *They gave us a tin cup*: Author's interview with Bill Baird.

66 *He was in there for thirty-six days*: Author's interview with Myra MacPherson.

11. What Was I Wearing?

67 *I came back to school*: Author's interview with Marilyn Webb, January 22, 2020.

68 *I'd left Chicago and*: Author's interview with Lee Webb.

68 *I moved to Washington*: Author's interview with Marilyn Webb, January 22, 2020.

69 *Getting a PhD was*: Author's interview with Lee Webb.

69 *Lee was at the Institute*: Author's interview with Marilyn Webb, January 22, 2020.

69 *Marilyn Webb was the one*: Author's interview with Charlotte Bunch, April 13, 2021.

12. Black Power—The Patterns Were Very Similar

70 *The idea was to make*: Faith Ringgold, *We Flew Over the Bridge: The Memoirs of Faith Ringgold* (1995; repr., Durham, NC: Duke University Press, 2005), 154.

71 *In 1967, Mother wasn't*: Author's interview with Michele Wallace, December 7, 2021.

71 *My first one-person show*: Ringgold, *We Flew Over the Bridge*, 154–55.

71 *My mother taught art*: Author's interview with Michele Wallace.

71 The Flag Is Bleeding *was eight feet*: New Museum (New York, NY), *Faith Ringgold: American People* (New York: Phaidon Press, in association with New Museum, 2022), 208; Ringgold, *We Flew Over the Bridge*, 156.

72 *The lack of reception*: Author's interview with Michele Wallace.

72 *The opening party*: Ringgold, *We Flew Over the Bridge*, 159.

72 *Flo Kennedy came*: Author's interview with Michele Wallace.

72 *I had called Flo*: Ringgold, *We Flew Over the Bridge*, 175.

73 *I could understand feminism*: Flo Kennedy, interview by Jacqueline Ceballos, February 18, 1991, transcript, 9, Tully-Crenshaw Feminist Oral History Project, Schlesinger Library, Radcliffe Institute for Advanced Study, Cambridge, MA.

73 *Flo was constantly egging*: Author's interview with Michele Wallace.

74 *Stokely Carmichael, who then*: Author's interview with Heather Booth, October 15, 2019.

74 *I attended all four*: Flo Kennedy, *Color Me Flo: My Hard Life and Good Times* (1976; repr., New York: Simon & Schuster, 2017), 62.

75 *My own view is that SNCC*: Frances Beal, interview by Loretta J. Ross, March 18, 2005, transcript, 38, Voices of Feminism Oral History Project, Sophia Smith Collection, Smith College, Northampton, MA.

75 *When Black Power was announced*: Author's interview with Michele Wallace.

75 *One of the many reasons*: Author's interview with Heather Booth, October 15, 2019.

76 *By the time I moved*: Author's interview with Jo Freeman.

76n *The National Conference*: Alice Echols, *Daring to Be Bad: Radical Feminism in America, 1967–1975* (Minneapolis: University of Minnesota Press, 1989), 46–47.

76 *At the New Politics Conference*: Ti-Grace Atkinson, interview by Jacqueline Ceballos, 101–103; Ti-Grace Atkinson, *Amazon Odyssey* (New York: Links Books, 1974), 97.

77 *The people at this conference*: Author's interview with Jo Freeman.

77 *I went around to get*: Ti-Grace Atkinson, interview by Jacqueline Ceballos; Atkinson, *Amazon Odyssey*, 97.

77n *The original women's resolution*: Echols, *Daring to be Bad*, 48; Evans, *Personal Politics*, 198.

77 *We passed out all these*: Author's interview with Jo Freeman.

78 *Out of this caucus came*: Atkinson, *Amazon Odyssey*, 98.

13. Newsweek's Good Girls

79 *When* Newsweek *started in '33*: Author's interview with Lynn Povich, November 17, 2021.

79 *I worked on the school newspaper*: Nora Ephron, *I Remember Nothing: And Other Reflections* (New York: Vintage Books, 2010), 15.

80 *I graduated from Vassar*: Author's interview with Lynn Povich.

80 *I graduated from Radcliffe*: Author's interview with Lucy Howard, January 31, 2022.

81 *I knew I wanted to be*: Author's interview with Peter Goldman, February 16, 2022.

81 *The man who interviewed me*: Ephron, *I Remember Nothing*, 15.

81 *We'd get these bags*: Abigail Pogrebin, "How Do You Spell Ms.," *New York*, October 28, 2011.

82 Newsweek *was really fun*: Author's interview with Lynn Povich.

82 *Then there was the Elliott girl*: Author's interview with Lucy Howard.

82 *I was the Elliott girl*: Ephron, *I Remember Nothing*, 17.

82 *So, we sort of accepted this*: Author's interview with Lynn Povich.

82 *After a few months*: Ephron, *I Remember Nothing*, 19.

83 *When I arrived at* Newsweek: Author's interview with Susan Brownmiller.

83 *It was the first time*: Author's interview with Peter Goldman.

83 *In the mid-'60s*: Author's interview with Lynn Povich; Pogrebin, "How Do You Spell Ms."

84 *Some of the stuff*: Author's interview with Lucy Howard.

84 *Many guys looked at us*: Author's interview with Lynn Povich; Pogrebin, "How Do You Spell Ms."

14. NOW Swings into Action

85 *In 1961, I went to Alverno College*: Mary Jean Collins, interview by Noreen Connell, February 1992, transcript, 17, Tully-Crenshaw Feminist Oral History Project, Schlesinger Library, Radcliffe Institute for Advanced Study, Cambridge, MA; author's interview with Mary Jean Collins, May 29, 2020.

86 *The 1967 NOW convention*: Friedan, *It Changed My Life*, 104.

86 *In NOW at that time*: Aileen Clarke Hernandez, interviewed by Larry Crowe, session 1, tape 6, story 5.

86 *Alice Rossi, who was a sociologist*: Mary Jean Collins, interview by Noreen Connell, 18.

86 *The first rift in the movement*: Atkinson, *Amazon Odyssey*, 96.

86 *Vote on the Resolution*: "Minutes from the Second National Conference of NOW," National Organization for Women, https:/350fem.blogs.brynmawr.edu/1967/11/19/national-conference-of-now-minutes/.

87 *I must say, I thought*: Author's interview with Muriel Fox.

87 *A bunch of people*: Author's interview with Mary Jean Collins.

87 *Labor union women were among*: Author's interview with Muriel Fox.

87 *The unions did not want*: Aileen Clarke Hernandez, interviewed by Larry Crowe, session 1, tape 6, story 6.

88 *The organization limped out*: Mary Jean Collins, interview by Noreen Connell, 19.

88 *Two of our most important*: Muriel Fox, "How It Began: Betty Friedan and the Modern Women's Movement," speech, April 24, 2009, Elizabeth A. Sackler Center for Feminist Art, Brooklyn Museum, New York, NY, video, 1:36:10, https://www.brooklynmuseum.org/eascfa/video/videos/how-it-began-betty-friedan-and-the-modern-women-s-movement.

89 *People would file complaints*: Author's interview with Sonia Pressman Fuentes.

89 *I was chairman*: Marguerite Rawalt, interview by Verta A. Taylor, October 15, 1979, transcript, 40, Tully-Crenshaw Feminist Oral History Project, Schlesinger Library, Radcliffe Institute for Advanced Study, Cambridge, MA; "Minutes from the Second National Conference of NOW."

90 *There weren't very many women*: Mary Eastwood, interview by Muriel Fox.

90 *Sue Sellers was the ringleader*: Marguerite Rawalt, interview by Verta A. Taylor.

15. A Program for Radical Women

92 *Five thousand women*: Author's interview with Charlotte Bunch, April 13, 2021; Charlotte Bunch, *Passionate Politics: Essays, 1968–1986; Feminist Theory in Action* (New York: St. Martin's Press, 1987), 6.

92 *We knew that this demonstration*: Author's interview with Marilyn Webb, February 3, 2020.

93 *Most of the women*: Author's interview with Charlotte Bunch, April 13, 2021.

93 *We were between the ages*: Author's interview with Marilyn Webb, February 3, 2020.

93 *From the beginning we felt*: Shulamith Firestone, "The Women's Rights Movement in the U.S.: A New View," in *Notes from the First Year*, by New York Radical Women (New York: New York Radical Women, 1968).

93 *At our meeting on Sunday night*: Author's interview with Marilyn Webb, February 3, 2020; Marilyn Salzman Webb, "Towards a Radical Women's Movement," from the files of Marilyn Webb.

93 *I gave a speech*: Author's interview with Charlotte Bunch, April 13, 2021.

94 *We staged an actual funeral*: Firestone, "The Women's Rights Movement in the U.S."

94 *We were the radical-left*: Rosalyn Fraad Baxandall, interview by Jacqueline Ceballos, February 1991, transcript, 14, Tully-Crenshaw Feminist Oral History Project, Schlesinger Library, Radcliffe Institute for Advanced Study, Cambridge, MA.

94 *Finally, by way of*: Firestone, "The Women's Rights Movement in the U.S."

94 *The weekend of the*: Author's interview with Charlotte Bunch, April 13, 2021.

95 *We spent months*: Bunch, *Passionate Politics*, 6.

95 *I was a little bit skeptical*: Author's interview with Cathy Wilkerson, February 11, 2021.

95 *Most of us gradually changed*: Author's interview with Charlotte Bunch, April 13, 2021.

95 *We began teaching classes*: Author's interview with Marilyn Webb, February 3, 2020.

96 *The New York Radical Feminist*: Rosalyn Fraad Baxandall, interview by Jacqueline Ceballos.

96 *By sharing personal experiences*: Joy Press, "The Life and Death of a Radical Sisterhood," The Cut, *New York*, November 15, 2017.

96 *We were talking about sex*: Press, "The Life and Death of a Radical Sisterhood."

96 *I went to a meeting*: Author's interview with Susan Brownmiller.

97 *NOW was the first group*: Author's interview with Anselma Dell'Olio, July 6, 2020.

97 *Sheila Cronan and I*: Author's interview with Barbara Mehrhof, March 3, 2020.

98 *That article came at a time*: Author's interview with Muriel Fox.

99 *Ti-Grace Atkinson*: Author's interview with Muriel Fox.

99 *By June 1968*: Author's interview with Marilyn Webb, February 3, 2020

99 *They sent notice*: Author's interview with Jo Freeman.

99 *Kathie Sarahchild and Roxanne Dunbar*: Author's interview with Marilyn Webb, February 3, 2020.

16. Wimbledon—The Men Get All the Money

101 *I don't remember when*: Author's interview with Rosie Casals, March 30, 2022.

101 *I started Stanford in 1962*: Author's interview with Julie Heldman, March 19, 2022.

102 *I was one of the lucky*: Author's interview with Billie Jean King, March 16, 2022; Billie Jean King, *All In: An Autobiography* (New York: Alfred A. Knopf, 2021), 136–37.

103 *My first year in '66*: Author's interview with Rosie Casals.

103 *I was in Australia*: King, *All In*, 138.

103 *When Wimbledon went pro*: Author's interview with Julie Heldman, March 18, 2022.

103 *I quickly landed my first*: King, *All In*, 141.

104 *One thing that Billie Jean*: Author's interview with Rosie Casals.

104 *When we won Wimbledon*: Author's interview with Billie Jean King, March 16, 2022.

17. Colleges Desegregate—I Am Now a Living Relic

105 *Our guidance counselor thought*: Author's interview with Barbara Smith.

107 *I grew up in a family*: Author's interview with Linda Burnham; Linda Burnham, interview by Loretta J. Ross, March 18, 2005, transcript, Voices of Feminism Oral History Project, Sophia Smith Collection, Smith College, Northampton, MA.

108 *I was born in 1949*: Author's interview with Margo Okazawa-Rey.

109 *I graduated from Vassar*: Author's interview with Brenda Feigen, May 18, 2021.

18. Messing with Miss America

111 *It was out of that*: Robin Morgan, *Going Too Far: The Personal Chronicle of a Feminist* (New York: Random House, 1977), 62.

111 *The idea came out*: Carol Hanisch, "What Can Be Learned: A Critique of the Miss America Protest; The 1968 Classic with Some New Introductory Thoughts," https://carolhanisch .org/CHwritings/MissACritique.html.

112 *The pageant was chosen*: Morgan, *Going Too Far*, 64.

112 *No one threw herself*: Susan Brownmiller, *In Our Time: Memoir of a Revolution* (1999; repr., New York: Dell, 2000), 35–36.

112 *I was living with my boyfriend*: Author's interview with Judy Gumbo, October 16, 2019, and Judy Gumbo, *Yippie Girl: Exploits in Protest and Defeating the FBI* (New York: Three Rooms Press, 2022), 67.

113 *I can still remember*: Morgan, *Going Too Far*, 62–63.

113 *I'd been on tryout*: Press, "The Life and Death of a Radical Sisterhood."

114 *We planned the Freedom Trash Can*: Author's interview with Alix Kates Shulman, February 27, 2020.

114 *The bras were not burned*. Author's interview with Susan Brownmiller.

114 *I had my eyes and ears on*: Author's interview with Jacqueline Ceballos, June 24, 2020.

114 *Because the [radical women] cut*: Friedan, *It Changed My Life*, 138.

115 *We decided, in DC*: Author's interview with Marilyn Webb, February 3, 2020.

115 *The New York group*: Author's interview with Charlotte Bunch, April 13, 2021.

115 *We assembled in Union Square*: Press, "The Life and Death of a Radical Sisterhood."

115 *About ten buses lined up*: Author's interview with Jacqueline Ceballos.

115 *Women came from as far away*: Morgan, *Going Too Far*, 64.

115 *Instead of running a pig*: Author's interview with Judy Gumbo.

116 *There were naysayers*: Press, "The Life and Death of a Radical Sisterhood."

116 *I wrote a biography*: Author's interview with Alix Kates Shulman.

116 *I attended the Atlantic City*: Kennedy, *Color Me Flo*, 62.

117 *I offered to pay for tickets*: Press, "The Life and Death of a Radical Sisterhood."

117 *Then when it came time*: Author's interview with Jacqueline Ceballos.

117 *The new Miss America*: "Up Against the Wall Miss America," Newsreel Films, Roz Payne Sixties Archive, https://rozsixties.unl.edu/items/show/836.

117 *At night, an "inside squad"*: Morgan, *Going Too Far*, 65.

117 *I was one of the four*: Press, "The Life and Death of a Radical Sisterhood."

117 *Although the television cameras*: Author's interview with Alix Kates Shulman.

117 *When I was growing up*: Press, "The Life and Death of a Radical Sisterhood."

118 *Shortly before ten Saturday night*: "Up Against the Wall Miss America."

118 *I watched the end*: Press, "The Life and Death of a Radical Sisterhood."

118 *There's an untold story*: Robin Morgan, *Saturday's Child: A Memoir* (New York: W. W. Norton, 2001), 262.

118 *Everybody knew about NOW*: Author's interview with Barbara Mehrhof.

118 *The radical feminist protest*: Michele Wallace, *Dark Designs and Visual Culture* (Durham, NC: Duke University Press, 2004), 102.

119 *Bras were big, overbuilt*: Author's interview with Sallie Bingham, February 20, 2020.

119 *People can laugh about*: Frances Beal, interview by Loretta J. Ross, 42.

120 *The pageant has been called*: Press, "The Life and Death of a Radical Sisterhood"; Morgan, *Going Too Far*, 62.

120n *All these groups:* Author's interview with Robin Morgan.

19. The Indomitable Shirley Chisholm

121 *By 1964 there was a vacancy*: Shirley Chisholm, *Unbought and Unbossed*, ed. Scott Simpson, expanded 40th anniversary ed. (Washington, DC: Take Root Media, 2010), 47.

122 *Starting in February 1968*: Transcript of *Chisholm '72: Unbought & Unbossed*, a documentary produced and directed by Shola Lynch (Realside Productions, 2004), in Shirley Chisholm '72 Collection, Archives & Special Collections, Brooklyn College Library; Chisholm, *Unbought and Unbossed*, 85.

122 *She ran a door-to-door campaign*: Transcript of *Chisholm '72*.

122 *Her primary opponent*: Author's interview with Barbara Winslow, December 16, 2019.

123 *When they counted the primary votes*: Chisholm, *Unbought and Unbossed*, 87.

123 *James Farmer was tall and handsome*: Author's interview with Barbara Winslow.

123 *Farmer's campaign was well oiled*: Chisholm, *Unbought and Unbossed*, 88.

124 *Something like 60 to 75 percent*: Author's interview with Barbara Winslow.

125 *So I went and contacted*: Transcript of *Chisholm '72*; Chisholm, *Unbought and Unbossed*, 92.

125 *Another thing that was interesting*: Transcript of *Chisholm '72*.

125 *I beat him*: Chisholm, *Unbought and Unbossed*, 94.

1. Take Her Off the Stage and Fuck Her

130 *When we got to the rally*: Author's interview with Marilyn Webb, February 3, 2020.

130 *Dave Dellinger introduces the rally*: Ellen Willis, "Up from Radicalism: A Feminist Journal," in *The Essential Ellen Willis*, ed. Nona Willis Aronowitz (Minneapolis: University of Minnesota Press, 2014).

130 *It was cold and the tent*: Author's interview with Marilyn Webb, February 3, 2020.

130 *What I remember very distinctly*: Author's interview with Paul Lauter, February 12, 2021.

131 *Marilyn spoke kind of haltingly*: Author's interview with Derek Shearer, February 8, 2020.

131 *I was terrified*: Author's interview with Marilyn Webb, February 3, 2020.

131 *When Marilyn said something*: Author's interview with Barbara Mehrhof.

131 *Her speech is just fairly*: Willis, "Up from Radicalism."

132 *It was very loud*: Author's interview with Paul Lauter.

132 *My memory of it*: Author's interview with Lee Webb.

132 *Now, I think, obviously*: Author's interview with Cathy Wilkerson; Cathy Wilkerson, *Flying Close to the Sun: My Life and Times as a Weatherman* (New York: Seven Stories Press, 2007), 243.

132 *I think there was a little bit*: Author's interview with Paul Lauter.

132 *These were the people*: Author's interview with Barbara Mehrhof.

133 *The guys in the front rows*: Author's interview with Marilyn Webb, February 3, 2020.

133 *When Shulamith Firestone, who*: Willis, "Up from Radicalism."

133 *Then Dave Dellinger came over*: Author's interview with Marilyn Webb, February 3, 2020.

133 *I am not sure*: Author's interview with Paul Lauter.

134 *I was standing there*: Author's interview with Marilyn Webb, February 3, 2020.

134n *Five months later:* Author's interview with David Harris, March 2013.

134 *Marilyn's description of me*: Author's interview with Jonathan Lerner, November 8, 2018.

135 *I was not at Marilyn's speech*: Author's interview with Cathy Wilkerson.

135n *In response to the*: Ward Churchill and Jim Vander Wall, *The COINTELPRO Papers: Documents from the FBI's Secret Wars Against Dissent in the United States*, 2nd ed. (Cambridge, MA: South End Press, 2002).

135 *Years later I was*: Author's interview with Marilyn Webb, February 3, 2020.

2. Mrs. Chisholm Goes to Washington

136 *She went to Congress*: Author's interview with Barbara Winslow.

137 *When I got there*: Transcript of *Chisholm '72*.

137 *She is just extraordinarily*: Transcript of *Chisholm '72*.

137 *I had [American] Indians on the staff*: Transcript of *Chisholm '72*.

137 *She's a lady*: Transcript of *Chisholm '72*.

137 *My staff loved the way*: Transcript of *Chisholm '72*.

138 *The famous story*: Author's interview with Barbara Winslow.

138 *The first big event*: Chisholm, *Unbought and Unbossed*, 99.

139 *I walked right down*: Transcript of *Chisholm '72*; Chisholm, *Unbought and Unbossed*, 100.

139 *Members of Congress made*: Author's interview with Barbara Winslow.

139 *One day Brock Adams*: Transcript of *Chisholm '72*; Chisholm, *Unbought and Unbossed*, 110.

140 *She decided to devote*: Barbara Winslow, *Shirley Chisholm: Catalyst for Change* (New York: Routledge, 2018), 80.

3. Shattering the Abortion Silence

141 *Women's liberation put*: Author's interview with Barbara Mehrhof, March 3, 2020.

142 *On the morning of the*: Brownmiller, *In Our Time*, 107.

142 *At the hearing, I was nervous*: Willis, "Up from Radicalism."

142 *Joyce Ravitz began to declaim*: Brownmiller, *In Our Time*, 107.

142 *They locked us out*: Rosalyn Fraad Baxandall, interview by Jaqueline Cebellos.

142 *Shulie had just*: Author's interview with Barbara Mehrhof.

143 *We decided to hold our own*: Willis, "Up from Radicalism."

143 *When Redstockings did their first*: Author's interview with Susan Brownmiller.

143 *We all wore dresses*: Author's interview with Barbara Mehrhof.

143 *I was not a testifier*: Author's interview with Alix Kates Shulman.

144 *I went to cover*: Gloria Steinem, interview by Evelyn C. White, September 28, 2007, transcript, 25, Voices of Feminism Oral History Project, Sophia Smith Collection, Smith College, Northampton, MA.

145 *It was fantastic*: Author's interview with Alix Kates Shulman.

145 *I became pregnant*: Speaker 1, Redstockings Abortion Speak-Out, "Found at Last, 1994: Full Audio of the First Abortion Speakout—1969," Redstockings, audio recording, 00.03, http://redstockings.org/index.php/main/taking-stock#Audio1969.

146 *The reason we have the laws*: Speaker 2, Redstockings Abortion Speak-Out, 04:54.

146 *You are really alone*: Speaker 4, Redstockings Abortion Speak-Out, 15:36.

147 *I was just so transformed*: Gloria Steinem, interview by Evelyn C. White.

147 *The Redstockings abortion speak-out*: Brownmiller, *In Our Time*, 109.

4. Slave of a Slave—Black Women's Liberation

148 *Jim Forman, the former executive*: Author's interview with Frances Beal.

148n *Published in March 1968*: Eldridge Cleaver, *Soul on Ice* (New York: Dell, 1968).

149 *After the student revolt*: Author's interview with Brian Flanagan, February 13, 2022.

149 *He was the minister*: Author's interview with Brian Flanagan.

150 *Women in the Panthers*: Author's interview with Ericka Huggins, August 26, 2021.

151 *People went crazy*: Author's interview with Michele Wallace.

151 *Statement on Birth Control*: This letter, which was written and distributed in September 1968, was published in *Sisterhood Is Powerful: An Anthology of Writings from the Women's Liberation Movement*, ed. Robin Morgan (New York: Vintage Books, 1970), 360. The working papers of the Pat Robinson Group (another name for the Mount Vernon women's group) were published in *The Black Woman: An Anthology*, ed. Toni Cade Bambara (1970; repr., New York: Washington Square Press, 2005), 239.

151n *Started in 1960*: Rosalyn Baxandall, "Re-Visioning the Women's Liberation Movement's Narrative: Early Second Wave African American Feminists," *Feminist Studies* 27, no. 1 (Spring 2001): 225–45.

152 *As women got together*: Frances Beal, interview by Loretta J. Ross, 37; author's interview with Frances Beal.

154 *Unfortunately, there seems to be*: Frances M. Beal, "Double Jeopardy: To Be Black and Female," first issued in a pamphlet in 1969, and then published in two collections, *The Black Woman* (ed. Toni Cade Bambara) and *Sisterhood Is Powerful* (ed. Robin Morgan).

154 *I didn't know anything*: Author's interview with Margo Jefferson.

154 *The Black Women's Caucus*: Linda Burnham, interview by Loretta J. Ross, 20.

155 *And so the concept*: Author's interview with Frances Beal.

155 *What set us apart*: Author's interview with Margo Jefferson.

155 *And then a number of women*: Author's interview with Frances Beal.

156 *. . . perhaps the most outlandish act*: Beal, "Double Jeopardy."

156 *About six months after forming*: Author's interview with Frances Beal; Frances Beal, interview by Loretta J. Ross, 50.

156n *Involuntary and coerced sterilization*: For information on forced sterilization, see: Felicia Kornbluh, *A Woman's Life Is a Human Life: My Mother, Our Neighbor, and the Journey from Reproductive Rights to Reproductive Justice* (New York: Grove Press, 2023); Jennifer Nelson, *Women of Color and the Reproductive Rights Movement* (New York: New York

University Press, 2003); Dorothy Roberts, *Killing the Black Body: Race, Reproduction, and the Meaning of Liberty* (1997; repr., New York: Vintage Books, 2017); Andrea Smith, *Conquest: Sexual Violence and American Indian Genocide* (2005; repr., Durham, NC: Duke University Press, 2015).

157 *The Third World Women's Alliance*: Linda Burnham, interview by Loretta J. Ross.

5. Our Bodies, Ourselves

158 *In May of 1969*: Author's interview with Nancy Miriam Hawley.

158 *Emmanuel College was run by*: Author's interview with Paula Doress-Worters, October 30, 2019.

159 *During the conference*: Author's interview with Nancy Miriam Hawley.

159 *We met in a huge room*: Author's interview with Paula Doress-Worters.

159 *I led a workshop called*: Author's interview with Nancy Miriam Hawley.

160 *There were a lot of talks*: Author's interview with Paula Doress-Worters.

160 *After the workshop*: Author's interview with Nancy Miriam Hawley.

160 *I had the best doctors*: Author's interview with Jane Pincus, November 15, 2019.

161 *I was pregnant*: Author's interview with Norma Swenson, October 30, 2019.

161 *When Gina was born*: Author's interview with Nancy Miriam Hawley.

162 *I was born in a hospital:* Author's interview with Louise "Mama Bear" Herne.

162 *Our grandmother was a midwife:* Author's interview with Beverly Kiohawiton Cook, October 1, 2021.

162 *I grew up here:* Author's interview with Jeanne Shenandoah, September 15, 2021.

162 *When I was in nursing school:* Author's interview with Beverly Kiohawiton Cook.

163 *We went to different:* Author's interview with Jeanne Shenandoah.

164 *After Hannah was born*: Author's interview with Paula Doress-Worters.

164 *We wrote up something*: Author's interview with Jane Pincus.

164 *So in the lounges at MIT*: Author's interview with Nancy Miriam Hawley.

164 *The first class was about sexuality*: Author's interview with Jane Pincus.

164 *There was this huge drawing*: Author's interview with Joan Ditzion.

165 *The revolution had been going on*: Author's interview with Nancy Miriam Hawley.

165 *The New England Free Press guys*: Author's interview with Jane Pincus.

165 *It truly was collectively written*: Author's interview with Joan Ditzion.

165 *In December of 1970*: Author's interview with Nancy Miriam Hawley.

166 *My job was sending out copies*: Author's interview with Jane Pincus.

167 *I was just amazed*: Author's interview with Byllye Avery, September 22, 2021.

167n *Founded by Marilyn Webb*: Author's interview with Marilyn Webb, February 3, 2020.

167 *I was noticing the demands*: Author's interview with Demita Frazier, August 4, 2021.

168 *We also read*: Author's interview with Torie Osborn.

168 *It was as though*: Author's interview with Sallie Bingham.

169 Our Bodies, Ourselves *was just so*: Author's interview with Barbara Smith.

6. NOW Lesbians Come Out

170 *We kind of knew*: Jacqueline Ceballos, interview by Mary Jean Tully, March 17, 1992, transcript, 184, Tully-Crenshaw Feminist Oral History Project, Schlesinger Library, Radcliffe Institute for Advanced Study, Cambridge, MA.

170 *I went to a meeting*: Dolores Alexander, interview by Kelly Anderson, 17.

171 *I got a scholarship at NYU*: Author's interview with Rita Mae Brown, December 5, 2022.

171 *Rita Mae never stopped*: Dolores Alexander, interview by Kelly Anderson, 17.

171 *I thought, Wow, wow, wow!*: Barbara J. Love, interview by Kelly Anderson, March 6, 2008, transcript, 16, Voices of Feminism Oral History Project, Sophia Smith Collection, Smith College, Northampton, MA.

171 *She was this beautiful young girl*: Jacqueline Ceballos, interview by Mary Jean Tully, 185.

171 *The problem was that*: Judith V. Branzburg, *The Liberation of Ivy Bottini: A Memoir of Love and Activism* (Fairfield, CA: Bink Books, 2018), 105.

172 *It was a question*: Author's interview with Muriel Fox.

172 *I figured why don't you*: Author's interview with Rita Mae Brown.

172 *Rita Mae had worked for me*: Author's interview with Anselma Dell'Olio.

172 *Betty called me a redneck*: Author's interview with Rita Mae Brown.

173 *From the beginning*: Rosalyn Fraad Baxandall, interview by Jacqueline Ceballos, 44.

173 *What can I say?*: Author's interview with Jacqueline Ceballos; Jacqueline Ceballos, interview by Mary Jean Tully, 186, 194.

173 *Betty was awful about it*: Dolores Alexander, interview by Kelly Anderson, 19.

173 *I was considered square*: Betty Friedan, "Up from the Kitchen Floor," *New York Times Magazine*, March 4, 1973.

174n *At the First Congress*: Rachel Shteir, *Betty Friedan: Magnificent Disrupter* (New Haven, CT: Yale University Press, 2023), 143–45.

174 *Over the months*: Dolores Alexander, interview by Kelly Anderson, 20.

174 *I decided it was time*: Branzburg, *The Liberation of Ivy Bottini*, 106.

174 *Ivy Bottini, a mother*: Rita Mae Brown, *Rita Will: Memoir of a Literary Rabble Rouser* (New York: Bantam Books, 1997), 227.

174 *In the summer of 1969*: Branzburg, *The Liberation of Ivy Bottini*, 106.

175 *Ivy was kind of matronly*: Barbara J. Love, interview by Kelly Anderson, 9.

175 *When I opened the NOW*: Branzburg, *The Liberation of Ivy Bottini*.

7. Code-Name Jane

177 *By 1968, there were too many*: Author's interview with Heather Booth, October 26, 2018.

177 *I had a friend in college*: Author's interview with Laura Kaplan, October 30, 2018.

178 *I was a mom with four children*: Author's interview with Martha Scott, November 1, 2018.

178 *First, we had counselor-training*: Author's interview with Laura Kaplan.

178 *The way it worked is you*: Author's interview with Martha Scott.

178 *We had "the front" and then*: Author's interview with Laura Kaplan.

179 *I lived in a big house*: Author's interview with Martha Scott.

179 *I had gone to the University*: Author's interview with Alice Fox, November 1, 2018.

180 *After I had joined the Service*: Author's interview with Martha Scott.

180 *As the service evolved*: Author's interview with Judith Arcana, October 21, 2018.

180 *It was an apprenticeship*: Author's interview with Martha Scott.

181 *Then in 1971, he disappeared*: Author's interview with Judith Arcana.

181 *Once he was gone, we dropped*: Author's interview with Laura Kaplan.

181 *When it was just the group*: Author's interview with Martha Scott.

181 *We had these people's lives*: Author's interview with Judith Arcana.

181 *There was a real sense*: Author's interview with Laura Kaplan.

8. The Next Great Moment in History Is Theirs

182 *I got a job at the* Village Voice: Author's interview with Vivian Gornick, February 10, 2022.

183 *It was like a moment of:* Author's interview with Vivian Gornick.

184 *After the article was published:* Author's interview with Vivian Gornick.

9. The Boston Tea Party of Women's Health

185 *I first learned about the dangers:* Jewish Women's Archive, "Barbara Seaman," The Feminist Revolution, https://jwa.org/feminism/seaman-barbara.

186 *When I was in Chicago:* Author's interview with Marilyn Webb, February 3, 2020.

186 *In about 1950:* Barbara Seaman, "The Pill and I: 40 Years On, the Relationship Remains Wary," *New York Times,* June 25, 2000.

186 *One of the early demonstrations:* Author's interview with Alice Wolfson, April 22, 2020; Alice Wolfson, "Clenched Fist, Open Heart," in *The Feminist Memoir Project: Voices from Women's Liberation,* ed. Rachel Blau DuPlessis and Ann Barr Snitow (1998; repr., New Brunswick, NJ: Rutgers University Press, 2007).

187 *I was pretty much:* Author's interview with Marilyn Webb, February 3, 2020.

187 *In those days:* Author's interview with Alice Wolfson.

187 *We sat there for a bunch:* Author's interview with Marilyn Webb, February 3, 2020.

187 *As the testimony unfolded:* Wolfson, "Clenched Fist, Open Heart."

188 *One by one, different women:* Author's interview with Jan Fenty, February 11, 2020.

188 *The cameras turned to us:* Author's interview with Alice Wolfson.

188 *They ushered us out:* Author's interview with Marilyn Webb, February 3, 2020.

188 *I remember meeting the next day:* Author's interview with Jan Fenty.

188 *Of all the witnesses:* Seaman, "The Pill and I."

189 *The demonstrations, with national:* Wolfson, "Clenched Fist, Open Heart," 275.

189 *Alice Wolfson and her colleagues:* Seaman, "The Pill and I."

10. Goodbye to All That

190 *So there I was one day:* Author's interview with Robin Morgan.

191 *This literally nauseated me:* Author's interview with Robin Morgan.

192 *You have to remember:* Author's interview with Robin Morgan.

193 *So we published it:* Author's interview with Robin Morgan.

193 *I recall Stew [Albert] storming:* Gumbo, *Yippie Girl,* 187.

194 *I remember I was living:* Author's interview with Michael Kazin, January 31, 2014.

194 *I could never have imagined:* Author's interview with Robin Morgan.

11. Newsweek Girls Revolt

195 *We did it in the ladies' room:* Author's interview with Lynn Povich; Lynn Povich, *The Good Girls Revolt: How the Women of* Newsweek *Sued Their Bosses and Changed the Workplace* (New York: PublicAffairs, 2012), 80.

196 *I was assistant legal director:* MAKERS, "Eleanor Holmes Norton: The *Newsweek* Lawsuit," March 20, 2013, documentary video, 00:02:17, https://www.youtube.com/watch?v=y0ae1v1JrkY; author's interview with Eleanor Holmes Norton.

196 *Eleanor was perfect for us:* Author's interview with Lynn Povich; Povich, *The Good Girls Revolt,* 85.

197 *I must say it took some meetings*: Author's interview with Eleanor Holmes Norton.

197 *Then we opened it up*: Author's interview with Lynn Povich.

197 *These women understood*: Author's interview with Eleanor Holmes Norton.

198 *There were five or six*: Author's interview with Lynn Povich.

198 *There was a feeling*: Diane Camper, as quoted in Povich, *The Good Girls Revolt*, 76.

198 *There were two Black women*: Author's interview with Lynn Povich.

198 *In March 1970,* Newsweek *ran*: Osborn Elliott, *The World of Oz* (New York: Viking, 1980), 144.

199 *I was the only woman writer*: Author's interview with Lynn Povich.

199 *Helen had come up in an era*: Author's interview with Peter Goldman.

199 *The moment that* Newsweek *said*: Author's interview with Lynn Povich.

200 *We wanted it to be a surprise*: Author's interview with Lucy Howard.

200 *The women sent their letter*: Elliott, *The World of Oz*, 146.

201 *I was away at the time*: Katharine Graham, *Personal History* (1997; repr., New York: Vintage Books, 1998), 425.

201 *When we went into the office*: Author's interview with Lucy Howard.

201 *Some of the correspondents*: Povich, *The Good Girls Revolt*, 99.

201 *My attitude was, go for it*: Author's interview with Peter Goldman; Povich, *The Good Girls Revolt*, 100.

202 *When I went in to meet*: Author's interview with Eleanor Holmes Norton.

202 *A couple of days after*: Elliott, *The World of Oz*, 147.

202 Newsweek *eventually reached out*: Author's interview with Eleanor Holmes Norton.

203 *Two months after we filed*: Povich, *The Good Girls Revolt*, 9.

12. Betty's Last Stand

204 *I was going to step down*: Friedan, *It Changed My Life*, 176.

204 *I got asked by members*: Aileen Clarke Hernandez, interviewed by Larry Crowe, session 1, tape 6, story 2.

205 *It was a legitimate change*: Author's interview with Muriel Fox.

205 *One of my goals*: Aileen Clarke Hernandez, interviewed by Larry Crowe, session 1, tape 6, story 2.

205 *I joined NOW after I went*: Brenda Feigen, *Not One of the Boys: Living Life as a Feminist* (New York: Alfred A. Knopf, 2000), 27.

206 *The media was still treating*: Friedan, *It Changed My Life*, 177.

206 *At the end of our conference*: Author's interview with Muriel Fox.

206 *Our Movement toward true equality*: Betty Friedan, "Call to Women's Strike for Equality," in *It Changed My Life*, 180.

207 *This was March 31*: Author's interview with Mary Jean Collins.

207 *I was told that I spoke*: Friedan, *It Changed My Life*, 178.

13. Shut Out of Academia

208 *I had always wanted to be a professor*: Bernice Sandler, interview by Julia Lamber and Jean Robinson, June 28, 2004, transcript, 4–6, Papers of Bernice Resnick Sandler, Schlesinger Library, Radcliffe Institute for Advanced Study, Cambridge, MA.

209 *One of the first times*: Edith Green, interview by Shirley Tanzer, March 18, 1980, 101,

included with other transcripts of oral history interviews with her, 1979–1980, in Green, Edith, folder 11, box II:6, Transcripts, Former Members of Congress, Inc., Oral History Interviews.

210 *I called the Office*: Bernice Sandler, interview by Julia Lamber and Jean Robinson, 6–7, 12–15, 66–67.

211 *I was also keenly aware*: Edith Green, interview by Shirley Tanzer, 102.

211 *I started in '69*: Bernice Sandler, interview by Julia Lamber and Jean Robinson, 17–18, 68.

212 *So, I'm filing complaints like mad*: Bernice Sandler, interview by Julia Lamber and Jean Robinson, 20.

212 *We started a series of hearings*: Edith Green, interview by Shirley Tanzer, 102.

213 *When Edith Green held her hearings*: Bernice Sandler, interview by Julia Lamber and Jean Robinson, 30.

213 *The subcommittee will come to order*: United States Congress House Committee on Education and Labor Special Subcommittee on Education. *Discrimination Against Women: Hearings Before the Special Subcommittee on Education of the Committee on Education and Labor, House of Representatives, Ninety-First Congress, Second Session, on Section 805 of H.R. 16098.* Washington, DC: US Government Printing Office, 1970. https://catalog .hathitrust.org/Record/011394695.

216 *In 1970, when Congress begins hearings*: Author's interview with Susan Rennie, April 6, 2021.

14. Congress Hears the ERA

217 *Shortly after I assumed*: Author's interview with Brenda Feigen; Feigen, *Not One of the Boys*, 28.

218 *I think it is fair to say*: United States Congress Senate Committee on the Judiciary Subcommittee on Constitutional Amendments. *The "Equal Rights" Amendment: Hearings Before the Subcommittee on Constitutional Amendments of the Committee on the Judiciary, United States Senate, Ninety-first Congress, Second Session, on S.J. Res. 61 to Amend the Constitution So as to Provide Equal Rights for Men and Women. May 5, 6, and 7, 1970.* Washington, DC: US Government Printing Office, 1970. https://babel.hathitrust.org /cgi/pt?id=uc1.$b643809&view=1up&seq=7.

219 *I reviewed the transcripts*: Author's interview with Brenda Feigen.

219 *My name is Aileen Hernandez:* Senate ERA hearing, May 5, 1970.

219 *I was young, just twenty-six*: Author's interview with Brenda Feigen; Feigen, *Not One of the Boys*, 31.

219 *My name is Brenda Feigen Fasteau:* Senate ERA hearing, May 5, 1970.

15. New York Legalizes Abortion

222 *I graduated from UC Berkeley:* Author's interview with Nancy Stearns, October 21, 2019.

223 *Nancy Stearns was "ready":* Brownmiller, *In Our Time*, 110.

223 *The summer of '69*: Author's interview with Nancy Stearns.

223 *Stearns proposed that*: Author's interview with Susan Brownmiller.

224 *At that point there had been*: Author's interview with Nancy Stearns.

225 *Stearns enlisted four more*: Brownmiller, *In Our Time*, 112.

225 *The* Abramowicz *case*: Diane Schulder and Florynce Kennedy, *Abortion Rap* (New York: McGraw-Hill, 1971), 92.

225 *We packed the Southern District*: Author's interview with Nancy Stearns.

226   *Under the Fourteenth Amendment*: Schulder and Kennedy, *Abortion Rap*, 208.

226   *I joined the legal team*: Author's interview with Emily Goodman, October 3, 2019.

226   *The lawyers for the women's suit*: Author's interview with Susan Brownmiller; Brownmiller, *In Our Time*, 112.

227   *The all-woman lawyer team*: Flo Kennedy, *Pathology of Oppression*, unpublished manuscript, 200; *Pathology of Oppression*, 17.14–18.2, Papers of Florynce Kennedy, 1915–2004, Schlesinger Library, Radcliffe Institute for Advanced Study, Cambridge, MA.

227   *The following testimony*: Schulder and Kennedy, *Abortion Rap*, 20.

228   *A successful court case*: "An Abortion Rights Champion of the 1970s on Life Before and After Roe," *The Daily*, podcast, hosted by Sabrina Tavernise, July 1, 2022, https://www .nytimes.com/2022/07/01/podcasts/the-daily/abortion-rights-nancy-stearns-roe.html.

228   *It was not until New York*: Schulder and Kennedy, *Abortion Rap*, 178–79.

229   *A week before the Cook*: Brownmiller, *In Our Time*, 114.

230   *The new law mooted out*: Author's interview with Emily Goodman.

231   *I started working closely*: Author's interview with Nancy Stearns, "An Abortion Rights Champion of the 1970s on Life Before and After Roe" (podcast).

231n *After the new law went into effect*: David Harris, Donna O'Hare, Jean Pakter, and Frieda G. Nelson, "Legal Abortion, 1970–1971—The New York City Experience," *American Journal of Public Health* 63, no. 5 (May 1973): 409–18.

232   *I may have been one*: Author's interview with Elizabeth Spahn.

232n *The lawsuit argued that*: Greenhouse and Siegel, eds., *Before* Roe v. Wade*: Voices That Shaped the Abortion Debate Before the Supreme Court's Ruling*, 177.

232n *Spahn was in the first*: Anne Gardiner Perkins, *Yale Needs Women: How the First Group of Girls Rewrote the Rules of an Ivy League Giant* (Naperville, IL: Sourcebooks, 2019), 38.

232   *I heard about the case:* Author's interview with Nancy Stearns, "An Abortion Rights Champion."

233   *I took comfort in the knowledge*: Sarah Weddington, *A Question of Choice*, 40th anniversary edition, revised and updated (New York: Feminist Press at the City University of New York, 2013), 49.

233   *In January 1970, a friend*: Author's interview with Susan Brownmiller.

233   *She had never finished*: Weddington, *A Question of Choice*, 57.

234   *The main argument was that*: Linda Coffee, interview by Patricia Duke, April 17, 1973, transcript, 5, Baylor University Institute for Oral History, Waco, TX.

234   *On March 2, 1970, Linda and I*: Weddington, *A Question of Choice*, 57.

16. We Are Your Worst Nightmare, Your Best Fantasy

235   *The Second Congress to Unite Women*: Karla Jay, *Tales of the Lavender Menace: A Memoir of Liberation* (New York: Basic Books, 1999), 143.

235   *The organizers of the second congress*: Brown, *Rita Will*, 236; author's interview with Rita Mae Brown.

235   *What happened was we had our*: Martha Shelley, interview by Kelly Anderson, October 12, 2003, transcript, 42, Voices of Feminism Oral History Project, Sophia Smith Collection, Smith College, Northampton, MA.

236   *I was planted in the middle*: Jay, *Tales of the Lavender Menace*, 143.

236   *We ran up and grabbed*: Martha Shelley, interview by Kelly Anderson, 41–42.

236   *I said, "There wasn't much light"*: Author's interview with Rita Mae Brown.

237 *They then led a speak-out*: Author's interview with Phyllis Chesler, December 2, 2019; Phyllis Chesler, *A Politically Incorrect Feminist: Creating a Movement with Bitches, Lunatics, Dykes, Prodigies, Warriors, and Wonder Women* (New York: St. Martin's Press, 2018), 64.
237 *When they rushed the stage*: Author's interview with Anselma Dell'Olio.
237 *Our position paper*: Brown, *Rita Will*, 236.
237 *By virtue of being brought up*: Radicalesbians, "The Woman-Identified Woman," 3, Duke University Libraries, Sallie Bingham Center for Women's History & Culture, Women's Liberation Movement Print Culture.
238 *"Women-Identified Woman" became*: Jay, *Tales of the Lavender Menace*, 141.
238 *Only women can give*: Radicalesbians, "The Woman-Identified Woman," 3–4.
238 *Though the manifesto was*: Jay, *Tales of the Lavender Menace*, 141.
238 *Many people said*: Author's interview with Muriel Fox.
238 *The congress shot me up*: Brown, *Rita Will*, 237.
239 *I call it the Congress*: Author's interview with Susan Brownmiller; Brownmiller, *In Our Time*, 98.
239 *The Chinese Cultural Revolution*: Author's interview with Phyllis Chesler.
239 *My accusers, some of whom*: Author's interview with Susan Brownmiller; Brownmiller, *In Our Time*, 98.

17. The Whitney Isn't With-It

240 *It was not until 1970*: Ringgold, *We Flew Over the Bridge*, 174; Faith Ringgold, interview by Doloris Holmes, 1972, transcript, Art World in Turmoil Oral History Project, Archives of American Art, Smithsonian Institution, Washington, DC.
241 *In the fall of 1969*: Wallace, *Dark Designs and Visual Culture*, 103; author's interview with Michele Wallace.
241 *I first met Faith Ringgold*: Lucy R. Lippard, "Hot from Her Soul: Faith Ringgold's Art Activism," in *Faith Ringgold: American People*, ed. Massimiliano Gioni and Gary Carrion-Murayari (New York: Phaidon Press, in association with the New Museum, New York, 2022), 10.
241 *So the Ad Hoc committee*: Author's interview with Michele Wallace.
242 *The percentage of women artists*: Author's interview with Lucy Lippard, February 18, 2020.
242 *I wrote from WSABAL to the Whitney*: Author's interview with Michele Wallace.
242 *[Betye] Saar and [Barbara] Chase-Riboud*: Ringgold, *We Flew Over the Bridge*, 179.
242n *In 1969, only 8 of the 143*: Lucy R. Lippard, *From the Center: Feminist Essays on Women's Art* (New York: Dutton, 1976), 29.
242 *There were whistles*: Author's interview with Michele Wallace.
243 *The women came toward*: Ringgold, *We Flew Over the Bridge*, 180.
243 *We picketed every Saturday*: Author's interview with Lucy Lippard.
244 *We would go into the museums*: Author's interview with Michele Wallace.
244 *We really went at MoMA*: Author's interview with Lucy Lippard.
244 *We had nothing to lose*: Author's interview with Lynn Hershman Leeson, February 5, 2021.
244 *The women's art movement*: Author's interview with Michele Wallace.
244 *One of the things that grew*: Author's interview with Harmony Hammond, May 6, 2020.
244 *A Women's Art Registry*: Lippard, *From the Center*, 37.

18. An Idea Whose Time Has Come

245 *The ERA simply stated*: Branzburg, *The Liberation of Ivy Bottini*, 119.

246 *When I went to Hale Boggs*: Martha W. Griffiths, interview by Fern S. Ingersoll, October 29, 1979, 81; October 30, 1979, 108, 111.

248 *I felt that I was going to win*: Martha W. Griffiths, interview by Fern S. Ingersoll, October 29, 1979, 88.

249 *Another one of our significant actions*: Branzburg, *The Liberation of Ivy Bottini*, 120–21.

249 *We didn't have any trouble*: Author's interview with Jacqueline Ceballos.

249 *As I looked up*: Branzburg, *The Liberation of Ivy Bottini*, 121.

249 *Then they raised their fists*: Branzburg, *The Liberation of Ivy Bottini*, 120–21.

250 *Bella Abzug was running*: Author's interview with Jacqueline Ceballos.

250 *When I moved to New York*: Author's interview with Sherrye Henry, March 11, 2022.

251 *One of our big issues*: Author's interview with Muriel Fox.

251 *One evening, soon after*: Author's interview Sherrye Henry.

252 *Another cause we adopted*: Author's interview with Muriel Fox.

253 *NOW fought this*: Author's interview with Muriel Fox.

19. Don't Iron While the Strike Is Hot—Women's Strike for Equality

254 *The August 26 Women's Strike*: Branzburg, *The Liberation of Ivy Bottini*, 122.

255 *We didn't know whether*: Author's interview with Alix Kates Shulman.

255 *We didn't even know*: Author's interview with Mary Jean Collins.

256 *It started at Columbus Circle*: Author's interview with Alix Kates Shulman, which included Shulman's reading from pages 288 to 289 of her book *Burning Questions: A Novel* (1978).

256 *We demonstrated all morning*: Author's interview with Jacqueline Ceballos.

257 *I joined Pat Lawrence and Marion Gannet*: "Carole De Saram," Veteran Feminists of America, https://www.veteranfeministsofamerica.org/legacy/Carole_DeSaram.htm.

257 *Carole De Saram, who was up*: Author's interview with Jacqueline Ceballos.

257 *The police tried to stop us*: "Carole De Saram."

257 *Mayor Lindsay wouldn't close*: Friedan, "Up from the Kitchen Floor."

258 *There were women like Dale Williams*: Author's interview with Jacqueline Ceballos.

258 *Redstockings and the feminists*: Author's interview with Alix Kates Shulman, which included Shulman's reading from pages 288 to 289 of her *Burning Questions: A Novel* (1978).

259 *It was amazing when I watched*: Author's interview with Brenda Feigen.

259 *I mean it was wall to wall*: Author's interview with Howardena Pindell, December 27, 2020.

259 *I was there and it was thrilling*: Author's interview with Vivian Gornick.

259 *Gloria and I decided*: Author's interview with Brenda Feigen.

259 *On the sidewalks*: Author's interview with Alix Kates Shulman, which included Shulman's reading from pages 288 to 289 of her *Burning Questions: A Novel* (1978).

260 *We, the Third World Women's Alliance*: Frances Beal, interview by Loretta J. Ross, 46.

260 *I marched down Fifth Avenue*: Author's interview with Eleanor Holmes Norton.

261 *Eleanor became the city*: Author's interview with Lynn Povich.

261 *I was exultant and deeply moved*: Branzburg, *The Liberation of Ivy Bottini*, 124.

261 *The march in Chicago*: Author's interview with Heather Booth, October 15, 2019.

262 *I was the master of ceremonies*: Author's interview with Mary Jean Collins.

262 *Our group had one speaker*: Author's interview with Heather Booth, October 15, 2019.

262 *We had Black speakers*: Author's interview with Mary Jean Collins.

263 *UNITED STATES DEPARTMENT*: Pogrebin Research FBI Files on Women's Lib, June 1977, Sophia Smith Collection of Women's History, Smith College Libraries, Northampton, MA.

264 *I went to the rally*: Author's interview with Ginny Berson, April 8, 2021.

264 *We went down to Bryant Park*: Author's interview with Lynn Povich.

265 *When we got to the*: Author's interview with Jacqueline Ceballos.

265 *After tonight, the politics*: Friedan, *It Changed My Life*, 192.

266 *It was in all the papers*: Author's interview with Muriel Fox.

266 *It transformed the women's movement*: Author's interview with Mary Jean Collins.

266 *On August 26, it suddenly became*: Friedan, "Up from the Kitchen Floor."

266n *NOW's membership grew*: Katherine Turk, *The Women of NOW: How Feminists Built an Organization That Transformed America* (New York: Farrar, Straus and Giroux, 2023), 193, 220.

20. Women's Lob—The Tennis Boycott

267 *Well, I did not participate*: Author's interview with Rosie Casals.

267 *Rosie was ready to have*: King, *All In*, 159.

268 *After tennis became open*: Author's interview with Rosie Casals.

268 *Everybody knew the name*: Author's interview with Julie Heldman, March 19, 2022.

268 *Throughout that whole summer*: Author's interview with Rosie Casals.

268 *We learned that the men's*: King, *All In*, 165.

269 *Because there were so few*: Author's interview with Julie Heldman.

269 *He planned to offer*: King, *All In*, 166.

269 *The men's winner will make*: Author's interview with Julie Heldman; Julie Heldman, *Driven: A Daughter's Odyssey* (Middletown, DE: Julie Heldman, 2018), 265.

269 *So, we decided that we would*: Author's interview with Judy Dalton, March 21, 2022.

269 *Of the 278 people who returned*: King, *All In*, 168–69.

270 *Billie Jean would come*: Author's interview with Rosie Casals.

270 *Rosie and I started polling*: King, *All In*, 168.

270 *My mother, Gladys Heldman*: Author's interview with Julie Heldman, March 18, 2022.

271 *We told Gladys Heldman*: Author's interview with Rosie Casals.

271 *Gladys was a brilliant, self-made*: King, *All In*, 168–69.

271 *Within days, my mother*: Author's interview with Julie Heldman, March 19, 2022.

271 *Fortunately, Gladys's friend*: Author's interview with Rosie Casals.

272 *My mother said, "I have a sponsor"*: Author's interview with Julie Heldman.

272 *The next day, Rosie, Ceci*: King, *All In*, 170.

272 *Once again, most of the top*: King, *All In*, 170.

273 *I wasn't about to remain quiet*: King, *All In*, 170.

273 *I was not planning to play*: Author's interview with Julie Heldman.

273 *The Houston Racquet Club*: Author's interview with Rosie Casals.

273 *Then Stan Malless said*: Author's interview with Julie Heldman, March 19, 2022.

274 *Every five seconds*: Author's interview with Billie Jean King.

274 *The meeting went on*: Author's interview with Julie Heldman.

274 *I talked to Gladys*: Author's interview with Billie Jean King.

274 *The day that all hell*: Author's interview with Julie Heldman.

275 *We lined up and*: King, *All In*, 174.

275 *I've always regretted*: Heldman, *Driven*, 272.

275 *That's how the "Original Nine"*: Author's interview with Rosie Casals.

275 *The only way to really join*: Author's interview with Julie Heldman.

275 *I'm happy to say*: Author's interview with Rosie Casals.

276 *During the tournament*: Heldman, *Driven*, 273; author's interview with Julie Heldman.

276 *Two weeks after*: King, *All In*, 177.

21. Making Cunt Art

277 *Back in the end of the sixties*: Getty Research Institute, "Judy Chicago Oral History," April 13, 2011, 01:37:50, https://www.youtube.com/watch?v=7NVRl2lWpmU; *Judy Chicago & the California Girls*, a documentary produced and directed by Judith Dancoff (1971; California Girl Productions, 2008), DVD.

278 *I ended up at Fresno State*: Suzanne Lacy, interview by Moira Roth, March 16, 1990, transcript, Archives of American Art, Smithsonian Institution, Washington, DC.

279 *And then Judy Chicago*: Faith Wilding, interview by Lynn Hershman, May 30, 1990, Women Art Revolution: Videotape Interviews by Lynn Hershman-Leeson for Film, 1990–2008, Stanford University Libraries, Department of Special Collections and University Archives, Stanford, California, https://exhibits.stanford.edu/women-art-revolution/catalog/vp168cy8117.

279 *I applied that spring*: Suzanne Lacy, interview by Moira Roth.

279 *It was like a little experimental*: Faith Wilding, interview by Lynn Hershman.

279 *Judy would give us assignments*: Suzanne Lacy, interview by Moira Roth.

279 *We would meet every week*: Faith Wilding, interview by Lynn Hershman.

280 *When people put people down*: *Judy Chicago & the California Girls*.

280 *In her efforts to explore*: Faith Wilding, "The Feminist Art Programs at Fresno and CalArts, 1970–75," in *The Power of Feminist Art: The American Movement of the 1970s, History and Impact*, ed. Norma Broude and Mary D. Garrard (1994; repr., New York: Harry N. Abrams, 1996), 35.

280 *Ti-Grace Atkinson came to Fresno*: Suzanne Lacy, interview by Moira Roth.

281 *I felt that it was important*: Judy Chicago, *Through the Flower: My Struggle as a Woman Artist* (Garden City, NY: Doubleday, 1975), 86.

281 *We had a series of courses*: Suzanne Lacy, interview by Moira Roth.

281 *So here I am in Fresno*: "Judy Chicago Oral History."

282 *Well, in the interim*: Miriam Schapiro, interview by Ruth Bowman, September 10, 1989, transcript, Archives of American Art, Smithsonian Institution, Washington, DC.

282 *Mimi and [her husband] Paul*: Chicago, *Through the Flower*, 81; "Judy Chicago Oral History."

282 *I remember driving through*: Faith Wilding, interview by Lynn Hershman.

282 *At CalArts we were to have*: Chicago, *Through the Flower*, 103.

283 *Womanhouse was spectacular*: Author's interview with Christina Schlesinger, May 12, 2020.

283 *Womanhouse with its sickly*: Faith Wilding, *By Our Own Hands: The Woman Artist's Movement, Southern California, 1970–1976* (Santa Monica, CA: Double X, 1977), 27.

283 *The kitchen that had eggs*: Author's interview with Christina Schlesinger.

283 *There was Judy Chicago's*: Linda Nochlin, *Women Artists: The Linda Nochlin Reader*, ed. Maura Reilly (New York: Thames and Hudson, 2015), 197.

283 *We resolved to put together*: Chicago, *Through the Flower*, 86.

284 *CalArts had a weekend*: Author's interview with Christina Schlesinger.

284 *I went to Arlene Raven's:* Author's interview with Judy Baca, June 3, 2020.

22. Sexual Politics Lights a Fuse

285 *The year 1970 hit like a meteor*: Author's interview with Robin Morgan; Morgan, *Saturday's Child*, 289.

286 *I was called by Robin Morgan*: Author's interview with Frances Beal.

286 *My old friend from SNCC days*: Morgan, *Saturday's Child*, 285.

287 *I called up Betty Prashker*: Kate Millett, Introduction to *Sexual Politics* (1970; repr., New York: Simon & Schuster, 1990).

287 *I was about to publish*: Author's interview with Letty Cottin Pogrebin.

288 *Her face was on the cover*: Author's interview with Jo Freeman.

289 *Kate Millett's pivotal book*: Alix Kates Shulman, "Alix Kates Shulman," in Catharine R. Stimpson, Alix Kates Shulman, and Kate Millett, "'Sexual Politics': Twenty Years Later," *Women's Studies Quarterly* 19, nos. 3–4 (Winter 1991): 34.

290 *I ordered the hardback*: Author's interview with Margo Jefferson.

290 *That particular Christmas*: Author's interview with Barbara Smith.

290 *I stood up in the Sheridan*: Author's interview with Phyllis Chesler.

290 *Reading* Sexual Politics *was like*: Author's interview with Honor Moore, February 18, 2021.

291 *Reading* Sexual Politics: Shulman, "Alix Kates Shulman," 35.

291 *Marilyn and I were:* Author's interview with Lee Webb.

291 *It was in 1970*: Wallace, *Dark Designs and Visual Culture*, 151; originally published in the *Voice Literary Supplement*, November 7, 1995.

292 *That was a lot*: Author's interview with Margo Jefferson.

292 *Toni Cade had seen*: Author's interview with Frances Beal.

292 *This . . . is a beginning*: Bambara, *The Black Woman*, 4–7.

292 *For a long time*: Author's interview with Margo Okazawa-Rey.

293 *In fiction at that time*: Author's interview with Margo Jefferson.

294 *Toni Morrison was one*: Author's interview with Margo Okazawa-Rey.

294 *The steady flow of novels*: Wallace, *Dark Designs and Visual Culture*, 151; originally published in the *Voice Literary Supplement*, November 7, 1995.

23. We Are One

295 *When the forthcoming publication*: Jay, *Tales of the Lavender Menace*, 232.

296 *Kate had a consciousness-raising*: Author's interview with Anselma Dell'Olio.

296 *Radicalesbians determined not to let her*: Jay, *Tales of the Lavender Menace*, 232.

296 *First, she said*: Author's interview with Margo Jefferson.

296 *Suddenly Kate was no longer*: Jay, *Tales of the Lavender Menace*, 232.

297 Time *magazine first put me*: Kate Millett, interview by Jacquelyn Ceballos, 53–54.

297 *Many feminists, including me*: Branzburg, *The Liberation of Ivy Bottini*, 115.

297 *First thing I know*: Flo Kennedy, *Politics of Oppression*, unpublished manuscript, 135.

298 *Finally, we said*: Kate Millett, interview by Jacquelyn Ceballos, 32.

298 *We made a very fine*: Kate Millett, interview by Jacquelyn Ceballos, 32.

299 *I was there*: Branzburg, *The Liberation of Ivy Bottini*, 115.

299 *Even if the statement*: Kate Millett, interview by Jacquelyn Ceballos, 61.

299 *That afternoon, after the news*: Branzburg, *The Liberation of Ivy Bottini*, 115.

299 *Kate used her royalties*: Author's interview with Jo Freeman.

300 *I stayed friends with Kate*: Author's interview with Anselma Dell'Olio.

24. The Military Is Only for Men

301 *I was born in 1947*: Author's interview with Sharron Frontiero-Cohen.

302 *I have a pretty clear recollection*: Author's interview with Joe Levin.

302 *I was still insistent*: Author's interview with Sharron Frontiero-Cohen.

303 *She had tried all of the*: Author's interview with Joe Levin.

303 *I didn't do it because*: Author's interview with Sharron Frontiero-Cohen.

303 *We filed it in the district*: Author's interview with Joe Levin.

304 *In 1970, students at Rutgers*: Ruth Bader Ginsburg and Barbara Flagg, "Some Reflections on the Feminist Legal Thought of the 1970's," University of Chicago Legal Forum 1, article 3 (1989): 9–21. Judge Ginsburg delivered this speech as the keynote address for the University of Chicago Legal Forum Symposium held October 14–15, 1988.

1. You've Come a Long Way, Baby

307 *We knew this would be one*: Author's interview with Billie Jean King.

307 *What happened was the marketing*: Author's interview with Julie Heldman, March 19, 2022.

307 *The first tournament was in*: Author's interview with Billie Jean King.

308 *My Mom was like the Wizard of Oz*: Author's interview with Julie Heldman, March 19, 2022.

308 *We racked up fourteen tournaments*: King, *All In*, 182.

308 *The tournaments were tough*: Author's interview with Judy Dalton.

308 *The players were willing to do*: Author's interview with Billie Jean King.

309 *It was definitely an uphill battle*: Author's interview with Rosie Casals.

309 *Six months into the tour*: Author's interview with Julie Heldman, March 19, 2022.

309 *All of it was packaging*: Author's interview with Rosie Casals.

310 *In December of 1970*: Author's interview with Billie Jean King; King, *All In*, 182.

310 *Behind the scenes*: Author's interview with Rosie Casals.

310 *We protected each other*: King, *All In*, 218.

310 *Every one of the players*: Author's interview with Rosie Casals.

310 *It was not only not okay*: Author's interview with Julie Heldman, March 19, 2022.

311 *It's hard to convey how oppressive*: King, *All In*, 218.

2. In the Room Where It Happened

312 *I had been running political*: Author's interview with Esther Newberg, June 3, 2020.

312n *For comparison*: Center for American Women and Politics, Rutgers University Eagleton Institute of Politics.

313 *My slogan for my first campaign*: Bella Abzug, interview by Fern Ingersoll, August 27, 1979, in Abzug, Bella S., Tape, Former Members of Congress, Inc., Oral History Interviews.

314 *The National Women's Political Caucus*: Author's interview with Gloria Steinem, April 15, 2022.

314 *We needed to be in the room*: Author's interview with Jill Ruckelshaus, June 19, 2020.

314 *When my book*: Author's interview with Letty Cottin Pogrebin, July 1, 2021.

315 *A phone call from Shana Alexander*: Liz Carpenter, *Getting Better All the Time* (New York: Simon & Schuster, 1987), 121, 125, 127.

316 *Gloria Steinem, Shirley Chisholm*: Bella S. Abzug, *Bella! Ms. Abzug Goes to Washington*, ed. Mel Ziegler (New York: Saturday Review Press, 1972), 160.

316 *I think Bella liked Gloria*: Author's interview with Esther Newberg.

317 *Betty felt that Bella and Gloria*: Carpenter, *Getting Better All the Time*, 127.

317 *On July 10, 1971*: Bella Abzug with Mim Kelber, *Gender Gap: Bella Abzug's Guide to Political Power for American Women* (Boston: Houghton Mifflin, 1984), 22.

317 *Bella turns up at the Hilton*: Author's interview with Letty Cottin Pogrebin.

317 *After an early appointment*: Abzug, *Bella!*, 198; Abzug, *Gender Gap*, 22.

318 *Now, something has got to break*: Fannie Lou Hamer, *The Speeches of Fannie Lou Hamer: To Tell It Like It Is*, ed. Maegan Parker Brooks and Davis W. Houck (Jackson: University Press of Mississippi, 2010), 138.

318 *No one gives away political power*: Speech quoted in the *New York Times*, July 13, 1971, "Goals Set by Women's Political Caucus" (Special to the *New York Times*).

319 *This is no simple reform*: "Address to the Women of America: Gloria Steinem," Speaking While Female Speech Bank, https://speakingwhilefemale.co/womens-lives-steinem/.

319 *Women who have done*: Friedan, *It Changed My Life*, 214.

319 *At the end of the day*: Author's interview with Letty Cottin Pogrebin.

320n *One month after the NWPC*: Carolyn G. Heilbrun, *The Education of a Woman: The Life of Gloria Steinem* (New York: Dial Press, 1995), 190.

320 *I had been "drafted" by Shana*: Carpenter, *Getting Better All the Time*, 128–30.

321 *Meanwhile, in San Clemente*: Carpenter, *Getting Better All the Time*, 131.

321 *"Obviously," I commented*: Abzug, *Gender Gap*, 26.

3. The Past Is Studded with Sisters

323 *I was getting my master's*: Author's interview with Sally Roesch Wagner, May 26, 2021; Sally Roesch Wagner, "How Native American Women Inspired the Women's Rights, Suffrage Movement," *Ms.*, August 18, 2020.

324 *Shortly after my return*: Nochlin, "Starting from Scratch," 188.

324 *Back in 1970*: Author's interview with Brenda Feigen.

325 *A few months later*: Nochlin, "Starting from Scratch," 188.

325 *January of '71 I was walking*: Author's interview with Brenda Feigen.

325 *Women's history didn't exist*: Author's interview with Elizabeth Spahn.

326 *Holy moly*: Author's interview with Elizabeth Spahn.

327 *One part of my course*: Author's interview with Sally Roesch Wagner.

327n *Susan B. Anthony*: Elisabeth Griffith, *Formidable: American Women and the Fight for Equality, 1920–2020* (New York: Pegasus Books, 2022), 5.

328 *When I was a kid*: Wallace, *Dark Designs and Visual Culture*, 154.

328 *African American literature*: Author's interview with Barbara Smith.

329 *When I started teaching*: Alice Walker, *In Search of Our Mothers' Gardens: Womanist Prose* (San Diego: Harcourt Brace Jovanovich, 1983), 260.

330 *Fast-forwarding to summer*: Author's interview with Barbara Smith.

331 *That fall of '72 is when I*: Author's interview with Barbara Smith.

331 *When I began*: Florence Howe, "Feminist Scholarship: The Extent of the Revolution," *Change: The Magazine of Higher Learning* 14, no. 3 (1982); "Florence Howe, Feminist Teacher, Activist, Editor, Publisher, Writer, [. . .]," Veteran Feminists of America, https://www.veteranfeministsofamerica.org/legacy/florence%20howe.htm; Alice Murray, "Feminist Press Creating What It Couldn't Find," *New York Times*, December 10, 1972.

332 *And then slightly later*: Author's interview with Paul Lauter.

332 *By 1973, I was hunting*: Florence Howe, *A Life in Motion* (New York: Feminist Press at the City University of New York, 2011), 303.

333 *As part of my five-year fellowship*: Author's interview with Ruth Rosen, May 25, 2021.

333 *When I came to New York*: Honor Moore, ed., Introduction to *Poems from the Women's Movement* (New York: Library of America, 2009); author's interview with Honor Moore.

334 *At various events around town*: Author's interview with Michele Wallace.

335n *In 1977, Alice Walker*: Courtney Thorsson, *The Sisterhood: How a Network of Black Women Writers Changed American Culture* (New York: Columbia University Press, 2023), 8.

335 *What is happening here*: Kirsten Grimstad and Susan Rennie, eds., *The New Woman's Survival Sourcebook* (New York: Alfred A. Knopf, 1975), 110.

335 *I was teaching German*: Author's interview with Kirsten Grimstad, March 23, 2021.

336 *I was at the Barnard*: Author's interview with Susan Rennie.

4. Reed v. Reed and the Birth of Feminist Jurisprudence

338 *At the same time*: Ruth Bader Ginsburg, interview by Trevor W. Morrison, July 5, 2016, transcript, IJA Oral History of Distinguished American Judges, Institute of Judicial Administration, New York University School of Law, New York, NY; Ruth Bader Ginsburg, "Constitutional Adjudication in the United States as a Means of Advancing the Equal Stature of Men and Women Under the Law," *Hofstra Law Review* 26, no. 2 (Winter 1997): 263–71; Ginsburg and Flagg, "Some Reflections on the Feminist Legal Thought of the 1970's" (speech symposium held October 14–15, 1988).

340 *I was a vice president of NOW*: Author's interview with Brenda Feigen.

340 *It became more and more clear*: Gloria Steinem, interview by Evelyn C. White; "Feminists Come in Pairs, Like Nuns," podcast, hosted by Abigail E. Disney, episode 10, November 19, 2021, https://abigaildisney.com/podcast/all-ears-podcast-gloria-steinem/; Gloria Steinem, *Outrageous Acts and Everyday Rebellions*, 2nd ed. (New York: Henry Holt, 1995), 8.

341 *The Action Alliance was going on*: Author's interview with Brenda Feigen; Feigen, *Not One of the Boys*, 46.

342 *All of us who were writing*: Gloria Steinem, interview by Evelyn C. White.

342 *Every woman you'd ever seen*: Author's interview with Brenda Feigen.

342 *Radical feminists like me*: Abigail Pogrebin, "How Do You Spell Ms.?," *New York*, October 28, 2011.

342 *In trying to think of a title*: Gloria Steinem, interview by Evelyn C. White.

343 *Then I got a call*: Author's interview with Brenda Feigen; Feigen, *Not One of the Boys*, 72.

5. Ms. and the Cultural Click

344 *My friendship with Gloria Steinem*: Graham, *Personal History*, 422.

344 *Clay Felker at* New York *magazine*: Gloria Steinem, interview by Evelyn C. White.

345 *To give Clay credit*: Author's interview with Jane O'Reilly, October 28, 2019.

345 *I remember Clay saying*: Author's interview with Nancy Newhouse, July 11, 2021.

345 *I remember sitting*: Author's interview with Jane O'Reilly.

346 "*The Housewife's Moment of Truth*": Jane O'Reilly, "Click! The Housewife's Moment of Truth," *Ms.*, Spring 1972.

346 *Jane described a moment*: Pogrebin, "How Do You Spell Ms."

346 *The "click" idea just came*: Pogrebin, "How Do You Spell Ms."

346 *Sometime in late 1971*: King, *All In*, 188, 201–2; "Gutting 'Roe' Would Devastate Millions of Americans—and the Court Itself," *Washington Post*, December 1, 2021.

347 *The abortion petition was*: Author's interview with Barbaralee Diamonstein-Spielvogel, February 2, 2023.

347 *I remember that Gloria*: Pogrebin, "How Do You Spell Ms."

348 *I thought it was especially*: Pogrebin, "How Do You Spell Ms."

348 *Several people, as you*: Author's interview with Barbaralee Diamonstein-Spielvogel.

348 *I said, okay, that*: King, *All In*, 201.

348 *Last year, 343 prominent*: "We Have Had Abortions," *Ms.*, Spring 1972.

349 *Letty was a friend of mine*: Author's interview with Suzanne Levine, February 21, 2022.

350 *I was blindsided*: King, *All In*, 202.

350 *I remember that story*: Author's interview with Julie Heldman, March 19, 2022.

351 *I had no idea that Billie*: Author's interview with Barbaralee Diamonstein-Spielvogel.

351 *When the first edition*: Author's interview with Julie Heldman, March 19, 2022.

351 *For the first six days*: Author's interview with Barbaralee Diamonstein-Spielvogel.

351 *It was chaotic and scary*: Gloria Steinem, interview by Evelyn C. White.

352 *We were quivering*: Author's interview with Letty Cottin Pogrebin.

352 *But it sold out*: Gloria Steinem, interview by Evelyn C. White.

352 *We had a deal*: Author's interview with Letty Cottin Pogrebin.

352 *My story was on the cover*: Author's interview with Jane O'Reilly.

352 *We had no money*: Pogrebin, "How Do You Spell Ms."

352 *When the first issue*: Author's interview with Demita Frazier, August 18, 2021.

353 *We got these reports back*: Author's interview with Letty Cottin Pogrebin.

354 *I think that Ms. was seen*: Author's interview with Letty Cottin Pogrebin.

354 *People in Redstockings*: Pogrebin, "How Do You Spell Ms."

354 *Vivian Gornick speaks intelligently*: Author's interview with Margo Jefferson.

354 *Ms. came along as the super*: Author's interview with Charlotte Bunch, April 14, 2021.

355 *The hardest consideration*: Author's interview with Suzanne Levine.

355 *Literally thousands of letters*: Author's interview with Jane O'Reilly.

355 *The letters came in big*: Author's interview with Suzanne Levine.

355 *We were getting much*: Gloria Steinem, interview by Evelyn C. White.

355 *Ms. acted like a bulletin board*: Author's interview with Ruth Rosen.

6. National Childcare—Nixon Says No

356 *I held a special hearing*: Abzug, *Bella!*, 38; Abzug, *Gender Gap*, 20.

357 *One of the things*: Ida Lewis and Aileen Hernandez, "Conversation," *Essence*, February 1971, 24.

357 *The Republicans worked with us*: Patsy T. Mink, interview by Fern S. Ingersoll, March 26, 1979, 49, included with other transcripts of oral history interviews with her, 1968–1981, in Mink, Patsy T., folder 11, box II:11, Transcripts, Former Members of Congress, Inc., Oral History Interviews.

358 *Well, we did it*: Abzug, *Bella!*, 279.

358 *The most conservative member*: Patsy T. Mink, interview by Fern S. Ingersoll, 49.

358 *Worse than the veto*: Walter F. Mondale with David Hage, *The Good Fight: A Life in Liberal Politics* (New York: Scribner, 2010), 99.

7. Shirley Chisholm Runs for President

360 *The primary campaign to nominate*: Theodore H. White, *The Making of the President 1972* (1973; repr., New York: Harper Perennial, 2010), 18–23.

360 *Running for President*: Shirley Chisholm, *The Good Fight* (New York: Harper and Row, 1973), 13.

361 *Shirley Chisholm basically*: Transcript of *Chisholm '72*.

361 *You have to remember*: Transcript of *Chisholm '72*.

361 *Young radicals failed*: Transcript of *Chisholm '72*.

361 *She said, "I think I'm going*: Transcript of *Chisholm '72*.

362 *I interned for Chisholm*: Transcript of *Chisholm '72*.

362 *I thought she was out*: Transcript of *Chisholm '72*.

362 *I realized at the moment*: Shirley Chisholm, interview by Edward Thompson III, May 2, 1973, transcript, Gale Cengage Learning, Ralph J. Bunche Oral Histories Collection on the Civil Rights Movement.

362 *The voting age had just*: Transcript of *Chisholm '72*.

363 *While the Women's Caucus*: Abzug, *Bella!*, 219.

363 *Shirley Chisholm knew*: Transcript of *Chisholm '72*.

363 *I am not the candidate*: Frank Lynn, "New Hat in Ring: Mrs. Chisholm's," *New York Times*, January 26, 1972.

364 *One surprise came from*: Chisholm, *The Good Fight*, 74.

364 *Bella wasn't really*: Author's interview with Esther Newberg.

365 *Shirley announced her run*: Author's interview with Jill Ruckelshaus.

365 *Shirley Chisholm won*: Friedan, *It Changed My Life*, 225.

365 *Florynce Kennedy and I*: "The Shirley Chisholm Project," Brooklyn Women's Activism, 1945 to the Present, Archives and Special Collections, Brooklyn College, City University of New York, https://chisholmproject.com.

365n *Friedan actively campaigned*: Chuck Andrews, "Politics Is Black," (New York) *Amsterdam News*, July 1, 1972; Florynce Kennedy, interview by Marcia Cohen, 1983, transcript, Tully-Crenshaw Feminist Oral History Project, Schlesinger Library, Radcliffe Institute for Advanced Study, Cambridge, MA.

366 *Shirley Chisholm is fabulous*: Florynce Kennedy, interview by Marcia Cohen, transcript, 27.

366 *We were absolutely*: Author's interview with Michele Wallace.

366 *In the spring of 1972*: Ringgold, *We Flew Over the Bridge*, 195.

367 *We wore Shirley Chisholm*: Author's interview with Michele Wallace.

367 *Two of the most prominent*: Chisholm, *The Good Fight*, 76.

367 *I never understood*: Gloria Steinem, interview by Carolyn Heilbrun, June 1991, transcript, 8, Tully-Crenshaw Feminist Oral History Project, Schlesinger Library, Radcliffe Institute for Advanced Study, Cambridge, MA.

367 *There was not a single*: Author's interview with Barbara Winslow.

368 *At the National Black Political*: Transcript of *Chisholm '72*.

368 *I didn't attend that meeting*: Transcript of *Chisholm '72*.

368 *A young man at the Gary*: Author's interview with Barbara Winslow.

368 *I didn't pay them any mind*: Transcript of *Chisholm '72*.

368n *The National Black Political*: Anastasia C. Curwood, *Shirley Chisholm: Champion of Black Feminist Power Politics* (Chapel Hill: University of North Carolina Press, 2022), 259.

369 *So, I'm twenty-one years old*: Jackson Landers, "'Unbought and Unbossed': When a Black Woman Ran for the White House," *Smithsonian*, April 25, 2016.

370 *I served her as a staff*: Transcript of *Chisholm '72*.

370n *Wallace and Chisholm were*: Curwood, *Shirley Chisholm*, 255.

370 *I must have gone to*: Transcript of *Chisholm '72*.

371 *She had a speech impediment*: Transcript of *Chisholm '72*.

371n *Chisholm could draw big crowds*: Curwood, *Shirley Chisholm*, 249.

371 *In her campaign*: Transcript of *Chisholm '72*.

371 *I had a Washington office*: Transcript of *Chisholm '72*.

8. The ERA Passes with Flying Colors

373 *When we got the ERA*: Martha W. Griffiths, interview by Fern S. Ingersoll, October 29, 1979, 96.

373 *The Equal Rights Amendment*: Freeman, *The Politics of Women's Liberation*, 217.

374n *Dubbed "Crater's Raiders"*: Flora Davis, *Moving the Mountain: The Women's Movement in America Since 1960* (1991; repr., Urbana: University of Illinois Press, 1999), 131.

374 *Then I went to see senator*: Martha W. Griffiths, interview by Fern S. Ingersoll, October 29, 1979, 92.

375n *By September 1972*: Donald T. Critchlow, *Phyllis Schlafly and Grassroots Conservatism* (Princeton, NJ: Princeton University Press, 2005), 219; Donald G. Mathews and Jane Sherron De Hart, *Sex, Gender, and the Politics of ERA* (New York: Oxford University Press, 1990), 51.

375n *In the days leading up*: Mathews and De Hart, *Sex, Gender, and the Politics of ERA*, 49.

377 *I remember being in*: Author's interview with Jill Ruckelshaus.

377n *President Nixon quietly endorsed*: Freeman, *The Politics of Women's Liberation*, 219.

378 *The next day I was sent*: Martha W. Griffiths, interview by Fern S. Ingersoll, October 29, 1979, 103.

378 *There was no organized*: Freeman, *The Politics of Women's Liberation*, 217.

378n *By April 1973*: Leslie W. Gladstone, *Equal Rights Amendment (Proposed)* (Washington, DC: Library of Congress, Congressional Research Service, 1982).

378 *Phyllis Schlafly was a defense person*: Author's interview with Jill Ruckelshaus.

378n *Married to a lawyer*: Critchlow, *Phyllis Schlafly and Grassroots Conservatism*, 217.

379 *The ERA was not considered*: Author's interview with Muriel Fox.

379 *It was not controversial*: Author's interview with Jill Ruckelshaus.

379 *Phyllis Schlafly, she is one*: Birch Bayh interview by Julia Lamber, February 19–20, 2004, and February 18, 2005, "A Forgotten History: The Women Who Brought Us Title IX," Indiana University–Bloomington, Maurer School of Law Digital Repository.

9. Bill Baird's Supreme Court Victory

381 *I was in the courtroom*: Author's interview with Bill Baird.

381 *It took from the beginning*: Author's interview with Myra MacPherson.

382 *My case affected millions*: Author's interview with Bill Baird.

382 *One would think*: Author's interview with Myra MacPherson.

10. Ginsburg Stuns the Supreme Court

383 *We lost the* Frontiero *case*: Author's interview with Joe Levin, March 3, 2022.

383 *Joe took the case*: Author's interview with Sharron Frontiero-Cohen, February 28, 2022.

384 *Ruth and I continued*: Author's interview with Brenda Feigen.

384 *At that time, we*: Author's interview with Joe Levin.

384 *We wanted the Court*: Author's interview with Brenda Feigen; Feigen, *Not One of the Boys*, 80.

386 *I got a subsequent call*: Author's interview with Joe Levin.

386 *For the upcoming argument*: Author's interview with Brenda Feigen.

386 *There was a lot of tension*: Author's interview with Joe Levin.

387 *The first case I argued*: Ruth Bader Ginsburg, interview by Trevor W. Morrison.

387 *Then Ruth was asked*: Author's interview with Brenda Feigen.

388 *There was not a single*: Author's interview with Brenda Feigen.

388 *As it turned out*: Ruth Bader Ginsburg, interview by Trevor W. Morrison.

389 *I've subsequently seen*: Author's interview with Brenda Feigen.

11. Who Are These Girls?

390 *It was May 3, 1972*: Author's interview with Judith Arcana.

391 *We were at this apartment*: Author's interview with Martha Scott.

391 *That day, there was one*: Author's interview with Judith Arcana; *The Janes*, a documentary directed by Tia Lessin and Emma Pildes; produced by Emma Pildes, Daniel Arcana, and Jessica Levin (HBO Documentary Films, 2022).

391 *There was a loud knock*: Author's interview with Martha Scott.

392 *I don't know how long*: Author's interview with Judith Arcana.

392 *We were put in a holding cell*: Author's interview with Martha Scott.

392 *They said to us*: Author's interview with Judith Arcana.

393 *The other women in*: Author's interview with Judith Arcana.

393 *During the time between*: *The Janes*.

393 *Then the seven interviewed*: Laura Kaplan, *The Story of Jane: The Legendary Underground Feminist Abortion Service* (1995; repr., Chicago: University of Chicago Press, 1997), 246.

394 *This is what Jo-Anne*: *The Janes*.

394 *By the time we got busted*: Author's interview with Laura Kaplan, October 30, 2018.

394 *Because* Roe v. Wade *was*: Author's interview with Judith Arcana.

12. On the Chisholm Trail

395 *I was an activist*: "A Conversation with Barbara Lee," John F. Kennedy Presidential Library and Museum, https://www.jfklibrary.org/node/392391.

396 *In '72, I was a junior transfer*: Transcript of *Chisholm '72*.

396 *Shirley came out and she*: "A Conversation with Barbara Lee."

397 *What she was saying*: Transcript of *Chisholm '72*.

397 *I went back and I talked*: "A Conversation with Barbara Lee."

397 *I had come home*: Transcript of *Chisholm '72*.

397 *What attracted me to Shirley*: Transcript of *Chisholm '72*.

398 *I went on to the Democratic*: "A Conversation with Barbara Lee."

398 *I was told that I would*: Transcript of *Chisholm '72*.

398 *Our campaign office was*: Transcript of *Chisholm '72*.

398 *The Black Panther Party*: Transcript of *Chisholm '72*.

398 *The rivalry between Black men*: Chisholm, *The Good Fight*, 102.

399 *The Black Panthers were evolving*: Transcript of *Chisholm '72*.

399 *I don't think a lot of people*: Transcript of *Chisholm '72*.

400 *She came to California*: Transcript of *Chisholm '72*.

400 *Then there was the biggest*: Transcript of *Chisholm '72*.

400 *Later, I found out*: Transcript of *Chisholm '72*.

400n *G. Gordon Liddy*: Rick Perlstein, *Nixonland: The Rise of a President and the Fracturing of America* (New York: Scribner, 2008), 637.

401 *The office of special prosecutor*: Pogrebin, "How Do You Spell Ms."; Pogrebin Research FBI Files on Women's Lib.

401 *I had a visit from a couple*: Transcript of *Chisholm '72*.

401 *No other candidate had*: Author's interview with Barbara Winslow; Winslow, *Shirley Chisholm*, 125.

402 *She had never been audited*: Transcript of *Chisholm '72*.

402 *We did surprisingly well*: Transcript of *Chisholm '72*.

13. The Education Act's Surprise—Title IX

403 *The 1972 Education Act*: Edith Green, interview by Shirley Tanzer, 102.

403 *We tried to get a civil rights bill*: *Congressional Record*, July 26, 1999, 17795.

403 *The main reason I got*: "Interview with Birch Bayh," 26.

404 *So, what happened*: Bernice Sandler, interview by Julia Lamber and Jean Robinson, 30–31.

404n *By the time the amendment*: Sherry Boschert, *37 Words: Title IX and Fifty Years of Fighting Sex Discrimination* (New York: New Press, 2022), 43.

404 *When Title IX passed*: Bernice Sandler, interview by Julia Lamber and Jean Robinson, 25–26, 34–35.

405 *Without the word "activity"*: Author's interview with Billie Jean King.

405 *The athletic groups didn't*: Author's interview with Donna de Varona, November 19, 2021.

406 *In '72 they didn't know*: Bernice Sandler, interview by Julia Lamber and Jean Robinson, 52–53.

406 *Dear Bunny!*: Pauli Murray to Bernice Sandler, August 8, 1970, Papers of Bernice Resnick Sandler, 1963–2008, Box 7, folder 9, Schlesinger Library, Radcliffe Institute for Advanced Study, Cambridge, MA.

14. Woman Power 1972 at the Democratic Convention

408 *Gloria, Marc, my brother*: Author's interview with Brenda Feigen; Feigen, *Not One of the Boys*, 62.

408 *The National Women's Political*: White, *The Making of the President 1972*, 168.

408 *I went to both conventions*: Friedan, *It Changed My Life*, 224; Feigen, *Not One of the Boys*, 62.

409 *The Women's Caucus at the*: Transcript of *Chisholm '72*.

410 *WE WANT SHIRLEY!*: Vivien Leone, "The Elusive Miami Beach Democratic National Transitory Soap Button Opera (A Cavalcade in 43 Buttons)," *Off Our Backs*, September 30, 1972, 6.

411 *Into the meeting*: Leone, "The Elusive Miami Beach Democratic National Transitory Soap Button Opera."

412 *We started shouting*: Transcript of *Chisholm '72*.

412 *He closed his book*: Transcript of *Chisholm '72*.

413 *Afterwards, you could hear*: Transcript of *Chisholm '72*.

413 *We still had to convince*: Feigen, *Not One of the Boys*, 63.

413 *We were on the floor*: Author's interview with Brenda Feigen.

414 *I was on the floor*: Author's interview with Myra MacPherson.

415 *That was a page one story*: Author's interview with Myra MacPherson.

415n *The* Washington Post *and*: Ellen Goodman, "Women Delegates Caucus Hopefuls Woo Their Votes," *Boston Globe*, July 11, 1972.

415 *At first the McGovern*: Chisholm, *The Good Fight*, 129.

416 *Then came the question*: Gloria Steinem, interview by Carolyn Heilbrun, 15.

417 *Through all of this*: Chisholm, *The Good Fight*, 129.

417 *Chisholm ended up with*: Author's interview with Barbara Winslow.

417n *On the first-ballot roll*: White, *The Making of the President 1972*, 183; author's interview with Jo Freeman.

417 *When I got to the convention*: Transcript of *Chisholm '72*.

15. Exhibiting Art by and for Themselves

418 *Shirley Chisholm had really*: Ringgold, *We Flew Over the Bridge*, 195, 261.

419n *In the summer of 1971*: Kay Brown, "'Where We At' Black Women Artists," *Feminist Art Journal*, April 1972.

419 *Women artists were just not*: Author's interview with Harmony Hammond.

419 *The art world was almost*: Author's interview with Howardena Pindell.

419 *We rented a space in SoHo*: Author's interview with Harmony Hammond.

420 *A.I.R. was a ground-floor*: Author's interview with Howardena Pindell.

420 *The gallery began to form*: Author's interview with Harmony Hammond.

420n *Founding artists were*: "A Short History," A.I.R., https://www.airgallery.org/history.

420 *The feminist movement was*: Author's interview with Howardena Pindell.

420 *A bunch of us traversed*: Author's interview with Harmony Hammond.

421 *On November 28, 1973*: Chicago, *Through the Flower*, 201.

421 *The Women's Building*: Suzanne Lacy, interview by Moira Roth.

421 *I came out to the Women's*: Author's interview with Lucy Lippard.

421 *When the building opened*: Chicago, *Through the Flower*, 202.

422 *I became friends*: Author's interview with Judy Baca.

16. The Supreme Court Legalizes Abortion

424 *Monday, January 22*: Weddington, *A Question of Choice*, 158.

425 *There were spontaneous*: Weddington, *A Question of Choice*, 163.

425 *The downtown feminist*: Brownmiller, *In Our Time*, 134, 168.

425 *The copy of the* Roe *opinion*: Weddington, *A Question of Choice*, 167.

426 *If the Court hadn't used*: Linda Coffee, interview by Patricia Duke, 15.

426 *It was fabulous*: Author's interview with Nancy Stearns; "An Abortion Rights Champion of the 1970s on Life Before and After Roe" (podcast).

426 Roe *was a very, very*: Author's interview with Brenda Feigen.

427 *At the time of* Roe v. Wade: Jeffrey Rosen, *Conversations with RBG: Ruth Bader Ginsburg on Life, Love, Liberty, and Law* (New York: Henry Holt, 2019), 60.

17. Ginsburg (Nearly) Wins *Frontiero* Big

429 *On May 14, 1973*: Ruth Bader Ginsburg, "The Need for the Equal Rights Amendment," *American Bar Association Journal* 59, no. 9 (September 1973).

429 *In* Frontiero, *in which Rehnquist*: Ruth Bader Ginsburg, interview by Trevor W. Morrison.

430 *We won on the merits*: Author's interview with Brenda Feigen.

430 *This is before cable news*: Author's interview with Joe Levin.

431 *Ruth was still determined*: Author's interview with Brenda Feigen.

431*n* *After Frontiero*: Jane Sherron De Hart, *Ruth Bader Ginsburg: A Life* (New York: Alfred A. Knopf, 2018), 333–48.

18. FBI Closes Its WLM Files

432 Pogrebin Research FBI Files on Women's Lib.

19. The Battle of the Sexes

435 *Bobby Riggs tapped into*: Author's interview with Julie Heldman, March 19, 2022.

435 *Bobby Riggs was one of*: Author's interview with Billie Jean King.

436 *Bobby Riggs went after*: Author's interview with Rosie Casals.

436 *I said to Larry*: Author's interview with Billie Jean King.

436 *At that stage*: Author's interview with Julie Heldman, March 19, 2022.

436 *Margaret was not a feminist*: Author's interview with Rosie Casals.

436 *Margaret had no idea*: Author's interview with Julie Heldman, March 19, 2022.

436 *She really did not prepare*: Author's interview with Rosie Casals.

437 *As soon as Margaret*: Author's interview with Judy Dalton.

437 *He threw her junk*: Author's interview with Julie Heldman, March 19, 2022.

437 *Billie Jean and myself:* Author's interview with Rosie Casals.
437 *He beats her badly:* Author's interview with Julie Heldman, March 19, 2022.
437 *So Margaret loses:* Author's interview with Billie Jean King.
438 *First of all:* Author's interview with Julie Heldman, March 19, 2022.
438 *I won the triple crown:* Author's interview with Billie Jean King.
438 *Billie Jean took it in:* Author's interview with Rosie Casals.
438 *All these things:* Author's interview with Billie Jean King.
438n *In 1973, approximately:* King, *All In*, 263.
439 *We had to give way:* Author's interview with Julie Heldman, March 19, 2022.
439 *At that time, of course:* Author's interview with Rosie Casals.
440 *It was men versus women:* Author's interview with Julie Heldman, March 19, 2022.
440 *Before the match:* Author's interview with Rosie Casals.
440 *I think there were thirty-seven thousand:* Author's interview with Julie Heldman, March 19, 2022.
440 *Bobby was exhausted:* Author's interview with Rosie Casals.
440 *When she saw that:* Author's interview with Julie Heldman, March 19, 2022.
441 *I was up in the ABC booth:* Author's interview with Rosie Casals.
442 *Every single day since:* Author's interview with Billie Jean King.

20. A Model for Political Action

443 *The state of Illinois:* Author's interview with Judith Arcana.
443 *The state didn't need:* Author's interview with Laura Kaplan.
443 *It was an enormous relief:* Author's interview with Martha Scott.
443 *After New York legalized:* Author's interview with Laura Kaplan.
444 *Between 1965, when I:* Author's interview with Heather Booth, October 15, 2019.
444 *After we folded:* Author's interview with Laura Kaplan.
444 *If you think about:* Author's interview with Alice Fox.
445 *The problem was:* Author's interview with Nancy Stearns.

21. We Were Beautiful Black Women

446 *By 1973, I had not yet found:* Author's interview with Margo Jefferson.
447 *Flo Kennedy was:* Author's interview with Margo Jefferson.
447 *We broke down into:* Author's interview with Margo Jefferson.
448 *Ironically, I don't really think:* "Margaret Sloan on Black Sisterhood," *Woman*, interview by Sandra Elkin, WNED, New York, August 4, 1974, American Archive of Public Broadcasting, https://americanarchive.org/catalog/cpb-aacip-81-47rn8v5q.
448 *Margaret Sloan left Chicago:* Author's interview with Demita Frazier, August 4, 2021.
448 *One of the biggest changes:* Karla Jay, "Double Trouble for Black Women: An Interview with Margaret Sloan," *The Tide*, July 1974.
449 *We loved that we got:* Author's interview with Demita Frazier.
449 *That summer, the media:* "Margaret Sloan on Black Sisterhood."
451 *We never expected to get:* "Margaret Sloan on Black Sisterhood."
451 *I was living in New York:* Author's interview with Beverly Smith, July 30, 2021.
451 *Beverly told me that:* Author's interview with Barbara Smith.
451 *It was wonderful:* Author's interview with Beverly Smith.

451 *It was amazing*: Author's interview with Barbara Smith.

452 *It just felt like this*: Author's interview with Beverly Smith.

452 *Because my sister and I*: Author's interview with Barbara Smith.

452 *I realized at the National Black*: Alice Walker, "A Letter to the Editor of *Ms.*," in *In Search of Our Mothers' Gardens*, 273.

453 *At the conference at Riverside*: Author's interview with Michele Wallace.

453 *The central core*: Barbara Smith, "Black Feminists Organize Nationally," *Women's Studies Quarterly* (1974): 2.

453 *I thought about friends*: Walker, "A Letter to the Editor of *Ms.*"

454 *This was prior to coming out*: Author's interview with Barbara Smith.

455 *So the people who were there*: Author's interview with Barbara Smith.

455 *And then to hear Shirley Chisholm*: Walker, "A Letter to the Editor of *Ms.*"

456 *And we talked and we discussed*: Walker, "A Letter to the Editor of *Ms.*"

Author's Interviews

(listed chronologically)

The following is a list of people I interviewed for this book. Though not all are quoted, everyone contributed to my understanding of this time in history.

———————————

The interviews conducted before 2019 were originally for Witness to the Revolution *and two magazine articles.*

———————————

Cathy Wilkerson 10/25/12, 8/18/22
Heather Booth 1/8/13, 10/26/18,
    10/15/19
Vivian Rothstein 3/24/13, 3/26/13
Michael Kazin 1/31/14
Robin Morgan 3/5/14
Emily Goodman 3/25/15, 10/3/19
Ericka Huggins 9/16/15, 7/26/21
Eleanor Stein Raskin 1/22/18
Karla Spurlock-Evans 1/30/18
Judith Arcana 10/21/18
Laura Kaplan 10/30/18
Alice Fox 11/1/18
Margery Tabankin 11/1/18
Martha Scott 11/1/18

Jonathan Lerner 11/8/18
Leslie Reagan 11/14/18
Susan Brownmiller 9/24/19
Judy Gumbo 10/16/19
Nancy Stearns 10/21/19
Jane O'Reilly 10/28/19
Joan Ditzion 10/28/19
Miriam Hawley 10/30/19
Paula Doress-Worters 10/30/19
Norma Swenson 10/30/19
Bobbi Gibb 10/31/19
Jane Pincus 11/16/19
Phyllis Chesler 12/2/19, 2/5/19
Barbara Winslow 12/16/19
Marilyn Webb 1/22/20, 2/3/20

Lee Webb 1/31/20

Derek Shearer 2/8/20

Norma Lesser 2/11/20

Jan Fenty 2/11/20

Myra MacPherson 2/11/20

Lucy Lippard 2/18/20

Sallie Bingham 2/20/20

Alix Kates Shulman 2/27/20

Barbara Mehrhof 3/3/20

Jo Freeman 3/11/20

Bill Baird 4/15/20

Alice Wolfson 4/22/20

Muriel Fox 4/28/20, 5/26/20

Harmony Hammond 5/6/20

Christina Schlesinger 5/12/20

Sonia Pressman Fuentes 5/15/20

Nancy Fried 9/19/20

Mary Jean Collins 5/29/20

Mary Pat Laffey-Inman 6/1/20

Judy Baca 6/3/20

Jill Ruckelshaus 6/19/20

Jacqueline Ceballos 6/24/20

Esther Newberg 6/3/20

Sheila Tobias 7/2/20

Ronnie Eldridge 7/3/20

Anselma Dell'Olio 7/6/20

Adele Simmons 7/17/20

Bobby (Robert) Paul 7/24/20

Arthur Morey 7/25/20

Elizabeth Spahn 7/27/20

Kit McClure 7/29/20

Paul Stephan 8/1/20

Constance Royster 8/13/20

Faye Wattleton 11/18/20

Natasha Dellinger Singer 12/7/20

Howardena Pindell 12/27/20

Susanne Jackson 1/23/21

Torie Osborn 2/4/21

Lynn Hershman Leeson 2/5/21

Tom Gardner 2/6/21

Paul Lauter and Doris Friedenshohn
    2/12/21

Honor Moore 2/18/21

Judy Norsigian 3/3/21

Kirsten Grimstad 3/23/21

Susan Rennie 4/6/21

Ginny Berson 4/8/21

Charlotte Bunch 4/13/21, 4/14/21,
    4/21/21

Patricia Ireland 4/15/21

Holly Near 4/19/21

Kumea Shorter-Gooden 4/20/21

Joanne Parrent 5/17/21

Brenda Feigen 5/18/21

Linda Burnham 5/20/21

Frances Beal 5/21/21

Ruth Rosen 5/25/21, 6/8/21

Sally Wagner 5/26/21

Susan Griffin 6/4/21

Margo Okazawa-Rey 6/7/21

Margo Jefferson 6/9/21

Barbara Smith 6/14/21

Letty Cottin Pogrebin 7/1/21

Nancy Newhouse 7/11/21

Beverly Smith 7/27/21, 7/30/21, 8/3/21

Demita Frazier 8/4/21, 8/18/21

Louise "Mama Bear" Herne 9/13/21

Jeanne Shenandoah 9/15/21

Byllye Avery 9/22/21

Beverly Kiohawiton Cook 10/1/21

Lynn Povich 11/17/21

Donna de Varona 11/19/21

Michele Wallace 12/7/21

Eleanor Holmes Norton 1/25/22

Lucy Howard 1/31/22

Vivian Gornick 2/10/22

Brian Flanagan 2/13/22

Peter Goldman 2/16/22

Suzanne Levine 2/21/22

Sharron Frontiero Cohen 2/28/22

Stephen Wiesenfeld 3/1/22

Joe Levin 3/3/22

Sherrye Henry 3/11/22

Billie Jean King 3/16/22

Julie Heldman 3/18/22, 3/19/22

Judy Dalton 3/21/22

Rosie Casals 3/30/22

Gloria Steinem 4/15/22

Ted Bent 9/13/22

Margaret McQuade 9/30/22

Rita Mae Brown 12/5/22

Barbaralee Diamonstein-Spielvogel
  2/2/23

Barbara Lee 3/21/23

Bibliography

BOOKS

Abbott, Sidney, and Barbara Love. *Sappho Was a Right-On Woman: A Liberated View of Lesbianism*. New York: Stein and Day, 1972.

Abzug, Bella S. *Bella! Ms. Abzug Goes to Washington*. Edited by Mel Ziegler. New York: Saturday Review Press, 1972.

———, with Mim Kelber. *Gender Gap: Bella Abzug's Guide to Political Power for American Women*. Boston: Houghton Mifflin, 1984.

Allen, Paula Gunn. *The Sacred Hoop: Recovering the Feminine in American Indian Traditions*. Boston: Beacon Press, 1986.

Antler, Joyce. *Jewish Radical Feminism: Voices from the Women's Liberation Movement*. New York: New York University Press, 2018.

Arcana, Judith. *Hello. This Is Jane*. O'Brien, OR: Left Fork, 2020.

Atkinson, Ti-Grace. *Amazon Odyssey*. New York: Links Books, 1974.

Bambara, Toni Cade. *Deep Sightings and Rescue Missions: Fiction, Essays, and Conversations*. Edited by Toni Morrison. 1996. Reprint, New York: Vintage Books, 1999.

———. *The Salt Eaters*. 1980. Reprint, New York: Vintage Books, 1992.

———, ed. *The Black Woman: An Anthology*. 1970. Reprint, New York: Washington Square Press, 2005.

Barber, David. *A Hard Rain Fell: SDS and Why It Failed*. Jackson: University Press of Mississippi, 2008.

Barry, Kathleen. *Femininity in Flight: A History of Flight Attendants*. Durham, NC: Duke University Press, 2007.

Baumgardner, Jennifer, and Amy Richards. *Manifesta: Young Women, Feminism, and the Future*. 2000. Reprint, New York: Picador, 2020.

Baxandall, Rosalyn, and Linda Gordon, eds. *Dear Sisters: Dispatches from the Women's Liberation Movement.* New York: Basic Books, 2000.

Beauvoir, Simone de. *The Second Sex.* Translated by Constance Borde and Sheila Malovany-Chevallier. New York: Vintage Books, 2011 (originally published in US 1953).

Bell, Janet Dewart. *Lighting the Fires of Freedom: African American Women in the Civil Rights Movement.* New York: New Press, 2018.

Bennetts, Leslie. *The Feminine Mistake: Are We Giving Up Too Much?* New York: Voice/Hyperion, 2007.

Berry, Daina Ramey, and Kali Nicole Gross. *A Black Women's History of the United States.* Boston: Beacon Press, 2020.

Berson, Ginny Z. *Olivia on the Record: A Radical Experiment in Women's Music.* San Francisco: Aunt Lute Books, 2020.

Bingham, Clara. *Witness to the Revolution: Radicals, Resisters, Vets, Hippies, and the Year America Lost Its Mind and Found Its Soul.* New York: Random House, 2016.

———. *Women on the Hill: Challenging the Culture of Congress.* New York: Times Books, 1997.

Bird, Caroline, with Sara Welles Briller. *Born Female: The High Cost of Keeping Women Down.* New York: David McKay, 1968.

B[iren], J[oan] E. *Eye to Eye: Portraits of Lesbians.* 1979. Reprint, New York: Anthology Editions, 2021.

Blain, Keisha N. *Set the World on Fire: Black Nationalist Women and the Global Struggle for Freedom.* Philadelphia: University of Pennsylvania Press, 2018.

———. *Until I Am Free: Fannie Lou Hamer's Enduring Message to America.* Boston: Beacon Press, 2021.

Boschert, Sherry. *37 Words: Title IX and Fifty Years of Fighting Sex Discrimination.* New York: New Press, 2022.

Boston Women's Health Book Collective. *Our Bodies, Ourselves: A Book by and for Women.* 1971. Reprint, New York: Simon & Schuster, 1973.

Bradley, Patricia. *Mass Media and the Shaping of American Feminism, 1963–1975.* Jackson: University Press of Mississippi, 2003.

Braeman, Katherine M., and Gladys E. Henrikson. *Carol Burris and the Women's Lobby: The Untold Story of a Shoestring Lobbyist.* Oakton, VA: Justitia Publishing, 2019.

Branzburg, Judith V. *The Liberation of Ivy Bottini: A Memoir of Love and Activism.* Fairfield, CA: Bink Books, 2018.

Breines, Winifred. *The Trouble Between Us: An Uneasy History of White and Black Women in the Feminist Movement.* Oxford, UK: Oxford University Press, 2007.

Bronx Museum of the Arts. *Division of Labor: "Women's Work" in Contemporary Art.* Bronx, NY: Bronx Museum, 1995.

Broude, Norma, and Mary D. Garrard, eds. *The Power of Feminist Art: The American*

Movement of the 1970s, History and Impact. 1994. Reprint, New York: Harry N. Abrams, 1996.

Brown, Elaine. *A Taste of Power: A Black Woman's Story.* New York: Pantheon, 1992.

Brown, Rita Mae. *A Plain Brown Rapper.* Oakland, CA: Diana Press, 1976.

———. *Rita Will: Memoir of a Literary Rabble-Rouser.* New York: Bantam Books, 1997.

———. *Rubyfruit Jungle.* 1973. Reprint, New York: Bantam Books, 1988.

Brownmiller, Susan. *In Our Time: Memoir of a Revolution.* 1999. Reprint, New York: Dell, 2000.

———. *Shirley Chisholm: A Biography.* 1970. Reprint, New York: Pocket Books, 1972.

Bufwack, Mary A., and Robert K. Oermann. *Finding Her Voice: Women in Country Music, 1800–2000.* Nashville: Country Music Foundation Press and Vanderbilt University Press, 1993.

Bunch, Charlotte. *Passionate Politics: Essays, 1968–1986; Feminist Theory in Action.* New York: St. Martin's Press, 1987.

Butler, Cornelia H., and Alexandra Schwartz, eds. *Modern Women: Women Artists at the Museum of Modern Art.* New York: Museum of Modern Art, 2010.

Carmon, Irin, and Shana Knizhnik. *Notorious RBG: The Life and Times of Ruth Bader Ginsburg.* New York: Dey Street Books, 2015.

Carpenter, Liz. *Getting Better All the Time.* New York: Simon & Schuster, 1987.

Chafe, William H. *The Road to Equality: American Women Since 1962.* New York: Oxford University Press, 1994.

Chesler, Phyllis. *A Politically Incorrect Feminist: Creating a Movement with Bitches, Lunatics, Dykes, Prodigies, Warriors, and Wonder Women.* New York: St. Martin's Press, 2018.

———. *Woman's Inhumanity to Woman.* 2001. Reprint, Chicago: Lawrence Hill Books, 2009.

———. *Women and Madness.* 1972. Reprint, New York: Lawrence Hill Books, 2018.

Chicago, Judy. *The Flowering: The Autobiography of Judy Chicago.* New York: Thames and Hudson, 2021.

———. *Institutional Time: A Critique of Studio Art Education.* New York: Monacelli Press, 2014.

———. *Through the Flower: My Struggle as a Woman Artist.* Garden City, NY: Doubleday, 1975.

Chisholm, Shirley. *The Good Fight.* New York: Harper and Row, 1973.

———. *Shirley Chisolm: The Last Interview and Other Conversations.* Brooklyn: Melville House, 2021.

———. *Unbought and Unbossed.* Edited by Scott Simpson. Expanded 40th anniversary edition. Washington, DC: Take Root Media, 2010.

Christian, Barbara. *Black Feminist Criticism: Perspectives on Black Women Writers*. 1985. Reprint, New York: Teachers College Press, 1997.

Churchill, Ward, and Jim Vander Wall. *The COINTELPRO Papers: Documents from the FBI's Secret Wars Against Dissent in the United States*. 2nd ed. Cambridge, MA: South End Press, 2002.

Cleaver, Eldridge. *Soul on Ice*. New York: Dell, 1968.

Cobble, Dorothy Sue. *The Other Women's Movement: Workplace Justice and Social Rights in Modern America*. Princeton, NJ: Princeton University Press, 2003.

————, Linda Gordon, and Astrid Henry. *Feminism Unfinished: A Short, Surprising History of American Women's Movements*. New York: Liveright, 2014.

Cohen, Marcia. *The Sisterhood: The Inside Story of the Women's Movement and the Leaders Who Made it Happen*. 1988. Reprint, Santa Fe: Sunstone Press, 2009.

Collins, Gail. *When Everything Changed: The Amazing Journey of American Women from 1960 to the Present*. New York: Little, Brown, 2009.

Collins, Patricia Hill. *Black Feminist Thought: Knowledge, Consciousness, and the Politics of Empowerment*. New York: Routledge, 1990.

Colman, David. *Judy Chicago: Roots of the Dinner Party: History in the Making*. New York: Salon 94, 2019.

Coontz, Stephanie. *A Strange Stirring:* The Feminine Mystique *and American Women at the Dawn of the 1960s*. New York: Basic Books, 2010.

Corea, Gena. *The Hidden Malpractice: How American Medicine Mistreats Women*. Updated ed. New York: Harper and Row, 1985.

Cott, Nancy F. *The Grounding of Modern Feminism*. New Haven, CT: Yale University Press, 1987.

Court, Margaret. *Margaret Court: The Autobiography*. Sidney, NSW: Pan Macmillan Australia, 2016.

Craig, Barbara Hinkson, and David M. O'Brien. *Abortion and American Politics*. Chatham, NJ: Chatham House, 1993.

Critchlow, Donald T. *Phyllis Schlafly and Grassroots Conservatism*. Princeton, NJ: Princeton University Press, 2005.

Crow, Barbara A. *Radical Feminism: A Documentary Reader*. New York: New York University Press, 2000.

Crowhurst, Anna-Marie. *Badly Behaved Women: The Story of Modern Feminism*. London: Welbeck, 2020.

Curwood, Anastasia C. *Shirley Chisholm: Champion of Black Feminist Power Politics*. Chapel Hill: University of North Carolina Press, 2022.

Cushman, Clare, ed. *Supreme Court Decisions and Women's Rights: Milestones to Equality*. Washington, DC: CQ Press, 2000.

Daly, Mary. *Beyond God the Father: Toward a Philosophy of Women's Liberation*. Boston: Beacon Press, 1973.

————. *Gyn/Ecology: The Metaethics of Radical Feminism.* Boston: Beacon Press, 1978.

Davidson, Sara. *Loose Change: Three Women of the Sixties.* 1977. Reprint, Berkeley: University of California Press, 1997.

Davis, Angela Y. *Angela Davis: An Autobiography.* 3rd ed. Chicago: Haymarket Books, 2021.

————. *Women, Culture, and Politics.* 1989. Reprint, New York: Vintage Books, 1990.

————. *Women, Race, and Class.* 1981. Reprint, New York: Vintage Books, 1983.

————, Gina Dent, Erica R. Meiners, and Beth E. Richie. *Abolition. Feminism. Now.* Chicago: Haymarket Books, 2022.

Davis, Flora. *Moving the Mountain: The Women's Movement in America Since 1960.* 1991. Reprint, Urbana: University of Illinois Press, 1999.

Davis, Kathy. *The Making of "Our Bodies, Ourselves": How Feminism Travels Across Borders.* Durham, NC: Duke University Press, 2007.

Davis, Rebecca Harding. *Life in the Iron Mills and Other Stories.* Edited by Tillie Olsen. Rev. and expanded. ed. New York: Feminist Press, 1993.

De Hart, Jane Sherron. *Ruth Bader Ginsburg: A Life.* New York: Alfred A. Knopf, 2018.

DeWolf, Rebecca. *Gendered Citizenship: The Original Conflict over the Equal Rights Amendment, 1920–1963.* Lincoln: University of Nebraska Press, 2021.

Didion, Joan. *Let Me Tell You What I Mean.* New York: Alfred A. Knopf, 2021.

————. *The White Album.* 1979. Reprint, New York: Farrar, Straus and Giroux, 2009.

Dodson, Betty. *Sex by Design: The Betty Dodson Story.* California: CreateSpace, 2016.

————. *Sex for One: The Joy of Selfloving.* 1987. Reprint, New York: Three Rivers Press, 1996.

DuBois, Ellen Carol, and Lynn Dumenil. *Through Women's Eyes: An American History with Documents.* Boston: Bedford/St. Martin's, 2005.

Dunbar-Ortiz, Roxanne. *Outlaw Woman: A Memoir of the War Years, 1960–1975.* Rev. ed. Norman: University of Oklahoma Press, 2014.

————. *Red Dirt: Growing Up Okie.* 1997. Reprint, Norman: University of Oklahoma Press, 2006.

DuPlessis, Rachel Blau, and Ann Barr Snitow, eds. *The Feminist Memoir Project: Voices from Women's Liberation.* 1998. Reprint, New Brunswick, NJ: Rutgers University Press, 2007.

Echols, Alice. *Daring to Be Bad: Radical Feminism in America, 1967–1975.* Minneapolis: University of Minnesota Press, 1989.

Ehrenreich, Barbara, and Deirdre English. *Witches, Midwives, and Nurses: A History of Women Healers.* 2nd ed. New York: Feminist Press at the City University of New York, 2010.

Eisenstein, Zillah R., ed. *Capitalist Patriarchy and the Case for Socialist Feminism.* New York: Monthly Review Press, 1978.

Elliott, Osborn. *The World of Oz.* New York: Viking, 1980.

Ephron, Nora. *Crazy Salad: Some Things About Women.* 1975. Reprint, New York: Modern Library, 2000.

———. *I Remember Nothing: And Other Reflections.* New York: Vintage Books, 2010.

———. *Wallflower at the Orgy.* New York: Viking Press, 1970.

Evans, Mari, ed. *Black Women Writers, 1950–1980: A Critical Evaluation.* Garden City, NY: Anchor Press/Doubleday, 1984.

Evans, Sara. *Born for Liberty: A History of Women in America.* New York: Free Press, 1989.

———. *Personal Politics: The Roots of Women's Liberation in the Civil Rights Movement and the New Left.* 1979. Reprint, New York: Vintage Books, 1980.

———. *Tidal Wave: How Women Changed America at Century's End.* New York: Free Press, 2003.

Faderman, Lillian. *The Gay Revolution: The Story of the Struggle.* New York: Simon & Schuster, 2015.

Fahs, Breanne. *Firebrand Feminism: The Radical Lives of Ti-Grace Atkinson, Kathie Sarachild, Roxanne Dunbar-Ortiz, and Dana Densmore.* Seattle: University of Washington Press, 2018.

———. *Valerie Solanas: The Defiant Life of the Woman Who Wrote SCUM (and Shot Andy Warhol).* New York: Feminist Press at the City University of New York, 2014.

———, ed. *Burn It Down: Feminist Manifestos for the Revolution.* London: Verso, 2020.

Farrell, Amy Erdman. *Yours in Sisterhood:* Ms. *Magazine and the Promise of Popular Feminism.* Chapel Hill: University of North Carolina Press, 1998.

Farrell, Kate, Linda Joy Myers, and Amber Lea Starfire, eds. *Times They Were A-Changing: Women Remember the '60s and '70s.* Berkeley, CA: She Writes Press, 2013.

Fasteau, Marc Feigen. *The Male Machine.* New York: McGraw Hill, 1974.

Feigen, Brenda. *Not One of the Boys: Living Life as a Feminist.* New York: Alfred A. Knopf, 2000.

Felsenthal, Carol. *The Biography of Phyllis Schlafly: The Sweetheart of the Silent Majority.* 1981. Reprint, Chicago: Regnery Gateway, 1982.

Feminist Book Society, ed. *This Is How We Come Back Stronger: Feminist Writers on Turning Crisis into Change.* New York: Feminist Press at the City University of New York, 2021.

Finch, Annie, ed. *Choice Words: Writers on Abortion*. Chicago: Haymarket Books, 2020.

Firestone, Shulamith. *The Dialectic of Sex: The Case for Feminist Revolution*. 1970. Reprint, New York: Farrar, Straus and Giroux, 2003.

Flexner, Eleanor, and Ellen Fitzpatrick. *Century of Struggle: The Woman's Rights Movement in the United States*. Enlarged ed. Cambridge, MA: Belknap Press of Harvard University Press, 1996.

Flomenhaft, Eleanor. *Faith Ringgold, a 25 Year Survey: April 1 to June 24, 1990, FAMLI, Fine Arts Museum of Long Island*. Hempstead, NY: Fine Arts Museum of Long Island, 1990.

Frankfort, Ellen. *Vaginal Politics*. New York: Bantam Books, 1972.

Freedman, Estelle B. *No Turning Back: The History of Feminism and the Future of Women*. New York: Ballantine Books, 2002.

Freeman, Jo. *The Politics of Women's Liberation: A Case Study of an Emerging Social Movement and Its Relation to the Policy Process*. Indiana: iUniverse, 1975.

———. *Women: A Feminist Perspective*. Palo Alto, CA: Mayfield Publishing, 1975.

Fried, Marlene Gerber, ed. *From Abortion to Reproductive Freedom: Transforming a Movement*. Boston: South End Press, 1990.

Friedan, Betty. *The Feminine Mystique*. 20th anniversary edition. New York: Dell, 1984.

———. *It Changed My Life: Writings on the Women's Movement*. 1976. Reprint, Cambridge, MA: Harvard University Press, 1998.

Friedman, Danielle. *Let's Get Physical: How Women Discovered Exercise and Reshaped the World*. New York: G. P. Putnam's Sons, 2022.

Fuentes, Sonia Pressman. *Eat First—You Don't Know What They'll Give You: The Adventures of an Immigrant Family and Their Feminist Daughter*. Indiana: Xlibris, 1999.

Garrow, David J. *Liberty and Sexuality: The Right to Privacy and the Making of Roe v. Wade*. Updated ed. Berkeley: University of California Press, 1998.

Gaskin, Ina May. *Spiritual Midwifery*. Summertown, TN: Book Publishing, 1975.

Gay, Roxane. *Bad Feminist: Essays*. New York: Harper Perennial, 2014.

Giardina, Carol. *Freedom for Women: Forging the Women's Liberation Movement, 1953–1970*. Gainesville: University Press of Florida, 2010.

Gibb, Bobbi. *Wind in the Fire*. N.p.: Institute for the Study of Natural Systems Press, 2016.

Giddings, Paula. *When and Where I Enter: The Impact of Black Women on Race and Sex in America*. New York: William Morrow, 1984.

Gilbert, Sandra M., and Susan Gubar. *Still Mad: American Women Writers and the Feminist Imagination, 1950–2020*. New York: W. W. Norton, 2021.

Ginsburg, Ruth Bader, and Amanda L. Tyler. *Justice, Justice Thou Shalt Pursue: A Life's Work Fighting for a More Perfect Union*. Oakland: University of California Press, 2021.

Ginsburg, Ruth Bader, with Mary Hartnett and Wendy W. Williams. *My Own Words*. New York: Simon & Schuster, 2016.

Gioni, Massimiliano, and Gary Carrion-Murayari, eds. *Faith Ringgold: American People*. New York: Phaidon Press, in association with the New Museum, New York, 2022.

———, and Margot Norton, eds. *Judy Chicago: Herstory*. London: Phaidon Press, 2023.

Giovanni, Nikki. *Gemini: An Extended Autobiographical Statement on My First Twenty-Five Years of Being a Black Poet*. 1971. Reprint, New York: Penguin Books, 1976.

———. *The Prosaic Soul of Nikki Giovanni*. New York: Perennial, 2003.

Glick, Brian. *War at Home: Covert Action Against U.S. Activists and What We Can Do About It*. Boston: South End Press, 1989.

Godfrey, Mark, and Allie Biswas, eds. *The Soul of a Nation Reader: Writings by and about Black American Artists, 1960–1980*. New York: Gregory R. Miller, 2021.

Gordon, Linda. *The Moral Property of Women: A History of Birth Control Politics in America*. 3rd ed. Urbana: University of Illinois Press, 2002.

Gore, Dayo F., Jeanne Theoharis, and Komozi Woodard, eds. *Want to Start a Revolution?: Radical Women in the Black Freedom Struggle*. New York: New York University Press, 2009.

Gorney, Cynthia. *Articles of Faith: A Frontline History of the Abortion Wars*. New York: Simon & Schuster, 1998.

Gornick, Vivian. *The End of the Novel of Love*. 1997. Reprint, New York: Picador, 2020.

———. *Essays in Feminism*. New York: Harper and Row, 1978.

———. *Fierce Attachments: A Memoir*. New York: Farrar, Straus and Giroux, 1987.

———. *The Men in My Life*. Cambridge, MA: MIT Press, 2008.

———. *The Odd Woman and the City: A Memoir*. New York: Farrar, Straus and Giroux, 2015.

———. *Taking A Long Look: Essays on Culture, Literature, and Feminism in Our Time*. London: Verso, 2021.

———, and Barbara K. Moran, eds. *Woman in Sexist Society: Studies in Power and Powerlessness*. New York: Basic Books, 1971.

Gottlieb, Annie. *Do You Believe in Magic?: Bringing the Sixties Back Home*. 1987. Reprint, New York: Simon & Schuster, 1988.

Graham, Katharine. *Personal History*. 1997. Reprint, New York: Vintage Books, 1998.

Grant, Linda. *Sexing the Millennium: Women and the Sexual Revolution*. New York: Grove Press, 1994.

Green, Robin. *The Only Girl: My Life and Times on the Masthead of* Rolling Stone. New York: Little, Brown, 2018.

Greer, Germaine. *The Female Eunuch*. 1970. Reprint, New York: McGraw Hill, 1981.

Griffin, Susan. *Woman and Nature: The Roaring Inside Her*. California: Counterpoint, 1978.

Griffith, Elisabeth. *Formidable: American Women and the Fight for Equality, 1920–2020*. New York: Pegasus Books, 2022.

Grimstad, Kirsten, and Susan Rennie, eds. *The New Woman's Survival Sourcebook*. New York: Alfred A. Knopf, 1975.

———, and Rachel Valinsky, eds. *The New Woman's Survival Catalog: A Woman-Made Book*. 1973. Reprint, New York: Primary Information, 2019.

Gumbo, Judy. *Yippie Girl: Exploits in Protest and Defeating the FBI*. New York: Three Rooms Press, 2022.

Guy-Sheftall, Beverly, ed. *Words of Fire: An Anthology of African American Feminist Thought*. New York: New Press, 1995.

Hamer, Fannie Lou. *The Speeches of Fannie Lou Hamer: To Tell It Like It Is*. Edited by Maegan Parker Brooks and Davis W. Houck. Jackson: University Press of Mississippi, 2010.

Hammond, Harmony. *Lesbian Art in America: A Contemporary History*. New York: Rizzoli, 2000.

Hampton, Henry, and Steve Fayer, comps. *Voices of Freedom: An Oral History of the Civil Rights Movement from the 1950s Through the 1980s*. New York: Bantam Books, 1990.

Harris, Ann Sutherland, and Linda Nochlin. *Women Artists, 1550–1950*. 1976. Reprint, Los Angeles: Los Angeles County Museum of Art; New York: Alfred A. Knopf, 1977.

Harrison, Cynthia Ellen. *On Account of Sex: The Politics of Women's Issues, 1945–1968*. Berkeley: University of California Press, 1989.

Hay, Carol. *Think Like A Feminist: The Philosophy Behind the Revolution*. New York: W. W. Norton, 2020.

Height, Dorothy. *Open Wide the Freedom Gates: A Memoir*. New York: PublicAffairs, 2003.

Heilbrun, Carolyn G. *The Education of a Woman: The Life of Gloria Steinem*. New York: Dial Press, 1995.

Heldman, Julie. *Driven: A Daughter's Odyssey*. Middletown, DE: Julie Heldman, 2018.

Hennessee, Judith. *Betty Friedan: Her Life*. New York: Random House, 1999.

Henry, Sherrye. *The Deep Divide: Why American Women Resist Equality*. New York: Macmillan, 1994.

Hershman-Leeson, Lynn. *Civic Radar*. Edited by Peter Weibel. Ostfildern, Germany: Hatje Cantz, 2016.

Hessel, Katy. *The Story of Art Without Men*. New York: W. W. Norton, 2023.

Hewitt, Nancy A., ed. *No Permanent Waves: Recasting Histories of U.S. Feminism.* New Brunswick, NJ: Rutgers University Press, 2010.

Hirshman, Linda. *Sisters in Law: How Sandra Day O'Connor and Ruth Bader Ginsburg Went to the Supreme Court and Changed the World.* New York: Harper Perennial, 2016.

Hoff-Wilson, Joan, ed. *Rights of Passage: The Past and Future of the ERA.* Bloomington: Indiana University Press, 1986.

Hogshead-Makar, Nancy, and Andrew Zimbalist, eds. *Equal Play: Title IX and Social Change.* Philadelphia, PA: Temple University Press, 2007.

Hole, Judith, and Ellen Levine. *Rebirth of Feminism.* New York: Quadrangle Books, 1971.

Holladay, Hilary. *The Power of Adrienne Rich: A Biography.* New York: Nan A. Talese / Doubleday, 2020.

Holsaert, Faith S., et al., eds. *Hands on the Freedom Plow: Personal Accounts by Women in SNCC.* Urbana: University of Illinois Press, 2010.

Holton, Curlee Raven, with Faith Ringgold. *Faith Ringgold: A View from the Studio.* Boston: Bunker Hill Publishing, 2005.

hooks, bell. *Ain't I a Woman: Black Women and Feminism.* 2nd ed. New York: Routledge, Taylor and Francis Group, 2015.

———. *Bone Black: Memories of Girlhood.* New York: Henry Holt, 1996.

———. *Feminism Is for Everybody: Passionate Politics.* 2nd ed. New York: Routledge, 2015.

———. *Feminist Theory: From Margin to Center.* New ed. New York: Routledge, 2015.

———. *Talking Back: Thinking Feminist, Thinking Black.* New ed. New York: Routledge, Taylor and Francis Group, 2015.

Horn, Miriam. *Rebels in White Gloves: Coming of Age with Hillary's Class, Wellesley '69.* New York: Times Books, 1999.

Horowitz, Daniel. *Betty Friedan and the Making of "The Feminine Mystique": The American Left, the Cold War, and Modern Feminism.* Amherst: University of Massachusetts Press, 1998.

Howe, Florence. *A Life in Motion.* New York: Feminist Press at the City University of New York, 2011.

Howe, Louise Kapp. *Pink Collar Workers: Inside the World of Women's Work.* New York: Avon, 1978.

Hughes, Dorothy Pitman. *Wake Up and Smell the Dollars! Whose Inner-City Is This Anyway!: One Woman's Struggle Against Sexism, Classism, Racism, Gentrification, and the Empowerment Zone.* Phoenix, AZ: Amber Books, 2000.

Hull, Akasha Gloria, Patricia Bell-Scott, and Barbara Smith, eds. *All the Women Are White, All the Blacks Are Men, But Some of Us Are Brave: Black Women's Studies.* 2nd ed. New York: Feminist Press at the City University of New York, 2015.

Hunter-Gault, Charlayne. *In My Place*. 1992. Reprint, New York: Vintage Books, 1993.

Ireland, Patricia. *What Women Want*. New York: Dutton, 1996.

Jay, Karla. *Tales of the Lavender Menace: A Memoir of Liberation*. New York: Basic Books, 1999.

——, and Allen Young, eds. *Lavender Culture*. 1979. Reprint, New York: New York University Press, 1994.

Jefferson, Margo. *Constructing a Nervous System: A Memoir*. New York: Pantheon Books, 2022.

——. *Negroland: A Memoir*. New York: Pantheon Books, 2015.

Jeffreys, Sheila. *Anticlimax: A Feminist Perspective on the Sexual Revolution*. 2nd ed. North Melbourne, Australia: Spinifex Press, 2011.

Joffe, Carole. *Doctors of Conscience: The Struggle to Provide Abortion before and after Roe v. Wade*. Boston: Beacon Press, 1995.

Jolly, Margaretta. *Sisterhood and After: An Oral History of the UK Women's Liberation Movement, 1968–Present*. New York: Oxford University Press, 2019.

Jones, Alethia, and Virginia Eubanks, eds., with Barbara Smith. *Ain't Gonna Let Nobody Turn Me Around: Forty Years of Movement Building with Barbara Smith*. Albany: SUNY Press, 2014.

Jones, Radhika, ed., with David Friend. *Vanity Fair's Women on Women*. New York: Penguin Press, 2019.

Jong, Erica. *Fear of Flying*. New York: Holt, Rinehart and Winston, 1973.

Jordan, June. *Civil Wars*. 1981. Reprint, New York: Simon & Schuster, 1995.

——. *The Essential June Jordan*. Edited by Jan Heller Levi and Christoph Keller. London: Penguin Books, 2021.

——. *Some of Us Did Not Die: New and Selected Essays of June Jordan*. New York: Basic/Civitas Books, 2002.

Joseph, Gloria I., and Jill Lewis. *Common Differences: Conflicts in Black and White Feminist Perspectives*. 1981. Reprint, Boston: South End Press, 1986.

Kanowitz, Leo. *Women and the Law: The Unfinished Revolution*. Albuquerque: University of New Mexico Press, 1969.

Kantor, Jodi, and Megan Twohey. *She Said: Breaking the Sexual Harassment Story That Helped Ignite a Movement*. New York: Penguin Press, 2019.

Kaplan, Laura. *The Story of Jane: The Legendary Underground Feminist Abortion Service*. 1995. Reprint, Chicago: University of Chicago Press, 1997.

Kelly, Kate. *Ordinary Equality: The Fearless Women and Queer People Who Shaped the U.S. Constitution and the Equal Rights Amendment*. Layton, UT: Gibbs Smith, 2022.

Kempton, Sally. *Awakening Shakti: The Transformative Power of the Goddesses of Yoga*. Boulder, CO: Sounds True, 2013.

Kennedy, Flo. *Color Me Flo: My Hard Life and Good Times*. 1976. Reprint, New York: Simon & Schuster, 2017.

Kessler-Harris, Alice. *In Pursuit of Equity: Women, Men, and the Quest for Economic Citizenship in Twentieth-Century America*. Oxford, UK: Oxford University Press, 2001.

King, Billie Jean. *All In: An Autobiography*. New York: Alfred A. Knopf, 2021.

———, with Christine Brennan. *Pressure Is a Privilege: Lessons I've Learned from Life and the Battle of the Sexes*. New York: LifeTime Media, 2008.

Kleinhenz, Elizabeth. *Germaine: The Life of Germaine Greer*. London: Scribe Publications, 2018.

Kornbluh, Felicia. *A Woman's Life Is a Human Life: My Mother, Our Neighbor, and the Journey from Reproductive Rights to Reproductive Justice*. New York: Grove Press, 2023.

Kunz, Anita. *Original Sisters: Portraits of Tenacity and Courage*. New York: Pantheon, 2021.

Lader, Lawrence. *Abortion II: Making the Revolution*. Boston: Beacon Press, 1973.

Larson, Kate Clifford. *Walk with Me: A Biography of Fannie Lou Hamer*. New York: Oxford University Press, 2021.

Lauter, Paul. *Our Sixties: An Activist's History*. Rochester, NY: University of Rochester Press, 2020.

Lerner, Gerda. *The Creation of Patriarchy*. New York: Oxford University Press, 1986.

———, ed. *Black Women in White America: A Documentary History*. 1972. Reprint, New York: Vintage Books, 1973.

Lessing, Doris. *The Golden Notebook*. New York: Simon & Schuster, 1962.

Lester, Joan Steinau. *Fire in My Soul*. New York: Atria Books, 2004.

Levin, Gail. *Becoming Judy Chicago: A Biography of the Artist*. New York: Harmony Books, 2007.

Levine, Suzanne, and Harriet Lyons, eds. *The Decade of Women: A Ms. History of the Seventies in Words and Pictures*. New York: G. P. Putnam's Sons, 1980.

Levine, Suzanne Braun, and Mary Thom. *Bella Abzug: How One Tough Broad from the Bronx Fought Jim Crow and Joe McCarthy, Pissed Off Jimmy Carter, Battled for the Rights of Women and Workers, Rallied Against War and for the Planet, and Shook Up Politics Along the Way; An Oral History*. New York: Farrar, Straus and Giroux, 2007.

Levy, Alan H. *The Political Life of Bella Abzug, 1920–1976: Political Passions, Women's Rights, and Congressional Battles*. Lanham, MD: Lexington Books, 2013.

Lewis, Thabiti. *"Black People Are My Business": Toni Cade Bambara's Practices of Liberation*. Detroit: Wayne State University Press, 2020.

———, ed. *Conversations with Toni Cade Bambara*. Jackson: University Press of Mississippi, 2012.

Lichtenstein, Grace. *A Long Way, Baby: Behind the Scenes in Women's Pro Tennis*. New York: William Morrow, 1974.

Linden, Robin Ruth, ed. *Against Sadomasochism: A Radical Feminist Analysis*. East Palo Alto, CA: Frog in the Well, 1982.

Lippard, Lucy R. *From the Center: Feminist Essays on Women's Art*. New York: Dutton, 1976.

———. *The Pink Glass Swan: Selected Essays on Feminist Art*. New York: New Press, 1995.

———. *Six Years: The Dematerialization of the Art Object from 1966 to 1972* [. . .]. 1973. Reprint, Berkeley: University of California Press, 1997.

Lipsyte, Robert. *The Masculine Mystique*. New York: New American Library, 1966.

Lobo, Susan, Steve Talbot, and Traci L. Morris. *Native American Voices: A Reader*. 3rd ed. Abingdon, Oxfordshire, UK: Routledge, 2016.

Lorde, Audre. *A Burst of Light, and Other Essays*. 1988. Reprint, Mineola, NY: Ixia Press, 2017.

———. *Sister Outsider: Essays and Speeches*. Trumansburg, NY: Crossing Press, 1984.

———. *Zami, A New Spelling of My Name: A Biomythography*. Trumansburg, NY: Crossing Press, 1982.

Love, Barbara J. *There at the Dawning: Memories of a Lesbian Feminist*. N.p.: Lulu, 2021.

———, ed. *Feminists Who Changed America, 1963–1975*. Urbana: University of Illinois Press, 2006.

Lovett, Laura L. *With Her Fist Raised: Dorothy Pitman Hughes and the Transformative Power of Black Community Activism*. Boston: Beacon Press, 2021.

MacAdams, Cynthia. *Rising Goddess*. Dobbs Ferry, NY: Morgan and Morgan, 1983.

MacKinnon, Catharine A. *Sexual Harassment of Working Women: A Case of Sex Discrimination*. New Haven, CT: Yale University Press, 1979.

MacLean, Nancy. *The American Women's Movement, 1945–2000: A Brief History with Documents*. London: Palgrave Macmillan, 2009.

MacPherson, Myra. *The Scarlet Sisters: Sex, Suffrage, and Scandal in the Gilded Age*. New York: Twelve, 2014.

Mailer, Norman. *The Prisoner of Sex*. Boston: Little, Brown, 1971.

Mansbridge, Jane J. *Why We Lost the ERA*. Chicago: University of Chicago Press, 1986.

Marotta, Toby. *The Politics of Homosexuality*. Boston: Houghton Mifflin, 1981.

Marston, William Moulton. *Wonder Woman*. New York: Bonanza Books, 1972.

Martin, Del, and Phyllis Lyon. *Lesbian/Woman*. New York: Bantam Books, 1972.

Mathews, Donald G., and Jane Sherron De Hart. *Sex, Gender, and the Politics of ERA*. New York: Oxford University Press, 1990.

Medsger, Betty. *The Burglary: The Discovery of J. Edgar Hoover's Secret FBI Files*. New York: Alfred A. Knopf, 2014.

Melnick, R. Shep. *The Transformation of Title IX: Regulating Gender Equality in Education*. Washington, DC: Brookings Institution Press, 2018.

Miller, Isabel. *Patience and Sarah*. 1969. Reprint, Vancouver, Canada: Arsenal Pulp Press, 2005.

Millett, Kate. *A.D.: A Memoir*. New York: W. W. Norton, 1995.

———. *Flying*. New York: Alfred A. Knopf, 1974.

———. *Sexual Politics*. 1970. Reprint, Urbana: University of Illinois Press, 2000.

Mills, Kay. *This Little Light of Mine: The Life of Fannie Lou Hamer*. New York: Plume Books, 1994.

Mitchell, Juliet. *Psychoanalysis and Feminism: A Radical Reassessment of Freudian Psychoanalysis*. 1974. Reprint, New York: Basic Books, 2000.

Mondale, Walter F., with David Hage. *The Good Fight: A Life in Liberal Politics*. New York: Scribner, 2010.

Moore, Honor. *Darling*. New York: Grove Press, 2001.

———. *Memoir: Poems*. Goshen, CT: Chicory Blue Press, 1988.

———. *Our Revolution: A Mother and Daughter at Midcentury*. New York: W. W. Norton, 2020.

———, ed. *The New Women's Theatre: Ten Plays by Contemporary American Women*. New York: Vintage Books, 1977.

———, ed. *Poems from the Women's Movement*. New York: Library of America, 2009.

Moraga, Cherríe, and Gloria Anzaldúa, eds. *This Bridge Called My Back: Writings by Radical Women of Color*. 40th anniversary ed. New York: State University of New York Press, 2021.

Morgan, Robin. *The Demon Lover: The Roots of Terrorism*. 1988. Reprint, New York: Washington Square Press, 2001.

———. *Going Too Far: The Personal Chronicle of a Feminist*. New York: Random House, 1977.

———. *Monster: Poems*. New York: Random House, 1972.

———. *Saturday's Child: A Memoir*. New York: W. W. Norton, 2001.

———. *The Word of a Woman: Feminist Dispatches, 1968–1992*. New York: W. W. Norton, 1992.

———, ed. *Sisterhood Is Powerful: An Anthology of Writings from the Women's Liberation Movement*. New York: Vintage Books, 1970.

Morrill, Rebecca, Karen Wright, and Louisa Elderton, eds. *Great Women Artists*. London: Phaidon, 2019.

Morris, Bonnie J., and D-M Withers. *The Feminist Revolution: The Struggle for Women's Liberation*. Washington, DC: Smithsonian Books, 2018.

Morris, Catherine, and Rujeko Hockley, eds. *We Wanted a Revolution: Black Radical Women, 1965–85; A Sourcebook*. Brooklyn: Brooklyn Museum, 2017.

Morrison, Tony. *Beloved*. New York: Alfred A. Knopf, 1987.

———. *The Bluest Eye*. 1970. Reprint, New York: Vintage International, 2007.

———. *The Source of Self-Regard: Selected Essays, Speeches, and Meditations*. 2019. Reprint, New York: Vintage International, 2020.

Murray, Pauli. *Proud Shoes: The Story of an American Family*. 1956. Reprint, Boston: Beacon Press, 1999.

———. *Song in a Weary Throat: Memoir of an American Pilgrimage*. 1987. Reprint, New York: Liveright, 2018.

Near, Holly, with Derk Richardson. *Fire in the Rain—Singer in the Storm: An Autobiography*. New York: William Morrow, 1990.

Nelson, Jennifer. *Women of Color and the Reproductive Rights Movement*. New York: New York University Press, 2003.

Neuwirth, Jessica. *Equal Means Equal: Why the Time for an Equal Rights Amendment Is Now*. New York: New Press, 2015.

New York Radical Women. *Notes from the First Year*. New York: New York Radical Women, 1968.

Newhouse, Nancy R., ed. *Hers, Through Women's Eyes*. New York: Villard Books, 1985.

Nies, Judith. *The Girl I Left Behind: A Personal History of the 1960s*. New York: Harper Perennial, 2009.

Nochlin, Linda. *Women Artists: The Linda Nochlin Reader*. Edited by Maura Reilly. New York: Thames and Hudson, 2015.

Oliver, Susan. *Betty Friedan: The Personal Is Political*. New York: Pearson Longman, 2008.

Olsen, Tillie. *Silences*. 1978. Reprint, New York: Feminist Press at the City University of New York, 2003.

Oral History and Art: Sculpture; Interviews with Alexander Calder, Judy Chicago, Walter De Maria, Donald Jud and Robert Smithson. London: MuseumsETC, 2015.

Orleck, Annelise. *Rethinking American Women's Activism*. New York: Routledge, 2014.

Paterson, Judith Hillman. *Be Somebody: A Biography of Marguerite Rawalt*. Austin, TX: Eakin Press, 1986.

Patton, Gwendolyn. *My Race to Freedom: A Life in the Civil Rights Movement*. 2019. Reprint, Montgomery, AL: NewSouth Books, 2020.

Perkins, Anne Gardiner. *Yale Needs Women: How the First Group of Girls Rewrote the Rules of an Ivy League Giant*. Naperville, IL: Sourcebooks, 2019.

Perkins, Margo V. *Autobiography as Activism: Three Black Women of the Sixties*. Jackson: University Press of Mississippi, 2000.

Perlstein, Rick. *Nixonland: The Rise of a President and the Fracturing of America*. New York: Scribner, 2008.

Piercy, Marge. *Small Changes*. 1973. Reprint, New York: Random House, 1997.

Pierpont, Julia. *The Little Book of Feminist Saints*. New York: Random House, 2018.

Plath, Sylvia. *Ariel: The Restored Edition*. New York: HarperCollins, 2004.

Pogrebin, Letty Cottin. *Deborah, Golda, and Me: Being Female and Jewish in America*. New York: Crown, 1991.

———. *How to Make It in a Man's World*. New York: Bantam Books, 1970.

Poletti, Frances, and Kristina Yee. *The Girl Who Ran: Bobbi Gibb, the First Woman to Run the Boston Marathon*. Seattle: Compendium, 2017.

Povich, Lynn. *The Good Girls Revolt: How the Women of Newsweek Sued Their Bosses and Changed the Workplace*. New York: PublicAffairs, 2012.

Prager, Joshua. *The Family Roe: An American Story*. New York: W. W. Norton, 2021.

Princenthal, Nancy. *Unspeakable Acts: Women, Art, and Sexual Violence in the 1970s*. 2019. Reprint, New York: Thames and Hudson, 2022.

Raines, Howell. *My Soul Is Rested: Movement Days in the Deep South Remembered*. 1977. Reprint, New York: Penguin Books, 1983.

Randolph, Sherie M. *Florynce "Flo" Kennedy: The Life of a Black Feminist Radical*. Chapel Hill: University of North Carolina Press, 2015.

Reckitt, Helena, ed. *The Art of Feminism: Images That Shaped the Fight for Equality, 1857–2017*. San Francisco: Chronicle Books, 2018.

Redstockings, Inc. *Feminist Revolution*. Edited by Kathie Sarachild. New York: Random House, 1978.

Rich, Adrienne. *Of Woman Born: Motherhood as Experience and Institution*. New York: W. W. Norton, 1976.

———. *On Lies, Secrets, and Silence: Selected Prose, 1966–1978*. New York: W. W. Norton, 1979.

———. *The Will to Change: Poems, 1968–1970*. New York: W. W. Norton, 1971.

Ringgold, Faith. *Faith Ringgold*. New York: Walther Koenig Books, 2020.

———. *A Letter to My Daughter, Michele: In Response to Her Book, "Black Macho and the Myth of the Superwoman."* North Charleston, SC: CreateSpace, 2015.

———. *We Flew over the Bridge: The Memoirs of Faith Ringgold*. 1995. Reprint, Durham, NC: Duke University Press, 2005.

———, Michele Wallace, and Kirsten Weiss. *Faith Ringgold: Politics/Power*. Edited by Elena Cheprakova. New York: Weiss Publications, 2022.

Risen, Clay. *The Bill of the Century: The Epic Battle for the Civil Rights Act*. New York: Bloomsbury Press, 2014.

Roberts, Dorothy. *Killing the Black Body: Race, Reproduction, and the Meaning of Liberty*. 1997. Reprint, New York: Vintage Books, 2017.

Roberts, Selena. *A Necessary Spectacle: Billie Jean King, Bobby Riggs, and the Tennis Match That Leveled the Game*. New York: Crown, 2005.

Robertson, Nan. *The Girls in the Balcony: Women, Men, and The New York Times*. New York: Random House, 1992.

Roiphe, Katie. *The Morning After: Sex, Fear, and Feminism*. Boston: Back Bay Books, 1994.

Romney, Patricia. *We Were There: The Third World Women's Alliance and the Second Wave*. New York: Feminist Press at the City University of New York, 2021.

Rosen, Jeffrey. *Conversations with RBG: Ruth Bader Ginsburg on Life, Love, Liberty, and Law*. New York: Henry Holt, 2019.

Rosen, Ruth. *The World Split Open: How the Modern Women's Movement Changed America*. New York: Viking, 2000.

Rosenberg, Rosalind. *Jane Crow: The Life of Pauli Murray*. New York: Oxford University Press, 2017.

Rosenthal, Michael. *Barney: Grove Press and Barney Rosset, America's Maverick Publisher and His Battle Against Censorship*. New York: Arcade, 2017.

Rossi, Alice S., and Ann Calderwood, eds. *Academic Women on the Move*. New York: Russell Sage Foundation, 1973.

Roth, Benita. *Separate Roads to Feminism: Black, Chicana, and White Feminist Movements in America's Second Wave*. Cambridge, UK: Cambridge University Press, 2004.

Roth, Moira, ed. *The Amazing Decade: Women and Performance Art in America, 1970–1980*. Los Angeles: Astro Artz, 1983.

Sanchez, Sonia. *Collected Poems*. Boston: Beacon Press, 2021.

———. *Homegirls and Handgrenades*. 1984. Reprint, Buffalo, NY: White Pine Press, 2007.

Schneir, Miriam, ed. *Feminism in Our Time: The Essential Writings, World War II to the Present*. New York: Vintage Books, 1994.

Schoen, Johanna. *Abortion after Roe*. Chapel Hill: University of North Carolina Press, 2015.

Schulder, Diane, and Florynce Kennedy. *Abortion Rap*. New York: McGraw Hill, 1971.

Seaman, Barbara. *The Doctor's Case Against the Pill*. London: Michael Joseph, 1970.

Shange, Ntozake. *For Colored Girls Who Have Considered Suicide, When the Rainbow Is Enuf: A Choreopoem*. New York: Scribner, 1997.

Shteir, Rachel. *Betty Friedan: Magnificent Disrupter*. New Haven, CT: Yale University Press, 2023.

Shulman, Alix Kates. *Burning Questions: A Novel*. New York: Alfred A. Knopf, 1978.

———. *A Marriage Agreement and Other Essays: Four Decades of Feminist Writing*. New York: Open Road Integrated Media, 2012.

———. *Memoirs of an Ex-Prom Queen: A Novel*. New York: Alfred A. Knopf, 1972.

———, and Honor Moore, eds. *Women's Liberation!: Feminist Writings That Inspired a Revolution and Still Can*. New York: Library of America, 2021.

Smith, Andrea. *Conquest: Sexual Violence and American Indian Genocide*. 2005. Reprint, Durham, NC: Duke University Press, 2015.

Smith, Barbara. *The Truth That Never Hurts: Writings on Race, Gender, and Freedom*. New Brunswick, NJ: Rutgers University Press, 1998.

———, ed. *Home Girls: A Black Feminist Anthology*. 1983. Reprint, New Brunswick, NJ: Rutgers University Press, 2000.

Smith-Stewart, Amy. *Harmony Hammond: Material Witness; Five Decades of Art*. Ridgefield, CT: Aldrich Contemporary Art Museum; New York: Gregory R. Miller, 2019.

Spender, Dale. *Women of Ideas and What Men Have Done to Them: From Aphra Behn to Adrienne Rich*. London: Routledge and Kegan Paul, 1982.

Springer, Kimberly. *Living for the Revolution: Black Feminist Organizations, 1968–1980*. Durham, NC: Duke University Press, 2005.

———, ed. *Still Lifting, Still Climbing: Contemporary African American Women's Activism*. New York: New York University Press, 1999.

Srinivasan, Amia. *The Right to Sex: Feminism in the Twenty-First Century*. New York: Farrar, Straus and Giroux, 2021.

Steinem, Gloria. *Moving Beyond Words*. New York: Simon & Schuster, 1994.

———. *My Life on the Road*. New York: Random House, 2015.

———. *Outrageous Acts and Everyday Rebellions*. 2nd ed. New York: Henry Holt, 1995.

———. *Revolution from Within: A Book of Self-Esteem*. Boston: Little, Brown, 1992.

———. *The Truth Will Set You Free, But First It Will Piss You Off!: Thoughts on Life, Love, and Rebellion*. New York: Random House, 2019.

Stern, Sydney Ladensohn. *Gloria Steinem: Her Passions, Politics, and Mystique*. Secaucus, NJ: Birch Lane Press, 1997.

Stevenson, Prudence, Susan Mackie, Anne Robinson, and Jess Baines. *See Red Women's Workshop Feminist Posters, 1974–1990*. 2nd printing. London: Four Corners Books, 2017.

Strebeigh, Fred. *Equal: Women Reshape American Law*. New York: W. W. Norton, 2009.

Studio Museum in Harlem. *Faith Ringgold: Twenty Years of Painting, Sculpture, and Performance (1963–1983)*. New York: Studio Museum in Harlem, 1984.

Swerdlow, Amy. *Women Strike for Peace: Traditional Motherhood and Radical Politics in the 1960s*. Chicago: University of Chicago Press, 1993.

Swinth, Kirsten. *Feminism's Forgotten Fight: The Unfinished Struggle for Work and Family*. Cambridge, MA: Harvard University Press, 2018.

Tanner, Leslie B., comp. and ed. *Voices from Women's Liberation*. New York: New American Library, 1971.

Taylor, Keeanga-Yamahtta, ed. *How We Get Free: Black Feminism and the Combahee River Collective*. Chicago: Haymarket Books, 2017.

Thom, Mary. *Inside Ms.: 25 Years of the Magazine and the Feminist Movement*. New York: Henry Holt, 1997.

———, ed. *Letters to Ms., 1972–1987*. New York: Henry Holt, 1987.

Thomas, Gillian. *Because of Sex: One Law, Ten Cases, and Fifty Years That Changed American Women's Lives at Work*. New York: St. Martin's Press, 2016.

Thompson, Hunter S. *Fear and Loathing on the Campaign Trail '72*. 40th anniversary ed. New York: Simon & Schuster, 2012.

Thompson, Mary Lou, ed. *Voices of the New Feminism*. Boston: Beacon Press, 1970.

Thorsson, Courtney. *The Sisterhood: How a Network of Black Women Writers Changed American Culture*. New York: Columbia University Press, 2023.

Tobias, Sheila. *Faces of Feminism: An Activist's Reflections on the Women's Movement*. Boulder, CO: Westview Press, 1997.

Tolchin, Susan, and Martin Tolchin. *Clout: Womanpower and Politics*. New York: Coward, McCann and Geoghegan, 1974.

Tone, Andrea. *Devices and Desires: A History of Contraceptives in America*. New York: Hill and Wang, 2002.

Traister, Rebecca. *Good and Mad: The Revolutionary Power of Women's Anger*. New York: Simon & Schuster, 2018.

Tribe, Laurence H. *Abortion: The Clash of Absolutes*. New York: W. W. Norton, 1990.

Turk, Katherine. *The Women of NOW: How Feminists Built an Organization That Transformed America*. New York: Farrar, Straus and Giroux, 2023.

Ulrich, Laurel Thatcher. *Well-Behaved Women Seldom Make History*. 2007. Reprint, New York: Vintage Books, 2008.

Wagner, Sally Roesch. *Sisters in Spirit: Haudenosaunee (Iroquois) Influence on Early American Feminists*. Summertown, TN: Native Voices, 2001.

Walker, Alice. *Gathering Blossoms Under Fire: The Journals of Alice Walker, 1965–2000*. Edited by Valerie Boyd. New York: Simon & Schuster, 2022.

———. *In Love and Trouble: Stories of Black Women*. 1973. Reprint, San Diego: Harcourt Brace Jovanovich, 1974.

———. *In Search of Our Mothers' Gardens: Womanist Prose*. San Diego: Harcourt Brace Jovanovich, 1983.

Wallace, Michele. *Black Macho and the Myth of the Superwoman*. 1979. Reprint, London: Verso, 1990.

———. *Black Popular Culture*. Edited by Gina Dent. Seattle: Bay Press, 1992.

———. *Dark Designs and Visual Culture*. Durham, NC: Duke University Press, 2004.

———. *Invisibility Blues: From Pop to Theory*. London: Verso, 1990.

Ware, Cellestine. *Woman Power: The Movement for Women's Liberation*. New York: Tower Publications, 1970.

Wattleton, Faye. *Life on the Line*. New York: Ballantine Books, 1996.

Webb, Marilyn. *The Good Death: The New American Search to Reshape the End of Life*. New York: Bantam Books, 1997.

Weddington, Sarah. *A Question of Choice*. 40th anniversary edition, rev. and updated. New York: Feminist Press at the City University of New York, 2013.

Wells, Susan. *"Our Bodies, Ourselves" and the Work of Writing*. Stanford, CA: Stanford University Press, 2010.

Whitaker, Mark. *Saying It Loud: 1966–The Year Black Power Challenged the Civil Rights Movement*. New York: Simon & Schuster, 2023.

White, Theodore H. *The Making of the President 1972.* 1973. Reprint, New York: Harper Perennial, 2010.

Wilding, Faith. *By Our Own Hands: The Woman Artist's Movement, Southern California, 1970–1976.* Santa Monica, CA: Double X, 1977.

Wilkerson, Cathy. *Flying Close to the Sun: My Life and Times as a Weatherman.* New York: Seven Stories Press, 2007.

Willis, Ellen. *The Essential Ellen Willis.* Edited by Nona Willis Aronowitz. Minneapolis: University of Minnesota Press, 2014.

Winslow, Barbara. *Shirley Chisholm: Catalyst for Change.* New York: Routledge, 2018.

Winterson, Jeanette. *Oranges Are Not the Only Fruit.* 1985. Reprint, New York: Grove Press, 1997.

Wolbrecht, Christina. *The Politics of Women's Rights: Parties, Positions, and Change.* Princeton, NJ: Princeton University Press, 2000.

Woloch, Nancy. *A Class by Herself: Protective Laws for Women Workers, 1890s–1990s.* Princeton, NJ: Princeton University Press, 2015.

Wu, Judy Tzu-Chun, and Gwendolyn Mink. *Fierce and Fearless: Patsy Takemoto Mink, First Woman of Color in Congress.* New York: New York University Press, 2022.

Wulfhart, Nell McShane. *The Great Stewardess Rebellion: How Women Launched a Workplace Rebellion at 30,000 Feet.* New York: Doubleday, 2022.

Zarnow, Leandra Ruth. *Battling Bella: The Protest Politics of Bella Abzug.* Cambridge, MA: Harvard University Press, 2019.

DOCUMENTARIES

Boston. A documentary produced and directed by Jon Dunham. La Roma Films, 2017. 1 hr., 54 min.

Chisholm '72: Unbought & Unbossed. A documentary produced and directed by Shola Lynch. Realside Productions, 2004. 1 hr., 17 min.

The Janes. A documentary directed by Tia Lessin and Emma Pildes; produced by Emma Pildes, Daniel Arcana, and Jessica Levin. HBO Documentary Films, 2022. 1 hr., 41 min.

Judy Chicago & the California Girls. A documentary produced and directed by Judith Dancoff, 1971. California Girl Productions, 2008. 24 min. DVD.

She's Beautiful When She's Angry. A documentary produced and directed by Mary Dore, coproduced by Nancy Kennedy. MusicBox Films, 2014. 1 hr., 32 min.

Town Bloody Hall. A documentary directed by Chris Hegedus and D. A. Pennebaker; produced by Shirley Broughton and Edith Van Slyck. Janus Films, 1979. 1 hr., 25 min.

W.A.R.!: Women Art Revolution. A documentary directed by Lynn Hershman Leeson; produced by Sarah Peter. Zeitgeist Films, 2010. 1 hr., 23 min. DVD.

Index

This page constitutes a continuation of the copyright page:

———————

Bella Abzug, excerpts from *Gender Gap: Bella Abzug's Guide to Political Power for American Women*. Copyright © 1984 by Bella Abzug. Reprinted by permission of HarperCollins Publishers and Creative Artists Agency.

Frances M. Beal, excerpts from "Double Jeopardy: To Be Black and Female" from *Sisterhood Is Powerful: An Anthology of Writings from the Women's Liberation Movement*, edited by Robin Morgan (New York: Random House, 1970). Reprinted with the permission of the author.

Liz Carpenter, excerpt from *Getting Better All the Time* (Simon & Schuster, 1987). Copyright © 1987 by Liz Carpenter. Reprinted by permission of Christy Carpenter.

Shirley Chisholm, excerpts from *Unbought and Unbossed*. Copyright © 1970 by Shirley Chisholm. Excerpts from *The Good Fight*. Copyright © 1973 by Shirley Chisholm. Both reprinted by permission of HarperCollins Publishers.

Nora Ephron, excerpts from "Journalism: A Love Story" from *I Remember Nothing and Other Reflections* (Knopf, 2010). Copyright © 2010 by Heartburn Enterprises, Inc. Reprinted by permission of Heartburn Enterprises, Inc.

Betty Friedan, excerpts from *"It Changed My Life": Writings on the Women's Movement* (Random House, 1976). Copyright © 1976 by Betty Friedan. Reprinted by permission of Curtis Brown, Ltd. All rights reserved.

Germaine Greer, excerpts from "McGovern the Big Tease" from *Harper's Magazine* (October 1972). Reprinted with the permission of the author.

Flo Kennedy, excerpt from *Politics of Oppression* (unpublished ms). Reprinted with the permission of the President and Fellows of Harvard College for the Schlesinger Library.

Billie Jean King, excerpts from *All In: An Autobiography* by Billie Jean King with Johnette Howard and Maryanne Vollers. Copyright © 2021 by Billie Jean King Enterprises, Inc. Used by permission of Alfred A. Knopf, an imprint of the Knopf Doubleday Publishing Group, a division of Penguin Random House LLC. All rights reserved.

Faith Ringgold, excerpts from *We Flew Over the Bridge: The Memoirs of Faith Ringgold* (Little, Brown, 1995). © 2024 Faith Ringgold / Artists Rights Society (ARS), New York.